T0203202

Qualitative Spatial and Temporal Reasoning

Qualitative Spatial and Temporal Reasoning

Gérard Ligozat

First published 2012 in Great Britain and the United States by ISTE Ltd and John Wiley & Sons, Inc.

ISTE Ltd
27-37 St George's Road
London SW19 4EU
UK

www.iste.co.uk

John Wiley & Sons, Inc.
111 River Street
Hoboken, NJ 07030
USA

www.wiley.com

© ISTE Ltd 2012

Library of Congress Cataloging-in-Publication Data

Ligozat, Gérard.
 Qualitative spatial and temporal reasoning / Gérard Ligozat.
   p. cm.
 Includes bibliographical references and index.
 ISBN 978-1-84821-252-7
 1. Qualitative reasoning. 2. Spatial analysis (Statistics) 3. Space and time--Mathematical models. 4. Logic, Symbolic and mathematical. I. Title.
 Q339.25.L54 2011
 511.3--dc23
                                                                                    2011029658

British Library Cataloguing-in-Publication Data
A CIP record for this book is available from the British Library
ISBN 978-1-84821-252-7

Printed and bound in Great Britain by CPI Group (UK) Ltd., Croydon, Surrey CR0 4YY

Table of Contents

Introduction

Qualitative Reasoning

Why do we need qualitative reasoning formalisms? Let us consider an example of [LIG 05a], which represents a "spatial" version of what we will call the *Point calculus* in this book. This example describes a boat race (Figure 1) that is conducted on a river, which we represent as a directed axis giving the direction of the race.

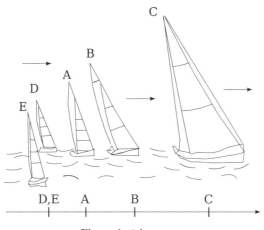

Figure 1. *A boat race*

An observer positioned on the river bank transmits a telephonic message to his correspondent to inform him about the state of the competition. His initial message would be:

1) A is behind B;

2) C is in front of B;

3) D is behind B;

4) E is at the same level as D.

Let us assume then that a second informant gives the following indication:

5) C is behind E.

The manner in which the observers formulate their messages shows that they have implicitly adopted a "qualitative" view point: they do not try to give indications of distance, but only information that is related to the order of the competitors. A listener who would like to make a graphical representation of the situation could perfectly content himself with representing the river as a directed line, and the boats by points located on it. Using such an abstraction, the message would need only three relations: *in front of, behind*, and *at the same level*. The selected level of description makes it clear that there are only three possible relations between two boats (one precedes or follows the other, or they are at the same level), and that these relations are exclusive of each other. We are in the presence of three qualitative relations which constitute what is known as a *JEPD set* of relations, *jointly exhaustive* (whose reunion is exhaustive) and *pairwise disjoint* (pairwise exclusive).

In the context of qualitative reasoning, these three relations are called *basic relations*.

Let us notice that the relation *at the same level*, in terms of points on the line, is the *equality* relation. In the same manner, *in front of* and *behind* correspond to the relations *greater than* and *smaller than* between points. The two relations *in front of* and *behind* are what one calls *inverse* relations of each other: for each pair (x, y) of elements, x is *in front of* y if, and only if, y is *behind* x. Obviously, the relation *at the same level* is its own inverse.

Using the concept of inverse, the listener has a possibility of reasoning on the information he gets from the informant, where "reasoning" means deriving new pieces of information. For instance, knowing that " C is *in front of* B"(a piece of information he has been given), he can derive by inversion that "B is *behind* C" (which is a new piece of information). More interestingly, the listener can use another operation to derive new information: he can *compose* relations. For instance, from the fact that A is *behind* B and B is *behind* C, the listener can deduce that A is *behind* C. By doing so, the listener implicitly uses the fact that the relation *behind* is a transitive relation, i.e. that, for each 3-tuple (x, y, z) of elements, x *behind* y and y *behind* z imply that x *is behind* z. This (composing the relation *behind* with itself) is a typical case of *composition* of two relations. For this operation, it is clear that the relation *at the same level* is what is called a neutral element.

The fact is that D is *behind B* is equivalent to B being *in front of* D. What can we say about the position of D from the fact that A is *behind B* and that B is *in front of D*? Nothing at all, i.e. we can have *A behind D*, or A *at the same level as D*, or *A in front of D*. We can express this fact by saying that the composition of *behind* and *in front of* is the relation known as the universal relation, which is the union of the three basic relations.

This last example of composition of relations shows that the composition operation leads us to consider, in addition to the three basic relations, subsets of the set of basic relations. Such subsets will be called *disjunctive relations*, or, in short, *relations*.

In our case, it is natural to represent the three relations *behind*, *in front of*, and at *at the same level* by the symbols $<$, $>$, and eq respectively. On doing this, we notice that most of the subsets of the set $\{<, eq, >\}$, interpreted as disjunctions, have usual "names": for example, $\{<, eq\}$ corresponds to the relation denoted by $\leq$, and $\{<, >\}$ to the relation denoted by $\neq$.

At this stage we could rewrite the information about the race provided by the first observer in the following way:

1) $A < B$;

2) $C > B$;

3) $D < B$;

4) E eq D.

The information given by the second informant would then be written as:

5) $C < E$.

But we will use a different kind of representation, namely a representation in terms of constraint networks. This is a key move which will allow us to establish a connection to the domain of constraint-based reasoning.

The data consisting of the five objects and of the relations between them can be represented by a directed graph having five vertices $A, \ldots, E$, and whose arcs are labeled according to the relations provided by the informants. In our case, the content of the message from the first informant is represented by the graph (a) of Figure 2, and that from the two informants brought together by graph (b); these graphs are called the associated *constraint networks*.

When no indication is provided on the relation between two vertices, the arc in question will not be drawn, but it is clear that one could equivalently use the universal relation as a label. In a similar manner, it is equivalent to label an arc by a relation, or to label the opposite arc by the inverse relation. It is generally assumed that either one of the two arcs has been selected, and that the inverse relation on the opposite arc is implicitly assumed.

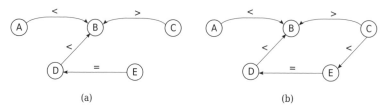

Figure 2. *Representation in the form of constraint networks of the messages of the two informants: (a) conditions 1) to 4); (b) conditions 1) to 5)*

This representation has the advantage of considering the basic operations in terms of path-following on the graph. The inversion operation corresponds to replacing one arc by the opposite arc, and that of composition to combining two successive arcs, first from x to y, and then from y to z, to get a path from x to z.

Let us consider the recipient of the telephone messages. Can he graphically represent the five boats as points on the directed line, based on the information received from the two informants? In order to do so, it is necessary that the provided information be *consistent*, i.e. represents a possible *configuration*. However, this is not the case. In fact, from $C > B$, we can deduce that $B < C$ (by inversion on the arc (B, C)), then by composition of $D < B$ (going from D to B) and $B < C$ (going from from B to C) we deduce that $D < C$, which cannot be the case, since in addition $C < E$ and D eq E imply that $C < D$. The information provided by the two informants taken together is thus contradictory, and the network considered is an *inconsistent* network. That would not have been the case if the message from the second informant (C precedes E) had not been taken into account. The corresponding network would then be that of Figure 2 (b). Perhaps the second informant wanted to say that, actually, it is E which precedes C. In that case, the information would be correct, but redundant: owing to the fact that E eq D, $E < C$ is implied by the constraints 1) to 4). A network is called *consistent* if there is a configuration compatible with its constraints.

Let us consider what happens if we do not take into account the information provided by the second informant, i.e. leave out constraint 5). The corresponding network is the network (b) of Figure 2, obtained from (a) by removing the constraint $<$ from the arc (C, E) (which amounts to replacing it by the universal constraint). Now this network is consistent. Figure 3 then represents the three possible qualitative configurations.

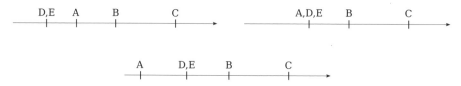

Figure 3. *The three configurations of points satisfying the constraints 1) to 4) of Figure 2 (a)*

A fundamental problem in the domain of qualitative reasoning will be to determine whether a given constraint network is consistent. If this is the case, we may, like the recipient of the messages in our example, be interested in describing a configuration, or all possible configurations.

A configuration, conversely, can be represented by a constraint network which has the peculiarity that each one of its arcs is labeled by a basic relation. Such a network is called a *scenario* or an *atomic network*. A general question will be to determine whether a given scenario is a consistent network. For example, three consistent scenarios correspond to the three configuration of Figure 3. Rather than representing them in graphic form, we can use a tabular representation as in Table 1.

	A	B	C	D	E
A	eq	<	<	>	>
B	>	eq	<	>	>
C	>	>	eq	>	>
D	<	<	<	eq	eq
E	<	<	<	eq	eq

Table 1. *A tabular representation of the first scenario*

The example of the boat race had enabled us to introduce some of the basic notions used in qualitative reasoning: one considers *constraint networks*, whose vertices correspond to spatial or temporal entities (here, points of a directed line), and whose arcs are labeled by relations (unions of basic relations). In particular, a *scenario* is a network where all the labels are basic relations. The central problem is to determine whether a given network (and in particular a scenario), is consistent, i.e. if it corresponds to a configuration of the entities in question.

We have chosen in this presentation to consider the points of the line as spatial entities (abstractions of the position of a boat). However, the formalism whose definition we have outlined is interpreted in general in a temporal manner: the entities in question are *time points* on the time axis, the relation $A < B$ is read "time point A precedes time point B", and the relation eq is the concomitance relation. For this reason, we will, from now onwards, refer to this formalism as to the *Point calculus*.

The Point calculus thus provides a language which allows us to express qualitative constraints on configurations of points. The constraint propagation operations allow a simple type of inference.

We will see that the problem of determining whether a given network is consistent can be solved by simple algorithms whose time-cost is polynomial with regard to the size of the network.

More generally, in this book, we will be interested in qualitative reasoning on various types of temporal or spatial entities. In our example, these entities could be considered as points of a directed axis. In the temporal case, they can be time points, time intervals, or more complex entities. In the spatial case, the nature of the entities considered can vary widely: points of the plane, regions of the plane, but also points, pairs of points, or regions of a Euclidean space, or even abstract entities such as subspaces of a topological space.

The temporal or spatial entities are elements of a certain universe U, and one is interested in finite sets of relations of a fixed arity r between the entities (arity 2 for binary relations, arity 3 for ternary relations). In the example of the boat race, U can be represented by the real line $\mathbb{R}$. The relations considered are three binary relations, hence, from the mathematical point of view, three subsets of $\mathbb{R}^2$:

  – the relation denoted by $<$, i.e. $\{(x, y)|\mathbb{R}^2|x < y\}$;
  – its inverse, the relation denoted by $>$, i.e. $\{(x, y)|\mathbb{R}^2|x > y\}$;
  – the equality relation denoted by eq, i.e. $\{(x, x)|x \in \mathbb{R}\}$.

This set **B** of relations, known as the set of basic relations, constitutes a finite partition of all r-ary relations on U (this is the property known as the JEPD property), i.e. these relations are non-empty and any r-tuple of elements of U belongs to one and only one of these basic relations. The reasoning machinery uses the set **A** of all subsets of **B**, whose elements are called (disjunctive) relations, as constraints. It makes use of the inversion and composition operations, which are defined on **B**, and by extension on **A**, for propagating the constraints.

Structure of the book

Chapter 1 deals with *Allen's calculus* [ALL 83], which corresponds to a choice of entities more complex than punctual entities: in the temporal domain, they are (closed and bounded) intervals in the real line; such intervals are characterized by their starting and ending points.

The relations considered are the 13 possible qualitative relations between two intervals, i.e. they correspond to all possible orderings of two pairs of distinct points in a linear order.

These relations, known as basic relations, constitute a JEPD (Jointly Exhaustive and Pairwise Disjoint) set of relations. Their algebraic structure is similar to the one we have described for points; in particular, there exists inversion and composition operations on the set $\mathbf{B}_2$ of basic relations. The composition of two basic relations takes its values in the set $\mathbf{A}_2$ of subsets of $\mathbf{B}_2$, which is called the set of Allen's interval relations. The operations of inversion and composition extend to $\mathbf{A}_2$ and provide it with an algebraic structure which makes it a relation algebra. Equipped with this structure, $\mathbf{A}_2$ is known as Allen's Interval algebra (or IA).

In this chapter we examine the definition and the basic properties of constraint networks on Allen's Interval algebra. Any finite configuration of intervals can be described by such a network (whose labels are then basic relations). The fundamental problem, known as the consistency problem, is to determine, conversely, whether there are configurations of intervals described by a given constraint network. A necessary condition for consistency is that the network should be algebraically closed, a condition which can be checked in polynomial time. However, the general problem is NP-complete, and the existing algorithms have to use backtracking techniques.

Chapter 2 is devoted to the study of *polynomial subclasses of Allen's Interval algebra*. In fact, in view of the NP-completeness of the general consistency problem, an important part of the research in this domain has been devoted to the determination of subsets of relations known as *tractable* subsets, i.e. for which the consistency problem can be solved in polynomial time, relative to the size of the network. In this case, the question also arises for determining whether the algebraic closure condition provides a sufficient criterion for consistency.

The techniques used for the determination of tractable classes are related to two types of approach: techniques of a geometrical type and techniques of a syntactic nature. In this chapter, we focus on the first, which exploit the possibility of associating two particular structures to the set of basic relations: a partial order structure, which makes it a distributive lattice, and a geometrical structure which reflects the fact that relations can be regarded as regions of the plane.

Using these two representations, we describe three particular subclasses of relations: *convex*, *pointizable* and *pre-convex* relations. The geometrical techniques enable us to show that the criterion of algebraic closure can be used for pre-convex relations, and that these relations constitute the only maximal tractable subset containing all basic relations.

We also show that the class of pre-convex relations of Allen's algebra coincides with the class of ORD-Horn relations, a class originally characterized by syntactic methods. We end this chapter with a description of all the tractable subclasses of Allen's algebra.

Chapter 3 describes the framework of *generalized intervals*, which contains and generalizes a wide class of calculi including the Point calculus, Allen's calculus, as well as Vilain's Point-and-interval calculus [VIL 82].

The encoding used for the relations highlights the lattice structure from which they inherit in a natural manner. This lattice plays a significant role in the study of subclasses of relations. In the same way, the interpretation of the relations in terms of regions of a Euclidean space highlights their geometrical and topological properties (concepts of dimension, closure).

Representing relations in terms of lattices and regions of a Euclidean space makes it possible to develop a geometrical approach to the study of complexity based on defining convex, pointizable, and pre-convex relations, and leads to a general result of polynomial complexity for the *strongly* pre-convex relations. We show that these strongly pre-convex relations are precisely the relations characterized in a syntactic way as ORD-Horn relations, which shows that for generalized intervals the geometrical and syntactic approaches result in two alternative characterizations of the same polynomial subclass.

Chapter 4 continues with the investigation of new *binary qualitative formalisms* by presenting some of the many works devoted to temporal or spatial qualitative formalisms, which have appeared during the last two decades. Some of these formalisms can be considered as variations on Allen's calculus (for example, the Directed interval calculus, which can also be interpreted in a spatial way, as we have done earlier for the Point calculus). A special role in this category is played by the INDU formalism, which is a refinement of Allen's calculus by the introduction of a concept of relative duration, but whose study shows profound differences with Allen's formalism.

The variation can also relate to the nature of the ambient space: for example, the latter can be circular, which makes it possible to develop a formalism called the Cyclic interval calculus.

With regard to those calculi that clearly relate to spatial entities, we will mainly deal with two families: the first is that of "product" formalisms, which use the fact that the n-dimensional Euclidean space is the product of n 1D spaces. This projection-based approach, introduced by Güesgen [GÜS 89], has spawned many variants besides the prototypical "Rectangle calculus", such as the n-point calculi and the n-block calculi.

The 2-point calculus coincides with the standard Cardinal relation calculus, which is concerned with relations between points in the Euclidean plane. Its extension to relations between regions has given rise to a Calculus of cardinal relations between regions which, in addition to the fact that its expressiveness is higher than that of the Rectangle calculus, presents interesting properties. We describe recent results concerning the consistency problem for constraints networks in this formalism.

A second important family of formalisms is concerned with the study of binary topological relations between regions. They are spatial formalisms developed in the context of mereotopological theories. The theory known as RCC (*region connection calculus*) enables us to define a qualitative calculus called RCC–8 whose composition table coincides with that of the formalism developed by Egenhofer under the name of

"9-intersection calculus". We present the basic elements of this formalism here. We end this chapter by describing a proposal, due to Galton [GAL 99], for a discrete analog of this calculus.

Chapter 5 is dedicated to the study of *qualitative formalisms of arity higher than 2*: the relations considered are not binary any more, but of arity higher than 1. Indeed, if the formalisms considered up to now concerned relations between pairs of entities, it appears that the restriction to binary relations is no longer justified in many cases: for example, on a circle, the relation "the points x, y, z are met in this order when one traverses the circle in the counterclockwise direction" is the most natural relation of orientation for points on the circle; it is a ternary relation. Similarly, in space, important concepts such as "x is between y and z" correspond to ternary relations. As a last example, consider spatial entities in the plane: if a global frame of reference is not available, describing the orientation of x with respect to y requires the introduction of a third object z as a reference. We describe some well-known qualitative formalisms using ternary relations: Freksa's Double-cross calculus [FRE 92b], and calculi based on the alignment relation between regions, including the so-called 5-intersection calculus.

Chapter 6 presents what we call *hybrid formalisms*, for which one leaves the strictly qualitative framework to approach aspects of metric type. Indeed, a presentation limited to describing only purely qualitative formalisms would conceal the fact that, right from the early works of the 1980s, an interest in the study of formalisms integrating qualitative knowledge and metric knowledge had emerged. Such an integration is required in many applications, in particular those related to natural language processing. Typical cases in this direction include the works of Kautz and Ladkin [KAU 91] and those of Meiri [MEI 91, MEI 96] at the beginning of the 1990s, which have defined formalisms for reasoning about knowledge that is at the same time qualitative (like, for example, what can be deduced from the assertion "The stay of x precedes that of y") and metric (as in the assertion "The departure of x precedes that of y by 30 to 35 minutes"). This chapter is dedicated to a presentation of some of the main hybrid formalisms in the literature.

Chapter 7 approaches the domain of *fuzzy qualitative reasoning*. In fact, the qualitative formalisms that we have considered up to now make it possible to describe incomplete knowledge (for example, "interval x and interval y are disjoint", therefore one precedes the other, without knowing which one comes first), but they are not adequate to take into account knowledge where this ignorance is weighted (as in the assertion "There is a 90% chance that x precedes y"). Another type of difficulty arises when the entities considered are defined in a fuzzy manner, whether it is in the temporal domain or in the spatial domain: when does the period of the Renaissance start and end? What about Picasso's "Blue period"? Where do the suburbs of a big city end?

A possible approach to treat these questions is provided by fuzzy logic. We have chosen to describe three types of approaches: the use of fuzzy interval relations, Allen's calculus between fuzzy intervals, and an extension of the RCC–8 calculus to relations between fuzzy regions.

A – somewhat sweeping – but striking and encouraging conclusion of the results in this direction is that several complexity results in the "classical" case can be carried over to the fuzzy context.

Chapter 8 revisits the *foundations of the geometrical approach to the study of complexity* in qualitative formalisms, with a view to determining to what extent this approach can be used for general qualitative formalisms. We show that the geometrical representations can be regarded as particular instances of "theoretical" conceptual spaces, in the sense of Gärdenfors [GÄR 04].

Then we examine the case of the INDU calculus and the problem of determining its polynomial classes. We show that the use of syntactic methods on the one hand, and of geometrical methods on the other hand, enables us to characterize different polynomial classes, contrary to what was the case for generalized intervals.

Chapters 9, 10 and 11 focus on determining the models of a formalism, and on studying the structures satisfying a given constraint network. To this end, we use the concept of a *weak representation* of the algebra associated with a formalism. This concept corresponds to the intuitive idea of a "weak" interpretation of the composition table, and generalizes the concept of algebraically closed scenario.

As an introduction to the topic of weak representations, let us examine the case of the Point calculus. A weak representation of the Point algebra is basically a linear order. The models of the Point calculus, in this sense, are all linear orders. In addition, a constraint network which is an algebraically closed scenario is a weak representation of the Point algebra, and there is exactly one linear ordering on the set of vertices of the network such that all the constraints are satisfied. In other words, in this case, a consistent scenario describes one, and only one, qualitative configuration. We will see that a similar result holds in the case of Allen's formalism. On the other hand, the situation is much more complex in many other cases.

Chapter 9 is devoted to the study of *weak representations* and to their relation with the *configurations* that they can describe.

We begin this study with the case of the weak representations of generalized intervals, which includes in particular the Point calculus, Allen's calculus, and the Point-and-interval calculus. We also study the weak representations of the formalisms presented in the preceding chapter that can be considered as product calculi of generalized calculi. This applies in particular to the Cardinal direction calculus, the n-point calculus, and the n-block calculus.

For all these formalisms, we show that we can define a concept of closure in such a way that any weak representation is embedded in a natural way in a closed weak representation, called its closure, and that a closed weak representation is entirely equivalent to a well-defined configuration. For example, in the case of generalized intervals, a weak representation defines a set of implicit bounding points for each generalized interval it contains, and the ordering of all bounding points is completely determined by the weak representation considered.

To prove these results, Ligozat [LIG 90, LIG 01] uses the language of category theory. A basic component of the proof is a construction which, given a weak representation for a calculus based on complex entities, associates to it a weak representation of the Point algebra. This construction can be interpreted as a functor which is left-adjoint to the natural functor associated with the construction of complex entities from points.

Using the same techniques, we also prove that the relation algebras associated to those calculi share the following property with the Point algebra: there is a unique countable representation of this algebra up to isomorphism. This also implies that the first-order theories associated to the algebras are $\aleph_0$ categorical.

Chapter 10 deals with the *weak representations* of RCC–8. It describes in particular recent research which made it possible to clarify the following question: to what extent does a weak representation of RCC–8 correspond to a representation of the algebra, i.e. how far can the composition table be interpreted in an extensional manner (that is, as giving necessary and sufficient conditions)? It turns out that, if natural interpretations of RCC–8 (closed circles of the plane for example) constitute representations, we cannot find an RCC model which has this property. Results of Li *et al.* [LI 03b] make it possible to characterize for each entry of the composite table its "defect" of extensionality.

The description of the models of RCC was largely facilitated by its reformulation in terms of connection algebras. It has been of great help for determining which among them are associated with topological spaces. Using a generalization of the concept of connection algebra, one can moreover study the construction of finite or countable models.

As already mentioned, a qualitative formalism defines a Boolean algebra with operators, which in many classical cases, including that of Allen's calculus, is a relation algebra. However, the example of the INDU calculus, whose algebra is not associative, shows that more general algebras have to be considered. On the other hand, the relation algebra associated with a calculus has only a loose relationship with the properties of the constraint networks, for which the properties of the interpretation domain have a prime importance. In the case of RCC–8, the entities whose relations one describes can be of very varied nature. In general, with regard to the relations between the various concepts of consistence, the domain of interpretation intervenes in a fundamental way:

for example, an algebraically closed scenario on the Point algebra is consistent for an interpretation in terms of integers, but it is not 3-consistent.

Chapter 11 proposes an answer to the general question: *what is a qualitative formalism?*

The main result is that a qualitative formalism is built on the basis of what we call a partition scheme. For example, the real line, together with the three relations $<, >$, and eq, define such a partition scheme.

A partition scheme naturally gives rise to a Boolean algebra equipped with operations of inversion and composition (known as weak composition) which make it a non-associative algebra (a concept which generalizes that of relation algebra). The map which, to each basic relation symbol, associates the corresponding relation of the partition scheme, constitutes a weak representation of this algebra. In this way we get a very general definition answering our initial question: a qualitative formalism is defined as non-associative algebra together with a weak representation of it.

Using once more the language of category theory, one sees that the consistency condition for a network corresponds to the existence of a morphism between two objects in the category of weak representations: the network, on the one hand and, on the other hand, the weak representation which defines the formalism.

We end this chapter by a discussion of the various notions of consistency in a qualitative formalism: besides "mere" consistency, definable in terms of the existence of a morphism, we have to consider properties such as k-consistency (possibility of extension to k variables of an instantiation of $(k-1)$ variables), strong k-consistency, and global consistency.

Chapter 12 presents *an alternative approach to the study of the complexity of qualitative constraint-based formalisms*. In the preceding chapters we saw how the use of algebraic techniques made it possible to clarify the nature of the formalisms and in certain cases to describe their complexity properties. In this use from the algebraic point of view, the main role is played by the algebra of basic relations of the formalism.

Another aspect of the algebraic study of satisfaction problems was highlighted by the works of Krokhin *et al.* [KRO 03]: the complexity of a constraint language is directly related to the properties of what is called its associated *operation clones*. In this context, relational structures are considered, which consist of a relational signature together with an interpretation of this signature. For example, the Point calculus can be considered as associated to the signature containing the eight symbols corresponding to the disjunctions of $<, >$, and eq, and the usual interpretations of these symbols as binary relations on $\mathbb{Q}$. The operations in question are the operations on $\mathbb{Q}$ which preserve these relations, and, in an intuitive manner, the complexity is correlated with the existence of certain types of operations. Moreover, these methods make it possible to study the conditions under which k-consistency for a certain k guarantees global consistency.

The consideration of relations of various arities, other than those of the basic relations, can be compared to the use of disjunctive constraints, using constraint families of which the reduced complexity is known in order to combine them into constraints which, under certain assumptions, preserve this reduced complexity. We describe these techniques, as well as their use by the refinement method, which allows us to a certain extent to automate the discovery of polynomial subclasses. These techniques make it possible in particular to give alternative proofs of known results for Allen's Interval algebra, the RCC–8 algebra, and the Point-and-interval algebra.

Chapter 13 is devoted to some aspects of *the use of modal languages for spatial reasoning*. A key element in proving the consistency of weak representations of RCC–8 is the use of an interpretation of RCC–8 in terms of modal logic. The links between the modal logic S4 and topology have been known and used right from the 1940s, and a fundamental result of McKinsey and Tarski [MCK 44] asserts that S4 is in a very precise way the modal logic of topology. We recall this result, and describe some recent research which uses the connection with the modal logics to explore questions of expressiveness, as well as extension of modal logics incorporating notions such as convexity.

Chapter 14 departs from the domain of theory. It provides a *list of applications* of the techniques described in the book in various domains. It also contains short descriptions of *software libraries* which have been developed with the aim of providing researchers with generic tools for qualitative reasoning.

The term of application can be understood, in our opinion, in at least three different ways:

– on the one hand, in terms of transposition of a domain of research in another. For example, the RCC–8 reasoning techniques for the spatial domain can be used in a "space" which is a conceptual space, and the relations considered will be of relations of topological type between concepts. The application, in this case, remains on the same theoretical level;

– on the other hand, we could use the term of modular applications of spatio-temporal reasoning to refer to the integration of "ready-for-use" spatio-temporal modules in various kinds of systems: spatial or temporal database management systems, planning systems;

– finally, a third type of application corresponds to systems in which the reasoning on time and/or space is closely integrated into the system itself. Many examples are provided by systems incorporating natural language processing components, such as components providing event recognition or event sequencing in textual sources.

In this chapter, rather than making a choice of applications which could only be arbitrary, we simply provide the reader with a substantial set of bibliographical references.

As for software libraries, we present three of them: QAT, SparQ, and GQR.

Chapter 15 presents *research directions* which appear important and promising to us. We retain three of them:

– the first relates to the problem of combining several qualitative calculi on the same domain: an example is the INDU calculus, which can be considered as a combination of Allen's calculus and of the Point calculus. Two general questions arise in this context: first, determining to what extent consistency in the composed calculus can be deduced from consistency in each component; secondly, determining the complexity of the consistency problem for the composed calculus;

– the second is that of the elaboration of spatio-temporal calculi, either as full-fledged calculi (the basic entities are then elements of space-time), or as combinations of spatial and temporal calculi. In this last case, the general problems of combination also arise;

– the third is related the development of efficient methods for solving qualitative constraint satisfaction problems. The question is the following: can one hope to increase efficiency by translating the qualitative problems in terms of formalisms for which one currently has very powerful techniques, such as finite CSPs or the SAT problem?

Appendices

For the convenience of the reader, we give in the appendices short reviews of three domains, so that the reader can refer to them while reading this book:

– appendix A: basic concepts and results of topology;

– appendix B: elements of universal algebra and of category theory;

– appendix C: disjunctive linear relations (DLRs).

A reading grid of the book

It may be useful to view the project represented by this book in the general perspective of the elaboration and the study of formalisms for representation and reasoning.

Such an undertaking typically comprises a certain number of stages which will be addressed in the course of the book:

1) defining the representation language; here, the language considered will be predominantly the language of constraint networks;

2) studying the expressiveness of this language;

3) defining reasoning techniques; in the present case, the main reasoning techniques are based on constraint propagation;

4) characterizing the reasoning complexity: are the main problems decidable, solvable in polynomial time? What are the possible compromises in terms of expressivity versus complexity?

5) elaborating effective algorithms, and studying their theoretical and empirical properties;

6) studying the models of the formalism: having been devised to represent a certain state of affairs (the expected model), can the formalism have other models, and if such is the case, can one give a description of these alternative models?

Acknowledgments

During the AAAI, IJCAI, and ECAI conferences of these last decades, we organized with Frank Anger, Rita Rodriguez, and Hans Guesgen, a series of "workshops" dealing with the qualitative reasoning on time and space. I owe to these colleagues, to their support and their friendship, the idea of writing a book which would take stock of the advancement of research on qualitative spatial and temporal reasoning.

The European network "SPACENET", of which my laboratory, the LIMSI, was a participant, was a great opportunity for promoting research on space cognition and circulating ideas and projects in the European context. Many thanks to Tony Cohn, Christian Freksa, and to all those who took part in this network.

I would also like to thank the many colleagues with whom I had the chance to have many stimulating exchanges, in particular: Philippe Balbiani, Peter van Beek, Christian Bessière, Brandon Bennett, Maroua Bouzid, Myriam Bras, Christophe Claramunt, Jean-François Condotta, Ivo Düntsch, Geoffrey Edwards, Anthony Galton, Alfonso Gerevini, Amar Isli, Robert Jeansoulin, Lina Khatib, Peter Ladkin, Florence Le Ber, Sanjiang Li, Debasis Mitra, Robert Morris, Till Mossakowski, Bernard Moulin, Amitabha Mukerjee, Bernhard Nebel, Odile Papini, Jochen Renz, Christoph Schlieder, John Stell, Kathleen Stewart Hornsby, Zygmunt Vetulani, Laure Vieu, Stefan Wölfl.

Thanks also to Patrick Paroubek, who gave the initial impulse to write this book, then followed the writing constantly.

The throes of writing a book are undoubtedly a minor nuisance compared with those that the author's entourage must undergo. I must thus particularly thank my family for their support and understanding during that time.

Chapter 1

Allen's Calculus

1.1. Introduction

The story of qualitative temporal and spatial reasoning begins with the publication of Allen's 1983 paper [ALL 83]. In this chapter and the following one, we give an introduction to Allen's calculus, and take stock of the current state of knowledge on the subject. The past 25 years have witnessed a steady development of results and techniques for reasoning about time and space in a qualitative way. For a view of the state of knowledge on this subject by the late 1980s, the reader can refer to [BES 89b].

1.1.1. *"The mystery of the dark room"*

In [ALL 83], Allen introduces his calculus by using the following anecdote:

1) John was not in the room when I touched the switch to turn on the light;

2) But John was in the room later while the light went out.

1.1.1.1. *Representation*

These two sentences refer to three events, which in turn correspond to three time intervals: Let S (for "switch") be a short time interval during which the switch was pressed, an interval L (for "light") corresponding to the period when the light was on, and an interval R (for "room") during which John was present in the room. Moreover, the two sentences provide qualitative (qualitative, i.e. not involving measurements) information about the relationships between the three time intervals I, L, and J.

What indeed can we deduce from these sentences?

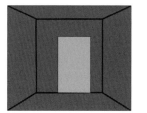

Figure 1.1. *When I pressed the switch . . .*

According to sentence 1, there is no overlapping of the time intervals S and R. Moreover, our common sense informs us that the light was on in the room at a time soon after I started to press the switch and also not later than the time when I released the pressure on the switch.

If we consider all possible relations between two intervals based only on the relative orderings of their starting and ending points, we get the 13 relations represented in Figure 1.2. These 13 relations are called Allen's *basic relations*.

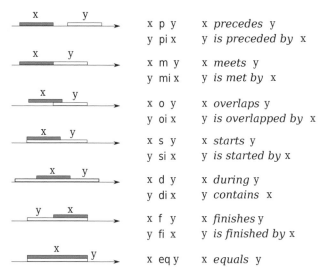

Figure 1.2. *Allen's 13 basic relations between interval x (in gray) and interval y (in white)*

The information obtained from sentence 1 of Allen's example is not sufficiently precise to be expressed in terms of Allen's basic relations, but only in terms of disjunctions between these relations. These disjunctions are noted as subsets of the basic relations. For example, from sentence 1, we can deduce that the relationship between S and R corresponds to the set $\{p, m, pi, mi\}$ (expressing the fact that I and J are disjoint), and that the relationship between S and L corresponds to the set $\{o, m\}$.

In a similar manner, from sentence 2, we can deduce that the relationship between L and R corresponds to the set $\{o, s, d\}$.

More precisely, we will express our knowledge about the existing relations in terms of constraint networks. In our case, we will consider a network with three nodes representing the time intervals S, L, and R, and arcs labeled by subsets of Allen's basic relations to express the constraints between these intervals. Hence we get the following labels:

- on the arc (S, R), the constraint $\{p, m, pi, mi\}$;
- on the arc (S, L), the constraint $\{m, o\}$;
- on the arc (L, R), the constraint $\{o, s, d\}$.

Figure 1.3 (a) represents the network thus obtained.

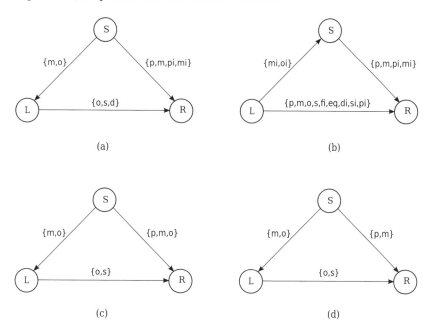

Figure 1.3. *The dark room: initial constraints between the three intervals S, L, and R (a); constraint on the arc (L, R) by composition (b); after intersection, the constraint on (L, R) is $\{o, s\}$; by composition, $\{p, m, o\}$ on (S, R) is obtained (c); after intersection with the initial constraint on (S, R) (d)*

1.1.1.2. *Reasoning: constraint propagation*

In a manner similar to what we discussed for the time point calculus in the Introduction, two natural operations are possible for Allen's relations: the inversion operation and the composition operation. For example, by inverting the constraint $\{m, o\}$ on the arc (S, L), the constraint $\{mi, oi\}$ on the arc (L, S) can be deduced. We now have a set of possible basic relations between L and S, and another set of possible basic relationships between S and R. The operation of composition will allow us to infer a set of possible relations between L and R from this knowledge. The results of the composition of two basic relations can be tabulated, resulting in a table called the *composition table* of Allen's calculus (originally called *table of transitivity* by Allen). Using the composition table, we get the constraint $\{p, m, o, s, fi, eq, di, si, pi\}$ on the arc (L,R) (Figure 1.3 (b)). We already had the constraint $\{o, s, d\}$, so that intersecting the two constraints results in the set $\{o, s\}$ on the arc (L, R) (Figure 1.3 (c)) As the label of arc (L, R) has changed, we can use this to deduce that the relationship between S and R must be in the set $\{p, m, o\}$, by composition of $\{m, o\}$ on the arc (S, L) and by that of $\{o, s\}$ on the arc (L, R). We can finally obtain $\{p, m\}$ by intersection with the constraint $\{p, m, pi, mi\}$. The network thus obtained cannot be simplified further by applying inversion or composition, as shown in Figure 1.3 (d).

1.1.1.3. *Going further*

At this juncture, the method of constraint propagation does not provide any further information about the possible relationships between the three intervals. We still have to decide whether there exist configurations of intervals as described by sentences 1 and 2. However, constraint propagation has allowed us to restrict the scope of research: we may replace the network (a) of Figure 1.3 by the network (d) without changing the problem.

In order to proceed, we will now examine each one of the various possible cases. If the relation on the arc (S, L) is o, then oi is on the arc (L, S), and we can deduce the constraint $\{p, m, o, fi, di\}$ on the arc (L, R) by composition and thus deduce the constraint $\{o\}$ by intersection with the constraint $\{o, s\}$. There exist two "scenarios", or configurations, verifying the constraints. They are represented in (a) and (b) of Figure 1.4.

Since we have already found two scenarios, we now know that the constraints can indeed be satisfied. If we are interested in determining all possible scenarios, we proceed with the examination of other possibilities. Consider the case where the relation on the arc (S, L) is m. In that case, constraint propagation does not bring any new knowledge, and we have to consider each of the basic relations on the arc (S,R) successively. If the constraint on the arc (S, R) is $\{m\}$, then the composition of mi with m is $\{s; eq, si\}$, and the only possible relation on the arc (L, R) is s, which corresponds to the configuration (c) of Figure 1.4.

Finally, if the constraint on the arc (S, R) is $\{p\}$, the fact that the composition of mi with p is $\{p, m, o, fi, di\}$ excludes s from the constraint on (L, R). This configuration is represented in part (d) of Figure 1.4.

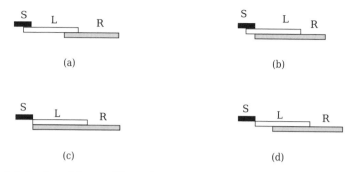

Figure 1.4. *Review of the possible configurations according to the relationship between S and L: relation o in cases (a) and (b), and relation m in cases (c) and (d)*

1.1.2. Contributions of Allen's formalism

Allen's approach introduces several original points into the domain of qualitative temporal reasoning:

– the choice of time intervals, rather than of time points, as basic temporal entities;

– the introduction of 13 basic relations which constitute a partition of the set of possible relations between pairs of (closed and finite) intervals on the real number line;

– the ability to represent partial knowledge (for example, by considering the fact that two time intervals are disjoint, irrespective of the precedence among the intervals), using disjunctions of basic relations;

– the use of the constraint propagation methods which were successfully introduced by Waltz [WAL 75] for image recognition;

– the adaptation for constraint propagation of algorithms used in the field of CSPs (Constraint Satisfaction Problems).

In other words, Allen's formalism provides the following:

– a language to represent qualitative temporal knowledge, including incomplete knowledge;

– a reasoning mechanism to infer the resulting knowledge which is not explicitly represented;

– efficient algorithms to implement the mechanisms of deduction.

With the last point, we touch upon the well-known opposition in the field of knowledge representation between, on the one hand, the expressivity of formalism and on the other hand, the possibility of an effective automatic processing. This opposition has been eloquently described in an article by Brachman and Levesque [BRA 85]. In fact, after 1983, a significant part of the work consisted of exploring in a precise manner the borderline between expressiveness and what is called "tractability", i.e. the existence of polynomial-time algorithms.

1.2. Allen's interval relations

1.2.1. *Basic relations*

1.2.1.1. *Definition of the basic relations*

To make things precise, let us consider time as represented by the real number line $\mathbb{R}$. A *time interval* A time interval, in Allen's sense, is a pair $x = (x_1, x_2)$ of real numbers, where $x_1 < x_2 : x_1$ is the upper limit of x, and x_2 is its lower limit[1].

We will only consider qualitative relationships between pairs of time intervals. More precisely, a pair of intervals being given, we will only consider the way in which their limits are ordered. For example, if the upper limit x_2 of x strictly precedes the lower value y_1 of y, it implies that x precedes y, i.e. interval x entirely precedes interval y. In this case, the relationship between x and y is denoted as p (for *precedence*)[2]. Conversely, the relationship between y and x is the inverse of precedence, denoted as[3] pi.

Similarly, if the upper limit of x coincides with the lower limit of y, then x *meets* y, and the corresponding relation is denoted as m.

In this manner, the 13 relations known as *basic relations* are obtained. Apart from the relation of equality (when the two intervals coincide), the remaining relations can be ordered as pairs of relations inverse to each other.

We refer the reader to Table 1.1 and Figure 1.2 which summarize the above discussion.

We note that for each basic relation other than the equality relation eq, the notation adopted makes explicit the correspondence between pairs of inverse relations such as p and pi.

1.2.1.2. *The JEPD property*

An important property of the 13 basic relations is that they constitute a *partition* of the set of all the possible relationships between two intervals. In less mathematical terms, this means that, given two intervals, there exists exactly one basic relation that

---

1 That means, in particular, that we do not consider intervals of infinite duration, and that we do not make the usual distinction between open, closed and half-open intervals. All the intervals are bounded and closed.

2 Also denoted as b (before), or $<$.

3 Also denoted as a (after), or $>$.

x p y	x pi y	$x_1 < x_2 < y_1 < y_2$
x m y	x mi y	$x_1 < x_2 = y_1 < y_2$
x o y	x oi y	$x_1 < y_1 < x_2 < y_2$
x s y	x si y	$x_1 = y_1 < x_2 < y_2$
x d y	x di y	$y_1 < x_1 < x_2 < y_2$
x f y	x fi y	$y_1 < x_1 < x_2 = y_2$
	x eq y	$x_1 = x_2$ and $y_1 = y_2$

Table 1.1. *Definition of Allen's basic relations between an interval*
$x = (x_1, x_2)$ *and an interval* $y = (y_1, y_2)$

holds between these two intervals. Of course, this property is a consequence of the fact that two time points of the real line either coincide, or one of them precedes the other one.

As already mentioned in the Introduction, this property is generally called the *JEPD* property in the literature: the 13 relations are exhaustive (*Jointly Exhaustive*) and pairwise incompatible (*Pairwise Disjoint*)[4].

1.2.2. *Disjunctive relations*

The basic relations enable us to express "precise" information between temporal intervals. For example, the fact that x starts y, and that y is strictly contained in z, can be written as: x s y and x d z.

In addition, we can introduce the possibility of representing certain vague information: the fact that x and y are disjoint, for example, which is the disjunction of x p y and x pi y, can be written as x $\{p, pi\}$ y, by introducing sets of basic relations which are interpreted in a disjunctive manner: xRy, where R is a set of basic relations, signifies that for some basic relation $r \in R$, we have $x r y$.

In particular, if R is the set of all basic relations (whose union is the *universal* relation, which by definition contains all the pairs of intervals), we can express that the position of x relative to y is completely unknown. If R is the empty set, a contradiction can be expressed.

DEFINITION 1.1.– A disjunctive relation, *or in short a* relation, *is a subset of the set of all the 13 basic relations.*

---

4 Let us note that JEPD is also an acronym used in the biblical exegesis literature: Following work on the origins of the Bible in the 19th Century, historians have adopted the practice of referring to the J (Jehovah), E (Elohim), P (Priestly), and D (Deuteronomic) sources. It would seem that the fact that the two acronyms are the same is entirely coincidental!

We will denote by B_2 the set of basic relations, and by A_2 the set of disjunctive relations.

When no ambiguity is possible, we will consider basic relations as particular cases of disjunctive relations, i.e. we will consider B_2 as a subset of A_2.

1.3. Constraint networks

1.3.1. *Definition*

Knowledge, in Allen's language, is most often expressed in terms of *constraint networks*, and not in logical terms: in this kind of representation by labeled directed graphs, the vertices of the graph represent intervals, and the arcs are labeled by Allen's relations. In general, the arcs labeled by the universal relation are not represented.

DEFINITION 1.2.– *A temporal constraint network for Allen's calculus is a pair $\mathcal{N} = (N, C)$, where N is a finite set of vertices (or nodes), and $N: N \times N \to \mathbf{A}_2$ a map which to each pair (i, j) of vertices associates an element $C(i, j)$ of $\mathbf{A}_2$. The Allen relation $C(i, j)$ is called the* constraint *on the arc* (i, j).

EXAMPLE 1.1.– The network in Figure 1.5 represents information on four intervals, where the four intervals correspond to four processes p_1, p_2, p_3, and p_4, for which we know that:

– p_2 starts after p_1 begins;

– p_1 happens during p_3;

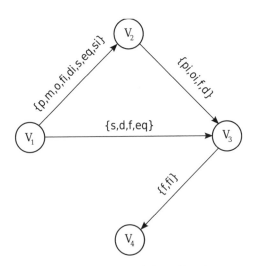

Figure 1.5. *A constraint network describing four processes*

– p_3 starts before p_2 and its end does not coincide with the start of p_2;

– p_4 ends p_3, or p_3 ends p_4.

A network of constraints on Allen's algebra therefore represents knowledge about a set of intervals which constitutes what is known as a *configuration* of intervals:

DEFINITION 1.3.– A configuration of intervals *is a finite set of (bounded and closed) intervals*.

Given a configuration of intervals, we can use Allen's language to associate to it a qualitative description in terms of a constraint network whose labels are basic relations.

EXAMPLE 1.2.– The configuration of four intervals, as shown in Figure 1.6, has an associated network of constraints which is represented in the upper part of this figure.

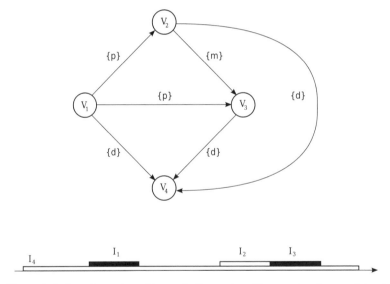

Figure 1.6. *A configuration of intervals (bottom) and its associated network (top)*

By convention, in the graphical representation of a constraint network, we assume that, if the arc (i, j) is labeled by $C(i, j)$, then the arc (j, i) is labeled by the inverse relation $C(i, j)^{-1}$, and that the arcs (i, i) have the relation eq as an associated constraint. In other words, we assume, unless otherwise specified, that the network represented is normalized:

DEFINITION 1.4.– *A network of constraints is normalized if:*

– *for any* $i \in N, C(i, j) =$ eq;

– *for any pair* $(i, j) \in N \times N, C(j, i) = C(i, j)^{-1}$.

1.3.2. *Expressiveness*

1.3.2.1. *Point networks*

It will be informative at this juncture to consider a similar but simpler situation, which leads us to define the Time Point calculus.

Let us consider the real line $\mathbb{R}$ again as a model of the flow of time. The elements of this line represent (time) points.

Any pair of points of the line is contained in one, and only one, of the following three relations:

- the relation $<$, defined by $< = \{(x,y) \in \mathbb{R} \times \mathbb{R} | x < y\}$;
- the relation $>$, defined by $> = \{(x,y) \in \mathbb{R} \times \mathbb{R} | x > y\}$;
- the relation eq, defined by $\text{eq} = \{(x,y) \in \mathbb{R} \times \mathbb{R} | x = y\}$.

We can thus consider the three relations $<, >$, and eq as the three basic relations of a qualitative formalism. Here, most of the disjunctive relations have conventional symbols associated with them: the relation $\{<, \text{eq}\}$ is denoted by $\leq$, the relation $\{>, \text{eq}\}$ is denoted by $\geq$, and $\{<, >\}$ is denoted by $\neq$.

The composition of $<$ with $>$, and that of $>$ with $<$ coincide with the universal relation, i.e. the union of $<, >$, and eq. Again we note that this is a full equality of sets, and not just a containment. The exercise is worth doing at least once, so we do it now.

PROPOSITION 1.1.– *We have* $(< \circ >) = (> \circ <) = \{<, \text{eq}, >\}$.

Let us assume that $x < y$ and $y > z$. This condition is consistent with $z < x, z = x$, and z between x and y, and therefore $z > x$. Consequently, $(< \circ >) \subseteq \{<, \text{eq}, >\}$ (i.e. the universal relation is required). Conversely, let us verify that $< \subseteq (< \circ >)$: if $x < y$, it is sufficient to consider z such that $z > y$ for $x < z$ and $z > y$. Let us verify in a similar manner that $> \subseteq (< \circ >)$ and that $\text{eq} \subseteq (< \circ >)$. Notice that we only use the fact that we can always find a point between two distinct points (property of density), and that given any point, there exists one point which precedes it and one point which follows it.

In addition, we can verify that, for the same reasons, we have not only the inclusions of elements $(< \circ <) \subseteq <$ and $(> \circ >) \subseteq >$, which express the transitivity of $<$ and $>$, but also $(< \circ <) = <$ and $(> \circ >) = <$. Again, this follows from the density property.

It is convenient to represent the composition of the basic relations by a composition table which is by definition a two-way table, where each row and each column correspond to a basic relation. The entry in the row corresponding to r and the column corresponding to s, is the composition $(r \circ s)$ of the two relations r and s.

	<	eq	>
<	<	<	1
eq	<	eq	>
>	1	>	>

Table 1.2. *Composition table of the point algebra*

The composition table of the Point algebra comprises nine entries (Table 1.2), where 1 denotes the universal relation.

Similar to the case of Allen's algebra, we can also consider constraint networks on the Point algebra.

We will now see that some of Allen's networks are equivalent to point networks.

1.3.2.2. *Pointizable relations*

First, any constraint network on Allen's algebra can be translated in terms of constraints on the ends of the intervals considered: we associate to each vertex V of the network a pair of points (V_1, V_2) which respectively represent the beginning and end of the interval V, with the constraint $V_1 < V_2$, and then translate the relations of Allen in terms of constraints on the beginnings and ends of the intervals using (Table 1.1). However, the formula thus obtained cannot in general be represented as a point network.

EXAMPLE 1.3.– Let us consider a network of two intervals x and y, with the constraint $x\{\mathsf{p}, \mathsf{pi}\}y$. If $x = (x_1, x_2)$ and $y = (y_1, y_2)$, the network results in the logical formula $x_1 < x_2 \wedge y_1 < y_2 \wedge (x_2 < y_1 \vee y_2 < x_1)$. This formula is equivalent to the formula $(x_1 < x_2 \wedge y_1 < y_2 \wedge x_2 < y_1) \vee (x_1 < x_2 \wedge y_1 < y_2 \wedge y_2 < x_1)$, but the latter cannot be expressed in terms of a single network on the point algebra.

EXAMPLE 1.4.– Let us consider a network of two intervals x and y, as before, with the constraint $x\{\mathsf{p}, \mathsf{o}, \mathsf{s}, \mathsf{di}, \mathsf{si}\}y$. This formula is equivalent to the formula $(x_1 < x_2 \wedge y_1 < y_2 \wedge x_1 \leq y_1 \wedge x_2 \neq y_1 \wedge x_2 \neq y_2)$. In this case, the network of intervals is equivalent to a point network with four vertices (Figure 1.7).

Those among Allen's relations which can be expressed in terms of constraint networks over the point algebra are called pointizable relations.

DEFINITION 1.5.– *A relation of Allen is* pointizable *if it can be defined by a point network on the starting and ending points of the intervals involved.*

The relation $\{\mathsf{p}, \mathsf{o}, \mathsf{s}, \mathsf{di}, \mathsf{si}\}$ is therefore pointizable, whereas the relation $\{\mathsf{p}, \mathsf{pi}\}$ is not.

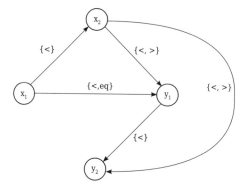

Figure 1.7. *A point network which is equivalent to the interval network* $x\{\mathsf{p, o, s, di, si}\}y$

The pointizable relations are defined in [VIL 86], and are discussed explicitly by Ladkin and Maddux [LAD 88, LAD 94]. There are 167 pointizable relations. We will further see (proposition 2.5) an extremely simple characterization of these relations.

1.3.2.3. *Expressiveness properties compared*

The language of Allen's networks therefore makes it possible to express on a set of intervals some constraints which could not be expressed in terms of point networks corresponding to the beginnings and ends of these intervals. In that sense, Allen's language is strictly more expressive than the language of time points. Allen's relations allow us to express an additional degree of uncertainty through disjunctive relations. For example, we can express the fact that two intervals x and y do not have common subintervals, by using the relation $\{\mathsf{p, m, pi, mi}\}$ on the arc (x, y).

However the possibility of representing disjunctions offered by Allen's language is not sufficient to represent all kinds of qualitative knowledge. For instance the fact that an interval x is situated between two intervals y and z can only be expressed by writing that either $y\mathsf{p}x$ and $x\mathsf{p}z$, or $z\mathsf{p}x$ and $x\mathsf{p}y$, which cannot be reduced to a conjunction using Allen's disjunctive relations.

1.3.2.4. *Expressiveness and complexity*

A general theme in the domain of Knowledge Representation is the search for a compromise between expressiveness and ease of processing. The problem of determining whether a point network corresponds to a configuration can be solved in polynomial time, for example, by using the Van Beek CSPAN algorithm of Van Beek [BEE 90a]. This is no longer true for the similar problem for constraint networks on Allen's algebra: Vilain and Kautz [VIL 86, VIL 89] showed that this problem is a NP-complete problem. The language restricted to pointizable relations is equivalent to a sublanguage of the language of points, which implies that for these relations this problem can be solved in polynomial time. However, to restrict oneself to pointizable relations implies a severe limitation of the expressiveness: since there are 13 basic relations, there are in total $2^{13} = 8,192$ relations in Allen's algebra whereas there are only 167 pointizable relations.

We will further discuss (section 2.2.7) the work of Nebel and Bürckert [NEB 94b, NEB 95] which describes precise conditions for the consistency problem to remain polynomial.

1.3.3. *Consistency*

Any configuration of intervals is associated with a constraint network. Conversely, given a constraint network, the question of whether the network is associated with a configuration (in which case, it is associated with an infinity of configurations that are qualitatively indistinguishable) arises. This is the fundamental concept of *consistency*:

DEFINITION 1.6.– *A network of constraints is* consistent *if there exists a configuration of intervals such that the network is associated to it.*

Clearly, there exist constraint networks that are not consistent. For example, a network of three vertices V_1, V_2, V_3, with the constraints $C(V_1, V_2) = \{p\}, C(V_2, V_3) = \{p\}$, and $C(V_1, V_3) = \{pi\}$ is not consistent: in any configuration where V_1 precedes V_2 and V_2 precedes V_3, V_1 will precede V_3, which is not consistent with the requirement that V_1 should follow V_3.

In fact, much of the theoretical research concerning Allen's formalism (and more generally, other qualitative formalisms) has been devoted to various aspects of the following question: how can we efficiently decide if a given network of constraints is consistent or not?

It is, in any case, intuitively plausible that, given a network in which all the labels are basic relations, we can decide whether this network is consistent or not. This is indeed the case, and we will further discuss (section 1.5.1) one of the algorithms which can be used for this purpose. The difficulty in the general case, for an arbitrary network labeled by disjunctions of basic relations, is that deciding whether it is consistent implies considering all basic relations in the disjunctive relations, which leads to an exponential growth of the number of basic networks to be considered.

We will discuss all these points in a precise manner further in the chapter.

A configuration of intervals is described by a normalized constraint network (Definition 1.4) in which moreover all the labels are basic relations. Such a network is called a *scenario*. In general, a network satisfying the last condition is called an *atomic network*[5].

_____

5 It would be more logical to call it a basic network.

DEFINITION 1.7.– *A constraint network* (N, C) *is* atomic *if for any pair* $(i, j) \in N \times N$ *the constraint* $C(i, j)$ *is a basic relation. A* scenario *is a normalized atomic network.*

NOTE.– When representing a network of constraints, it is common not to represent the arcs on which the constraint is the universal constraint, since, strictly speaking, in this case there is no constraint to be satisfied. It is therefore important to make the difference between atomic networks (all arcs are labeled by basic relations) and networks whose explicitly labeled arcs are labeled by basic relations.

1.3.3.1. *From configurations to networks*

Let us recall that a configuration is a finite set of intervals, i.e. of pairs $x^i = (x_1^i, x_2^i)$, with $x_1^i < x_2^i, i = 1, \ldots n$.

Given a configuration of n intervals, we can associate with it a network of constraints in the following natural manner: this network has n vertices $X_1, \ldots X_n$. For any pair $i, j, 1 \leq i, j \leq n$, the pair (x^i, x^j) is in one and only one of Allen's basic relations, say $R_{i,j}$. We define the associated network as the network with vertices $X_1, \ldots X_n$ and, for each pair (i, j), the constraint $C(i, j) = R_{i,j}$ on the arc (X_i, X_j).

The network obtained in this way is obviously atomic and normalized. We will say that it describes the configuration.

1.3.3.2. *From networks to configurations*

Conversely, given a network of constraints (N, C), what are the conditions under which it can describe a configuration? Consider an arbitrary network. Let us denote by *Int*($\mathbb{R}$ the set of (bounded and closed) intervals of $\mathbb{R}$.

DEFINITION 1.8.– *An* instantiation *of a network* (N, C) *is a map* $m : N \rightarrow Int(\mathbb{R})$.

An instantiation thus defines a configuration of intervals.

DEFINITION 1.9.– *An instantiation* m *of a network* (N, C) satisfies *the network, or is a* solution *of the network if for any pair* $(i, j)?N \times N$, *the pair of intervals* $(m(i), m(j))$ *is in one of the basic relations contained in* $C(i, j)$.

EXAMPLE 1.5.– Let us consider the normalized network shown in Figure 1.8, which has four vertices $V_1, \ldots V_4$, such that $C(V_1, V_2) = \{si, d\}, C(V_1, V_3) = \{di, mi\}$, $C(V_1, V_4) = \{f, fi\}, C(V_2, V_3) = \{m, s, d\}, C(V_2, V_4) = \{p, m\}$, and $C(V_3, V_4) = \{s, oi\}$.

The instantiation $m(V_1) = [0, 4]$, $m(V_2) = [0, 2]$, $m(V_3) = [2, 3]$, and $m(V_4) = [2, 4]$ satisfies this network.

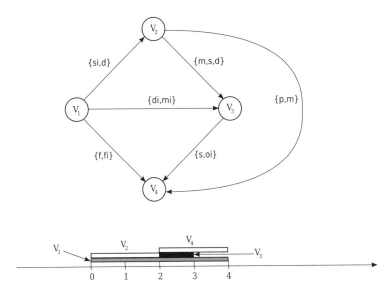

Figure 1.8. *A network and an instantiation which satisfies it*

The definition of network consistency (Definition 1.6) can be reformulated in a more precise manner as follows:

DEFINITION 1.10.– *A network is* consistent *if there is an instantiation which satisfies it.*

1.3.3.3. *Refinements, minimal network*

DEFINITION 1.11.– *A network* (N, C') *is a* refinement *of a network* (N, C) *if, for any* $(i, j) \in N \times N$, *the relation* $C'(i, j)$ *is a subset of* $C(i, j)$.

A consistent network is thus a network that admits a refinement which is a consistent scenario (atomic and normalized subnetwork).

EXAMPLE 1.6.– Let us consider Example 1.1 (Figure 1.5) again. A refinement of the original network is the scenario depicted on the right side (b) of Figure 1.9. This scenario is consistent, as shown by the instantiation m represented in the bottom (c) of Figure 1.9.

DEFINITION 1.12.– *A network* (N, C) *is* minimal *if, for any* $(i, j) \in N \times N$ *and for any basic relation* $r \in C(i, j)$, *there exists a refinement* (N, C') *which is a consistent scenario such that* $C'(i, j) = \{r\}$.

Informally speaking, a minimal network is a consistent network in which all the basic relations labeling the arcs are necessary, since each one of them appears in one of the instantiations satisfying the network. If we consider the network as a system of

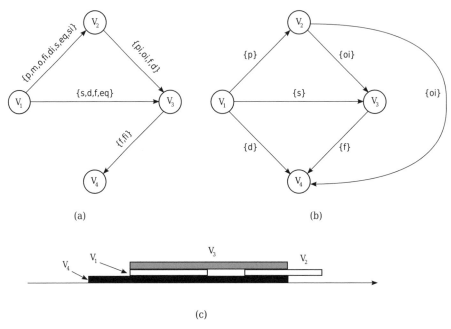

Figure 1.9. *A network of constraints (a), a refinement which is a scenario (b), and an instantiation of the scenario (c)*

equations, then a minimal network is an "economic" form of the system, in which all the symbols used are useful.

The following result is due to Montanari [MON 74]:

PROPOSITION 1.2.– *Any consistent network has a refinement which is minimal; this minimal refinement is unique.*

EXAMPLE 1.7.– Let us consider the network on the left-hand side of Figure 1.10. The network on the right-hand side is a refinement of this network, and constitutes the associated minimal network. In fact, it can be easily verified that each basic relation is part of a consistent scenario. Let us check this for the basic relations in $C(V_1, V_2)$:

– let us choose the relation s in $C(V1, V2)$, m in $C(V1, V3)$, and o in $C(V2, V4)$. The resulting scenario is a consistent refinement;

– let us choose the relation f in $C(V1, V2)$, f in $C(V1, V3)$, and o in $C(V2, V4)$. The resulting scenario is a consistent refinement;

– let us choose the relation eq in $C(V1, V2)$, p in $C(V1, V3)$, and o in $C(V2, V3)$. The resulting scenario is a consistent refinement.

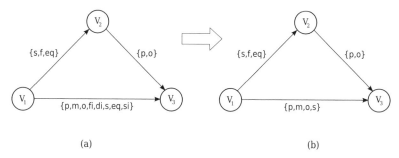

Figure 1.10. *A network of constraints (a) and its minimal network (b)*

1.3.3.4. *Fundamental problems*

Given an arbitrary network, the fundamental problems which we consider are the following:

– determining if the network is consistent;
– if this is the case:
    - finding an instantiation which satisfies it,
    - finding a consistent scenario,
    - computing the minimal network.

The problem of consistency, as we have already seen, is NP-complete, in general. The other problems are polynomially reducible to it and hence also NP-complete.

Given these results, three types of approach evolve if we consider the practical resolution of these problems. We may consider one of the three types of approaches as follows:

– complete algorithms, but with exponential time cost;
– polynomial, but incomplete, algorithms;
– specific algorithms which are complete only in certain cases.

We will describe further in detail each one of these approaches.

1.4. Constraint propagation

The technique of constraint propagation is based on the use of two operations: inversion and composition.

1.4.1. *Operations: inversion and composition*

Any basic relation has an inverse relation. More generally, we define the inverse of a relation (disjunction of a set of basic relations) as the disjunction of the basic relations within it.

This definition generalizes the one used for basic relations: a relation R is true between i and j if, and only if, R is true between i and j for a basic relation $r \in R$, which is equivalent to the fact that r^{-1} is true for a basic relation $r^{-1} \in R^{-1}$.

Recall that, in general, if R and S are two binary relations on U, the *composition* of R and S, denoted as $R \circ S$, is the binary relation which is defined as follows:

$$R \circ S = \{(x, y) \in U \times U \mid \exists z \in U \text{ such that } (x, z) \in R \text{ and } (z, y) \in S\}$$

In terms of constraints, the fact that the constraint $C(i, j)$ holds on the arc (i, j) while the constraint $C(j, k)$ holds on the arc (j, k) makes it possible to deduce a constraint on the arc (i, k). This is expressed in terms of *composition* of relations.

EXAMPLE 1.8.– Let us consider three intervals I_1, I_2, I_3. Let us assume that I_1 overlaps I_2 and that I_2 is strictly contained in (*during*) I_3. Now, can we determine the relationship between I_1 and I_3?

If all the possibilities are examined (as illustrated in Figure 1.11), we can note that there are exactly three possible cases: I_1 overlaps with I_3, or I_1 initiates I_3, or I_1 is strictly contained in I_3. In other words, $C(1, 2) = \{o\}$ and $C(2, 3) = \{d\}$ imply that $C(1, 2) = \{o, s, d\}$.

Figure 1.11. *The three configurations for which we have I_1 o I_2 and I_2 d I_3; in that case either I_1 o I_3, or I_1 s I_3, or and I_1 d I_3; hence the composition of the relations o and d is the relation $\{o, s, d\}$*

A remarkable property of Allen's formalism is that the implication illustrated by this example is in fact an equivalence, in the following sense:

If I_1, I_3 are two intervals on the real line such that either I_1 o I_3, or I_1 s I_3, or I_1 d I_3, then there exists an interval I_2 such that I_1 o I_2 and I_2 d I_3. This can be easily checked, the only property used in the proof being the fact that given two distinct points on the real line, a third point can be found between them.

1.4.2. *Composition table*

The systematic review, for each pair of basic relations, of the implications obtained by composition can be expressed by the so-called Allen's *composition table* (Table 1.3). Moreover we can easily verify that for each pair of basic relations, the disjunction of the relations listed in the table coincides exactly with the composition of these relations.

Table 1.3. *Allen's composition table*

○	p	m	o	s	d	fi	eq	f	di	si	oi	mi	pi
p	p	p	p	p	[p, d]	p	p	[p, d]	p	p	[p, d]	[p, d]	[p, pi]
m	p	p	p	m	[o, d]	p	m	[o, d]	p	m	[o, d]	[s, si]	[d, pi]
o	p	p	[p, o]	o	[o, d]	[p, o]	o	[o, d]	[p, di]	[o, di]	[o, oi]	[d, oi]	[d, pi]
s	p	p	[p, o]	s	d	[p, o]	s	d	[p, di]	[s, si]	[d, oi]	mi	pi
d	p	p	[p, d]	d	d	[p, d]	d	d	1	[d, pi]	[d, pi]	pi	pi
fi	p	m	o	o	[o, d]	fi	fi	[fi, f]	di	di	[di, oi]	[di, oi]	pi
eq	p	m	o	s	d	fi	eq	f	di	si	oi	mi	pi
f	p	m	[o, d]	d	d	[fi, f]	f	f	[di, pi]	[oi, pi]	[oi, pi]	pi	pi
di	[p, di]	[o, di]	[o, di]	[o, di]	[o, oi]	di	di	[di, oi]	di	di	[di, oi]	[di, oi]	[di, pi]
si	[p, di]	[o, di]	[o, di]	[s, si]	[d, oi]	di	si	oi	di	si	oi	mi	pi
oi	[p, di]	[o, di]	[o, oi]	[d, oi]	[d, oi]	[di, oi]	oi	oi	[di, pi]	[oi, pi]	[oi, pi]	pi	pi
mi	[p, di]	[s, si]	[d, oi]	[d, oi]	[d, oi]	mi	mi	mi	pi	pi	pi	pi	pi
pi	[p, pi]	[d, pi]	[d, pi]	[d, pi]	[d, pi]	pi	pi	pi	pi	pi	pi	pi	pi

The following notations are used:

[p, o] = {p, m, o}	[p, d] = {p, m, o, s, d}	[p, di] = {p, m, o, fi, di}	[p, pi] = all relations
[d, oi] = {d, f, oi}	[d, pi] = {d, f, oi, mi, pi}	[s, si] = {s, eq, si}	[o, di] = {o, fi, di}
[o, oi] = {o, s, d, fi, eq, f, di, si, oi}	[o, d] = {o, s, d}	[di, pi] = {di, si, oi, mi, pi}	[di, oi] = {di, si, oi}
[oi, pi] = {oi, mi, pi}	[fi, f] = {fi, eq, f}		

This notation in terms of intervals is justified by the existence of a lattice structure on the set of basic relations (see section 2.2.4).

Once the composition of two basic relations is defined, we can extend this definition to arbitrary relations:

DEFINITION 1.13.– *The composition $(R \circ S)$ of two relations is the union of the sets $(r \circ s)$, where $r \in R$ and $s \in S$.*

Also, it is clear that the above definition is compatible with the natural semantics of the language used.

1.4.3. *Allen's algebra*

So far we have considered Allen's relations as actual, "concrete" binary relations, that is, as sets of pairs of intervals on the real line and the operations of inversion and composition are the usual operations on binary relations. Equipped with these operations, Allen's relations form an *algebra of binary relations* (see Appendix B).

Let us now change our perspective and consider the set of 13 symbols which refer to the basic relations, i.e. the set $\{p, m, o, s, d, f, eq, pi, mi, oi, si, di, fi\}$. We still use the notation B_2 for this set. Let A_2 be the Boolean algebra of all subsets of B_2. If we equip A_2 with the inversion operation and the composition operation as defined by the table of composition, we get an abstract algebra which is a relation algebra in the sense of Tarski [TAR 41, JÓN 52].

This abstract algebraic structure A_2 is called Allen's algebra. In this way, we may consider the algebra of Allen relations between intervals as a representation of the abstract algebra A_2 (see Appendix B).

In a similar manner, the Boolean A_1 of all subsets of the set $B_1 = \{<, eq, >\}$ (considered independently of its interpretation as a set of binary relations on the real line), equipped with the operations of inversion and composition, is an abstract algebra A_1 which is a relation algebra in the sense of Tarski.

1.4.4. *Algebraic closure*

We will use the term *algebraic closure* to refer to the property which is usually called "path consistency" in the literature. The term "path consistency" is derived from the field of constraint satisfaction problems or CSPs. These problems involve variables which assume their values in finite domains, and many techniques known as filtering techniques are used to restrict the set of the values of the variables.

The property of *algebraic closure* corresponds to the intuitive idea that the various constraints between two given variables must be compatible in order for the network to be consistent. In particular, the constraints which can be deduced between i and j while following two different paths from i to j should not be incompatible. In fact, this boils down to a condition which can be verified on subnetworks with three vertices: for any three vertices (i, j, k), the constraint $C(i, j)$ must be compatible with the composite of the constraints $C(i, k)$ and $C(k, j)$:

$$C(i,j) \cap (C(i,k) \circ C(k,j)) \neq \emptyset$$

This implies that we do not change the problem of the consistency of a network by replacing the original relation $C(i, j)$ by $C(i,j) \cap (C(i,k) \circ C(k,j))$. If this intersection is empty, the network cannot be consistent. If it is equal to $C(i, j)$, taking the intersection does not change the label. In all other cases, taking the intersection removes some basic relations from the set C(i,j), which is a set with at most 13 elements. Hence, clearly, repeating the operation of composition and intersection eventually terminates, either because an empty intersection arises, or because we get a stable network which is no longer changed. This network, then, is equivalent to the original network, and it verifies the condition of algebraic closure.

DEFINITION 1.14.– *A constraint network* (N, C) *is* algebraically closed *(or* path consistent*) if for any three vertices* $i, j, k \in N$ *we have:*

$$C(i,j) \subseteq (C(i,k) \circ C(k,j))$$

1.4.4.1. *Path-consistency and k-consistency*

In the domain of finite CSPs, which correspond to constraint networks for which the domains of values of the variables are finite sets, the concept of k-consistency was introduced by Freuder.

DEFINITION 1.15.– *Let k be an integer, where $k \geq 1$. A network of constraints is k-consistent if for any k-tuple of variables $(V_1, \ldots, V_k)$ and for any consistent instantiation of $(k-1)$ variables $(V_1, \ldots, V_{k-1})$, there exists a value v such that instantiating V_k to v yields a consistent instantiation.*

DEFINITION 1.16.– *A network of constraints is said to be* strongly k-consistent *if it is i-consistent for any integer i, $1 \leq i \leq k$.*

For the qualitative networks of Allen's algebra, k-consistency is verified for $1 \leq k \leq 2$: more precisely, any network which does not contain the empty label is 1-consistent and 2-consistent, hence strongly 2-consistent. The property of 2-consistency, for example, asserts that given an interval of the real line $\mathbb{R}$, it is always possible to find an interval which is in one of the 13 basic relations with respect to the first. Let us simply note that this is true because $\mathbb{R}$ is dense and unlimited on the left and on the right. In particular, this would remain true if $\mathbb{R}$ was replaced by the line of the rationals $\mathbb{Q}$.

For 3-consistency, we have the following important result:

PROPOSITION 1.3.– *A network of constraints on Allen's algebra is 3-consistent if, and only if, it is algebraically closed.*

Proof. 3-consistency implies algebraic closure: for any triangle with vertices i, j, k, the choice of two intervals $m(i)$ and $m(j)$ such that any basic relation t of $C(i, j)$ is verified implies that we can find an interval $m(k)$, such that $m(i)$ is in a relation $r \in C(i, k)$ with respect to $m(k)$ and that $m(k)$ is in a relation $s \in C(k, j)$ with respect to $m(k)$. Thus $t \in (r \circ s)$, and *a fortiori* $t \in C(i, k) \circ C(k, j)$. Since this is true for arbitrary t in $C(i, j)$, we have $C(i, j) \subseteq (C(i, k) \circ C(k, j))$.

Conversely, let us consider instantiations $m(i)$ and $m(j)$ such that $C(i, j)$ is verified, i.e. $m(i)\ t\ m(j)$ for a basic relation $t \in C(i, j)$. Given that $t \in (C(i, k) \circ C(k, j))$, we have to find an instantiation $m(k)$ of k. However, $t \in (C(i, k) \circ C(k, j))$ implies that there exists $r \in C(i, k)$ and $s \in C(k, j)$ such that $t \in (r \circ s)$. But, as already seen in section 1.4, the last statement is true, since $\mathbb{R}$ is dense and unlimited on the left- and right-hand sides. The same would hold true if $\mathbb{R}$ was replaced by $\mathbb{Q}$.

1.4.5. *Enforcing algebraic closure*

Given a network of constraints on Allen's algebra, it is always possible to replace this network by an equivalent network (i.e. having the same set of solutions) which is algebraically closed. The definition of the property of algebraic closure suggests a way of doing it. In the literature, the corresponding algorithms are called algorithms for enforcing path consistency (or algebraic closure).

As already mentioned, enforcing path consistency is based on repeatedly performing the following operation on 3-tuples of vertices (i, j, k):

$$C(i, j) \leftarrow C(i, j) \cap (C(i, k) \circ C(k, j))$$

Since each label contains a maximum of 13 basic relations, it is clear that stability is achieved after a finite number of operations.

This operation can be defined in a clear and elegant way using a matrix product [MON 74, MAC 77, LAD 88, LAD 94].

More precisely, consider a constraint network (N, C). Choose an ordering on the set of vertices N, so that we may assume that $N = \{1, \ldots, n\}$. We associate with the network the matrix M_N, where the matrix element $M_N(i, j)$ is $C(i, j)$. In this way, we get a square matrix whose elements are Allen relations.

We define the matrix product in the usual manner, with the difference that the product is replaced by composition, and the sum by intersection: if M and M' are two $n \times n$ matrices, the product $M \circ M'$ is defined by:

$$(M \circ M')(i,j) = \bigcap_{k=1}^{k=n} (M(i,k) \circ M'(k,j))$$

where M^k denotes the matric product $M \circ \ldots \circ M$ (k times).

PROPOSITION 1.4.– *Let M_N be the matrix associated with a network with contraints N. The* algebraic closure *of N is the network whose associated matrix is the matrix* $\lim_{k=1}^{\infty} M^k$.

NOTE 1.1.– If all the relations of the algebraic closure are empty relations, then the network is not consistent. Therefore, the matrix of the algebraic closure should be non-empty for achieving consistency.

We must emphasize the fact that non-empty algebraic closure provides a necessary, but not sufficient condition for network consistency: if the algebraic closure of a network contains the empty relation, we can conclude that the original network is not consistent. On the other hand, if that is not the case, so that the path consistent network obtained has all its labels non-empty, we cannot, in general, conclude that the network is consistent. We still have to examine all the atomic subnetworks to arrive at a conclusion.

EXAMPLE 1.9.– Consider the following network (Figure 1.12 (a)):
$C(V_1, V_2) = \{p, m, o, s, di, fi, eq, si\}$, $C(V_1, V_3) = \{s, f, eq\}$, $C(V_2, V_3) = \{pi, oi\}$, $C(V_2, V_4) = \{pi, oi, di, si\}$, and $C(V_3, V_4) = \{f, fi\}$

The composition of $C(V_1, V_3) \circ C(V_3, V_2)$ is $\{p, o, m, d, s\}$. Its intersection with $C(V_1, V_2)$ is $\{p, m, o, s\}$. We thus obtain an equivalent network by replacing $C(V_1, V_2)$ by $\{p, m, o, s\}$.

Similarly, $C(V_2, V_3) \circ c(V_3, V_4)$ is $\{pi, oi, di, si\}$, and is thus equal to $C(V_2, V_4)$. Hence path-consistency already holds for this particular triangle and no change has to be made.

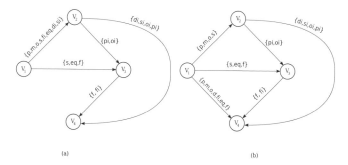

(a)   (b)

Figure 1.12. *A network (a) and its algebraic closure (b)*

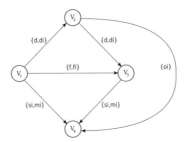

Figure 1.13. *An algebraically closed network which is not consistent*

In this case we can easily see that the associated matrix M verifies $M^2 = M^3$. The network associated with M^2 is the algebraic closure of the network considered. This algebraic closure is shown in part (b) of Figure 1.12.

EXAMPLE 1.10.– Let us consider the following network (Figure 1.13):
$C(V_1, V_2) = \{d, di\}, C(V_1, V_3) = \{f, fi\}, C(V_1, V_4) = \{si, mi\}, C(V_2, V_3) = \{d, di\},$
$C(V_2, V_4) = \{oi\}, C(V_3, V_4) = \{si, mi\}$

We can easily check that this network is algebraically closed. However, it is not consistent. According to Allen [ALL 83], this counter-example is due to Kautz.

The above example shows that, in general, the property of algebraic closure of a non-empty network is not sufficient to guarantee its consistency. However, this holds true for atomic networks.

1.4.5.1. *PC type algorithms*

The calculation of the successive powers of a matrix is obviously not the most effective way to determine the algebraic closure of a network of constraints.

First of all, it is clear that the network is inconsistent if there is an empty relationship between two vertices; in matrix terms, this implies that the limit matrix has all its elements equal to the empty relation. We can therefore stop the calculation once the empty relation appears.

The algorithms used for the calculation of algebraic closure are adaptations of PC algorithms (PC for *path consistency*), which are used in the field of finite CSPs. These algorithms use a function called REVISE which, given any three vertices (i, j, k) of a network, returns **true** if following the path from i to j via k results in a change of the constraint between i and j, and **false** if it does not. In the first case, the constraint between i and j and that between j and i are actually modified (the REVISE function thus has a side effect).

Data: A constraint network (V, C) and three vertices (i, j, k) of this network
Result: Returns **true** if $C(i, j)$ is changed, **false** otherwise
if $C(i, k)$ *or* $C(k, j)$ *is the universal relation* **then**
| **return** *false*
end
$S \leftarrow \emptyset$
for each $a \in C(i, k)$ **do**
| **for each** $b \in C(k, j)$ **do**
| | $S \leftarrow S \cup (a \circ b)$
| **end**
end
if $S \supseteq C(i, j)$ **then**
| **return** *false*
end
$C(i, j) \leftarrow (C(i, j) \cap S)$
$C(j, i) \leftarrow C(i, j)^{-1}$
return *true*

Figure 1.14. *The function* REVISE

Figure 1.14 shows the function in question. The various versions used in the literature use this function [ALL 83, VIL 86, DEC 91, BEE 92]. A more advanced version of this function, due to Bessière, skillfully avoids the full computation of the composition of $C(i, k)$ and $C(k, j)$ [BES 96].

Figure 1.15 shows algorithm PC_{IA} as described in [DEC 91].

Data: A network of constraints (V, C) with n vertices
repeat
| $change \leftarrow$ **false**
| **for all** $k, i, j \leftarrow 1$ *to* n **do**
| | **if** (i, j, k) *are all distinct* **then**
| | | **if** REVISE(i, k, j) **then**
| | | | **if** $C(i, j) = \emptyset$ **then**
| | | | | **exit** on inconsistency
| | | | **end**
| | | | $change \leftarrow$ **true**
| | | **end**
| | **end**
| **end**
until *change false*

Figure 1.15. *The algorithm* $PC1_{IA}$

For a detailed description (in French) of the various versions of PC algorithms, the reader can refer to [LEB 07], section 7.3.

1.5. Consistency tests

1.5.1. *The case of atomic networks*

We will first examine the consistency problem for atomic networks. Our aim, therefore, is to determine if a given atomic network is consistent or not. We will see that the problem can be solved in polynomial time. More precisely, we present an algorithm in Figure 1.16, whose temporal cost is $O(n^2)$, if n is the number of vertices of the network.

Data: An atomic network of constraints (V, C) of vertices $V_1, \ldots, V_n$
Result: An instantiation of the variables if the network is consistent
initialization
$V_1 \leftarrow (x_1, y_1)$; $min \leftarrow x_1 - 1$; $max \leftarrow y_1 + 1$
for $i \leftarrow 2$ **a** n **do**
    $posXi \leftarrow [min, max]$; $posYi \leftarrow [min, max]$
    for $j \leftarrow 1$ **a** $i - 1$ **do**
        update $posXi$ and $posYi$ while using $C(i, j)$
        if $posXi$ or $posYi$ *empty* **then**
         | **return** *inconsistent*
        end
    end
    $x_i \leftarrow$ any value in $posXi$
    $y_i \leftarrow$ any value in $posYi$ such that $x_i < y_i$
end
return $(x_1, y_1), \ldots (x_n, y_n)$

Figure 1.16. *Consistency of atomic networks: the* CONSATOM *algorithm*

EXAMPLE 1.11.– Let us consider the network shown in Figure 1.17, which is defined by the constraints $C(V_1, V_2) = \{p\}, C(V_1, V_3) = \{s\}, C(V_1, V_4) = \{p\}, C(V_2, V_3) = \{oi\}, C(V_2, V_4) = \{o\}$, and $C(V_3, V_4) = \{m\}$.

Let us choose the interval $[1, 10]$ as an instantiation of V_1. We therefore have $Min = 0$ and $Max = 11$. The process then enters the main loop. Initially, we have $posX2 = posY2 = [0, 11]$. Since $C(1, 2)$ is p, we update $posX2$ to $(10, 11]$, and $posY2$ to $(10, 11]$. Let us choose $x_2 = 10.5$ and $y_2 = 10.7$.

Again, the value of $posX3$ and $posX4$ is $[0, 11]$. The constraint $C(1, 3) = $ s results in $posX3 = [1, 1]$ and $posY3 = (10, 11]$. Then, the constraint $C(2, 3) = $ oi results in $posX3 = [1, 1]$ and $posY3 = (10.5, 10.7]$. Let us choose $x_3 = 1$ and $y_3 = 10.6$.

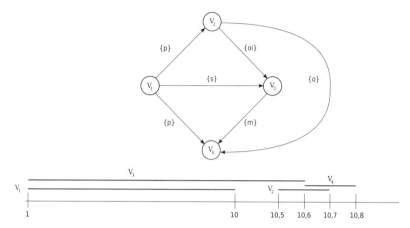

Figure 1.17. *Usage of the ConsAtom algorithm*

Finally, we initialize $posX4$ and $posY4$ to $[0, 11]$, and consider the three constraints $C(1, 4), C(2, 4)$, and $C(3, 4)$. Since $C(1, 4) = $ p, we set $posX4 = posY4 = [10, 11]$. Since $C(2, 4) = $ o, we update $posX4$ to $(10.5, 10.7)$ and $posY4$ to $(10.7, 11]$. Also, since $C(3, 4) = $ m, we obtain $posX4 = [10.6, 10.6]$ and $posY4 = (10.7, 11]$. Ultimately, we can choose $x_4 = 10.6$ and $y_4 = 10.8$. The instantiation thus obtained is shown in the lower part of Figure 1.17. It is a solution of the network.

1.5.2. *Arbitrary networks*

We are now in a position to outline complete algorithms for solving the consistency problem and, if applicable, of determing the minimal network of an arbitrary network:

Consistency: Generate all the atomic subnetworks of the given network and test the consistency of each subnetwork, by using, for example, the ConsAtom algorithm.

Minimal network: For each constraint $C(i, j)$, and for each atomic relation r in $C(i, j$, replace $C(i, j)$ by r, and test for consistency; if the network obtained is consistent, then r is part of the minimal network for the arc (i, j); if not, delete r from the corresponding label.

It is clear that these methods are complete, but they are of exponential cost. Their implementation assumes an effective management of the way in which the atomic subnetworks are generated.

1.5.3. *Determining polynomial subsets*

Since solving the consistency problem for arbitrary networks on Allen's algebra leads to exponential costs, researchers have explored another approach to the study of consistency which consists in limiting *a priori* the type of constraints used in a network. For example, we have seen that certain relations, the pointizable relations, correspond to networks on the point algebra. Since for these networks, determining consistency is a problem of polynomial cost in time, the same holds for networks on Allen's algebra whose labels are pointizable relations.

We are now led to asking the general question of determining all subsets S of relations in Allen's algebra such that restricting the labels of constraint networks to S guarantees that the consistency problem can be solved in polynomial time. Such a subset is called *tractable* in the literature. In that case, the question is: which polynomial algorithms allow us to determine if a given network is consistent? In particular, are the filtering algorithms such as those which enforce algebraic closure sufficient? The next chapter addresses these issues.

Chapter 2

Polynomial Subclasses of Allen's Algebra

2.1. "Show me a tractable relation!"

Since the set of basic relations in Allen's algebra contains 13 elements, the disjunctive relations are $2^{13} = 8,192$ in number. Up to the beginning of the year 1994, only 168 relations among these 8,000 odd relations were known to be tractable relations, i.e. relations for which the consistency problem can be solved by using a polynomial algorithm. Then Nebel and Bürckert published a watershed paper [NEB 94b] in which they characterized a set of more than 800 tractable relations: the ORD-Horn relations.

So far so good, but can we decide in a simple way whether a given relation is an ORD-Horn relation? The answer is "Yes! Just take a look at it!"

Indeed, Ligozat's [LIG 94b], characterization of the ORD-Horn relation in terms of pre-convex relations makes it possible to immediately answer this question by

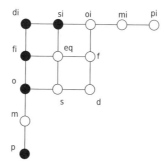

Figure 2.1. *Is the relation* $\{p, o, fi, di, si\}$ *tractable?*

using the lattice structure of the set of basic relations. For example, the relation $\{p, o, fi, di, si\}$ is pre-convex, hence an ORD-Horn relation. As shown in Figure 2.1, this relation is obtained from the convex relation $[p, oi]$ by removing three basic relations of dimensions 0 or 1. Hence, according to definition 2.10, it is pre-convex.

More generally, the characterization, the study, and the applications of tractable relations are the main themes of this chapter.

2.2. Subclasses of Allen's algebra

The consideration of constraint networks and the use of algebraic closure type methods lead us to concentrate on three operations: inversion, composition, and intersection. These are the three operations used by the algebraic closure algorithms. It is thus convenient to introduce a specific concept of subclass of relations:

DEFINITION 2.1.– *A subclass S of Allen's algebra is a set of relations closed under the inversion, intersection, and composition operations.*

If S is an arbitrary subset of Allen's algebra, there is a smallest subclass containing S, which we denote by $\hat{S}$.

Now if we consider a network on a set S, i.e. such that the relations labeling the arcs are elements of S, and if S is a subclass, then the application of the algebraic closure method results in a network whose relations belong to S.

As for the question of complexity, Nebel and Bürckert [NEB 95] show that if a set S of relations contains the relation eq and the universal relation, then the consistency problem of a network on $\hat{S}$ has a polynomial translation into the consistency problem of a network on S. In particular, the first problem is polynomial if, and only if, the second problem is polynomial.

Before we concentrate on the study of important subclasses of Allen's algebra, we must make a detour to introduce two fundamental representations of Allen's relations: the geometrical representation and the lattice representation.

2.2.1. *A geometrical representation of Allen's relations*

Let us recall the definition of an interval in Allen's sense: an interval is a pair of real numbers $x = (x_1, x_2)$, where $x_1 < x_2$. Hence the set *Int* ($\mathbb{R}$) of intervals on $\mathbb{R}$ can be represented in a natural way as the set of points in the plane $\mathbb{R} \times \mathbb{R}$ having this property, that is, as the upper half-plane $\mathbf{H}$ bounded from below by the first bisector (Figure 2.2): $\mathbf{H}$ is defined by the equation $X_1 < X_2$.

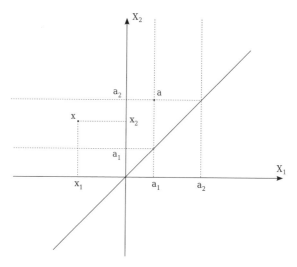

Figure 2.2. *Intervals as points in the upper half-plane. Here, the interval* $x = (x_1, x_2)$ *is in the relation* o *with respect to the interval* $a = (a_1, a_2)$, *since* $x_1 < a_1$ *and* $a_1 < x_2 < a_2$

Let us consider a fixed interval $a = (a_1, a_2)$. We have $a_1 < a_2$. Where in the half-plane are the intervals which are in each one of the basic relations with respect to a? The question is easily answered. For example:

– an interval $x = (x_1, x_2)$ is such that $(x, a) \in$ p if, and only if, $x_2 < a_1$, hence if the point x is in the part of **H** situated below the horizontal line $X_2 = a_1$;

– an interval $x = (x_1, x_2)$ is such that $(x, a) \in$ m if, and only if, $x_2 = a_1$, hence if the point x is in the horizontal half-line which is the intersection of **H** and of the line $X_2 = a_1$;

– an interval $x = (x_1, x_2)$ is such that $(x, a) \in$ o if, and only if, $x_1 < a_1$ and $x_2 > a_1$, hence if the point x is in the zone above the horizontal line $X_2 = a_1$, below the horizontal line $X_2 = a_2$, and located on the left of the vertical line $X_1 = a_1$;

– similar descriptions for other basic relations;

– in particular, the relation eq corresponds to the point a itself.

We thus get the representation of the basic relations shown in Figure 2.3. The 13 relations define an "a-centered" partition $\mathcal{P}_a$ of the the open half-plane **H** into 13 regions. The inversion operation is easily interpreted in geometrical terms: it corresponds the symmetry with respect to the line $X_1 + X_2 = a_1 + a_2$.

Also, let us note that the choice of another reference interval $b = (b_1, b_2)$ results in a partition centered on b of the same geometrical structure. More precisely, $\mathcal{P}_b$ can be deduced from $\mathcal{P}_a$ by carrying out a homothety and a translation. The two partitions are thus similar in a geometrical sense.

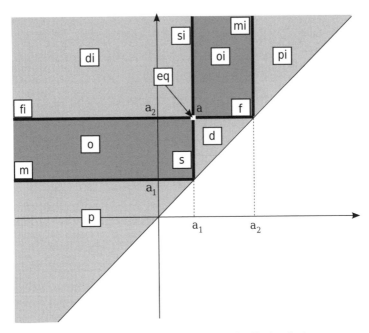

Figure 2.3. *The regions associated with Allen's relations*

2.2.1.1. *Dimension and topological closure*

Based on this geometrical interpretation of relations in terms of regions of the upper half-plane, all topological and geometrical concepts are available for Allen's relations, in particular:

DEFINITION 2.2.–

    – *The* dimension *dim*(r) *of a relation r is the dimension of its corresponding region*;

    – *The* topological closure *$Cl(r)$ of a relation r is the smallest closed set of* **H** *containing (the region representing) this relation*;

    – *A relation is* closed *if it is equal to its topological closure.*

Let us consider the 13 basic relations. The relation eq is of dimension 0, and it is the only relation of dimension 0. The relations of dimension 1 are m, s, f, mi, si, and fi. The 6 remaining relations are of dimension 2. Clearly, the dimension of a basic relation reflects the intuitive concept of *degree of freedom* implied by this relation: consider a fixed interval of reference, and an interval whose bounding points may move slightly; the equality relation has no degree of freedom, since any perturbation of the equality of the bounding points of the movable interval leads to a relation other than equality. In the case of a relation of dimension 1, we can slightly move one of the bounding points without changing the relation, and in the case of a relation of dimension 2, the same holds true for a simultaneous move of both bounding points.

Now consider topological closure. Notice that the topological closure of any basic relation (at least the part of it contained in the half-plane) is a finite union of basic relations.

The relation eq is represented by a point, hence it is closed: it is its own closure.

The region representing p is an open cone in the plane. The corresponding closed cone in the plane contains the borders of this cone, which are represented as a half-line carried by the first bisector and by the region representing m: the closure of p is thus the relation $\{p, m\}$, which is the intersection of the closed cone with $\mathbf{H}$.

A similar reasoning shows that the relation m is closed.

In the case of the relation o, we note that the closure operation adds the relations m, s, fi, and eq to the relation o itself.

We can summarize the results of this discussion in Table 2.1.

Relation	p	m	o	s	d	f
Closure	$\{p, m\}$	m	$\{m, o, s, fi, eq\}$	$\{s, eq\}$	$\{s, d, eq, f\}$	$\{f, eq\}$
Relation	pi	mi	oi	si	di	fi
Closure	$\{pi, mi\}$	mi	$\{mi, oi, si, f, eq\}$	$\{si, eq\}$	$\{si, di, eq, fi\}$	$\{fi, eq\}$

Table 2.1. *Topological closures of the basic relations*

2.2.2. *Interpretation in terms of granularity*

We have mentioned the interpretation of dimension in terms of degrees of freedom of the relations. Topological closure can be interpretated in terms of granularity: let us consider for example, two intervals i and j such that i *slightly* precedes j (relation p): i is very close to j. If we now move away from the pair (i, j) (we zoom out, in cinematographic terms), we will not be able to distinguish the small interval which separates i from j, and we will conclude that i meets j (relation m). The situation is illustrated in part (a) of Figure 2.4 (a).

In a similar manner, if i *slightly* overlaps j (relation o) (the intersection of i and j is very small), and if we zoom out, we will again conclude that i meets j (relation m, case (b) of Figure 2.4). But it is also possible that i overlaps j in such a way that the amount of time between the end of i and that of j is quite short: zooming out leads to conclude that i is finished by j (relation fi, case (c)); it may also be that j starts *very shortly after*

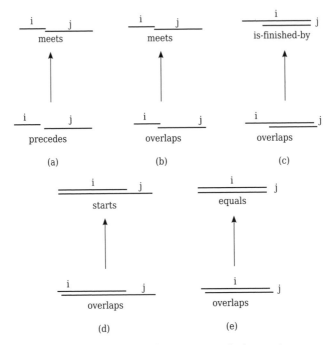

Figure 2.4. *Zooming out: the situation at the bottom is seen as that at the top when we move away from it sufficiently*

i starts, so that zooming out makes the delay unnoticeable, and leads us to conclude that *i* begins *j* (relation s, case (d)); and finally, if the conditions of cases (c) and (d) are both met (the beginnings of *i* and *j* are very close, and the same holds true for their ends), then zooming out leads us to conclude to the equality (relation eq, case (e)).

With these examples, which reflect a general phenomenon, we see that the topological closure can be interpreted in terms of zooming out.

Conversely, this interpretation makes obvious an interpretation of the reverse transformation in terms of zooming in: for example, if we start with the relation s (*i* starts *j*) and if we zoom in, we may discover that the beginnings of *i* and *j* were in fact distinct, and that what we considered as a s relation is actually a case of *i* overlapping *j* (relation o), or of *i* taking place during *j* (relation d). Figure 2.5 illustrates these two cases.

For other basic relations, the reader may refer to Table 2.1 again for the result of this reverse transformation.

To conclude this discussion of the zooming effects, it should be noted that there is still a way of using this idea of very short durations (which we have just used for the

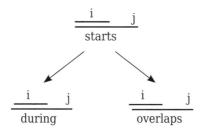

Figure 2.5. *Zooming in: when we come close to it, the situation at the top may reveal itself to be one of the two situations at the bottom*

durations separating the bounding points of two distinct intervals), by applying it this time to the intervals themselves: a "very short" interval, after zooming out, becomes a point, and relations between intervals (infinitesimal or not) will become relations between points (and intervals). We will not elaborate on this idea for the moment, and refer to the works of Hobbs [HOB 85] and Euzenat [EUZ 96, EUZ 01], as well as to Chapter 6.

2.2.2.1. *Formal properties of topological closure*

Let us denote by $Cl(r)$ the topological closure of a relation r. We can easily prove the following properties:

PROPOSITION 2.1.– *For any pair of relations r, s:*
- $Cl(r^{-1}) = Cl(r)^{-1}$;
- $Cl(r) \supseteq r$;
- $dim(Cl(r) \setminus r) < dim(r)$;
- $Cl(Cl(r)) = Cl(r)$;
- r *is closed if, and only if,* $Cl(r) = r$;
- *if* $r \subseteq s$ *then* $Cl(r) \subseteq Cl(s)$;
- $Cl(r \circ s) \supseteq Cl(r) \circ Cl(s)$.

Let us emphasize the last point: In all cases, we have $Cl(r \circ s) \supseteq Cl(r) \circ Cl(s)$, but no equality in general. A counterexample is the case where $r = s = $ m. We have $Cl(\mathsf{m}) = \{\mathsf{m}\}$ and $Cl(\mathsf{p}) = \{\mathsf{p}, \mathsf{m}\}$. Thus, $Cl(\mathsf{m} \circ \mathsf{m}) = Cl(\mathsf{p}) = \{\mathsf{p}, \mathsf{m}\}$, which strictly contains $Cl(\mathsf{m}) \circ Cl(\mathsf{m}) = \{\mathsf{p}\}$.

2.2.3. *Convex and pre-convex relations*

To make things easier, let us from now agree, on the model of definition 2.2, to make no explicit distinction between Allen's relations and the regions representing them when discussing geometrical or topological properties.

Let us recall that in topology, a subspace Y of a topological space X is *connected* (see Appendix A) if it is not a disjoint union of two non-empty closed subsets (or equivalently, of two non-empty open sets). In intuitive terms, this means that Y is "in one piece".

Assuming a basic knowldge of geometry makes it clear that the 13 basic relations are connected. General, disjunctive relations may be connected or not: for example, the disjunctive relation $\{p, pi\}$ is not connected (it is in two pieces, or, in mathematical terms, it has two connected components). The relation $\{p, o, d\}$ is also not connected (it has three connected components). The disjunctive relation $\{m, o, eq\}$ is connected, since the three basic regions which correspond to it are in contact. Similarly, the relation $\{o, fi, di, si, oi\}$ is connected, for the same reason.

A region Y of the plane is called *convex* if, when it contains two points x and y, it also contains the line segment connecting x to y. The concept of convexity corresponds to the usual use of this term (no concavity).

Again, we can easily note that the 13 basic relations are convex relations, and that it is not necessarily the case of general relations. A general result is that convexity implies connectedness, but the reverse is not true: for example, the relation $\{o, fi, di, si, oi\}$ is connected, but not convex.

The concept of convexity can be deduced from the ternary relation of *betweenness* for points (see for example [GÄR 00]): a set is convex if, when it contains x and y, also contains the points which are "between" x and y. For the usual Euclidean distance relation, the points lying between x and y are precisely those of the line segment connecting x to y.

Let us consider two intervals i and j and the points in the plane x_i and x_j which represent them. It is not obvious to interpret what it means for a third interval k to be positioned between i and j in the Euclidean sense, i.e. to have its representative point on the segment $[x_i, x_j]$. On the other hand, it is natural to use the following definition:

DEFINITION 2.3.– *An interval k is* between *two intervals i and j, which we denote by $B(i, k, j)$, if its starting point is located between those of i and j and its ending point between those of i and j.*

In terms of representation in the plane, this means that the set of intervals located between i and j is represented by the intersection of the closed rectangle of diagonal (i, j) with **H**.

It is also clear that we thus obtain the points in the plane located between i and j for the *Manhattan metric* (see Appendix A.32), which is defined in the plane by: $\rho_p(i, j) = |i_1 - j_1| + |i_2 - j_2|$.

Let us recall (see A.32) that generally, in a metric space equipped with a metric ρ, a point y is located between two points x and z, which we write $B(x, y, z)$, if we have $\rho(x, z) = \rho(x, y) + \rho(y, z)$.

DEFINITION 2.4.– *(see Appendix A.33) In a metric space, a region Y is* convex *if the fact that $x, y \in Y$ implies that for any z such that $B(x, z, y)$, we have $z \in Y$.*

Let pr_1 and pr_2 denote the projections of the plane on the coordinate axes X_1 and X_2, respectively. If Y is a region in the plane, we may consider the region $\mathrm{pr}_1\,(Y) \times \mathrm{pr}_2\,(Y)$, called the closure of Y by projection. In general, this set contains Y but does not coincide with Y. Taking the closure by projection is an operation which is a closure operation (see Appendix A.1.2).

DEFINITION 2.5.– *A region Y is* closed by projection *if it coincides with the product $pr_1(Y) \times pr_2(Y)$.*

Let us now come back to Allen's basic relations. Each one of these relations is defined in the plane by a conjunction of (in)equalities. For example, the relation m is defined by $i_2 = j_1$ and the relation o by $i_1 < j_1 \wedge j_1 < i_2 \wedge i_2 < j_2$.

DEFINITION 2.6.– *A relation Y is* closed by projection *if it coincides with $(pr_1(Y) \times pr_2(Y)) \cap \mathbf{H}$.*

We can easily deduce from the definition of basic relations in terms of (in)equalities that each of these relations is closed by projection.

We will also use the term *M-convexity* to refer to the convexity for Manhattan metric.

We can now define *convex relations*:

DEFINITION 2.7.– *An Allen's relation r is* convex *if it satisfies one of the following equivalent conditions:*

    – *the region associated with r is convex for the Manhattan metric (M-convex);*

    – *the region associated with r is convex and is closed by projection.*

Proof. ($\Rightarrow$) Let us show that M-convexity implies convexity and closure by projection. The first point is clear, since the rectangle rect (i, j) with diagonal (i, j) and sides parallel to the coordinates axes contains the segment $[i, j]$. For the second point, let us consider a region Y which is M-convex and an interval k whose projections k_1 and k_2 are contained in the projections $\mathrm{pr}_1(Y)$ and $\mathrm{pr}_2(Y)$ of Y, respectively. Hence there is a point y' in Y whose first coordinate y_1' is k_1. Similarly, there is a point $y'' \in Y$ such that $y_2'' = k_2$. The M-convexity of Y implies that rect $(y', y'') \cap \mathbf{H}$ is contained in Y. But rect (y', y'') is the Cartesian product of [inf (y_1', y_1''), sup (y_1', y_1'')] and [inf (y'_2, y''_2), sup (y'_2, y''_2)], with $y'_1 = k_1$ and $y''_1 = k_2$. Consequently, inf $(y'_1, y''_1) \leq k_1 \leq \sup (y'_1, y''_1)$ and inf $(y'_2, y''_2) \leq k_2 \leq \sup (y'_2, y''_2)$, hence $(k_1, k_2) \in \text{rect}(y', y'')$. Since $k \in \mathbf{H}$, we can conclude that $k \in Y$, and that Y is closed by projection.

($\Leftarrow$) Assume that Y is convex and closed by projection. Let us show that Y is M-convex. Since convexity is preserved by continuous maps, $I = \text{pr}_1(Y)$ and $J = \text{pr}_2(Y)$ are convex in $\mathbb{R}$, hence they are two (not necessarily open or closed) intervals in $\mathbb{R}$.

We have $Y = (I \times J) \cap \mathbf{H}$. Let $u, v \in Y$. We have to show that the rectangle rect (u, v) is contained in $I \times J$. But this is clearly the case, since inf (u_1, v_1) and sup (u_1, v_1) are in I, and inf (u_2, v_2) and sup (u_2, v_2) are in J. □

In accordance with the unanimous tradition in this field, when dealing with Allen's relations, we will henceforth use the term "convex" as meaning "convex for the Manhattan metric".

EXAMPLE 2.1.– The empty relation is trivially convex.

EXAMPLE 2.2.– The region in the plane corresponding to the relation $\{o, eq\}$ is convex in the ordinary sense: first, each one of the two regions which correspond to o and eq; then, consider line segments having one extremity which is the point corresponding to eq and the other in the region associated with o; clearly, such a segment is entirely contained in the region associated with $\{o, eq\}$.

However, this relation is not M-convex: if j is a reference interval, and i is in the relation o with respect to j, the intervals between i and j include intervals contained in the relations fi and s, so that the smallest M-convex relation containing $\{o, eq\}$ is the relation $\{o, s, fi, eq\}$.

2.2.4. The lattice of Allen's basic relations

The set of intervals, considered as a set of points in $\mathbb{R}^2$, inherits a partial ordering from the natural ordering of on $\mathbb{R}$. We now introduce an encoding for basic relations which highlights the lattice structure that this ordering implies for them.

Let $J = (j_1, j_2)$ be a reference interval. This interval defines five successive zones in the temporal line, which we number from 0 to 4 (Figure 2.6):

– zone 0 is the infinite open interval $(-\infty, j_1)$;
– zone 1 is the point $\{j_1\}$;
– zone 2 is the open interval (j_1, j_2);
– zone 3 is the point $\{j_2\}$;
– zone 4 is the infinite open interval $(j_2, +\infty)$.

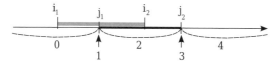

Figure 2.6. *An interval $j = (j_1, j_2)$ defines five zones numbered from 0 to 4. To each atomic relation is associated a pair of integers; for example, $i = (i_1, i_2)$ is with j in the relation o, which corresponds to the pair $(0, 2)$*

Now the Allen relation of an interval i with respect to j is entirely determined by the pair of integers giving the numbers of the zones containing i_1 and i_2, respectively. For example, p corresponds to the pair $(0, 0)$, m to the pair $(0, 1)$, o to the pair $(0, 2)$, etc. Table 2.2 gives the correspondence for the 13 basic relations. We may thus encode the basic relations in terms of pairs of integers between 0 and 4. More precisely:

PROPOSITION 2.2.– *A pair of integers (m, n) between 0 and 4 corresponds to a basic Allen's relation if, and only if,* m $\leq$ n *and no odd integer occurs more than once in the pair.*

p	m	o	s	d	f	eq
$(0,0)$	$(0,1)$	$(0,2)$	$(1,2)$	$(2,2)$	$(2,3)$	$(1,3)$
pi	mi	oi	si	di	fi	
$(4,4)$	$(3,4)$	$(2,4)$	$(1,4)$	$(0,4)$	$(0,3)$	

Table 2.2. *The basic relations as pairs of integers*

As a consequence, the natural order relation on the integers induces a partial ordering on the basic relations which provides them with the structure of a distributive lattice: by definition, two basic relations (m_1, m_2) and (n_1, n_2) are such that $(m_1, m_2) \leq (n_1, n_2)$ if $m_1 \leq n_1$ and $m_2 \leq n_2$.

Figure 2.7 represents the lattice of basic relations. This representation turns out to be extremely useful for a convenient visualization of the general relations. A first application is an easy characterization of convex relations.

First, let us recall that in a partial order, given a and b such that $a \leq b$, the interval defined by (a, b), denoted as $[a, b]$, is the set $\{x \mid a \leq x \leq b\}$ has. We then have:

PROPOSITION 2.3.– *A relation is convex if, and only if, it is empty or if it corresponds to an interval in the lattice of basic relations.*

Allen's algebra contains 83 convex relations. Using either the geometrical or the lattice characterization, it is easily shown that the intersection of two convex relations is convex.

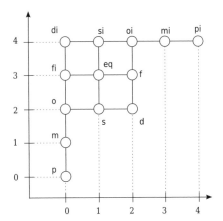

Figure 2.7. *The lattice of Allen's relations*

2.2.4.1. *Dimension and topological closure*

The dimension of a basic relation is easily deduced from its representation as a pair of integers: it is equal to the number of even integers in the encoding of this relation.

The topological closure itself can be expressed easily by using an operation which we call the *edge operation*, which we denote by ∂: by definition, the edge $\partial(r)$ of the basic relation r is the set of relations that can be obtained by increasing or decreasing the even coordinates of r by 1. For example, ∂ (d) $= \partial$ $((2,2))$ contains $(1,2)$ and $(2,3)$. In turn, the edge of $(1,2)$ is $(1,3)$, and the edge of $(1,3)$ is empty. The edge of $(2,3)$ is also $(1,3)$.

The topological closure of a relation is the relation obtained by iterating the edge operation and by adding all the basic relations obtained in this way to the initial relation. The procedure is illustrated by Figure 2.8: using the edge operation, we can compute the topological closure of a relation by "following the arrows".

2.2.4.2. *Convex closure*

The intersection of two convex relations being convex, there is a smallest convex relation containing an arbitrary relation:

DEFINITION 2.8.– *The* convex closure $I(r)$ *of a relation r is the smallest convex relation containing r.*

With regard to composition, we can easily check that the composition of two convex relations is convex. Actually, we have a more precise result:

PROPOSITION 2.4.– *Let $[a,b]$ and $[c,d]$ be two (non-empty) convex relations. The composition $[a,b] \circ [c,d]$ is the relation $[\inf (a \circ c), \sup (b \circ d)]$.*

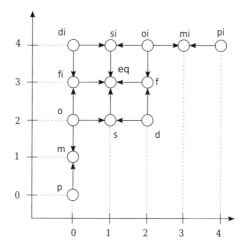

Figure 2.8. *Edge operation and topological closure: the topological closure of a relation is obtained by adding to it all the relations obtained by iterating the edge operation (represented by the arrows); for example, the edge of* d *contains* s *and* f*; the edge of* s *and* f *is* {eq}*; the topological closure of* d *is thus the relation* {d, s, f, eq}

As a consequence, using Allen's composition table, we can compute the composition of two convex relations by carrying out only two table lookups, regardless of the number of basic relations contained in the two relations.

2.2.4.2.1. Formal properties of convex closure

The following properties can be easily proved, for any pair of relations r, s:

– $I(r^{-1}) = I(r)^{-1}$;

– $I(r) \supseteq r$;

– $I(I(r)) = I(r)$;

– r is convex if, and only if, $I(r) = r$;

– If $r \subseteq s$ then $I(r) \subseteq I(s)$;

– $I(r \circ s) = I(r) \circ I(s)$.

2.2.4.3. *Convex relations in the lattice*

A non-empty convex relation is thus an interval of the lattice; equivalently, it can be defined in the lattice as the product of its projections, which are intervals in $\mathbb{N}$. For example, the relation [m, si] is characterized by its projections $[0, 1]$ and $[1, 4]$. Using X_1 and X_2 as coordinate axes in $\mathbb{N} \times \mathbb{N}$, this relation is defined by $X_1 \leq 1$ and $X_2 \geq 1$.

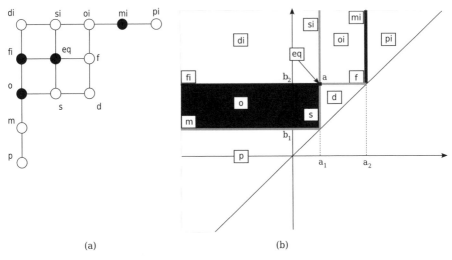

(a)   (b)

Figure 2.9. *A non-convex relation; the region of the plane which represents it is not connected, and a fortiori non-convex*

EXAMPLE 2.3.– The relation {o, fi, eq, mi} is not a convex relation (Figure 2.9). This can be seen on its representation as a subset of the lattice, and similarly on its representation in terms of regions in the plane: the associated region is not connected and *a fortiori* not convex.

The relation {o, fi, eq} is also not a convex relation (Figure 2.10), although its associated region is convex in the usual sense; but it is not M-convex. Its convex closure is the relation [o, eq] = {o, s, fi, eq}.

EXAMPLE 2.4.– The relation p is defined by $X_1 = 0$ and $X_2 = 0$. The relation [s, mi] has as projections [1, 3] and [2, 4], and is hence defined by $1 \leq X_1 \leq 3$ and $2 \leq X_2 \leq 4$.

More generally, a convex relation can be defined by equalities and inequalities involving the X_1 coordinate and the X_2 coordinate separately.

A consequence of this fact is that any convex relation is a pointizable relation.

Since they describe intervals of $\mathbb{N}$, the (in)equalities defining the convex relations do not have to use the relation $\neq$.

2.2.4.4. *A characterization of pointizable relations*

The lattice representation provides a nice characterization of the pointizable relations:

DEFINITION 2.9.– *Let r be an Allen's relation. An* odd cut *of r is a subrelation of r defined by a (possibly empty) conjunction of inequalities of type $X_i \neq \varpi$, where $i \in \{1, 2\}$ and $\varpi \in \{1, 3\}$.*

PROPOSITION 2.5.– *A relation is pointizable if, and only if, it is an odd cut of a convex relation.*

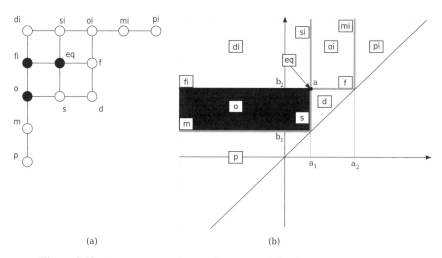

(a)   (b)

Figure 2.10. *A non-convex relation; the region of the plane which represents it is convex, but not M-convex*

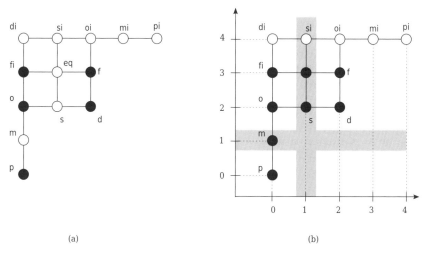

(a)   (b)

Figure 2.11. *A pointizable relation (a); it is obtained from its convex closure as the odd cut defined by $X_1 \neq 1$ and $X_2 \neq 1$ (b)*

EXAMPLE 2.5.– Let us consider (Figure 2.11, part (a)) the relation $r_1 = \{p, o, d, fi, f\}$. It is not convex. Its convex closure $C(r)$ is the relation $[p, f]$. We obtain r_1 (Figure 2.11, part (b)) by adding the conditions $X_1 \neq 1$ and $X_2 \neq 1$.

Similarly, the relation $r_2 = \{s, d, si, oi, pi\}$, whose convex closure is $[s, pi]$, is obtained as an odd cut of $[s, pi]$ by adding the inequalities $X_1 \neq 3$ and $X_2 \neq 3$.

These two relations are thus pointizable.

2.2.5. *Tractability of convex relations*

The convex relations constitute a subclass for which the consistency problem is polynomial. This is a consequence of the fact that they are themselves pointizable. More precisely, based on the above description, it is clear that a constraint network can be translated in terms of a constraint network on the Point algebra involving the boundary points of these intervals, and moreover, in such a way that the equalities and inequalities used *do not contain the relation* $\neq$.

PROPOSITION 2.6.– *For convex constraint networks, the algebraic closure method is complete for the problems of* consistency *and* minimality.

In other words, a convex network which is algebraically closed and which does not contain the empty relation is consistent and minimal.

We can thus use the algebraic closure algorithms that we discussed above to solve these problems.

The point concerning consistency extends to the subclass of pointizable relations: a pointizable network which is algebraically closed (and does not contain the empty relation) is consistent. On the other hand, as shown by van Beek [BEE 92], minimality cannot be achieved by the algebraic closure alone.

The counterexample of van Beek is the time-point network shown in Figure 2.12 which is defined by:

$$C(V_1, V_2) = C(V_1, V_3) = C(V_1, V_4) = C(V_2, V_4) = C(V_3, V_4) = \{\leq\}$$
$$C(V_2, V_3) = \{\neq\}$$

This network is algebraically closed, but it is not minimal. The algebraic closure property can be easily verified. The network is not minimal, since the equality on the arc $(1, 4)$ would imply the equality of all the vertices, which is not compatible with the constraint on the arc $(2, 3)$. Hence the minimal network should not contain the equality relation on the arc $(1, 4)$.

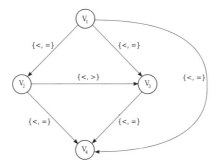

Figure 2.12. *A time-point network which is algebraically closed and consistent, but not minimal*

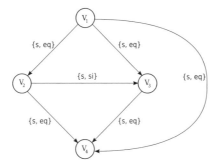

Figure 2.13. *An interval network which is algebraically closed and consistent, but not minimal*

Analogous counterexamples can easily be exhibited for interval networks. For example, the network in Figure 2.13 is algebraically closed, but not minimal.

Another example is the network:

$$C(V_1, V_2) = C(V_1, V_3) = C(V_1, V_4) = C(V_2, V_4) = C(V_3, V_4) = \{\mathsf{o}, \mathsf{fi}\}$$
$$C(V_2, V_3) = \{\mathsf{o}, \mathsf{di}\}$$

Van Beek [BEE 92] shows that in the case of time-point networks, any counterexample contains a subnetwork such as the one considered above. Using this fact, he describes an algorithm which computes the minimal network in $O(n^4)$ time.

2.2.6. Pre-convex relations

The subclass of convex relations contains less than 1% of the set of all relations, and about twice as many pointizable relations. The existence of larger subclasses of tractable relations was not known until 1994, when Nebel and Bürckert [NEB 94c, NEB 95] discovered a subclass of relations which they called the ORD-Horn relations. This subclass contains more than 10% of the set of relations, and the same authors showed that the consistency problem for this subclass can be solved in polynomial time by using the algebraic closure method. Moreover, this subclass is the only maximal tractable subclass containing all basic relations.

This subclass may also be defined in geometric terms as the class of pre-convex relations [LIG 94b, LIG 96]. This is what we will now proceed to do.

The intuitive idea of the definition of pre-convex relations is that the "almost" convex relations obtained by removing some basic relations of strictly smaller dimension from a convex relation of a given dimension are "almost as tractable" as convex relations. An example is provided by the pointizable relations, which, as seen before (proposition 2.5), are obtained from convex relations by removing basic relations of smaller dimension, using the odd cut operation.

EXAMPLE 2.6.– Let us consider the relation $\{o, s, fi\}$, which is of dimension 2. We obtain it by excluding the relation eq, of dimension 0 from the convex relation $[o, eq]$. This relation is not pointizable. On the other hand, it is a typical example of a pre-convex relation.

DEFINITION 2.10.– A relation r is pre-convex if it satisfies one of the following equivalent conditions:

  – the topological closure $Cl(r)$ is a convex relation;
  – $Cl(r) \supseteq I(r)$;
  – $dim\ (I(r) \setminus r) < dim(r)$;
  – r can be obtained from a convex relation by removing some of its basic relations dimension 0 or 1.

Let $\mathcal{P}(\mathbf{A}_2)$ denote the class of pre-convex relations.

Clearly, the definition of pre-convex relations provides an immediate criterion for pre-convexity using the lattice representation. Given a pre-convex relation, it is also very easy to determine the set of pre-convex relations that it contains.

EXAMPLE 2.7.– Let us start from the convex relation $r = [p, si]$ (Figure 2.14 (a)). It is of dimension 2 and contains four basic relations of dimension 1, namely m, s, fi, si and one relation of dimension 0, namely eq. Hence it contains $2^5 - 1 = 31$ pre-convex relations other than itself.

The set of pre-convex relations is set of relations which contains the pointizable relations. Actually, it is a subclass of relations:

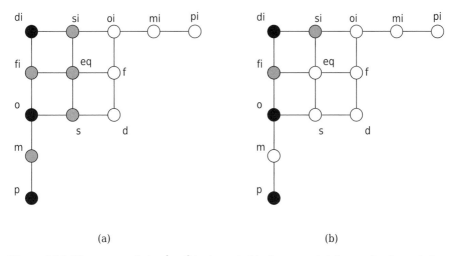

(a)   (b)

Figure 2.14. *The convex relation* [p, si] *is shown in black or gray, (a). It contains four relations of dimension 1 or 0 (in gray); on the right (b), we find one of the 31 pre-convex relations that can be deduced from it; here, we have excluded* m, s, *and* eq

PROPOSITION 2.7.– *The set of pre-convex relations is a subclass of relations: it is closed under the inversion, composition, and intersection operations.*

Proof. The fact that the inverse of a pre-convex relation is itself pre-convex is easily checked: for example, it is a consequence of the fact that r and r^{-1} are of the same dimension, and of the last condition of definition 2.10.

Let us show the stability under composition. Let r and s be two pre-convex relations. In order to show that their composition is itself pre-convex, we will show that $Cl(r \circ s)$ contains $I(r \circ s)$. We know (proposition 2.1) that $Cl(r \circ s) \supseteq Cl(r) \circ Cl(s)$. In addition, we deduce from $Cl(r) \supseteq I(r)$ and $Cl(s) \supseteq I(s)$ that $Cl(r) \circ Cl(s) \supseteq I(r) \circ I(s)$. Since moreover $I(r \circ s) = I(r) \circ I(s)$, we obtain the desired result.

The last point is the fact that the intersection of two pre-convex relations r and s is itself pre-convex. This is not as obvious as it appears, but is true, and it can be proved by using the last characterization: if $r \cap s$ is empty, it is pre-convex. If not, we can obtain $r \cap s$ by removing a certain number of relations of dimension 0 or 1 from the relation $I(r \cap s) = I(r) \cap I(s)$, which shows that this relation is pre-convex. □

2.2.7. *Polynomiality of pre-convex relations*

The following result is shown in [LIG 96]:

PROPOSITION 2.8.– *A network (N, C) which is pre-convex, algebraically closed and does not contain the empty relation is a consistent network. Moreover, it is generically* minimal *in the following sense: if $b \in C(i,j)$ is a basic relation such that dim $(b) =$ dim$(C(i,j))$, then there is a consistent scenario for which the relation b holds between i and j.*

The previous result suggests the following method to build a consistent scenario, starting from a network which is pre-convex and algebraically closed: on a first arc, we choose a basic relation of maximum dimension in the constraint. We know that the subnetwork obtained by replacing the initial constraint by this basic relation is consistent. We compute the algebraic closure of this subnetwork, which is consistent and contains the basic relation selected on the arc considered. We then choose a second arc and a basic relation of maximal dimension on it, and repeat the same procedure. We may thus continue as long as all the constraints are not reduced to basic relations. When this condition is met, we get a consistent scenario for the initial network. The instantiation obtained in this way is a *maximal instantiation*:

DEFINITION 2.11.– *Let $(\mathcal{N} = N, C)$ be a consistent network. An instantiation m of the variables of this network is a* maximal instantiation *if for any pair (i,j), the dimension of the relation between m (i) and m (j) is equal to the dimension of $C(i,j)$.*

2.2.7.1. *Maximality of pre-convex relations*

The subclass $\mathcal{P}(\mathbf{A_2})$ of pre-convex relations contains all basic relations, and it is tractable. It is in fact the only maximal subclass among all the subclasses having these two properties. More precisely, the following result is shown in [LIG 98a]:

PROPOSITION 2.9.– *Let r be an Allen's relation which is not pre-convex. Then, the consistency problem for the relations of the set $\mathcal{P}(\mathbf{A_2}) \cup \{r\}$ is NP-complete.*

The subclass $\mathcal{P}(\mathbf{A_2})$ is thus the only maximal subclass among the tractable subclasses containing the basic relations to possess these properties.

The proof of this proposition uses a detailed analysis of the geometrical properties (in the lattice of basic relations) of those relations that are not pre-convex. It involves four specific relations called *corner relations* (see Figure 2.15).

DEFINITION 2.12.– *The* corner relations *of Allen's algebra are the four relations $N_o = \{\text{di, fi, o, s, d}\}$, $N_{di} = \{\text{oi, si, di, fi, o}\}$, $N_{oi} = \{\text{d, f, oi, si, di}\}$ and $N_d = \{\text{o, s, d, f, oi}\}$.*

The corner relations are not pre-convex relations. They have the following property:

PROPOSITION 2.10.– *Any subclass of relations which contains all the basic relations and which also contains a relation that is not pre-convex contains at least two corner relations.*

Proof. Let S be a subclass which contains all basic relations as well as a relation α that is not pre-convex. Let $I(\alpha)$ be the convex closure of α. The starting point of the proof

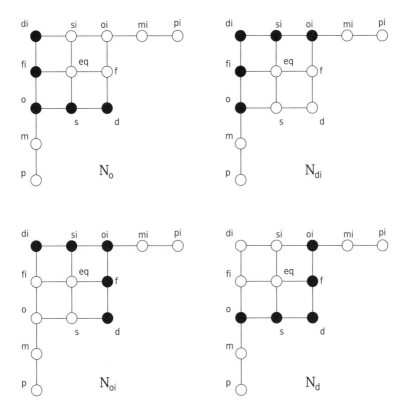

Figure 2.15. *The four corner relations N_o, N_{di}, N_{oi}, and N_d*

is to notice that $I(\alpha) \setminus \alpha$ must then contain a basic relation of dimension 2, hence one of the six relations p, o, d, pi, oi, and di.

Now, this relation cannot be p because, if α does not contain p, α is contained in the convex relation [m, pi], and the same holds true for its convex closure $I(\alpha)$. A similar argument shows that it cannot be pi either.

Let us then suppose that this basic relation of dimension 2 is o. Let us partition the set of basic relations other than o into four subsets $A_1 = [\text{p}, \text{m}]$, $A_2 = [\text{s}, \text{d}]$, $A_3 = [\text{fi}, \text{di}]$, and $A_4 = [\text{eq}, \text{pi}]$ (Figure 2.16 (a)).

If α does not contain any element of A_1, it must necessarily contain a basic relation of A_2 and one of A_3. It can be easily verified that $((\alpha \cap A_2) \circ \text{oi})$ is either [d, oi], or [d, pi], and that $((\alpha \cap A_3) \circ \text{oi}) = [\text{di}, \text{oi}]$. As $((\alpha \cap A_4) \circ \text{oi})$ is contained in [oi, pi], we conclude that $(\alpha \circ \text{oi}) \cap [\text{o}, \text{oi}]$ is the corner relation N_{oi}. However, oi and $[\text{o}, \text{oi}] = (\text{di} \circ \text{d})$ are elements of S. Consequently, S contains N_{oi}.

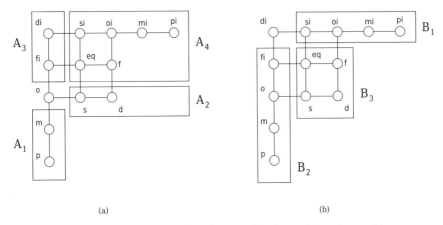

(a)   (b)

Figure 2.16. *A partition of the relations other than* o *(a), and a partition*
of the relations other than di *(b)*

If α contains an element of A_1, as well as an element of A_2, then $[p, d] \cap \alpha$ is an element α' of S (since $[p, d] = (p \circ oi)$) which intersects A_1 and A_2. We can easily verify that $(\alpha' \cap A_1) \circ oi$ is $[p, d]$ or $[o, d]$, and that $(\alpha' \cap A_2) \circ oi$ is $[d, oi]$ or $[d, pi]$. Consequently, $(\alpha' \circ oi) \cap [o, oi] = N_d$ is an element of S.

If α contains an element of A_1, as well as an element of A_3, then $[p, di] \cap \alpha$ is an element α'' of S (since $[p, di] = (o \circ di)$) which intersects A_1 and A_3. We can easily verify that oi $\circ (\alpha'' \cap A_1)$ is $[p, di]$ or $[o, di]$, and that oi $\circ (\alpha'' \cap A_2)$ is $[di, oi]$ or $[di, pi]$. Consequently, $(oi \circ \alpha'') \cap [o, oi] = N_{di}$ is an element of S.

If α contains an element of A_1 but does not intersect neither N_2 nor N_3, α contains an element of N_4. We can easily verify that $(\alpha \cap A_1) \circ [d, oi]$ is $[p, d]$ or $[o, d]$, and that $(\alpha \cap A_4) \circ [d, oi]$ is $[d, oi]$ or $[d, pi]$. Thus, $(\alpha \circ [d, oi]) \cap [o, oi]$ is the relation N_d.

Let us suppose now that $I(\alpha) \setminus \alpha$ contains di. Let us partition the set of basic relations other than o into three subsets $B_1 = [si, pi]$, $B_2 = [p, fi]$, and $B_3 = [s, f]$ (Figure 2.16 (b)).

This time, α must have a non-empty intersection with B_1 and B_2. We can easily verify that $(\alpha \cap B_1) \circ d$ contains $[d, oi]$, and that $(\alpha \cap B_2) \circ d$ contains $[o, d]$. On the other hand, $(B_3 \circ d) = \{d\}$. We conclude from it that $(\alpha \circ d) \cap [o, oi]$ is the relation N_d, which is thus an element of S.

The cases where $I(\alpha) \setminus \alpha$ contains oi or d can be deduced from the previous cases.   □

It is then easy to prove NP-completeness by showing that the 3-SAT problem can be encoded in terms of relations belonging to S [NEB 95].

2.2.8. ORD-Horn relations

As mentioned above, these results have an equivalent formulation in terms of ORD-Horn relations.

Rather than starting from the original definitions of Nebel and Bürckert, we will make use of the lattice of Allen's relations. We consider this lattice in the frame of reference centered at $O = (0,0)$ with coordinate axes X_1 and X_2.

We begin by defining the language of ORD-Horn clauses:

– a *positive literal* is an expression of the form $X_i \leq \varpi$, $X_i \geq \varpi$ or $X_i = \varpi$, where $i \in \{1, 2\}$ and $\varpi \in \{1, 3\}$ is an odd integer between 0 and 4;

– a *negative literal* is an expression of the form $X_i \neq \varpi$, where $i \in \{1, 2\}$ and $\varpi \in \{1, 3\}$;

– an *ORD-clause* is a disjunction of literals;

– an *ORD-Horn clause* is an ORD-clause containing at most one positive literal.

We can now define the ORD-Horn relations in the lattice:

DEFINITION 2.13.– *A relation is an* ORD-Horn relation *if it can be defined in the lattice of relations by an ORD-Horn clause.*

It becomes clear that the convex relations are ORD-Horn relations if we notice that inequalities such as $X_i \leq k$ and $X_i \geq k$, where k is equal to 0 or 2, can be replaced by conditions involving odd integers only, and that the same holds true for strict inequalities.

EXAMPLE 2.8.– The convex relation [o, oi] whose projection is $[0, 2] \times [2, 4]$, is thus naturally defined by $X_1 \leq 2$ and $X_2 \geq 2$ (Figure 2.17 (a)). We may replace the first condition by $(X_1 \leq 3)$ and $(X_1 \neq 3)$, and the second condition by $(X_2 \geq 1)$ and $(X_2 \neq 1)$. The four clauses obtained in this way are thus ORD-Horn clauses.

EXAMPLE 2.9.– The relation $r = \{o, s, fi\}$ is obtained by removing the relation eq from the convex relation [o, eq] (Figure 2.17 (b)). The latter is defined by $X_1 \leq 1$, $X_2 \geq 1$, $X_2 \neq 1$ and $X_2 \leq 3$. Consequently, the relation r is defined by the five clauses: $X_1 \leq 1$, $X_2 \geq 1$, $X_2 \neq 1$, $X_2 \leq 3$ and $(X_1 \neq 1) \vee (X_2 \neq 3)$, which are all Horn clauses. It is thus an ORD-Horn relation.

In Chapter 3, we will see that the concept of pre-convex relation can be defined within a more general framework. In the case of Allen's relations, the geometrical concept of pre-convex relation and the syntactic concept of ORD-Horn relation define the same relations:

PROPOSITION 2.11.– *A relation is an ORD-Horn relation if, and only if, it is pre-convex.*

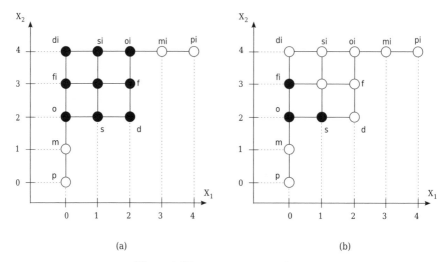

Figure 2.17. *Two ORD-Horn relations*

2.3. Maximal tractable subclasses of Allen's algebra

The subclass of pre-convex relations (or ORD-Horn relations) is thus the only maximal subclass which contains all basic relations.

More generally, let us leave out the last condition, and focus on all the maximum tractable subclasses of Allen's algebra. These subclasses were determined by Krokhin, Jeavons, and Jonsson [KRO 03], who showed that there are exactly 18 maximal tractable subclasses.

2.3.1. *An alternative characterization of pre-convex relations*

The 18 maximal tractable subclasses can all be characterized by conditions of the following type: "if a relation intersects such-and-such relations fixed in advance, then it necessarily contains such basic relation".

In particular, the subclass of pre-convex relations can be characterized in the following way. The pre-convex relations are those relations which satisfy the following conditions:

1) if r meets $[o, s]$ and $[f, oi]$, then it contains d;

2) if r meets $[s, d]$ and $[fi, di]$, then it contains o;

3) if r meets $[p, m]$ and $[o, d]$, then it contains o;

4) the three conditions obtained by replacing the relations in the preceding conditions by their inverses.

For example, the last condition means that, along with the condition 1), the relation must also verify the condition 1′) which we will refer to as the dual condition of 1): 1′). That is, if r meets [si, oi] and [o, fi], then it contains di.

Figure 2.18 represents these conditions in a pictorial way: if a relation intersects the black relation and the gray relation, then it contains the atomic relation pointed to by the arrow.

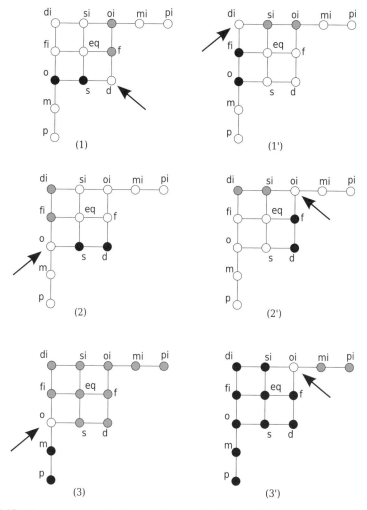

Figure 2.18. *The pre-convex relations are characterized by conditions 1), 2), 3) and conditions 1′), 2′), 3′): they are those which, when intersecting both a black relation and a gray relation, also contain the relation pointed to by the arrow*

2.3.2. *The other maximal polynomial subclasses*

In addition to the subclass of pre-convex relations, denoted by $\mathcal{H}$ in [KRO 03], the list of maximal tractable subclasses contains 17 more subclasses, which we will describe by using Figures 2.19, 2.20, 2.21, 2.22, 2.23 and 2.24.

To make things easier to understand, let us agree that the *dual condition* of the statement "if r intersects S, then r contains the atomic relation a" is the condition "if r intersects S^{-1}, then r contains the atomic relation a^{-1}".

The class $\mathcal{A}$ is formed by the empty relation and all the relations which contain eq; here, the condition is: "if r intersects the universal relation, i.e. is non-empty, then it contains eq".

Three subclasses denoted by $\mathcal{S}_\mathrm{p}, \mathcal{S}_\mathrm{o},$ and $\mathcal{S}_\mathrm{d}$ are defined, respectively, as follows (Figure 2.19):
  – "if r intersects [p, di], then it contains p", and its dual condition;
  – "if r intersects [p, di], then it contains o", and its dual condition;
  – "if r intersects [p, di], then it contains d", and its dual condition.

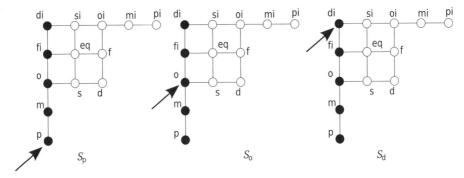

Figure 2.19. *The subclasses $\mathcal{S}_\mathrm{p}, \mathcal{S}_\mathrm{o}, \mathcal{S}_\mathrm{d}$: if the relation contains one of the relations in black, it contains the relation pointed to by the arrow (dual conditions are not shown)*

Four subclasses $\mathcal{A}_1, \mathcal{A}_2, \mathcal{A}_3,$ and $\mathcal{A}_4$ are defined, respectively, as follows (Figure 2.20):
  – "if r intersects [p, di], then it contains si", and its dual condition;
  – "if r intersects [p, di], then it contains s", and its dual condition;
  – "if r intersects $\{p, m, o, d, f\}$, then it contains s", and its dual condition;
  – "if r intersects $\{p, m, o, d, fi\}$, then it contains s", and its dual condition.

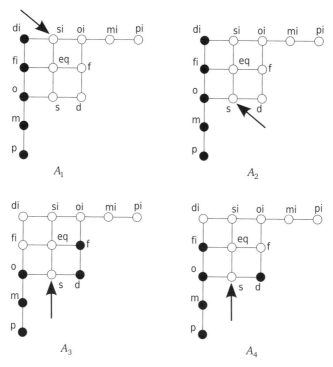

Figure 2.20. *The subclasses A_i, for $i = 1, \ldots, 4$: if the relation contains one of the relations in black, it contains the relation pointed to by the arrow (dual conditions not shown)*

Four subclasses $\mathcal{B}_1, \mathcal{B}_2, \mathcal{B}_3$, and $\mathcal{B}_4$ are defined, respectively, as follows (Figure 2.21):

- "if r intersects $[p, d]$, then it contains fi", and its dual condition;
- "if r intersects $[p, d]$, then it contains f", and its dual condition;
- "if r intersects $\{p, m, o, di, si\}$, then it contains fi", and its dual condition;
- "if r intersects $\{p, m, o, di, s\}$, then it contains fi", and its dual condition.

Three subclasses $\mathcal{E}_p, \mathcal{E}_o$, and $\mathcal{E}_d$ are defined, respectively, as follows (Figure 2.22):

- "if r intersects $[p, d]$, then it contains p", and its dual condition;
- "if r intersects $[p, d]$, then it contains o", and its dual condition;
- "if r intersects $[p, d]$, then it contains d", and its dual condition.

The subclass $\mathcal{E}^*$ is defined by the conjunction of the conditions (Figure 2.23):

- "if r intersects $\{p, m, o, d\}$, then it contains s" and its dual condition;
- "if r intersects $\{fi, f\}$, then it contains eq.

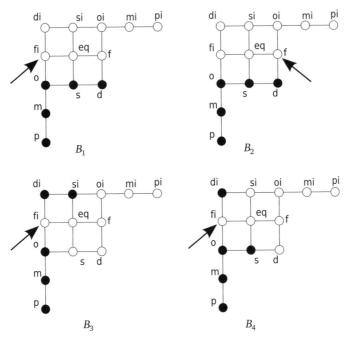

Figure 2.21. *The subclasses B_i, for $i = 1, \ldots, 4$: if the relation contains one of the relations in black, it contains the relation pointed to by the arrow (dual conditions are not shown)*

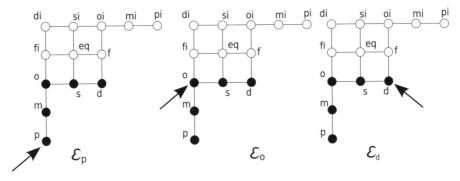

Figure 2.22. *The subclasses $\mathcal{E}_p, \mathcal{E}_o, \mathcal{E}_d$: if the relation contains one of the relations in black, it contains the relation pointed to by the arrow (dual conditions are not shown)*

The subclass $\mathcal{S}*$ is defined by the conjunction of the conditions (Figure 2.24):

– "if r intersects $\{p, m, o, di\}$, then it contains fi", and its dual condition;

– "if r intersects $\{s, si\}$, then it contains eq".

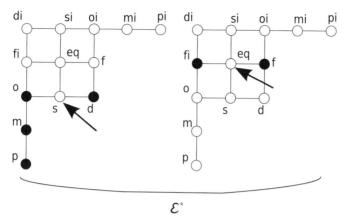

Figure 2.23. *The subclass $\mathcal{E}^*$: if the relation contains one of the relations in black, it contains the relation pointed to by the arrow (dual conditions are not shown)*

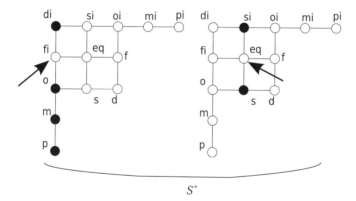

Figure 2.24. *The subclass S^*: if the relation contains one of the relations in black, it contains the relation pointed to by the arrow (dual conditions are not shown)*

2.4. Using polynomial subclasses

2.4.1. *Ladkin and Reinefeld's algorithm*

Let us come back to the consistency problem for constraint networks. When the relations considered are arbitrary, the algebraic closure method is not enough to solve the problem; it only provides a technique for reducing the given network.

The naive method for deciding consistency, then, consists in checking whether, for each choice of a basic relation as a label on each arc, the corresponding subnetwork is consistent and, in the event of failure, to backtrack and make another choice, until one consistent subnetwork is found (success), or all choices have been examined without success (failure).

EXAMPLE 2.10.– Let us consider the network of Example 1.10. For the convenience of the reader, we give its description in Figure 2.25. The naive method would consist in successively examining the 32 possibilities of choice of an atomic relation on the five arcs whose labels are not basic relations.

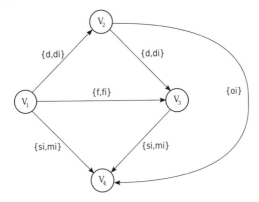

Figure 2.25. *A non-zero algebraically closed network which is not consistent (see Example 1.10)*

We make the search simpler by using the algebraic closure operation: if for example, we choose the relation d on the arc (V_1, V_2), we note that the corresponding subnetwork has an algebraic closure which contains the empty relation, and that the same holds true for the choice of di. We thus conclude that the network is not consistent by using a single backtrack.

This process of filtering using the algebraic closure is applied by Ladkin and Reinefeld [LAD 92]. In the same chapter, the authors notice that the set of basic relations can be replaced by any subclass for which the algebraic closure method is complete (i.e. for which a non-zero algebraically closed network is consistent). This is in particular the case of the subclass of convex relations, of the pointizable relations, and of the subclass of pre-convex relations. The advantage is that the branching factor is reduced *a priori* at the time of a backtrack. For example, an arbitrary relation is the union of at most 5 pre-convex relations, so that the branching factor is reduced from 13 to 5 if we use pre-convex relations rather than basic relations.

Ladkin and Reinefeld's algorithm [LAD 92, NEB 97] is shown in Figure 2.26. The notation S denotes a subclass of relations for which the algebraic closure method is complete. The function **Alg-clos** associates its algebraic closure with a network. Nebel shows in [NEB 97] that the algorithm is complete when the subclass S has the property of completeness.

Data: A constraint network $N = (V, C)$
Result: Returns **true** if the network is consistent
function CONSISTENT (C)
Alg-clos (N)
if C *contains the empty constraint* **then**
| **return** *false*
else
| **choose** an unprocessed label C (i, j) and
| decompose it into $r_1, \ldots, rk$ such that $r_l \in \mathcal{S}$
| **if** *no label can be decomposed* **then**
| | **return** *true*
| **end**
| **for each** $r_l (1 \leq i \leq k)$ **do**
| | $C(i, j) \leftarrow r_l$
| | **if** *consistent* (C) **then**
| | | **return** *true*
| | **end**
| **end**
| **return** *false*
end

Figure 2.26. *The* CONSISTENT *algorithm. It uses the function **Alg-clos** which associates its algebraic closure with a network*

2.4.2. *Empirical study of the consistency problem*

Several works have studied the effectiveness of the various methods for solving the NP-complete consistency problem for arbitrary Allen's networks.

Ladkin and Reinefeld [LAD 97] show that problems of sizes going up to 500 variables are quickly solved by using the algebraic closure method as a filtering technique. They describe several techniques for optimizing the computation of the composition and algebraic closure, and study the influence of the branching factor when the subclasses used are those of pointizable relations and of pre-convex relations.

A general phenomenon for NP-complete problems is the presence of very hard instances of the problem in the *phase transition* region [CHE 91, SEL 95]. A characterization of the latter is proposed in [LAD 97].

Van Beek and Manchak [BEE 96] have developed the techniques of Ladkin and Manchak and studied the potential benefits of using the class of pre-convex relations instead of the class of pointizable relations.

Nebel [NEB 97] provides a characterization of the phase transition region, and shows that, as opposed to what could have been expected from previous studies, the use of the class of pre-convex relations in fact makes it possible to deal more efficiently with the very hard instances encountered in this region.

2.5. Models of Allen's language

2.5.1. *Representations of Allen's algebra*

Let us refer back to the reading grid that we proposed in the Introduction for a formalism. The last point is concerned with the question of the models of the formalism. Intuitively, it is a matter of answering the question: what does the formalism talk about? The implicit assumption is that there may be other possible interpretations than those that motivated contructing the formalism in the first place.

In the case of Allen's calculus, we consider a language which uses 13 symbols, and whose axioms are the JEPD property and the axioms expressed by the composition table of Allen's algebra.

Let us recall (see section 1.4.3) the dual use me make of the basic relation symbols. We have used these symbols p, m, etc. to denote binary relations on the set of (bounded and closed) intervals of the real line, and noted that this particular interpretation of the symbols constitutes a binary relation algebra. Consequently, if we forget about the interpretation and retain only the algebraic abstraction, the set of all subsets of this set of symbols, equipped with the relevant operations, is a relation algebra which we denoted by A_2. We thus have a representation of this abstract algebra with a specific interpretation in terms of intervals. We also noted that the intervals (ordered pairs of distinct points) of the rational line would have as well fit the bill.

We will use the framework of relation algebras to formulate the question of the models of Allen's calculus. Then the question is: what are the representations of Allen's algebra? We will examine the issue in detail in Chapter 9.

2.5.2. *Representations of the time-point algebra*

In the study of models as we understand it here, the case of the Point algebra is particularly enlightening. Recall (refer to Appendix B for the general definition of a representation of a relation algebra) that a representation of the relation algebra A_1 is a pair (U, ϕ) such that U is a non-empty set and ϕ a map which associates to the symbol $<$, a binary relation R verifying the following conditions:

– the relations R, Δ, R^{-1} constitute a partition of $U \times U$;

– R is transitive, dense, and unlimited on the left and on the right.

Consequently, a representation of the Point algebra is simply a dense linear order, unlimited on the left and on the right. In particular, there is no finite representation, and any countable representation is isomorphic to the linear order $\mathbb{Q}$, according to a theorem of Cantor.

The first order theory associated with the Point algebra thus has the $\aleph_0$-categoricity property.

2.5.3. $\aleph_0$-categoricity of Allen's algebra

In his thesis, Ladkin shows [LAD 87], by using the method of elimination of quantifiers, that the theory associated with Allen's algebra is $\aleph_0$-categorical. This implies that it is decidable.

As mentioned earlier, we will see in Chapter 9 that this result can be generalized: the Point algebra and Allen's algebra are two particular cases of generalized interval algebras, and we will show that the result extends to a whole family of formalisms based on linear orders.

2.6. Historical note

The original proof by Nebel and Bürckert [NEB 95] of the fact that the consistency problem is polynomial for ORD-Horn relations makes an essential use of the general properties of Horn theories. The fact that the algebraic closure algorithm can be used for deciding their consistency is also proved. The maximality of the class of ORD-Horn relations and its uniqueness are also shown in the chapter by an exhaustive exploration using a computer program.

In the alternative geometrical approach, the proof of the fact that pre-convex and algebraically closed networks are consistent is a consequence of a geometrical property of pre-convex relations: they are "almost" closed by projection (see definition 2.5): if we project them on the axes of coordinate, then consider the product of the projections, we obtain (after intersecting with the half-plane **H**) a relation which, in general, strictly contains the initial relation, but which only adds to it basic relations of *strictly smaller dimensions*. It is this property which makes it possible to build an instantiation which "avoids" the prohibited zones, as explained in [LIG 96].

The proof of the maximality property for pre-convex relations, of which we gave a quick presentation in this chapter, is described in detail in [LIG 98a]. The same technique is used in [LIG 98b] for the cardinal relation calculus (see Chapter 4).

Chapter 3

Generalized Intervals

3.1. "When they built the bridge ... "

In their analysis of the semantics of temporal expressions, Moens and Steedmann [MOE 88] consider the following example:

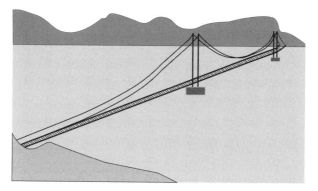

Figure 3.1. *When they built the bridge ...*

"When they built the 39th Street bridge ... ,

1) ... a local architect drew up the plans;

2) ... they used the best materials;

3) ... they solved most of their traffic problems".

What are the mechanisms which help us to understand that 1) refers to the preparatory period of the construction, 2) refers to the period of construction itself, and 3) refers to the state of affairs resulting from the completion of the construction? To answer this question, the authors propose to analyze each event in terms of entities which occupy two contiguous temporal intervals: a *preparatory process*, followed by a *culmination point*, which in turn is followed by a *resulting state* (Figure 3.2).

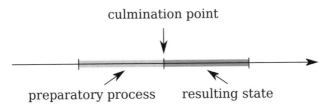

Figure 3.2. *A sequence containing a preparatory process, a culmination point, and a resulting state is associated with each event*

Thus, a temporal entity is associated with an event and this temporal entity comprises not two (its beginning and its end) but three successive points, since a culmination point is added between the first two.

Other types of analyses of the *linguistic semantics* of time result in the introduction of ordered sequences of points. For example, the analysis of tenses by Reichenbach [REI 66] involves a time of event (E), a time of reference (R), and a time of speech (S). Introducing a representation which generalizes these concepts, Bestougeff and Ligozat [BES 89b] refer to the structures associated with texts in natural language as *temporal sites*. The desire for reasoning about the constraints involved in the construction of these sites is the initial motivation for introducing ordered sequences of points, which are considered as fully-fledged temporal entities.

3.1.1. *Towards generalized intervals*

If we move from the field of linguistics to that of the constitution of temporal databases, we may be interested in activities whose temporal support is actually an interval, but which, in addition to their beginnings and ends, contain intermediate points. For example, we may consider medical records mentioning a date of admission, a date of intervention, and a date of release.

Conversely, we can also, while reasoning about intervals, consider time points, which may or may not be the extremities of the intervals. We then deal with two types of identities, and the qualitative relations that we consider are point to point, point to interval, interval to point, and interval to interval. We thus obtain a formalism, the *point-and-interval calculus*, which has been introduced and studied in particular by Vilain [VIL 82] and Meiri [MEI 96].

Finally, many protracted processes have a temporal support that splits into several intervals separated by interruptions: consider for example the meeting periods of a committee, or the successive periods of activity of a computer. The temporal support of such processes is thus formed by a sequence of intervals. Ladkin [LAD 86] refers to the temporal entities containing several connected components (which are intervals themselves) as *non-convex intervals*. A natural way to study the relations between non-convex intervals is to associate with them the sequence of their bounding points, which is an increasing sequence of an even number of points. Figure 3.3 shows, for example, how an increasing sequence of six points (called a 6-interval) is associated with a non-convex interval consisting of three connected components.

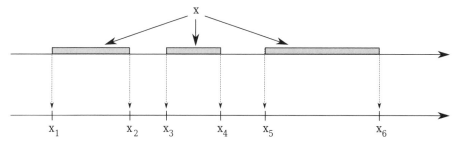

Figure 3.3. *A non-convex interval (here, formed by three disjoint intervals) can be represented by an increasing sequence of points (here, six points)*

Allen's calculus, which was discussed in the previous chapters, deals with intervals represented as ordered pairs of points. The Time Point calculus is its analog for punctual temporal entities. We have seen that these two formalisms have similar properties, and we have shown how the language of constraint networks allowed a type of reasoning which benefits from the use of constraint propagation methods.

In this chapter, we will show that many concepts introduced for Allen's calculus can be extended to the general framework of entities made up of finite sequences of points, and we will use the analysis grid considered in the introduction: definition of a language and study of its complexity. The question of models will be discussed in a broader context in Chapter 9.

3.2. Entities and relations

Without further ado, let us define the temporal entity which will generalize points and intervals: let T be a linear order representing the temporal structure. For example, T can be $\mathbb{N}$, $\mathbb{Q}$, or $\mathbb{R}$.

DEFINITION 3.1.– *Let p be a positive integer. A p-interval x in T is a strictly increasing sequence $(x_1, \ldots x_p)$ of points of T. A generalized interval is a p-interval, for some*

p. If $x = (x_1, \ldots x_p)$ is a p-interval, we will say that $x_i (1 \leq i \leq p)$ is its i-th boundary.

If T is a finite set with K elements (thus isomorphic to the subset $[0, K-1]$ of $\mathbb{N}$), then clearly the only possible p-intervals are those for which $p \leq K$.

Hence, a 1-interval is a point, a 2-interval is an interval, in Allen's sense.

Let $Int_p(T)$ denote the set of p-intervals of T.

As in the cases of points and intervals, we focus on the qualitative relations between the generalized intervals which result from possible orderings of the points constituting these generalized intervals. To do this, it is convenient to use the above-mentioned technique for Allen's intervals.

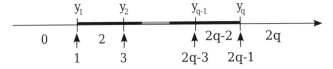

Figure 3.4. *Encoding (p, q)-relations: a q-interval $y = (y_1, \ldots, y_q)$ defines $(2q + 1)$ zones numbered from 0 to $2q$*

Given a q-interval of reference $y = (y_1, \ldots, y_q)$, we thus define in T, a set of $(2q + 1)$ zones numbered from 0 to $2q$ (Figure 3.4)

– zone 0 is defined as $\{t \in T \mid t < y_1\}$;
– zone 1 is defined as $\{y_1\}$;
– zone $2k$ is defined as $\{t \in T \mid y_k < t < y_{k+1}\}(0 \leq k < q)$;
– zone $2k + 1$ is defined as $\{y_{k+1}\}$;
– zone $2q$ is defined as $\{t \in T \mid t > y_q\}$.

In particular, a point defines three zones numbered from 0 to 2. An interval defines five zones as already discussed in section 2.2.4.

Let y be a q-interval and x be a p-interval in T. The relations that we focus on are entirely determined by the list of the numbers of the zones (defined by y) that contain the successive boundaries $(x_1, \ldots, x_p)$ of x. Clearly, this list is a non-decreasing sequence of p integers, and moreover, the zones with odd numberings being points, the same odd integer cannot appear more than once in the list.

Conversely, it can be easily be seen that such a sequence defines a possible qualitative relation. This motivates the following definition:

DEFINITION 3.2.– *Let p and q be two positive integers. A basic (p, q)-relation is a nondecreasing sequence of p integers ranging between 0 and $2q$, such that no odd integer appears more than once in the sequence.*

The set of basic (p, q)-relations is denoted by $\Pi_{p,q}$. An element of $\Pi_{p,q}$ is thus a sequence of integers (indexed by (p, q), if there is any ambiguity).

EXAMPLE 3.1.– For $p = q = 1$, we obtain three relations $(0)_{1,1}$, $(1)_{1,1}$, and $(2)_{1,1}$ corresponding to precedence, equality, and the inverse of precedence between points.

When $p = q = 2$, we find the encoding of Allen's basic relations, as introduced in section 2.2.4.

EXAMPLE 3.2.– Let us simultaneously consider points (1-intervals) and 2-intervals. In addition to the relations between the entities of the same type, we have five possible relations between a point and an interval: $(0)_{1,2}$ (the point precedes the interval), $(1)_{1,2}$ (the point starts the interval), $(2)_{1,2}$ (the point is inside the interval), $(3)_{1,2}$ (the point ends the interval), and $(4)_{1,2}$ (the point follows the interval). Simultaneously, we have five relations between the intervals and points: $(0,0)_{2,1}$ (the interval is completely before the point), $(0,1)_{2,1}$ (the interval is finished by the point), $(0,2)_{2,1}$ (the interval contains the point), $(1,2)_{2,1}$ (the interval is started by the point), and $(2,2)_{2,1}$ (the interval follows the point).

The above example is a particular case of a general situation: if S is a subset of positive integers, we may consider the set $\Pi_S = \bigcup_{p,q \in S} \Pi_{p,q}$. This set is the set of qualitative relations between the generalized intervals of which the number of boundaries is an element of S. The set of relations between the points and intervals thus corresponds to $\Pi_{\{1,2\}}$, which is the union of $\Pi_{1,1}$ (3 elements), $\Pi_{1,2}$ (5 elements), $\Pi_{2,1}$ (5 elements), and $\Pi_{2,2}$ (13 elements), totalling 26 basic relations in all.

Do (p, q)-relations have the JEPD property?

We have previously introduced (section 1.2.1.2) the JEPD property in connection with Allen's relation. The essentially intensional definition of basic (p, q)-relations given here clearly implies that the various relations of $\Pi_{p,q}$ are pairwise disjoint, and that any pair formed by a p-interval and q-interval is exactly one of the relations of $\Pi_{p,q}$.

However, without any further assumption on the temporal structure T, it is possible that some of the basic (p, q)-relations are empty. For example, if T is the linear order with two elements, there are only two points and one 2-interval, which is started by the first point and finished by the second one. This means, in particular, that the three relations $(0)_{1,2}$, $(2)_{1,2}$, and $(4)_{1,2}$ are empty.

If T is infinite, no basic relation is empty:

PROPOSITION 3.1.– *If T is infinite, the relations of $\Pi_{p,q}(T)$ are non-empty and constitute a partition of $Int_p(T) \times Int_q(T)$.*

Proof. If T is infinite, it is easy to build a configuration according to the model defined by an element of $\Pi_{p,q}(T)$. It is sufficient to have $p + m$ distinct points, where m is the number of even integers in the encoding of the relation.

EXAMPLE 3.3.– Let us prove for example that the element $(0, 0, 4, 9)_{4,5}$ of $\Pi_{4,5}(T)$ is not empty. Choose a strictly increasing sequence of eight points $t_1, \ldots, t_8$ in T. It can be easily seen that the pair formed by the 4-interval (t_1, t_2, t_5, t_8) and the 5-interval $(t_3, t_4, t_6, t_7, t_8)$ belongs to the relation $(0, 0, 4, 9)_{4,5}(T)$, which is thus non-empty.

3.3. The lattice of basic (p, q)-relations

The elements of $\Pi_{p,q}$ are sequences of p integers (between 0 and $2q$). We can thus consider this set as a subset of $\mathbb{N}^p$ and provide it with the product ordering inherited from the usual ordering on $\mathbb{N}$ (as we did in the case of $p = q = 2$).

PROPOSITION 3.2.– *The set $\Pi_{p,q}$ provided with the product ordering is a distributive lattice. In fact, if $a = (a_1, \ldots, a_p)$ and $b = (b_1, \ldots, b_p)$ are two elements of $\Pi_{p,q}$, we have*

$$\inf(a, b) = (\inf (a_1, b_1), \ldots, \inf (a_p, b_p))$$

$$\sup(a, b) = (\sup (a_1, b_1), \ldots, \sup (a_p, b_p))$$

Proof. Let us first verify that $(\inf (a_1, b_1), \ldots \inf (a_p, b_p))$ is an element of $\Pi_{p,q}$. It is sufficient that this sequence of integers is non-decreasing and does not contain the same odd integer twice. However, $\inf (a_i, b_i) \leq \inf (a_{i+1}, b_{i+1})$, as is easily verified (four possible cases), which establishes that it is non-decreasing. Finally, we can deduce from the four cases that c_i is odd and $c_i = c_{i+1}$ would imply that either $c_i = a_i = a_{i+1}$, or $c_i = b_i = b_{i+1}$, which is impossible by assumption. Distributivity results from this explicit calculation.

Figure 3.5 represents the lattice $\Pi_{2,3}$ of the relations of a 2-interval with respect to a 3-interval. Figure 3.6 represents the lattice $\Pi_{3,3}$ of the relations between 3-intervals.

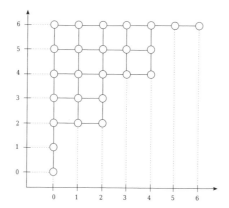

Figure 3.5. *The lattice $\Pi_{2,3}$ of the relations of a 2-interval with respect to a 3-interval*

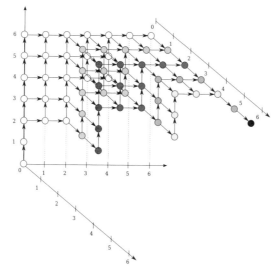

Figure 3.6. *The lattice $\Pi_{3,3}$ of the relations between 3-intervals. The elements of each vertical plane corresponding to each value of the first coordinate are uniformly colored*

3.4. Regions associated with basic (p, q)-relations

A p-interval of $\mathbb{R}$ corresponds to a point $x = (x_1, \ldots, x_p)$ such that $x_1 < \cdots < x_p$, and hence to a point located in the part of $\mathbb{R}^p$, that we will denote by Λ_p, which is the intersection of the half spaces $X_1 < X_2, \ldots X_{p-1} < X_p$. This intersection is the half-plane defined by $X_1 < X_2$ when $p = 2$. Given a fixed q-interval, $y = (y_1 < \cdots < y_q)$, the various basic (p, q)-relations define a partition of Λ_p into zones of dimensions varying from 0 to p.

EXAMPLE 3.4.– When $p = q = 1, \Lambda_1$ represents the entire real line. A fixed point y defines a partition of $\mathbb{R}$ into three zones $(-\infty, y)$, $\{y\}$, and $(y, +\infty)$.

EXAMPLE 3.5.– When $p = 1$ and $q = 2$, there is again a partition of the real line Λ_1. An interval (y_1, y_2) defines a partition of $\mathbb{R}$ into five zones $(-\infty, y_1)$, $\{y_1\}$, (y_1, y_2) $\{y_2\}$, and $(y_2, +\infty)$ (Figure 3.7 (a)).

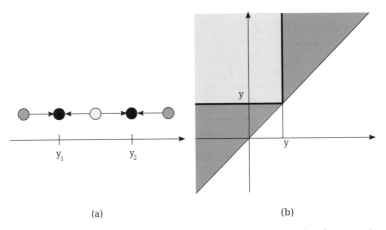

(a)   (b)

Figure 3.7. *The partition of the real line Λ_1 defined by an interval and its associated incidence graph (a); this graph is also the incidence graph associated with the partition $\Lambda_2 = \mathbf{H}$ define by a point y (b)*

The corresponding incidence graph is also represented in Figure 3.7 (a).

EXAMPLE 3.6.– When $p = 2$ and $q = 1$. In this case, Λ_2 is the upper half-plane $\mathbf{H}$ bounded by the first bisector. A point y defines a partition of $\mathbf{H}$ into five zones which are, respectively, defined by (i) $X_2 < y$; (ii) $X_2 = y$; (iii) $X_2 > y$ and $X_1 < y$; (iv) $X_1 = y$; (v) $X_1 > y$. These zones correspond to the relations $(0,0)_{2,1}$, $(0,1)_{2,1}$, $(0,2)_{2,1}$, $(1,2)_{2,1}$, and $(2,2)_{2,1}$, respectively (Figure 3.7 (b)).

The incidence graph is the same as in the previous case. This graph describes a topological situation between the zones of dimensions 2 and 1, whereas in the previous example they were of dimensions 1 and 0, but the incidence structure is the same.

This is a general phenomenon. For a given pair (p, q), the cone Λ_p, which is of dimension p, is cut out into zones of dimension less than or equal to p (the dimension of a relation being equal to the number of odd integers in the canonical representation in the form of p-tuples of integers). Similarly, the Λ_p cone is cut out into the same number of zones of maximum dimension q. The incidence graph associated with the first partition is isomorphic to the one associated with the second partition.

NOTE 3.1.– It is not surprising that the dimensions of the two partitions corresponding to $\Pi_{p,q}$, on the one hand, and to $\Pi_{q,p}$, on the other hand, are different, and this is consistent with the interpretation of dimension in terms of degrees of freedom. To illustrate this in the simplest case, there are five "qualitative" ways to choose an interval with respect to a given point. If none of the boundaries coincide with the point, there are two degrees of freedom (there can be a slight shift of one of the two boundaries). Alternatively, there are also five ways of choosing a point with respect to a given interval. But the degree of freedom, in the three cases where the points and boundaries are distinct, is only 1.

3.4.1. Associated polytopes

The incidence graph corresponding to the geometrical representation of $\Pi_{p,q}$ relations describes the incidence relations of the regions which represent the basic (p, q)-relations. We may also focus on the dual graph, which, as seen in [LIG 90], corresponds to the incidence graph of a polytope $P_{p,q}$ (thus a compact object), more precisely to a cell complex which is a union of basic cells of dimensions ranging from 0 to $\inf(p, q)$ (Figure 3.8). We can easily visualize this cell complex by considering the lattice of basic (p, q)-relations, seen as a graph in $\mathbb{R}^p$. The reader can refer to [BES 89b], Chapter 4, for the detailed description of a recursive construction of this polytope.

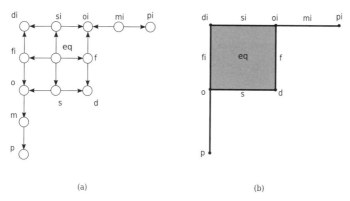

(a)   (b)

Figure 3.8. *The dual of the incidence graph of Allen's relations (a) is the incidence graph of a cell complex (b) denoted as $P_{2,2}$*

In an informal manner, we obtain $P_{p,q}$ by taking a copy of $P_{p-1,q}$ and a copy of $P_{p,q-1}$. Each of these two polytopes contains a copy of $P_{p-1,q-1}$. The product $P_{p-1,q-1} \times I$ of $P_{p-1,q-1}$ is obtained by a segment I. This product has two "faces" isomorphic to $P_{p-1,q-1}$. We paste the copy of P_{p-1}, on one face, along the polytope $P_{p-1,q-1}$ that it contains. Then we paste the copy of $P_{p,q-1}$ on the other face, along the polytope $P_{p-1,q-1}$ that this copy contains.

EXAMPLE 3.7.– For $p = q = 1$ the associated lattice has three elements 0, 1, and 2 in $\mathbb{R}$. The dual of the incidence graph is the incidence graph of the polytope $[0,1]$, which is the union of the cells $\{0\}$, $(0,1)$, and $\{1\}$.

When $p = 1, q = 2$, the dual of the incidence graph is the incidence graph of the cell complex $P_{1,2} = [0, 2]$, which is the union of the cells $\{0\}$, $(0,1)$, $\{1\}$, $(1,2)$, and $\{2\}$. The case of $p = 2, q = 1$ corresponds to the same polytope embedded in a different way in $\mathbb{R}^2$, reunion of the segments $[(0,0), (0,2)]$ and $[(0,2), (2,2)]$ (Figure 3.9, on the left).

EXAMPLE 3.8.– The case of the polytope corresponding to $p = q = 2$ provides a good illustration of the recursive construction of this polytope in the general case: a copy of $P_{1,2}$ and a copy of $P_{2,1}$ are pasted along the opposite faces of $P_{1,1} \times I$ which are isomorphic to $P_{1,1}$, where I is a segment (Figure 3.9).

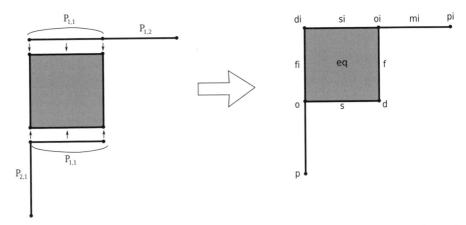

Figure 3.9. *We obtain $P_{2,2}$ by pasting a copy of $P_{1,2}$ and a copy of $P_{2,1}$ along the two faces of $P_{1,1} \times I$ isomorphic to $P_{1,1}$*

PROPOSITION 3.3.– *Let $p, q \geq 1$. The polytope $P_{p,q}$ is obtained by pasting a copy of $P_{p,q-1}$ and a copy of $P_{p-1,q}$ along the opposite faces of $P_{p-1,q-1} \times I$. As a result, the number of faces $h(p, q)$ of the polytope $P_{p,q}$, which is also the number of elements of $\Pi_{p,q}$, is given by the following formulas:*

$$h(p, 0) = h(0, q) = 1 \qquad\qquad [3.1]$$

$$h(p, q) = h(p - 1, q) + h(p, q - 1) + h(p - 1, q - 1) \qquad\qquad [3.2]$$

It is remarkable that the number $h(p, q)$ also corresponds to the number of points with integer coordinates in polytopes of $\mathbb{R}^p$ defined in a very simple manner:

PROPOSITION 3.4.– *Let us consider in $\mathbb{R}^p$, provided with the coordinates $(X_1, \ldots, X_p)$, the polytope defined by the equation:*

$$|X_1| + \cdots + |X_p| \leq q$$

Then $h(p, q)$ is the number of points with integer coordinates contained in this polytope.

Proof. It can be easily seen that the number of points with integer coordinates contained in the polytope defined by $|X_1| + \cdots + |X_p| \leq q$ verifies the same recurrence formulas as $h(p, q)$ (proposition 3.4).

3.4.2. *M-convexity of the basic relations*

We have seen (section 2.2.3) that for Allen's relations the zones of the plane which are associated with the basic relations satisfy a property stronger than convexity, referred to as M-convexity: these zones are convex in the usual sense and, moreover, they are closed by projection; or, such a zone, when containing two points, also contains the points which are located between these two points for the relation corresponding to the Manhattan metric.

PROPOSITION 3.5.– *The zones of Λ_p corresponding to the basic (p, q)-relations are M-convex.*

3.5. Inversion and composition

3.5.1. *Inversion*

Let us consider an element r of $\Pi_{p,q}$, which represents the position of a p-interval x relative to a q-interval y. The inversion operation corresponds to the interchange of the roles of x and y. To explicitly define this operation, it is necessary to determine which element of $\Pi_{p,q}$ represents the position of y relative to x.

The above question can easily be solved in a simple manner. To express it, let us provide a definition which will be reused in other circumstances:

DEFINITION 3.3.– *Given an element $r = (r_1, \ldots, r_p)$ of $\Pi_{p,q}$, the associated symbolic interval is a p-interval whose boundaries are labeled as $r_1, \ldots, r_p$.*

The symbolic p-interval associated with a p-relation r defines $(2p + 1)$ successive zones which are labeled as $0, \ldots, 2p$.

An explicit description of inversion is given by the following proposition:

PROPOSITION 3.6.– *The inverse $r^{-1} = s$ of r is the element of $\Pi_{q,p}$ obtained in the following way: let us consider the first q odd integers $1, \ldots, 2q - 1$. The i-th* *component s_i of s is the number of the zone in which the i-th odd integer $2i - 1$ should be placed if we want to retain the ascending order.*

EXAMPLE 3.9.– Let us consider the relation $(0, 0, 3, 6)_{4,3} \in \Pi_{4,3}$. The associated symbolic interval is represented in Figure 3.10. The inverse relation is an element of $\Pi_{3,4}$, hence a sequence of three integers between 0 and 8. The first three odd integers, namely, 1, 3, and 5 are in the zones 4, 5 and 6 of the symbolic interval, respectively. Hence, the required inverse is the relation $(4, 5, 6)_{3,4}$.

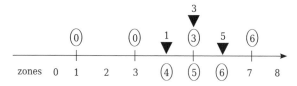

Figure 3.10. *The inverse of the (4, 3)-relation $(0, 0, 3, 6)_{4,3}$ is the (3, 4)-relation $(4, 5, 6)_{3,4}$: indeed, 4, 5 and 6 are the numbers of the zones containing the first three odd integers 1, 3, and 5*

The inversion operation is a bijective mapping of the lattice $\Pi_{p,q}$ on the lattice $\Pi_{q,p}$ which is decreasing (the orders are interchanged). In particular, if $p = q$, we obtain a decreasing involution of the lattice $\Pi_{p,p}$ on itself. This occurs in particular for Allen's relations.

EXAMPLE 3.10.– The lattice (actually a linear order) $\Pi_{1,2}$ contains the five relations $(0)_{1,2}, \ldots, (4)_{1,2}$, ordered in the usual manner. The lattice $\Pi_{2,1}$ (also a linear order) contains the five relations $(0, 0)_{2,1}$, $(0, 1)_{2,1}$, $(0, 2)_{2,1}$, $(1, 2)_{2,1}$ and $(2, 2)_{2,1}$. The inversion maps the smallest element $(0)_{1,2}$ of the first lattice on the largest element $(2, 2)_{2,1}$ of the second lattice[1], and so on in a decreasing order (Figure 3.11).

3.5.2. *Composition*

Let us consider a p-interval x, a q-interval y, and an r-interval z. If $r \in \Pi_{p,q}$ represents the position of x relative to y, and $s \in \Pi_{q,r}$ represents the position of y relative to z, what are the possible positions of x relative to z? The answer to this question defines the composition of the relations r and s, which will be denoted as $(r \circ s)$.

We will provide a general rule for computing this composition. Let us first introduce a convenient notation.

NOTATION.– Let $a, b \in \mathbb{N}$ be two integers, with $a \leq b$. We denote by $[a, b]$ the point $\{a\}$ if $a = b$, and if not, the largest interval of integers contained in $[a, b]$ whose bounding points are even integers.

---

1 Of course, this can be seen directly, without having to use Proposition 3.6!

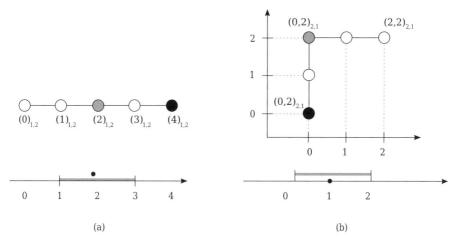

Figure 3.11. *The five relations between a point and an interval (a), and between an interval and a point (b). The inversion operation sends the black relation in (a) to the black one in (b), and similarly for the relations in gray*

For example: $[1, 2] = \{2\}, [0, 3] = [0, 2]$.

The following proposition [LIG 91] provides a rule for computing the composition of two basic relations.

PROPOSITION 3.7.– *Let* $r = (r_1, \ldots, r_p) \in \Pi_{p,q}$ *and* $s = (s_1, \ldots, s_q) \in \Pi_{q,r}$. *The composition* $(r \circ s)$ *is defined in the lattice* $\Pi_{p,r}$ *in the following way:*

– *consider the symbolic interval system associated with s (it defines* $2q + 1$ *zones);*

– *for i from 1 to p, let us consider the i-th component* r_i *of r;*

– *let* (a_i, b_i) *be the zone of the symbolic interval of s numbered as* r_i *(if* r_i *is 0,* $a_i = 0$ *and* $b_i = s_1$; *if it is* $2q$, *consider that* $a_i = r_p$ *and* $b_i = 2s$);

– *then the i-th projection of* $(r \circ s)$ *is* $[a_i, b_i]$.

EXAMPLE 3.11.– Let us compute the composition of $(2, 3)_{2,2}$ and $(1, 4)_{2,3}$. The result is thus a set of $(2, 3)$-relations, i.e. a pair of integers between 0 and 6.

The symbolic interval associated with $(1, 4)_{2,3}$ is represented in Figure 3.12. According to the given rule, the first component of the result corresponds to the zone 2 of this interval; it is thus an integer of $[1, 4] = [2, 4]$.

The second component corresponds to zone 3, and hence to the integer 4. The result is thus $[2, 4] \times \{4\}$, that is $\{(2, 4)_{2,3}, (3, 4)_{2,3}, (4, 4)_{2,3}\}$.

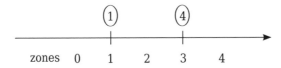

Figure 3.12. *The symbolic interval associated with the relation $(1,4)_{1,3}$*

NOTE 3.2.– The explicit definition of composition shows that, in all cases, the composition of two basic relations is an interval in the lattice. In addition, this interval has projections which are either points, or intervals with even bounding points.

Let us use this remark in the case of Allen's algebra.

Consider the lattice of the basic relations (Figure 3.13):

– first of all, an interval of the lattice whose two projections (horizontal and vertical) are punctual is hence a single basic relation: we thus obtain the 13 basic relations, which indeed occur as entries in the composition table, in particular, as compositions with the relation eq;

– let us then consider the relations whose projection on the horizontal axis is punctual, and the projection on the vertical axis is an interval with even bounding points. There are five such relations, namely: [p, o], [p, di], [o, di], [s, si], and [d, oi];

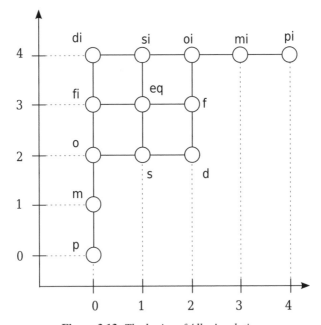

Figure 3.13. *The lattice of Allen's relations*

– let us consider in a similar way the relations whose projection on the vertical axis is punctual, and the projection on the horizontal axis an interval with even bounding points. The situation is symmetrical, thus there are five relations, namely: [di, pi], [oi, pi], [fi, f], and [o, d];

– finally, let us consider the relations whose two projections are intervals with even bounding points. On each component, there are three possibilities: [0, 2], [0, 4], and [2, 4], and six corresponding relations, namely: [p, d], [p, oi], [o, oi], [p, pi], [o, pi], and [d, pi].

We thus ultimately obtain a total of 29 relations which are *a priori* likely to appear in the composition table. If we refer to the latter (Table 1.3), we note that 27 of these relations occur as entries in the table, the exceptions being the two relations [p, oi] and [o, pi], which do not correspond to the composition of two atomic relations.

3.5.2.1. *Composition and inversion*

The composition operation and the inversion operation interact in the following way:

PROPOSITION 3.8.– *Let* $a \in \Pi_{p,q}$ *and* $b \in \Pi_{q,r}$. *We have* $a \circ (a \circ b)^{-1} = (b^{-1} \circ a^{-1})$.

3.5.3. *The algebras of generalized intervals*

Let us consider a subset S of positive integers. We have previously introduced the notation Π_S to denote the union of $\Pi_{p,q}$, for $p, q \in S$.

DEFINITION 3.4.– *An S-relation is a subset of* Π_S. *Let us denote by* $\mathbf{A}_S$ *the set of S-relations.*

The above considerations show that in addition to the set operations of union, intersection, and complement, the set of S-relations is naturally provided with two operations, inversion and composition, induced by the operations of the same name on the (p, q)-relations.

Also note that for each positive integer p, $\Pi_{p,p}$ contains a particular element, which we will denote as $\mathbf{1}'_{p,p}$: this element is the sequence of the first p odd numbers $(1, \ldots, (2_p - 1))$. It corresponds to the equality relation between two p-intervals. This is the neutral element for the composition with an arbitrary element of $\Pi_{p,q}$ on the right, and on the left with an arbitrary element of $\Pi_{q,p}$. When $p, q, r, s \in S$ is such that $q \neq r$, the composition of $a \in \Pi_{p,q}$ and $b \in \Pi_{r,s}$ is considered as the empty set, also denoted as $\mathbf{0}$ in this context (this set is the smallest element of $\Pi_{p,s}$).

Using these notations, we note that the union of $\mathbf{1}'_{p,p}$ for $p \in S$, denoted as $\mathbf{1}'_S$, is a neutral element for composition in the set of S-relations.

Let us recall the definition of a relation algebra in Tarski's sense [TAR 41] (see Appendix B.6):

DEFINITION 3.5.– *A relation algebra* $(A, +, -, 0,1,1', \smile, ;)$ *is an algebra of signature* $(+, -, 0, 1, 1', \smile, ;)$ *such that the following conditions are satisfied:*

- $(A, +, -, 0, 1)$ *is a Boolean algebra;*
- *the symbol ; denotes an associative binary operation, i.e.:*

$$x; (y; z) = (x; y); z \tag{3.3}$$

- *we have the following properties:*

$$(x + y); z = x; z + y; z \tag{3.4}$$

$$x; \mathbf{1}' = x \tag{3.5}$$

$$(x^\smile)^\smile = x \tag{3.6}$$

$$(x + y)^\smile = x^\smile + y^\smile \tag{3.7}$$

$$(x; y)^\smile = y^\smile ; x^\smile \tag{3.8}$$

- *we have Pierce's law:*

$$(x; y) \cdot z^\smile = \mathbf{0} \text{ if, and only if, } (y; z) \cdot x^\smile = \mathbf{0} \tag{3.9}$$

Let us consider the set $\mathbf{A}_S$ of S-relations, and interpret the successive elements of the signature as the union, the complement, the empty set, the set $\mathbf{A}_S$, the element 1', the inversion, and the composition, respectively. We then have a general result:

THEOREM 3.1.– $\mathbf{A}_S$ *is a relation algebra.*

Proof. It is sufficient to note that the definitions given for the abstract algebra $\mathbf{A}_S$ describe the operations of the concrete algebra of relations consisting of the S-relations between the generalized intervals on the real line $\mathbb{R}$.

EXAMPLE 3.12.– Let p be a positive integer. We denote by $\mathbf{A}_p$ the algebra corresponding to $S = \{p\}$. In particular, $\mathbf{A}_1$ is the time-point algebra, and $\mathbf{A}_2$ is Allen's algebra.

EXAMPLE 3.13.– Let us consider the particular case of $S = \{1, 2\}$ again (Example 3.2). We have seen that the union of the basic generalized relations contains 26 relations. This is a simple example of a relation algebra which is not *integral*, i.e. in which the composition of two non-zero elements can be zero.

3.6. Subclasses of relations: convex and pre-convex relations

We now have two types of representation of basic (p, q)-relations: a representation as elements of a lattice, and another as regions in a cone Λ_p of $\mathbb{R}^p$ which form a partition of this cone.

As a consequence, as done previously for Allen's relations, we can use concepts related to the lattice structure (for example, that of interval in a lattice), as well as geometrical and topological concepts (convexity, M-convexity, dimension, topological closure, etc.).

We will use these concepts to extend the concepts of convex and pre-convex relations to the (p, q)-relations (which are the unions of basic (p, q)-relations).

3.6.1. (p, q)-relations

Given p, q, the set $\Pi_{p,q}$ of basic (p, q)-relations is the generalization of the basic relations of Allen's algebra. Similarly as for Allen's relations, we consider (p, q)-relations which are subsets of $\Pi_{p,q}$, and which will be interpreted in the context of constraint networks as disjunctions.

DEFINITION 3.6.– A (p, q)-relation *is a subset of* $\Pi_{p,q}$.

Here again, we will not differentiate between basic (p, q)-relations and their corresponding (p, q)-relations (sets with one element), except when ambiguity may arise.

We extend the inversion and composition operations to relations in the usual way:

DEFINITION 3.7.– *If α and β are two relations,* $\alpha^{-1} = \{a^{-1} \,|\, a \in \alpha\}$, *and* $\alpha \circ \beta = \{(a \circ b) \,|\, a \in \alpha, b \in \beta\}$.

We can easily check that all the properties stated in proposition 3.8 still hold for arbitrary relations.

3.6.2. Convex relations

DEFINITION 3.8.– *A* convex (p, q)-relation *is either an interval of the* $\Pi_{p,q}$ *lattice, or the empty relation.*

If $a, b \in \Pi_{p,q}$ are two basic (p, q)-relations such that $a \leq b$, we will continue to denote by $[a, b]$ the interval defined by a and b. We can easily verify that under these conditions, $[a, b]^{-1} = [b^{-1}, a^{-1}]$.

Let $[a, b]$ and $[c, d]$ be two non-empty convex relations.

PROPOSITION 3.9.– *Let* $[a, b] \subseteq \Pi_{p,q}$ *and* $[c, d] \subseteq \Pi_{q,r}$ *be two non-empty convex relations. Then the composition* $[a, b] \circ [c, d]$ *is the relation* $[\inf(a \circ c), \sup(b \circ d)]$.

EXAMPLE 3.14.– For $p = q = 1$, we obtain three relations $(0)_{1,1}$, $(1)_{1,1}$, and $(2)_{1,1}$ corresponding to precedence, equality, and inverse of precedence between two points.

When $p = q = 2$, we obtain the encoding of Allen's relations defined in section 2.2.4.

Clearly, convex relations are closed under intersection. The properties just discussed show that these relations are also closed under inversion and composition.

PROPOSITION 3.10.– *A* (p, q)-*relation is* convex *if it satisfies one of the following equivalent conditions:*

- *the associated subset is an interval of the lattice;*
- *the associated region of* Λ_p *is M-convex;*
- *the associated region of* Λ_p *is convex and is closed by projection.*

As in the particular case of Allen's relations, given a (p, q)-relation r, we denote by $Cl(r)$ its topological closure, and by $I(r)$ its convex closure (which is the smallest interval containing r). We then have the following properties which generalize those discussed in Chapter 2 for Allen's relations:

PROPOSITION 3.11.– *For any pair of relations* r, s:

- $Cl(r^{-1}) = Cl(r)^{-1}$;
- $Cl(r) \supseteq (r)$;
- $dim(Cl(r) \setminus r) < dim(r)$;
- $Cl(Cl(r)) = Cl(r)$;
- r *is closed if, and only if,* $Cl(r) = r$;
- *if* $r \subseteq s$, *then* $Cl(r) \subseteq Cl(s)$;
- $Cl(r \circ s) \supseteq Cl(r) \circ Cl(s)$.

We also have:

- $I(r^{-1}) = I(r)^{-1}$;
- $I(r) \supseteq (r)$;
- $I(I(r)) = I(r)$;
- r *is convex if, and only if,* $I(r) = r$;
- *if* $r \subseteq s$ *then* $I(r) \subseteq I(s)$;
- $I(r \circ s) = I(r) \circ I(s)$.

In particular, the set of convex relations is closed under inversion, composition, and intersection.

3.6.3. *Pre-convex relations*

DEFINITION 3.9.– *A relation r of* $\Pi_{p,q}$ *is* pre-convex *if it satisfies one of the following equivalent conditions:*

- *the topological closure Cl(r) of r is a convex relation*;
- *Cl(r)* $\subseteq$ *I(r)*;
- *dim(I(r)\r)* < *dim(r)*.

It follows from the properties of proposition 3.11 that the set of pre-convex relations is closed under inversion and composition.

However, the set of pre-convex relations, in general, is not closed under intersection, as shown by the following counter-example:

EXAMPLE 3.15.– Consider the lattice of $(2, 3)$-relations. It is a subset of pairs of integers ranging between 0 and 6 (Figure 3.14). Let us consider in the lattice the relation $r = [(0, 2)_{2,3}, (2, 6)_{2,3}] \setminus \{(1, 4)_{2,3}\}$. It is a pre-convex relation, since it is obtained from the convex relation $I(r) = [(0, 2)_{2,3}, (2, 6)_{2,3}]$ by removing the relation $(1, 4)_{2,3}$

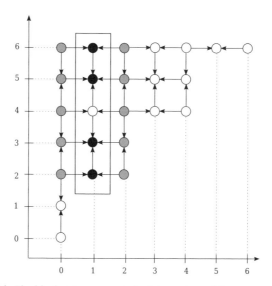

Figure 3.14. *The black dots represent the intersection of the pre-convex relation* $[(0, 2)_{2,3}, (2, 6)_{2,3}]\setminus\{(1, 4)_{2,3}\}$ *and the convex relation* $[(1, 2)_{2,3}, (1, 6)_{2,3}]$; *this intersection is not a pre-convex relation*

which belongs to the closure of r (it is on the edge of $(0, 4)_{2,3}$ and on that of $(2, 4)_{2,3}$). As for the relation $s = [(1, 2)_{2,3}, (1, 6)_{2,3}]$, it is obviously convex.

However, the intersection $r \cap s$ is the relation:

$$\{(1, 2)_{2,3}, (1, 3)_{2,3}, (1, 5)_{2,3}, (1, 6)_{2,3}\}$$

which *is not pre-convex*. In fact, the relation is closed $(Cl(r \cap s) = r \cap s)$ but not convex. $(I(r \cap s) = (r \cap s) \cup \{(1, 4)_{2,3}\})$

The set of pre-convex relations thus does not constitute a subclass according to the definition 2.1.

This leads us to define a more restricted class of relations called strongly pre-convex relations:

DEFINITION 3.10.– *A relation r of* $\Pi_{p,q}$ *is strongly pre-convex* if it is pre-convex *and if its intersection with any convex relation is pre-convex.*

We will further see (section 3.8.1) that strongly pre-convex relations have an equivalent definition in terms of ORD-Horn relations.

3.7. Constraint networks

Let us consider the general case where S is a set of positive integers. A *constraint network* on $\mathbf{A}_S$ is a pair (N, C), where N is a finite set of vertices (or variables) representing p-intervals, for $p \in S$, and, for each pair $(i, j) \in N \times N, C(i, j)$ is an element of $\mathbf{A}_S$.

Although in a more general framework, the number of bounding points of a vertex would not be given (it would only be known that it belongs to S), we will assume from now on that a given vertex represents a p-interval for a predetermined p and that, if (i, j) are two vertices, the constraint $C (i, j)$ is a (p, q)-relation, where p and q are determined by i and j, respectively.

All definitions previously used for networks on Allen's algebra and on the Point algebra can easily be extended to this wider context.

In particular, we will use the algebraic definition of the algebraic closure of a network.

Let M be the matrix associated with a normalized network having n vertices, and let us consider the successive powers of M for the relational product. Then there is a smallest integer k such that $M^k = M^{k+1}$. By definition, the network associated with M^k is the algebraic closure of the network considered.

It is this algebraic closure that is computed by the algorithms called "path consistency (PC)" algorithms. We use the term algebraic closure to emphasize that this computation involves only the purely algebraic structure of the formalism, regardless of the concrete interpretations of the constraint networks considered.

If a network is consistent, its algebraic closure is necessarily non-zero, but the reverse assertion does not hold. In spite of this "incompleteness" (we use this term when we deal with a necessary but not sufficient condition for consistency), the computation of the algebraic closure of a network often involves a process of effective filtering, which can be implemented in polynomial time (in cubic time) as seen for Allen's algebra.

The general question is to determine under what circumstances the computation of the algebraic closure is sufficient to determine consistency. We will now discuss this point further.

3.8. Tractability of strongly pre-convex relations

PROPOSITION 3.12.– *Let $(\mathcal{N} = N, C)$ be a network on $\mathbf{A}_S$ which is algebraically closed and non-zero and whose constraints are pre-convex relations. Then $\mathcal{N}$ is consistent. Moreover, it is generically minimal: if $b \in C(i, j)$ is a basic relation such that $dim(b) = dim(C(i, j))$, then there is a consistent scenario for which the relation b holds between i and j.*

Proof. The proof is similar to that given in [LIG 96] in the case of Allen's algebra. It uses the crucial fact that pre-convex relations are "almost" closed by projection.

However, we cannot conclude that any pre-convex network whose algebraic closure is non-zero is consistent: in fact, because of the instability of pre-convex relations under intersection, there is no guarantee that the algebraic closure of a pre-convex network is itself pre-convex.

Nevertheless, the result is true for strongly pre-convex relations:

PROPOSITION 3.13.– *Let $(\mathcal{N} = N, C)$ be a network on $\mathbf{A}_S$ whose constraints are strongly pre-convex relations. Then N is consistent if, and only if, its algebraic closure is non-zero.*

For strongly pre-convex relations, the computation of the algebraic closure is thus a procedure for testing consistency.

EXAMPLE 3.16.– The Point-and-interval calculus corresponds to the case of $S = \{1, 2\}$. In this case, it is easy to determine the pre-convex relations. They form the only maximal subclass of tractable relations containing all basic relations [LIG 94b]. In particular, the subclass denoted by $\mathcal{V}^{23}$ in [JON 99], an article in which Jonsson *et al.* determine all the tractable subclasses of the set of point-and-interval relations, is characterized as the class of all subsets of $\Pi_{1,2}$ which are pre-convex relations: more precisely, non pre-convex relations are those relations which do not contain the relation $(2)_{1,2}$ (Figure 3.11, (a)) while not being contained either in $[(0)_{1,2}, (1)_{1,2}]$ or in $[(3)_{1,2}, (4)_{1,2}]$.

3.8.1. *ORD-Horn relations*

The definition of ORD-Horn relations given in section 2.2.8 can be easily extended to the relations between generalized intervals.

We consider relations (subsets of the basic relations) in the lattice $\Pi_{p,q}$:

– a *positive literal* is an expression of the form $X_i \leq \varpi, X_i \geq \varpi$, or $X_i = \varpi$ where $i \in \{1, \ldots, p\}$ and $\varpi \in \{1, 3, \ldots, 2q - 1\}$ is an odd integer between 0 and $2q$;

– a *negative literal* is an expression of the form $X_i \neq \varpi$, where $i \in \{1, \ldots, p\}$ and $\varpi \in \{1, 3, \ldots, 2q - 1\}$;

– an *ORD-clause* is a disjunction of literals;

– an *ORD-Horn clause* is an ORD-clause containing at the most one positive literal.

We can now define the ORD-Horn relations in the lattice $\Pi_{p,\, q}$:

DEFINITION 3.11.– *A relation is an* ORD-Horn relation *if it can be defined in the lattice of relations by an ORD-Horn clause.*

The following proposition [BAL 00b] states that the syntactic definition of ORD-Horn relations is in fact equivalent to the geometrical definition of the strongly pre-convex relations:

PROPOSITION 3.14.– *A relation is an* ORD-Horn relation *if, and only if, it is strongly pre-convex.*

Proof. It can be easily seen that an ORD-Horn relation is strongly pre-convex. The difficult part is to show the reverse inclusion. The reader can refer to [BAL 00b] for a full proof.

3.9. Conclusions

The qualitative reasoning formalisms about points, Allen's algebra, and the Point-and-interval algebra belong a group of formalisms which can be subsumed as the group of generalized intervals. For these formalisms, we have shown that several techniques and several results which are known for Allen's algebra have analogs within this general framework.

One of the advantages of this fact is the possibility of clarifying what is specific to the framework defined by Allen, and what is – more or less straightforwardly – generalizable. One of the aims of the field of qualitative reasoning about time and space is to develop formalisms that can be used to give an account of specific aspects of knowledge about time and/or space (duration, orientation, topology). In order not to have to start again from scratch when developing these new formalisms, it is advantageous to have general techniques which can be applied to them.

We will see in Chapter 11 how this search for generality leads to a general concept of qualitative formalism.

3.10. Historical note

The formalism of generalized intervals was introduced in [LIG 90, LIG 91]. The definition of the Point-and-interval algebra, as seen previously, is due to Vilain [VIL 82] and Meiri [MEI 96]. Pre-convex relations have been introduced in [LIG 94b], where it is also shown that the subclass of the pre-convex relations in the Point-and-interval algebra is tractable, and that computing the algebraic closure provides a decision procedure for the consistency of a pre-convex network. The fact that pre-convex relations are not closed under intersection is due to Balbiani and Condotta. The equivalence between the syntactic definition, in terms of ORD-Horn relations, and the geometrical definition, in terms of strongly pre-convex relations, is shown in [BAL 00b] in the context of some of the formalisms (n-point and n-block calculus) which we will discuss later. The proof for generalized intervals does not seem to have been published previously.

Balbiani *et al.* [BAL 98b] call "generalized intervals" temporal entities which are basically sets of (ordinary) intervals.

The topic of non-convex intervals introduced by Ladkin in 1986 [LAD 86] has been further developed by Morris, Shoaff, and Khatib [MOR 91, MOR 93b, MOR 95]. More recently, Claramunt [CLA 00] has considered extending Ladkin's algebra to the spatial domain.

Chapter 4

Binary Qualitative Formalisms

4.1. "Night driving"

It's a dark night, and I am driving on a two-lane highway. From my point of view as a driver, the other cars on the same highway are divided into different classes:

– they are either in front of me, or behind me, or at the same level as me;

– they run either in the same direction as that of mine (I see their tail lights shining red if they are in front of me; and their headlights shining white, if they are behind me), or in the opposite direction (the lights are reversed in this case).

Figure 4.1. *Night driving*

The kind of attention that I must pay to other cars on the same road that night depends on this classification: I must not forget to put the headlights on low-beam when a car approaches me, or I must anticipate the fact that a car which is now following me may intend to overtake me, and so on.

We started this book with the example of a boat race, where the boats were represented by points on a line directed by the direction of the race. It was not necessary then to specify in which direction a boat moved: it was implicitly moving in the direction of the race.

Several elements have changed in the case of night driving:

– the road does not have any preferred direction, even if I may decide to assign it (for instance, the direction which leads from my departure point toward my destination). We may thus consider ourselves to be in an undirected 1D universe.

– the entities constituted by the cars have a direction of movement which must be taken into account;

– the selected point of view is local: there is no external observer on the roadside for taking note of the passing cars. I can only describe my relationship to other cars with respect to my point of view.

We used the boat race example to motivate the definition of the Point calculus. In a similar way, the night driving example leads us to choose the following type of representation: the entities are points provided with a direction (directed points) which move along a line. The relationship of a directed point A (another car) and of another directed point B (my car) will be classified according to my own point of view:

– either A is in front of me, or behind me, or at the same level as me;

– either A moves in the same direction as me, or in the opposite direction.

At the price of some simplification (we consider only moving cars, for instance), we obtain a formalism which has eight basic relations, that we may denote by r^ε, where r is one of the three relations < (precede), > (follow) and eq (same level), and ε can be either + (same direction) or − (opposite directions).

The various possibilities that this formalism allows us to represent are shown in Figure 4.2. We will refer to the formalism as to the *1D directed point* calculus. In

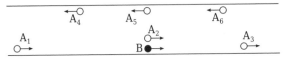

Figure 4.2. *From my point of view (I am driving car B), the other cars are in one of the six positions illustrated by the six cars $A_1, \ldots, A_6$. Using the notation introduced in the text, we have for instance $A_4 <^- B$ and $A_3 >^+ B$*

Figure 4.2, the six directed points $A_1, \ldots, A_6$ illustrate each of the six basic relations of a directed point with respect to B.

We will come back to the 1D directed point calculus below.

4.1.1. *Parameters*

In [LIG 93a], we propose a list of some of the parameters according to which we can distinguish the various qualitative formalisms:

– the nature of the entities considered: regions, geometric objects such as points, vectors, rectangles, and so on;

– the possession of an intrinsic direction by the entities;

– the presence of physical properties such as rigidity or, on the contrary, deformability, the possibility for the entities of overlapping;

– the nature and dimension of the ambient space: 1D or 2D Euclidean space, abstract topological space, and so on;

– the availability of a global frame of reference;

– the arity of the relations considered: binary, ternary relations, or relations of arity greater than 2;

– the use of relative or absolute orientations.

These are parameters which are features of the formalism and not of what it represents. For example, the spatial reasoning may deal with directional relations, topological relations, qualitative distance and so on.

The example of directed points in dimension 1 illustrates one of the possible configurations of these parameters: the entities are points provided with an intrinsic direction; "overlapping" is possible (in the representation, not advisable on the road!), the ambient space is 1D, it is not necessarily provided with a direction, the relations considered are binary and model relative orientations.

4.1.2. *A panorama of the presented formalisms*

4.1.2.1. *Terminology*

The main kinds of spatial and temporal entities we will consider in this chapter are *points* (in a Euclidean space), *directed points* (i.e. data consisting of a point in some Euclidean space together with an direction represented by a non-zero vector), *dipoles* (pairs of distinct points), geometrical objects such as *rectangles* in $\mathbb{R}^2$, and more generally, blocks in $\mathbb{R}^n$, as well as "*regions*". We deliberately leave vague the precise meaning of the term "region", which according to the context will denote either regions satisfying various properties in Euclidean spaces, or more generally, subspaces of a topological space. Figure 4.3 represents some of these entities.

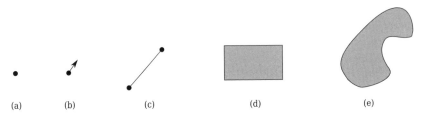

(a)   (b)   (c)   (d)   (e)

Figure 4.3. *Some of the entities considered: a point (a), a directed point (b), a dipole (c), a rectangle (d), and a region in the plane (e)*

We will distinguish between the case where the formalism uses an absolute frame of reference (for example, in the Euclidean plane, a fixed direction giving the north direction), and the case where the formalism does not depend on such a frame of reference.

That being said, we can summarize all the formalisms presented in this chapter and the following chapter in Table 4.1. In this table, the entry "relations" represents the number of basic relations.

Name of the calculus	Entities	Space	Relations	Arity	Absolute
Point	1D points	$\mathbb{R}$	3	binary	yes
Allen	1D intervals	$\mathbb{R}$	13	binary	yes
1D directed point	1D directed points	$\mathbb{R}$	6	binary	no
Directed interval	1D dipoles	$\mathbb{R}$	26	binary	no
$\mathcal{OPRA}_m$	2D directed points	$\mathbb{R}^2$	$4m(4m+1)$	binary	no
2D dipole	2D dipoles	$\mathbb{R}^2$	16	binary	no
Cardinal direction	points	$\mathbb{R}^2$	9 relations	binary	yes
Cardinal direction	regions	$\mathbb{R}^2$	218^1	binary	yes
Rectangle	rectangles	$\mathbb{R}^2$	$13^2 = 169$	binary	yes
n-point	points	$\mathbb{R}^n$	3^n	binary	yes
n-block	blocks	$\mathbb{R}^n$	13^n	binary	yes
INDU	intervals	$\mathbb{R}$	25	binary	yes
n-star	points	$\mathbb{R}^2$	$4n+1$ relations	binary	yes
Cyclic interval	dipoles	circle S^1	16	binary	no
RCC-8	regions	variable	8	binary	no
Discrete RCC-8	regions	plane	8	binary	yes
Cyclic point	points	circle S^1	6	ternary	no
Double cross	points	$\mathbb{R}^2$	17	ternary	no
Qualitative triangulation	points	$\mathbb{R}^2$	variable	ternary	no
5-intersection	regions	plane/sphere	34/42	ternary	no

Table 4.1. *The main formalisms discussed in this chapter*

4.1.2.2. *An attempt of classification*

In Chapter 3, we have seen how the various formalisms such as Allen's calculus, the Point calculus, and the point-and-interval calculus could be considered as particular demonstrations of the same general formalism, which is the formalism of generalized intervals.

The research activity in the field of qualitative spatial and temporal reasoning resulted in the emergence of many formalisms which, under many aspects, present strong analogies with Allen's calculus.

An initial group consists of formalisms based on the use of temporal formalisms in order to reason about spatial data. The first example, to our knowledge, is the definition of a 2D Allen's calculus [GÜS 89] by Guesgen, a formalism which was later referred to as to the "Rectangle calculus". The complexity properties of this calculus have been studied by Balbiani, Condotta and Fariñas del Cerro [BAL 99a, CON 00]. The shift from dimension 2 to dimension $n \geq 3$ resulted in the emergence of the "n-block calculus". Similarly, a "Cardinal direction calculus" representing a 2D extension of the time point calculus has been introduced by Frank [FRA 92a] and studied in-depth by Ligozat [LIG 98b]. The n-dimensional version of this formalism is what we call the "n-point calculus", which will be discussed later.

A second group of formalisms brings together, in a less systematic way, what could be considered as local variations on existing formalisms: for example, one considers directed intervals in a 1D universe which is similar to the time line. One thus obtains the "Directed interval" calculus [REN 01b] (due to its reference to space, we could have also classified this formalism in the first group). Alternatively, rather than assuming a *linear* 1D space, we can consider a cyclic one, so that we get a "cyclic" version of the interval calculus, a calculus whose intervals are intervals on a directed circle. This "Cyclic interval calculus" has been defined and studied in particular by Balbiani and Osmani [OSM 99b, BAL 00a]. In the same category, we should also mention the research on points or intervals in a temporal structure which is not a linear order [ANG 98, BRO 99, BRO 00a, BRO 02]. We will not deal with these formalims in this book.

Another type of variation on Allen's calculus which is apparently a minor one, consists in making a difference between the cases when the duration of i is smaller, equal, or greater, than that of j. For instance, this leads to decomposing p into three basic subrelations.

The resulting calculus, called INDU by its developers, independently of its intrinsic interest, has played an important role in the context of qualitative reasoning. Studying its properties, it quickly became evident that most of the "nice" properties possessed by Allen's calculus are not valid for the INDU calculus. This realization, and the theoretical questions that it gave rise to [LIG 04a], motivated an in-depth study of the formalisms, and led to the clarification of a question raised in particular by Mitra: what ultimately is a "qualitative formalism", and what are the relations of such a formalism with the various "algebras" it involves? The outcome of this inquiry will be examined in the subsequent chapters.

From our point of view, a third group is represented by the formalisms which revolve around the approach known as RCC (*region connection calculus*) approach. Based originally on the work of Clarke [CLA 81, CLA 85], and developed vigorously by the Leeds school, under the influence and guidance of Cohn, it is representative of a body of research advocating a "pointless" approach of spatial reasoning. This approach, which led to the development of a whole range of formalisms such as RCC–5, RCC–8, also RCC–6, etc. eventually came to meet with the research on the formalization of geographical data, and specifically with Egenhofer's independently developed "4-intersection" and "9-intersection" calculi.

We will come back to these points in detail later. A significant feature of this line of research is that it has practical applications in the field of geographical information systems (GIS). However, another important aspect is of theoretical nature, in connection with the questions raised above regarding the INDU formalism: the question arose to determine the precise nature of the models these formalisms relate to, since they have been primarily defined in a purely syntactic way in terms of axiomatic theories. The answers to these questions, for the RCC formalisms, have been provided in particular by Renz, Nebel, Li *et al.* and Düntsch, whose results will be discussed in Chapter 10.

For the time being, we will only introduce a part of these three groups of formalisms in this chapter by quickly mentioning the state of knowledge for each one of them. This overview will further allow us to place concrete images behind our examination of formalisms, and provide concrete examples for the study of arbitrary "qualitative formalisms".

4.2. Directed points in dimension 1

We have already introduced this calculus above. Let us recall that it deals with directed points on the line, and that we consider six basic relations.

Clearly, these relations have the JEPD property: for any pair of directed points (A, B), there is exactly one basic relation containing (A, B).

Let $\mathbf{B}_{1\varepsilon}$ denote the set of basic relations. We will say that the basic relations $<^+$, eq^+, and $>^+$ are positive, whereas the others are negative. A subset of $\mathbf{B}_{1\varepsilon}$ is called a (disjunctive) relation. A relation is positive (negative, respectively) if it contains only positive relations (negative, respectively). A *homogeneous* relation is a relation which is either positive or negative.

4.2.1. *Operations*

The effect of the inversion operation is summarized in Table 4.2. In a nutshell: the relations between directed points of the same direction behave as in the Point calculus. The other relations are invariable by inversion. In other words: inversion interchanges $<^+$ and $>^+$ and leaves all other basic relations fixed.

relation	$<^+$	eq^+	$>^+$	$<^-$	eq^-	$>^-$
inverse	$>^+$	eq^+	$<^+$	$<^-$	eq^-	$>^-$

Table 4.2. *The inversion operation*

To define the composition operation, it is convenient to introduce the *time reversal* operation [BES 89a] for relations between the points. The intuition is that this operation expresses what happens when the temporal axis is reversed.

DEFINITION 4.1.– *The* time reversal *operation on the basic relations between points* $\{<, eq, >\}$ *is the operation which interchanges* $<$ *and* $>$ *and leaves* eq *fixed.*

The definition extends to disjunctive relations. Let r^u denote the transform of a relation r by time reversal. If R is a relation of the time point algebra, R^+ (R^-, respectively) will denote the union of the relations r^+ (r^-, respectively) for $r \in R$.

The composition operation can then be described in a very simple manner:

PROPOSITION 4.1.– *Let* $r^\in$ *and* s^η *be two basic relations. Then the composition* $(r^\in \circ s^\eta)$ *is the relation* $(r \circ s)^\in$ *if* $\in = +$, *and* $(r^u \circ s)^{-\in}$ *if* $\eta = -$.

EXAMPLE 4.1.– The composition of $<^+$ and $<^+$ is the relation $(< \circ <)^+ = <^+$. The composition of $>^+$ and $<^+$ is the relation $(> \circ <)^+ = 1^+$, i.e. the relation $\{<^+, eq^+, >^+\}$.

The composition of $<^+$ and $<^-$ is the relation $(<^u \circ >)^-$, that is, $(> \circ <)^- = 1^-$; that of $>^+$ and $<^-$ is the relation $(>^u \circ >)^-$, that is, $(< \circ <)^- = <^-$.

DEFINITION 4.2.– *The algebra* $\mathbf{A}_{1\in}$ *associated with the 1D directed point calculus is the Boolean algebra of subsets of the six basic relations equipped with the inversion and composition operations.*

4.2.2. *Constraint networks*

The usual definitions of constraint networks are applicable here. A constraint network (N, C) for the directed points in dimension 1 is a graph whose arcs are labeled by elements of $\mathbf{A}_{1\in}$.

A main question is that of the consistency problem: given a constraint network, can we find a consistent instantiation of this network?

EXAMPLE 4.2.– A network with four vertices is the network with vertices $(V_1, \ldots, V_4)$ and the constraints

$$C(V_1, V_2) = \{<^-\} \qquad\qquad C(V_1, V_3) = \{\mathsf{eq}^-\}$$
$$C(V_1, V_4) = \{<^+, \mathsf{eq}^+, <^-, >^-\} \qquad C(V_2, V_3) = \{<^+, \mathsf{eq}^+, >^+, \mathsf{eq}^-\}$$
$$C(V_2, V_4) = \{\mathsf{eq}^+, >^+, \mathsf{eq}^-, >^-\} \qquad C(V_3, V_4) = \{\mathsf{eq}^+, <^-, \mathsf{eq}^-\}$$

The algebraic closure method provides a necessary condition for consistency. Thus, it can be easily seen that the algebraic closure of the network of Example 4.2 contains the empty relation, which shows that this network is not consistent.

4.2.3. Networks reducible to point networks

When a network contains only constraints which are either homogeneous constraints, or the universal relation, it can be easily seen that the consistency problem can be reduced to a problem for a point network. In order to do that, we will use the method used by Renz in the case of directed intervals [REN 01b] (see below).

If A is a directed point, the *opposite* $\bar{A}$ of A is the directed point whose underlying point is the one of A, but whose direction is opposite to that of A.

LEMMA 4.1.– *Let A and B be two directed points in dimension 1. If A is in the relation $r^\in$ with respect to B, then $\bar{A}$ is in the relation $r^{-\in}$ with respect to B, and A is in the relation $(r^u)^{-\in}$ with respect to $\bar{B}$.*

Let (N, C) be a network whose constraints are homogeneous or equal to the universal relation.

The intuitive idea is to choose a vertex which sets a global direction, and then replaces the other vertices which would not be directed in the same direction by the opposite vertices.

More precisely:

1) consider the following relation on the set N of vertices: two vertices $i, j \in N$ are equivalent if $i = j$ or if there is a path connecting i to j whose arcs are labeled by constraints other than the universal relation (these labels are thus, homogeneous relations);

2) the equivalence classes of this relation are subnetworks, for which we can search for solutions in an independent manner;

3) for each subnetwork, select a vertex i, and propagate the following operation starting from i: if $C(i, j)$ is negative, replace j by $\bar{j}$, so that $C(i, \bar{j})$ is positive. If this leads to contradictions, then the network is not consistent;

4) once this operation is over, if no contradiction has been met, then we have network whose constraints are all positive. We can thus apply a resolution technique for the corresponding point network.

EXAMPLE 4.3.– Let us consider the network of Figure 4.4 (a), which has six vertices, and whose non-trivial constraints are

$$C(V_1, V_2) = \{<^+, \mathsf{eq}^+\} \quad C(V_1, V_3) = \{<^-, \mathsf{eq}^-\} \quad C(V_1, V_4) = \{<^+\}$$
$$C(V_3, V_4) = \{<^-, >^-\} \quad C(V_5, V_6) = \{<^-\}$$

The equivalence relation considered in point 1) above subdivides the network into two subnetworks: on the one hand, $(V_1, \ldots, V_4)$, and on the other hand, (V_5, V_6), which can be considered separately. Let us choose V_1 as a starting point. By substituting V_3 by $\bar{V}_3$, we obtain $C(V_1, \bar{V}_3) = \{>^+, \mathsf{eq}^+\}$. Thus, $C(\bar{V}_3, V_4) = \{<^+, >^+\}$, and the set of non-trivial constraints on this subgraph contains only positive constraints. It can also be noted that if the constraint $C(V_1, V_4)$ had been negative, this would have led to a contradiction.

The point subnetwork which corresponds to the vertices $V_1, \ldots, V_4$ (Figure 4.4 (b)) is consistent and has several solutions; one of them is represented in Figure 4.5, in the

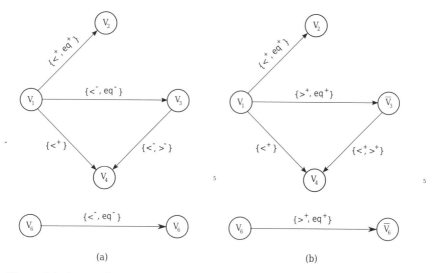

(a)   (b)

Figure 4.4. *A network whose non-trivial constraints are homogeneous (a); the equivalent network after replacing the vertices V_3 and V_6 by their opposite vertices (b)*

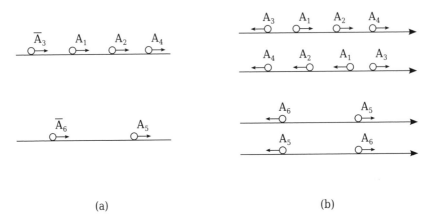

(a)   (b)

Figure 4.5. *Solutions of the network after transformation (a); for each one, there are two possible embeddings in the directed line (b)*

upper part of (a). Each one of the solutions can be embedded in two different ways in the real line, since the direction of V_1 can be selected in two ways (Figure 4.5, upper part of (b)).

In a similar way, we may choose V_5 as a starting point. In this case, we replace V_6 by $\bar{V}_6$, so that $C(V_5, \bar{V}_6)] = \{>^+\}$. Here again, the solution for the time point network can be embedded in two ways in the real line, regardless of the choices made for the first subnetwork (Figure 4.5).

A network that can be transformed in this manner is equivalent to a network on the point algebra. Hence, the corresponding algorithms can be used to answer the question of consistency.

Let us note that the algebraic closure property, if it holds, ensures that the situation of contradiction in stage 3) cannot occur: if the relation between i_1 and j is negative and that between i_1 and k is positive, then the relation between k and $\bar{j}$ cannot be negative, since if it were so, the relation between k and j would be positive, and the triangle (i_1, j, k) would contain only one negative label, which contradicts the algebraic closure property.

Hence we get the following result:

PROPOSITION 4.2.– *For directed point networks whose constraints are homogeneous or equal to the universal relation, the consistency problem can be solved in polynomial time. In particular, such a network is consistent if it is algebraically closed and non-zero.*

4.2.4. *Arbitrary directed point networks*

In the general case, we could adapt the results obtained by Renz [REN 01b] for directed intervals. However, since directed points networks do not seem to have been considered independently in the literature, we will directly pass on to the more complex case of directed intervals.

4.3. Directed intervals

A dipole in $\mathbb{R}$ is a pair of distinct points (x_1, x_2) in $\mathbb{R}$. Following Renz [REN 01b], we will consider this entity as a directed interval: in the positive direction if $x_1 < x_2$, and in the negative in the contrary case.

The entities are thus *directed intervals* on the line. We can therefore distinguish for $i_1 \neq i_2$, two directed intervals $i = (i_1, i_2)$ and (i_2, i_1).

Our study of directed points may be regarded as propaedeutics in this context. To define the basic relations between two directed intervals, we apply the same principle used in the case of directed points: let $j = (j_1, j_2)$ be a directed interval of reference $(j_1 \neq j_2)$ and $i = (i_1, i_2)$ $(i_1 \neq i_2)$ an arbitrary directed interval. The interval with bounding points $\{i_1, i_2\}$, with respect to the interval with bounding points $\{j_1, j_2\}$, is in one of Allen's basic relations, say r. We denote the relation of i with respect to j by r^+ if $(i_2 - i_1)(j_2 - j_1) > 0$, and by r^- in the contrary case.

Let $\mathbf{B}_{2\varepsilon}$ denote the set of basic relations between directed intervals.

NOTE 4.1.– Our choice of notations is different from the one used by Renz. The correspondence of our notation with his notation is given in Table 4.3.

here	p	m	o	s	d	f	eq	fi	di	si	oi	mi	pi
Renz	b	mb	ob	cb	c	cf	eq	eb	e	ef	of	mf	f

Table 4.3. *Correspondence between the notation used here, and the notation of [REN 01b]. In addition, Renz uses $=$ ($\neq$ resp.) in subscript, whereas we use $+$ ($-$, respectively) in superscript*

EXAMPLE 4.4.– In Figure 4.6, we consider three directed intervals A, B, and C. The intervals A and B are both directed in the positive direction. Hence, A s$^+$ B. The interval C is directed in the negative direction. Hence, A d$^-$ C and B o$^-$ C.

Figure 4.6. *The directed interval calculus; here, we have A s$^+$ B, A d$^-$ C and B o$^-$ C*

4.3.1. *Operations*

As was the case for directed points, introducing the operation of time reversal is useful for expressing the operations of inversion and composition.

Time reversal, which we will denote here by u, acts on Allen's basic relations by interchanging p and pi, m and mi, o and oi, s and f, si and fi, and leaving d, di, and eq fixed (see Figure 4.7).

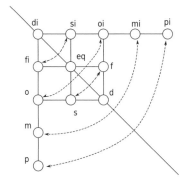

Figure 4.7. *The effects of time reversal, denoted by u, on Allen's basic relations. For example, we have* $s^u = f, d^u = d$

PROPOSITION 4.3.– *Let r be one of the 13 Allen's basic relations:*

– the inverse of the relation r^+ *is the relation* r^{-1+}, *and that of relation* r^+ *is the relation* r^{-1^u+}. *In particular, the relations r for which* $r^{-1} = r^u$ *are their own inverses;*

– the composition of $(r^\varepsilon \circ s^\eta)$ *is the relation* $(r \circ s)^\varepsilon$ *if* $\varepsilon = +$, *and* $(r^u \circ s)^{-\varepsilon}$ *if* $\eta = -$.

Equipped with these operations, the directed interval algebra $\mathbf{A}_2\varepsilon$, is a relation algebra which contains 26 atoms.

4.3.2. *Constraint networks and complexity*

A constraint network on the directed interval algebra is a graph whose vertices represent the directed intervals, and whose arcs are labeled by the elements of the algebra $\mathbf{A}_2\varepsilon$.

The consistency problem arises in a way similar to what was seen in the simpler case of directed points. Clearly, this problem is NP-hard since the consistency problem for intervals is NP-hard.

We may again consider the homogeneous relations. The natural transformation in this case allows us to transform a network, of which all the non-trivial relations are homogeneous, into a network whose labels are all positive. The following result holds:

THEOREM 4.1.– ([REN 01b], th. 5.2) Let S be a tractable subset of Allen's algebra which is stable under the time reversal operation. Then the set $S^{\pm} = \{r^+ \mid r \in S\} \cup \{r^- \mid r \in S\} \cup \{1\}$ is a tractable subset of the directed interval algebra.

This result applies in particular to the basic relations. It also applies to the pre-convex relations of Allen's algebra, since these relations are obviously stable by time reversal.

In addition, in the case of the subclass associated with pre-convex relations $\mathcal{H}$, the algebraic closure method yields a decision method for the consistency problem:

THEOREM 4.2.– ([REN 01b], th. 5.4) Any non-zero algebraically closed $\mathcal{H}^{\pm}$ network is consistent.

In the case of non-homogeneous relations, the examination of subnetworks for all the possible directions of variables can be expressed in the form of an instance of the 3SAT problem, and hence as an NP-hard problem. However, Renz shows that for a particular subset of the algebra, the consistency of a 3-tuple of variables depends only on the direction of two of them, which implies that the corresponding instance is an instance of 2SAT, which is a polynomial problem. More precisely, let $\mathcal{B}_2$ denote the set $\{\{r^+, r^-\} \mid r \in \mathbf{B}_2\}$, which is thus a set of 13 non-homogeneous relations. We then have the following theorem:

THEOREM 4.3.– ([REN 01b], th. 5.3) Let $(N = \{V1, \ldots, V_n\}, C)$ be a constraint network such that $C(i, j)$ contains a constraint of $\mathcal{B}_2$ if, and only if, $i < j$. Then the consistency of N can be determined in polynomial time.

4.4. The $\mathcal{OPRA}$ direction calculi

The $\mathcal{OPRA}$ [MOR 05, MOR 06] calculi are concerned with directed points in the plane. They are relative calculi which do not use an external reference in the plane: as in the case of dimension 1, each directed point is located with respect to a "local" reference defined by the other. Finally, these calculi are parametrized: they make use of subdivisions of the plane with varying degrees of fineness.

More precisely, let A and B be two directed points in the plane (Figure 4.8). The $\mathcal{OPRA}_m$ calculus (where m is an integer ≥ 2) uses m lines passing through A, making angles equal to a multiple of $\pi/2m$ with the vector of A. We thus obtain a partition of the plane into a point (the point A), $2m$ half-lines with A as a starting point, and

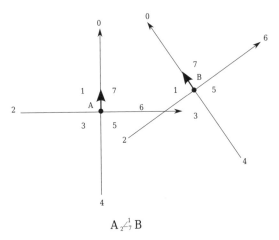

$$A_2 \overset{1}{\angle}_7 B$$

Figure 4.8. *The $\mathcal{OPRA}_2$ calculus. The directed point A defines eight zones numbered from 0 to 7 which form a partition of the plane centered at A. The integer i (here $i = 7$) defines the zone in which B is located. Symmetrically, the integer j (here $j = 1$) defines the zone in which A is located with respect to B. The configuration thus corresponds to the pair (7, 1). If A and B coincide, we use the position of the vector of B with respect to A*

$2m$ sectors. We number the half-lines 0 (this is the half line containing the direction of A), $2, \ldots, 4m - 2$ and the sectors $1, 3, \ldots, 4m - 1$ (following the counterclockwise direction). If a point B is distinct from point A, it lies in exactly one of these $4m - 1$ regions, and we associate to B the corresponding integer i, which identifies the position of B with respect to A. We then reverse the roles of A and B: this time, B defines a partition of the plane, and we obtain a second integer ranging between 0 and $4m - 1$ for A, which identifies the position of A with respect to B.

By definition, the pair (i, j) denotes the relation of A with respect to B in the $\mathcal{OPRA}_m$ calculus.

In the particular case where A and B coincide, the position of A with respect to B is identified by the region i to which the direction of B belongs with respect to A (which in turn determines the region to which the direction of A with respect to B belongs, namely the region $(4m - i)$). Thus, we ultimately obtain $4m(4m + 1)$ basic relations.

4.5. Dipole calculi

The 1D dipole calculus is a relative calculus, but the choice of a direction is reduced to two possibilities. In dimension 2, the situation becomes more complex. Several dipole calculi have been introduced in the literature by Schlieder [SCH 95, MOR 00, DYL 04]. The simplest calculus is the $\mathcal{DRA}_c$ calculus (coarse dipole calculus). We will simply describe its basic relations.

In the plane, a dipole (A, B) defines a line and a direction on this line. The points which are not on the line either belong to the open half-plane on the left side (symbol l for *left*), or to the open half-plane on the right side (symbol r for *right*) of the directed line defined by AB. We also consider the possibility that a point coincides with the starting point A (s for starts) or the ending point B (e for ends) of the dipole AB.

Let (C, D) be a reference dipole. If (A, B) is a dipole in a general position, i.e. no 3-tuple in $\{A, B, C, D\}$ is made up of aligned points, we identify the position of (A, B) with respect to (C, D) by a chain of four symbols from the set $\{l, r\}$ which successively indicate:

- the half-plane in which C is located relative to (A, B);
- the half-plane in which D is located relative to (A, B);
- the half-plane in which A is located relative to (C, D);
- the half-plane in which B is located relative to (C, D).

EXAMPLE 4.5.– Let us consider Figure 4.9. Point C, with respect to (A, B), is in the right half-plane defined by the latter, and D in the left half-plane; if we reverse the roles, we see that A and B are both in the left half-plane defined by (C, D). Thus, *rlll* will denote the relation of (A, B) with respect to (C, D).

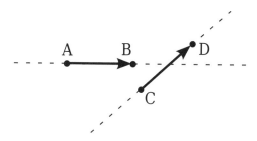

Figure 4.9. *The dipole calculus. Here, the relation of* (A, B)
with respect to (C, D) *is the relation rlll*

4.6. The Cardinal direction calculus

The Cardinal direction calculus is a 2D version of the Point calculus. It uses nine basic relations to locate the relative position of a point in the plane with respect to another point.

A point in the plane defines nine regions in the plane, as shown in Figure 4.10 (a). The incidence graph of these regions is shown in (c). As in the case of Allen's calculus, the linear orders in the East-West and South-North directions also induce a lattice structure on these relations, as shown in (b).

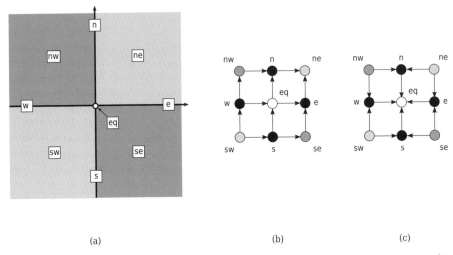

(a)   (b)   (c)

Figure 4.10. *The Cardinal direction calculus; in (a), the nine regions defined by a point; in (b), the lattice structure of the basic relations; in (c), the incidence graph of the nine regions*

We can give a precise meaning [LIG 98b] to the assertion that this calculus is a 2D version of the time point calculus: each basic relation is characterized, by projection on the axes, by a pair of basic relations between points, hence as a pair of elements of $\{<, eq, >\}$ (Table 4.4). The inversion and composition operations may be computed component-wise. In particular, the composition table is easily derived from that of the Point algebra.

eq	n	s	e	w	ne	nw	se	sw
(eq, eq)	$(eq, >)$	$(eq, <)$	$(>, eq)$	$(<, eq)$	$(>, >)$	$(<, >)$	$(>, <)$	$(<, <)$

Table 4.4. *Cardinal directions as pairs of relations between points*

4.6.1. *Convex and pre-convex relations*

The Cardinal direction calculus behaves in a very similar manner to that of Allen's calculus. In a way, it is a simpler version of Allen's calculus. As already mentioned, its set of basic relations has a natural structure of a lattice. This lattice is the product of two linearly ordered sets; it may explicitly be embedded in $\mathbb{N} \times \mathbb{N}$ (Figure 4.10 (b)).

Given a point (a_1, a_2) in the plane, the nine basic relations obviously correspond to nine regions which constitute a partition of the plane (Figure 4.10 (a)). We may thus refer to the dimension and closure of a basic relation, and more generally, to the dimension and closure of an arbitrary (disjunctive) relation, that is, of a union of basic relations. The incidence graph of the nine regions is represented in Figure 4.10 (c). We may note that the dual graph is that of the cell complex consisting of a square, formed by the union of nine cells: a 2D cell, which is the interior of the square, labeled eq, four 1D cells, which are the sides of the square, labeled n, w, s and eA, and four 0D cells, which are the vertices of the square, labeled nw, sw, se, and ne (Figure 4.11).

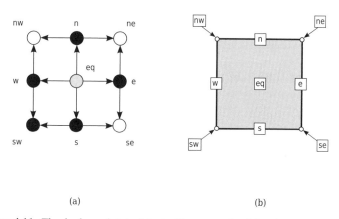

(a)   (b)

Figure 4.11. *The dual graph (a) of the incidence graph of the nine regions is the incidence graph of the cell complex (b)*

We can now define a convex relation by the condition that it corresponds to an interval of the lattice, or equivalently to a convex region which is closed by projections. The set of convex relations is a subclass in the Cardinal direction algebra (an algebra with $2^9 = 512$ elements).

More generally, a pre-convex relation is a relation whose closure is convex. Any pre-convex relation is obtained by removing 0D or 1D relations from a convex relation. The pre-convex relations also constitute a subclass in the algebra.

4.6.2. *Complexity*

It can be shown [LIG 98b] that the consistency problem of a constraint network on the Cardinal direction algebra is NP-complete. The complexity of this formalism is hence as high as the complexity of Allen's calculus. And in fact, results exactly similar to those we know for Allen's calculus also hold for the Cardinal direction calculus.

First of all, the subclass of pre-convex relations is of polynomial complexity and, more precisely, a pre-convex network whose algebraic closure is non-zero is a consistent network. We can thus decide consistency by using an algebraic closure algorithm.

Moreover, such a network is generically minimal (see proposition 2.8).

Finally, just like for Allen's calculus, the subclass of pre-convex relations is the only maximal subclass among the polynomial subclasses containing all basic relations. In fact, we show in [LIG 98b] that any subclass containing the pre-convex relations and at least one relation that is not pre-convex, is necessarily NP-complete. The proof uses "corner" relations similar to those of Allen's algebra.

We refer to [LIG 98b] for the description of two methods of construction of a consistent scenario associated with a non-zero pre-convex network. The first method uses the generic property of minimality and has a time-cost of $O(n^3)$. The second method consists in first replacing the network by its convex closure, then considering its two projections, which are point networks, and using van Beek's algorithm [BEE 90a].

4.7. The Rectangle calculus

Just as the Cardinal direction calculus is the 2D version of the Point calculus, the rectangle calculus is a "2D" version of Allen's calculus [GÜS 89, BAL 98a, BAL 99c, BAL 99a].

More precisely, we consider spatial entities which are rectangles with their axes parallel to the coordinate axes (orthoaxial rectangles) in the plane. Such a rectangle is entirely determined by its projections on the coordinate axes, which are closed and bounded intervals on each of these axes.

The qualitative relation between two given rectangles is defined by a pair of Allen's relations. We thus obtain a set of basic relations $\mathbf{B}_{rec}$ with 169 elements. Clearly, this set of basic relations constitutes a partition of the set of all relations. Here again, the inversion and composition operations can be computed component-wise.

EXAMPLE 4.6.– In the example of Figure 4.12, there are two rectangles A and B. The projection a_1 of A on the horizontal axis is an interval which overlaps the projection b_1 of B (relation o). The projection of A on the vertical axis is overlapped by that of B (relation oi). Thus, A (o, oi) B.

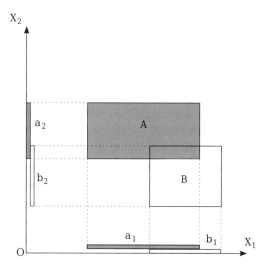

Figure 4.12. *The Rectangle calculus: the gray rectangle A is in the relation (o, oi) with respect to the white rectangle B*

4.7.1. *Convex and pre-convex relations*

Balbiani *et al.* [BAL 99c, BAL 99a] have shown how to define convex and pre-convex relations in this context:

– a basic relation of the rectangle calculus is a pair of basic relations of Allen's algebra. Using the lattice structure of the latter, we provide the basic relations of the rectangle calculus with the product structure, i.e. if (r, s) and (r', s') are two elements of $\mathbf{B}_{rec}$, we have $(r, s) \leq (r', s')$ if, and only if, $r \leq r'$ and $s \leq s'$. Equipped with this partial order, $\mathbf{B}_{rec}$ is a lattice;

– a relation is convex if it corresponds to an interval of the lattice, or if it is the empty relation;

– the convex closure $I(R)$ of a relation R is, by definition, the smallest convex relation containing R;

– the dimension of a basic relation (r, s) is the sum of the dimensions of r and s (intuitively, the degree of freedom of (r, s)). For example, it is 0 for $(\mathrm{eq}, \mathrm{eq})$, 3 for (p, m), 4 for $(\mathrm{p,pi})$;

– the topological closure of (r, s) is the Cartesian product of the topological closures of r and s, i.e. the set of pairs $(r', s') \in \mathbf{B}_{rec}$ such that $r' \in Cl(r)$ and $s' \in Cl(s)$;

– a relation is pre-convex[1] if, and only if, $I(R) \subseteq Cl(R)$.

---

1 Balbiani, Condotta and Fariñas del Cerro [BAL 99a] use the term "weak pre-convexity" to refer to what we call "pre-convexity" here.

PROPOSITION 4.4.– *[BAL 99a] The following conditions are equivalent for a relation R:*

  – *R is pre-convex*;
  – *the dimension of $(I(R) \setminus R)$ is strictly less than that of R*;
  – *the topological closure $Cl(R)$ of R is convex.*

The convex relations form a subclass: they are stable by inversion, composition, and intersection.

The pre-convex relations are also stable by inversion and composition; but the intersection of two pre-convex relations is not necessarily pre-convex. A counterexample is provided by the pre-convex relations $\{(\mathsf{o}, \mathsf{o}), (\mathsf{eq}, \mathsf{s}), (\mathsf{s}, \mathsf{eq})\}$ and $\{(\mathsf{d}, \mathsf{d}), (\mathsf{eq}, \mathsf{s}), (\mathsf{s}, \mathsf{eq})\}$ whose intersection $\{(\mathsf{eq}, \mathsf{s}), (\mathsf{s}, \mathsf{eq})\}$ is not pre-convex.

4.7.2. *Complexity*

The complexity results for the rectangle calculus [BAL 99c, BAL 99a] are quite similar to the results known for Allen's calculus.

THEOREM 4.4.– *Let N be a constraint network whose constraints are all non-empty convex relations, and which is algebraically closed. Then, there exists a maximal instantiation of N.*

In the case of pre-convex relations, the authors introduce a technique called the *weak path-consistency method*, which consists in iterating the following operation (where $I(r)$ indicates the convex closure of the relation r):

$$C(i, j) \leftarrow C(i, j) \cap I(C(i, k) \circ C(k, j))$$

The pre-convex relations contain a subset of relations which constitute a subclass:

DEFINITION 4.3.– *A relation is* strongly pre-convex *if it is pre-convex and if its intersection with any convex relation is pre-convex.*

PROPOSITION 4.5.– *The set of strongly pre-convex relations is stable by inversion, composition, and intersection.*

4.8. The *n*-point calculus

Similarly as for the Cardinal direction calculus, a 2D version of the Point calculus, we can consider a dimension $n \geq 3$. In this way we get a calculus referred to as the n-point calculus [BAL 99b].

The entities considered in this formalism are thus points in the n-dimensional Euclidean space $\mathbb{R}^n$, and the relations between pairs of points are n-tuples of elements of the set $\{<, \text{eq}, >\}$. The inverse and composition operations are computed component-wise.

4.8.1. *Convexity and pre-convexity*

Convex and pre-convex relations, when $n \geq 3$, can be defined in a way similar to their definitions for the Cardinal direction calculus.

However, for $n \geq 3$, it is no longer true that the intersection of two pre-convex relations is necessarily a pre-convex relation, as shown by the following example.

EXAMPLE 4.7.– Let us consider (Figure 4.13) in the lattice of relations between 3-points[2], the relation $r = [(0,0,0),(2,2,2)] \setminus \{(2,1,2)\}$ (r is thus the entire lattice from which the relation $(2,1,2)$ is removed). The topological closure of r contains $(2,1,2)$, since this relation is for instance in the topological closure of $(2,2,2)$, hence this topological closure is the whole lattice. The relation r is thus pre-convex. In addition, let us consider the convex relation $s = [(0,1,0),(2,1,2)]$ (represented in Figure 4.13 by the shaded square). The intersection of r and s is the relation $s \setminus \{(2,1,2)\}$ which is not pre-convex since the relation $(2,1,2)$ is not in the topological closure of any of the relations of $r \cap s$.

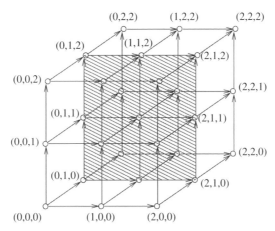

Figure 4.13. *The lattice of 3-points; the intersection of the pre-convex relation* $[(0,0,0),(2,2,2)] \setminus \{(2,1,2)\}$ *and the convex relation* $[(0,1,0),(2,1,2)]$ *(shaded) is not a pre-convex relation*

---

2 We use the notations 0,1, and 2 to indicate the relations $<$, eq, and $>$ respectively between points, in accordance with the notations introduced for the generalized intervals.

The problem is the same problem we encountered in the case of generalized intervals (see section 3.6). We can solve it in a similar way by introducing a concept of strong pre-convexity. Let us recall the corresponding definition:

DEFINITION 4.4.– *A relation is* strongly pre-convex *if it is pre-convex and if its intersection with any convex relation is also pre-convex.*

4.9. The *n*-block calculus

The *n*-block calculus is the *n*-dimensional version of Allen's calculus, in the same way as the Rectangle calculus is its 2D version. In the *n*-dimensional Euclidean space we consider *n*-blocks, which are cartesion products of closed intervals on each coordinate. Hence a 1-block is an interval on the line, and a 2-block is an orthoaxial rectangle in the plane. Figure 4.14 represents two 3-blocks in $\mathbb{R}^3$.

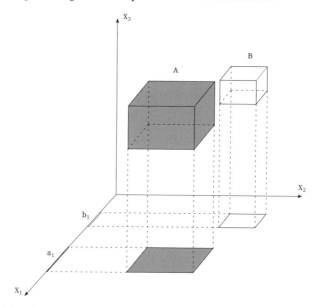

Figure 4.14. *The calculus of 3-blocks; the relation between A and B is represented by a 3-tuple of Allen's relations; in this case, the first component of this 3-tuple is* pi, *since* a_1 pi b_1

A basic relation, for this calculus, is thus an *n*-tuple of Allen's relations. The inverse and composition operations can be computed component-wise.

4.9.1. *Convexity and pre-convexity*

We define convex and pre-convex relations, when $n \geq 3$, in a way similar to their definitions for the rectangle calculus.

However, here again, for $n \geq 2$, pre-convex relations are no longer preserved by intersection, which implies that they do not constitute a subclass in the algebra. Hence, we are led to define a subclass that is strictly smaller, the subclass of strongly pre-convex relations.

4.10. Cardinal directions between regions

The CDC formalism, which was introduced by Goyal and Egenhofer [GOY 97, GOY 00, GOY 01], has also been studied by Skiadopoulos and Koubarakis [SKI 01, SKI 02, SKI 04, SKI 05]. It deals with relative directions between regions in the plane. A region in this context is a subset of the plane which is bounded, closed and regular (it coincides with the closure of its interior). In the version of the calculus that we present here, it is further assumed that these regions are connected.

Cicerone and Di Felice [CIC 04] have studied the problem of pairwise consistency (that is the determination of possible pairs $(\text{dir}(A, B), \text{dir}(B, A))$, see below for the notations).

4.10.1. *Basic relations*

Let B be a bounded, closed, regular and connected region in $\mathbb{R}^2$. Its projections $\text{pr}_1(B)$ and $\text{pr}_2(B)$ on the coordinate axes are two intervals which are closed and bounded (since the projections, which are continuous, preserve the connectedness and boundedness of B and that, since B is compact, its projection is closed).

The product $\text{mbr}(B) = \text{pr}_1(B) \times \text{pr}_2(B)$ is a rectangle in the plane called the *minimal bounding rectangle* of B. Clearly, it is actually the smallest orthoaxial[3] rectangle containing B. The four lines containing the sides of $\text{mbr}(B)$ devide the plane into nine regions called *tiles*, of which $\text{mbr}(B)$ is the only bounded one. We denote these nine tiles by the symbols (inspired by the names of the cardinal directions) $NW(B), N(B), NE(B), W(B), O(B), E(B), SW(B), S(B)$, and $SE(B)$ (we may leave out the symbol B when no ambiguity is possible).

These nine tiles do not constitute a partition of the plane, but they cover it, and the intersection of two distinct tiles has a maximum dimension of 1 (we use the convention whereby the empty set is of dimension-1). It is convenient to represent the list of tiles in matrix form, and $B_{1,1}, B_{1,2}, \ldots B_{3,1}, B_{3,2}, B_{3,3}$ will denote the nine tiles taken in the order used above (that is, from north to south and from west to east).

If a region B is selected as a reference region, and if A is a region to be located, we define the Boolean 3×3-matrix $(\text{dir}(A, B))$ as the matrix whose element $(\text{dir}(A, B))_{i,j}$

---

3 Recall that a rectangle is orthoaxial if its axes are parallel to the coordinate axes.

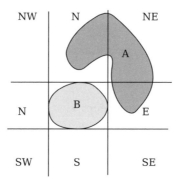

Figure 4.15. *Cardinal directions between regions*

in row i and column $j(1 \leq i, j \leq 3)$ is to 1 if $\mathring{A} \cap B_{i,j} \neq \emptyset$, and 0 otherwise. We refer to this matrix as to the *direction matrix* of A with respect to B.

For example, in the configuration illustrated in Figure 4.15, the matrix dir(A, B) is the matrix:

$$\begin{pmatrix} 0 & 1 & 1 \\ 0 & 0 & 1 \\ 0 & 0 & 0 \end{pmatrix}$$

It is also usual to represent dir(A, B) by the Boolean vector which is the concatenation of the rows of this matrix, and also, in a symbolic manner, by the list of the tiles with which the interior of A has a non-empty intersection. In the case shown in Figure 4.15, we would get the vector $(0, 1, 1, 0, 0, 1, 0, 0, 0)$, and the list $(N : NE : E)$.

Notice that with this definition, dir(B, B) is the matrix:

$$\begin{pmatrix} 0 & 0 & 0 \\ 0 & 1 & 0 \\ 0 & 0 & 0 \end{pmatrix}$$

The number of possible relations is *a priori* $2^9 - 1 = 511$. The fact that we are considering only connected regions implies that not all these possibilities are realized. In fact, we have the following criterion:

PROPOSITION 4.6.– *[GOY 00] A (3 × 3) Boolean matrix is a direction matrix if, and only if, it is non-zero and 4-connected.*

The property of 4-connectedness means that two non-zero squares can be connected by a path formed by vertically or horizontally adjacent non-zero squares.

There are 218 distinct matrices satisfying this condition.

DEFINITION 4.5.– *A relation is called a* single-tile relation *if it is represented by a matrix containing only a single occurrence of 1. Otherwise, it is a* multi-tile relation.

The set $\mathbf{B}_{CDC}$ of basic relations of the CDC formalism is thus made up of nine single-tile relations, and 209 multi-tile relations. We may relate this number of basic relations to that of the rectangle calculus, which consists of 169 basic relations.

As usual, we use the term *relation* to refer to arbitrary subsets of $\mathbf{B}_{CDC}$. The set of corresponding relations, which we will denote by $\mathbf{A}_{CDC}$, is thus a Boolean algebra whose elements are interpreted in disjunctive terms.

4.10.2. *Operations*

Clearly, the basic relations have the JEPD property. A peculiarity of the calculus is that a basic relation may not have a unique inverse: knowing $\text{dir}(A, B)$ is not enough in general to determine $\text{dir}(B, A)$. This fact is illustrated in Figure 4.16, which shows that a matrix $\text{dir}(A, B)$ may correspond to several matrices $\text{dir}(B, A)$.

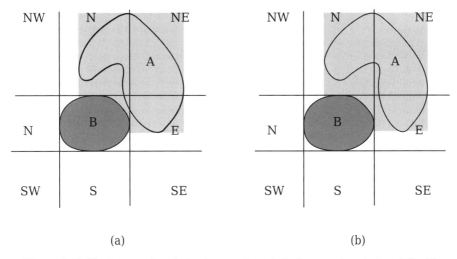

(a)   (b)

Figure 4.16. *The inverse of a relation is not unique: in both cases, the relation of B with respect to A is the relation $W : O : SW : S$, whereas that of A with respect to B is $N : NE : O : E$ in case (a) and $N : NE : E$ in case (b)*

Determining all pairs of matrices (M, M') such as $M = \text{dir}(A, B)$ and $M' = \text{dir}(B, A)$, for two connected regions A and B, is a particular case of the general consistency problem called *pairwise consistency problem*. This problem has been studied by Cicerone and Di Felice [CIC 04].

The problem of weak composition is to determine, for two matrices M and M', the set of matrices M'' such that there are connected regions A, B, and C, such that $M = \text{dir}(A, B)$, $M' = \text{dir}(B, C)$, and $M'' = \text{dir}(A, C)$. This problem has been studied by Skiadopoulos and Koubarakis [SKI 01, SKI 04].

4.10.3. *Consistency of basic networks*

In [ZHA 08], Zhang, Liu, Li, and Ying proved the following result:

THEOREM 4.5.– *The consistency problem for a basic CDC network is tractable in cubic time.*

More precisely, [ZHA 08] describes a cubic algorithm which, given a basic CDC network, constructs in $O(n^3)$ time an instantiation which satisfies the network if this network is consistent, or concludes that it is inconsistent.

NOTE 4.2.– To say that a network $(N, C(i, j), 1 \leq i, j \leq n)$ with n vertices is a basic network means that, for each pair $(i, j), 1 \leq i, j \leq n$, both $C(i, j)$ and $C(j, i)$ are basic relations $\text{dir}(N_i, N_j)$ and $\text{dir}(N_j, N_i)$.

The proof of this result is crucially based on relating the CDC calculus to Allen's calculus and to the Rectangle calculus. It also introduces interesting properties of solutions. In what follows, we describe some of the main ingredients of the proof. We refer the reader to [ZHA 08] and [LIU 10] for more details about the proof and for the extension of the result to other variants of the CDC calculus.

4.10.3.1. *A 1D CDC*

Let us suppose that we want to define a formalism analogous to the CDC calculus, but in dimension 1. The "regions" are bounded and closed intervals, hence intervals in Allen's sense. An interval $B = [b_1, b_2]$ defines three regions which are the equivalents of the nine 2D tiles: the half-line $B_1 = (-\infty, b_1]$, the interval itself $B_2 = B$ and the half-line $B_3 = [b_2, +\infty)$.

Using the same ideas we used in dimension 2, we choose an interval of reference $B = (b_1, b_2)$, and we associate to each interval $A = [a_1, a_2]$ its direction vector $\text{dir}(A, B)$, which is a boolean vector of length 3 whose i-th component, for $1 \leq i \leq 3$, is equal to 1 if the interior (a_1, a_2) of A meets B_i, and 0 if it does not.

Clearly, among the eight boolean vectors of length 3, two are excluded, namely $(0, 0, 0)$ and $(1, 0, 1)$. The remaining six vectors correspond to a partition of Allen's basic relations into 6 convex relations):

  – $(1, 0, 0)$ corresponds to $[\mathsf{p}, \mathsf{m}] = \{\mathsf{p}, \mathsf{m}\}$;
  – $(1, 1, 0)$ corresponds to $[\mathsf{o}, \mathsf{fi}] = \{\mathsf{o}, \mathsf{fi}\}$;

- $(0, 1, 0)$ corresponds to $[\mathsf{s}, \mathsf{f}] = \{\mathsf{s}, \mathsf{d}, \mathsf{eq}, \mathsf{f}\}$;
- $(1, 1, 1)$ corresponds to $\{\mathsf{di}\}$;
- $(0, 1, 1)$ corresponds to $[\mathsf{si}, \mathsf{oi}] = \{\mathsf{si}, \mathsf{oi}\}$;
- $(0, 0, 1)$ corresponds to $[\mathsf{mi}, \mathsf{pi}] = \{\mathsf{mi}, \mathsf{pi}\}$.

This 1D CDC is coarser than Allen's calculus. However, if for two intervals A and B, dir (A, B) and dir (B, A) are both known, we can infer a well-defined basic Allen's relation between A and B, except in the case where the vectors considered are $(1, 0, 0)$ and $(0, 0, 1)$. This is a consequence of the effect of the inversion operation on the basic relations, as illustrated in Figure 4.17.

EXAMPLE 4.8.– For example, if we know that $r \in \{\mathsf{o}, \mathsf{fi}\}$, this implies that $r^{-1} \in \{\mathsf{oi}, \mathsf{f}\}$. Since the class containing r^{-1} is also known, which can be only be $\{\mathsf{oi}, \mathsf{si}\}$ or $\{\mathsf{s}, \mathsf{d}, \mathsf{eq}, \mathsf{f}\}$, we can conclude that $r = \mathsf{o}$ in the first case, and $r = \mathsf{fi}$ in the second case.

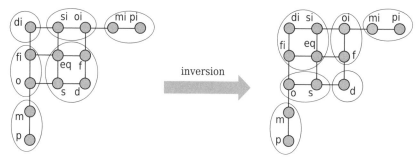

Figure 4.17. *The partition corresponding to the Boolean vectors (on the left) and the effect of inversion on this partition (on the right). The intersection of the two partitions subdivides the set of basic relations into nine classes containing one element each, and two classes with two elements, namely $\{\mathsf{p}, \mathsf{m}\}$ and $\{\mathsf{pi}, \mathsf{mi}\}$*

Let us now come back to CDC networks. Given a *basic* CDC network, we know the direction vectors on the two projections, as well as their inverses (note 4.2). Using this knowledge, what we have just discussed concerning 1D vectors shows that we can deduce from the CDC network two constraint networks on Allen's algebra which are "almost" basic networks, the only non-atomic relations being $[\mathsf{p}, \mathsf{m}]$ and $[\mathsf{mi}, \mathsf{pi}]$.

However, we can leave out m or mi from these non-atomic constraints without changing the problem. We are justified to do so, because a network N of intervals on the set of relations $S = \{\{\mathsf{p}, \mathsf{m}\}, \{\mathsf{pi}, \mathsf{mi}\}, \mathsf{o}, \mathsf{s}, \mathsf{d}, \mathsf{f}, \mathsf{oi}, \mathsf{si}, \mathsf{di}, \mathsf{fi}, \mathsf{eq}\}$ is consistent if, and only if, the network N' obtained by replacing $\{\mathsf{p}, \mathsf{m}\}$ by p, and $\{\mathsf{pi}, \mathsf{mi}\}$ by pi is consistent.

This can be shown as follows: First, N' is a refinement of N: its constraints are stronger, so that if N' is consistent, N is consistent *a fortiori*. If N is consistent, its algebraic closure is a network which does not contain the empty constraint, and whose constraints are convex relations, since {p, m} and {pi, mi} are convex. Since it is a subnetwork of N, the only possible relations are elements of S. But we know that, more generally, any algebraically closed network not containing $\emptyset$ on the set of pre-convex relations accepts a maximal instantiation, that is such that a basic relation of maximum dimension is instantiated for each pair of vertices (proposition 2.8). In this particular case, this result shows the existence of a solution where m and mi no longer appear.

A direct demonstration of this result can also be found in [LIU 10].

DEFINITION 4.6.– *Let $N, C(i,j), 1 \leq i, j \leq n$ be a basic CDC constraint network. The projected networks of N are the two atomic networks of intervals $pr_1(N)$ and $pr_2(N)$ obtained by replacing the constraints* {p, m} *by* p, *and* {pi, mi} *by* pi.

Using this definition, we can now state the following theorem:

THEOREM 4.6.– *For a basic CDC network to be consistent, it is necessary that its projected networks are consistent.*

4.10.3.2. *Configurations and constraint networks*

Let us begin with a finite configuration of (closed, regular, and connected) regions in the plane. Using the CDC formalism, we can give a description of this configuration in terms of a basic constraint network.

EXAMPLE 4.9.– Consider the configuration of regions on the left part of Figure 4.18. It is described in the following way in the CDC formalism:

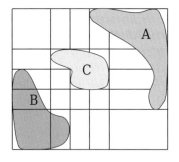 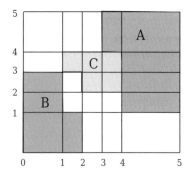

Figure 4.18. *A configuration (on the left) and its regularization (on the right). Both configurations have the same description in the CDC formalism*

$$\text{dir}(A, B) = \begin{pmatrix} 0 & 0 & 1 \\ 0 & 0 & 1 \\ 0 & 0 & 0 \end{pmatrix} \qquad \text{dir}(C, B) = \begin{pmatrix} 0 & 1 & 1 \\ 0 & 0 & 1 \\ 0 & 0 & 0 \end{pmatrix}$$

$$\text{dir}(A, C) = \begin{pmatrix} 0 & 1 & 1 \\ 0 & 0 & 1 \\ 0 & 0 & 1 \end{pmatrix} \qquad \text{dir}(B, C) = \begin{pmatrix} 0 & 0 & 0 \\ 1 & 0 & 0 \\ 1 & 1 & 0 \end{pmatrix}$$

$$\text{dir}(B, A) = \begin{pmatrix} 0 & 0 & 0 \\ 1 & 0 & 0 \\ 1 & 0 & 0 \end{pmatrix} \qquad \text{dir}(C, A) = \begin{pmatrix} 0 & 0 & 0 \\ 1 & 1 & 0 \\ 0 & 0 & 0 \end{pmatrix}$$

Conversely, let us assume now that we are given this description, and that we have to determine whether this given set of constraints has a solution.

Let a_1, b_1, c_1 (a_2, b_2, c_2, respectively) denote the first (resp. second) projection of the regions A, B, and C. We now proceed to construct the two projected networks. We can compute the direction vectors by taking the Boolean union of the rows of the matrix (for the first projection) and the Boolean union of its columns (for the second projection).

– The rows of the matrix $\text{dir}(A, B)$ yield the vector $(0, 0, 1)$, hence the constraint $\{\text{pi}, \text{mi}\}$. Those of the matrix $\text{dir}(B, A)$ yield the vector $(1, 0, 0)$, hence the constraint $\{\text{p}, \text{m}\}$. Thus, we get the constraint $\{\text{pi}, \text{mi}\}$ between a_1 and b_1. Using our definition of the projected networks, we leave out mi and keep pi as the constraint on the arc (a_1, b_1).

– The rows of the matrix $\text{dir}(A, C)$ yield the vector $(0, 1, 1)$, hence the constraint $\{\text{oi}, \text{si}\}$. Those of the matrix $\text{dir}(C, A)$ yield the vector $(1, 1, 0)$, hence the constraint $\{\text{o}, \text{fi}\}$. This is only compatible (refer to Figure 4.17) with the constraint oi on the arc (a_1, c_1).

– The rows of the matrix $\text{dir}(B, C)$ yield the vector $(1, 1, 0)$, hence the constraint $\{\text{o}, \text{fi}\}$. Those of the matrix $\text{dir}(C, B)$ yield the vector $(0, 1, 1)$, hence the constraint $\{\text{oi}, \text{si}\}$. Again, this means that we have the constraint o on the arc (b_1, c_1).

Using the same procedure, we compute the second projected network. The projected networks obtained in this way are shown in Figure 4.19.

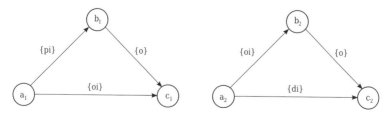

Figure 4.19. *The two projected networks corresponding to Example 4.9*

Notice that the consistency of the projected networks is also equivalent to that of the basic network of rectangles which they define.

NOTE 4.3.– Zhang *et al.* also that 3-consistency alone does not imply consistency for basic CDC constraint networks. More generally, for any k, we can build counterexamples which are networks such that all the subnetworks of size k are consistent without the network itself being consistent.

4.10.3.3. *Properties of configurations*

Let us now consider the Rectangle calculus. Given a configuration of connected regions, it allows us to describe this configuration in terms of basic networks labeled by pairs of Allen's basic relations. Clearly, this description depends only on the minimal bounding rectangles of the regions.

The first point to note is that, in a similar way, the description of a configuration of regions in terms of the CDC formalism depends only on regions containing them which are unions of orthoaxial rectangles. This remark leads to the definition of the *regularization* of a configuration.

4.10.3.3.1. Regularized configurations

Let us consider a finite configuration of regions in the plane. The first and second projections of each region are closed and bounded intervals. Let us consider the set of bounding points of the intervals defined on the first axis by the first projection, and similarly the set of bounding points on the second axis defined by the second projection.

We can now consider the vertical lines passing through the points defined in this way on the first axis, and similarly the horizontal lines passing through the points on the vertical axis. Finally, we get a rectangle which is subdivided in a finite set of rectangular cells defined by these lines. This rectangle is the minimal bounding rectangle containing all the regions considered. Zhang *et al.* refer to this rectangle as to the *frame* of the configuration. Notice that if the configuration contains n regions, this frame contains at most $4n^2$ cells.

In the case of Example 4.9, the construction of the frame and its subdivision into cells is illustrated in the left part of Figure 4.18.

The *regularization* procedure consists in replacing each region by the union of all the cells which meet the interior of this region.

In a graphic way, we can think of the procedure of regularization as a filling process, similar to what is done by the "paint bucket" tool of drawing applications: a specific color is associated with each region. If a cell intersects the interior of a region, we fill the entire cell with the color of the region (we may thus have overlapping colors if a cell contains interior points of several regions).

Figure 4.18 represents the initial configuration of Example 4.9 (on the left) and the configuration obtained by regularization (on the right).

It can be easily seen that the description of the set of regularized regions in terms of CDC relations is the same as that of the initial configuration: intuitively, extending the regions by filling does not lead to change this description.

Let us define a *regular* configuration as a configuration which coincides with its regularization. Then, as a consequence of this construction, we get the fact that a CDC constraint network which is consistent necessarily has a solution which is a regular configuration. To determine whether a given network is consistent, it will thus be enough to determine whether it has regular solutions.

4.10.3.3.2. Meet-free configurations

We have seen that the knowledge about $\text{dir}(A, B)$ and $\text{dir}(B, A)$ for two regions A and B determines Allen's relations between the projected intervals of A and B only if these relations do not contain connection relations (the two relations m and mi).

Let us consider again a finite configuration. If the set of vertically or horizontally projected intervals introduce connection relations, we can modify the configuration without changing its description in terms of CDC relations in such a way that this is no longer the case. Such a configuration is called a *meet-free* configuration. We refer the reader to [LIU 10] for the description of a procedure which achieves this result. Thus, we can restrict ourselves to the search of meet-free configurations to find the solutions.

4.10.3.3.3. Canonical solutions

In the case of Allen's calculus, any basic constraint network with n variables which is consistent has a solution such that the bounding points of the intervals of this solution constitute an initial segment $[0, \ldots, k]$ of $\mathbb{N}$, with $k \le 2n$. The proof of this fact is quite elementary: the set of intervals of a solution with n intervals has at most $2n$ bounding points, which can be numbered in an ascending way by the successive integers of an initial segment of $\mathbb{N}$. We thus obtain a solution known as the *canonical solution*, which is unique. We may also see this property as a consequence of the construction of left adjoint functors described in Chapter 9.

A set of finite intervals is *canonical* if the set of its bounding points is the initial segment $[0, N]$ of $\mathbb{Z}$, for some $N \in \mathbb{N}$. We define a *canonical solution* as a solution whose set of intervals is canonical.

If a basic CDC network of size n is consistent, then each of the projected networks has a canonical solution.

Consider a configuration which is regular and meet-free. The cells of this solution are defined by vertical and horizontal lines which form a finite rectangular grid in $\mathbb{R}^2$.

It is intuitively clear that, by moving this grid in such a way that its lower left corner is placed at the origin, and carrying out a series of horizontal and vertical deformations, we can get a configuration where the defining vertical lines are the lines $X = 0, 1, \ldots, M$, while the defining horizontal lines are lines $Y = 0, 1, \ldots, N$, for integers M and N such that $0 < M, N \leq 2n - 1$.

In particular, once this transformation has been made, the horizontal and vertical projections in the regions are canonical solutions of the projected networks.

Clearly, the description of the configuration in terms of CDC relations is not changed by this transformation.

Here again, we refer the reader to [LIU 10] for a detailed and rigorous description of this process.

Let us now define a *pixel* in $\mathbb{R}^2$ as a region $[i, i + 1] \times [j, j + 1]$, for $i, j \in \mathbb{Z}$. A region is a *digital* region if it is a union of pixels.

DEFINITION 4.7.– *A finite configuration of regions is* canonical *if it is digital, regular, meet-free, and if the set of its horizontal (vertical resp.) projections is canonical.*

If a configuration of regions is canonical, the configurations of intervals constituted by the horizontal and vertical projections in the regions are canonical configurations of intervals.

As a result of the preceding discussion, the following theorem is obtained:

THEOREM 4.7.– *Any consistent basic CDC network accepts a canonical solution.*

EXAMPLE 4.10.– Let us reconsider the configuration of Example 4.9. This configuration is a meet-free configuration. Its regularization is a configuration of regions in a frame containing 25 rectangular cells. Each region is the union of a finite number of cells. We obtain a canonical configuration by replacing this configuration by a regular configuration whose frame is $[0, 5] \times [0, 5]$. Each region is replaced by a union of pixels (five for A, and four for B and C), as shown in Figure 4.20.

It should be noted that the definition of a canonical configuration does not imply its uniqueness: in general, a constraint network may accept several *canonical* solutions. However, any canonical solution is *contained* in a *maximal canonical solution*, which is the canonical solution built by the algorithm described below for solving the consistency problem.

4.10.3.4. *The consistency problem*

Let us come back to the problem of consistency for a basic CDC network. Let $(N, C(i, j))$ be a basic CDC constraint network. Hence, for any pair $(i, j) \in N^2$, there is a matrix $\text{dir}(i, j)$ which defines the relation between the vertices i and j.

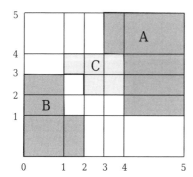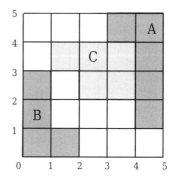

Figure 4.20. *A regular configuration (on the left) and its associated canonical configuration (on the right). In the latter, each region is a union of pixels*

Since we know $\mathrm{dir}(i, j)$ and $\mathrm{dir}(j, i)$ for each pair $(i, j) \in N^2$, we can determine its projected networks, which are networks which do not involve the meet relation.

For the CDC network to be consistent, it is necessary that these two projected networks be consistent. Therefore, the first stage is to determine whether they are consistent. If they are consistent, they have canonical solutions. If not, we can conclude right away that the CDC network is inconsistent.

Let us assume that the projected networks are consistent. For each $i \in N$, let I_i and J_i be the horizontal and vertical intervals corresponding to i. The rectangle $M_i = I_i \times J_i$ is a union of pixels which, in the case where the network is consistent, is the minimal bounding rectangle of the region corresponding to i.

The problem of consistency is then equivalent to determining whether there are connected digital regions satisfying the constraints and whose minimal bounding rectangles are the solution rectangles.

EXAMPLE 4.11.– Let us again consider Example 4.9, where we now change our point of view: we assume that the network with three vertices whose constraints are defined by the six matrices is given. Our aim is to build a canonical solution of this network.

In this case, the three enclosing rectangles associated with A, B, and C in the grid $[0, 5] \times [0, 5]$ are the rectangles $[3, 5] \times [1, 5]$, $[0, 2] \times [0, 3]$, and $[1, 4] \times [2, 4]$, respectively (left part of Figure 4.21).

4.10.3.5. *Determining the disallowed pixels*

A canonical solution, if available, consists of digital regions whose minimal bounding rectangles are known. The problem therefore is to determine, for each pixel of each of the minimal bounding rectangles whether the constraints allow it to belong to a solution.

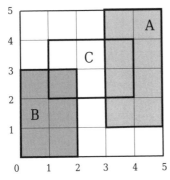
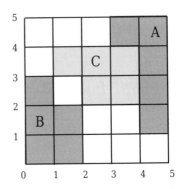

Figure 4.21. *Construction of a maximal canonical solution by removal of disallowed pixels. One gets each region from its enclosing rectangle by removing pixels: pixels $[3, 4] \times [1, 4]$ for A, pixel $[1, 2] \times [2, 3]$ for B, and pixel $[1, 2] \times [2, 3]$ for C*

DEFINITION 4.8.– *A pixel p of M_i is disallowed by $dir(i, i)$ if it is in one of the tiles defined by M_j of which $dir(i, j)$ states that it does not contain a subregion of the region corresponding to i.*

For each $i \in N$, let R_i be the region obtained from M_i after removal of the disallowed pixels. There is no guarantee that R_i is a connected region, but if a canonical solution exists, the region corresponding to i is a connected subregion of R_i whose minimal bounding rectangle is M_i.

EXAMPLE 4.12.– Let us consider again the case of Example 4.9. First, we note that the matrices $dir(A, B)$ and $dir(B, A)$ do not enforce any constraint on A and B.

If we then examine the matrix $dir(A, C)$, we realize that the three pixels of the rectangle $[3, 4] \times [1, 4]$ cannot be contained in A. We note that A deprived of these three pixels remains convex, and that its minimal bounding rectangle does not change.

Coming now to the matrix $dir(B, C)$, we see that it prohibits B from containing the pixel $[1.2] \times [2.3]$. Hence we remove it. Here again, the resulting region is still connected, and its minimal bounding rectangle does not change.

The matrix $dir(C, A)$ does not lead to any removal. On the other hand, we notice that the matrix $dir(C, B)$ does not allow pixel $[1, 2] \times [2, 3]$ to belong to C, so we remove it from C.

The remaining three regions contain all the five pixels. They constitute a canonical configuration which is represented on the right side of Figure 4.21.

For this configuration to be a solution, we still have to check that the associated description is the network we started with. One part is clear: if a pixel is disallowed in a region (a 0 value in the matrix), then it does not appear in the region we have obtained, by construction. But conversely, it should be checked that an occurrence of the value 1 in the matrix corresponds to the presence of at least one pixel.

In this example, we can verify that this is indeed the case. Thus, the configuration we have constructed is a canonical solution. In fact, it is the *maximal canonical solution*, which contains all canonical solutions. Non-maximal canonical solutions can be easily derived from it: for example, removing pixel $[2, 3] \times [2.3]$ from C and/or pixel $[1, 2] \times [1, 2]$ from B, would still yield a canonical solution. It should be noted that the initial configuration we started from (refer to Figure 4.18) corresponds to a canonical configuration which is not maximal and thus is strictly contained in the one we have just built.

In Example 4.9, the regions obtained by the elimination of the disallowed pixels are all connected regions. However, this is not true in the general case. If the subregion R_i' of the minimal bounding rectangle M_is is not connected, we have to determine whether it contains a subregion R_i such that:

– $R_i \subset R_i'$ is connected;
– the minimal bounding rectangle of R_i is M_i.

If this is not the case, the network does not have a solution. Otherwise, we still have to determine whether the direction matrix $\mathrm{dir}(R_i, M_j)$, for $j \neq i$ is the matrix $\mathrm{dir}(N_i, N_j)$ of the network.

EXAMPLE 4.13.– In the example considered above, the maximal canonical solution we have constructed has three connected regions of five pixels each, and we have checked that the matrices describing this configuration are the matrices given at the outset.

4.10.3.6. *A decision algorithm*

The algorithm presented in [LIU 10] then consists of the following sequence of operations:

1) build the projected networks; if they are not consistent, return failure;

2) compute canonical solutions of the projected networks;

3) for each region, remove all disallowed pixels from the corresponding rectangle;

4) if the region obtained in this way does not have a connected component having the rectangle as its minimal bounding rectangle, return failure;

5) otherwise, check whether this connected component is a solution.

The algorithm obtained in this way has a time cost of $O(n^4)$, but the authors describe a coding trick which makes it possible to reduce this cost to $O(n^3)$.

The consistency problem for arbitrary disjunctive relations is thus in NP. It is also NP-hard, since an instance of the consistency problem for Allen's algebra can be encoded in terms of CDC. Consequently, the consistency problem for CDC is NP-complete.

4.10.4. *Applications of the algorithm*

4.10.4.1. *Computing inverse relations*

We have seen that a basic CDC relation has in general more than one inverse. The algorithm described above can be used to answer the question of determining all inverses of a given basic relation r: it amounts to examine all networks with two vertices, for which the constraint $C(N_1, N_2)$ is r, and $C(N_2, N_1)$ each one of the basic relations.

The calculation shows that there are 757 pairs of basic relations which are in the inverse relation. Among the 218 basic relations, 119 have a single inverse, 68 have 2 inverses, 6 have 4 inverses, 20 have 8 inverses, 4 have 30 inverses, and 1 has 198 inverses.

The problem of determining the consistency of networks with two nodes is called the *pairwise consistency* problem.

4.10.4.2. *Computing the composition table*

The authors of [LIU 10] have also computed the weak composition table of the CDC calculus. This time, the task consists in using the algorithm for a set of networks with three nodes. Recall that the weak composition table answers the question: if the basic constraints $C(i, j) = r$ and $C(j, k) = s$ are known, what about $C(i, k)$? Since the knowledge of $C(i, j)(C(j, k)$, respectively) does not uniquely determine that of $C(j, i)(C(k, j)$, respectively), the results of pairwise consistency have to be used first in order to determine all the possible values for the basic relations $C(j, i)$ $(C(k, j)$, respectively). Then the consistency algorithm is used for the resulting three-node networks.

4.10.4.3. *Non-necessarily connected regions, simple regions*

The methods used for the version of the CDC calculus we have presented, which is a calculus dealing with connected regions, can also be applied to the version of the calculus which operates with regions that are not necessarily connected.

They can also be applied to Goyal and Egenhofer's version of the CDC calculus, which deals with simple regions, that is, regions homeomorphic to the closed disk. The algorithm, properly adapted, can be used to solve the consistency problem, again in cubic time.

Again, we refer the reader to [LIU 10] for a full presentation of these topics.

4.11. The INDU calculus

We now introduce the INDU calculus [PUJ 99a, VIJ 02] briefly. This formalism, similarly to Allen's calculus, considers intervals (let us say on the real number line $\mathbb{R}$) conceived as pairs $x = (x_1, x_2)$, with $x_1 < x_2$. For a basic relation relation r which indicates the relation of an interval x with regard to a reference interval y, we now distinguish three cases: the case where the duration of interval x is smaller than that of interval y (we denote by r^+ denote the corresponding relation), the case where it is the same (this is denoted by $r^=$), and the case where it is greater (denoted by $r^>$).

Clearly, not all basic relations will be partitioned into three subrelations: for example, the relation d implies that the duration of x is strictly smaller than that of y, and thus only d^- has to be considered.

It is quite convenient in many situations to consider the set of basic relations as a subset of pairs (r, s), where r is a basic relation of Allen's algebra, and s is one of the three basic relations $\{<, eq, >\}$ between points. We will then consider, for example, that d^- corresponds to the relation $(d, <)$.

4.11.1. *Inversion and composition*

In this way, we obtain 25 basic relations which form a partition (this is the JEPD property, see 1.2.1.2) of the set of binary relations between intervals (see Figure 4.23 also for a geometrical depiction of these relations). Let $\mathbf{B}_{\mathsf{INDU}}$ denote the set of these basic relations.

The inversion and composition operations are defined in a way similar to what we have seen for Allen's relations. In addition, they can be easily computed:

– *the inverse* of a basic INDU relation (r, s), where r is a relation of Allen's algebra, and s a basic relation between points, is the relation (r^{-1}, s^{-1});

– *the composition* of two basic relations (r, s) and (r', s') is the intersection of $(r \circ r') \times (s \circ s')$ with $\mathbf{B}_{\mathsf{INDU}}$.

EXAMPLE 4.14.– The inverse of the relation $p^<$ is the relation $pi^>$. The composition of $(di, >)$ and of $(p, >)$ is the intersection with $\mathbf{B}_{\mathsf{INDU}}$ of the relation $[p, di] \times \{>\}$, that is the relation $\{p^>, m^>, o^>, fi^>, di^>\}$.

4.11.2. *The lattice of* INDU *relations*

As a subset of the product of $\Pi_{2,2}$ and $\Pi_{1,1}$ (we use the notations introduced in Chapter 3), the set of basic $\mathbf{B}_{\mathsf{INDU}}$ relations has a partial order structure, of which it is easy to see that it is in fact a lattice structure: any pair of basic relations has a greatest lower bound (glb) and a least upper bound (lub). We may see this lattice as a subset of the Cartesian product of the lattice of Allen's basic relations and of the lattice of basic relations between points. In this product, which consists of $3 \times 13 = 39$ pairs, only 25 relations represent the elements of INDU. The other pairs, such as $(s, >)$ for example, are "virtual relations". Figure 4.22 represents the set of relations of the product of the two lattices, where the virtual relations are represented in white.

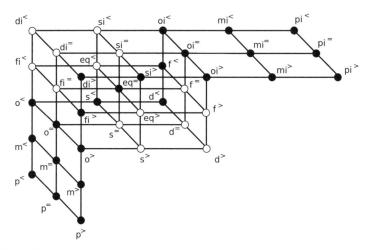

Figure 4.22. *The lattice of basic* INDU *relations (black vertices), seen as a subset of the product of Allen's lattice and of the lattice of basic relations between the points; the vertices represented in white are "virtual relations"*

4.11.3. *Regions associated with* INDU *relations*

Allen's basic relations correspond to regions in the plane. The basic relations of the INDU formalism correspond to a refinement of this set of regions. More precisely, we have the following interpretation, which is illustrated by Figure 4.23: given an interval $y = (y_1, y_2)$, as an interval of reference, we consider the regions corresponding to the 13 basic relations of Allen's calculus. Now, the line parallel to the first bisector which passes through y subdivides six of these regions into three subregions: the subregions located above this line correspond to relations of type $>$, those contained in the line correspond to those of type $=$, and those located below the line correspond to those of type $<$. The remaining seven basic relations are not affected.

We thus check geometrically the fact that we get $(3 \times 6) + 7 = 25$ basic relations.

We are also naturally led to define topological and geometrical concepts within this framework, such as the dimension of a relation, the topological closure of a relation, and the concepts of convexity and pre-convexity.

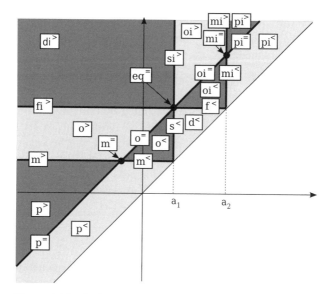

Figure 4.23. *The basic relations of the* INDU *calculus as regions*

Let us only note for the time being that the 2D relations of Allen's algebra are subdivided into two 2D relations and one 1D relation. This is illustrated by the subdivision of p into $p^>$, $p^<$ (of dimension 2) and $p^=$ (of dimension 1).

4.11.4. *A non-associative algebra*

We define the set $\mathbf{A}_{INDU}$ of INDU *relations* as the set of all subsets of $\mathbf{B}_{INDU}$, similarly to what was done for the other qualitative formulations. The composition of two basic relations is, in general, an element of $\mathbf{A}_{INDU}$. We naturally extend the inversion and composition operations to $\mathbf{A}_{INDU}$.

As an algebra of subsets, $\mathbf{A}_{INDU}$ is a Boolean algebra with a union, an intersection, and a complement operation. Moreover, inversion and composition are two additional operations which make it a Boolean algebra with operators. The relation $eq^=$ is a neutral element for composition, and we easily verify that most of the properties which define a relation algebra (refer to Appendix B) are satisfied. However, one property is lacking: composition is not associative.

EXAMPLE 4.15.– We have $(pi^> \circ mi^>) \circ m^> = \{oi^>, mi^>, pi^>\}$, a relation which strictly contains $pi^> \circ (mi^> \circ m^>) = \{pi^>\}$.

PROPOSITION 4.7.– *The Boolean algebra with operators* $\mathbf{A}_{INDU}$ *is a non-associative algebra in Maddux's sense [MAD 82, HIR 02]. More precisely, it is a semi-associative algebra [LIG 04b].*

Proof. The required properties are easily verified, using, for example, the representation of basic relations as pairs of Allen's and point relations. The semi-associativity is a consequence of the fact that the basic relations are serial[4] (see proposition 11.1). □

We will see below that the situation illustrated by the INDU formalism is, in a certain manner, typical: in general, for a "qualitative formalism", we should not expect the corresponding algebra to be associative. This point will be examined in detail in Chapter 11. Hence, formalisms such as Allen's calculus are not typical in that sense. This realization, in turn, raises the general question of determining which of the qualitative formalisms have associative algebras associated to them.

4.12. The $2n$-star calculi

We have noted above that the n-point calculi (for $n \geq 3$) are generalizations of the cardinal direction calculus to spaces of higher dimensions. Now the cardinal direction calculus, as indicated by its name, is in fact a formalism that is concerned with directions rather than points in the plane: all points lying in the same direction with respect to a reference point y are by definition in the same relation with respect to y.

The $2n$-star calculi are other types of generalization of the cardinal direction calculus, where the underlying space is still the plane, but where the basic relations are considered as directional relations with various degrees of refinement.

Let n be a positive integer. Let us fix a reference point y in the plane $\mathbb{R}^2$ with coordinates (O, X_1, X_2). Consider the half-lines passing through y and making angles of $k\pi/n$ (for $k = 0, \ldots, n$) with the semi-axis (O, X_1). Let $D_{2k+1}(y)$ be the semi-axis of angle $k\pi/n$ (y not included, and $D_0(y) = \{y\}$).

Let $D_{2k+2}(y)$, for $k = 0, \ldots, n$ be the open sector of the plane of angle π/n which lies between $D_{2k+1}(y)$ and $D_{2k+3}(y)$ (between $D_{2n+1}(y)$ and $D_1(y)$ if $k = n$) which is generated by rotating $D_{2k+1}(y)$ around y in the counterclockwise direction.

DEFINITION 4.9.– *The $2n$-star calculus has the $4n + 1$ relations defined by $D_i(y)$, for $i = 0, \ldots, 4n$, as basic relations.*

Thus, this formalism has a 0D basic relation D_0 (the point y), $2n$ 1D basic relations, and $2n$ 2D basic relations. These $4n + 1$ basic relations form a partition of the plane.

---

4 A binary relation R is serial if, for any x, there exists y such that $R(x, y)$.

EXAMPLE 4.16.– Let us consider the case where $n = 1$. We may interpret the corresponding calculus as the one that defines a "full east" region D_1 and a "full west" region D_3, both of dimension 1, and two 2D regions D_2 (north) and D_4 (south) (Figure 4.24).

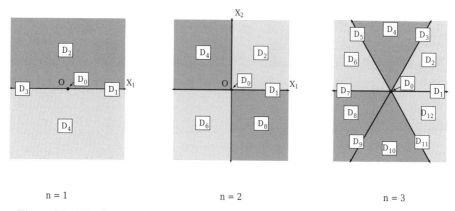

n = 1   n = 2   n = 3

Figure 4.24. *The 2n-star calculus, for $n = 1, n = 2, n = 3$. The 4-star calculus coincides with the cardinal direction calculus*

EXAMPLE 4.17.– The case where $n = 2$ defines a partition of the plane into nine zones, and the corresponding calculus is none other than the Cardinal direction calculus, the relation D_0 being eq and the relations D_i, for $1 \leq i \leq 8$, corresponding to e, n, nw, w, sw, s, and se, respectively.

EXAMPLE 4.18.– The case where $n = 3$ is also illustrated in Figure 4.24. This 6-star calculus has 13 basic relations.

4.12.1. *Inversion and composition*

The inversion and composition operations are defined in the usual way. They can be described explicitly in a simple way:

PROPOSITION 4.8.– *Let D_i and D_j be two basic relations of the 2n-star calculus:*

– the basic relations D_i and $D_{2n+i}(1 \leq i \leq 4n)$ are inverses to one another; D_0 is its own inverse;

– the composition of D_i and D_j is the set of basic relations which are contained in the interior of the convex closure of $D_i \cup D_j$ if this convex closure is of dimension 2, and in this convex closure itself otherwise.

EXAMPLE 4.19.– Let us consider the case $n = 3$ (Figure 4.25). The inverse of D_3 is D_9; the composition of D_3 and D_9 is $\{D_3, D_0, D_9\}$; in fact, the convex closure of $D_3 \cup D_9$

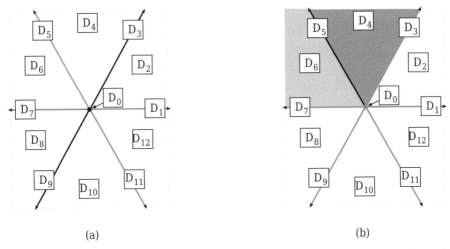

Figure 4.25. *Composition in the 6-star calculus: in (a), composition of the relations D_3 and D_9; in (b), composition of D_3 and D_7*

is the line containing these two relations; the composition of D_3 and D_7 is formed by the relations contained in the interior of the convex closure of $D_3 \cup D_7$. The latter is $D_0 \cup D_3 \cup D_4 \cup D_5 \cup D_6 \cup D_7$, so that the desired composition is $\{D_4, D_5, D_6\}$.

NOTE 4.4.– The cardinal direction calculus is identical to the 4-star calculus. We know that its composition table can be deduced from the composition table of the Point calculus. But, as a particular case of $2n$−star calculus, it can also be obtained by using proposition 4.8.

EXAMPLE 4.20.– The composition of se and n (Figure 4.24 and Figure 4.10) corresponds to the interior of the convex closure of the union of regions corresponding to these two relations. This convex closure is the relation $\{n, eq, ne, e, se, s\}$. The desired result is therefore the relation $\{ne, e, s\}$.

4.13. The Cyclic interval calculus

The Cyclic interval calculus is a qualitative formalism for intervals on a circle. As was the case for Allen's calculus, these intervals are characterized by their starting and ending points. If $\mathbf{S}^1$ is a circle (directed in the counterclockwise direction), an interval $A = (A_1, A_2)$ is defined by its starting point $A_1 \in \mathbf{S}^1$ and its ending point $A_2 \in \mathbf{S}^1$, with $A_1 \neq A_2$. In particular, (A_1, A_2) and (A_2, A_1) are two complementary intervals, whose union is the entire circle, and whose intersection is the set $\{A_1, A_2\}$.

Similarly again to Allen's calculus, the basic relations between the intervals are defined by distinguishing the various possible configurations of the bounding points.

Here, a relevant relation is the ternary relation between points on a circle which we denote by $\prec$: by definition, $\prec (P, Q, R)$ means that, starting from P and moving in the counterclockwise direction, we pass through Q before reaching R.

We get in this way 16 basic relations between cyclic intervals. Table 4.5 gives the definition of ten of these relations in terms of the relation $\prec$ and the equality relation. Six of them, namely m, o, s, d, f, and moi have inverse relations denoted, respectively, by mi, oi, si, di, fi, and omi. Four relations ppi, ooi, mmi, and eq are their own inverses (symmetrical relations).

$m(A, B)$	$o(A, B)$	$s(A, B)$	$d(A, B)$	$f(A, B)$
$\prec (A_1, B_1, B_2)$	$\prec (A_1, B_1, A_2)$	$\prec (A_1, A_2, B_2)$	$\prec (A_2, B_2, B_1)$	$\prec (A_1, A_2, B_1)$
$A_2 = B_1$	$\prec (A_2, B_2, A_1)$	$A_1 = B_1$	$\prec (A_1, A_2, B_2)$	$A_2 = B_2$
$ppi(A, B)$	$ooi(A, B)$	$mmi(A, B)$	$moi(A, B)$	$eq(A, B)$
$\prec (A_1, A_2, B_1)$	$\prec (A_1, B_2, B_1)$	$A_1 = B_2$	$\prec (A_2, A_1, B_2)$	$A_1 = B_1$
$\prec (A_1, B_1, B_2)$	$\prec (A_2, A_1, B_1)$	$A_2 = B_1$	$A_2 = B_1$	$A_2 = B_2$

Table 4.5. *Definition of the basic relations between cyclic intervals in terms of the ternary relation $\prec$ and the equality relation ($\prec (P, Q, R)$ means that the P, Q, and R are met in this order when traversing the circle in the counterclockwise direction)*

Figure 4.26 represents the sixteen basic relations of the Cyclic interval calculus (we use the notations of [OSM 99b, BAL 00a]).

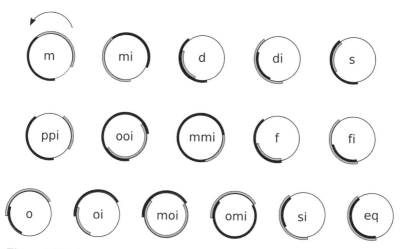

Figure 4.26. *The sixteen basic relations between cyclic intervals: the gray interval is in the relation indicated with respect to the black interval*

4.13.1. *Convex and pre-convex relations*

As usual, a (disjunctive) *relation* is by definition a subset of the set of basic relations. Consider the left part of Figure 4.27. It allows us to associate a basic relation with each pair of integers between 0 and 8. Balbiani and Osmani [BAL 00a] use this representation to define several classes of interesting relations.

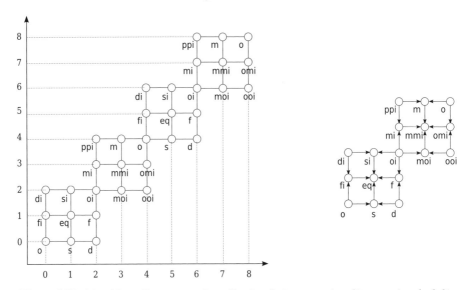

Figure 4.27. *A (multivocal) representation of basic relations as pairs of integers (on the left); on the right, the topological closure relation. For example, the topological closure of the basic relation* oi *is the relation* {eq, f, si, oi, moi, mi, mmi}

DEFINITION 4.10.– *A convex relation is a relation which can be defined as the product of two intervals of* ℕ.

For example, the relation {ppi, m, o, s, d} is convex, since it can be defined by the product [2, 6] × [6, 6].

Now let us consider the right part of the same figure. We use it to define the topological closure of a relation.

DEFINITION 4.11.– *A pre-convex relation is a relation whose topological closure is a convex relation.*

For example, the relation {fi, f, di, oi} has a convex relation as its topological closure, namely the relation {fi, eq, f, di, si, oi, moi, mi, mmi}, which is defined by the product [0, 2] × [4, 5]. It is hence a pre-convex relation.

As in the case of Allen's relations, we can associate a dimension with a basic relation. This dimension corresponds to its degree of freedom. In the representation in the form of pairs of integers, this dimension is equal to the number of even integers in the pair. For example, eq and mmi are 0D relations, s is a 1D relation, and o is a 2D relation.

The convex relations are stable under inversion and composition. But they are not stable under intersection: Balbiani and Osmani give the example of the relations $\{d, f, oi, moi, ooi\}$ and $\{ooi, omi, o, s, d\}$, whose intersection $\{d, ooi\}$ is not a convex relation.

However, a subclass of the algebra is constituted by the set of *nice* relations:

DEFINITION 4.12.– *A* nice *relation is either a 0D or a 1D pre-convex relation, or a 2D convex relation which contains at most two basic relations.*

Nice relations are stable by inversion, composition, and intersection. Hence the algebraic closure of a nice constraint network is itself a nice network.

4.13.2. *Complexity of the consistency problem*

On the algebra of cyclic intervals, there are non-zero algebraically closed networks which are not consistent, and even algebraically closed *scenarios* which are inconsistent.

The authors of [BAL 00a] show the following two theorems:

THEOREM 4.8.– *The consistency problem for cyclic interval networks is an NP-complete problem.*

THEOREM 4.9.– *The consistency problem for nice cyclic interval networks is a polynomial problem which can be solved by the algebraic closure method.*

The proof of theorem 4.9 is based on a representation of the basic relations in terms of regions in a punctured disk. We refer the reader to [BAL 00a] for this proof. In Chapter 8, we will describe a geometrical representation of the relations which is topologically equivalent to the punctured disk representation used in [BAL 00a].

4.14. The RCC–8 formalism

The RCC–8 formalism originates from two distinct sources: the first source is based on work by Cohn and his collaborators [RAN 92a, BEN 94, COH 97, REN 97, REN 99a], and corresponds to a specific approach to geometry, and more generally to topology, which is related to Leśniewski's mereology [LEŚ 92]. The second source is related to the work of Egenhofer and his collaborators [EGE 89, EGE 90, EGE 91b] in the context of the formalization of reasoning about space and geographic entities, in connection with domains of application such as cartography and geographical information systems (GIS).

4.14.1. Basic relations

Let us start with the second approach, which is simpler to present. We will consider the first approach in depth in Part 1 of Chapter 10. Egenhofer considers 2D regions[5] in the 2D space $\mathbb{R}^2$. Such a region A has an interior $\overset{\circ}{A}$ and a boundary ∂A. If B is another region, *the 4-intersection calculus* considers the pairwise intersections of the four sets $\overset{\circ}{A}, \partial A, \overset{\circ}{B}, \partial B$ and associates with them a matrix called the 4-intersection matrix:

$$\mathcal{I}_4(A, B) = \begin{pmatrix} \overset{\circ}{A} \cap \overset{\circ}{B} & \overset{\circ}{A} \cap \partial B \\ \partial A \cap \overset{\circ}{B} & \partial A \cap \partial B \end{pmatrix}$$

From the 4-intersection matrix, we only retain whether the intersections in its entries are empty or not. We thus have *a priori* $2^4 = 16$ possible Boolean matrices. But, it can be shown that when A and B are homogeneous 2D regions with connected boundaries, only eight Boolean matrices are possible, which correspond to the eight situations illustrated in Figure 4.28.

The same author has also considered the 9-intersection calculus, in which we consider, for each region A, in addition to its interior and boundary, its exterior A^-.

In the RCC-8 formalism, the spatial objects considered are regions, or more generally subspaces of a topological space satisfying specific restrictions (for example, regular closed subspaces). The formalism has eight basic relations:

– four symmetrical relations, denoted by DC (*disconnected*), EC (*externally connected*), PO (*partial overlap*), and the equality relation, denoted by EQ;

– two relations of inclusion, TPP (*tangential proper part*) and NTPP (*not tangential proper part*);

– two relations which are the inverse relations of the latter, and are denoted as TPPI (tangentially contains) and NTPPI (contains in a non-tangential way).

Figure 4.28 illustrates the meaning of the eight basic relations for regions which are disks in the plane.

---

5 More precisely, the bounded regions delimited in the plane by Jordan curves; see Chapter 10 for more on this subject.

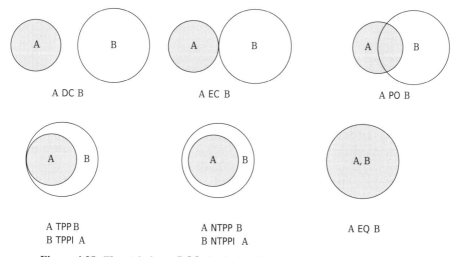

Figure 4.28. *The eight basic* RCC–8 *relations between the two disks in the plane*

A simpler formalism of the same type is the RCC−5 calculus. It corresponds to consider the union of DC and EC as a single basic relation DR, and similarly for TPP and NTPP, which are combined into a single basic relation PP (*proper part*); consequently the inverses TPPI and NTPPI are regrouped in a basic relation PPI. The resulting calculus has five basic relations, hence its name.

4.14.2. *Allen's relations and* RCC−8 *relations*

Now, the reader is entitled to ask the following question: since the intervals are particular regions of the real line, they constitute a domain of interpretation of the RCC−8 formalism; what then is the relationship between Allen's language and the RCC−8 language?

An answer to this question may be as follows: Moving from Allen's language to that of RCC−8 corresponds to forgetting the orientation of the time axis; moving in the opposite direction, obviously, corresponds to introducing an orientation on a line. Hence the relation DC corresponds to the union of p and pi, the relation EC to that of m and mi, and PO to that of o and oi. Similarly, TPP is the union of s and f, and NTPP, for its part, is d. The operation of inversion is interpreted in an obvious way.

A visually suggestive way of clarifying this correspondence is to consider the lattice of Allen's relations, in its canonical embedding in $\mathbb{N} \times \mathbb{N}$ (see Figure 4.29). The change of direction corresponds to the symmetry with respect to the line defined by $X_1 + X_2 = 4$. This symmetry interchanges p and pi, m and mi, o and oi, s and f, fi and si, and leaves the basic relations d, di, and eq fixed. Quotienting by this symmetry, we get for the

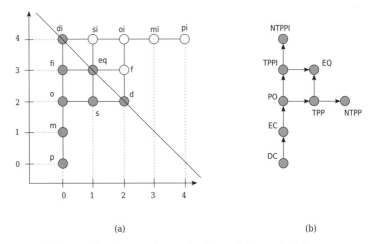

(a)   (b)

Figure 4.29. *The semi-lattice (b) deduced from Allen's lattice*
(a) by "forgetting" the direction of time

set of basic RCC−8 relations an ordered structure, as shown in Figure 4.29 (b). This structure is no longer a lattice, but only a lower semi-lattice (each pair of relations has a greatest lower bound).

4.14.3. *Operations*

Here, as in Allen's formalism, the inversion operation is "hardcoded" in the notation. The composition of two relations can be computed by hand, at least for these formalisms which involve a small number of basic relations. The general question of determining the composition table in an automatic way was initiated by Bennett [BEN 97b, BEN 97a].

EXAMPLE 4.21.– If $EC(x, y)$ and $EC(y, z)$, then the relations between x and z leave out the relations $NTPP(x, z)$ and $NTPPI(z, x)$. The composition EC ∘ EC is hence the relation $\{DC, EC, PO, TPP, TPPI, EQ\}$. Let us note that this relation is an interval in the semi-lattice, namely the set of relations located between DC and EQ. We may thus denote it by $[DC, EQ]$.

To give a concise description of the composition table, we use the remark made in the above example. If r and s are two basic relations such that $r \leq s$, we denote by $[r, s]$ denotes the corresponding interval. In addition, for any relation r, $[r, \omega]$ denotes the set of relations s such that $s \geq r$.

Using those conventions, the composition table of the RCC−8 calculus is as shown in Table 4.6.

	DC	EC	PO	TPP	NTPP	TPPI	NTPPI
DC	[DC, ω]	[DC, NTPP]				DC	
EC	[DC, NTPPI]	[DC, EQ]	[DC, NTPP]	[EC, NTPP]	[PO, NTPP]	[DC, EC]	DC
PO	[DC, NTPPI]		[DC, ω]	[PO, NTPP]		[DC, NTPPI]	
TPP	DC	[DC, EC]	[DC, NTPP]	[TPP, NTPP]	NTPP	[DC, EQ]	[DC, NTPPI]
NTPP	DC		[DC, NTPP]	NTPP		[DC, NTPP]	[DC, ω]
TPPI	[DC, NTPPI]	[EC, NTPPI]	[PO, NTPPI]	[PO, EQ]	[PO, NTPP]	[TPPI, NTPPI]	NTPPI
NTPPI	[DC, NTPPI]	[PO, NTPPI]			[PO, ω]	NTPPI	

Table 4.6. *The* RCC−8 *composition table. For example, if x* TPP *y and y* PO *z, then x is in one of the five relations of* [DC, NTPP] = {DC, EC, PO, TPP, NTPP} *with regard to z (row* TPP*, column* PO *of the table)*

4.14.4. *Maximal polynomial classes of* RCC−8

We will see later (Chapter 10) that any algebraically closed scenario is consistent, and that the RCC−8 algebra contains three maximal tractable subclasses of relations containing all the basic relations.

Representing the basic RCC−8 relations as a semi-lattice allows us to give a visually simple description of the three maximal classes identified by Renz [REN 99a].

In order to do this, let us first consider Figure 4.30. Let M_1 be the set of relations which contain at least one of the black relations and one of the gray relations, but which do not contain the relation PO. There are thus $3 \times 2^3 = 72$ relations in this set.

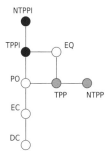

Figure 4.30. *Black and gray relations used for defining* M_1

We also need to consider the four-element set M_2 containing the relations represented in Figure 4.31.

Let B be the complement of the union of M_1 and M_2. It is hence a set of $256 - 76 = 180$ elements.

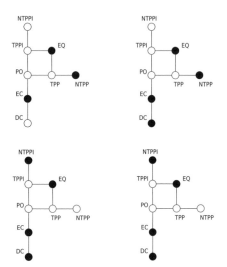

Figure 4.31. *The set M_2*

PROPOSITION 4.9.– *The three maximal tractable sub-classes of* RCC−8 *containing all basic relations are the following:*

– $\hat{\mathcal{H}}_8$ is the set obtained from B by removing all relations which contain EQ *and* NTPP *, but not* TPP*, as well as those which contain* EQ *and* NTPPI *but not* TPPI *(Figure 4.32 (a) and (b));*

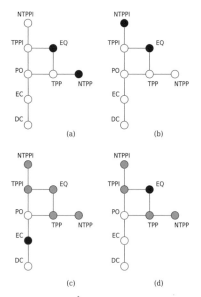

Figure 4.32. *The sub-classes $\hat{\mathcal{H}}_8$ (a), (b), class C_8 (c) and class Q_8 (d)*

– the class C_8 is the set obtained from B by removing all relations which have the following property: they contain EC. *and one of the five relations in gray, but do not contain* PO *(Figure 4.32 (c))*;

– the class Q_8 is the set obtained from B by removing all relations which have the following property: they contain EQ *and one of the four relations in gray, but do not contain* PO *(Figure 4.32 (d))*.

4.15. A discrete RCC theory

4.15.1. *Introduction*

When processing geographical data (for example, when exploitating satellite pictures), one often has to deal with discrete digital data (large arrays of pixels), whereas the qualitative formalizations refer to continuous models of space. In [GAL 99], Galton proposes a formal framework for reasoning instead (in terms of RCC-like calculus) about regions formed by finite unions of cells. Such regions may arise as the set of pixels of a picture, or as regions in a universe consisting of an orthogonal, hexagonal, or triangular tessellation of the plane, or more generally of one of the tessellations used in the field of GIS [WOR 95].

Galton rejects the solution which would consist in adopting the framework of *digital topology* [KON 89, KRO 92], and in using for example topological models such as the *Khalimsky spaces* (refer to Appendix A for the definition of these spaces), on the ground that this would imply the introduction of several kinds of primitive entities (for example, in dimension 2, of edges and of vertices, in addition to the basic cells). In what follows, we give an outline of Galton's proposal.

4.15.2. *Entities and relations*

There are two kinds of primitive entities in Galton's theory: *cells* and *regions*. These entities are related by two binary basic relations: the membership relation between a cell and a region, denoted by "∈", and an adjacency relation between two cells, denoted by "**A**". The formula $x \in X$ is read as *cell x belongs to region X*, or *region X contains cell x*. The formula $\mathbf{A}xy$ **is read as** *the cells x and y are adjacent*. The adjacency relation is symmetrical:

$\forall x \mathbf{A}xx$

$\forall xy(\mathbf{A}xy \rightarrow \mathbf{A}yx)$

In addition, there are two particular regions: the empty region ∅, which does not contain any cell, and the universal region $\mathcal{U}$ which contains all of them.

Regions are set of cells, so that set-theoretic concepts are available. In particular, for any cell x, there is a region referred to as *atomic* $\{x\}$ which contains only this cell.

4.15.3. *Mereology*

In order to define mereologic relations such as the "part-of", we use the set-theoretic definition:

$$X \subseteq Y \overset{\text{def}}{=} \forall x(x \in X \rightarrow x \in Y)$$

The relations of the RCC−5 type are defined in a natural way. We thus have:

$$X \; \mathsf{P} \; Y \overset{\text{def}}{=} X \subseteq Y \wedge X \neq \emptyset$$

$$X \; \mathsf{PP} \; Y \overset{\text{def}}{=} X \; \mathsf{P} \; Y \wedge X \neq Y$$

Two regions overlap (the *overlap* relation) if they have at least one cell in common. If not, they are disjoint (the *discrete* relation). They overlap partially if they overlap, but none of them contains the other:

$$X \; \mathsf{O} \; Y \overset{\text{def}}{=} X \cap Y \neq \emptyset$$

$$X \; \mathsf{DC} \; Y \overset{\text{def}}{=} X \cap Y = \emptyset$$

$$X \; \mathsf{PO} \; Y \overset{\text{def}}{=} \mathsf{O}XY \wedge \neg \mathsf{P} \; XY \wedge \neg \mathsf{P}YX$$

The relations DC, PO and the equality relation, denoted by EQ, are symmetrical. PPI denotes the inverse of PP.

Under these conditions, the five relations DC, PO, EQ, PPI, and PP are pairwise disjoint and exhaustive on the set of all the pairs of *non-empty* regions. For a given model of the theory, as long as each one of them is non-empty, we obtain a partition of the set of these pairs.

4.15.4. *Concept of contact and* RCC−8 *relations*

Now let us define what will play the role of topology, in order to obtain the mereotopological aspect of the theory. To this aim, we define a notion of connection between two regions: two regions are *connected* if some cell of the first is adjacent to some cell of the second:

$$\mathbf{C}XY \overset{\text{def}}{=} \exists xy(x \in X \wedge y \in Y \wedge \mathbf{A}xy)$$

In particular, two regions which have a common cell are in contact. But two disjoint regions may also be connected: the relation EC is defined in that way:

$$X \; \mathsf{EC} \; Y \overset{\text{def}}{=} \neg(X \; \mathsf{O} \; Y) \wedge \mathbf{C}XY$$

Three more basic relations are defined as follows:

$$\mathsf{DC}\, Y \stackrel{\text{def}}{=} \neg \mathbf{C} XY$$

$$X\, \mathsf{TPP}\, Y \stackrel{\text{def}}{=} X\, \mathsf{PP}\, Y \wedge X\, \mathsf{EC}\, (\mathcal{U} \setminus Y)$$

$$X\, \mathsf{NTPP}\, Y \stackrel{\text{def}}{=} X\, \mathsf{DC}\, (\mathcal{U} \setminus Y)$$

Lastly, the relations TPPI and NTPPI are defined as the inverses of TPP and NTPP, respectively.

The eight relations DC, DC, DC, DC, DC, DC, DC, and DC (here again provided that each one of them is non-empty) constitute a partition of the set of pairs of non-empty regions.

4.15.5. *Closure, interior and boundary*

The starting point is to consider, for a given cell, its *immediate neighborhood*, which is the region formed by the cells adjacent to it:

$$N_x \stackrel{\text{def}}{=} \{y \mid \mathbf{A}xy\}$$

EXAMPLE 4.22.– Let us consider the tessellation of the plane $\mathbb{R}^2$ that consists of the set of pixels $[i, i+1] \times [j, j+1]$, where $i, j \in \mathbb{Z}$. A region is a set of pixels. If the adjacency relation is 4-connectedness (the pixels adjacent to a given pixel are, in addition to itself, those located immediately on its left or its right, or immediately above or below), then the immediate neighborhood of a pixel contains five elements. On the other hand, if we consider 8-connectedness (we add the diagonal neighbors to the previous pixels), the immediate neighborhood has nine elements.

Using this definition, we define the *closure* $\mathrm{Cl}(X)$, the *interior* $\mathrm{Int}(X)$, and the *boundary* $\mathrm{Fr}(X)$ of a region X. The first contains all cells whose immediate neighborhood meets X. The second contains the cells whose immediate neighborhood is entirely contained in X. The third is formed by the cells whose immediate neighborhood meets both X and its complement:

$$\mathrm{Cl}(X) \stackrel{\text{def}}{=} \{x \mid N_x \cap X \neq \emptyset\}$$

$$\mathrm{Int}(X) \stackrel{\text{def}}{=} \{x \mid N_x \subseteq X\}$$

$$\mathrm{Fr}(X) \stackrel{\text{def}}{=} \{x \mid N_x \cap X \neq \emptyset \wedge N_x \setminus X \neq \emptyset\}$$

It should be noted that the behavior of the closure, interior, and boundary operations is only partially similar to that of their topological equivalents. In particular, closure and interior are not idempotent operations.

EXAMPLE 4.23.– Let us again consider the previous example, where the plane is subdivided into pixels, with the 4-connectedness relation as an adjacency relation. If $X = \{x\}$ is reduced to a pixel, $Cl(X)$ contains 5 pixels, $Cl(Cl(X))$ contains 13 pixels, and the successive closures add cells indefinitely (Figure 4.33).

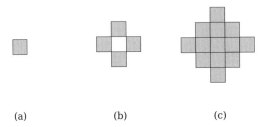

(a)   (b)   (c)

Figure 4.33. *A pixel (a); its closure (b); the closure of its closure (c)*

A property which definitely does not hold in the topological context is the following:

LEMMA 4.2.– *(lemma 6 of [GAL 99]) We have for any region X:*

$$Cl(Int(X)) \subseteq X \text{ and } X \subseteq Int(Cl(X))$$

EXAMPLE 4.24.– Let $X = [0,1)$ be the semi-open interval of the real line. The topological closure of its interior is $[0,1]$, which is not contained in X; neither is X contained in the interior of its topological closure, which is $(0,1)$.

4.15.6. *Self-connectedness*

A non-empty region X is *self-connected* if any proper subregion of X is connected to its complement relative to this region. The intuition is that, if X, for example consists of two disjoint pieces Y and Z, the complement Z of Y with respect to X and Y itself, are not connected (Figure 4.34).

$$\mathrm{Conn} X \stackrel{\mathrm{def}}{=} X \neq \emptyset \wedge \forall Y (Y \, \mathrm{PP} \, X \rightarrow \mathbf{C} Y (X \setminus Y))$$

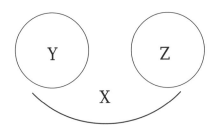

Figure 4.34. *If X is not self-connected, there is a sub-region Y*
such that Y and $X \setminus Y = Z$ are not adjacent

A *connected component* of X is a *maximal* connected subregion of X. If $x \in X$ is a given cell, it belongs to one of the connected components of X, and we may build the latter by successive closures:

THEOREM 4.10.– *(theorem 15 of [GALL 99]) Let $x \in X$. There is a connected component X_x of X containing X, and we have $X_x = \bigcup_{k=1}^{\infty} X_x^k$, where X_x^k is defined in a recursive manner: $X_x^0 = \{x\}$ and $X_x^{k+1} = X \cap Cl(X_x^k)$ for $k > 0$.*

In other words, we expand $\{x\}$ by successive closures.

4.15.7. *Paths, distance, and arc-connectedness*

In the context of regions formed by the cells, we may define the concept of a *path* connecting a cell x with a cell y: it is a sequence $\{x_i\}_{0 \le i \le n}$ of adjacent cells connecting x with y, hence such that $x_0 = x, x_n = y$, and such that for any i such that $0 \le i < n$, we have $\mathbf{A} x_i x_{i+1}$.

Such a path is called a path of length n.

DEFINITION 4.13.– *The distance $d(x,y)$ between two cells x and y is the smallest length of all paths connecting x with y, if any. Otherwise, it is infinite.*

Using the concept of path, a concept similar to that of arc-connectedness in topology may be defined in this context; let $\mathbf{L}xyX$ denote the fact that there is a path connecting x with y formed by cells contained in X:

DEFINITION 4.14.– *A region X is arc-connected by arcs if for any pair of cells $x, y \in X$, we have $\mathbf{L}xyX$.*

Here, contrary to what happens in general topology, the concept of arc-connectedness coincides with that of self-connectedness:

THEOREM 4.11.– *A region is self-connected if, and only if, it is arc-connected.*

Thus, in a model which is self-connected, we have a well-defined distance for any pair of cells. The following result is easily verified:

PROPOSITION 4.10.– *If $\mathcal{U}$ is self-connected, the function d is a metric, that is we have for all x, y, and z:*

– $d(x,y) = 0$ *if, and only if, $x = y$;*
– $d(x,y) = d(y,x)$;
– $d(x,y) \le d(x,z) + d(y,z)$.

4.15.8. *Distance between regions*

Galton also shows that we may define a distance between regions, which is similar to that of the Hausdorff distance in topology.

We could define this distance by considering all paths connecting a cell of one of the regions to a cell of the other, if any. But an interesting way to proceed is to define a concept of "almost equality" between regions:

DEFINITION 4.15.– *Two regions X and Y are* almost equal *if each one of them is contained in the closure of the other:*

$$X \subseteq Cl(Y) \wedge Y \subseteq Cl(X)$$

EXAMPLE 4.25.– Let X be any region. Then, $Cl(X) \backslash X$ and $X \backslash \mathrm{Int}(X)$ are almost equal.

Figure 4.35 illustrates the case of a region whose interior is non-empty. We have represented, respectively, in (a) the region itself, in (b) the region $Cl(X) \backslash X$, and in (c) the region $X \backslash \mathrm{Int}(X)$. It is easily verified that each of the regions (b) and (c) is contained in the closure of the other.

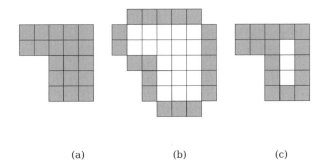

(a)   (b)   (c)

Figure 4.35. *A region X (a); in gray, $Cl(X) \backslash X$ (b); in gray, $X \backslash Int(X)$ (c); here the interior of X is not empty*

Figure 4.36 illustrates the same situation, but with a region whose interior is empty.

If X and Y are two regions such that there is a sequence $X_i, 0 \le i \le n$ such that $X_0 = X, X_n = Y$, and that for any $0 \le i < n$, we have X_i almost equal to X_{i+1}, we define the distance $\Delta(X, Y)$ between X and Y as the smallest n such that there is such a sequence.

The distance defined in this way is analogous to the Hausdorff metric:

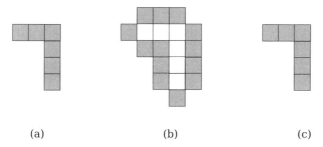

(a)   (b)   (c)

Figure 4.36. *A region X (a); in gray, $Cl(X)\backslash X$ (b); in gray, $X\backslash Int(X)$ (c);
here the interior of X is empty*

PROPOSITION 4.11.– *If $\mathcal{U}$ is self-connected, Δ is a metric, i.e. we have for all x, y, z:*

   – $\Delta(x, y) = 0$ *if, and only if, $x = y$;*

   – $\Delta(x, y) = \Delta(y, x)$;

   – $\Delta(x, y) \leq \Delta(x, z) + \Delta(y, z)$.

Moreover, as stated before, we may define the distance between two regions in terms of cells contained in these regions (which is not so in the continuous case):

THEOREM 4.12.– *If $\Delta(X, Y)$ is defined and is equal to n, then n is the smallest integer such that any cell of each of the regions is at a distance of at most n of a cell in the other region.*

4.15.9. *Conceptual neighborhoods*

Galton also shows how the concept of almost equal regions makes it possible to approach the definition of conceptual neighborhoods of basic relations. The idea is the following: if we think of regions which may change with time, two relations are neighbors if two regions can be found in the first relation at a time point, and in the second relation at the next time point.

More precisely, we define the concept of conceptual neighborhood in the following way:

DEFINITION 4.16.– *The relation r_1 is a conceptual neighbor of the relation r_2 if there are regions X, Y, and Z such that we have r_1 between X and Y, r_2 between X and Z, and Y and Z are almost equal.*

Galton shows that the conceptual neighborhoods thus defined coincide with the neighborhoods of the usual RCC-8 theory, provided that the regions considered have a non-empty interior.

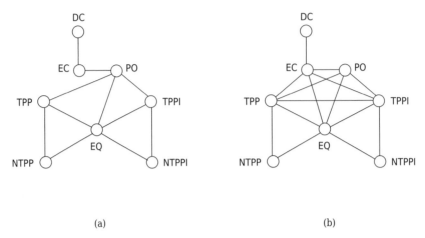

(a)   (b)

Figure 4.37. *The conceptual neighborhood structure of* RCC−8 *relations in the classical case (a) and in the discrete theory (b) (according to Galton [GAL 99])*

On the other hand, in the case of general regions, the relations TPP, EQ, and TPPI are conceptual neighbors of the relation EC. Similarly, the relations TPP and TPPI are conceptual neighbors. The situation is summarized in Figure 4.37.

Chapter 5

Qualitative Formalisms of Arity Greater than 2

5.1. "The sushi bar"

The scene takes place in a sushi bar (Figure 5.1). The restaurant has only two customers at the moment, me (M) and another person (N). Each sushi runs in an endless loop in the anti-clockwise direction.

The question is: Will I be able to grab my favorite sushi S_2 before the other customer can grab it?

The path followed by the sushis can be considered as a circle. No obvious binary relation can be defined on this circle. By contrast, three distinct points such as M, N, S_1

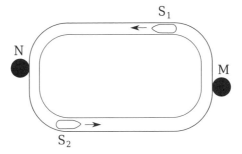

Figure 5.1. *The sushi bar. The sushis in the relation of type S_1 can be selected first by N, those which are of type S_2 will be available to M first. Note that this holds true even though S_1 is closer to M, and S_2 to N*

on the one hand, and M, N, S_2 on the other hand, are distinguished by the fact that, starting from S_1, we reach N before M, and that the reverse holds true if we start from S_2.

Let us use the notation $\prec (x, y, z)$ (see section 4.13) to express that x, y, z are distinct and that, starting from x, we meet y before z, we will have $\prec (S_1, N, M)$ and $\prec (S_2, M, N)$. Consequently, the sushis S such that $\prec (S, M, N)$, are the ones that I am interested in!

With $\prec (x, y, z)$ and the relation defined by exchanging the roles of y and z, we have two mutually exclusive ternary relations between distinct points on the cercle. If we add the possibility that two points coincide (for example, M or N grabs a sushi, or M and N team up), and all three points coincide (M and N team up and grab a sushi), then we will have considered all the possibilities: the reader will have recognized the set of ternary relations thus defined as a finite partition of the set of 3-tuples of points on the circle. This partition into six relations has the JEPD property; it contains the relation $\prec$, the relation $\succ$ defined by $\succ (x, y, z) = \prec (x, z, y)$, three relations eq_{12}, eq_{13}, and eq_{23}, where $eq_{12}(x, y, z)$ means that $x = y \neq z, eq_{13}(x, y, z)$ means that $x = z \neq y, eq_{23}(x, y, z)$ means that $y = z \neq x$, and the relation eq_{123}, which is true if $x = y = z$.

We have thus entered the field of qualitative formalisms for ternary relations. This chapter will be dedicated to a presentation of some representative formalisms of this type.

5.2. Ternary spatial and temporal formalisms

5.2.1. *General concepts*

In this chapter, we are mainly concerned with relations between 3-tuples of temporal or spatial entities. Similarly to the case of binary relations, which deal with pairs of entities, we consider a finite set of ternary relations, that is, of sets of 3-tuples of entities.

DEFINITION 5.1.– *Let D be a set of temporal or spatial entities, also called the domain of the formalism. A finite set of non-empty ternary relations* **B**, *called basic relations is a JEPD set if* **B** *is a partition of D^3: any 3-tuple (x, y, z) of elements of D belongs to one, and only one, element of* **B**.

5.2.1.1. *Operations*

If σ is a permutation of three elements (x, y, z) and ρ is a ternary relation, we obtain another ternary relation ρ^σ by setting $\rho^\sigma(x, y, z) = \rho(\sigma(x, y, z))$. Among the five operations (excluding the identity) that we obtain, three are, in general, considered in the literature: the *inverse*, *shortcut*, and *homing* operations.

DEFINITION 5.2.– *The* inverse, shortcut, *and* homing *of ρ are defined in the following way:*

- *inverse:* $\rho^i(x, y, z) = \{(y, x, z) \mid \rho(x, y, z)\}$;
- *shortcut:* $\rho^s(x, y, z) = \{(x, z, y) \mid \rho(x, y, z)\}$;
- *homing:* $\rho^h(x, y, z) = \{(y, z, x) \mid \rho(x, y, z)\}$.

A general concept of composition is defined in [CON 06c] for n n-ary relations (≥ 2). In the case of ternary relations, we get in this way a definition of the composition $\circ(R, S, T)$ of *three* ternary relations R, S, T:

DEFINITION 5.3.– *Let R, S, T be three ternary relations. The composition $\circ(R, S, T)$ is defined by:*

$$\circ(R, S, T) = \{(x, y, z) \mid (\exists u) R(x, y, u) \wedge S(x, u, z) \wedge T(u, y, z)\}$$

We will use the term *classical composition* to refer to this composition.

Freksa [FRE 92b] defines the composition of two (not three) ternary relations R and S in the following way:

$$(R \circ S) = \{(x, y, z) \mid (\exists u) R(x, y, u) \wedge S(x, u, z)\}$$

Let us note that this composition, which we will refer to as to the *binary composition*, is a particular case of the classical composition. In fact, if U indicates the universal ternary relation (i.e. D^3, if D is the domain considered), then $(R \circ S) = \circ(R, U, S^i)$.

5.2.2. *The Cyclic point calculus*

5.2.2.1. *Basic relations*

We have introduced the six basic relations of this formalism above. Clearly, by construction, these relations constitute a partition of the set of ternary relations: any 3-tuple of points (x, y, z) belongs to exactly one of them.

5.2.2.2. *Operations*

5.2.2.2.1. Inverse, shortcut, and homing

It can be easily seen that the inverse and shortcut operations interchange the basic relations $\prec$ and $\succ$, whereas the homing operation leaves them stable.

The inverse operation interchanges eq_{13} and eq_{23}, and leaves the relation eq_{12} fixed. The shortcut operation interchanges eq_{12} and eq_{13}, and leaves eq_{23} fixed. Finally, the homing operation leaves the relations $\prec$ and $\succ$ fixed, and operates in a cyclic way on the three relations of partial equality: $eq_{12}^h = eq_{13}, eq_{13}^h = eq_{23}$, and $eq_{23}^h = eq_{12}$.

Finally, eq_{123} is left fixed by the three unary operations of inverse, shortcut, and homing.

5.2.2.2.2. Binary composition

The binary composition table for this set of relations is given in Table 5.1.

	$\prec$	$\succ$	$eq_{1,2}$	$eq_{1,3}$	$eq_{2,3}$	$eq_{1,2,3}$
$\prec$	$\{\prec, \succ, eq_{1,3}\}$	$\prec$	0	$eq_{1,3}$	$\prec$	0
$\succ$	$\succ$	$\{\prec, \succ, eq_{1,3}\}$	0	$eq_{2,3}$	$\prec$	0
$eq_{1,2}$	$eq_{1,2}$	$eq_{1,2}$	0	$eq_{1,2,3}$	$eq_{1,2}$	0
$eq_{1,3}$	$\succ$	$\prec$	0	$eq_{1,3}$	$eq_{1,3}$	0
$eq_{2,3}$	0	0	$\{\prec, \succ\}$	$eq_{2,3}$	$eq_{2,3}$	$eq_{2,3}$
$eq_{1,2,3}$	0	0	$eq_{1,2}$	$eq_{1,2,3}$	$eq_{1,2,3}$	$eq_{1,2,3}$

Table 5.1. *Points on a circle: binary composition*

Let us note, in particular, the possibility of obtaining zero compositions (contradictions, denoted as 0 in the table). They are impossible configurations. For example, if $\prec (A, B, C)$ and $eq_{1,2}(B, C, D)$, the latter implies that $B = C$, which contradicts $\prec (A, B, C)$.

5.2.3. *The Double-cross calculus*

The *Double-cross calculus* has first been defined by Freksa [FRE 92b]. Its domain considered is the Euclidean plane $\mathbb{R}^2$. If A and B are two distinct points in this plane, the formalism considers the vector $\overrightarrow{AB}$ and, with respect to this vector, 15 distinct regions of the plane that a third point C may belong to: two of them correspond to the coincidence with A or B; three other regions to the fact that C belongs to the directed line from A to B, either behind A, or between A and B, or in front of B; now if C does not belong to the line defined by A and B, we consider the two perpendiculars to this line at A and B, which in turn define four regions of dimension 1: with respect to the direction AB, the half-line to the left of A, the half-line to the right of A, the half-line to the left of B, and the half-line to the right of B; the two perpendiculars further define three 2D regions, according to the same direction: a region which is to the left of and behind A, one to the left of and between A and B, and one to the left of and in front of B. Similarly, considering now the right side of the directed line AB, five more regions are defined in a similar way. We thus get 15 possible relations in all, assuming that A and B are distinct. The left part of Figure 5.2 illustrates the definition of these relations.

Clearly, given 3 arbitrary points A, B, and C in the plane, either all three of them coincide, which we will denote by $eq(A, B, C)$, or two of them are distinct, and the third point, with respect to these two points, is in one of the 15 relations considered above. We will denote the *Double-cross calculus* by $\mathcal{DCC}$.

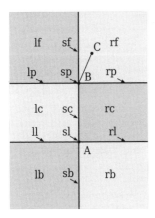 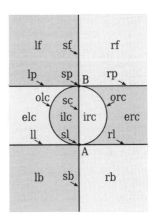

Figure 5.2. *The basic relations of the Double-cross calculus (on the left); the basic relations after refinement (on the right). The 3-tuple (A, B, C) is the basic relation denoted by rf (for right and front)*

To ensure compliance with the general framework of the formalisms considered until now, and to obtain JEPD relations, we have to also consider all possible cases of coincidence. Consequently, we consider the case where $A = B$. We will denote this by $eq_{12}(A, B, C)$ if $C \neq A$, and by $seq_{123}(A, B, C)$ if $A = B = C^1$. The set of ternary relations $\mathbf{B}_{DCC}$ thus defined constitutes a JEPD set of 17 basic relations.

5.2.3.1. *Unary operations*

Among the basic relations, those which correspond to the equality of two points are either stable or permuted by the unary operations.

EXAMPLE 5.1.– For example, we can easily check that $eq_{12}^i = eq_{12}, eq_{12}^s = sl$ (it would be consistent to adopt the notation eq_{13} for sl, and the notation eq_{23} for sp), and that $eq_{12}^h = f$, that is eq_{23}.

However, Scivos and Nebel [SCI 01] point out that this is not the case for all basic relations. For example, the shortcut operation sends the relation lf into the a *proper subset* of the relation rc.

To obtain a set of stable basic relations by the unary operations, it is necessary to refine each one of the two relations rc and lc into three subrelations, corresponding to the part of these subrelations located on the interior, the boundary, and the exterior of the disk of diameter (AB) (right part of Figure 5.2).

---

1 These relations are denoted respectively as *ex* and *eq* by Scivos and Nebel [SCI 01].

The relation lc is thus divided into three relations denoted by elc (exterior), olc (semi-circle on the left), and ilc (interior), and similarly for rc, which is subdivided into erc, orc, and irc. We thus obtain a set $\mathcal{RD}$ of 21 basic relations.

PROPOSITION 5.1.– *The $\mathcal{RD}$ set of basic relations is stable under the unary operations.*

5.2.3.2. *Weak composition*

With regard to composition, Scivos and Nebel [SCI 01] show that in general, the composition of two basic $\mathcal{RD}$ relations is not a union of basic relations, and that it is not possible to find a finite refinement for this to happen:

PROPOSITION 5.2.– *The $\mathcal{RD}$ relations are not closed by composition and intersection, and there is no finite refinement of these relations for which this property would hold.*

Thus we must be content with considering the *weak composition* of two basic relations:

DEFINITION 5.4.– *Let R and S be two basic relations of the $\mathcal{DCC}$ calculus. The weak composition of R and S, denoted as $(R \diamond S)$, is the union of the smallest subset of basic relations whose union contains $r \circ s$.*

What we have just seen implies that the composition table used by Freksa [FRE 92b] is a weak $\mathcal{DCC}$ composition table.

We could hope to develop a useful formalism based on weak composition, in so far as tractable subsets could be characterized. But again, this is not the case:

THEOREM 5.1.– *([SCI 01], theorem 2) The consistency problem of networks on the set $\{sf, 1\}$ is NP-difficult.*

In other words, even if we restrict ourselves to networks whose only non-trivial label is the relation sf, the problem is NP-difficult.

Proof. The proof uses the *betweenness problem*, which can be stated as follows: given a set M and m 3-tuples (a, b, c) of distinct elements of M, is it possible to define a linear ordering $t\colon M \to [0, \dots, m-1]$ on M such that for any 3-tuple (a, b, c), we have either $t(a) < t(b) < t(c)$, or $t(c) < t(b) < t(a)$ (intuitively, all bs are *between* the as and cs)?

Given an instance of the betweenness problem, we can associate a network with it. The vertices of this network are the elements of $M \cup \{x, y\}$, with the constraint $sf(x, y, m)$ for each element m of M, which enforces the elements of a solution to be on the line (x, y), so that they are aligned, and for each 3-tuple (a, b, c), the constraint $sf(a, b, c)$ which states that b is between b and a. Clearly, under these conditions, the problem is solvable if, and only if, the network is consistent. $\square$

In fact, even for networks in which all the constraints are basic relations, the problem is NP-difficult:

THEOREM 5.2.– *([SCI 01], theorem 3) The consistency problem for networks on the set of basic $\mathcal{RD}$ relations is NP-difficult.*

An outline of the proof is given in [SCI 01]. The full proof can be found in [SCI 00].

5.2.3.3. *Decidability*

Nevertheless, the consistency problem can be solved by using a translation in terms of inequalities involving polynomials with integer coefficients. Indeed, each basic relation can be expressed in polynomial terms.

EXAMPLE 5.2.– The relation $rf(A, B, C)$ may be expressed by writing that the scalar product $\overrightarrow{AB}.\overrightarrow{BC}$ is positive, and that the vector product $\overrightarrow{AB} \wedge \overrightarrow{BC}$ is negative. If $A = (a_1, a_2)$, $B = (b_1, b_2)$, and $C = (c_1, c_2)$, this is written as:

$$(b_1 - a_1)(c_1 - b_1) + (b_2 - c_2)(c_2 - b_2) > 0$$
$$(b_1 - a_1)(c_2 - b_2) - (b_2 - a_2)(c_1 - b_1) < 0$$

Using this translation and the results of [REN 92], Scivos and Nebel prove the following theorem:

THEOREM 5.3.– *([SCI 01], theorem 4) The consistency problem for networks on $\mathcal{RD}$ relations is in* PSPACE.

5.2.4. *The Flip-flop and $\mathcal{LR}$ calculi*

The Double-cross calculus is a member of a family of calculi obtained by choosing a finite number of directions in the plane. In particular, the simplest calculus of this family is the *Flip-flop calculus* introduced by Ligozat [LIG 93b]. We can see it as a coarser version of the Double-cross calculus, in which the five relations "C is to the right of AB" are combined into one single relation "to the left", and similarly for the five relations corresponding to the right side. Thus, in the case of A and B being distinct points, we have seven possible basic relations instead of 15. Conversely, we may express this by saying that the Double-cross calculus is a refinement of the Flip-flop calculus. Figure 5.3 represents the seven basic relations obtained in this way.

Here again, in order to get a JEPD set of basic relations, we must add the two ternary relations eq_{12} and $_{123}$. Equipped with the seven basic relations and the relations eq_{12} and eq_{123}, the Flip-flop calculus becomes the $\mathcal{LR}$ calculus defined by Scivos and Nebel [SCI 04].

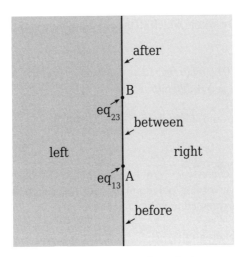

Figure 5.3. *The Flip-flop calculus*

5.2.5. *Practical and natural calculi*

Scivos and Nebel propose a general framework for the study of ternary formalisms whose domain is the Euclidean plane [SCI 04]. In particular, they have introduced the concept of a "practical" calculus:

DEFINITION 5.5.– *A qualitative formalism is* practical *if it has a finite JEPD set of basic relations and if the relations are closed under the unary operations and under composition.*

DEFINITION 5.6.– *A ternary formalism with the plane as its domain is called an RST formalism if its relations are preserved by rotation, translation, and positive homothety.*

For a given formalism, the *representation* of a basic relation r is the region in the complex plane formed by complex numbers z such that $r(0, 1, z)$, holds. This definition thus precludes that the relations eq_{12} and eq_{123} could be represented. However, the representation of eq_{12} is $\{\infty\}$ by convention.

DEFINITION 5.7.– *A ternary RST formalism is* natural, *if for any representable basic relation r, the associated region and its complement are connected regions.*

EXAMPLE 5.3.– The $\mathcal{LR}$ calculus is practical: the stability of its basic relations under unary operations and by composition is easily verified. Its basic relations other than eq_{12} are represented by the open half-line $(-\infty, 0)$, the point $\{0\}$, the open interval $(0, 1)$, the point $\{1\}$, and the open half-line $(0, +\infty)$ of the real line, by the half-plane of complex numbers whose imaginary part is strictly positive, and by the half-plane of complex numbers whose imaginary part is strictly negative.

Clearly, all the relations are invariable by rotation, translation, and positive homothety. Thus, the $\mathcal{LR}$ calculus is also an RST calculus.

Finally, it is straightforward that the $\mathcal{LR}$ calculus is a natural calculus. Scivos and Nebel show that the $\mathcal{LR}$ calculus is characterized by these properties:

THEOREM 5.4.– *([SCI 04], theorem 1) The $\mathcal{LR}$ formalism does not have any other practical and natural refinement other than itself.*

5.2.6. *The consistency problem*

The complexity of the consistency problem for the $\mathcal{LR}$ calculus and the search for methods to solve it are considered in [LÜC 08].

First, an $\mathcal{LR}$ adaptation of the methods used in [SCI 00] allows the authors to show that the NP-complete problem referred to as NOT-ALL-EQ-3SAT can be encoded in the $\mathcal{LR}$ language. Hence, one gets the theorem:

THEOREM 5.5.– *([LÜC 08], theorem 12) The consistency problem for the $\mathcal{LR}$ calculus is NP-difficult.*

It is also proved that the consistency problem cannot be solved by using the algebraic closure method for the binary composition operation.

This last point is an easy consequence of the examination of the binary composition table (Table 5.2), which shows that for the relations l, r, all the entries of the composition subtable contain the relations l and r; hence the following proposition:

	l	r
l	$\{b, s, i, l, r\}$	$\{f, l, r\}$
r	$\{f, l, r\}$	$\{b, s, i, l, r\}$

Table 5.2. *The binary composition subtable of the $\mathcal{LR}$ calculus. The relations l and r appear in each of the entries*

PROPOSITION 5.3.– *([LÜC 08], theorem 13) Any network which does not contain the empty relation and which only uses the relations l and r is necessarily algebraically closed for the binary composition.*

NOTE 5.1.– The $\mathcal{LR}$ calculus reduced to the two relations l and r involves points in the plane which are in a general position.

In view of what we have just seen, exhibiting a specific network which verifies the conditions of proposition 5.3 and which is not consistent is enough to prove the following theorem:

THEOREM 5.6.– ([LÜC 08], theorem 14) *There are algebraically closed networks (not containing the empty relation) for binary composition on the $\mathcal{LR}$ calculus which are not consistent.*

Proof. The constraint network defined by: $r(A,B,C), r(A,E,D),\ r(D,B,A),$ $r(D,C,A), r(D,C,B), r(D,E,B), l(D,E,C), r(E,B,A), r(E,C,A), r(E,C,B)$ is not consistent.

The proof uses the encoding of the relations l and r in terms of the vector product, as described in section 5.2.3.3.   □

This situation is not improved if we consider the ternary composition instead of the binary one. Indeed, we also have:

THEOREM 5.7.– ([LÜC 08], theorem 15) *There are algebraically closed networks (not containing the empty relations) for ternary composition on the $\mathcal{LR}$ calculus which are not consistent.*

Proof. Here again, the examination of the ternary composition subtable, along with the examination of the 4-tuples which are involved in the algebraic closure method, lead to the conclusion. The same counterexample as before can be used here again.   □

5.2.6.1. *Convex ternary relations*

In spite of these negative results, it is possible for formalisms of arity greater than 2 to make use of Helly's theorem about convex sets [HEL 23] to derive useful results. Such an application is described in [LÜC 08].

DEFINITION 5.8.– *A ternary relation r in $\mathbb{R}^n$ is convex if, for any pair of points x, y, the set $\{z \in \mathbb{R}^n \mid r(x,y,z)$ is a convex part of $\mathbb{R}^n$.*

The authors show that in the case of the $\mathcal{LR}$ calculus, 7-consistency implies global consistency for convex networks. As a consequence, determining the global consistency of a convex network is a polynomial problem.

However, global consistency is a very strong property, and in the case of the $\mathcal{LR}$ calculus, it is not equivalent to consistency: there are consistent scenarios which are not globally consistent.

EXAMPLE 5.4.– The network defined by:

$$r(A,B,C), r(A,B,D), r(C,D,A), r(C,D,B), r(A,B,E), r(C,D,E)$$

is consistent, as shown in the left part (a) of Figure 5.4. On the other hand, the right part (b) of the figure represents an instantiation of four variables which cannot be extended to a solution of the network.

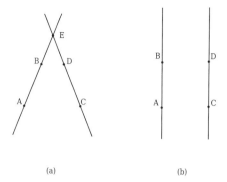

(a)   (b)

Figure 5.4. *A consistent instantiation (a) of the network of Example 5.4; the partial consistent instantiation (b) cannot be extended consistently*

5.3. Alignment relations between regions

5.3.1. *Alignment between regions of the plane: the 5-intersection calculus*

5.3.1.1. *Basic relations*

Billen and Clementini define a ternary calculus which describes directional relations between simple regions of the plane [BIL 04, BIL 05]. Two such regions define five regions (in the first case) or two regions (in the second case) depending on whether their convex closures are disjoint or not, as shown in Figures 5.5 and 5.6.

Let B and C be two simple regions. In the first case, given a third region A, we can associate a Boolean vector of length 5 with the triplet (A, B, C). This Boolean vector indicates, for each of the five regions, whether the interior of A meets each of the five

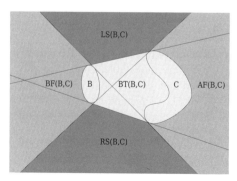

Figure 5.5. *The 5-intersection calculus: when the convex closures of B and C are disjoint, the external and internal tangents determine five regions: $BF(B,C)$ (before), $BT(B,C)$ (between), $AF(B,C)$ (after), $LS(B,C)$ (left side), and $RS(B,C)$ (right side)*

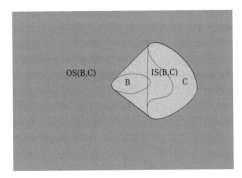

Figure 5.6. *The 5-intersection calculus: when the convex closures of B and C are not are disjoint, we can only distinguish two regions: IS (B, C) (inside) and OS(B, C) (outside)*

regions. We thus obtain $2^5 - 1 = 31$ vectors (referred to as "5-intersection matrices"). Similarly, in the second case, we define a Boolean vector of length 2, so that we have $2^2 - 1 = 3$ possibilities. Ultimately, the formalism thus defined comprises 34 basic relations, of which 7 are "uni-tile" relations, the other 27 being "multi-tile" relations (we use the terminology defined previously for the cardinal relation calculus between the regions). Only a subset of these relations may appear if A is further assumed to be connected.

5.3.1.2. *Computing relations between polygonal regions*

An interesting aspect of the research using this formalism is the development of algorithms for the effective computation of the relations when the regions considered are polygonal regions in the plane [CLE 09]. This computation can be achieved $O(n \log n)$ time, if n is the maximum number of vertices of the polygons considered. Clementini has developed a software program, that allows the user to draw polygonal objects in the plane and that subsequently computes the ternary relations between these objects.

5.3.1.3. *composition tables*

Another original contribution of this research is the idea to use a random approach [CLE 09] to compute the composition tables: one randomly generates 4-tuples of polygons $A, B, C,$ and D, and then determine the ternary relations thus obtained, for instance, $r = (A, B, C), s = (B, C, D)$ and $t = (A, C, D)$. One thus gets a 3-tuple (r, s, t) of relations which has to occur in the composition table.

5.3.2. *Ternary relations between solids in space*

A principle similar to that used for defining 5-intersections in the plane can be used to describe ternary relations between 3D objects in the 3D space ([CLE 09], Chapter 6). Since the third dimension allows an additional degree of freedom, there are only four distinct regions when B and C have disjoint convex closures. The natural extension of the principle is to consider the quaternary relations between the four objects $A, B, C,$ and D.

5.3.3. *Ternary relations on the sphere*

5.3.3.1. *Alignment on the sphere*

Geographical applications constitute one of the main motivations for the development of spatial formalisms. These applications deal with (portions of) the surface of the Earth, which is itself a spherical object. This justifies the attempt to define for the sphere a formalism similar to the 5-intersection formalism. This has been done by Clementini in [CLE 09].

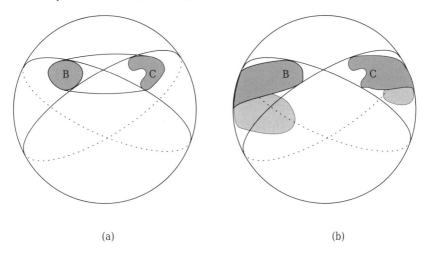

(a)   (b)

Figure 5.7. *Two regions B and C of the sphere which have internal tangents; the external tangents exist in the case (a), but not in the case (b), where the regions are not contained in the same hemisphere*

On a spherical surface, the equivalents of lines are great circles. A great circle divides the sphere into two hemispheres. We can define polygons by means of great circles. For two arbitrary points which are not antipodal (that is, aligned with the center of the sphere) only one great circle passes through them. If these points are antipodal, there is an infinite number of great circles containing them. Two distinct great circles intersect at two antipodal points.

Among the polygons, there are polygons which have two sides; two distinct great circles meet at two antipodal points, and divide the surface of the sphere into four regions called lunes, which are polygons having two vertices (which are two antipodal points).

Here also, we consider simple regions. If A is a region contained in a hemisphere (or equivalently, a region which does not contain two antipodal points), its convex closure is, by definition, the intersection of the hemispheres containing it.

Given two regions B and C on the sphere contained in the same hemisphere, the same procedure that was employed for the plane can be applied here: if the convex closures of the two regions do not meet, the internal tangents of B and C exist and define four regions, a fifth one being the convex closure of $B \cup C$; if not, this convex closure and its exterior constitute two regions. Thus in that case the situation is similar the planar situation (Figure 5.7 (a)).

If the two regions B and C are not contained in the same hemisphere, there are no external tangents of B and C. If their convex closures are disjoint, there are internal tangents of B and C which define four lunes: one contains B, another contains C, and the other two are two opposite lunes. Three regions are defined in this manner (Figure 5.7 (b)).

Finally, if B and C are not contained in the same hemisphere and if their convex closures are not disjoint, there are neither internal tangents nor external tangents, and the sphere constitutes a single region with respect to B and C which are said to be *entwined*.

5.3.3.2. *Basic ternary relations*

The above analysis shows that depending on the relative positions of two regions B and C, we can have:

– five tiles, hence 31 multi-tile relations;

– two tiles, hence 3 multi-tile relations;

– three tiles, hence 7 multi-tile relations;

– a single tile, where we have a relation known as the entwinement relation.

Ultimately, the spherical calculus thus obtained has a total of 42 basic relations, of which 11 are uni-tile relations.

5.4. Conclusions

In the domain of ternary qualitative relations, the state of knowledge about the topics which have been the main objects of research for binary relations (composition tables, complexity, algorithms, models) is less advanced. We should also refer the reader to [ISL 00] for an example of the use of relation algebras in this context. Clementini's thesis [CLE 09] contains extensive information about the properties of the alignment relations for various entities considered in the modeling of geographical data.

Chapter 6

Quantitative Formalisms, Hybrids, and Granularity

6.1. "Did John meet Fred this morning?"

Let us consider the following example taken from Meiri's paper [MEI 96]:

"John and Fred work for a company that has local and main offices in Los Angeles. They usually work at the local office, in which case it takes John less than 20 minutes and Fred 15-20 minutes to get to work. Twice a week John works at the main office, in which case his commute to work takes at least 60 minutes. Today John left home between 7:05-7:10 a.m., and Fred arrived at work between 7:50-7:55 a.m.".

This kind of example motivates the introduction of time points representing the departures and the arrivals of the two characters, and of a language for expressing *quantitative* constraints between these points. Such a language is provided by the formalisms called TCSPs (*temporal constraint satisfaction problems*).

Coming back to the example, consider the following question: could John and Fred have met on their way to work? This is a question of a *qualitative* nature; it can be expressed in a natural way by introducing the temporal intervals corresponding to John and Fred's respective journeys to work, and asking: do these two intervals have a common part?

If we do so, we will have to consider two types of entities (time points and intervals) and three types of relations:

– metric relations (durations between two time points);

– qualitative relations between intervals (such as two intervals having a common part);

– relations between a time point and an interval (a time point being the beginning or the end of an interval).

6.1.1. *Contents of the chapter*

In what follows, we start with a presentation of the works carried out in the context of metric relations between time points. We use the term *hybrid* formalisms to indicate the simultaneous representation of metric relations and qualitative relations. We describe two of the main approaches, which could be termed as the integrated approach (a single network representing the hybrid knowledge), and the parallel approach, where two networks, one qualitative and the other metric, are used. The first approach is illustrated by the work of Kautz and Ladkin, while the second approach is exemplified by Meiri's work. More recently, formalisms which generalize these early propositions have been proposed. The study of the complexity properties of those formalisms has gained a powerful tool with the introduction of disjunctive linear relations (DLR) done independently by Jonsson and Bäckström [JON 98] and by Koubarakis [KOU 96, KOU 01] (see Appendix C).

The simultaneous consideration of entities of different nature is closely related to the issue of granularity: the question of considering an event as a point or as an interval depends on the point of view adopted. A city will be represented by a point in a small scale map and by a region in a large-scale map. Furthermore, many temporal (and spatial) phenomena combine multiple granularities (centuries, years, days, hours, minutes, etc.) and regular recurrence (seasons, festivals). How can the constraint-based reasoning be combined with the use of multiple granularities? We end the chapter by a presentation of some representative works devoted to this question.

6.2. TCSP metric networks

TCSP (*temporal constraint satisfaction problems*) networks [DEC 91] are *quantitative* constraint networks. The temporal entities considered are points (of the real line). The constraints are binary constraints, which can be *simple* or *complex*. If $i, j \in N$ are two vertices, a simple constraint is of the form $a_1 \leq X_j - X_i \leq b_1$, where a_1, a_2 are real numbers such that $a_1 \leq b_1$. This constraint is written as $C(i, j) = [a_i, b_i]$. A complex constraint is a disjunction of simple constraints, i.e. a constraint of the form $a_1 \leq X_j - X_i \leq b_1 \vee \ldots a_k \leq X_j - X_j \leq b_k$, with $k > 1$. This constraint is written as $C(i, j) = \{[a_1, b_1], \ldots, [a_k, b_k]\}$.

In other words, the networks considered have vertices which represent points, and arcs labeled either by intervals of the real line (simple networks), or by sets of intervals of this line (complex networks).

EXAMPLE 6.1.– Consider again the example given in the beginning of this chapter. Let us introduce variables V_1, V_2, V_3, V_4 to denote, respectively, the departure and the arrival of John, and the departure and the arrival of Fred. In order to represent absolute times by binary constraints, we introduce V_0, which corresponds to 07:00.

We can then represent the given information by:
- $(0 \leq V_2 - V_1 \leq 20) \vee (V_2 - V_1 \geq 60$ (travel time of John);
- $(15 \leq V_4 - V_3 \leq 20)$ (travel time of Fred);
- $(5 \leq V_1 - V_0 \leq 10)$ (departure of John);
- $(50 \leq V_4 - V_0 \leq 55)$ (arrival of Fred).

Figure 6.1 represents the associated network.

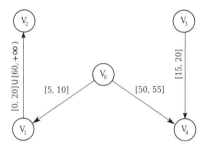

Figure 6.1. *A TCSP network representing the knowledge about John and Fred: V_1 and V_2 represent the departure and the arrival of John, V_3 and V_4 represent the departure and the arrival of Fred; V_0 represents 07:00*

We use the term STP *(simple temporal problems)* networks to refer the subclass of TCSP networks whose constraints are simple constraints.

6.2.1. *Operations*

The basic operations of inversion, intersection, and composition are easily described for simple constraints:

– if I and J are two intervals representing the constraints between i and j, the intersection is the constraint $I \cap J$;

– the inverse of the constraint $I = [a, b]$ is the constraint $-I = [-b, -a]$;

– the composition of $[a, b]$ on (i, j) and of $[c, d]$ on (j, k) is the interval $[a+c, b+d]$ on (i, k).

The corresponding operations for complex constraints can be derived from these descriptions.

EXAMPLE 6.2.– From the knowledge of the constraints $[5, 10]$ on (V_0, V_1) and $[50, 55]$ on (V_0, V_4), we deduce by inversion $[-10, -5]$ on (V_1, V_0) and then, by composition, $[40, 50]$ on (V_1, V_4): the departure of Fred thus took place between 40 and 50 minutes after the departure of John.

6.2.2. *The consistency problem*

The consistency problem for TCSP networks is NP-complete [DEC 91], even when we restrict ourselves to complex relations having no more than two component intervals.

On the other hand, in the case of simple networks, the consistency problem and the problem of determining the minimal subnetwork can be solved in $O(n^3)$ time. Indeed, we can associate to a STP network its *distance graph* in the following way: the distance graph is a directed graph which has the same vertices as that of the STP network; if the constraint between i and j is the interval $[a, b]$, the distance graph has an arc (i, j) labeled b, and an arc (j, i) labeled $-a$.

EXAMPLE 6.3.– Let us consider the situation of the example of John and Fred, and suppose that we know that "John went to the local branch". Then the corresponding network becomes a simple network whose distance graph is represented in the right part of Figure 6.2.

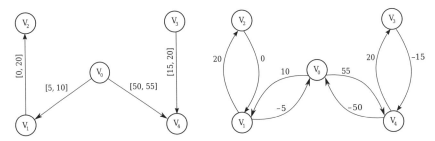

Figure 6.2. *The distance graph associated to the network of the example of John and Fred (right), if we assume that the constraint on the arc (V_1, V_2) is $[0, 20]$ (left)*

Now, an STP network is consistent if, and only if, the associated distance graph does not contain a negative cycle. We can determine the consistency and build the minimal network by using a minimal distance algorithm, for example that of Floyd-Warshall [COR 01].

The algorithm allows the computation of the minimal distances $d_{i,j}$, for $i, j \in N$. The case of a negative cycle results in the appearance of a negative distance $d_{i,i}$.

Otherwise, the minimal graph is the one for which the constraint on the arc (i, j) is $[-d_{j,i}, d_{i,j}]$.

EXAMPLE 6.4.– The incidence matrix of the distance graph for our example is the matrix:

$$\begin{pmatrix} 0 & 10 & \infty & \infty & 55 \\ -5 & 0 & 20 & \infty & \infty \\ \infty & 0 & 0 & \infty & \infty \\ \infty & \infty & \infty & 0 & 20 \\ -50 & \infty & \infty & -15 & 0 \end{pmatrix}$$

Applying the Floyd-Warshall algorithm results in the following matrix for the minimal distances:

$$\begin{pmatrix} 0 & 10 & 30 & 40 & 55 \\ -5 & 0 & 20 & 35 & 50 \\ -5 & 0 & 0 & 35 & 50 \\ -30 & -20 & 0 & 0 & 20 \\ -50 & -40 & -20 & -15 & 0 \end{pmatrix}$$

Consequently, the network considered is consistent, and its minimal graph has the following constraints:

$C(V_0, V_1) = [5, 10], C(V_0, V_2) = [5, 30], C(V_0, V_3) = [30, 40], C(V_0, V_4) = [50, 55]$

$C(V_1, V_2) = [0, 20], C(V_1, V_3) = [20, 35], C(V_1, V_4) = [40, 50]$

$C(V_2, V_3) = [-0, 35], C(V_2, V_4) = [20, 50]$

$C(V_3, V_4) = [15, 20]$

In the case of STP networks, the determination of the minimal distances is equivalent to the enforcement of path-consistency for the network. Hence path-consistency is a necessary and sufficient condition for the global consistency of these networks.

6.2.2.1. $STP^{\neq}$ networks

Gerevini and Cristani [GER 95] and Koubarakis [KOU 97] have introduced an extension of the STP formalism, called the $STP^{\neq}$ formalism, which allows constraints of the type $X_j - X_j \neq a$, where a is a real constant.

This formalism subsumes the formalism of the Point calculus (a qualitative formalism). Indeed, the relations $<, \leq, =, >, \geq, \neq$ of the Point algebra correspond to the constraints $(0, +\infty), [0, +\infty), [0, 0], (-\infty, 0), (-\infty, 0], (-\infty, +\infty) \backslash \{0\}$.

The consistency of an $STP^{\neq}$ network can still be tested in $O(n^3)$ time, by an easy modification of the search for minimal distances. For these networks, strong 5-consistency is a necessary and sufficient condition for global consistency [KOU 97].

6.3. Hybrid networks

Two main approaches have been used to combine qualitative temporal reasoning with quantitative reasoning. The first approach is that of Meiri [MEI 91, MEI 96], which represents quantitative constraints (between points) and qualitative constraints (between intervals) in the same constraint network. By contrast, the second approach, by Kautz and Ladkin [KAU 91], uses two distinct networks, one qualitative, the other quantitative, and defines ways of managing the interactions of the two types of constraints. We shall start our presentation with the latter.

6.3.1. *Kautz and Ladkin's formalism*

Kautz and Ladkin's [KAU 91] model manages separately a time point network with metric constraints between the points, and an interval network which defines qualitative constraints in terms of Allen relations.

More precisely, we consider a linearly ordered time, modeled by the set $\mathbb{Q}$ of rational numbers. Time points are elements of $\mathbb{Q}$, and intervals are pairs of points $(i-, i+) \in \mathbb{Q}^2$ such that $i- < i+$.

Relations between points are the two relations $<$ and $\leq$, and relations between the intervals are Allen relations.

The link between the two types of entities is ensured by the two projection functions which associate with an interval i, its lower bound $i-$ and its upper bound $i+$, respectively.

The model thus considers an interval network (N_A, C_A) and a time point network (N_M, C_M) separately, where N_M is the set of bounding points of the intervals of N_A. It is not possible to directly express constraints between an interval and points, but only between the bounding points of this interval and points.

The constraints of the two networks are put into correspondance by using two translation functions: one whose role is to determine what constraints between intervals are associated to the constraints given between the points (transition from points to intervals), and another one which makes the connection in the other direction (transition from intervals to points).

6.3.1.1. *The constraint languages*

The constraint language L used is the union of two sublanguages L_M (metric) and L_A which is the first order language using Allen relations.

More precisely, L_M uses atomic formulas $i^\varepsilon < j^{\varepsilon'}$ and $i^\varepsilon \leq j^{\varepsilon'}$ (where $\varepsilon \in \{+, -\}$) called *simple metric constraints*, which are used to express:

– constraints on the duration of an interval, such as, for example, $i^- - i^+ < -2$ (duration strictly greater than 2), $i^+ - i^- \leq 3$ (duration 3 at most);

– the time elapsed between two intervals, for example $i^- - j^+ < 5$;

– (after introducing an interval of origin j0), the distance to the beginning of time: $i^- - j_0^- < 5$.

NOTE 6.1.– Each one of Allen's basic relations may be defined by using conjunctions of simple metric constraints. For example, the relation m is defined by $i^+ - j^- \leq 0 \wedge j^- - i^+ \leq 0$, the relation d by $j^- - i^- < 0 \wedge i^+ - j^+ < 0$, and so on.

6.3.1.2. *Minimal models*

The first stage of processing is to determine an equivalent minimal network for each of the two networks.

In the case of the time point network, an adaptation of the method used by Dechter, Meiri, and Pearl may be used. It allows the determination of the minimal network in $O(n^3)$ time. In the case of the interval network, an approximate method is used, for example, a k-consistence algorithm, for $k \geq 3$.

6.3.1.3. *From quantitative to qualitative*

Given a quantitative time point network whose points are bounding points of intervals, we want to determine the Allen constraints that it induces on the intervals. We cannot simply restrict ourselves to associate with each metric constraint the constraint that it implies. Doing so would, for example, associate with the condition $i^- - j^- < -3$, the condition $i^- - j^- < 0$, which defines Allen's relation $X_1 < 1$ in the lattice, that is $[\mathsf{p}, \mathsf{di}] = \{\mathsf{p}, \mathsf{m}, \mathsf{o}, \mathsf{fi}, \mathsf{di}\}$. This consequence is correct, but the following example shows that it is not sufficient:

EXAMPLE 6.5.– Let us consider the network with two intervals i and j. Asssume that there is no Allen constraint between i and j, but that we have the constraints $i^- - i^+ < -3$ and $j^+ - j^- < 2$ on the bounding points of these two intervals: the duration of i is greater than 3, and that of j less than 2. The consideration of the induced metric constraints alone does not lead to any non-trivial constraint, whereas a consequence of the duration relations is that the relation of j with i can only be one of the basic relations compatible with a lower duration of j, which excludes the relations si, di, fi and eq.

The important point is that, in order to detect the consequences with a minimal loss of information, we may restrict ourselves to considering all *pairs of intervals*.

Kautz and Ladkin use this observation to define an algorithm named METRIC-TO-ALLEN (Figure 6.3) to determine the constraints induced by the metric network on the Allen network.

Data: A simple metric network N_M
Result: An Allen network expressing the strongest constraints implied by N_M
Let N'_M be the minimal network associated with N_M
if N'_M *is inconsistent* **then**
  | **return** *an inconsistent network*
end
$C_A \leftarrow \emptyset$
for each *pair* (i, j) *of intervals* **do**
  | Let S be the subnetwork $\{i^-, i^+, j^-, j^+\}$ of N'_M
  | $R \leftarrow \emptyset$
  | **for each** *Allen basic relation* r **do**
  | | $S' \leftarrow S \cup \{m \mid$
  | | m is a simple metric constraint in the definition of $i(r)j\}$
  | | **if** S' *is consistent* **then**
  | | | $R \leftarrow R \cup \{r\}$
  | | **end**
  | **end**
  | $C_A \leftarrow C_A \cup \{i(R)j\}$
end
return C_A

Figure 6.3. *The* METRIC-TO-ALLEN *algorithm*

EXAMPLE 6.6.– Consider example 6.5. The metric network is minimal. In the inner loop of the algorithm, we successively test all the networks obtained by adding (the constraint induced by) each Allen basic relation. We retain this constraint only if the 4-point network obtained in this way remains consistent. Clearly, we are led to reject the four relations si, di, fi, and eq.

Hence the associated network has the relation containing all basic relations except si, di, fi, and eq as a constraint between i and j.

THEOREM 6.1.– *The* METRIC-TO-ALLEN *algorithm is correct and causes a minimal loss of information in the following sense: for any interval network* (N_A, C_A) *and for any metric network* $(N_M, C_M), C_M$ *implies A if, and only if,* METRIC-TO-ALLEN (N_M) *implies A.*

Clearly, the algorithm has a time cost of $O(n^2)$, where n is the number of vertices of the network.

6.3.1.4. *From qualitative to quantitative*

We now consider the inverse problem: given an Allen network, we want to determine the metric constraints it implies.

To do so, Kautz and Ladkin introduce the ALLEN-TO-METRIC algorithm (Figure 6.4).

Data: An Allen network N_A
Result: a metric network which expresses the strongest constraints implied by
      N_A
Let N'_A be the minimal network associated with N_A
if N'_A *is inconsistent* **then**
  | **return** *an inconsistent metric network*
end
$C_M \leftarrow \emptyset$
for each *pair* (i, j) *of intervals* **do**
    Let R be the Allen relation between i and j in N'_A
    $S \leftarrow \{m \mid m$ is of the form $x - y < 0$ or $x - y \leq 0$ and
    $x, y \in \{i^-, i^+, j^-, j^+\}$
    for each *Allen basic relation* $r \in R$ **do**
      | $S \leftarrow S \cap \{m \mid m$ is a simple metric constraint implied by $i(r)j\}$
    end
    $C_M \leftarrow C_M \cup S$
end
return C_M

Figure 6.4. *The ALLEN-TO-METRIC algorithm*

EXAMPLE 6.7.– Consider example 6.5. The interval network is trivially minimal. We can check without too much difficulty that the set S computed in the inner loop of the ALLEN-TO-METRIC algorithm does not enforce any condition on the quantities $i^- - j^-, i^- - j^+, i^+ - j^-$, and $i^+ - j^+$. Consequently, the only metric constraints are the duration constraints of the initial network.

THEOREM 6.2.– *The ALLEN-TO-METRIC algorithm is correct and causes a minimal loss of information in the following sense: for any interval network (N_A, C_A) and for any metric network, (N_M, C_M), C_A implies M if, and only if, ALLEN-TO-METRIC (N_A) implies M.*

Here, the temporal cost of the algorithm depends on the time necessary for the calculation of the minimal network. If this cost is e, then the algorithm requires a time of $O(e + n_2)$.

6.3.1.5. *Network synchronization algorithm*

The management of the two networks is based on an algorithm that we may informally describe as follows:

– compute the minimal networks (or an approximation) of N_M and N_A;

– determine the Allen constraints implied by the metric constraints, and add them to the interval network;

– determine the metric constraints implied by Allen constraints, and add them to the metric constraints;

– iterate the previous operations for the new networks as long as a change takes place.

More precisely, the COMBINED-METRIC-ALLEN algorithm is as described in Figure 6.5.

Data: A simple metric network M and an Allen network A
Result: Networks M' and A' implied by the conjunction of the constraints of
    M and A
repeat
| $A' \leftarrow$ Metric-to-Allen$(M) \cup A$
| $M' \leftarrow$ Allen-to-Metric$(A') \cup A$
| $M \leftarrow M'; A \leftarrow A'$
until $A = A'$ and $M = M'$

Figure 6.5. *The* COMBINED-METRIC-ALLEN *algorithm*

In the case of the example described above, the procedure terminates after the first round. In general, we have the following theorem:

THEOREM 6.3.– *The* COMBINED-METRIC-ALLEN(M, A) *algorithm is correct. It has a time-cost of* $O(n^2(e+n^3))$, *where n is the number of intervals, and e the time necessary for the calculation of the minimal network of A.*

6.3.1.6. *Assessment of the approach*

A problem with this approach is the need to compute the minimal network. In the particular case of convex relations, we know that this determination can be done in $O(n^3)$ time by using the algebraic closure method. Hence, in this case, the total cost of the combined algorithm is $O(n^5)$. When pre-convex networks are considered, this cost is $O(n^7)$.

6.4. Meiri's formalism

Meiri's formalism [MEI 91, MEI 96], contrary to that of Kautz and Ladkin, uses only one constraint network which contains two kinds of temporal entities: points and intervals. The possible constraints are either qualitative binary constraints, which may be between two intervals — hence Allen relations — or constraints between

b	s	d	f	a	bi	si	di	fi	ai
$(0)_{1,2}$	$(1)_{1,2}$	$(2)_{1,2}$	$(3)_{1,2}$	$(4)_{1,2}$	$(2,2)_{2,1}$	$(1,2)_{2,1}$	$(0,2)_{2,1}$	$(0,1)_{2,1}$	$(0,0)_{2,1}$

Table 6.1. *Correspondence between Meiri's notations and the notations of Chapter 3: for example, the relation denoted as b by Meiri (a point precedes an interval) is the relation denoted as $(0)_{1,2}$ in Chapter 3; its transpose, denoted as bi by Meiri, is the relation $(2,2)_{2,1}$ of $\mathbf{B}_{2,1}$*

a point and an interval; thus, qualitatively speaking, we are in the context of the "point-and-interval" algebra studied in Chapter 3. In particular, the composition tables of qualitative relations can be computed in the way described for arbitrary generalized intervals (section 3.5.2). Table 6.1 gives the correspondence between the notations used by Meiri and the notations defined in Chapter 3 for (p, q)-relations (here $1 \leq p, q \leq 2$).

6.4.1. *Temporal entities and relations*

In this formalism, the time-model is the real line $\mathbb{R}$. The temporal entities are points and intervals, defined as pairs of points (P_1, P_2), where $P_1 < P_2$.

The basic relations considered may be qualitative (between intervals and points) or quantitative (between points):

– between intervals: Allen's basic relations;

– between points and intervals: they are the basic relations of $\mathbf{B}_{1,2}$ and $\mathbf{B}_{2,1}$ introduced in Chapter 3. There are five elements in each of these sets;

– between points: the qualitative relations are the three elements of $\mathbf{B}_{1,1}$, which are the three atoms of the Point algebra;

– between points: the basic metric relations are those of the TCSP formalism (section 6.2).

Here again, the inversion, intersection, and composition operations of the qualitative relations are particular cases of those described for arbitrary generalized intervals in Chapter 3.

EXAMPLE 6.8.– The composition of the qualitative relation $<$, aka $(0)_{1,1}$, between two points, and of the relation d, aka $(2)_{1,2}$, is the $(1, 2)$ relation whose unique coordinate is $[0, 2]$ (section 3.7), that is the relation $\{(0)_{1,2}, (1)_{1,2}, (2)_{1,2}\}$, or, in Meiri's notations, the relation $\{b, s, d\}$ between a point and an interval (see Table 3 of [MEI 96]).

Similarly, the composition of the relation di between an interval and a point, and of the relation a between a point and an interval results in a (disjunctive) Allen relation, which can be computed using the general formula for composition: di is $(0, 2)_{2,1}$ and a is $(4)_{1,2}$. Hence, according to proposition 3.7, the result of the composition is the set of elements of $\mathbf{B}_{2,2}$ defined by $[0, 4] \times [4, 4]$, that is the convex relation [di, pi] (see Table 5 of [MEI 96]).

6.4.1.1. QUAN *and* QUAL

There is a natural translation QUAN of the qualitative relations in terms of metric relations: for example, the precedence relation $P_1 < P_2$ results in the metric constraint $P_2 - P_1 \in (0, +\infty)$, and the constraint $P_1 \neq P_2$ results in the disjunctive constraint $P_2 - P_1 \in (-\infty, 0) \cup (0, +\infty)$.

Somewhat less trivially, a translation QUAL of the metric relations into qualitative terms can also be defined; more precisely, if the constraint between two intervals is defined by the real intervals $(I_1, \ldots, I_k)$:

– if one of the intervals contains 0, add equality to the qualitative constraints;

– if one of the intervals contains a strictly positive number, add $<$ to the qualitative constraints;

– if one of the intervals contains a strictly negative number, add $>$ to the qualitative constraints.

6.4.2. *Constraint networks*

We thus consider networks whose vertices represent either points or intervals, and whose arcs are labeled by the qualitative and metric constraints described above.

EXAMPLE 6.9.– Let us consider the example of John and Fred again, supplemented with some additional information: we also know that Fred and John met at a traffic light on their way to work.

Using Meiri's formalism, we can represent our knowledge about the situation by the network of Figure 6.6: to the previous point network, we add two intervals J and F, corresponding to the respective journeys of John and Fred; we indicate that V_1 starts J, that V_2 finishes it, while V_3 starts F and V_4 finishes it, and add the new information that one of the two intervals J and F have a common subinterval.

6.4.3. *Constraint propagation*

The way of propagating constraints between temporal objects (points or intervals) depends on the type of constraints. When these constraints are qualitative, we are in the context of the algebra $\mathbf{A}_{\{1,2\}}$, and we use the operations of this algebra. Similarly, if the constraints are metric, we use the TCSP operations.

Since the metric constraints are defined only for pairs of points, the question of composition of a qualitative relation and of a metric relation can arise only in two cases:

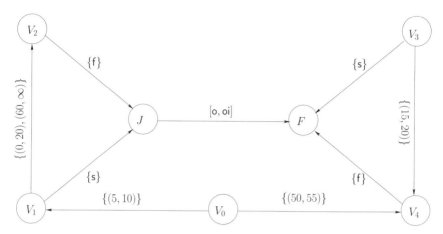

Figure 6.6. *Meiri's example: the metric constraint network (Figure 6.1) is supplemented by introducing two intervals J (John's journey) and F (Fred's journey) and adding that these two intervals have a common part, and that V_1 and V_2 (respectively, V_3 and V_4) are the ends of J (respectively, of F)*

– we have three points a, b, and c, a qualitative constraint r between a and b, and a metric constraint s between b and c. In this case, the qualitative constraint s is equivalent to a metric constraint QUAN(s), and the result of the composition is metric. We adopt the same method when r is metric and s is qualitative;

– we have two points a, b and an interval, with a metric constraint r between the two points. The expected result for the composition of the constraints is necessarily qualitative. In this case, we replace the constraint r by relation QUAL(r), and we carry out the composition in the qualitative algebra.

EXAMPLE 6.10.– Let us consider the network of Figure 6.6.

An example of composition of metric constraints: since the constraints between V_1 and V_0, and between V_0 and V_4 are $(-10, -5)$ and $(50, 55)$, respectively, we have the constraint $(40, 50)$ between V_1 and V_4. Since the constraint between V_4 and V_3 is $(-20, -15)$, we can conclude that the one between V_1 and V_3 is $(20, 35)$.

An example of composition of qualitative constraints: the composition of the relation f, i.e. $(3)_{1,2}$ between V_2 and J, and of [o, oi], or $[(0, 2)_{2,2}, (2, 4)_{2,2}]$ between J and F results in the constraint $[(2)_{1,2}, (4)_{1,2}]$ between V_2 and F, then, by composition with the constraint si, that is $(1, 2)_{2,1}$ between F and V_3, we get the constraint $(2)_{1,1}$ between V_2 and V_3. In other words, $V_2 > V_3$. This calculation only verifies the fact that for any pair of intervals J and F having a common subinterval, the end of J appears after the beginning of F. Or, in the lattice of Allen relations, the fact that the interval [o, oi] is contained in the part of the lattice defined by $X_2 > 1$.

An example of mixed composition with three points: we know that the constraint between V_1 and V_3 is $(20, 35)$ and that $V_3 < V_2$. This last constraint $<$ is equivalent to the metric constraint $\text{QUAN}(<) = (0, +\infty)$ between V_3 and V_2. By composition, we obtain the constraint $(20, +\infty)$ between V_1 and V_2. The intersection of this interval with $\{(0, 20) \cup (60, +\infty)$ is $(6, +\infty)\}$, which becomes the new constraint between V_1 and V_2.

We may thus infer that it took John more than 60 minutes to go to work, so that he must have worked in the central office.

In this way, we can get rid of the disjunctive constraint between V_1 and V_2: now all the explicit constraints in the network are convex relations.

6.4.4. *Tractability issues*

Meiri's formalism generalizes Allen's calculus, the Point calculus and the TCSP formalism at the same time.

In the case of the Point calculus, the consistency problem is polynomial: the consistency of a network with n vertices can be determined in $O(n^2)$ time. For Allen's calculus and for the TCSP formalism, this problem is NP-complete.

The qualitative Point-and-interval calculus is also NP-complete (the fact that it is NP-difficult results from a reduction of the *betweenness problem* ([MEI 96], theorem 4.3)).

Thus, Meiri's formalism itself is NP-complete, and Meiri poses the question of determining "islands of tractability" inside this formalism. Such a fragment is constituted by the Point calculus. In the case of Allen's algebra, the single tractable maximal subclass containing the basic relations is that of pre-convex relations. For the Point-and-interval calculus, the geometrical approach in terms of pre-convex relations provides a tractable subclass of relations:

THEOREM 6.4.– *In the algebra* $\mathbf{A}_{1,2}$ *of relations between points and intervals, the subclass formed by pre-convex relations is polynomial [LIG 94b]. Any pre-convex and non-zero algebraically closed network is consistent.*

Jonsson, Drakengren and Bäckström [JON 99] have subsequently determined *all* the tractable subclasses of this algebra. The subclass of pre-convex relations, denoted by $\mathcal{V}^{23}$ in [JON 99], is in fact the only tractable subclass containing all the basic relations. It is hence maximal.

As for metric relations, we again have a tractable subclass which is that of "singleton" relations, where the constraints are reduced to a single interval.

6.4.4.1. *Augmented qualitative networks*

Meiri's paper [MEI 96] describes in detail the complexity of subclasses called *augmented qualitative networks*, which are *qualitative* time point networks in which we may add unary constraints on the value of the variables. More precisely, the class PA is the class of time point networks, provided with qualitative constraints and quantitative constraints on the domains, and the class CPA is the subclass of the previous class for which the qualitative constraints are convex. Lastly, the IPA networks have qualitative constraints between points and intervals.

For each of these classes, the domains considered are of three types:

– *discrete domains*: each variable can take only a finite number of values;

– *domains limited to a single interval*: the values of each variable constitute an interval; more generally, the domains almost limited to an interval are those for which the acceptable values constitute an interval possibly without a finite number of points;

– *domains of multiple intervals*: the acceptable values are unions of intervals; this case generalizes the first two cases.

The results of Meiri's study are summarized in Table 6.2 (taken from [MEI 96]), in which AC and PC stand for arc-consistency and path-consistency, respectively, and where n denotes the number of vertices, e, the number of arcs, and k, the maximum number of points (in the discrete case) or intervals (in the case of multiple intervals):

	discrete	**single interval**	**multiple intervals**
CPA networks	AC $(O(ek))$	AC + PC $(O(n^2))$	AC + PC $(O(n^2k))$
PA networks	NP-complete	AC + PC $(O(en))$	NP-complete
IPA networks	NP-complete	NP-complete	NP-complete

Table 6.2. *Complexity of consistency (after [MEI 96])*

When the consistency problem is polynomial, the complexity of the determination of the minimal domains for the same classes is summarized in Table 6.3 (also taken from [MEI 96]).

	discrete	**single interval**	**multiple intervals**
CPA networks	AC + PC $(O(n^2k))$	AC + PC $(O(n^2))$	AC + PC $(O(n^2k))$
PA networks		AC + PC $(O(en^2))$	

Table 6.3. *Complexity of the computation of minimal domains (after [MEI 96])*

6.5. Disjunctive linear relations (DLR)

6.5.1. *A unifying formalism*

In the late 1990s, Jonsson and Bäckström [JON 98] and Koubarakis [KOU 96, KOU 01] independently introduced *disjunctive linear relations* as a formalism which subsumes most of the constraint-based temporal reasoning formalisms, for qualitative as well for metric constraints.

The reader may refer to Appendix C for the definition of DLRs and Horn DLRs. The main result with regard to complexity is summarized by the following theorem:

THEOREM 6.5.– *The satisfiability problem for a set of DLRs is NP-complete. The satisfiability problem of a set of Horn DLRs can be solved in polynomial time.*

In particular, the language of DLRs makes it possible to express:
– Allen's algebra;
– the universal language of Kautz and Ladkin;
– Meiri's qualitative algebra;
– Meiri's hybrid formalism.

Horn DLRs, for their part, subsume many tractable classes:
– the pre-convex or ORD-Horn relations in Allen's algebra;
– the relations considered by Koubarakis in [KOU 92];
– the simple temporal constraints (STC) of Dechter, Meiri and Pearl [DEC 91];
– the simple metric constraints of Kautz and Ladkin;
– the simple constraints of Meiri's hybrid formalism;
– the constraints defined by $TG - II$ formulas studied by Gerevini, Schubert and Schaeffer [GER 93];
– the tractable relations studied by Barber [BAR 00];
– the subclass $\mathcal{F}$ of the INDU algebra (Chapter 8).

6.5.2. *Allen's algebra with constraints on durations*

More recently, Krokhin, Jeavons, and Jonsson [KRO 04] solved the problem of determining all the subsets of Allen's algebra which result in a tractable consistency problem when, to Allen constraints, constraints involving the durations of intervals expressible in terms of Horn DLRs are added; such constraints on durations are for instance:
– the duration of x is less than a constant;

– the duration of x is strictly less than that of y;

– the duration of x is less than the sum of durations of y and z.

Angelsmark and Jonsson [ANG 00] have shown the following result for the 18 maximal tractable subclasses of Allen's algebra (section 2.2.8):

PROPOSITION 6.1.– *The satisfiability problem with Horn constraints on durations is tractable for the 3 subclasses $\mathcal{H}, \mathcal{S}_\mathsf{p}, \mathcal{E}_\mathsf{p}$, and NP-complete for the 15 other classes.*

Krokhin, Jeavons, and Jonsson explicitly determine seven other subclasses of relations for which the problem is tractable ([KRO 04], Table 4), and prove a dichotomy theorem:

THEOREM 6.6.– *For any subset S of Allen's algebra, the satisfiability problem with Horn constraints on durations is either strongly NP-complete, or polynomial, in which case S is contained in one of the 10 subclasses.*

6.5.3. *Conclusions*

DLRs provide a constraint language sufficiently expressive to subsume many languages which have been considered in domain of temporal and spatial reasoning, while guaranteeing that a specific sublanguage, that of Horn DLRs, has a polynomial consistency problem.

That being said, a number of tractability results do not seem to be reducible to the Horn property. This is the case of some of the tractable subclasses of Allen's algebra [GOL 93, DRA 98]. This is also the case of some tractable subclasses of the RCC−8 algebra (see proposition 4.9), and of the INDU algebra (Chapter 8).

Let us note that the use of DLRs takes us out of the domain of *binary* constraints, so that it raises the question of extending the constraint propagation techniques developed in the binary case to relations with arity greater than 2.

In addition, the resolution of qualitative problems by linear programming techniques poses problems of effectiveness, since it can be expensive in terms of computation time.

6.6. Generalized temporal networks

Generalized Temporal Networks (GTNs) have been proposed by Staab [STA 01] as a way of extending constraint-based temporal reasoning to constraints with arity greater than 2. Staab defines a general framework which extends conventional constraint propagation techniques, and examines the problems of testing consistency and determining the minimal network.

6.6.1. *Motivations*

The objective proposed by Staab is to define a formalism which generalizes several qualitative calculi (the Point calculus, Allen's calculus), quantitative calculi (Dechter, Meiri and Pearl's calculus), as well as hybrid calculi (Kautz and Allen's calculus, Meiri's calculus), and which could allow the representation and reasoning with non-binary constraints. The latter appear in a natural way, in particular when rules have to be expressed, such as for example:

"If John arrives at 03:00 pm, then Fred arrives two hours later. If not, both arrive at 6:00 pm".

Such generalized formalisms have to specify how the constraint propagation methods developed for the binary relations may be extended or adapted in this general context, in order to solve basic constraint reasoning problems such as the consistency problem or the search for a minimal network.

The GTN formalism generalizes several known formalisms. A distinctive point is that it conceives the set of formalisms as constituting a hierarchy, according to the level at which they operate. The consequence for processing is a concept of "variable depth" reasoning, which means that reasoning may operate at various granularities: if a coarse granularity is sufficient, a corresponding coarse calculus can be used which is in general simpler, less expressive, and which, by virtue of the expressiveness — complexity tradeoff, has a lower processing cost. The idea is that a higher granularity is only considered when necessary.

6.6.2. *Definition of GTN*

A GTN is defined by a finite set X of variables and a set C of constraints. The variables are interpreted as points of the rational line $\mathbb{Q}$ (time points). The constraints C are sets (interpreted as conjunctions) of disjunctions of constraints, where each constraint is itself a conjunction of constraints called *primitive* constraints. More precisely:

DEFINITION 6.1.– *A* primitive *constraint between two variables* $x, y \in X$ *is a constraint of the form* (x, I, y), *where* I *is an interval of the rational line* $\mathbb{Q}$. *The interpretation of this constraint is the fact that* $y - x \in I$.

EXAMPLE 6.11.– The expression $(t_0, [3, 3], t_1)$ is a primitive constraint. If t_0 refers to 00:00 and t_1 refers to the arrival of John, this formula can be used to express that John arrives at 03:00.

DEFINITION 6.2.– *A generalized temporal graph (GTN)* (X, C) *consists of a linearly ordered finite set* X *of vertices (or variables) and a finite set of constraints* C_k:

– *for each* C_k, *there exists a finite subset of arcs, namely* $E_k \subseteq X \times X$;

– $C_k = \bigcup_{n=1,\dots,L_k} \bigcap_{(x,y)\in E_k} \varphi_{k,n,x,y}$ *where* $\varphi_{k,n,x,y}$ *is a primitive constraint between* x *and* y.

The data consisting of the set of E_ks is called the *topology of the network*.

EXAMPLE 6.12.– Let us consider the network containing three points t_0, t_1, t_2 representing 0:00, the arrival of John and the arrival of Fred, respectively. The formula:

$$\varphi = ((t_0, [3,3], t_1) \cap (t_1, [2,2], t_2)) \cup ((t_0, [6,6], t_1) \cap (t_1, [0,0], t_2))$$

expresses the rule mentioned above.

6.6.3. *Expressiveness*

It can be easily seen that this formalism generalizes all the formalisms we mentioned in the beginning of this section. Among the expressive possibilities offered by the language, we have the following ones (taken from Table 1 of [STA 01]):

– interval $A = (A^-, A^+)$ meets interval $B = (B^-, B^+)$ with a tolerance of d units of time

$$(A^+, (-d,d), B^-) \cap (A^-, (0,+\infty), B^-) \wedge (A^+, (0,+\infty), B^+);$$

– interval $A = (A^-, A^+)$ is located between interval $B = (B^-, B^+)$ and interval $C = (C^-, C^+)$

$$(A^-, (-\infty,0), B^+) \wedge (A^+, (0,+\infty), C^-))$$
$$\vee (A^-, (-\infty,0), C^+) \wedge (A^+, (0,+\infty), B^-));$$

– interval A is at a distance of at least n units of time from B

$$(A^+, [n,+\infty), B^-) \vee (A^-, (-\infty,-n], B^+);$$

– if time point a precedes time point b, then time point c precedes time point d

$$((a, (0,+\infty), b) \wedge (c, (0,+\infty), d)) \vee (a, (-\infty,0], b);$$

– time point a is located between time points b and c

$$((a, (-\infty,0), b) \wedge (a, (0+\infty), c)) \vee ((a, (0+\infty), b) \wedge (a, (-\infty,0), c)).$$

6.6.4. *Constraint propagation*

The relations represented in GTNs generally are of an arity greater than 2. If Y is a subgraph of X, the operator π_Y selects the constraints relative to Y. Considering example 6.12 again, we have, for example $\pi_{\{(t_1,t_2)\}}(\varphi) = (t_1, [2, 2], t_2) \vee (t_1, [0, 0], t_2)$.

We have thus a general operator for decreasing the arities of the constraints we consider.

Another possibility offered by the formalism is to consider various interval structures (sets of intervals which are stable under composition and intersection). For example, besides the set of intervals on $\mathbb{Q}$, we may consider the substructure formed by the convex unions of the three intervals $(-\infty, 0)$, $[0, 0]$, and $(0, +\infty)$. The operator μ, which is essentially Meiri's QUAL operator (section 6.4.1.1) allows us to abstract a constraint so as to retain only its qualitative consequence.

The composition operation of the binary framework is replaced by a composition which uses the composition of binary projections.

In this way, Staab defines a property of weak path-consistency, and shows how to use an adaptation of the classical path-consistency algorithms to enforce weak path-consistency: the relations of the network are projected on the binary relations they imply, using the π operator, then the usual path-consistency procedure is applied.

Weak path-consistency is a necessary, but not sufficient condition for consistency.

EXAMPLE 6.13.– Consider the network containing six points $t_0, \dots, t_5$ whose constraints are the following ones:

$$C_1 = ((t_0, [1, 1], t_1) \wedge (t_0, [2, 2], t_2)) \vee ((t_0, [2, 2], t_1) \wedge (t_0, [1, 1], t_2))$$
$$C_2 = ((t_1, [0, 0], t_3) \wedge (t_2, [0, 0], t_4))$$
$$C_3 = ((t_3, [1, 1], t_5) \wedge (t_2, [1, 1], t_4)) \vee ((t_3, [2, 2], t_5) \wedge (t_2, [2, 2], t_4))$$

This network is weakly path-consistent, but it is inconsistent. In fact, the binary projections of the constraints are the following:

$$\pi_{\{t_0,t_1\}}(C_1) = (t_0, [1, 1], t_1) \vee (t_0, [2, 2], t_1)$$
$$\pi_{\{t_0,t_2\}}(C_1) = (t_0, [2, 2], t_2) \vee (t_0, [1, 1], t_2)$$
$$\pi_{\{t_1,t_3\}}(C_2) = (t_1, [0, 0], t_3)$$
$$\pi_{\{t_2,t_4\}}(C_2) = (t_2, [0, 0], t_4)$$
$$\pi_{\{t_3,t_5\}}(C_1) = (t_3, [1, 1], t_5) \vee (t_3, [2, 2], t_5)$$
$$\pi_{\{t_0,t_2\}}(C_1) = (t_4, [1, 1], t_5) \vee (t_4, [2, 2], t_5)$$

It is can be easily checked that the corresponding binary network is path-consistent. On the other hand, the initial system is not path-consistent.

In this framework, the constraint propagation techniques provide only the necessary conditions.

Staab also examines the problem of determining the minimal network. This requires the definition of a subsumption relation between networks. The definition of minimality depends on the granularity considered.

6.6.5. *Conclusions*

The GTN formalism is a generalization of binary formalisms which subsumes most of the classical formalisms. The extension of constraint propagation techniques to this generalized framework makes it possible to extend notions such as that of weak path-consistency, and to define algorithms which, although not complete in the general case, are correct and provide useful pre-processing filtering methods for solving standard problems such as the consistency problem or the problem of computing the minimal network. The interpretation of the networks on interval structures of variable complexity provides a consistent implementation of the concept of reasoning at variable degrees of granularity. It also highlights the fact that there exists a continuity between qualitative and metric concepts which may be used profitably for reasoning.

6.7. Networks with granularity

6.7.1. *Introduction*

The term *granularity* refers to the general question of determining at what level of detail we should consider the spatial or temporal entities we intend to reason about. We started this book with the example of boats which we considered as punctual entities. If, on second thoughts, we decide to treat them as intervals, we carry out a change of (spatial) granularity, by "zooming in" on these entities. The inverse operation, a zoom out, corresponds to an abstraction which is another example of granularity change. In the temporal domain, we usually have to use various units such as seconds, minutes, hours, years ... or centuries. These different units may have complex behaviors: for example, in general, months are not composed of entire weeks; or, the working days in a given week may vary in number, if this week contains extra "holes" due to holidays other than weekends, etc.

The granularity problem has been recognized and addressed by [HOB 85]. In [EUZ 96], Euzenat shows how the behavior under granularity change of algebras such as Allen's algebra and the Point algebra can be deduced from *a priori* specifying algebraic properties for the corresponding operations.

In this chapter, we introduce the very general formalism proposed by Bettini *et al.* [BET 98a, BET 98b, BET 02] for representing temporal granularity. We then briefly indicate how the same authors use constraint propagation methods in this generalized framework. Rather than giving a detailed description of this research, we emphasize the points which introduce specific difficulties and the techniques proposed to overcome these difficulties.

6.7.2. Granularities and granularity systems

Let us consider the general concepts introduced in [BET 98a]: let $(T, \leq)$ be a linear order representing time (for example, T can be the set of natural integers $\mathbb{N}$, that of relative integers $\mathbb{Z}$, the rational line $\mathbb{Q}$, the real line $\mathbb{R}$ provided with the usual relations). The data of $(T, \leq)$ is called a *temporal domain*.

DEFINITION 6.3.– *A granularity on T is a map $g \colon \mathbb{Z} \to \mathcal{P}(T)$ of the set of integers in the set of all subsets of T which satisfies the following conditions:*

– *if $i < j$ and if $g(i)$ and $g(j)$ are non-empty, $g(i)$ globally precedes $g(j)$: for any $t \in g(i)$ and any $t' \in g(j)$, we have $t < t'$;*

– *if $i < k < j$ and if $g(i)$ and $g(j)$ are non-empty, then $g(k)$ is non-empty.*

EXAMPLE 6.14.– Let T be the set of the 365 days of a given year. The map $g \colon \mathbb{Z} \to T$ which consists in associating with each integer $i \in \{1, \ldots, 365\}$ the one-element set containing the i-th day of this year, and the empty set to all other integers, is a granularity on a discrete temporal domain.

Let us now consider the business weeks (in the UK) of the same year (a business week is the set of working days it contains), and let us number them sequentially, starting from 1. We obtain in this way another granularity on the same domain.

The non-empty sets $g(i)$ are called the *granules* of the granularity. More precisely, $g(i)$ is the granule of index i. The first condition in definition 6.3 expresses the fact that the granules are disjoint, and ordered by their indices. The second means that the inverse image of $\mathcal{P}(T) \setminus \emptyset$ is a connected subset of $\mathbb{Z}$.

The *image* of a granularity g is by definition the set $\bigcup_{i \in \mathbb{Z}} g(i)$. As exemplified in the previous example, this image may contain "gaps", i.e. elements of T located between two granules and which are not contained in any granule.

The *extension* of a granule g is by definition the smallest interval of T containing all the granules.

What characterizes those situations in which the concept of granularity is useful is the fact that one has to consider several granularities simultaneously.

6.7.2.1. *Relations between granularities*

The granularities defined on the same temporal domain have a rich relational structure. The main relations are the following [BET 98a].

DEFINITION 6.4.– *Let g and h be two granularities defined on the same temporal domain T*:

– *granularity g is* finer *than granularity h, which is denoted by $g \preceq h$, if for any index i, there exists an index j such that $g(i) \subseteq h(j)$*;

– *granularity h groups* into *g, denoted by $g \trianglerighteq h$, or $h \trianglelefteq g$, if for any i, there exists a subset S_i of integers such that $g(i) = \bigcup_{j \in S_i} h(j)$*;

– *granularity h periodically groups* into *g, if $g \trianglerighteq h$ and if there exists $m, n \in \mathbb{Z}^+$, where n is less than the number of non-empty granules of g, such that for any $i \in \mathbb{Z}$, if $g(i) = \bigcup_{i=0}^{k} h(j_r)$ and $g(i+n) \neq \emptyset$, then $g(i+n) = \bigcup_{i=0}^{k} h(j_r + m)$*;

– *granularity g is a* subgranularity *of granularity h, denoted by $g \sqsubseteq h$, if for any index i there exists an index j such that $g(i) \subseteq h(j)$*;

– *granularities g and h are* shift *equivalent, denoted by $g \leftrightharpoons h$, if there exists an integer k such that, for any index i such that $g(i) \neq \emptyset$, we have $g(i) = h(i+k)$*;

– *granularity g* partitions *granularity h, denoted by $g \sqsubseteq h$, if we have $g \trianglelefteq h$ and $g \sqsubseteq h$*.

If $g \sqsubseteq h$, then $g \preceq h$. None of the two conditions $g \preceq h$ and $g \trianglelefteq h$ implies the other.

The three relations $\sqsubseteq$, $\preceq$, and $\trianglelefteq$ are reflexive and transitive on the set of granularities on a fixed domain. The relation $\leftrightharpoons$ is an equivalence relation, and, on the equivalence classes it defines, the three preorders induce order structures.

EXAMPLE 6.15.– Let us consider Figure 6.7. In (a), granularity h groups into g: each granule of g is a union of granules of h. In (b), h is finer than g: each granule of g is a subset of a granule of h. In (c), h partitions g.

In (d), granularity h periodically groups into g. Here, the integers of the definition are $m = 3$ and $n = 2$: to build g, every three granules of h, we repeat the pattern formed by two granules of $h (g(0) = h(0) \cup h(1))$ followed by a granule of $h (g(1) = h(2))$.

In practice, additional properties may be enforced on the granularities considered. For example, we may enforce that the granules should be intervals, or that two successive granules should be contiguous. We may also enforce that the granules should entirely cover T, or that all granules should have the same size, and so on.

We may also enforce that a given system of granularities should not comprise more than one granularity up to shift (the shift relation is then the identity in the system). We

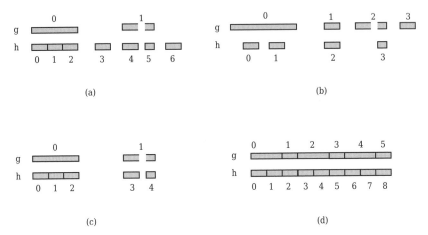

Figure 6.7. *Relations between granularities: in (a), h groups into g; in (b)
h is finer than g, and in (c), it partitions g; in (d), h periodically groups into g*

may also enforce that the system should not contain two incomparable granularities for a given relation. For example, the granularity associated with months and that associated with weeks are not comparable for the relation $\preceq$, since no week can contain a month, and since one week may overlap two months. A similar remark holds for the relations $\lhd$ and $\sqsubseteq$.

6.7.3. *Constraint networks*

Bettini *et al.* present an extension of the STP formalism to the context of multigranularity [BET 98b, BET 02]. We now give a brief sketch of this extension.

In what follows, we consider a system of granularities with values in $\mathbb{Z}$ treated as a set of seconds. The granularity second corresponds to the identical map. Moreover, we assume that all the granularities of the system regroup seconds: for any g, we have seconds $\lhd g$.

DEFINITION 6.5.– *Let $m \leq n$ be two integers and g, a granularity. The temporal constraint with granularity $[m, n]g$ is the binary relation on $\mathbb{N}$ defined in the following way: $(a, b) \in [m, n]g$ if, and only if*:

1) *there is a granule $g(t_a)$ of g containing a, and a granule $g(t_b)$ of g containing b;*

2) *we have $m \leq t_b - t_a \leq n$.*

The first condition states that the "points" a and b are contained each in a granule (which is hence unique) of g; the second expresses that the difference between the indices of these granules is an integer of $[m, n]$, called the (*range*) of the constraint.

EXAMPLE 6.16.– The constraint [0, 0] days is satisfied by two time points which belong to the same day. The constraint [−1, 1] hours expresses that two time points are separated by one hour at most. In general, a constraint cannot be expressed in terms of seconds. For example, the constraint [0, 0] days implies that two points are separated by a number of seconds ranging from 0 to 86,399 seconds, but the converse is not true, since two points located in two consecutive days may also differ by less than 24 hours.

DEFINITION 6.6.– *A constraint network with granularities is denoted by* (N, A, C) *where* N *is a finite set of vertices (called variables),* $A \subseteq N \times N$ *is a set of arcs, and* C *is a map of* A *in finite sets of constraints with granularity.*

The interpretation of a finite set of constraints with granularities is conjunctive: it is mandatory that all the constraints are satisfied simultaneously. This convention is to be contrasted with the disjunctive interpretation adopted in most of the formalisms studied in this book.

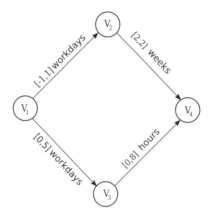

Figure 6.8. *A constraint network with granularities (taken from [BET 98b])*

EXAMPLE 6.17.– Figure 6.8 ([BET 98b], Figure 2) is an example of a constraint network with granularities. The four vertices represent the events V_1, V_2, V_3, V_4, with the constraints that:

– V_1 and V_2 should take place either on the same working day, or in two successive working days;

– V_3 should take place in the five working days following V_1;

– V_4 should occur in the 8 hours which follow V_3, and in the second week following V_2.

A constraint network with granularities is consistent if there is an interpretation of variables in terms of integers such that all the constraints are satisfied.

6.7.4. Complexity of the consistency problem

THEOREM 6.7.– *The consistency problem for networks with arbitrary granularities is a NP-difficult problem.*

The authors of [BET 98b] prove this result by using the subset sum problem[1]. The intuitive reason for this complexity is that, contrary to what could be expected, the introduction of granularities may introduce disjunctive constraints.

For example, let us consider the network with four vertices $V_1, \ldots, V_4$ of Figure 6.9:

$$C(V_1, V_2) = \{[11, 11]\text{month}, [0, 0]\text{year}\} \qquad\qquad [6.1]$$

$$C(V_1, V_3) = \{[0, 12]\text{month}\} \qquad\qquad [6.2]$$

$$C(V_3, V_4) = \{[11, 11]\text{month}, [0, 0]\text{year}\} \qquad\qquad [6.3]$$

The events V_1 and V_2 must belong to the same year and differ by 11 months, which implies that the first event must take place in January. For the same reason, V_3 must also take place in January. Consequently, the distance between V_1 and V_3 is either 0 month, or 12 months.

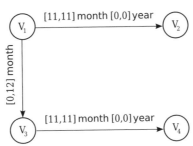

Figure 6.9. *A network whose consequences are disjunctive: a consequence of the constraints expressed by the network is that the events V_1 and V_3 either take place in the same month, or are separated by 12 months (from [BET 98b])*

6.7.5. Propagation algorithms

Bettini *et al.* propose an approximate algorithm using constraint propagation [BET 98b]. It is based on iterating the following operations:

– apply a path-consistency algorithm to each sub-network whose constraints have the same granularity;

---

1 The subset sum problem consists in determining if a given finite set of relative integers contains a non-empty subset whose sum is zero. This problem is NP-complete [GAR 79].

– express the constraints thus obtained in terms of other granularities which appear in the network.

This algorithm is correct but incomplete.

In [BET 02], the same authors consider constraint networks with granularities that involve unary constraints in addition to the binary constraints. The unary constraints are supposed to be of a periodic type (they are sets of granules with a granularity that periodically groups granules with a basic granularity).

Under these conditions, the authors describe an algorithm which is complete for the consistency problem. This algorithm, called AC-G, is a generalization of the path-consistency algorithm AC-3. It is polynomial in terms of variables and constraints, but exponential in terms of the number of granularities present in the network. Its implementation requires the explicit computation of the *normalization* of several periodic sets with different periods, as well as of the intersection of a periodic — or finite — set, and of another periodic set.

The main operation, denoted by $\uplus$, has a periodic — or finite — set as input (the domain of a variable X) and a set of constraints on the arc connecting X to another variable. Its output is a new finite or periodic set. We refer the reader to [BET 02] for a description of this operation, which is rather technical and complex.

It should also be mentioned that, as was the case for STP networks, the AC-G algorithm also provides a solution if the network is consistent. Indeed, the minimal values of the variable domains provide a solution.

Chapter 7

Fuzzy Reasoning

7.1. "Picasso's Blue period"

Picasso's "Blue period"[1] started by the beginning of the 20th Century. If I state that it begins at the very beginning of the 20th Century, I may see the "Blue period" as a temporal interval which is adjacent, or which closely follows, the interval constituted by the 19th Century (Figure 7.1). In terms of Allen's relations, the relation is a meeting relation between two intervals (m) or a precedence relation (p), but I tend to think that the second relation is more probable, and that the "Blue period" does not start as early as 1900. I would like to represent the vague knowledge I have of the relation between two well-defined intervals (Picasso's Blue period, and the 20th Century), and to express my preference. The framework of fuzzy relations between temporal intervals is a way of doing it. In that case, I consider that the "Blue period" is defined perfectly, and that the vagueness is linked to my imperfect knowledge about its temporal location: the relation between the beginning of the period and the year 1900 is not known precisely. Under these assumptions, the temporal entities are clearly defined, but the relations between them are "fuzzy" relations.

Now by searching on the Internet, I learn that the "Blue period" started in 1901 and ended in 1904. However, I am constituting a knowledge base on Picasso's work, but the many dates and periodizations that I was able to collect give me contradictory results. How can I reconcile this contradictory information? Upon reflection, I come to the conclusion that the definition of the "Blue period" as a well-defined interval has to be questioned: actually, this period is only defined in a vague manner: a painting assigned to the "Blue period" may have been painted in parallel with a painting assigned to another period. Do the corresponding days belong to the "Blue period" or not?

---

1 We take this example from [SCH 08a].

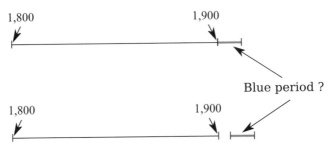

Figure 7.1. *The "Blue period" starts right at the beginning of the 20th Century.*
Does it start as early as 1900? Two assumptions

In this case, I must accept that not only the relations between temporal entities but also the temporal entities themselves, are vaguely defined.

What we have been saying for time periods may also be applied to spatial objects. Actually, vague spatial entities are constantly used in everyday life: for example, could we say precisely where the suburbs of a big city start and end? If we are not content with the fairly arbitrary definitions of these suburbs by the urban administrations, then the answer is probably that we cannot.

In this chapter, we will describe what solutions the formalism of fuzzy sets offers to the two types of problems we have highlighted: the problem of reasoning about *vague relations* between temporal or spatial entities, and the problem of reasoning about relations between entities which are themselves defined in a vague manner, that is, *vague entities*.

7.2. Fuzzy relations between classical intervals

7.2.1. *Motivations*

Let us consider the language of Allen's algebra. It allows to express a certain type of uncertainty with the help of disjunction of basic relations. For example, I may express the fact that the periods of two meetings I and J are disjoint by enforcing the constraint $\{p, pi\}$ between them. But I cannot express a *preference*, for example the fact that I p J is more appropriate to me than I pi J. I cannot express *priorities* between the constraints either, for example the fact that the constraint $\{p, pi\}$ between I and J is more important than the others, and that I am ready to relax some of these constraints to obtain a solution.

The construction of a fuzzy interval algebra is a response to these objectives. Our presentation is based on the work of Badaloni and Giacomin [BAD 06].

7.2.2. The fuzzy Point algebra

Before defining the fuzzy interval algebra, it is instructive to start by considering the simpler case of the fuzzy point algebra. In the same manner as an element of the point algebra is a subset of $\mathbf{B}_1 = \{<, \text{eq}, >\}$, an element of the *fuzzy* Point algebra is a fuzzy subset of $\mathbf{B}_1$:

DEFINITION 7.1.– *The domain of the algebra* $\mathbf{A}_1^{fuz}$ *is the set* $\Omega^{\mathbf{B}_1}$ *of maps* α: $\mathbf{B}_1 \rightarrow [0.1]$.

The set $\mathbf{B}_1$ contains the three relation symbols $<$, eq, and $>$. An element α of the algebra may thus be identified with a 3-tuple[2] $(\alpha_1, \alpha_2, \alpha_3) = (\alpha(<), \alpha(\text{eq}), \alpha(>))$ which is an element of $[0.1]^3$.

The inversion, intersection, and union operations are defined as follows:
– the inverse of $(\alpha_1, \alpha_2, \alpha_3)$ is $(\alpha_3, \alpha_2, \alpha_1)$;
– the conjunction of α and β is the function $(\alpha \wedge \beta)(r) = \inf(\alpha(r), \beta(r))$;
– the disjunction of α and β is the function $(\alpha \vee \beta)(r) = \sup(\alpha(r), \beta(r))$;
– the composition of α and β is defined in the following way: let α and β be two elements of the algebra. For each basic relation r, let S_r be the set of pairs (s, t) of basic relations such that $r \in (s \circ t)$. Then, $(\alpha \circ \beta)$ is the relation such that:

$$(\alpha \circ \beta)(r) = \sup_{(s,t) \in S_r} \inf(\alpha(s), \beta(t))$$

It can be easily seen that, in the case of the "classical" elements of $\mathbf{A}_1^{fuz}$, that is of functions whose only values are 0 or 1, these definitions coincide with the usual definitions. We may thus consider the Point algebra as a subalgebra of $\mathbf{A}_1^{fuz}$. In terms of 3-tuples, the eight coordinate elements are equal to 0 or 1 (Figure 7.2).

In the Point algebra, the subalgebra formed by the elements which do not contain the relation $\neq$, the subalgebra of convex relations, plays a special role. Its fuzzy analog is the algebra $\mathbf{A}_1^{fuz}{}_c$:

DEFINITION 7.2.– *The fuzzy convex relation algebra* $\mathbf{A}_1^{fuz}{}_c$ *is the subalgebra of* $\mathbf{A}_1^{fuz}$ *formed by the elements* $(\alpha_1, \alpha_2, \alpha_3)$ *such that* $\alpha_2 \geq inf(\alpha_1, \alpha_3)$.

Intuitively, the condition expresses that the degree of membership of eq to a disjunctive relation is at least equal to the smallest degree of membership of $<$ and $>$, and hence that, as long as a relation contains $<$ or $>$ (to some degree) it also contains $=$ (at this same degree). In Figure 7.2, the non-empty convex relations are those which do not belong to the interior of the pyramid in dark gray.

---

2 In the literature on the subject, the usual notation for this 3-tuple is $(< [\alpha_1], \text{eq} [\alpha_2], > [\alpha_3])$.

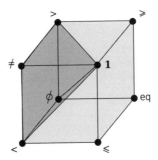

Figure 7.2. *The algebra* $\mathbf{A}_1^{fuz}$ *(in gray) contains the eight elements of the algebra* $\mathbf{A}_1$. *In an intuitive manner, an element of this algebra (a point of the cube) corresponds to choosing each basic relation weighted by a real number between 0 and 1. The element* $\emptyset$ *corresponds to choosing none of the three, and* $\mathbf{1}$ *to choose all of the three at the same time. The fuzzy convex relations are shown in light gray*

It can be easily checked that this condition defines a subalgebra: we have the stability under inversion, conjunction, and composition.

7.2.2.1. *a-cuts*

The analysis of the properties of a fuzzy algebra is facilitated by the use of its a-cuts (where $a \in (0, 1]$), which are elements of the "classical" algebra:

DEFINITION 7.3.– *Let* $a \in (0, 1]$, *and* $\alpha \in \mathbf{A}_1^{fuz}$. *The a-cut* α_a *of* α *is the set* $\alpha^{-1}([a, 1]) \subseteq \mathbf{B}_1$.

The a-cut of an element of the fuzzy Point algebra is hence a subset of $\mathbf{B}_1$, i.e. an element of $\mathbf{A}_1$.

The three operations of inversion, conjunction, and composition commute to the transition to the a-cut, for any $a \in (0, 1]$:

PROPOSITION 7.1.– *Let* $a \in (0, 1]$. *For all* $\alpha, \beta \in \mathbf{A}_1^{fuz}$, *we have:*

- $(\alpha_a)^{-1} = (\alpha^{-1})_a$;
- $(\alpha \wedge \beta)_a = \alpha_a \cap \beta_a$;
- $(\alpha \circ \beta)_a = \alpha_a \circ \beta_a$.

The a-cuts of sub-algebras of $\mathbf{A}_1^{fuz}$ are thus sub-algebras of the Point algebra. In particular, the a-cuts of the subalgebra of convex relations in A_1^{fuz} are subclasses of the class of convex relations between points.

7.2.3. *The fuzzy Interval algebra*

The domain of Allen's Interval algebra is the set $\Omega^{\mathbf{B_2}}$, where $\mathbf{B_2}$ is the set of the 13 symbols of Allen's relations, and $\Omega = \{0, 1\}$ is the set of truth-values, 0 (false) and 1 (true).

As in the case of the fuzzy Point algebra, we consider the fuzzy subsets of $\mathbf{B_2}$, i.e. Ω is replaced by the set [0,1] of fuzzy "truth-values":

DEFINITION 7.4.– *The domain of the algebra* $\mathbf{A}_2^{fuz}$ *is the set* $\Omega^{\mathbf{B_2}}$ *of maps* α: $\mathbf{B_2} \rightarrow$ $[0, 1]$.

An element of this algebra is denoted as $(\mathsf{p}[\alpha(\mathsf{p})], \ldots, \mathsf{pi}[\alpha(\mathsf{pi})])$ in [BAD 06]. If $\alpha(r) = 0$, we leave out $r[0]$. If $\alpha(r) = 1$, we denote $r[1]$ simply by r.

7.2.3.1. *Operations*

The inverse α^{-1} of an element α is defined by $\alpha^{-1}(r) = \alpha(r^{-1})$. In the classical case, where α only takes values 0 or 1, this definition coincides with the definition of inversion.

The intersection of two elements α and β is defined by $(\alpha \cap \beta)(r) = \inf(\alpha(r), \beta(r))$. Clearly, this definition reduces to the classical definition of intersection if α and β are classical elements.

Disjunction is defined in a similar way: $(\alpha \cup \beta)(r) = \sup(\alpha(r), \beta(r))$; here again, this definition reduces the classical definition of disjunction if α and β are classical elements.

Lastly, the composition of α and β is defined in a way similar to that used in the case of the Point algebra: let α and β be two elements of the algebra. For each Allen basic relation r, let S_r be the set of pairs (s, t) of basic relations such that $r \in (s \circ t)$. Then, $(\alpha \circ \beta)$ is the relation such that:

$$(\alpha \circ \beta)(r) = \sup_{(s,t) \in S_r} \inf(\alpha(s), \beta(t))$$

EXAMPLE 7.1.– Let $\alpha = (\mathsf{o}[0.5], \mathsf{m}[0.7])$, which is equal to 0.5 on o, 0.7 on m, and 0 on all the other basic relations. Let $\beta = (\mathsf{p}[0.9])$. To calculate $(\alpha \circ \beta)$, it is enough to consider the basic relations s and t such that $\alpha(s)$ and $\beta(t)$ are non-zero, hence the pairs $(s, t) = (\mathsf{o}, \mathsf{p})$ and $(s, t) = (\mathsf{m}, \mathsf{p})$. These two pairs are elements of S_p. We conclude that the required composition is the function which is zero for any basic relation other than p, and which, for p, has the value $\sup(\inf(0.5, 0.9), \inf(0.7, 0.9))$ that is $\sup(0.5, 0.7) = 0.7$, which in turn means the relation $(\mathsf{p}[0.7])$.

7.2.4. *Fuzzy constraint networks*

A fuzzy constraint network $\mathcal{N} = (N, C)$ on the algebra $\mathbf{A}_2^{fuz}$ consists of a finite set of vertices N and, for each pair $(i, j) \in N \times N$, of an element $C(i, j)$ of $\mathbf{A}_2^{fuz}$.

In the "classical" version of Allen's calculus, a scenario or atomic labeling of $\mathcal{N}$ consists of a basic relation $r_{i,j}$ for each pair $(i, j) \in N \times N$. The concept of a consistent scenario is the classical concept: there exists $m \colon N \to \mathbb{R}^2$ such that for any pair (i, j), the pair of intervals $(m(i), m(j))$ belongs to the relation $r_{i,j}$.

In the fuzzy case, we modify the definition of satisfaction in the following way: to each atomic subnetwork which is a consistent scenario, we assign a degree of satisfaction. Let $SL(\mathcal{N})$ denote the set of atomic subnetworks of $\mathcal{N}$; we refer to it as to the set of *solutions* of $\mathcal{N}$.

DEFINITION 7.5.– *Let $\mathcal{N} = (N, C)$ be a fuzzy constraint network on the algebra $\mathbf{A}_2^{fuz}$. The degree of satisfaction of an atomic subnetwork $s \colon N \times N \to \mathbf{B}_2$ of $\mathcal{N}$ is 0 if this scenario is not consistent. If it is consistent, it is equal to $inf_{(i,j)\in N^2}\alpha(s(i, j))$.*

EXAMPLE 7.2.– The network with three vertices for which $C(1, 2) = (\mathsf{m}[0.6])$, $C(1, 3) = (\mathsf{p}[0.9], \mathsf{m}[0.2])$, and $C(2, 3) = (\mathsf{m}[0.5], \mathsf{o}[0.7])$ has four atomic subnetworks. The subnetwork $C'(1, 2) = (\mathsf{m})$, $C'(1, 3) = (\mathsf{m})$, and $C'(2, 3) = (\mathsf{m})$ is not consistent. Its degree of satisfaction is therefore 0. The subnetworks $C'(1, 2) = (\mathsf{m})$, $C' = (1, 3) = (\mathsf{p})$, and $C'(2, 3) = (\mathsf{m})$ is consistent. Its degree of satisfaction is therefore 0.5.

The set of solutions of N, along with the map which associates to each solution its degree of satisfaction, defines a fuzzy subset of the set of solutions whose support is contained in the set of consistent scenarios. In the particular case where the network is a classical network, the classical set of solutions is precisely the set of consistent scenarios.

DEFINITION 7.6.– *Let $\mathcal{N} = (N, C)$ be a fuzzy constraint network on the algebra $\mathbf{A}_2^{fuz}$ which is consistent. An* optimal solution *is a solution whose degree of satisfaction is equal to that of the network.*

These definitions apply, *mutatis mutandis*, to the Point algebra.

The concept of a-cut itself applies to the two types of networks: if $\mathcal{N} = (N, C)$ is a constraint network on a fuzzy algebra, and $a \in (0, 1]$, the a-cut $\mathcal{N}_a$ is the classical network (N, C_a) such that, for any pair $(i, j) \in N^2$, the constraint $C_a(i, j)$ is the a-cut of the constraint $C(i, j)$.

NOTE 7.1.– A fuzzy constraint network is by definition a finite graph, which involves a finite number of constraints, and hence a finite number of degrees of membership. Consequently, only a finite number of a-cuts will be distinct.

7.2.5. Algorithms, tractable subclasses

The authors of [BAD 06] consider three types of algorithms. The first type involves algorithms derived from the classical algorithms PC1 and PC2 which make use of specific properties of fuzzy constraint networks. The second type corresponds to an adaptation of the AAC algorithm of van Beek and Cohen [BEE 90b], which ensures that all the subgraphs with four elements of a given network are minimal. Lastly, in the case of arbitrary networks, a *branch-and-bound* algorithm is proposed for the search of an optimal solution for a consistent network.

The subclass of convex relations of the fuzzy interval algebra can be defined in a way which is quite similar to its definition in the classical case. The pointizable subclass can also be defined. In the case of the first subclass, path-consistency makes it possible to decide consistency, and the network obtained, if non-zero, is a minimal network. In the case of the class of pointizable relations, the AAC algorithm ensures minimality.

Alternatively, the convex and pointizable subclasses can be defined in terms of a-cuts:

PROPOSITION 7.2.– *A relation of* $\mathbf{A}_2^{fuz}$ *is convex (respectively, pointizable) if, and only if, all its a-cuts, for* $a \in (0.1]$ *are convex (respectively, pointizable).*

Of course, here again, it should be noted that a given relation has only a finite number of distinct a-cuts. The classical criteria of recognition are thus easily applicable.

EXAMPLE 7.3.– Consider the relation:

$$(\mathsf{p}[0.7], \mathsf{m}[0.7], \mathsf{o}[0.5], \mathsf{s}[0.3], \mathsf{fi}[0.5], \mathsf{eq}[0.2])$$

Clearly, its distinct a-cuts correspond to $a < 0.2$ (empty relation), and to $a = 0.2, a = 0.3, a = 0.5$ and $a = 0.7$. These a-cuts are, respectively, $\{\mathsf{eq}\}$, $[\mathsf{s}, \mathsf{eq}]$, $[\mathsf{o}, \mathsf{eq}]$, and $[\mathsf{p}, \mathsf{eq}]$, which are all convex relations. It is therefore a convex relation.

We may in fact easily ascertain that the fuzzy network with four vertices on the fuzzy Point algebra which is defined by:

$$C(V_1, V_2) = (< [0.2], \mathsf{eq}[0], > [0])$$
$$C(V_1, V_3) = (< [0.5], \mathsf{eq}[0.2], > [0])$$
$$C(V_1, V_4) = (< [0.2], \mathsf{eq}[0], > [0])$$
$$C(V_2, V_3) = (< [0.7], \mathsf{eq}[0.7], > [0.2])$$

$$C(V_2, V_4) = (< [0.3], \text{eq}[0.2], > [0])$$
$$C(V_3, V_4) = (< [0.2], \text{eq}[0], > [0])$$

naturally corresponds to this relation: if we identify (V_1, V_2) with a first interval, and (V_2, V_3) with a second, then the various a-cuts define the required relations.

7.2.5.1. Pre-convex relations

The correspondence established by means of a-cuts between fuzzy concepts and classical concepts may also be used to define the subclass of fuzzy *pre-convex* relations:

DEFINITION 7.7.– *A relation of* $\mathbf{A}_2^{fuz}$ *is pre-convex if, and only if, all its a-cuts, for* $a \in (0.1]$ *are pre-convex.*

Here again, the correspondence with the classical concept ensures that this set of relations is a subclass.

Following Badaloni and Giacomin, let $\mathcal{H}^{fuz}$ denote the subclass of fuzzy pre-convex relations. The following proposition results from the correspondence established by the a-cuts between the fuzzy concepts and the classical concepts.

PROPOSITION 7.3.– *Let $\mathcal{N} = (N, C)$ be a fuzzy network which is algebraically closed and whose relations are pre-convex and non-empty. Then for each constraint $C(i, j)$ the maximal degree of $C(i, j)$ is equal to $\deg(\mathcal{N})$.*

As a consequence, we may determine an optimal solution for a fuzzy pre-convex network in cubic time:

– we use the path-consistency algorithm to build an equivalent algebraically closed network. The time-cost is $O(n^3 k)$, where k is the number of degrees of membership used by the network. If the network is non-zero;

– we note the maximal degree of membership of an arbitrary arc;

– we use the construction of a maximal solution: we can successively choose a relation of maximal dimension and of maximal degree of membership on each arc to arrive at a consistent scenario which is thus optimal. The time-cost is $O(n^2)$.

In the classical case, the pre-convex relations constitute the only maximal tractable subclass which contains all of Allen's basic relations.

A similar result also holds in the fuzzy case. In order to state it, we define the analogs of the basic relations as follows:

DEFINITION 7.8.– *An element α of $\mathbf{A}_2^{fuz}$ is a fuzzy basic relation if there is exactly one basic relation $r \in \mathbf{B}_2$ such that $\alpha(r) \neq 0$.*

In other words, the basic relations are precisely those relations whose all a-cuts are basic relations.

By using the correspondence established by the a-cuts once again, Badaloni and Giacomin prove in [BAD 06] the following theorem:

THEOREM 7.1.– *The subclass of fuzzy pre-convex relations $\mathcal{H}^{fuz}$ is the unique maximal tractable subclass of $\mathbf{A}_2^{fuz}$ which contains all fuzzy basic relations.*

7.2.6. *Assessment*

Badaloni and Giacomin's results show that most of the classical results concerning Allen's calculus may be extended to a fuzzy context in which fuzzy subsets of Allen's relations are considered. In particular, the unique maximal tractable class of relations containing all basic relations may be characterized in terms of pre-convex relations. This adds to the fact that, for specific subclasses of relations, such as those of convex relations and pointizable relations, classical results remain valid with regard to the search for minimal networks and optimal solutions. Moreover, algorithms which extend the classical algorithms in a suitable way can be used with a time-cost which is not fundamentally modified (the only complexifying factor is the number of degrees of membership present in the network).

7.3. Events and fuzzy intervals

We have previously discussed the reasons why, in the temporal domain, we may have to consider events whose limits are only vaguely defined, and hence whose temporal support is an interval whose limits are themselves vague.

In what follows, we present the approach of Schockaert *et al.* as it has been developed in a series of papers. In [SCH 06], the authors describe the basic idea of the approach, which is to give a fuzzy definition of binary relations between intervals such as the relation $bb^<(A, B)$ (the beginning of B precedes the beginning of A), $be^<(A, B)$ (the beginning of A precedes the end of B, etc.); they show how the formalism obtained in this way may be applied to the field of question-and-answer (QA) systems. In a more elaborate version, this formalism is extended to take into account metric aspects, by introducing relations of the type $bb_d^<(A, B)$ (the beginning of A precedes the end of B by a quantity of at least d temporal units).

7.3.1. *Fuzzy intervals and fuzzy relations*

A "classical" interval is a particular subset of the real line. Consequently, a fuzzy interval is a function $A: \mathbb{R} \to [0, 1]$ which checks the particular properties:

DEFINITION 7.9.– A fuzzy interval A is a normalized fuzzy subset of the real line $A :$ $\mathbb{R} \rightarrow [0,1]$ such that for any $a \in (0,1]$, the a-cut $A_a = A^{-1}[a,1]$ of A is a bounded and closed interval of $\mathbb{R}$ not reduced to a point.

The condition is equivalent to the fact that the function A, in addition to having a bounded support and of reaching the value 1, is also upper semi-continuous.

Relations between fuzzy intervals are defined by generalizing the definition of relations between the bounding points. In the case of two classical intervals $A = (A^-, A^+)$ and $B = (B^-, B^+)$, the condition $A^- < B^-$ (A starts before B) is characterized by the following formula:

$$A^- < B^- \Leftrightarrow (\exists x)(x \in A \wedge (\forall y)(y \in B \Rightarrow x < y) \quad [7.1]$$

In order to define a fuzzy equivalent of this relation, Schockaert and De Cock [SCH 08a] use the fuzzy equivalents of the right part of this equivalence: the conjunction $\varphi \wedge \psi$ has a T-norm as an equivalent. This T-norm defines a implicator I_T which represents the material implication $\varphi \Rightarrow \psi$. For technical reasons, the T-norm used here is the Łukasiewicz T-norm[3]. What corresponds to the universal quantification is inf, and sup corresponds to the existential quantification.

Thus, one arrives at the definition of what is denoted by $bb^\ll$ (in this formula, $L^\ll(x,y)$ denotes the Boolean function which is equal to 1 if $x < y$, and 0 otherwise):

$$bb^\ll(A, B) = \sup_{x \in \mathbb{R}} T(A(x), \inf_{y \in \mathbb{R}} I_T(B(y), L^\ll(x,y))) \quad [7.2]$$

In the classical case, we can easily check that $bb^\ll(A, B)$ corresponds indeed to the condition $A^- < B^-$, or again, in terms of Allen's relations, to the convex relation $[\mathsf{p}, \mathsf{di}]$.

Relations $ee^\ll(A, B), be^\ll(A, B)$, and $eb^\ll(A, B)$ are defined in a similar way:

$$ee^\ll(A, B) = \sup_{y \in \mathbb{R}} T(B(y), \inf_{x \in \mathbb{R}} I_T(A(x), L^\ll(x,y))) \quad [7.3]$$

$$be^\ll(A, B) = \sup_{x \in \mathbb{R}} T(A(x), \sup_{y \in \mathbb{R}} T(B(y), L^\ll(x,y))) \quad [7.4]$$

$$eb^\ll(A, B) = \inf_{x \in \mathbb{R}} I_T(A(x), \inf_{y \in \mathbb{R}} I_T(B(y), L^\ll(x, ydk))) \quad [7.5]$$

In the classical case, these are the three Allen relations $[\mathsf{p}, \mathsf{d}]$, $[\mathsf{p}, \mathsf{oi}]$, and $\{\mathsf{p}\}$, respectively.

Again, in the classical case, if $B^- < A^-$ is false, then $A^- \leq B^-$, which means that the relation between A and B is Allen's relation $[\mathsf{p}, \mathsf{si}]$. In the fuzzy case, this suggests to define a relation $bb^\preccurlyeq(A, B)$ by the following formula:

---

3 The Łukasiewicz T-norm T is defined by $T(x, y) = \sup(0, x + y - 1)$. The associated implicator I_T is $I_T(x, y) = \inf(1, 1 - x + y)$.

$$bb^{\preccurlyeq}(A, B) = 1 - bb^{\ll}(B, A) \qquad\qquad [7.6]$$

Relations $ee^{\preccurlyeq}(A, B)$, $be^{\preccurlyeq}(A, B)$, and $eb^{\preccurlyeq}(A, B)$ are defined in a similar way:

$$ee^{\preccurlyeq}(A, B) = 1 - ee^{\ll}(B, A) \qquad\qquad [7.7]$$

$$be^{\preccurlyeq}(A, B) = 1 - eb^{\ll}(B, A) \qquad\qquad [7.8]$$

$$eb^{\preccurlyeq}(A, B) = 1 - be^{\ll}(B, A) \qquad\qquad [7.9]$$

In the classical case, these three relations correspond to Allen's relations $[p, f]$, $[p, mi]$, and $[p, m]$, respectively.

NOTE 7.2.– As already mentioned, [SCH 08a] deals with a more general situation where a concept such as "the beginning of A precedes that of B" is replaced by the metric constraint "the beginning of A precedes that of B by at least d units. In the previous formulas, this amounts to replacing $L^{\ll}(x, y)$ by the function $L_d^{\ll}(x, y)$ which is equal to 1 if $y - x > d$, and to 0 otherwise.

Schockaert and De Cock then obtain fuzzy relations $bb_d^{\ll}(A, B)$ (whose intuitive meaning is that the beginning of A precedes that of B by at least d units), and so on for $ee_d^{\ll}(A, B)$, $be_d^{\ll}(A, B)$, and $eb_d^{\ll}(A, B)$. Similarly to what was done for $bb^{\ll}$, "negations" $bb_d^{\preccurlyeq}(A, B)$, $ee_d^{\preccurlyeq}(A, B)$, $be_d^{\preccurlyeq}(A, B)$, and $eb_d^{\preccurlyeq}(A, B)$ defined. For example:

$$bb^{\preccurlyeq}(A, B) = 1 - bb^{\ll}(B, A) \qquad\qquad [7.10]$$

It should be emphasized that the formula $bb^{\preccurlyeq}(A, B)$, for example, means that the beginning of A precedes that of B or, if that is not the case, it follows it by a quantity which does not exceed d temporal units.

7.3.2. *Fuzzy constraints*

The introduction of fuzzy intervals was motivated by the fact that, in many applications, precise definitions of the considered intervals are impossible. In terms of automatic reasoning, they cannot be used as strict constraints. An example is the constitution of knowledge bases from textual data that are collected from the Web: a rigid definition of temporal periods often leads to contradictions. Here, we consider again the example of [SCH 08a] which we have used in our introduction. This example deals with Picasso's "Blue", "Pink", and "Cubist" periods.

Since it has to manage constraints which, if interpreted in a classical way, often lead to contradictions, fuzzy reasoning will typically consist of determining to what extent a system with constraints on the degrees of satisfaction of basic constraints between intervals may be satisfied.

EXAMPLE 7.4.– Knowing that A, B, and C are three fuzzy intervals, is it possible that we can simultaneously have $bb^\ll(A, B) \geq 0.6$, $bb^\ll(B, C) \leq 0.5$, $be^\ll(B, C) \leq 0.8$, and $ee^\ll(A, C) \geq 0.3$? And if that is possible, then what can we say about the possible values of $be^\ll(A, C)$?

7.3.2.1. *Strategy adopted*

To solve the problems such as that of example 7.4, the strategy adopted in [SCH 08a] is to translate them in terms of constraints which are disjunctive linear relations (DLRs) (see Appendix C), and to make use of the complexity results which are known for DLRs, namely, NP-completeness of the satisfaction problem in the general case, and polynomiality for Horn DLRs.

When discussing networks on the fuzzy interval algebra, we have already observed that only those degrees of membership which appear in a given fuzzy constraint network actually intervene in the study of the satisfaction of this network. A general principle here (about which we will say more below) is that, in many cases, it is possible to restrict the values we consider to a finite set of values which constitute a finite subdivision of the interval $[0, 1]$. More precisely, let $M = \{0, \Delta, 2\Delta, \ldots, 1\}$, where $\Delta = \frac{1}{\rho}$, for $\rho \in \mathbb{N} \setminus \{0\}$; let M_0 denote the set $M \setminus \{0\}$ and M_1 the set $M \setminus \{0\}$. Then many questions will be reducible to considering values in M, for a suitable M.

The reader is advised to keep in mind these two points: the use of translations in terms of DLRs on the one hand, and the equivalence with constraints on a finite set of values on the other hand, as guidelines for understanding the following technical passages.

Our presentation closely follows [SCH 08a].

7.3.2.2. *FI-formulas, FI_M-formulas, and satisfaction*

In all definitions to follow, M is a fixed set.

DEFINITION 7.10.– *An atomic FI-formula on a set X of variables is an expression of the form $r(x, y) \geq l$ or $r(x, y) \leq k$, where $l \in M_0$, $k \in M_1$, $(x, y) \in X^2$, and where r is one of the relations $bb_d^\ll$, $ee_d^\ll$, $be_d^\ll$ $eb_d^\ll$. An FI-formula on X is a finite disjunction $\phi_1 \vee \ldots \vee \phi_n$ of atomic FI-formulas on X. We say that it is disjunctive if $n > 1$.*

NOTE 7.3.– Clearly, the constraint $bb_d^{\prec}(x, y) \geq l$, for example, is equivalent to the constraint $bb_d^{\prec}(x, y) \leq 1 - l$. Hence we do not have to consider explicitly formulas containing $bb^{\prec}$ and its analogs, except as possible abbreviations.

The definition of an interpretation (or FI-interpretation) and of the satisfiability of a set of FI-formulas, or *FI-satisfiability* are rather self-evident:

DEFINITION 7.11.– *An FI-interpretation m of a set of variables X is a map which, to each variable $x \in X$, associates a fuzzy interval $m(x)$. It is called an FI_M-interpretation if the degrees of membership $m(x)$ are elements of M.*

DEFINITION 7.12.– *A set Θ of FI-formulas on a set of variables X is FI-satisfiable (FI_M-satisfiable respectively) if there is an FI-interpretation (an FI_M-interpretation respectively) of X such that all the constraints of Θ are satisfied.*

As far as we only consider *finite* set of constraints, we may always reduce FI-satisfiability to FI_M-satisfiability:

PROPOSITION 7.4.– *Let Θ be a finite set of FI-formulas on a set of variables X. Then, Θ is FI-satisfiable if, and only if, it is FI_M-satisfiable.*

We will not enter into the details of the proof of this property. Clearly, it is enough to show that, if there is an FI-interpretation satisfying Θ, we can build a FI_M-interpretation having the same property.

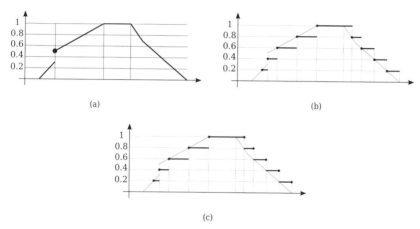

(a)

(b)

(c)

Figure 7.3. *From a fuzzy interval (a) to a step function (b) with values in M, then to a fuzzy interval (c) with values in M (after [SCH 08a]*

The construction may be described in a simple way in geometrical terms: for each interval $m(x)$ of the given interpretation, which is a function $m(x)\colon \mathbb{R} \rightarrow [0.1]$, we consider the graph of this fuzzy interval (refer to Figure 7.3). The function is upper semi-continuous. It has an increasing part, a constant part, and a decreasing part.

1) Consider the successive "horizontal slices" cut out by the elements of M, i.e. $0, \Delta, \ldots, 1$;

2) in the increasing part, for $k = 0, \ldots, \rho$, in the layer situated between the values $k\Delta$ and $(k+1)\Delta$, we project the corresponding part of the graph on the right semi-open interval of the line with abscissa $k\Delta$.

3) in the decreasing part, for $k = 0, \ldots, \rho$, in the layer situated between the values $k\Delta$ and $(k+1)\Delta$, we project the corresponding part of the graph on the right semi-open interval of the line with abscissa $(k+1)\Delta$.

The graph of $m(x)$ (refer to Figure 7.3(a)) is then replaced by the graph of a step function whose ascending steps are left-closed, and whose descending steps are also left-closed; the higher step corresponding to value 1 is also a left-closed interval; to get an interpretation that satisfies the definition of a fuzzy interval, we only have to replace the interval at the top by its closure, and to replace all semi-intervals of the descending part, which are left-closed, by their right-closed versions (Figure 7.3(c)).

Clearly, the a-cuts of $m(x)$ are closed intervals, and we thus have a FI_M-interpretation. It is tedious but easy to check that it satisfies the required constraints.

Thus, in order to study FI-satisfiabilty, it is enough to consider FI_M-satisfiability.

7.3.2.3. *Atomic formulas and DLRs*

The fundamental result which makes it possible to express fuzzy constraints in terms of disjunctive linear relations is that, for fuzzy intervals whose degrees of membership belong to M, the basic FI-formulas correspond to systems of linear equations on the set of variables constituted by the bounding points of the a-cuts of these intervals, for $a \in M$. More precisely, we have the following result for the relation $bb_d^{\lll}$ and its analogues:

PROPOSITION 7.5.– *Let A and B be two fuzzy intervals whose degrees of membership belong to the set M, and let $k \in M_1$ and $l \in M_0$. Then, we have the equivalences of Table 7.1.*

7.3.2.4. *Translation in terms of linear constraints*

At this point, a way of solving a system of atomic FI-formulas becomes apparent: given a set Θ on a set of variables X, one can proceed in the following way:

For each $x \in X$ (which denotes a fuzzy interval), introduce variables $x_\Delta^-, x_{2\Delta}^-, \ldots, x_1^-$ (which will stand for the left bounding points of the successive a-cuts of x, for $a = \Delta, 2\Delta, \ldots, 1$), and variables $x_\Delta^+, x_{2\Delta}^+, \ldots, x_1^+$ (which will stand for the right bounding points of these same a-cuts).

Enforce the conditions that these values should define intervals, hence that $x_1^- \leq x_1^+$, and that for any $m \in M_1 \backslash \{0\}$, one has $x_m^- \leq x_{m+\Delta}^-$ and $x_{m+\Delta}^+ \leq x_m^+$, so that the intervals $[x_m^-, x_m^+]$ may be effectively interpreted as the a-cuts of a fuzzy interval.

Proposition 7.5 can now be used to translate each of the constraints of Θ, which are atomic FI-formulas, in terms of linear inequalities.

$bb_d^{\ll}(A, B) \geq l \Leftrightarrow$

$$A_l^- < B_\Delta^- - d \vee A_{l+\Delta}^- < B_{2\Delta}^- - d \vee A_1^- \cdots \vee B_{1-l+\Delta}^- - d \qquad [7.11]$$

$bb_d^{\ll}(A, B) \leq k \Leftrightarrow$

$$B_\Delta^- \leq A_{k+\Delta}^- + d \wedge B_{2\Delta}^- \leq A_{k+2\Delta}^- + d \wedge \cdots \wedge B_{1-k}^- \leq A_1^- + d \qquad [7.12]$$

$ee_d^{\ll}(A, B) \geq l \Leftrightarrow$

$$A_\Delta^+ < B_l^+ - d \vee A_{2\Delta}^+ < B_{l+\Delta}^+ - d \vee A_{1-l+\Delta}^+ \cdots \vee_\Delta < B_1^+ - d \qquad [7.13]$$

$ee_d^{\ll}(A, B) \leq k \Leftrightarrow$

$$B_{k+\Delta}^+ \leq A_\Delta^+ + d \wedge B_{k+2\Delta}^+ \leq A_{2\Delta}^+ + d \wedge \cdots \wedge B_1^+ \leq A_{1-k}^+ + d \qquad [7.14]$$

$be_d^{\ll}(A, B) \geq l \Leftrightarrow$

$$A_l^- < B_1^+ - d \vee A_{l+\Delta}^- < B_{1-\Delta}^+ - d \vee \cdots \vee A_1^- < B_l^+ - d \qquad [7.15]$$

$be_d^{\ll}(A, B) \leq k \Leftrightarrow$

$$B_1^+ \leq A_{k+\Delta}^- + d \wedge B_{1-\Delta}^+ \leq A_{k+2\Delta}^- + d \wedge \cdots \wedge B_{k+\Delta}^+ \leq A_1^- + d \qquad [7.16]$$

$eb_d^{\ll}(A, B) \geq l \Leftrightarrow$

$$A_1^+ < B_{1-l+\Delta}^- - d \wedge A_{1-\Delta}^+ < B_{1-l+2\Delta}^- - d \wedge \cdots \wedge A_{1-l+\Delta}^+ < B_1^- - d \qquad [7.17]$$

$eb_d^{\ll}(A, B) \leq k \Leftrightarrow$

$$B_{1-k}^- \leq A_1^+ + d \vee B_{1-k+\Delta}^- \leq A_{1-\Delta}^+ + d \vee \cdots \vee B_1^- \leq A_{1-k}^+ + d \qquad [7.18]$$

Table 7.1. *The equivalences of the atomic relations for intervals with values in M (proposition 7.5)*

For example, if Θ contains the formula $bb_d^{\ll}(x, y) \leq k$, the following set of linear constraints is introduced:

$$\{y_\Delta^- \leq x_{k+\Delta}^- + d, y_{2\Delta}^- \leq x_{k+2\Delta}^- + d, \ldots, y_{1-k}^- \leq x_1^- + d\} \qquad [7.19]$$

Similarly, if Θ contains the formula $bb_d^{\ll}(x, y) \geq l$, the linear constraint is introduced:

$$x_l^- < y_\Delta^- - d \vee \leq x_{l+\Delta}^- < y_{2\Delta}^- - d \vee \ldots \vee x_1^- < y_{1-l+\Delta}^- - d \qquad [7.20]$$

If Ψ denotes the set of linear constraints obtained in this way, one has the following proposition:

PROPOSITION 7.6.– *The finite set of atomic FI-formula Θ is FI-satisfiable if, and only if, the system of linear constraints Ψ has a solution.*

NOTE 7.4.– Schockaert and De Cock's approach thus yields a general method for reducing the FI-satisfiability problem to a system of linear constraints. In addition, the equivalence is flexible enough to accomodate the enforcement of additional properties on the intervals; for instance, the condition that an interval x be a classic interval is expressed by the linear constraints $x_\Delta^- = x_{2\Delta}^-, x_{2\Delta}^- = x_{3\Delta}^-, \ldots, x_{1-\Delta}^- = x_1^-, x_\Delta^+ = x_{1-\Delta}^+, \ldots, x_{2\Delta}^+ = x_\Delta^+$, while the condition that x should not be punctual is expressed by adding $x_1^- < x_1^+$.

The preceding discussion shows that algorithms such as the linear programming algorithms (see Appendix C) may be used for testing FI-satisfiability. We may also use them to find solutions when the sets of FI-formulas are satisfiable.

7.3.3. An example of application

EXAMPLE 7.5.– To illustrate the use of these techniques, Schockaert and De Cock use the example of the periodization of Picasso's work. We follow the presentation given in [SCH 08a].

The problem consists of reasoning about the three following events:

– BFT: creation of "Bread and Fruit Dish on a Table";

– DMA: creation of "Les Demoiselles d'Avignon";

– AC: Picasso's Analytical Cubism period;

– C: Picasso's Cubist period.

The fact that the painting "Bread and Fruit Dish on a Table" marks the beginning of Picasso's "Analytical Cubism" period can be expressed by writing that each of the two periods BFT and AC begins (in the broad sense) before the other, and that the period BFT finishes before the period AC finishes. We can thus write:

$$bb^{\preceq}(BFT, AC) \geq \lambda_1 \qquad\qquad\qquad [7.21]$$

$$bb^{\preceq}(AC, BFT) \geq \lambda_2 \qquad\qquad\qquad [7.22]$$

$$ee^{\ll}(BFT, AC) \geq \lambda_3 \qquad\qquad\qquad [7.23]$$

keeping in mind that the three constants λ_1, λ_2, and λ_1 are as close to 1 as possible.

Similarly, the fact that "Les Demoiselles d'Avignon" mark the beginning of Picasso's Cubist period can be expressed by writing:

$$bb^{\preceq}(DMA, C) \geq \lambda_4 \qquad\qquad\qquad [7.24]$$

$$bb^{\preceq}(C, DMA) \geq \lambda_5 \qquad\qquad\qquad [7.25]$$

$$ee^{\ll}(DMA, C) \geq \lambda_6 \qquad\qquad\qquad [7.26]$$

Now the fact that the "Analytical Cubism" period is the first stage of the Cubist period can be written as:

$$bb^{\preceq}(AC, C) \geq \lambda_7 \tag{7.27}$$

$$bb^{\preceq}(C, AC) \geq \lambda_8 \tag{7.28}$$

$$ee^{\ll}(AC, C) \geq \lambda_9 \tag{7.29}$$

Lastly, we may introduce knowledge of a quantitative nature: "Les Demoiselles Avignon" was painted in 1907, "Bread and Fruit Dish on a Table" in 1909, and the "Analytical Cubism" period extends roughly from 1908 to 1912. Introducing a variable Z to represent the year 1900, we thus have:

$$bb_8^{\preceq}(Z, AC) \geq \lambda_{10} \tag{7.30}$$

$$bb_{-9}^{\ll}(AC, Z) \geq \lambda_{11} \tag{7.31}$$

$$ee_{12}^{\preceq}(Z, AC) \geq \lambda_{12} \tag{7.32}$$

$$ee_{-13}^{\ll}(AC, Z) \geq \lambda_{13} \tag{7.33}$$

$$bb_9^{\preceq}(Z, BFT) \geq \lambda_{14} \tag{7.34}$$

$$ee_{-10}^{\ll}(BFT, Z) \geq \lambda_{15} \tag{7.35}$$

$$bb_7^{\preceq}(Z, DMA) \geq \lambda_{16} \tag{7.36}$$

$$ee_{-8}^{\ll}(DMA, Z) \geq \lambda_{17} \tag{7.37}$$

Since Z represents a well-defined year, it is natural to assume that it is a classical non-fuzzy value and thus to add the constraints:

$$Z_{\Delta}^- = Z_{2\Delta}^- = \cdots = Z_1^- = Z_1^+ = \cdots = Z_{\Delta}^+$$

This example is typical of the fact that the choice of $\lambda_1 = \cdots = \lambda_{17} = 1$ often results in a system of constraints which is inconsistent. We then have to relax the constraints to arrive at a consistent system, then to reinforce them, parameter by parameter, in order to try to obtain an optimal situation.

Here, we can assume that the events indicated by Z, BFT, and DMA are not fuzzy, and enforce that $\lambda_{14} = \lambda_{15} = \lambda_{16} = \lambda_{17} = 1$. Without further information, one can start by supposing that the 13 other parameters are equal. Then Schockaert and De Cock show that, for $\Delta = 0.25$, a maximally FI-satisfiable representation is given by:

$$\lambda_{14} = \lambda_{15} = \lambda_{16} = \lambda_{17} = 1$$

$$\lambda_2 = \lambda_3 = \lambda_4 = \lambda_6 = \lambda_7 = \lambda_8 = \lambda_9 = \lambda_{10} = \lambda_{12} = \lambda_{13} = 1$$

$$\lambda_1 = \lambda_5 = \lambda_{11} = 0.5$$

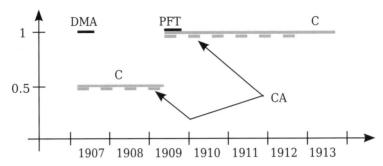

Figure 7.4. *A fuzzy interpretation: "Les Demoiselles d'Avignon" (DMA), "Bread and Fruit Dish on a Table" (BFT), the Cubism period ((C), in gray) and the Analytical Cubism period (AC), in gray dotted lines (after [SCH 08a])*

Figure 7.4 (taken from [SCH 08a]) illustrates this interpretation, in which the Cubism period and the Analytical Cubism period are represented by fuzzy intervals which have already started in 1907 (with a fuzzy truth-value equal to 0.5) and have fully started in 1909.

7.3.4. *Complexity*

We have seen that the satisfiability problem for FI-formulas on a set X of variables is equivalent to that of the satisfiability of a system of DLRs. For such systems, this problem is NP-complete when arbitrary disjunctions are allowed. If we have an oracle that lets us know which components of a disjunctive FI-formula must be satisfied, we get atomic FI-formulas, whose satisfiability problem is reducible in polynomial time to that of a system of linear constraints. The problem is thus an NP-complete problem.

Proposition 7.5 can be used to describe explicitly a subset the set of the FI-formulas on X which is assured to lead to non-disjunctive linear constraints.

Indeed:

– the formulas
$$bb_d^{\lll}(A, B) \leq k, \ ee_d^{\lll}(A, B) \leq k, \ be_d^{\lll}(A, B) \leq k \text{ and } eb_d^{\lll}(A, B) \geq l$$
correspond to conjunctions of linear relations;

– the formulas
$$bb_d^{\lll}(A, B) \geq 1, \ ee_d^{\lll}(A, B) \geq 1, \ be_d^{\lll}(A, B) \geq 1, \ eb_d^{\lll}(A, B) \leq 0$$
correspond to the constraints
$$A_1^- < B_\Delta^- - d, A_\Delta^+ < B_1^+ - d, A_1^- < B_1^+ - d \text{ and } B_1^- < A_1^+ + d, \text{ respectively.}$$

Consequently, the set $\mathcal{F}'_X$ defined by the following formula results in linear relations without disjunctions:

$$\mathcal{F}_X' = \bigcup_{(x,y)\in X^2} \bigcup_{d\in\mathbb{R}} (\{bb_d^{\lll}(x,y) \le k \mid k \in M_1\} \cup \{ee_d^{\lll}(x,y) \le k \mid k \in M_1\}$$

$$\cup \{be_d^{\lll}(x,y) \le k \mid k \in M_1\} \cup \{eb_d^{\lll}(x,y) \ge l \mid l \in M_0\}$$

$$\cup \{bb_d^{\lll}(x,y) \ge 1, ee_d^{\lll}(x,y) \ge 1, be_d^{\lll}(x,y) \ge 1, eb_d^{\lll}(x,y) \le 0\}$$

This implies that for the formulas in $\mathcal{F}_X'$ the satisfiability problem is tractable. More precisely, the resolution procedure described above is weakly polynomial (it depends on the choice of $\frac{1}{\Delta} = \rho$).

As already mentioned, the general problem is NP-complete; more precisely:

PROPOSITION 7.7.– *([SCH 08a], proposition 4) Let $k \in M_1 \setminus \{0\}$ and $d \in \mathbb{R}$. The satisfiability problem of a set $\mathcal{A}$ of FI-formulas is NP-complete if $\mathcal{A}$ contains at least one of the following sets of FI-formulas:*

$$\mathcal{F}_X' \bigcup_{(x,y)\in X^2} \{bb_d^{\lll}(x,y) \ge k\} \qquad [7.38]$$

$$\mathcal{F}_X' \bigcup_{(x,y)\in X^2} \{ee_d^{\lll}(x,y) \ge k\} \qquad [7.39]$$

$$\mathcal{F}_X' \bigcup_{(x,y)\in X^2} \{be_d^{\lll}(x,y) \ge k\} \qquad [7.40]$$

$$\mathcal{F}_X' \bigcup_{(x,y)\in X^2} \{eb_d^{\lll}(x,y) \le k\} \qquad [7.41]$$

The proof uses the fact that it is possible to encode the 3SAT problem in terms of these relations.

Hence, the atomic FI-formulas mentioned in proposition 7.7 cannot be used without losing the tractability property. A similar result holds for the disjunctive formulas considered in the following proposition:

PROPOSITION 7.8.– *([SCH 08a], proposition 5) Let $d \in \mathbb{R}$, and let $r_d, s_d \in \{bb_d^{\lll}, ee_d^{\lll}, be_d^{\lll}, eb_d^{\lll}\}$. The satisfiability problem of a set $\mathcal{A}$ of FI-formulas is NP-complete if $\mathcal{A}$ contains at least one of the following sets of FI-formulas:*

$$\mathcal{F}_X' \bigcup_{(x,y,z,t)\in X^4} \{r_{d_1}(x,y) \ge l_1 \vee s_{d_2}(z,t) \ge l_1\} \qquad [7.42]$$

$$\mathcal{F}_X' \bigcup_{(x,y,z,t)\in X^4} \{r_{d_1}(x,y) \ge l_1 \vee s_{d_2}(z,t) \le k_2\} \qquad [7.43]$$

$$\mathcal{F}'_X \bigcup_{(x,y,z,t)\in X^4} \{r_{d_1}(x,y) \leq k_1 \vee s_{d_2}(z,t) \leq k_2\} \qquad\qquad [7.44]$$

for all $d_1, d_2 \in \mathbb{R}, l_1, l_2 \in M_0$, and $k_1, k_2 \in M_1$.

7.3.4.1. *Horn FI-formulas*

An interesting example of a set of tractable relations, in view of the results in the classical case, is provided by the set of FI-formulas whose translations are Horn linear constraints.

DEFINITION 7.13.– *Let $\mathcal{G}_X$ be the set of FI-formulas defined in the following manner*:

$$\mathcal{G}_X = \bigcup_{(x,y)\in X^2} \bigcup_{d\in\mathbb{R}} \{bb_d^{\ll}(x,y) \geq \Delta \vee bb_{-d}^{\ll}(y,x) \geq \Delta$$

$$ee_d^{\ll}(x,y) \geq \Delta \vee ee_{-d}^{\ll}(y,x) \geq \Delta$$

$$be_d^{\ll}(x,y) \geq 1 \vee be_{-d}^{\ll}(y,x) \geq 1\}$$

DEFINITION 7.14.– *Let $\mathcal{H}_X$ be the set of FI-formulas recursively defined by*:
1) *if $\varphi \in \mathcal{F}'_X$, then $\varphi \in \mathcal{H}_X$*;
2) *if $\varphi_1 \in \mathcal{H}_X$ and $\varphi_2 \in \mathcal{G}_X$ then $(\varphi_1 \vee \varphi_2) \in \mathcal{H}_X$*;
3) *$\mathcal{H}_X$ does not contain any other element.*

Any formula of $\mathcal{H}_X$ corresponds to a set of Horn linear constraints, and is thus tractable.

When $\Delta = 1$, that is when the only elements of M are 0 and 1, we know that an FI-formula is satisfiable if, and only if, it accepts an interpretation in terms of *classical intervals* (proposition 7.4). In this case, $\mathcal{H}_X$ is exactly the set of Horn linear constraints on the bounding points of these intervals.

7.3.5. *Weak logical consequence*

An aspect of fuzzy reasoning which distinguishes it from classical reasoning has to do with the notion of logical consequence. According to the usual definition, if Θ is a set of FI-formulas on X, and γ is an FI-formula on X, we say that γ is a *logical consequence* of Θ, which is denoted by $\Theta \vDash \gamma$, if γ is true in any FI-model of Θ. Equivalently, this means that the set of formulas formed by Θ and the negation of γ is not satisfiable. However, the problem here is that the procedure to test satisfiability does not apply to strict inequalities.

For example, to decide whether $\Theta \vDash bb_d^{\ll}(x,y) \leq k$, it is necessary to determine the satisfiability of $\Theta \cup \{bb_d^{\ll}(x,y) > k\}$. However, it is obvious that $bb_d^{\ll}(x,y) > k$ if $bb_d^{\ll}(x,y) \leq k + \Delta$. Accordingly, Schockaert and De Cock introduce a concept of weak logical consequence:

DEFINITION 7.15.– *Let Θ be a set of FI-formulas on X, and γ an FI-formula on X. Then γ is a* weak logical consequence *of Θ, which is denoted by $\Theta \vDash_M \gamma$, if any FI_M-model of Θ is also an FI_M- model of γ.*

Weak logical consequence is reducible to FI-satisfiability in an obvious way:

PROPOSITION 7.9.– *Let Θ be a set of FI-formulas, and $r(x,y)$ one of the formulas $bb_d^{\ll}(x,y), ee_d^{\ll}(x,y), be_d^{\ll}(x,y)$ and $eb_d^{\ll}(x,y)$. For $k \in M_1$ and $l \in M_0$, we have the equivalences:*

1) $\Theta \vDash_M r(x,y) \geq l$ *if, and only if,* $\Theta \cup \{r(x,y) \leq l - \Delta\}$ *is not FI-satisfiable;*

2) $\Theta \vDash_M r(x,y) \geq k$ *if, and only if,* $\Theta \cup \{r(x,y) \geq k + \Delta\}$ *is not FI-satisfiable.*

Proof. This is an immediate consequence of the fact that for any FI_M-interpretation m, the condition $r(m(x), m(y)) < l$ implies that $r(m(x), m(y)) \leq l - \Delta$, and that $r(m(x), m(y)) > k$ implies $r(m(x), m(y)) \geq k + \Delta$. □

In general, the concept of weak logical consequence is weaker than the concept of logical consequence: if γ is a logical consequence of Θ, it is *a fortiori* a weak logical consequence of θ, but the converse is not true. However, it is a useful concept, as it allows a correct determination of consequences, as shown by the following proposition:

PROPOSITION 7.10.– *Let Θ be a set of FI-formulas, and $r(x,y)$ one of the formulas $bb_d^{\ll}(x,y), ee_d^{\ll}(x,y), be_d^{\ll}(x,y)$, and $eb_d^{\ll}(x,y)$. For $k \in M_1 \setminus \{1 - \Delta\}$ and $l \in M_0 \setminus \{Delta\}$, we have:*

1) *if* $\Theta \vDash_M r(x,y) \geq l$, *then* $\Theta \vDash r(x,y) \geq l - \Delta$;

2) *if* $\Theta \vDash_M r(x,y) \leq k$, *then* $\Theta \vDash r(x,y) \geq k + \Delta$.

The question arises to determine for which FI-formulas the concept of weak logical consequence coincides with that of logical consequence. A first result is given in [SCH 08a] for logical consequences which are upper bounds of $bb_d^{\ll}(x,y), ee_d^{\ll}(x,y), be_d^{\ll}(x,y)$ and lower bounds of $eb_d^{\ll}(x,y)$:

PROPOSITION 7.11.– *Let Θ be a set of* atomic *FI-formulas For $k \in M_1$ and $l \in M_0$; we have the following equivalences:*

1) $\Theta \vDash bb_d^{\ll}(x,y) \leq k$ *if, and only if,* $\Theta \cup \{bb_d^{\ll}(x,y) \geq k + \Delta\}$ *is not FI-satisfiable;*

2) $\Theta \models ee_d^{\ll}(x, y) \leq k$ *if, and only if,* $\Theta \cup \{ee_d^{\ll}(x, y) \geq k + \Delta\}$ *is not FI-satisfiable;*

3) $\Theta \models be_d^{\ll}(x, y) \leq k$ *if, and only if,* $\Theta \cup \{be_d^{\ll}(x, y) \geq k + \Delta\}$ *is not FI-satisfiable;*

4) $\Theta \models eb_d^{\ll}(x, y) \geq l$ *if, and only if,* $\Theta \cup \{eb_d^{\ll}(x, y) \leq l - \Delta\}$ *is not FI-satisfiable.*

In the case of lower bounds of $bb_d^{\ll}(x, y), ee_d^{\ll}(x, y), be_d^{\ll}(x, y)$ and upper bounds of $eb_d^{\ll}(x, y)$, the result obtained concerns the atomic formulas of the set $\mathcal{F}_X'$:

PROPOSITION 7.12.– *Let* Θ *be a set of atomic FI-formulas of* $\mathcal{F}_X'$. *For* $k \in M_1$ *and* $l \in M_0$, *we have the following equivalences:*

1) $\Theta \models be_d^{\ll}(x, y) \geq l$ *if, and only if,* $\Theta \cup \{be_d^{\ll}(x, y) \leq l - \Delta\}$ *is not FI-satisfiable;*

2) $\Theta \models eb_d^{\ll}(x, y) \leq k$ *if, and only if,* $\Theta \cup \{eb_d^{\ll}(x, y) \geq k + \Delta\}$ *is not FI-satisfiable;*

Moreover, for $l \in M_0 \setminus \{\Delta\}$, *we have the equivalences:*

3) $\Theta \models bb_d^{\ll}(x, y) \geq l$ *if, and only if,* $\Theta \cup \{bb_d^{\ll}(x, y) \leq l - \Delta\}$ *is not FI-satisfiable;*

4) $\Theta \models ee_d^{\ll}(x, y) \geq l$ *if, and only if,* $\Theta \cup \{ee_d^{\ll}(x, y) \leq l - \Delta\}$ *is not FI-satisfiable.*

7.3.6. *Assessment*

The framework for reasoning about fuzzy intervals presented by Schockaert and De Cock makes use of fuzzy relations which are analogs of the relations between the endpoints of classical intervals. A fundamental property of the approach is that it allows a reduction to fuzzy functions with finite domain. Translating the inequalities obtained in terms of disjunctive linear relations (DLRs) makes it possible to reformulate the satisfiability problem in terms of the satisfiability of DLRs, hence to solve it by using linear programming techniques, and to characterize tractable subclasses, including a tractable subclass which is the analog of ORD-Horn relations in the classical case.

Several of the topics which have arisen in our presentation of reasoning about fuzzy intervals will appear again in the fuzzy version of the RCC-8 calculus elaborated by Schockaert, De Cock, and Kerre which is presented in the following section.

7.4. Fuzzy spatial reasoning: a fuzzy RCC

7.4.1. *Motivations*

In the same way as many temporal entities have inherently vague extensions — recall the example of Picasso's Blue period — it is also a fact of everyday life that many spatial concepts are only vaguely defined: for instance, what do we precisely understand by "Central London", or the "Los Angeles region"? If we are interested in a commonsense definition of those expressions, rather than in an administrative one, we may be at a loss to decide whether a given location belongs to those regions. The problem is well known in the field of geographical applications, as testified by many publications [ERW 97, FIS 00, BEN 02b, BIT 02, MON 03, EVA 07, BEN 08c].

The solutions to this problem which have been proposed in the literature include the super evaluation semantics [BEN 02b, KUL 01, VAR 01], the theory of coarse sets [BIL 02], and the *egg-yolk theory* [COH 96]. In the framework of the egg-yolk theory, a vague region u is represented by a pair of regions $(\bar{u} \supseteq \underline{u})$; $\underline{u}$ is a region whose all points are definitely in u, while $\bar{u}$ is a region whose points are possibly in u. In the context of fuzzy set theory, as exemplified by [GOO 98, FIS 00, LI 04b, LIU 06, SHI 07], we may consider that these pairs of regions are particular cases of fuzzy sets in which the degree of membership is 1 for $\underline{u}$, 0.5 for $\bar{u}$, and 0 outside $\bar{u}$.

In what follows, we describe the approach of [SCH 08b, SCH 09], which is based on a fuzzy interpretation of the connection relation C of the RCC formalism.

7.4.2. *Fuzzy regions*

The precise nature of the regions considered in the formalism is deliberately left undefined. However, two types of models are predominantly targeted:

– the first type of models are the $(n; \alpha, \beta)$-models, to be defined hereafter. They involve bounded non-empty regions in the Euclidean space $\mathbb{R}^n$. In this case, the connection relation is defined by using fuzzy distance between the regions;

– the second type of models involves fuzzy regions whose degrees of membership belong to a finite set $M = \{\Delta, 2\Delta, \dots, 1\}$ (the situation is similar to that considered previously for fuzzy intervals). In this case, the regions are characterized by their a-cuts (for $a \in M$), and the connection relation can be expressed in classical terms.

The reason for leaving the precise nature of the models considered undefined is that most of the results of the study turn out to be valid irrespective of the models considered. In the meantime, we ask the reader to adopt an agnostic position toward the matter.

7.4.3. *Fuzzy* RCC *relations*

The starting point of [SCH 09] is a universe U of fuzzy regions, whose precise nature remains to be defined. A (fuzzy) region $u \in U$ is hence a function $u: D \to [0, 1]$, where D is some domain of classical "regions". On this universe, we consider a fuzzy binary connection relation C: $U \times U \to [0.1]$. This fuzzy relation is assumed to be reflexive and symmetrical:

$$(\forall u \in U)\mathsf{C}(u, u) = 1 \text{ and } (\forall u, v \in U)\mathsf{C}(u, v) = \mathsf{C}(v, u)$$

The fuzzy relations deduced from C are the 11 relations defined in Table 7.2, which also recalls the classical definitions of these relations. As described above (section 7.3), the T-norm used is the Łukasiewicz T-norm, and I_T indicates the implicator associated with this T-norm. It is shown in [SCH 08b] that the definitions of these relations coincide with the classical definitions when the regions are classical regions, i.e. the elements of U take their values from the set $\{0, 1\}$.

Relation	Classical definition	Fuzzy definition
$DC(u, v)$	$\neg C(u, v)$	$1 - C(u, v)$
$P(u, v)$	$(\forall w \in U)(C(w, u) \Rightarrow C(w, v))$	$\inf_{w \in U} I_T(C(w, u), C(w, v))$
$PP(u, v)$	$P(u, v) \wedge \neg P(v, u)$	$\inf(P(u, v), 1 - P(v, u))$
$EQ(u, v)$	$P(u, v) \wedge P(v, u)$	$\inf(P(u, v), P(v, u))$
$O(u, v)$	$(\exists w \in U)P(w, u) \wedge P(w, v)$	$\sup_{w \in U} T(P(w, u), P(w, v))$
$DR(u, v)$	$\neg O(u, v)$	$1 - O(u, v)$
$PO(u, v)$	$O(u, v) \wedge \neg P(u, v) \wedge \neg P(v, u)$	$\inf(O(u, v), 1 - P(u, v), 1 - P(v, u))$
$EC(u, v)$	$C(u, v) \wedge \neg O(u, v)$	$\inf(C(u, v), 1 - O(u, v))$
$NTP(u, v)$	$(\forall w \in U)(C(w, u) \Rightarrow O(w, v))$	$\inf_{w \in U} I_T(C(w, u), O(w, v))$
$TPP(u, v)$	$PP(u, v) \wedge \neg NTP(u, v)$	$\inf(PP(u, v), 1 - NTP(u, v))$
$NTPP(u, v)$	$PP(u, v) \wedge NTP(u, v)$	$\inf(1 - P(v, u), NTP(v, u))$

Table 7.2. *Classical and fuzzy definitions of the basic* RCC *relations*

Let us recall that, in accordance with the general definitions of fuzzy relations, the inverse R^{-1} of a fuzzy relation R is the relation defined by:

$$R^{-1}(u, v) = R(v, u)$$

Its complementary relation, denoted by coR, is the relation defined by:

$$coR(u, v) = 1 - R(u, v)$$

In addition, the relations defined in that way satisfy the following properties:

– O and P are reflexive relations;

– O is a symmetrical relation;

– for any pair of fuzzy regions $u, v \in U$, we have:

$$NTP(u, v) \le P(u, v) \le O(u, v) \le C(u, v)$$

Lastly, the analog of the classical composition table is a fuzzy "composition table" (Table 7.3), whose significance is the following: the entry K located in the line R and the column S is such that:

$$(\forall u, v, w \in U)T(R(u, v), S(v, w)) \le K(u, w)$$

	C	DC	P	P^{-1}	coP	coP^{-1}	O	DR	NTP	NTP^{-1}	coNTP	coNTP^{-1}
C	1	coP	C	1	1	1	1	coNTP	O	1	1	1
DC	coP^{-1}	1	coP^{-1}	DC	1	1	coP^{-1}	1	coP^{-1}	DC	1	1
P	1	DC	P	1	coP	coP^{-1}	1	DR	NTP	1	1	coNTP^{-1}
P^{-1}	C	coP	O	P^{-1}	1	1	O	coP	O	NTP^{-1}	coNTP	1
coP	1	1	1	coP	1	1	1	1	1	coP	1	1
coP^{-1}	1	1	coP^{-1}	1	1	1	1	1	coP^{-1}	1	1	1
O	1	coP	O	1	1	1	1	coP	O	1	1	1
DR	coNTP^{-1}	1	coP^{-1}	DR	1	coP^{-1}	coP^{-1}	1	coP^{-1}	DC	1	1
NTP	1	DC	NTP	1	1	coP^{-1}	1	DC	NTP	1	1	coP^{-1}
NTP^{-1}	0	coP	O	NTP^{-1}	coP	1	O	coP	O	NTP^{-1}	coP	1
coNTP	1	1	1	coNTP	1	1	1	1	1	coP	1	1
coNTP^{-1}	1	1	coNTP^{-1}	1	1	1	1	1	coP^{-1}	1	1	1

Table 7.3. A fuzzy analog of the RCC composition table: the entry K in row R and column S is such that, for any 3-tuple of regions (u, v, w), the T-norm of $R(u, v)$ and $S(v, w)$ is bounded from above by $K(u, w)$. For example (row 9, column 8), we have for all u, v, w
$$T(\text{NTP}(u, v), \text{DR}(v, w)) \leq \text{DC}(u, w)$$

7.4.3.1. *A fuzzy composition table*

Using those definitions, Schockaert *et al.* prove that the analog of the classical composition table is as shown in Table 7.3.

7.4.4. *Fuzzy* RCC *formulas*

Similarly to the temporal case, the fuzzy formulas considered here are formulas which express upper or lower bounds for the degrees of satisfaction of $R(x, y)$, where R is one of the relations considered in Table 7.3:

DEFINITION 7.16.– *An* atomic fuzzy RCC formula *is an expression of the form* $R(x, y) \leq \lambda$ *or* $R(x, y) \geq \lambda$, *where* R *is one of the 12 relations* C, DC, P, P^{-1}, *co* P, *co*P^{-1}, O, DR, NTP, NTP^{-1}, *co*NTP, *and co*NTP^{-1}.

DEFINITION 7.17.– *A* fuzzy RCC formula *is a disjunction* $\varphi \vee \ldots \vee \varphi_k$ *of atomic fuzzy* RCC *formulas.*

Introducing the relation NTP, which is not part of the relations considered in the classical case, is motivated by notational convenience. This relation is used to define *standard* sets of formulas:

DEFINITION 7.18.– *A set of fuzzy* RCC *formulas is called* standard *if it does not contain atomic formulas of the form* $NTP(x, y) \leq \lambda$ *or* $NTP(x, y) \geq \lambda$.

7.4.5. *Semantics*

An interpretation of fuzzy RCC formulas in a universe U of regions is defined as follows:

DEFINITION 7.19.– *An* interpretation *is a map* m *which associates a fuzzy region to each variable* $x \in X$, *and to* C *a fuzzy binary relation between regions.*

The definition of the satisfiability of a fuzzy RCC formula is what may be expected:

DEFINITION 7.20.– *An interpretation* m *satisfies the atomic formula* $R(x, y) \leq \lambda$ *($R(x, y) \geq \lambda$, respectively) if* $m(R)(m(x), m(y)) \leq \lambda$ *($m(R)(m(x), m(y)) \geq \lambda$, respectively). It satisfies the disjunctive formula* $\varphi_1 \vee \ldots \vee \varphi_k$ *if it satisfies at least one of the* φ_i, *for* $1 \leq i \leq k$. *It satisfies a set* Θ *of formulas if it satisfies each formula in* Θ.

NOTE 7.5.– If we examine the definitions of the fuzzy RCC relations other than C, we notice that the only relations among the 11 relations whose definition involves the fuzzy equivalent of a (universal or existential) quantification are the 3 relations P, O, and NTP. The other eight relations are defined by (the equivalent of) conjunctions of formulas using only the four relations C, P, O, and NTP.

As a consequence, any expression of the form $R(x, y) \leq \lambda$ or $R(x, y) \geq \lambda$ can be rewritten in an equivalent way as a fuzzy RCC formula which involves only the four relations C, P, O, and NTP. We may thus replace any set Θ of fuzzy RCC formulas by an equivalent set involving only these four relations.

EXAMPLE 7.6.– Let us consider the formula $EC(x, y) \leq 0.6$. According to the definition of EC, this condition is equivalent to the fact that the smallest of $C(x, y)$ and of $1 - O(x, y)$ is at most equal to 0.6, hence that either of these two expressions is at most equal to 0.6. We may thus replace $EC(x, y) \leq 0.6$ by $C(x, y) \leq 0.6 \vee O(x, y) \geq 0.4$.

Similarly, the formula $EC(x, y) \geq 0.6$ is equivalent to the formula $C(x, y) \geq 0.6 \wedge O(x, y) \leq 0.4$.

NOTE 7.6.– Note the somewhat paradoxical situation: on the one hand, constraint systems where NTP does not appear explicitly (called standard sets of formulas) play a central part in what follows. But, on the other hand, one makes use of the possibility of expressing these constraints by using only C, P, O ...and ... NTP!

A set of fuzzy RCC constraints will generally define only upper or lower bounds for the quantities $C(x, y)$, $P(x, y)$, $O(x, y)$, and $NTP(x, y)$, rather than definite values. When definite values are actually enforced by the constraints, one speaks of sets of normalized formulas. Note that, since the definition of atomic formulas uses only the symbols $\leq$ and $\geq$, we have to write $R(x, y) \geq 1$ to express that $R(x, y)$ is equal to 1, and $R(x, y) \leq 0$ to express that it is equal to 0. Similarly, the equality of $R(x, y)$ and λ is written as the conjunction of $R(x, y) \leq \lambda$ and $R(x, y) \geq \lambda$. Using this remark, we can now define normalized sets of formulas as follows:

DEFINITION 7.21.– *Let Θ be a set of fuzzy RCC formulas, and V the set of variables used in this set. The set Θ is normalized if, for any $R \in \{C, P, O, NTP\}$, and for any pair $(x, y) \in V^2$, Θ contains the formula $R(x, y) \geq 1$, or $R(x, y) \leq 0$, or both formulas $R(x, y) \leq \lambda$ and $R(x, y) \geq \lambda$, for some $\lambda \in (0, 1)$.*

Let us recall that in general, a set of constraints Θ_2 is a refinement of a set of constraints Θ_1 if, any interpretation satisfying Θ_2 satisfies Θ_1 *a fortiori*. In short, Θ_2 is stronger than Θ_1.

7.4.6. *Satisfying a finite set of normalized formulas*

If Θ is a set of normalized formulas, let n be the number of elements of the set V of variables which appear in the formulas of Θ. The set of constraints is then completely defined by the four $n \times n$-matrices which give the values of $C(x, y), P(x, y), O(x, y)$, and $NTP(x, y)$ for $(x, y) \in V^2$.

EXAMPLE 7.7.– Let $V = \{V_1, V_2, V_3\}$. The four matrices:

$$C(V) = \begin{pmatrix} 1 & 0.6 & 0.8 \\ 0.6 & 1 & 0.6 \\ 0.8 & 0.6 & 1 \end{pmatrix}$$

$$P(V) = \begin{pmatrix} 1 & 0.6 & 0 \\ 0 & 1 & 0 \\ 0.8 & 0.4 & 1 \end{pmatrix}$$

$$O(V) = \begin{pmatrix} 1 & 0.6 & 0.8 \\ 0.6 & 1 & 0.4 \\ 0.8 & 0.4 & 1 \end{pmatrix}$$

and:

$$NTP(V) = \begin{pmatrix} 0 & 0.6 & 0 \\ 0 & 0 & 0 \\ 0.4 & 0.4 & 0.6 \end{pmatrix}$$

define a normalized set of formulas on V.

A first necessary condition for such a normalized finite set to be satisfiable is that the entries in these four matrices satisfy the constraints corresponding to the following set of conditions $Cond$:

1) for all x, y, $NTP(x, y) \leq P(x, y) \leq O(x, y) \leq C(x, y)$;
2) for all x, y, $C(x, y) = C(y, x)$;
3) for all x, y, $O(x, y) = O(y, x)$;
4) for all x, $P(x, x) = O(x, x) = C(x, x) = 1$.

On the other hand, a set of conditions $Comp$ corresponding to the composition table is also a necessary condition for satisfiability. A detailed analysis of the table shows that it is in fact sufficient to check a subset $Comp$ of 31 "rules", whose general format is:

$$T_W(R_1(x, y), R_2(y, z)) \leq R_3(x, z) \tag{7.45}$$

Table 7.4 gives the list of 3-tuples (R_1, R_2, R_3) which appear in the set $Comp$.

Under these conditions, we have the proposition:

PROPOSITION 7.13.– *Let Θ be a finite normalized set of fuzzy RCC formulas. Assume that Θ does not contain any formula of the form $NTP(x, x) \geq 1$. Then Θ is satisfiable if, and only if, the conditions $Cond$ and $Comp$ are satisfied.*

R_1	R_2	R_1	R_1	R_2	R_3
C	DC	coP	C	P	C
C	DR	coNDP	C	NDP	O
DC	P	coP^{-1}	DC	P^{-1}	DC
DC	O	coP^{-1}	DC	NDP	coP^{-1}
DC	NDP^{-1}	DC	P	P	P
P	coP^{-1}	coP^{-1}	P	DR	DR
P	coNDP^{-1}	coNDP^{-1}	P	NDP	NDP
P^{-1}	NDP^{-1}	NDP^{-1}	P^{-1}	NDP	O
P^{-1}	coNDP	coNDP	P^{-1}	NDP	O
P^{-1}	DR	coP	P^{-1}	P	coP
P^{-1}	O	O	coP^{-1}	NDP	coP^{-1}
coP	NDP^{-1}	coP	O	DR	coP
O	NDP	O	DR	NDP^{-1}	DC
DR	NDP	coP^{-1}	NDP	NDP	NDP
NDP	NDP	coP^{-1}	NDP^{-1}	coNDP	coP
NDP^{-1}	coNDP^{-1}	O			
	NDP				

Table 7.4. *3-Tuples of relations defining the set Comp*

A more precise result (proposition 7.14) is proved in [SCH 09], namely that when the conditions *Cond* and *Comp* are satisfied, there exists a particular type of model of the set Θ: a $(n; \alpha, \beta)$-model.

7.4.7. $(n; \alpha, \beta)$-models

A $(n; \alpha, \beta)$-model, where n is a positive integer, and $\alpha, \beta \geq 0$, corresponds to an interpretation in the Euclidean space $\mathbb{R}^n$ (equipped with the Euclidean distance d). More precisely,

– the domain D is the family of *normalized* fuzzy sets of in $\mathbb{R}^n$ with *bounded support*;

– the function $\varphi_{\alpha,\beta}(t): \mathbb{R}^+ \to [0, 1]$ (for $\beta > 0$) is the continuous function which is equal to 1 on $[0, \alpha]$, 0 on $[\alpha + \beta, +\infty)$, and is linear on $[\alpha, \alpha + \beta]$ (Figure 7.5). When $\beta = 0$, $\varphi_{\alpha,0}$, denoted by φ_α, is equal to 1 on $[0, \alpha]$ and 0 on $(\alpha, +\infty)$. The proximity function $R_{\alpha,\beta}: \mathbb{R}^n \times \mathbb{R}^n \to [0, 1]$ is the composition of the Euclidean distance and of the function $\varphi_{\alpha,\beta}$:

$$R_{(\alpha,\beta)}(p, q) = \varphi_{\alpha,\beta}(d(p, q))$$

– let A and B be two elements of D (two regions). The connection degree $C_{\alpha,\beta}(A, B)$ is defined by the formula:

$$C_{(\alpha,\beta)}(A, B) = \sup_{p \in \mathbb{R}^n} T(A(p), \sup_{q \in \mathbb{R}} T(R_{(\alpha,\beta)}(p, q), B(q)))$$

Intuitively, two sets of $\mathbb{R}^n$ which are at a distance less than α are connected; they are partially connected if this distance is less than $\alpha + \beta$, and not connected at all if

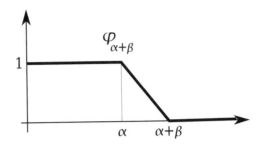

Figure 7.5. *The function $\varphi_{\alpha,\beta}$ is equal to 1 on $[0,\alpha]$, 0 on $[\alpha+\beta,\infty)$, and linearly decreases from 1 to 0 on the interval $[\alpha, +\alpha\beta]$*

it is greater than $\alpha + \beta$. In particular, two sets may be connected athough they do not "touch each other": a degree of tolerance α is accepted for the distance between the two sets.

DEFINITION 7.22.– *Let Θ be a set of fuzzy RCC formulas on a set of variables X. A $(n; \alpha, \beta)$-interpretation is an interpretation for which the variables are interpreted as regions of D, and C as the fuzzy relation $C_{\alpha,\beta}$.*

The more precise result mentioned above is the following:

PROPOSITION 7.14.– *Let Θ be a finite normalized set of fuzzy RCC formulas. Assume that Θ does not contain any formula of the form $NTP(x, x) \geq 1$. Let V be the set of variables appearing in Θ, and n the number of elements of V. Then if the conditions Cond and Comp are satisfied, Θ has a $(n; \alpha, 0)$-model for any $\alpha > 0$.*

Moreover, the effective construction of a model shows that, under these conditions, the a-cuts of the model can be assumed to be regular closed sets of $\mathbb{R}^n$.

Recall that standard sets of formulas are by definition sets of formulas that do not contain atomic formulas whose relation is NTP. We have already noted that these are the sets which are predominantly used in the applications, but that, however, it was natural to reduce arbitrary systems to equivalent sets of formulas where only the four relations C, P, O, and NTP appear. The apparent paradox actually has no incidence on the satisfiability problem:

PROPOSITION 7.15.– *Let Θ_0 be a finite standard set of fuzzy RCC formulas. We assume that the T-norm is the Łukasiewicz T-norm. If Θ_0 can be refined to a normalized set of fuzzy RCC formulas Θ_1 satisfying Cond and Comp, then Θ_0 has a $(n; \alpha, 0)$-model for any $\alpha > 0$.*

7.4.8. *Satisfiability and linear programming*

Let Θ be a finite standard set of fuzzy RCC formulas. Let $V = \{x_1, \ldots, x_n\}$ be the set of variables appearing in Θ. Θ can be replaced by an equivalent system Θ' in which the only relations are C, P, O, and NTP. The set Θ' is thus not standard any more, but it is equivalent to a standard system, and thus proposition 7.15 can be used.

The satisfiability problem for Θ hence boils down to determining whether there is a normalized refinement of Θ' — in other terms, a choice of degrees of satisfaction $\lambda_{i,j}^R = R(x_i, x_j)$, where $R \in \{C, P, O, NTP\}$ — such that the conditions $\mathcal{C}ond$ and $\mathcal{C}omp\ I, J$ are met.

We are in a situation where consider $4n^2$ real variables $\lambda_{i,j}^R$ are considered, subject to a series of conditions:

– the values of these variables are in the interval $[0.1]$:

$$0 \leq \lambda_{i,j}^R \leq 1$$

– each constraint of Θ' results in a disjunctive linear constraint. For example, if Θ' contains the fuzzy RCC formula $NTP(x_1, x_2) \geq 0.4 \vee O(x_3, x_4) \leq 0.7$, we will have the constraint $\lambda_{1.2}^{NTP} \geq 0.4 \vee \lambda_{3.4}^O \leq 0.7$;

– the conditions in $\mathcal{C}ond$ translate into linear constraints:

$$\lambda_{i,j}^{NTP} \leq \lambda_{i,j}^P \leq \lambda_{i,j}^O \leq \lambda_{i,j}^C, \lambda_{i,j}^C = \lambda_{j,i}^C, \lambda_{i,j}^O = \lambda_{j,i}^O, \text{ et} \lambda_{i,i}^P \geq 1$$

– similarly, the conditions $\mathcal{C}omp$ are easily translated in terms of disjunctive linear constraints.

Thus, we obtain a system of disjunctive linear constraints for which the existence of solutions is equivalent to the satisfiability of Θ. If this system does not contain disjunctions, it may be solved in polynomial time. The satisfiability problem is thus an NP-problem.

In the general case, the use of a solver for linear programming may be combined with backtracking techniques.

PROPOSITION 7.16.– *([SCH 09], proposition 3) The satisfiability problem of a set of fuzzy RCC formulas is NP-complete.*

This result is a consequence of the NP-completeness in the classical case, and of the fact that solving the problem in the classical case may be interpreted in the fuzzy context as solving the satisfiability problem for a set of fuzzy RCC formulas.

7.4.9. *Models with a finite number of degrees*

In the temporal case, we have already used the relations between general fuzzy models and models taking only a finite number of values. The same strategy may be used here. We use the notations introduced above: let ρ be a positive integer, $\Delta = \frac{1}{\rho}$, $M_\Delta = \{0, \Delta, 2\Delta, \ldots, 1 - \Delta, 1\}$, and $M_{\frac{\Delta}{2}} = \{0, \frac{\Delta}{2}, \Delta, \ldots, 1 - \frac{\Delta}{2}, 1\}$.

The main result is expressed by the following proposition:

PROPOSITION 7.17.– *([SCH 09], proposition 4) Let Θ be a satisfiable standard set of fuzzy RCC formulas whose degrees are elements of M_Δ. Assume that the T-norm used is that of Łukasiewicz. Let V be the set of variables appearing in Θ, and n the number of elements of V. Then, there exists a model of Θ in which the variables are interpreted as bounded and normalized fuzzy sets in $\mathbb{R}^n$ and whose degrees of membership are elements of $M_{\frac{\Delta}{2}}$.*

As in the temporal case, the satisfaction of fuzzy constraints involving only a finite number of values can be reduced to that of classical constraints. We will not develop this aspect here, and we only give an example.

Let A and B be two bounded and normalized fuzzy subsets of $\mathbb{R}^n$ whose degrees of membership are elements of $M_{\frac{\Delta}{2}}$. Let $\lambda \in M_{\frac{\Delta}{2}} \setminus \{1\}$.

LEMMA 7.1.– *We have the equivalence*:

$$\mathsf{C}_\alpha(A, B) \geq \lambda \Leftrightarrow \mathsf{C}_\alpha(A_1, B_\lambda) \vee \mathsf{C}_\alpha(A_{1-\frac{\Delta}{2}}, B_{\lambda+\frac{\Delta}{2}}) \vee \ldots \vee \mathsf{C}_\alpha(A_\lambda, B_1)$$

A proof of this equivalence, as well as of the seven similar equivalences (upper bound for $\mathsf{C}_\alpha(A, B)$, upper and lower bounds for the quantities $\mathsf{O}_\alpha(A, B), \mathsf{P}_\alpha(A, B)$ and $\mathsf{NTP}_\alpha(A, B)$) can be found in [SCH 09], Appendix D.

As a consequence:

PROPOSITION 7.18.– *Let Θ be a standard set of fuzzy RCC formulas whose degrees are elements of M_Δ, and let Γ be the set of RCC formulas obtained by using the equivalences considered above. Then, Θ is satisfiable if, and only if, Γ is satisfiable.*

7.4.10. *Links with the egg-yolk calculus*

As seen above (section 7.4.1), an *egg-yolk k-calculus* (generalized, if $k > 2$) considers nested sets $A = (A_1 \subseteq \ldots \subseteq A_k)$. Intuitively, the elements of A_1 definitely belong to the set considered, those of A_2 belong to it with less certainty, and so on, with decreasing degrees of certainty. The classical case is the case where $k = 2$; then A_1 is the yolk, and A_2 is the set (the whole egg) formed by the yellow and the white.

In the egg-yolk calculus, the relations between sets may be expressed in terms of the various combinations of relations between the various layers. For example, two sets are more or less in contact depending on whether their yolks are in contact, or whether the yolk of one set meets only the white of the other, or whether only the whites meet.

Intuitively, it is clear that a set of the k- calculus may be seen as a fuzzy set using k degrees. In the case of the 2-calculus, for example, the elements of the yolk have degree 1, those of the white have $\frac{1}{2}$, and the elements outside the egg have degree 0.

More generally, for a given k, we may see A_1 as the 1-cut, A_2 as the $\frac{k-1}{k}$-cut, and so on until A_k, which is the $\frac{1}{k}$-cut of a fuzzy set whose degrees are in $M_{\frac{1}{k}}$.

Let $n > 0$ and $k \leq 2$. Let us consider egg-yolk-regions, which are k-sequences of nested sets A_i of which each one is a non-empty regular bounded and closed subset of $\mathbb{R}^n$.

While the interpretation of the connection relation used up to now is in terms of $(n; \alpha, \beta)$-models, formalisms of the egg-yolk type use a classical concept of connection: in the case of two regular closed sets A and B of $\mathbb{R}^n$, $C(A, B)$ for example, implies that $A \cup B \neq \emptyset$.

In this context, Schockaert *et al.* define the concept of egg-yolk interpretation:

DEFINITION 7.23.– *An interpretation of a set of fuzzy RCC formulas is a (k, n)egg-yolk-interpretation, if each variable is interpreted by a k-egg-yolk region $(x_1, \ldots, x_k)$ of $\mathbb{R}^n$, and where the connection relation between $\bar{x} = (x_1, \ldots, x_k)$ and $\bar{y} = (y_1, \ldots, y_k)$ is defined in the following manner:*

1) if $C(x_i, y_j)$ is false for all $i, j \in \{1, \ldots, k\}$, then $C(\bar{x}, \bar{y}) = 0$;
2) otherwise, let $k' = inf\{i + j \mid C(x_i, y_j)\}$:
    - if $k' > k + 2$, then $C(\bar{x}, \bar{y}) = 0$,
    - else, $C(\bar{x}, \bar{y}) = 1 - \frac{k'-2}{k}$.

In this formula, the connection relation C considered between regions in $\mathbb{R}^n$ is the standard relation which holds if, and only if, the two regular closed sets have a point in common.

EXAMPLE 7.8.– Let us consider the case where $k = 2$. Then the definition of the connection relation means that $C((x_1, x_2), (y_1, y_2))$ is equal to 1 if the two yolks have a common point, $\frac{1}{2}$ if the yolk of one touches only the white of the other, and 0 otherwise.

Thanks to Renz [REN 02a], we know that a set of classical RCC constraints has a standard model in $\mathbb{R}^n$ for any $n \geq 1$. Hence, proposition 7.17 implies the following proposition:

PROPOSITION 7.19.– *Let* Θ *be a set of satisfiable fuzzy* RCC *formulas in which the degrees used are elements of the set* $\{0, \frac{2}{k}, \frac{4}{k}, \ldots, 1\}$ *for some positive integer* k. *Then,* Θ *has a* (k, n)-*egg-yolk-model for any* $n \geq 1$.

EXAMPLE 7.9.– Consider[4] the system of normalized fuzzy formulas defined by the following four matrices $C(x, y)$, $P(x, y)$, $O(x, y)$, and $NTP(x, y)$:

$$C(x, y) = \begin{pmatrix} 1 & 0.75 \\ 0.75 & 1 \end{pmatrix} \qquad P(x, y) = \begin{pmatrix} 1 & 0 \\ 0.5 & 1 \end{pmatrix}$$

$$O(x, y) = \begin{pmatrix} 1 & 0.5 \\ 0.5 & 1 \end{pmatrix} \qquad NTP(x, y) = \begin{pmatrix} 1 & 0 \\ 0.25 & 1 \end{pmatrix}$$

This system is satisfied by the $(1; 20,0)$ interpretation which sends x on A and y on B, where A, B are the fuzzy sets of Figure 7.6(a). The image of these fuzzy sets is the entire segment $[0, 1]$.

This system is normalized, and the degrees of membership it involves belong to the set $M_{0.25}$. There is thus a $(n; \alpha, 0)$-model using only degrees of membership of $M_{0.25}$. Figure 7.6(b) represents such a model, for $n = 1$ and $\alpha = 20$.

As for Figure 7.6(c), it represents the model:

$$x \mapsto A' = ([5, 30], [5, 40], [5, 100], [5, 120])$$

$$y \mapsto B' = ([60, 90], [60, 90], [60, 90], [60, 90])$$

for which C is represented in terms of distances. Due to the tolerance introduced by the function $\varphi_{20.0}$, two sets can be in contact without containing common points: here, this is the case of $[5, 40]$ and of $[60, 90]$ which are considered to be in contact because their distance does not exceed 20.

Lastly, Figure 7.6(d) represents the following *egg-yolk*-model:

$$x \mapsto A'' = ([100, 120], [90, 130], [60, 140], [50, 150])$$

$$y \mapsto B'' = ([60, 90], [60, 90], [60, 90], [60, 90])$$

In this case, C is defined as in definition 7.23, for which the connection of two regular closed regions implies a non-empty intersection.

The dissymmetry between the existence of models in a particular dimension and in any dimension is only apparent, and the following result is shown in [SCH 09]:

---

4 This example is taken from [SCH 09].

PROPOSITION 7.20.– *Let* Θ *be a standard set of fuzzy* RCC *formulas whose bounding on the degrees are finite. A set* Γ *of classical* RCC *formulas can be associated with* Θ *in such a way that the following statements are equivalent:*

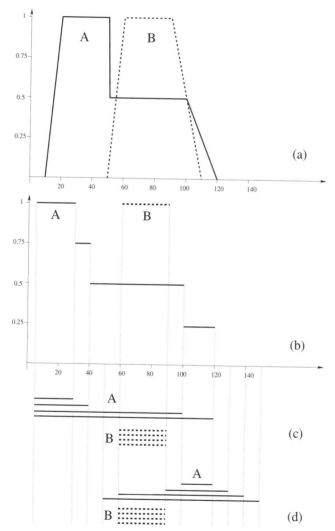

Figure 7.6. *Four fuzzy models which are solutions of the system considered in example 7.9; the first two, (a) and (b), are (1; 20.0)-models, in which the regions are bounded fuzzy regions in ℝ, and where the connection relation is defined from distance with a tolerance of 20 (section 7.4.7); the third (c) is a model of the egg-yolk type (four nested subregions) for the same connection relation; the fourth (d) is also of egg-yolk type, but it is an egg-yolk-interpretation which uses a "classical" concept of connection (definition 7.23) (this figure is taken from [SCH 09])*

1) Θ *is satisfiable*;

2) Γ *is satisfiable*;

3) Θ *has a normalized refinement which satisfies the constraints* Cont *and* Comp;

4) Θ *has an egg-yolk-model in some dimension*;

5) Θ *has an egg-yolk-model in any dimension*;

6) Θ *has a* $(n; \alpha, 0)$*-model for at least one* $\alpha > 0$ *and one positive integer* n;

7) Θ *has one* $(n; \alpha, 0)$*-model for any* $\alpha > 0$ *and any positive integer* n.

7.5. Historical note

The use of fuzzy techniques for temporal or spatial qualitative reasoning already has a rather long history. The reader will find many references in the three main sources [BAD 06, SCH 08a, SCH 09] which we have used in this chapter. The fuzzy constraint satisfaction problem (FCSP) in the temporal domain has been considered notably in [VIL 94, GOD 95, DUB 96, ROS 01, KHA 01, BOS 02, ROS 02, YOR 03, GUE 94]. For the spatial domain, we should also mention the work of Guesgen and his collaborators [GUE 01, GUE 02a, GUE 02b], as well as [BOD 03a, LI 04b, PAL 04, DU 05a, DU 05b, LIU 06, TAN 06, TAN 07].

Chapter 8

The Geometrical Approach and Conceptual Spaces

8.1. "What color is the chameleon?"

Three chameleons have entered the spindle representing the set of all colors (Figure 8.1). We know that each chameleon takes the color of its environment. For instance, the chameleon located at A — in an orange environment — is orange, and so is the one located at B in the same environment. Now, what color is the chameleon located at C?

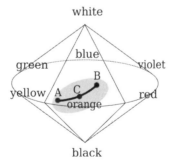

Figure 8.1. *Knowing that the chameleons A and B are in an orange environment, what is the color of the chameleon located at C?*

According to the theory of conceptual spaces [GÄR 04], the answer is as follows: since C is located *between* A and B, and since A and B are located in the orange colored region, C must also be orange, because the region representing a given color is a *convex* part of the color spindle, that is, if two points belong to this region, then any point located between them also belongs to it.

The geometrical theme of convexity is a main theme of the theory of Conceptual spaces, and a main theme of this chapter.

8.2. Qualitative semantics

Qualitative spatial reasoning about time and space, as we have presented it up to now, comes under the heading of the *symbolic approach* in Artificial Intelligence: for example, to reason about qualitative relations between intervals, we have introduced 13 symbols, leaving aside the question of measuring durations. Each symbol refers to an infinite number of possible quantitative relations between two intervals. Then, we defined a language which, although it is limited, is sufficiently expressive and non-ambiguous (this is the intuitive content of JEPD property); for this language, we introduced specific methods of inference, essentially based on the idea of composition of relations, interpreted in terms of constraint propagation on a graph.

If we leave it at that, Allen's calculus — and more generally, the set of formalisms which we have examined so far — may be considered as particular sublanguages of a logical language. Therefore, they could be assigned to a subfield of predicate logic as knowledge representation techniques for representing and reasoning about temporal or spatial knowledge in a more convenient way. Indeed, it is by building explicit bridges between those formalisms and more classical types of logic that complexity results such as those of Nebel and Bürckert [NEB 95] for Allen's interval algebra have been proved (using the properties of Horn theories); similarly, many results about the RCC−8 formalism have been established by using translations in terms of intuitionistic and modal logic, a strategy introduced by Bennett [BEN 94, BEN 95, BEN 96b].

The natural semantics of those formalisms is therefore the semantics of particular logical systems: it can be described *à la* Tarski, by using set-theoretic concepts, based on the classical concepts of models and interpretations.

However, it is intuitively quite clear that our qualitative understanding of temporal or spatial phenomena goes beyond the mere combinatorics of some basic concepts such as the concept of precedence for time points or Allen's relations between temporal intervals. Although it has been argued convincingly that Allen's relations and the RCC−8 relations have a good cognitive base [RAU 97, KNA 98, KNA 97], it is nonetheless clear that our time-models incorporate topological type of concepts, such as that of continuity, and geometrical concepts, like that of convexity.

This realization has led some researchers to introduce topological or geometrical concepts in their formalisms. An example of the introduction of a geometrical concept in a spatial language is provided by the enrichment of the RCC language by a primitive of convex closure [GOT 94], leading to the definition of more expressive formalisms.

Another way of introducing topological and geometrical aspects consists in incorporating part of the additional structuring implied by the specific properties of time or space into the formalisms. A case in point is the introduction by Freksa [FRE 91, FRE 92a] of the concept of *conceptual neighborhood*. Conceptual neighborhoods may be also understood in terms of phase spaces, as shown in [LIG 94a].

Now the enhancement of set-theoretic models by topological or geometrical concepts is one of the main ideas of Gärdenfors' theory of Conceptual spaces [GÄR 04]. In the context of building a very general framework for cognitive science, Gärdenfor defines an intermediate level between the symbolic level on the one hand — this is the level of logic and of its set-theoretic models — and the sub-symbolic level on the other hand. This level is called the *conceptual level* by Gärdenfors; it is based on the concept of *conceptual space*.

As witnessed by the preceding chapters of this book, one of the most studied and successful domains in qualitative spatial and temporal reasoning is that of complexity issues; for several formalisms, it has resulted in answering questions about the complexity of basic problems, such as: Is the consistency problem for such and such class of constraint networks decidable? Which complexity class does it belong to? Is it a polynomial problem? If not, are there polynomial subclasses? Can one characterize them?

We have seen, at least for a broad family of formalisms based on linear orders, that we could establish a link between the complexity classes and some topological and geometrical properties of the basic relations. The typical example is the characterization of the subclass of polynomial relations of Allen's interval algebra in terms of pre-convex relations, hence in terms of geometrical and topological properties of the regions in the half-plane associated to basic relations.

In this chapter, we will see that the geometrical representations we have been using for this family of formalisms may be considered as particular cases of conceptual spaces associated with those formalisms.

For several formalisms we consider, the geometrical approach to the study of complexity can be seen as competing with purely logical methods, as it provides alternative proofs of results which can be obtained by using the latter. However, on the specific example of the INDU formalism, we will see that the two approaches may also, in certain cases, provide complementary results, specifically, they allow the characterization of different tractable subclasses of relations. This provides a justification for using both types of approaches concurrently.

8.3. Why introduce topology and geometry?

Why is the introduction of topological and geometrical concepts into qualitative temporal or spatial formalisms a profitable move to make? We can see several reasons for doing so:

– *cognitive motivations*: human beings are able to make inferences quickly and effectively in the temporal and spatial domains, even on the basis of vague or incomplete knowledge. This remains true even when the inference processes are based on incorrect principles. The reader is referred to [RAU 97, KNA 98] for a study of the manner in which humans reason about temporal intervals, and to [KNA 97] for similar work in the spatial domain. Freksa [FRE 92a] proposes the idea that, in many cases, the most natural way to represent our knowledge about temporal intervals involves disjunctive relations that he interprets as relations between "semi-intervals". This is what he calls "coarse knowledge". In the same paper, he introduces several notions of "conceptual neighborhood". One of the motivations for introducing conceptual neighborhoods is related to perception: neighboring relations will tend to correspond to similar perceptive conditions;

– *physical reasons*: we may also justify the introduction of conceptual neighborhoods in terms of properties of the physical world. The neighborhood concepts of types A, B, C, introduced by Freksa correspond to different constraints on the intervals considered. Similar ideas had been introduced by [NÖK 88] in connection with the use of Allen's relations for diagnosis, and the term of "convex relations" is apparently due to him. The formulation of conceptual neighborhoods in terms of phase space [LIG 94a] prefigures the introduction of conceptual spaces;

– *conceptual gains*: Ligozat [LIG 97] illustrates what can be gained from the use of topological and geometrical representations of relations: it allows us to visualize many properties of these relations, and also to prove interesting results. A case in point is the analytical proof of the maximality of the subclass of pre-convex relations in Allen's interval algebra [LIG 98b], a result Ligozat obtains by a detailed analysis of the geometrical properties of relations in the lattice of Allen's relations;

– *an alternative approach to the study of complexity*: the last point, as already mentioned, results from the link established between topological and geometrical properties of the relations on the one hand, and complexity of the associated calculi on the other hand, a link of which the concept of pre-convexity is a typical example. This connection, although it came up somewhat unexpectedly, should probably be assigned to the intuitive idea that "convex" problems tend to be easier to solve. This is resonant with the central tenet of the theory of Conceptual spaces, namely the idea that adequate concepts of "convexity" characterize "natural" concepts, which in turn makes them easier to manipulate and reason about.

8.4. Conceptual spaces

Conceptual spaces, as defined by Gärdenfors [GÄR 00], are built from *domains*. Consider again the example in the introduction to this chapter. It refers to the *natural color system* (NCS) described in [HAR 81]. The NCS is a model of colors based on perception. A perceived color is described by means of three perceptual dimensions: hue, chromaticness (or saturation), and brightness.

The first dimension, hue, is represented by a color circle. Complementary colors are in antipodal position; for example, as the green is antipodal to red, and orange to blue.

The second dimension, chromaticness, varies from zero to maximal intensity. It can be represented by a segment. Consequently, hue and chromaticness are considered simultaneously and are represented by a disc on which colors are distinct at the periphery of the disk, and become less and less distinct when we get closer to the center of the disk.

The third dimension is brightness, which varies from white to black, and hence, can also represented by a segment. Brightness and chromaticness do not vary independently: the differences in chromaticness become less visible when brightness comes nearer either black or white. As a consequence, for a given hue, the set of pairs (chromaticness, brightness) describes a triangle.

When all three dimensions are simultaneously considered, we obtain a model which has the shape of a solid made up of two cones joined together by their bases, as shown in Figure 8.2; this solid shape may be referred to as the "color spindle". Gärdenfors discusses in detail the way in which the use of this model makes it possible to explain difficult semantic phenomena, such as the use of the terms of colors in natural language. A fundamental point is the "Convexity hypothesis", according to which linguistic terms referring to "natural" properties, for example, basic terms used for referring to colors, correspond to *convex* regions in the space of colors (for a suitable definition of convexity).

The NCS model is an example of a *phenomenal* conceptual space: it is associated with a perceptive category. Other conceptual domains and spaces are *theoretical*

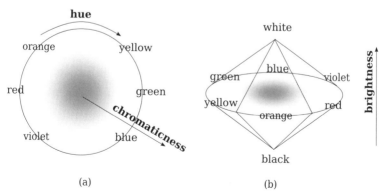

Figure 8.2. *The "Color spindle" in the NCS model (after [GÄR 04]). The two parameters of hue and chromaticness define a disk (a), and the third parameter, brightness, defines a "spindle" (b) in* $\mathbb{R}^3$

conceptual spaces: for example, the conceptual model of space in classical Newtonian physics is a three-dimensional Euclidean space, the temporal dimension being an independent or *separable* (in Gärdenfors' terminology) dimension. By contrast, the temporal dimension is an *integral* dimension of the four-dimensional Minkowski space: it cannot be considered independently from the spatial dimension.

8.4.1. *Higher order properties and relations*

In Gärdenfors' theory of semantics, the "Convexity hypothesis" applies in the first place to *properties* — that is, in logical terms, to monadic predicates — but Gärdenfors notes that the dimensions of a conceptual space may be used to describe higher order predicates. He gives the example of the relation "longer than" which, in the space of pairs of lengths may be represented in $(\mathbb{R}^+)^2$ by the region located above the first bisector ([GÄR 00], p. 92).

A similar idea will enable us to interpret the geometrical representations of basic relations of several qualitative formalisms in terms of conceptual spaces.

8.4.2. *Notions of convexity*

As already mentioned, the concept of convexity is central to the Gärdenfors' approach. We have also — *à propos* colors — alluded to the fact that other notions of convexity than Euclidean convexity may be involved. For example, consider once again the "Color spindle". If two colors have the same chromaticness and brightness, but correspond to different hues, the "shortest path" between them will be an arc of the circle located in the plane perpendicular to the axis of the spindle. The set of intermediate colors between the two considered colors is hence represented by an arc, and it is with regard to this particular concept of "betweenness" that this arc is convex (it is not convex in $\mathbb{R}^3$). The concept of convexity used in this case is a concept which is associated with the betweenness relation on a circle; more generally:

DEFINITION 8.1.– *A set X is* convex *if for any pair of points $x, y \in X$, the set of points located* between *x and y is contained in X.*

We will not discuss here the properties that a *betweenness* ternary relation has to satisfy, and we will only mention what is useful to us; we refer the reader to [GÄR 00] for a detailed discussion.

In particular, in a metric space (see Appendix A for this concept), a natural concept of betweenness is derived from the metric:

DEFINITION 8.2.– *Let X be a metric space equipped with a metric ρ. For any 3-tuple $x, y, z \in X$, we say that y is* between *x and z if $\rho(x, z) = \rho(x, y) + \rho(y, z)$.*

When d is the Euclidean metric in a Euclidean space, y is between x and z if, and only if, y belongs to the segment $[x, z]$, and the concept of convexity derived from this notion of betweenness is the usual concept.

On the other hand, if the Euclidean space is equipped with the Manhattan metric (Appendix A) defined in $\mathbb{R}^n$ by the following condition, for $x = (x_1, \ldots, x_n)$ and $y = (y_1, \ldots, y_n)$:

$$d(x, y) = \sum_{i=1}^{n} |x_i - y_i|$$

then the set of points located between two points is no longer a segment, but a n-block. If $n = 2$, and if the space considered is the Euclidean plane equipped with the Manhattan metric, then the set of points located between x and y is the set of points contained in the smallest orthoaxial rectangle containing these two points (Figure 8.3). This rectangle contains the segment $[x, y]$, and hence convexity for the Manhattan metric implies convexity for the Euclidean metric; this in fact remains true for a Euclidean space R_n of arbitrary dimension n.

More generally, Gärdenfors considers topological notions based on *closure structures* in the sense of [MOR 93a]. These structures involve the property of closure under projections, which can be expressed in the following manner: if $X \subseteq Y \times Z$ is a subset of a product space, and $pr_1: Y \times Z \rightarrow Y$, $pr_2: Y \times Z \rightarrow Z$ the canonical projections, then $X \subseteq pr_1(X) \times pr_2(X)$; a region X is *closed under projections* if $X = pr_1(X) \times pr_2(X)$. In other words, a region closed by the projections is entirely characterized by its projections. This definition can be extended in an obvious way to the product of an arbitrary number of spaces.

In the case of Euclidean spaces, we have the following proposition:

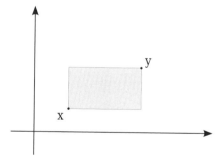

Figure 8.3. *For the Manhattan metric, the set of points located between x and y is an orthoaxial rectangle (possibly degenerated to a segment or a point) of which the segment $[x, y]$ is a diagonal*

PROPOSITION 8.1.– *In the Euclidean space* $\mathbb{R}^n (n \geq 1)$, *a region* X *is convex for the Manhattan metric if, and only if, it is convex for the Euclidean metric and closed under projections.*

8.4.3. *Conceptual spaces associated to generalized intervals*

In the case of Allen's formalism, we may consider that the representation of relations as regions in the plane constitutes the conceptual space attached to the formalism. We have previously seen that this conceptual space allows a simple characterization of the subclasses of tractable relations: for example, convex relations are basically those relations which are convex for the Manhattan metric.

The encoding of the (p, q)-relations as p-tuples of integers has enabled us to extend this kind of representation to the context of generalized intervals. The associated conceptual space in this case consists of a set of convex regions for the Manhattan metric which constitute a partition of a cone in some Euclidean space.

For instance, Figure 8.4 represents the conceptual space associated with $(2, 3)$-relations. The basic relations constitute a partition of the half-plane **H**.

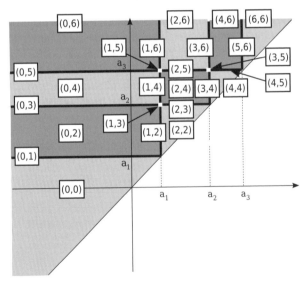

Figure 8.4. *The conceptual space associated with* (2, 3)*-relations (we have omitted the index* (2, 3) *in the notation of basic relations)*

8.4.4. *The conceptual space associated to directed intervals*

A directed interval of the real line is defined by a pair of two distinct real numbers. The set of directed intervals thus corresponds to the points in the plane which lie

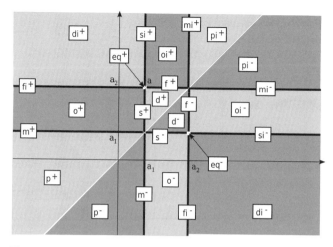

Figure 8.5. *The conceptual space associated with directed intervals*
(notations defined in section 4.3)

outside the first bisector. If such a point is fixed, the 26 regions corresponding to the basic relations are those of Figure 8.5; thus the conceptual space for directed intervals is essentially made of two copies of the partition defined by Allen's relations.

8.4.5. *Conceptual space associated with cyclic intervals*

An interval on a directed circle corresponds to the choice of two distinct points on the circle, hence to an element in the product of the circle by itself; the product of two circles is a torus. The condition that the two points are distinct eliminates a subset of this torus. We now describe the situation more precisely.

In order to do this, we choose an origin O on the circle and cut the circle at O (left side of Figure 8.6). We obtain a line segment $[O, L]$, where the extremity L must be identified with O to reconstitute the circle.

The product $[O, L] \times [O, L]$ is a square, and we obtain the required torus by pasting together the pair of opposite sides of this square. A cyclic interval corresponds to a point of the square which does not belong to the segment connecting (O, O) to (L, L). The set of cyclic intervals is represented by the remaining part of the square, or more correctly by the part of the torus which corresponds to it.

Let us consider now a reference interval B. We may assume that this interval begins at O and ends at a, with $a < L$. The point of the square which corresponds to it is hence the point $(0, a)$.

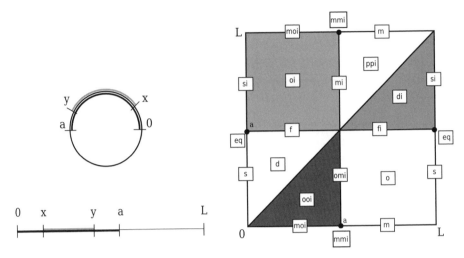

Figure 8.6. *Geometry of the 16 basic relations: after opening the circle, we obtain a segment* $[0, L]$. *The interval* $[0, a]$ *being fixed, an arbitrary interval is determined by its beginning* x *and its end* y, *with* $x \neq y$; *if we associate the point* (x, y) *of the square* $[0, L] \times [0, L]$ *with this interval, the basic relations correspond to the regions represented on the right side of the figure*

Consider now an arbitrary interval which begins at x and ends at y. What conditions does this interval have to satisfy for its relation relative to B to be a given basic relation? For example, for A to be in the relation d with respect to B, it is necessary that A starts after the beginning of B and ends before the end of B. Hence the region of the square corresponding to the relation d corresponds to the condition $0 < x < y < a$.

Proceeding in the same way for each basic relation, we obtain the 16 regions represented on the right side of Figure 8.6. It should be noted that the diagonal $[(0, 0), (L, L)]$ of the square must be excluded (since we consider intervals of non-zero duration), and that the left and right sides of the square must be identified, as well as the lower and upper sides.

To obtain a proper image of the geometry of relations, some cutting and pasting is still necessary. If we cut the square into two triangular pieces by removing the diagonal $[(0, 0), (L, L)]$, then paste together the vertical sides, we obtain the ribbon represented in Figure 8.7. We now paste together the horizontal sides, which results in a figure which is an open cylinder, or alternatively, after a continuous deformation, an open disc with a hole in it. The left part of Figure 8.8 represents the 16 relations after having carried out such an operation. On the right side of the same figure, the incidence graph corresponding to this partition of the open disk minus its center is represented.

As in the case of intervals on a line, the dual graph of the incidence graph (left side of Figure 8.9) describes a simple geometrical situation: two cellular complexes made

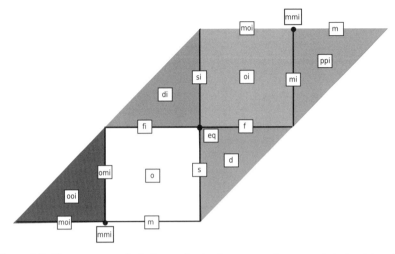

Figure 8.7. *The geometry of relations, after having cut out the square into two triangles, and having pasted the vertical sides together*

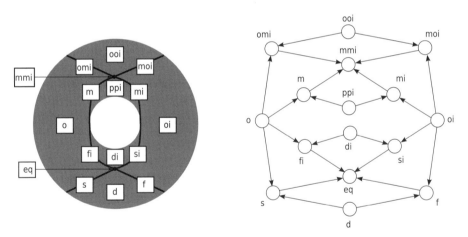

Figure 8.8. *After continuous deformation, the 16 regions correspond to a partition of an open disk with a hole in it (on the left); the corresponding incidence graph is represented on the right*

up of two squares, which are pasted at two of their diagonally opposite points. The first square has its interior labeled by mmi, and its four sides are labeled by m, mi, omi, and moi (right side of Figure 8.9); the second square has its interior labeled by eq, and its four sides are labeled by s, si, f, and fi. The sides m and omi of the first square meet at o, so that this point is the intersection of the sides s and fi of the second square. Similarly, the sides mi and moi of the first square meet at oi, and this point is the intersection of the sides si and f of the second square.

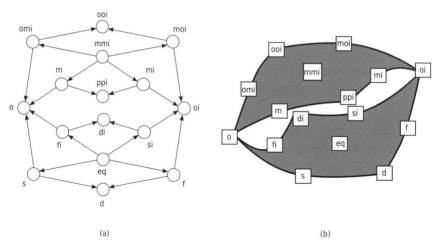

(a)   (b)

Figure 8.9. *The dual graph of the incidence graph of the basic relations (on the left)
is that of a cell complex formed by two squares pasted together at two
diagonally opposite corners (on the right)*

8.4.6. *Conceptual neighborhoods in Allen's relations*

The geometrical and topological structures of the relations of a formalism are
closely related to the concept of conceptual neighborhood. In what follows, we recall
the original definition of Freksa, then present a proposition of formalization of this
concept due to Galton.

Freksa [FRE 92a] gives the following definition of conceptual neighborhoods in
Allen's interval algebra:

DEFINITION 8.3.– *Two relations between pairs of events are* (conceptual) *neighbors
if they can be directly transformed into one another by continuously deforming (i.e.
shortening, lenghtening, moving) the events (in a topological sense).*

DEFINITION 8.4.– *A set of relations between pairs of events forms a   conceptual
neighborhood if its elements are path-connected through "conceptual neighbor"
relations.*

Freksa calls *semi-interval* the data corresponding to the beginning or the end of
an interval. Consequently, the relations between two semi-intervals are the disjunctive
relations which, in terms of the lattice representation of basic relations, correspond
to horizontal or vertical "slices" of the lattice cut out by conditions such as $X_1 < 1$
(the beginning of the first semi-interval precedes that of the second, which defines
the relation ol (*older*)), $X_1 = 1$ (both have the same beginning, which defines the

Name	Symbol	Relation
Older	ol	[p, di]
Head-to-head with	hh	[s, si]
Younger	yo	[d, pi]
Survived by	sb	[p, d]
Tail-to-tail with	tt	[fi, f]
Survives	sv	[di, pi]
Precedes	pr	[p, m]
Born before death of	bd	[p, oi]
Contemporary of	ct	[o, oi]
Died after birth of	db	[o, pi]
Succeeds	sd	[mi, pi]
Older & survived by	ob	[p, o]
Older contemporary of	oc	[o, di]
Surviving contemporary of	sc	[di, oi]
Survived by contemporary of	bc	[o, d]
Younger contemporary of	yc	[d, oi]
Younger & survives	ys	[d, oi]

Table 8.1. *Freksa's [FRE 92a] relations between semi-intervals*

relation hh (*head-to-head*)), etc. Table 8.1 gives the list of these relations and their representations as intervals in the lattice.

The definition of the conceptual neighborhood relation depends on the kinds of deformations allowed on the intervals when moving from one relation to another. If, starting from a relation between two intervals, we are only allowed to move one endpoint, we get what Freksa calls the concept of A-neighborhood. If the intervals are rigid intervals which are allowed to move without changing their durations, the corresponding concept is that of B-neighborhood. Lastly, we obtain a concept of C-neighborhood by leaving the middle point of one of the two intervals fixed and accepting changes in duration.

8.4.7. Dominance spaces and dominance diagrams

In [GAL 01], Galton introduces the concepts of *dominance* and *dominance space* to formalize the notion of continuous change in the context of qualitative representation. As a motivating example, he considers a variable X with real values (a quantitative entity). This variable may be described qualitatively by saying that it can be strictly positive (state P), strictly negative (N), or equal to zero (Z). The basic idea is that, if X varies in a continuous manner, if it is in state N on a some time interval I, and if it is in another state in one of the bounding points of I, then this other state can only be Z. The fact that this is possible only for Z is expressed by saying that N and Z are perturbations of each other, and the impossibility of having Z on an interval and N at an extremity of this interval by saying that Z dominates N.

More precisely, Galton's theory comprises a temporal theory in which we consider points and intervals, which are ordered pairs of points. It also uses a concept of states. A predicate $Holds-at$ links states and points: $Holds-at(S, t)$ expresses the fact that state S holds at point t. By definition, a state holds on an interval $i = [t_1, t_2]$, which is denoted by $Holds(S, i)$, if it holds at every point t of the open interval (t_1, t_2).

If S and S' are two states such that S holds on an interval i, and that S' holds at an endpoint of i, we say that each of the two states S and S' is a *perturbation* of the other.

DEFINITION 8.5.– *Let S and S' be two states. We say that S' dominates S, which is denoted by $S' \succ S$, if the following conditions are satisfied*:
– *there is an interval i such that Holds(S, i)*;
– *one endpoint t of i is such that Holds−at (S', t)*;
– *the roles of S and S' cannot be interchanged.*

For example, the continuity of the variable X considered above implies that the value zero may appear at an endpoint of an interval where X is strictly positive or negative, but the converse is not true: consequently, state Z dominates states P and N.

DEFINITION 8.6.– *A dominance space is a pair $(S, \succ)$, where S is a finite set of states, $\succ$ an irreflexive and asymmetrical relation on S, such that the following rule of temporal incidence is satified: for any pair of states (S, S'), if S is true on i, and S' is true at an endpoint t of i, then $S = S'$ or $S' \succ S$.*

The choice of the term dominance is motivated by the idea that incompatible states may be in competition at a point, and that it is the state which dominates the other which wins the game: for instance, if the continuous variable X is positive on an interval i, and zero on an interval j, and if i m j, then X is zero at the point where i meets j.

DEFINITION 8.7.– *Given a dominance space $(S, \succ)$, the associated dominance graph is the directed graph whose set of vertices is S, and such that there is an arc (S', S) if, and only if, S' dominates S.*

In the example of the three states of a continuous variable X, we may interpret the situation by noting that N, Z, and P correspond to the relations $<, eq$, and $>$ of the time point algebra, and that the topology on the corresponding graph is the quotient topology for which N and P are two open points whose closures contains Z. The dominance relation in this case is none other than the inverse relation of the edge relation ∂ (a relation whose reflexive and transitive closure is the topological closure relation): a relation r_1 dominates r_2 if, and only if, $r1 \in \partial r_2$.

Galton shows that a Cartesian product of dominance spaces equipped with the product relation is a dominance space.

In particular, this enables him to give a description of the conceptual neighborhoods associated with Allen's interval algebra, as well as of those associated with the RCC–8 formalism. In the case of the latter, the basic idea is to characterize the qualitative relation between two regions X and Y using the values of three parameters: the portion α of X contained in Y, the portion β of Y contained in X, and the fact that the borders of the two regions have a common part ($\gamma = 0$) or not ($\gamma = 1$). The first two parameters have three qualitative values, namely $\alpha = 0$, $\alpha = 1$, and $0 < \alpha < 1$, where the first two values dominate the third one. In the case of the last parameter, $\gamma = 0$ dominates $\gamma = 1$. The conceptual neighborhood graph is then obtained from the product dominance space of the three dominance spaces corresponding to the three parameters α, β, and γ.

The corresponding dominance graph is represented in Figure 8.10. This graph can also be interpreted as describing the topological closure operation in the quotient of the polytope associated with Allen's relations by the time reversal operation (Figure 4.29).

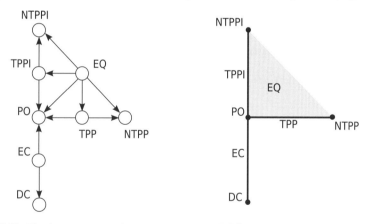

Figure 8.10. *The dominance graph associated with the* RCC−8 *formalism (on the left). We may also see it as the graph describing the topological closure operation in the quotient (on the right) of the polytope associated with Allen's relations by the time reversal operation (Figure 4.29)*

8.5. Polynomial relations of INDU

In what follows, we show how the geometrical approach can be used for determining tractable subclasses in the INDU algebra. For a more comprehensive presentation, the reader is referred to [BAL 06], of which this section is an extended summary.

A first point is concerned with the notion of consistency: the reader should be aware of the fact that the INDU formalism is one of the examples where various technical concepts of consistency are not equivalent. Let us recall that the *consistency* of a constraint network, for a given algebra, is relative to a particular domain of interpretation for the relation symbols of the algebra. In the case of INDU, this domain is the set $Int(\mathbb{R})$ of intervals on the real line $\mathbb{R}$, that is of pairs $x_1, x_2 \in \mathbb{R}$ such that $x_1 < x_2$, and the interpretation of the 25 basic relations of INDU is as defined previously in section 4.11.

8.5.1. *Consistency*

Let $\mathcal{N} = (N, C)$ be a network on the INDU algebra. By definition, $\mathcal{N} = (N, C)$ is *consistent* if there is an instantiation m such that, for any pair $(i, j) \in N \times N$, the pair $((m(i), m(j))$ belongs to the relation denoted by $C(i, j)$. Such an instantiation is called a *solution* of the network.

Recall that a network is called k-consistent (for $k \geq 1$) if any consistent partial instantiation defined on a subset of $k - 1$ vertices can be extended consistently to an arbitrary new vertex.

Now it should be emphasized that several properties which are true for Allen's interval algebra, are no longer true for the INDU algebra:

PROPOSITION 8.2.– *There are consistent networks on the* INDU *algebra which are not 3-consistent.*

Proof. The network with three vertices whose constraints are as follows:

$$C(V_1, V_2) = C(V_2, V_3) = C(V_1, V_3) = \mathsf{p}^=$$

is consistent: the instantiation $m(V_1) = [1, 2], m(V_1) = [1, 2], m(V_1) = [1, 2]$ is consistent. But the partial instantiation $m(V_1) = [1, 2], m(V_2) = [3, 4]$, which is consistent, cannot be extended to a consistent instantiation of the three vertices.   □

PROPOSITION 8.3.– *There are algebraically closed scenarios on the* INDU *algebra which are not consistent.*

Proof. Consider the network with four vertices of Figure 8.11, whose constraints are as follows:

$$C(V_1, V_2) = \mathsf{si}^>, C(V_1, V_3) = \mathsf{o}^= C(V_1, V_4) = \mathsf{o}^> =$$

$$C(V_2, V_3) = \mathsf{m}^<, C(V_2, V_4) = \mathsf{p}^=, C(V_1, V_4) = \mathsf{fi}^>$$

This network is algebraically closed: we may check this fact explicitly, or more simply note that firstly the corresponding Allen network (leaving aside the onstraints

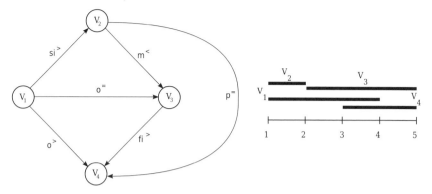

Figure 8.11. *A scenario on the* INDU *algebra which is algebraically closed but not consistent (left); a consistent instantiation of the corresponding Allen network (leaving aside duration constraints) (right)*

on durations) is consistent, since it has, for example, $m(V_1) = [1,4], m(V_2) = [1,2], m(V_1) = [2,5], m(V_1) = [3,5]$ as a consistent instantiation; and secondly that all duration constraints involving only three vertices are consistent. But these constraints on the durations imply that V_1 and V_3 have the same duration, and similarly that V_2 and V_4 also have the same duration. The sum of the durations of V_2 and V_3 is the total duration of the union of the four intervals, and it should also be the sum of the durations of V_1 and V_4. But the latter also have as a union the total union of the four intervals, and they overlap each other: the total duration of their union is hence strictly less than the sum of their durations. Thus, we have a contradiction.   □

In the case of Allen's interval algebra, a lemma due to Nebel and Bürckert [NEB 95] states that the complexity (for the consistency problem) of a set $\mathcal{E}$ of relations is the same as that of its closure $\hat{\mathcal{E}}$ under the inversion, composition, and intersection operations. This is a consequence of the fact that a network on $\hat{\mathcal{E}}$ may be replaced, if necessary, by an equivalent network on $\mathcal{E}$, by replacing pairs of vertices (i,j), where $C(i,j)$ is of the form $(r \circ s)$, by 3-tuples (i,j,k) with the constraints r for $C(i,k)$ and s for $C(k,j)$. But this is no longer unconditionally possible in the case of the INDU algebra, since the fact that two intervals I and J are in the relation $(r \circ s)$ does not guarantee the existence of an interval K such that IrK and KsJ.

The point here is that the operation of composition in the INDU algebra is actually a case of *weak composition* of relations:

DEFINITION 8.8.– *Let **B** be a set of binary relations on a domain D, called basic relations, which constitute a partition of $D \times D$. The weak composition $(r \diamond s)$ of two elements r and s of B is by definition the smallest set of basic relations whose union contains $(r \circ s)$.*

PROPOSITION 8.4.– *The operation of composition for the* INDU *algebra is the weak composition on the set of the basic relations of* INDU.

The composition operation on the *INDU* algebra is thus naturally interpreted in the set $Int(\mathbb{R})$ as the weak composition of basic relations. We will use the notation $(r \diamond s)$ for weak composition, especially when we will have to contrast it to the actual composition operation, also called strong composition.

EXAMPLE 8.1.– We should be aware of the fact that, in the context of qualitative reasoning, weak composition is the rule rather than the exception: it appears naturally in many contexts.

For example, let us consider the point calculus on a time isomorphic to the set $\mathbb{Z}$ of relative integers. The Point algebra, whose basic relations are $<$, eq, and $>$, can be used to describe configurations of points, and to reason using inversion and composition.

The three corresponding basic relations in the interpretation in terms of integer points are $R = \{(n, m) \in \mathbb{Z}^2 \mid n < m\}$, $\Delta = \{(n, n) \mid n \in \mathbb{Z}\}$, and R^{-1}. Admittedly, we have, for example, $R \circ R \subset R$, but this inclusion is not an equality, since in particular $(1, 2) \in R$, but there is no integer between 1 and 2 such that $1 < n < 2$. Relation R is merely the basic relation that contains $R \circ R$, hence the *weak* composition of R with itself.

The same observation, *mutatis mutandis*, holds for Allen's interval algebra if it is interpreted in terms of intervals on the integers $\mathbb{Z}$.

Let us return to the questions of complexity. In the case of the INDU algebra, we can no longer hope to reduce the complexity problems to subsets closed by inversion, composition, and intersection — those subsets we called *subclasses* of the algebra. However, we have the following fact:

PROPOSITION 8.5.– *Let $\mathcal{E}$ be a set of relations of the* INDU *algebra which is closed under inversion and which contains the relation* eq$^=$. *Then, the consistency problem for $\mathcal{E}$ is polynomial (respectively, NP-complete) if, and only if, it is polynomial (respectively, NP-complete) for $\mathcal{E}^*$, where $\mathcal{E}^*$ is the closure of $\mathcal{E}$ under intersection.*

Proof. If the network contains the constraint $r_1 \cap \ldots r_N$ between i and j, we add N vertices $k_1, \ldots, k_N$ with the constraints $C(i, k_1) = r_1, \ldots, C(i, k_N) = r_N$, and $C(k_i, k_j) =$ eq$^=$ for $1 \leq i, j \leq N$. □

We now concentrate on the problem of determining polynomial subsets of INDU. A first observation is that the knowledge of polynomial subsets of Allen's interval algebra allows us to determine some of them:

PROPOSITION 8.6.– *Let $\mathcal{E}$ be a subset of Allen's interval algebra for which the consistency problem is polynomial. Let $\mathcal{E}'$ be the set $\mathcal{E}' = \{r^\varepsilon \mid r \in \mathcal{E} \wedge \varepsilon \in \{+,=,-\} \wedge r^\varepsilon \in INDU\}$. Then, $\mathcal{E}'$ is polynomial.*

Proof. This is a consequence of the fact that for two intervals x and y, and for a relation r of Allen's interval algebra, the INDU constraint represented by $\{r^\varepsilon \mid \varepsilon \in \{+,=,-\} \wedge r^\varepsilon \in INDU\}$ is equivalent to r (since we accept all possible durations of x and y which are compatible with r).   □

It should be noted that the constraints used in example 8.3 are not of this type: the smallest network containing the network of example 8.3 and satisfying the conditions of proposition 8.6 is defined by:

$$C(V_1, V_2) = \mathsf{si}^>, C(V_1, V_3) = \{\mathsf{o}^=, \mathsf{o}^<, \mathsf{o}^>\}, C(V_1, V_4) = \{\mathsf{o}^=, \mathsf{o}^<, \mathsf{o}^>\}$$
$$C(V_2, V_3) = \{\mathsf{m}^=, \mathsf{m}^<, \mathsf{m}^>\}, C(V_2, V_4) = \{\mathsf{p}^=, \mathsf{p}^<, \mathsf{p}^>\}, C(V_1, V_4) = \mathsf{fi}^>$$

and this network, which actually does not enforce any condition on the relative durations of the four intervals, is consistent, as seen previously.

Hence, difficult problems only appear when we consider constraint networks which are not equivalent to networks on Allen's interval algebra.

In spite of the negative results mentioned at the beginning of this section, we will now see how the combined use of syntactic methods and of geometrical methods allows to progress further in the determination of tractable subsets.

8.5.1.1. *The lattice of INDU relations*

Recall (Chapter 4, section 4.11) that the set of basic relations of INDU has a natural structure of lattice. This lattice may be considered as a subset of the product of the lattices associated with the Point algebra and Allen's interval algebra. For the convenience of the reader, Figure 8.12 is a copy of Figure 4.22 in Chapter 4.

Let us also recall that we use the term *virtual* basic relations of INDU to refer to those elements of the product lattice (such as the relations $(1, 2, 1) = \mathsf{s}^=$, or $(1, 2, 2) = \mathsf{s}^>$) which do not belong to the basic relations of INDU.

The product lattice therefore contains *bona fide* basic relations of the INDU algebra, as for example the relation $\mathsf{f}^<$, which corresponds to the pair $(\mathsf{f}, <)$ (that is, in terms of 3-tuples of integers, to the 3-tuple $(2, 3, 0)$), and *virtual* relations, such as the pairs $(\mathsf{f}, =)$ or $(\mathsf{f}, >)$ (associated to the 3-tuples $(2, 3, 1)$ and $(2, 3, 2)$, respectively). Let INDU denote the set of basic relations of INDU, which is a subset of 25 elements inside the product lattice; the latter contains $3 \times 13 = 39$ elements. In Figure 4.22, the elements of INDU are represented by black vertices, while white vertices correspond to virtual relations.

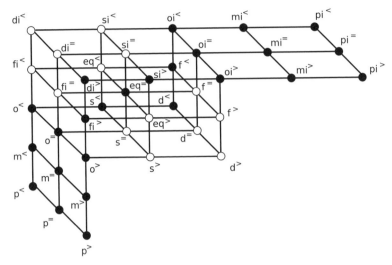

Figure 8.12. *The lattice of the basic relations of* INDU *(black vertices), seen as subsets of the product of Allen's lattice by the lattice of relations between points; the vertices represented in white are "virtual relations"*

8.5.1.2. *Convex relations*

Our goal is now to define convex and pre-convex relations; we then try to use these geometrical notions for determining polynomial subclasses of the INDU algebra, as we did for Allen's interval algebra and more generally for the various formalisms studied in Chapter 3.

The implementation of this program is somewhat tricky and will require a number of subsets of the INDU algebra to be defined in a precise way.

Recall that an *interval* in a lattice $(T, \prec)$ is either the empty set, or a set of the form $[m, M] = \{t \in T \mid m \preceq t \leq M\}$, where m and M are two elements of T such that $m \preceq M$.

DEFINITION 8.9.– *A convex relation of the* INDU *algebra is a relation which corresponds to the intersection of an interval of the* INDU *product lattice with* INDU.

A non-empty convex relation is hence of the form $[m, M] \cap$ INDU, where m and M are elements of the INDU product lattice.

Let $\mathcal{C}$ denote the set of convex relations in INDU. The set $\mathcal{C}$ is a subset of $\mathcal{P}(\text{INDU})$ (set of 2^{25} elements). It can be easily checked that it contains 240 elements.

EXAMPLE 8.2.– The relation $\{m^<, m^=, o^<, o^=\}$ is a convex relation.

The same is true for the relation $\{m^<, m^=, o^<, o^=, s^<\}$. This is an interesting case, as it corresponds to the intersection of INDU with the interval $[m^<, s^=]$, whose upper bound is a virtual relation.

We will use the conceptual space associated with INDU, that is, the representation of relations in terms of regions in the plane (Figure 8.13) which we have introduced above (Chapter 4, section 4.11). This conceptual space is a refinement of the conceptual space associated with Allen's calculus, in the sense that some of the regions[1] defining the basic relations of Allen's calculus are subdivided into three subregions by the line parallel of the first bisector which contains the point $eq^=$. For example, the region representing the relation p is divided into two-dimensional regions $p^<$ and $p^>$, and a one-dimensional region $p^=$.

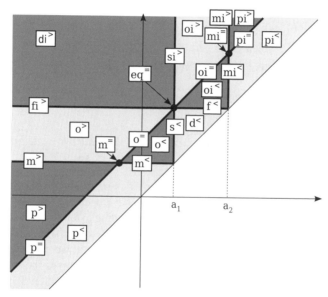

Figure 8.13. *The regions associated with the* INDU *formalism*

It follows from the definition of convex relations that a relation is convex if, and only if, it is of the form $r = (s \times t) \cap$ INDU, where s is a convex relation of Allen's interval algebra, and t a convex relation of the Point algebra.

---

1 These are the six regions associated with the relations p, m, o, pi, mi, and oi; each one of them splits into three subregions. The seven regions corresponding to the remaining seven basic relations are not affected.

EXAMPLE 8.3.– The relation $\{m^<, m^=, o^<, o^=\}$ is the intersection of $([m, o] \times [<, =])$ with INDU. The relation $\{m^<, m^=, o^<, o^=, s^<\}$ is the intersection of $([m, s] \times [<, =])$ with INDU

We will now discuss some geometrical consequences of this property.

First of all, let us note that among the eight relations of the time point algebra, seven are convex, the only non-convex one being the relation $\neq$, i.e. $\{<, >\}$. In terms of the regions that are cut out in the upper half-plane $\mathbf{H}$ by the parallel to the first bisector, the non-empty convex relations correspond to 6 regions:

– the upper half-plane $\mathbf{H}$ itself;

– the line parallel to the first bisector containing $eq^=$, which we will be denoted by $\mathbf{H}^=$;

– the region $\mathbf{H}^<$, which is the part of $\mathbf{H}$ located strictly below $\mathbf{H}^=$;

– the region $\mathbf{H}^\leq$, which is the union of $\mathbf{H}^<$ and $\mathbf{H}^=$;

– the region $\mathbf{H}^>$, which is the part of $\mathbf{H}$ located strictly above $\mathbf{H}^=$;

– the region $\mathbf{H}^\geq$, which is the union of $\mathbf{H}^>$ and $\mathbf{H}^=$.

The convex relations of INDU "are determined by their projections", in the sense of the following proposition:

PROPOSITION 8.7.– *A relation r is convex if, and only if, the associated region* $\mathrm{Reg}(r)$ *is such that* $r = (pr_1(r) \times pr_2(r)) \cap \mathbf{H}^c$, *where* $c \in \{<, eq, >, \leq, \geq, [<, >]\}^2$.

EXAMPLE 8.4.– The relation $\{m^<, m^=, o^<, o^=\}$ is represented (Figure 8.14(a)) by a right-angled triangle from which two vertices have been removed (the one on the parallel to the first bisector, and the vertex corresponding to the relation $eq^=$) and from which its vertical side (corresponding to the relation $s^<$) has also been removed. The two projections of this relation are right-open intervals, and we easily check that the intersection of the product of these two intervals with $\mathbf{H}^\leq$ gives the initial relation; hence the relation considered satisfies the conditions of Proposition 8.7, as it should since it is convex.

The relation $\{m^<, m^=, o^<, o^=, s^<\}$ is represented (Figure 8.14(b)) by a triangle which only differs from the previous triangle by the addition of the vertical open segment corresponding to the relation $s^<$. As a consequence, the projection of the triangle on the horizontal axis is now a closed interval (the right endpoint has been added to the right-open interval considered in the preceding example), and the vertical projection is the same as before. We obtain the relation considered by taking the intersection of $\mathbf{H}^\leq$ with the product of the two intervals, and intersecting the result with $\mathbf{H}^\leq$. Again, this gives a confirmation of the fact that the relation is convex.

---

2 We make the natural assumption that $\mathbf{H}^{[<,>]}$ denotes $\mathbf{H}$ itself.

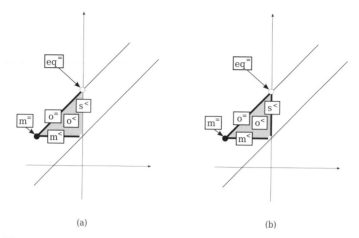

Figure 8.14. *Two convex relations: in* (a)*, the relation* $\{m^<, m^=, o^<, o^=\}$*;*
in (b)*, the relation* $\{m^<, m^=, o^<, o^=, s^<\}$

The set $\mathcal{C}$ of convex relations is closed by inversion and intersection. It is not closed by the weak composition operation, as shown by the following counterexample: the composition of $p^<$ with $\{d^<, o^<, o^=, o^>, s^<\}$ is the relation $\{p^<, p^=, d^>, o^<, m^<, s^<\}$, which is not a convex relation.

Hence, the set of convex relations is not a subclass of the INDU algebra. However, $\mathcal{C}$ contains a subset of relations which is a subclass, namely that of those relations which are "equivalent" to a convex relation of Allen's interval algebra, in the sense that they are non-committal with respect to durations:

DEFINITION 8.10.– *A convex relation* $r \in \mathcal{C}$ is transversal[3] *if it satisfies one of the following equivalent conditions:*

– $r = s \times \{<, =, >\}$, *where s is a convex relation of Allen's interval algebra;*

– $r = [a^<, b^>]$, *where a and b are basic relations of Allen's interval algebra.*

The set $\mathcal{C}_{IA}$ of transversal convex relations is in one-to-one correspondence with the set of convex relations of Allen's interval algebra. It contains 83 elements, and it is a subclass of the algebra, since in this case weak composition coincides with *bona fide* composition.

---

3 We use this term in connection with the geometrical representation of relations. In terms of the product lattice, such a relation is stable when we traverse the lattice in the direction of the coordinate axis which corresponds to the basic relations of the Point algebra.

8.5.2. *Convexity and Horn clauses*

The characterization of the convex relations of Allen's interval algebra and the Point algebra in terms of Horn clauses extends to a characterization of the convex relations of the INDU algebra:

PROPOSITION 8.8.– *An* INDU *relation is convex if, and only if, it can be expressed as a conjunction of unitary Horn clauses* Φ *such that, if* $u \neq v \in \Phi$, *then either* $u \leq v \in \Phi$, *or* $v \leq u \in \Phi$ *(where u and v denote endpoints of intervals or differences of endpoints of intervals).*

Proof. Indeed, if r is a convex relation, $r = (s \times t) \cap \mathsf{INDU}$, where s is a convex Allen relation, and t a convex relation between points. Consequently, s can be expressed as a conjunction Φ_s of unitary Horn clauses which satisfies the property that, if $u \neq v \in \Phi_s$, then either $u \leq v \in \Phi_s$, or $v \leq u \in \Phi_s$ (where u and v denote endpoints of intervals). Similarly, t can be expressed as a conjunction Φ_t of unitary Horn clauses which satisfies the property that, if $u \neq v \in \Phi_t$, either $u \leq v \in \Phi_t$ or $v \leq u \in \Phi_t$ (where u and v denote differences of endpoints). Hence the conjunction of Horn clauses $\Phi = \Phi_s \wedge \Phi_t$ is a formula which answers the question. ☐

EXAMPLE 8.5.– Let us again consider the convex relation $r = \{\mathsf{m}^<, \mathsf{m}^=, \mathsf{o}^<, \mathsf{o}^=\}$ between two intervals $x = (x_1, x_2)$ and $y = (y_1, y_2)$. We have $r = (s \times t) \cap \mathsf{INDU}$, where $s = [\mathsf{m}, \mathsf{o}]$ and $t = \{<, =\}$. Let us consider Allen's lattice in the plane with coordinate axes X_1, X_2. The relation $[\mathsf{m}, \mathsf{o}]$ is defined by the conditions $X_1 \leq 1, X_1 \neq 1, X_2 \leq 3, X_2 \neq 3, X_2 \geq 1$. The constraint s between x and y can be expressed by $\Phi_s = x_1 \leq y_1 \wedge x_1 \neq y_1 \wedge x_2 \leq y_2 \wedge x_2 \neq y_2 \wedge y_1 \leq x_2 \wedge x_1 \leq x_2 \wedge x_1 \neq x_2 \wedge y_1 \leq y_2 \wedge y_1 \neq y_2$. The constraint on the durations t, in turn, can be expressed as $\Phi_t = x_2 - x_1 \leq y_2 - y_1$. Thus, r can be expressed as $\Phi_s \wedge \Phi_t$.

Let us now consider the relation $\{\mathsf{m}^<, \mathsf{m}^=, \mathsf{o}^<, \mathsf{o}^=, \mathsf{s}^<\}$ (this is the previous relation to which the relation $\mathsf{s}^<$ has been added); it is also convex. And in fact, removing the literal $x_1 \neq y_1$ from the previous conjunction of Horn clauses is a way of expressing this relation.

NOTE 8.1.– Let us fix a reference interval y. In geometrical terms, unitary ORD-Horn clauses result in constraints enforcing a variable interval to lie in an intersection of (open or closed) horizontal or vertical half-planes. The conditions of durations, on the other hand, correspond to half-planes bounded by parallels of the first bisector. These conditions always correspond to unitary Horn clauses. But, they are no longer of the ORD type.

8.5.2.1. *Polynomiality of convex relations*

Due to their characterization in terms of Horn clauses, convex relations correspond to a polynomial consistency problem:

PROPOSITION 8.9.– *The consistency problem for the set $\mathcal{C}$ of convex relations is a polynomial problem.*

Indeed, a constraint network whose relations are in $\mathcal{C}$ can be translated in terms of a conjunction of Horn clauses. We may then apply the results known for DLRs (Appendix C) to solve the problem in polynomial time.

In the particular case of transversal convex relations, we have a set of relations which does not involve durations. The results known for Allen's interval algebra can be applied: the consistency problem for these relations is polynomial and, moreover, it can be resolved by using the $\diamond$-algebraic closure method.

8.5.3. *Pre-convex relations*

Once again, representing the INDU relations as regions in the plane enables us to associate geometrical and topological properties to them.

DEFINITION 8.11.– *The* dimension *of a relation r, denoted by dim (r), is the dimension of the corresponding region.*

By convention, the dimension of the empty relation is -1. It should be noted that the dimension of the relations $\mathsf{p}^=, \mathsf{m}^=, \mathsf{o}^=$ and their inverses is 1, contrary to that of the corresponding relations $\mathsf{p}^>, \mathsf{p}^<, \ldots$, which is 2. The dimension of a disjunctive relation is equal to the largest dimension of the relations it contains.

DEFINITION 8.12.– *The* topological closure *of a relation r, denoted by $C(r)$, is the relation whose corresponding region is the topological closure of the region representing r.*

The universal relation, which is the union of the 25 basic relations, is convex, and we have seen that the intersection of two convex relations is also convex. As a consequence, for any relation, there exists a smaller convex relation which contains it, namely the intersection of all convex relations containing it. We may thus define the convex closure of a relation:

DEFINITION 8.13.– *The* convex closure *of a relation r, denoted by $I(r)$, is the smallest convex relation containing r.*

The definition of convexity implies that the convex closure of a relation may be calculated component-wise, that is, if $r = (s \times t) \cap \mathsf{INDU}$, where $s \in \mathbf{A_2}$ and $t \in \mathbf{A_1}$, then $I(r) = (I(s) \times I(t)) \cap \mathsf{INDU}$.

We are now in a position to define pre-convex relations:

DEFINITION 8.14.– *A relation r is* pre-convex *if, and only if, it is the empty relation or if* $dim(I(r) \setminus r) < dim(r)$.

In particular, any convex relation, and *a fortiori*, any basic relation, is pre-convex.

NOTE 8.2.– The use of the term "pre-convex relation" (for Allen's relations) was originally motivated by the fact those relations are characterized by the fact that their topological closures are convex.

Let $\mathcal{P}$ denote the set of pre-convex relations. It is a set of relations which contains 88,096 elements. It is easily checked that this set is closed under inversion. But it is closed neither under intersection, nor under weak composition.

$\mathcal{P}$ is not closed under intersection: indeed, consider for example the relations $r_1 = \{p^<, p^=, o^<, eq^=\}$ and $r_2 = \{p^>, p^=, o^>, eq^=\}$. Both relations are pre-convex, since $I(r_1) \setminus r_1 = \{m^<, m^=, s^<\}$, which is of dimension 1, whereas r_1 is two-dimensional, and $I(r_2) \setminus r_2 = \{m^>, m^=, fi^>\}$ is also one-dimensional, whereas r_2 is two-dimensional. But the intersection $r_1 \cap r_2$ is the one-dimensional relation $r_3 = \{p^=, eq^=\}$ which is not pre-convex, because $I(r_3) = \{p^=, m^=, ^=, eq^=\}$, and hence $I(r_3) \setminus r_3 = \{m^=, ^=\}$, which is also one-dimensional.

Neither is $\mathcal{P}$ closed under weak composition: indeed, consider the relations $r_4 = p^<$ and $r_5 = \{d^<, o^<, o^>\}$. The basic relation r_4 is pre-convex. The relation r_5 is two-dimensional, and $I(r_5) \setminus r_5 = \{o^=, s^<\}$ is one-dimensional, hence r_5 is pre-convex. But, $r_4 \diamond r_5 = \{p^<, p^=, p^>, m^<, o^<, s^<, d^<\}$, which is not a pre-convex relation (since its convex closure contains the relation $o^>$ which is two-dimensional).

8.5.4. *NP-completeness of pre-convex relations*

The set of pre-convex relations (a set of 88,096 elements in a set of $2^{25} = 33,554,432$ elements) is neither closed under intersection nor under weak composition. Proposition 8.5 states that the complexity of $\mathcal{P}$ is the same as that of $\mathcal{P}^*$.

PROPOSITION 8.10.– *The consistency problem for networks on $\mathcal{P}^*$ relations is NP-complete.*

Proof. We refer the reader to [BAL 06], which describes in detail the reduction of the problem of 3-coloring of a graph to the consistency problem for networks on $\mathcal{P}^*$. □

8.5.5. *Strongly pre-convex relations*

Since the set of pre-convex relations of INDU is not closed under intersection, it is thus natural to try to apply the same strategy which we used in Chapter 4 for the formalism of generalized intervals and for product formalisms and to define a concept of strong pre-convexity:

DEFINITION 8.15.– *A relation r is* strongly pre-convex *if, for every convex relation $t \in C$, the relation $r \cap t$ is a pre-convex relation.*

Let $\mathcal{F}$ be the set of strongly pre-convex relations. We can check that, among the 88,096 elements of $\mathcal{P}$, 45,792 relations are strongly pre-convex. Any convex relation is strongly pre-convex, since C is closed by intersection, hence $C \subseteq \mathcal{F}$.

The set $\mathcal{F}$ satisfies the required condition with regard to intersection, but is not closed under weak composition:

PROPOSITION 8.11.– *The set $\mathcal{F}$ is closed under inversion and intersection. It is not closed under weak composition.*

Proof. The proof of this proposition results from an explicit computation using a computer program. As regards the negative result, a counterexample is provided by the relations $r_1 = \mathsf{p}^<$ and $r_2 = \{\mathsf{o}^<, \mathsf{o}^>, \mathsf{d}^>\}$. Indeed:

  – r_1 and r_2 are strongly pre-convex;

  – their weak composition $r_1 \diamond r_2 = \{\mathsf{p}^<, \mathsf{p}^=, \mathsf{p}^>, \mathsf{m}^<, \mathsf{o}^<, \mathsf{s}^<, \mathsf{d}^<\}$ is not strongly pre-convex.

The first point is clear for the basic relation r_1. The relation r_2 is the set of two-dimensional relations in the convex relation $([\mathsf{o}, \mathsf{d}] \times [<, >]) \cap \mathsf{INDU}$, and its intersections with a convex relation are clearly pre-convex.

The second point is also clear, as the convex closure of the weak composition contains the relation $\mathsf{o}^>$, which is two-dimensional.   □

PROPOSITION 8.12.– *The strongly pre-convex relations of* INDU *can be represented by conjunctions of Horn clauses.*

Proof. Let us consider a relation $r \in \mathcal{F}$. Since the convex closure $I(r)$ of r is convex, it can be represented by a Horn clause $\Phi_{I(r)}$. In general, $I(r) \setminus r$ will contain basic relations which also satisfy $\Phi_{I(r)}$. If a is one of these basic relations, we have to find a Horn clause excluding it, without excluding the basic relations contained in r.

As r is pre-convex, the eventual basic relations of $I(r) \setminus r$ are of dimension strictly less than that of r, hence 0 or 1-dimensional. Such a relation may be of two types: either it does not enforce equal durations, so that it is one of the 8 relations

$m^\varepsilon, mi^\varepsilon (\varepsilon \in \{<, >\}), s^<, f^<, si^>, fi^>$; or it is one of the seven basic relations in the convex relation $s = [p^=, pi^=]$.

Let $x = (x_1, x_2)$ and $y = (y_1, y_2)$ be two intervals.

The crux of the proof is that we have to remove all unwanted relations, and *only them*, by using Horn clauses, that is clauses which contain at most one positive literal.

For the 8 relations of the first type, this is easily done. Indeed, consider the following clauses:

$$\Phi_{m<} = (x_2 \neq y_1 \vee x_2 - x_1 \geq y_2 - y_1)$$
$$\Phi_{m>} = (x_2 \neq y_1 \vee x_2 - x_1 \leq y_2 - y_1)$$
$$\Phi_{mi<} = (y_2 \neq x_1 \vee x_2 - x_1 \geq y_2 - y_1)$$
$$\Phi_{mi>} = (y_2 \neq x_1 \vee x_2 - x_1 \leq y_2 - y_1)$$
$$\Phi_{s<} = (x_1 \neq y_1 \vee x_2 - x_1 \geq y_2 - y_1)$$
$$\Phi_{si>} = (x_1 \neq y_1 \vee x_2 - x_1 \leq y_2 - y_1)$$
$$\Phi_{f<} = (x_2 \neq y_2 \vee x_2 - x_1 \geq y_2 - y_1)$$
$$\Phi_{fi>} = (x_2 \neq y_2 \vee x_2 - x_1 \leq y_2 - y_1)$$

Each one of these 8 clauses is the negation of a conjunction which exactly defines the relation that we want to exclude. For example, $\Phi_{m<}$ is the negation of $(x_2 = y_1 \wedge x_2 - x_1 < y_2 - y_1)$, which exactly expresses the condition defining the relation $m^<$.

We then have to consider the seven relations which enforce equal durations. Finding suitable Horn clauses for five of them is straightforward:

$$\Phi_{p=} = (x_2 - x_1 \neq y_2 - y_1 \vee x_2 \geq y_1)$$
$$\Phi_{pi=} = (x_2 - x_1 \neq y_2 - y_1 \vee y_2 \geq x_1)$$
$$\Phi_{m=} = (x_2 - x_1 \neq y_2 - y_1 \vee x_2 \neq y_1)$$
$$\Phi_{mi=} = (x_2 - x_1 \neq y_2 - y_1 \vee y_2 \geq x_1)$$
$$\Phi_{eq=} = (x_1 \neq y_1 \vee x_2 \neq y_2)$$

We have to examine the case of relations $o^=$ and $oi^=$. The difficulty here is that the relation $o^=$, for example, is defined by the formula:

$$(x_1 < y_1 \wedge y_1 < x_2 \wedge x_2 < y_2 \wedge x_2 - x_1 = y_2 - y_1)$$

whose negation *is not* a Horn clause, since it reads:

$$(x_1 \geq y_1 \vee y_1 \geq x_2 \vee x_2 \geq y_2 \vee x_2 - x_1 \neq y_2 - y_1)$$

and the relation oi$^=$ poses a similar problem.

Let us consider the case of o$^=$. Assume that r is a strongly pre-convex relation, that $I(r)$ contains o$^=$, and that r does not contain o$^=$. The case of oi$^=$ is completely similar and so we will not elaborate on it.

Let us show that we have either $r \cap \{p^=, m^=\} = \varnothing$, or $r \cap \{eq^=, oi^=, mi^=, pi^=\} = \varnothing$. Indeed, if this was not the case, we would have $I(r \cap s) \ni o^=$, whereas o$^=$ is not contained in $r \cap s$. Hence, the dimension of $I(r \cap s) \setminus (r \cap s)$ is at least 1, the dimension of o$^=$. As, in addition, the dimension of $(r \cap s)$ is increased by that of s, which is 1, $(r \cap s)$ is not pre-convex, which contradicts the hypothesis that r is strongly pre-convex.

We thus know that the relation r meets at most one of the two subsets $\{p^=, m^=\}$ and $\{eq^=, oi^=, mi^=, pi^=\}$ of s: either it meets none of them, or it meets one and not the other; hence we have to examine three cases:

– $r \cap s = \varnothing$. This means that the relation r does not contain any element of s, but that $I(r)$ contains o$^=$. To get rid of o$^=$, we add the condition which excludes s, that is in this case, $\Phi_{o^=} = (x_2 - x_1 \neq y_2 - y_1)$. Of course, by doing this, we remove all the relations of s, but only the relation o$^=$ is removed from $I(r)$, which is precisely what we wanted to do;

– r has a non-empty intersection with $\{p^=, m^=\}$, but it does not contain any element of $\{eq^=, oi^=, mi^=, pi^=\}$. This time, removing the whole of s would actually result in removing o$^=$, but it would also mean removing this non-empty intersection. However, inside s, $\{p^=, m^=\}$ corresponds to the condition $x_2 \leq y_1$. We can thus remove only o$^=$ if we add $\Phi_{o^=} = (x_2 - x_1 \neq y_2 - y_1 \vee x_2 \leq y_1)$, which is a Horn clause;

– r has a non-empty intersection with $\{eq^=, oi^=, mi^=, pi^=\}$, but it does not contain any relation of $\{p^=, m^=\}$. This time, the subrelation $\{eq^=, oi^=, mi^=, pi^=\}$ is defined in s by the condition $x_2 \geq y_2$; we add it, and obtain a Horn clause which removes o$^=$, and only it: $\Phi_{o^=} = (x_2 - x_1 \neq y_2 - y_1 \vee x_2 \geq y_2)$.

It follows from the previous discussion that any $r \in \mathcal{F}$ can be represented by the conjunction of Horn clauses $\Phi_{I(r)} \wedge \bigwedge_{a \in (I(r) \setminus r)} \Phi_a$.   □

As a consequence, we have the following theorem:

THEOREM 8.1.– *The consistency problem for the set $\mathcal{F}$ is polynomial.*

8.5.6. The subclass $\mathcal{G}$

The various subsets of the INDU algebra we have considered so far are not subclasses, except for the subclass $\mathcal{C}_{IA}$ of transversal convex relations, which is basically a copy of the subclass of convex relations of Allen's interval algebra.

The class $\mathcal{G}$ that we are going to define uses the existence of this subclass in order to build a polynomial subclass inside the set of pre-convex relations.

DEFINITION 8.16.– *The set $\mathcal{G}$ is the set of relations r such that, for any transversal convex relation s, the intersection $r \cap s$ is pre-convex and the convex closure $I(r \cap s)$ of this intersection is a transversal convex relation: $I(r \cap s) \in \mathcal{C}_{IA}$.*

The universal relation INDU is a transversal convex relation, and consequently, a relation belonging to $\mathcal{G}$ is necessarily pre-convex. $\mathcal{G}$ is hence a subset of $\mathcal{P}$, and it is distinct from the set $\mathcal{F}$ of strongly pre-convex relations. Indeed, the relation $[\mathsf{m}^<, \mathsf{mi}^>] \setminus \{\mathsf{o}^=, \mathsf{oi}^=, \mathsf{s}^<, \mathsf{si}^>, \mathsf{f}^<, \mathsf{fi}^>\}$ belongs to $\mathcal{G}$, as can be easily verified (for this, we may use the representation of the product lattice of Figure 8.12). But it is not a strongly pre-convex relation, since its intersection with the convex relation $[\mathsf{m}^=, \mathsf{mi}^=]$ is the relation $\{\mathsf{m}^=, \mathsf{eq}^=, \mathsf{mi}^=\}$, which is not pre-convex.

The set $\mathcal{G}$ contains 11,854 elements.

NOTE.– What are the basic relations contained in $\mathcal{G}$? The definition immediately shows that they are the basic relations which are transversal, that is, the seven relations $\mathsf{eq}^=, \mathsf{s}^<, \mathsf{si}^>, \mathsf{f}^<, \mathsf{fi}^>, \mathsf{d}^<, \mathsf{di}^>$. Thus, $\mathcal{G}$ is a subclass which does not contain all basic relations.

PROPOSITION 8.13.– *The set $\mathcal{G}$ is closed under inversion, intersection, and weak composition. Hence, it is a subclass of the INDU algebra.*

Proof. The proof is based on an explicit computation using a computer program. The reader may refer to [BAL 06] for more details. ☐

We will now see that the consistency problem is polynomial for the subclass $\mathcal{G}$ and that, moreover, this problem may be solved by using the $\diamond$-algebraic closure method. The reason is that, in this case, we will be able to use the property of the existence of a maximal solution (see definition 2.11) for algebraically closed pre-convex constraint networks on Allen's interval algebra (proposition 2.8).

The definition of a maximal solution (definition 2.11) applies here. For example, if the constraint $C(i, j)$ is $\{\mathsf{m}^=, \mathsf{m}^>, \mathsf{o}^=, \mathsf{o}^<, \mathsf{p}^>\}$, and if m is a maximal solution, then the relation between $m(i)$ and $m(j)$ must be $\mathsf{o}^<$ or $\mathsf{p}^>$.

The following result expresses the fact that transversal convex relations, which constitute a copy of the convex relations inside the INDU relations, behave like the INDU relations with respect to the existence of maximal solutions:

PROPOSITION 8.14.– *Let* $\mathcal{N} = (N, C)$ *be a constraint network for* INDU *whose constraints are transversal convex constraints other than the empty constraint. Then, if* $\mathcal{N}$ *is non-empty and* $\diamond$-*algebraically closed,* $\mathcal{N}$ *has a maximal solution.*

Proof. The constraints of $\mathcal{N} = (N, C)$ are transversal convex relations, hence $\mathcal{N}$ is equivalent to the network $\mathcal{N}' = (N, C')$ on Allen's interval algebra that we get if we forget the constraints on durations. Let us choose a maximal solution m for the latter. Then, for all $i, j \in N$, an endpoint of $m(i)$ coincides with an endpoint of $m(j)$ only if *all* basic relations of $C(i, j)$ enforce this coincidence.

We cannot yet assert that m is a maximal solution for the INDU network. Indeed, if we remember that, for an Allen basic relation a of dimension 2 or 1, the dimension of a^ε is that of a for $\varepsilon =<$ and $\varepsilon =>$, but only $dim(a) - 1$ when ε is =, we see that it is *a priori* possible that two intervals $m(i)$ and $m(j)$ are of the same duration, so that the dimension of the corresponding relation in INDU is decreased by 1, although this is not enforced by the constraints. Since we are dealing with transversal convex constraints, the only constraint that can enforce the equality of durations has to be the constraint $C(i, j) = \mathsf{eq}^=$.

Hence, we have to show that m may be modified to yield an instantiation m' such that for any pair $i, j \in N$, the duration of $m'(i)$ is equal to that of $m'(j)$ if, and only if, $C(i, j) = \mathsf{eq}$. That follows from lemma 8.1 below. □

EXAMPLE 8.6.– If for example, the instantiation of a network with three vertices is $m(1) = [0, 1]$, $m(2) = [1, 3]$, $m(3) = [2, 4]$, there is an equality of duration between $m(2)$ and $m(3)$.

LEMMA 8.1.–

– *any constraint network* $\mathcal{N} = (N, C)$ *on Allen's interval algebra which is a consistent scenario has a solution* $m: N \rightarrow Int(\mathbb{R})$ *such that the set of endpoints of the intervals* $m(i), i \in N$ *is the set* $[0, \dots, M]$ *of non-negative integers* k *such that* $k \leq M$. *The corresponding solution is known as the* canonical model *of the network[4];*

– *under the same conditions,* $\mathcal{N}$ *has a solution such that* $m(i)$ *and* $m(j)$ *are of the same duration if, and only if,* $C(i, j) = \mathsf{eq}$.

---

4 The term was introduced by Zhang *et al.* in [ZHA 08]. See also Chapter 4, section 4.10.

Proof. The Part 1 follows immediately from the examination of a solution for a consistent network. If $M + 1$ is the cardinal of the set W of endpoints of this solution, W_{can} is isomorphic to $[0, \ldots, M]$ and the canonical map provides by composition a solution $m_{can} \colon N \to Int[0, \ldots, M]$ whose set of endpoints is $[0, \ldots, M]$.

Let us now prove the Part 2. Consider the canonical model $m_{can} \colon N \to Int(\mathbb{N})$. It satisfies the property that the set of endpoints of $m_{can}(N)$ is an initial segment $[0, M] = \{0, 1, \ldots, M\}$ of $\mathbb{N}$, with $2 \leq M \leq 2n - 1$.

Let $f \colon \mathbb{N} \to \mathbb{N}$ be defined by $f(t) = 2^t - 1$. This is a strictly increasing map, hence the map $(m' = m_{can} \circ (f \times f)) \colon N \to Int(\mathbb{N})$ is an instantiation of N corresponding to the same consistent scenario.

We now state that two intervals $m'(i)$ and $m'(j)$ may be of the same duration only if the constraint $C(i, j))$ is $\mathrm{eq}^=$.

Our statement could only be falsified for Allen relations of type eq, p, m, o, or their inverses, as the other relations enforce different durations. By changing the notations if necessary, we may assume that the beginning of i precedes that of j, or that both coincide, and hence that the relation of i with respect to j is one of the four relations eq, p, m, o, which means that the end of i precedes that of j, or coincides with it.

We thus have two intervals $m_{can}(i) = (i_1, i_2)$ and $m_{can}(j) = (j_1, j_2)$, with $i_1 \leq j_1$ and $i_2 \leq j_2$.

The duration of $m'(i)$ is $2^{i_2} - 2^{i_1} = 2^{i_1}(2^{i_2 - i_1} - 1)$. Similarly, that of $m'(j)$ is $2^{j_1}(2^{j_2 - j_1} - 1)$. Let $a = j_1 - i_1$, which is positive or zero. If these two durations are equal, then $2^{i_1}(2^{i_2 - i_1} - 1) = 2^{i_1 + a}(2^{j_2 - j_1} - 1)$. The second factors of the two members of this equality being odd, we conclude that $a = 0$, and hence that $j_1 = i_1$, and $j_2 = j_1$, which was to be proved. $\qquad\square$

The following proposition shows that some INDU relations have the same nice behavior as Allen's relations with respect to weak composition and convex closure:

PROPOSITION 8.15.– *Let $r, s \in$ INDU such that $I(r), I(s)$ and $I(r \diamond s)$ are transversal convex relations. Then $I(r \diamond s) \subseteq I(r) \diamond I(s)$.*

Proof. Since $r \subseteq I(r)$ and $s \subseteq I(s)$, we have $r \diamond s \subseteq I(r) \diamond I(s)$. Convex closure is an increasing function, which implies that $I(r \diamond s) \subseteq I(I(r) \diamond I(s))$. The set of transversal convex relations is closed under weak composition, hence $I(r) \diamond I(s)$ is a convex relation, so that it is equal to its convex closure. We conclude that $I(r \diamond s) \subseteq I(r) \diamond I(s)$. $\qquad\square$

PROPOSITION 8.16.– *Let $\mathcal{N} = (N, C)$ be a constraint network whose constraints are elements of $\mathcal{G}$. Let $\mathcal{N}^I = (N, C^I)$ be the network defined by $C^I(i, j) = I(C(i, j))$, for $i, j \in N$. If $\mathcal{N}$ is $\diamond$-algebraically closed, the network $\mathcal{N}^I$ is also $\diamond$-algebraically closed.*

Proof. By hypothesis, we have $C(i, j) \subseteq C(i, k) \diamond C(k, j)$ for any 3-tuple $i, j, k \in N$. Since $\mathcal{G}$ is closed under weak composition, $I(C(i, k) \diamond C(k, j))$ is a transversal convex relation. According to proposition 8.15, $I(C(i, k) \diamond C(k, j)) \subseteq I(r) \diamond I(s)$, which shows that $\mathcal{N}^I$ is $\diamond$-algebraically closed. □

We are now in a position to state the main result about the subclass $\mathcal{G}$:

THEOREM 8.2.– *For constraint networks on the subclass $\mathcal{G}$, the consistency problem can be solved by applying the $\diamond$-algebraic closure method.*

Proof. Let $\mathcal{N} = (N, C)$ be a constraint network whose constraints are elements of $\mathcal{G}$. After enforcing $\diamond$-closure, we get a network $\mathcal{N}' = (N, C')$ equivalent to $\mathcal{N}$, whose constraints are elements of $\mathcal{G}$, as $\mathcal{G}$ is a subclass. If $\mathcal{N}'$ contains the empty relation, it is not consistent. Otherwise, consider the network $\mathcal{N}'' = (N, C'')$ defined by $C''(i, j) = I(C'(i, j))$, for $i, j \in N$. This network is $\diamond$-algebraically closed (proposition 8.16). According to proposition 8.16, it has a maximal solution $m: N \to Int(\mathbb{R})$. But this maximal solution is also a maximal solution of $\mathcal{N}'$, since $dim(I(C'(i, j) \backslash C'(i, j)) < dim(C'(i, j))$ for any pair $i, j \in N$. □

NOTE 8.3.– Once again, let us recall that the subclass $\mathcal{G}$ contains only 7 of the 25 basic relations of the INDU algebra, namely those which are transversal relations, that is, the relations $eq^=, s^<, si^>, f^<, fi^>, d^<$, and $di^>$. We also know that the $\diamond$-algebraic closure method cannot be used for solving the consistency problem on INDU — even for atomic networks. The question may be raised of determining whether there are basic relations other than these seven relations for which the $\diamond$-algebraic closure method solves the consistency problem. The answer is a positive one:

THEOREM 8.3.– *Let $\mathcal{N}$ be a network whose constraints are basic relations belonging to the set $\mathsf{INDU}^= = \{p^=, m^=, o^=, eq^=, pi^=, mi^=, oi^=\}$. If $\mathcal{N}$ is closed by weak composition and does not contain the empty constraint, then $\mathcal{N}$ is consistent.*

The proof of this result is based on one observation and on a property of Allen's interval algebra: the observation is that given an arbitrary network on the INDU algebra, we may consider its projections on Allen's interval algebra and the Point algebra, and that this projection operation preserves the $\diamond$-closure property (which, for Allen's interval algebras and the Point algebra, coincides with closure by composition); the property is stated by the following proposition:

PROPOSITION 8.17.– *Let $\mathcal{N}$ be an atomic constraint network on Allen's interval algebra whose constraints belong to the set $S = \{\mathsf{p}, \mathsf{m}, \mathsf{o}, \mathsf{eq}, \mathsf{pi}, \mathsf{mi}, \mathsf{oi}\}$[5]. Then, if $\mathcal{N}$ is algebraically closed and does not contain the empty relation, there exists a solution of $\mathcal{N}$ whose intervals have the same common duration.*

We refer the reader to [BAL 06] for a proof of this result.

The projection operations of a network on the INDU algebra are those naturally induced by considering that the basic relations of INDU are pairs a^ε, where a is an Allen relation and ε is a relation between points:

DEFINITION 8.17.– *Let $\mathcal{N}$ b a constraint network on the INDU algebra. The projection of $\mathcal{N}$ on Allen's interval algebra (respectively, on the Point algebra) is the network $\mathcal{N}^{IA} = (N, C^{IA})$ on Allen's interval algebra (respectively, the network $\mathcal{N}^{PA} = (N, C^{PA})$ on the Point algebra) defined by $C^{IA}(i,j) = \{a \mid \exists \varepsilon \text{ such that } a^\varepsilon \in C(i,j)\}$ (respectively, $(C^{PA}(i,j) = \{\varepsilon \mid \exists a \text{ such that } a^\varepsilon \in C(i,j)\})$, for all $i, j \in N$.*

Obviously, the projections of a network may be consistent without the network itself being so.

PROPOSITION 8.18.– *If $\mathcal{N}$ is an atomic constraint network on the INDU algebra which is $\diamond$-algebraically closed, then its projections on Allen's interval algebra and on the Point algebra are algebraically closed.*

Proof. The demonstration essentially results from the definitions. Let us show the result for the projection on Allen's interval algebra. Let $i, j, k \in N$. If a is a basic relation in $C^{IA}(i,j)$, there exists by definition $\varepsilon \in \{<, =, >\}$ such that $a^\varepsilon \in C(i,j)$. By definition of $\diamond$, and due to the $\diamond$-algebraic closure of the network, we have $b^\eta \in C(i,k)$ and $c^\varsigma \in C(k,j)$ such that $a^\varepsilon \in (b^\eta \diamond c^\varsigma)$, that is $a^\varepsilon \in ((b \circ c) \times (\eta \circ \varsigma)) \cap$ INDU. Hence $a \in (C^{IA}(i,k) \circ C^{IA}(k,j))$ and $\varepsilon \in (C^{PA}(i,k) \circ C^{PA}(k,j))$. This shows that the projection on Allen's interval algebra is algebraically closed. The same reasoning using $\varepsilon \in C^{PA}(i,j)$ shows that the projection on the Point algebra is also algebraically closed. □

We now have all the elements required to prove theorem 8.3.

---

5 These are the six basic relations other than eq) which do not correspond to atomic transversal relations.

The Geometrical Approach and Conceptual Spaces   257

Proof. Let $\mathcal{N}$ be a network satisfying the assumptions of Theorem 8.3. Its projection on Allen's interval algebra is algebraically closed according to proposition 8.18. This projection does not contain the empty relation, and it satisfies the assumptions of proposition 8.17. Hence, it has a consistent instantiation for which all intervals are of the same duration, so that it is actually a consistent instantiation of $\mathcal{N}$ itself.   □

8.5.7. *A summary of complexity results for INDU*

We may summarize the results obtained for the complexity problem of the INDU algebra in Table 8.2.

Set	Cardinal	-1	$\cap$	$\diamond$	complexity	$\diamond$-closure
INDU	25	yes	no	no	polynomial	no
INDU$^=$	7	yes	no	no	polynomial	yes
$\mathcal{C}$	240	yes	yes	no	polynomial	no
$\mathcal{C}^{IA}$	83	yes	yes	yes	polynomial	yes
$\mathcal{P}$	88,096	yes	no	no	NP-complete	no
$\mathcal{F}$	45,792	yes	yes	no	polynomial	no
$\mathcal{G}$	11,854	yes	yes	yes	polynomial	yes

Table 8.2. *The subsets of the* INDU *algebra considered in this chapter, and their properties: cardinality, stability under inversion, intersection and weak composition, complexity of the consistency problem, and decidability by the $\diamond$-closure method*

Although most of the properties of Allen's calculus are no longer satisfied, it is all the same possible to characterize several sets of relations which result in a polynomial consistency problem. When this is the case, the $\diamond$-algebraic closure method is not always a test for consistency; but we have characterized several subsets of relations for which it is indeed such a test.

Two types of methods have been used: syntactic methods (using Horn clauses) and geometrical methods (using the lattice and geometrical representations of the relations). Note that the "syntactic" method can also be considered as geometric in nature, as far as it is based on the properties of convex sets in Euclidean spaces. In this regard, it does not fundamentally differ from the geometrical method.

The simultaneous use of both types of approaches has made it possible to determine different polynomial subsets, as opposed to what happens in the case of Allen's calculus (or more generally of generalized interval calculi) for which ORD-Horn relations and pre-convex relations prove to be the same polynomial subclass.

8.6. Historical note

The idea of systematically relating the geometrical approach to the study of complexity to the theory of conceptual spaces is exposed in [LIG 05b]. The simultaneous application of syntactic and geometrical techniques for the study of INDU relations is described in [BAL 03], of which [BAL 06] is an improved and completed version.

Chapter 9

Weak Representations

9.1. "Find the hidden similarity"

What is the hidden similarity between the two labeled graphs in Figure 9.1?

These two graphs represent two scenarios: the first one is a scenario (a) on the Point algebra $\mathbf{A}_1$, and the second one (b) on Allen's Interval algebra $\mathbf{A}_2$. As shown in the figure, these two networks are normalized – the label eq appears only on the arcs (i, i), and for any pair of vertices (i, j), the label on arc (i, j) is the inverse of the label on arc (i, j).

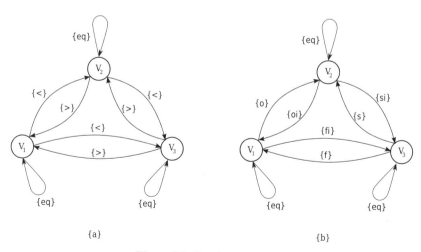

Figure 9.1. *Two labeled graphs*

The hidden similarity is the fact that these two scenarios are algebraically closed: if an arc (i, j) is labeled by a relation $C(i, j)$ and the arc (j, k) is labeled by a relation $C(j, k)$, then the arc (i, k) has one of the basic relations of $C(i, j) \circ C(j, k)$ as its label. For example, in the second graph, $C(V_1, V_2) = \{o\}$, and $C(V_2, V_3) = \{si\}$, and we note that the label $C(V_1, V_3) = \{fi\}$ is one of the elements of $(o \circ si) = \{o, fi, di\}$.

If we consider the set of basic relations $\mathbf{B}_1$ ($\mathbf{B}_2$, respectively) as sets of labels, we are dealing with particular labelings of the arcs of a graph by basic relations which we will refer to as a *weak representation* of the corresponding algebra.

The main topic of this chapter is to study the weak representations of the algebras of some of the qualitative formalisms we have previously presented.

In the two examples we considered at the outset, we know that the corresponding networks are consistent, which means that in the first case, we may interpret V_1, V_2, and V_3 in terms of three points on the line, so that $<$ is interpreted as the precedence relation, $>$ as its transpose, and eq as the equality. Similarly, for the second case, we may find three intervals which are in the specified relations. This property will not hold true for all formalisms.

Scenarios involve a finite number of nodes, but there is no reason for not extending the definition to infinite sets; for example, we may see the specification:

$$\varphi(<) = \{(i, j) \in \mathbb{R}^2 \mid (i < j)\}$$
$$\varphi(>) = \{(i, j) \in \mathbb{R}^2 \mid (i > j)\}$$
$$\varphi(eq) = \{(i, j) \in \mathbb{R}^2 \mid (i = j)\}$$

as a "labeling" of all pairs of real numbers by elements of $\mathbf{B}_1$, and the fact that this labeling is algebraically closed expresses the fact that $\mathbb{R}$ is a linear order for the usual relation.

Another way of looking at things is to consider that each labeling gives an image of the abstract algebra associated with the formalism. This image may be imperfect, but it is concrete, as it is formed by pairs of elements of a set.

More precisely, the "imperfection" of the image is due to the concrete composition operation, the composition of binary relations, which only reflects imperfectly the abstract composition:

EXAMPLE 9.1.– In the case of (a), we have $\varphi(<) = \{(V_1, V_2), (V_2, V_3), (V_1, V_3)\}$ and $\varphi(>) = \{(V_2, V_1), (V_3, V_2), (V_3, V_1)\}$. We see that the composition of these two relations is $\{(V_1, V_1), (V_2, V_2), (V_2, V_1), (V_1, V_2)\}$, a relation which contains only four out of the nine elements of $\varphi(< \circ >) = U \times U$. In other words, the image of the (abstract) composition of the two relations contains the (set-theoretical) composition of the images of these abstract relations, but it does not coincide with it.

If the image of the algebra is a "perfect" image, we say that the weak representation is a *representation*. In that case, the image of composition is the composition of the images. In particular, this is true for the representation of the Point algebra $\mathbf{A}_1$ in terms of pairs of points on the real line that we have just considered.

9.2. Weak representations

We come to the general definition of a weak representation (the reader may refer to Appendix B for the concepts and notations pertaining to relation algebras):

DEFINITION 9.1.– *A weak representation of a simple relation algebra* A *consists of a pair* (U, φ), *where:*

- U *is a non-empty set*;
- φ *is a map:* $\varphi \colon A \to \mathcal{P}(U \times U)$;
- φ *is a morphism of Boolean algebras*;
- $\varphi(1') = \Delta_U$;
- *for any* $x \in A, \varphi(x^\smile) = \varphi(x)^{-1}$;
- *for all* $x, y \in A, \varphi(x; y) \supseteq \varphi(x) \circ \varphi(y)$.

Let us comment on some immediate consequences of the definition:

– algebraically closed and normalized scenarios are particular cases of weak representations. In the general case, we do not enforce the set associated with a weak representation to be finite set;

– the representations (see Appendix B) of a relation algebra are particular cases of weak representations;

– in the case of the *finite* relation algebras that we will consider — which consequently are atomic — a weak representation of such an algebra $\mathbf{A}$ is entirely determined by its restriction to the set $\mathbf{B}$ of atoms of $\mathbf{A}$;

– more precisely, in this case, consider a weak representation (U, φ) of $\mathbf{A}$. Then, the set of $\varphi(b)$, for $b \in \mathbf{B}$ such that $\varphi(b) \neq \varnothing$, is a partition of $U \times U$ or, in other terms, a JEPD set of binary relations on U.

In order to illustrate the concept of weak representation more precisely, let us examine some examples.

9.2.1. *Weak representations of the Point algebra*

Consider the Point algebra $\mathbf{A}_1$. This algebra has three atoms $<$, eq, and $>$. A weak representation of $\mathbf{A}_1$ is a pair (U, φ), where U is a non-empty set and φ is a map which associates with each atom a binary relation on U such that the following constraints constraints are satisfied:

- the three relations $\varphi(<), \varphi(\text{eq})$, and $\varphi(<)$ are pairwise disjoint;
- $\varphi(\text{eq}+ <+>) = \varphi(<) \cup \varphi(\text{eq}) \cup \varphi(>) = U \times U$;
- $\varphi(\text{eq})$ is the diagonal relation;
- $\varphi(<) = R$ and $\varphi(>)$ are the two relations which are inverse of each other;
- $\varphi(< \circ <) = \varphi(<) \supseteq (<) \circ \varphi(<)$, i.e. $R \supseteq R \circ R$: the relation R is transitive.

Consequently, R must be a linear order on U. Conversely, a linear order on U defines a weak representation, by considering U as the subjacent set and $\varphi(<)$ as the order relation.

The concept of a weak representation of $\mathbf{A}_1$ thus coincides with that of a linear order.

9.2.1.1. *Representations of* $\mathbf{A}_1$

We may then ask the question of representations: what are the weak representations that are also representations? Two conditions have to be met: first, φ should be an injective map, which is the case. Moreover, we must have:

- $R \subseteq (R \circ R)$;
- $\Delta \subseteq (R \circ R^{-1})$;
- $\Delta \subseteq (R^{-1} \circ R)$.

The first condition implies that the linear order R is a *dense* order. The second condition implies that there is no greatest element in U (the order unlimited on the right), and the third condition implies that there is no smallest element. A representation is thus associated with such a linear, dense order unlimited on the left and right. Conversely, it is clear that such an order defines a representation.

A theorem of Cantor (see theorem 9.1, [CHA 77, HOD 93]) states that such a linear order, if it is countable, is in fact isomorphic to the linear order $\mathbb{Q}$ of the rational numbers. Hence there is no finite representation of $\mathbf{A}_1$, and there is only one countable representation of this algebra up to isomorphism.

We will subsequently see that this result extends to an entire class of algebras related to the Point algebra.

9.2.2. *Weak representations of Allen's interval algebra*

In the case of Allen's algebra $\mathbf{A}_2$, a weak representation is defined by a set U which we may consider as a set of abstract "intervals" and by a partition of $U \times U$ indexed by a subset of the 13 basic relations. This partition is subject to behaving "as required by the composition table", which means that for any 3-tuple (i, j, k) of elements of U, if (i, k) is labeled by $C(i, k)$ and (k, j) by $C(k, j)$, then (i, j) must be labeled by one of the basic relations contained in $C(i, k) \circ C(k, j)$.

Let us introduce a concept of configuration for Allen's calculus:

DEFINITION 9.2.– A configuration *for Allen's calculus consists of a linear order* W *and a subset* I *of intervals (in Allen's sense) of* W, *i.e.* $I \subseteq Int(W)$, *where* $Int(W) = \{(w_1, w_2) \mid w_1 < w_2\}$.

EXAMPLE 9.2.– Let $W = \{a, b, c, d, e\}$, ordered such that $a < b < c < d < e$ and $I = \{(a, c), (b, d), (c, e)\}$ (Figure 9.2). This a finite configuration.

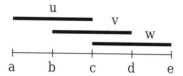

Figure 9.2. *A configuration for Allen's calculus: the linear order* W *is* $\{a, b, c, d, e\}$, *with* $a < b < c < d < e$, *and the configuration contains three intervals in* W: $u = (a, c)$, $v = (b, d)$, *and* $w = (c, e)$

Given a configuration, a weak representation of Allen's interval algebra is associated to it in a natural way: it is defined as the pair formed by I and by the map which, to each basic relation r of Allen's interval algebra, associates the set of pairs of elements of I which are in the relation r.

EXAMPLE 9.3.– In the example given above, we have a set I of three intervals, that are $u = (a, c)$, $v = (b, d)$, and $w = (c, e)$. The map φ is defined by $\varphi(\mathsf{o}) = \{(u, v), (v, w)\}$, $\varphi(\mathsf{m}) = \{(u, w)\}$, $\varphi(\mathsf{oi}) = \{(v, u), (w, v)\}$, $\varphi(\mathsf{mi}) = \{(w, u)\}$, and for relation eq, $(\mathsf{eq}) = \{(u, u), (v, v), (w, w)\}$. For all other basic relations r, we have $\varphi(r) = \varnothing$.

Moreover, given a configuration (W, I), we have a canonical map $p: I \rightarrow W \times W$ which associates the endpoints of this interval with each interval of the configuration.

EXAMPLE 9.4.– In the example above, we have $p(u) = (a, c), p(v) = (b, d)$, and $p(w) = (c, e)$.

So, each configuration defines a weak configuration. What about the converse: given a weak representation (U, φ) of Allen's interval algebra, can we find a configuration from which it is derived?

9.2.2.1. *From weak representations to configurations*

We will now see how, given a weak representation (U, φ) of Allen's interval algebra, it is possible to build a linear order W_{can} and an injective map $p_{can} \colon U \to W_{can} \times W_{can}$ which actually defines a map of U into the set of intervals of W_{can}, hence a configuration $(W_{can}, p_{can}(U) \subseteq Int(W_{can}))$, such that the given weak representation is associated with this configuration. We will say that this configuration is the canonical representation associated with the weak representation.

Why does this configuration deserve to be called "canonical"? The answer is that it has a property known as the property of universality. Indeed, if (W, I) is an arbitrary configuration such that its weak representation is isomorphic to (U, φ), then there exists a strictly increasing map $h \colon W_{can} \to W$ such that the triangle of Figure 9.3 is commutative:

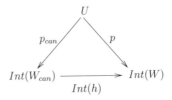

Figure 9.3. *Universality of the canonical configuration*

9.2.2.2. *Constructing the canonical configuration*

Let us start by clarifying what we wish to obtain. We start from a weak representation (U, φ) of Allen's interval algebra. Intuitively, we must consider U as a set of abstract intervals, and we have to find a way of exhibiting the virtual endpoints of these intervals as points in a linearly ordered set, so that the intervals appear as pairs of points in some way. To do this, we have to start with the images $\varphi(r)$ of Allen's relation r, which are (possibly empty) binary relations on U.

The idea of the construction is simply to make the (implicit) endpoints of the intervals appear explicitly, by using the properties of relations, then to build a linear order on this set. Allen and Hayes basically used the same idea in [ALL 85]; it also appeared in a slightly different form in [BES 89b].

We start by letting some Allen relations "do the talking". For example, Allen's relation $\mathbf{a}_{1,1} = (\mathsf{s} + \mathsf{eq} + \mathsf{si})$ says that two intervals have the same beginning. The relation $\mathbf{b}_{1,1} = (\mathsf{p} + \mathsf{m} + \mathsf{o} + \mathsf{fi} + \mathsf{di})$ says that the beginning of the first interval strictly precedes the beginning of the second one.

More precisely, let us consider the following relations:

- $\mathbf{a}_{1,1} = (\mathsf{s} + \mathsf{eq} + \mathsf{si})$;

- $\mathbf{a}_{2,2} = (\mathsf{f} + \mathsf{eq} + \mathsf{fi})$;
- $\mathbf{a}_{1,2} = \mathsf{mi}$;
- $\mathbf{a}_{2,1} = \mathsf{m}$.

Denote by U_1 and U_2 two copies of the set U, and consider the disjoint union $U_1 \sqcup U_2$ of these two sets. Intuitively, the set U_1 is used to build the points which are starting points of the intervals, and U_2, those points which are finishing points.

PROPOSITION 9.1.– *For $i, j \in \{1, 2\}$, the relation $\varphi(\mathbf{a}_{i,j})$ defines an equivalence relation α on $U_1 \sqcup U_2$.*

First of all, we should explain why $\varphi(\mathbf{a}_{i,j})$, which is *a priori* a binary relation on U, may be considered as a binary relation on $U_1 \sqcup U_2$. By definition of a direct union, an element of this last set is either an element of U_1, or an element of U_2. Consider now two elements (u, v) of $U_1 \sqcup U_2$: if both are in U_1, we consider that they belong to the relation α if $(u, v) \in \varphi(\mathbf{a}_{1,1})$; if $u \in U_1$ and $v \in U_2, (u, v) \in \alpha$ is true if $(u, v) \in \varphi(\mathbf{a}_{1,2})$, and so on.

We may also say in a simpler way that $(U_1 \sqcup U_2) \times (U_1 \sqcup U_2)$ is none other than $(U_1 \times U_1) \sqcup (U_1 \times U_2) \sqcup (U_2 \times U_1) \sqcup (U_2 \times U_2)$ and that in this disjoint union $\alpha = \varphi(\mathbf{a}_{1,1}) \sqcup \varphi(\mathbf{a}_{1,2}) \sqcup \varphi(\mathbf{a}_{2,1}) \sqcup \varphi(\mathbf{a}_{2,2})$.

The proof of proposition 9.1 is based on the following result:

LEMMA 9.1.– *For $i, j, k \in \{1, 2\}$, we have the following identities in Allen's algebra:*
- $\mathbf{a}_{i,i} \geq \mathsf{eq}$, *and* $\mathbf{a}_{1,1} \cap \mathbf{a}_{2,2} = \varnothing$;
- $\mathbf{a}_{i,j}^{-1} = \mathbf{a}_{j,i}$;
- $\mathbf{a}_{i,j}\mathbf{a}_{j,k} = \mathbf{a}_{i,k}$.

We are now in a position to prove proposition 9.1.

Proof. We have to prove that the relation α is reflexive, symmetrical, and transitive.

Reflexivity: Let $u \in U_1 \sqcup U_2$. If $u \in U_1, (u, u) \in U_1 \times U_1$, then $(u, u) \in \varphi(\mathbf{a}_{1,1})$, because $\mathbf{a}_{1,1} \geq \mathsf{eq}$ and because φ, which is a homomorphism of Boolean algebras, preserves this inequality, so that $\varphi(\mathbf{a}_{1,1}) \supseteq \varphi(\mathsf{eq}) = \Delta$. The proof is similar for the other three cases to be considered.

Symmetry: It should be verified that, if $(u, v) \in \alpha$, then $(v, u) \in \alpha$. Here again, four cases are to be considered. For example, let us consider the case where $u \in U_1$ and $v \in U_2$. By hypothesis, we have $(u, v) \in \varphi(\mathbf{a}_{1,2})$. Hence, $(v, u) \in \varphi(\mathbf{a}_{1,2})^{-1}$, or $(v, u) \in \varphi(\mathbf{a}_{1,2}^{-1}) = \varphi(\mathbf{a}_{2,1})$, which shows that $(v, u) \in \alpha$. The other cases are dealt with in a similar manner.

Transitivity: Let us consider the general case, and assume that $u \in U_i, v \in U_j$, and $w \in U_k$ are such that $(u, v) \in \alpha$ and $(v, w) \in \alpha$, with $1 \leq i, j, k \leq 2$. Thus, we have $(u, v) \in \varphi(\mathbf{a}_{i,j})$ and $(v, w) \in \varphi(\mathbf{a}_{j,k})$. According to the properties of weak representations, we also have $\varphi(\mathbf{a}_{i,j}) \circ \varphi(\mathbf{a}_{j,k}) \subseteq \varphi((\mathbf{a}_{i,j}) \circ (\mathbf{a}_{i,k}))$, therefore, according to the lemma, $(\mathbf{a}_{i,j}) \circ \varphi(\mathbf{a}_{i,k}) \subseteq (\mathbf{a}_{i,k})$. We conclude that $(u, w) \in \varphi(\mathbf{a}_{i,k})$, which is what we had to prove. $\qquad\square$

We can now define the set W_{can} of endpoints of the intervals in U as the quotient set of $U_1 \sqcup U_2$ by the equivalence relation α:

DEFINITION 9.3.– $W_{can} = (U_1 \sqcup U_2)/\alpha$.

We have accomplished part of the required work. We still have to define on W_{can}, an order relation and show that it is a linear order.

Here again, we will use the statements associated to Allen's relations. For example, the relation $\mathbf{b}_{1,1} = (\mathsf{p} + \mathsf{m} + \mathsf{o} + \mathsf{fi} + \mathsf{di})$ expresses the fact that the beginning of the first interval strictly precedes the beginning of the second one.

Consider the following relations (we use the notation of convex relations as intervals in the lattice of basic relations):

- $\mathbf{b}_{1,1} = [\mathsf{p}, \mathsf{di}]$;
- $\mathbf{b}_{2,2} = [\mathsf{p}, \mathsf{d}]$;
- $\mathbf{b}_{1,2} = [\mathsf{p}, \mathsf{oi}]$;
- $\mathbf{b}_{2,1} = \mathsf{p}$.

We will now use them to define an order relation on the set W_{can}.

In order to do so, we need the following lemma:

LEMMA 9.2.– *For $i, j, k, l \in \{1, 2\}$, we have the following identities in Allen's algebra:*

- $\mathbf{a}_{i,j} \circ \mathbf{b}_{j,k} \circ \mathbf{a}_{k,l} = \mathbf{b}_{i,l}$;
- $\mathbf{b}_{i,j} \circ \mathbf{b}_{j,k} = \mathbf{b}_{i,k}$;
- $\mathbf{b}_{i,j} \cdot \mathbf{b}_{j,i}^{-1} = \varnothing$;
- $\mathbf{b}_{i,j} + \mathbf{b}_{j,i}^{-1} + \mathbf{a}_{i,j} = 1$;
- $\mathbf{b}_{1,2} \geq \mathsf{eq}$.

Proof. Here again, we can easily check that the statements of the lemma are correct. We could also consider a "semantic" proof, as seen below for generalized intervals. $\qquad\square$

Let β be the binary relation defined on $U_1 \sqcup U_2$ by $\varphi(\mathbf{b}_{1,1})$ on $U_1 \times U_1$, by $\varphi(\mathbf{b}_{1,2})$ on $U_1 \times U_2$, by $\varphi(\mathbf{b}_{2,1})$ on $U_2 \times U_1$, and by $\varphi(\mathbf{b}_{2,2})$ on $U_2 \times U_2$.

By using lemma 9.2, it can be easily checked that the binary relation β induces a binary relation on the quotient set, i.e. that if $(u, u') \in \alpha$, and $(v, v') \in \alpha$, then $(u, v) \in \beta$ if, and only if, $(u', v') \in \beta$. Consequently β defines a binary relation $\prec_{can}$ on W_{can}. Another way of stating this result is that α is a congruence for the relation β:

PROPOSITION 9.2.– *The relation α is a congruence for β.*

Proof. Let u and u' be such that u and u' are equivalent modulo α. If $u \in U_j$ and $u' \in U_i (1 \leq i, j \leq 2)$, this means that $(u, u') \in \varphi(\mathbf{a}_{j,i})$. Let $v \in U_k$ and $w \in U_l (1 \leq k, l \leq 2)$ such that v and v' are equivalent, so that $(v, v') \in \varphi(\mathbf{a}_{k,l})$. If $(u, v) \in \beta$, i.e. if $(u, v) \in \varphi(\mathbf{b}_{j,k})$, we have $(u', u) \in \varphi(\mathbf{a}_{i,j})$, and $(v, v') \in \varphi(\mathbf{a}_{k,l})$, hence $(u', v') \in \varphi(\mathbf{a}_{i,j}) \circ \varphi(\mathbf{a}_{j,k}) \circ \varphi(\mathbf{a}_{k,l})$. Now, according to the properties of weak representations, $\varphi(\mathbf{a}_{i,j} \circ \mathbf{b}_{j,k} \circ \mathbf{a}_{k,l}) \supseteq \varphi(\mathbf{a}_{i,j}) \circ (\mathbf{a}_{j,k}) \circ \varphi(\mathbf{a}_{k,l})$. According to the lemma, we have $\varphi(\mathbf{b}_{i,l}) \supseteq \varphi(\mathbf{a}_{i,j}) \circ \varphi(\mathbf{a}_{j,k}) \circ \varphi(\mathbf{a}_{k,l})$, and thus $(u', v')\beta$. □

Consequently, β defines on W_{can} a relation which we denote by $\prec_{can}$.

We contend that this relation is a strict order relation: it is irreflexive and transitive:

PROPOSITION 9.3.– *The relation $\prec_{can}$ is a strict order on W_{can}.*

Proof. We must show that $\prec_{can}$ is irreflexive and transitive.

Irreflexivity: If we simultaneously have $(u, v) \in \beta$ and $(v, u) \in \beta$, with $u \in U_i$ and $v \in U_j (1 \leq i, j \leq 2)$, this means that $(u, v) \in \varphi(\mathbf{b}_{i,j})$ and that $(v, u) \in \varphi(\mathbf{b}_{j,i})$, so that $(u, v) \in \varphi(\mathbf{b}_{i,j})^{-1} = \varphi(\mathbf{b}_{i,j}^{-1})$. Thus, $(u, v) \in \varphi(\mathbf{b}_{i,j} \cdot \mathbf{b}_{i,j}^{-1}) = \varphi(\mathbf{0}) = \varnothing$, and we get a contradiction.

Transitivity: If $u \in U_i$, $v \in U_j$, and $w \in U_k$ are such that $(u, v) \in \beta$, and $(v, w) \in \beta$, hence $(u, v) \in \varphi(\mathbf{b}_{i,j})$ and $(v, w) \in \varphi(\mathbf{b}_{j,k})$, we have $(u, w) \in \varphi(\mathbf{b}_{i,j} \circ \mathbf{b}_{j,k}) = \varphi(\mathbf{b}_{i,k})$, hence $(u, w) \in \beta$. □

This strict order is also a linear order:

PROPOSITION 9.4.– *The relation $\prec_{can}$ is a linear order.*

Proof. Let $u \in U_i$ and $v \in U_j (1 \leq i, j \leq 2)$. We have $\varphi(\mathbf{1}) = U \times U$, therefore according to the lemma, $\varphi(\mathbf{b}_{i,j} + \mathbf{b}_{i,j}^{-1} + \mathbf{a}_{i,j}) = U \times U$. Consequently, either $(u, v) \in \beta$, or $(v, u) \in \beta$, or $(u, v) \in \alpha$. □

Ultimately, we have shown that $(W_{can}, \prec_{can})$ is a linear order. Moreover, since U_1 and U_2 are two copies of U, there exist two natural maps of U in $U_1 \sqcup U_2$: the first one simply associates to $u \in U$ the same u in U_1, while the second associates to u the same u in U_2. Choosing one or the other map makes a difference: in the first case, we are intuitively concerned with the starting point of the "interval" u, and in the second case, with its ending point.

Let us consider the first map $U \to U_1 \sqcup U_2$, and follow it by quotienting by the equivalence relation α. We thus obtain a composed map $\varphi_1: U \to W_{can}$. Doing the same for the second map, we get another map $\varphi_2: U \to W_{can}$.

In a schematic way:

$$\varphi_1: U \to U_1 \to (U_1 \sqcup U_2) \to (U_1 \sqcup U_2)/\alpha = W_{can}$$
$$\varphi_2: U \to U_2 \to (U_1 \sqcup U_2) \to (U_1 \sqcup U_2)/\alpha = W_{can}$$

LEMMA 9.3.– *For any $u \in U$, we have $\varphi(u) \prec_{can} \varphi_2(u)$.*

Proof. We simply have to check that (u, u), where the first u is considered as an element of U_1 and the second as an element of U_2, belongs to $\varphi(\mathbf{b}_{1,2})$. But this is true, because $\mathbf{b}_{1,2}$ contains eq, so that its image under φ contains the diagonal of $U \times U$.   □

Consequently, we may define a map $p_{can}: U \to Int(W_{can})$ by $p_{can}(u) = (\varphi_1(u), \varphi_2(u))$.

LEMMA 9.4.– *The map p_{can} is an injective map.*

Proof. We have to check that two distinct elements u and v of U have distinct images. If this was not the case, it would mean that $\varphi_1(u) = \varphi_1(v)$, and $\varphi_2(u) = \varphi_2(v)$, so that $(u, v) \in \varphi(\mathbf{a}_{1,1}) \cap \varphi(\mathbf{a}_{2,2}) = \varphi(\mathbf{a}_{1,1} \cap \mathbf{a}_{2,2}) = (eq) = \Delta$, hence $u = v$, a contradiction.   □

Thus, we ultimately have a configuration $(W_{can}, p_{can}(U))$, together with a map $p_{can}: U \to Int(W_{can})$.

Clearly, the weak representation associated with this configuration is isomorphic to the initial weak representation: its intervals are indexed by U, and for any pair of intervals u, v of U, the Allen relation between $p_{can}(u)$ and $p_{can}(v)$ is the unique basic relation r such that $(u, v) \in \varphi(r)$.

9.2.2.3. *Universality*

To conclude, let us show the universality property which expresses the intuitive idea that the configuration built in this way is the simplest and smallest possible configuration resulting in the weak representation we started from.

Assume that (W, I) is a configuration whose associated representation is isomorphic to (U, φ).

By assumption, then, a map $f\colon U \to Int(W)$ is given. This map $f = (f_1, f_2)$ is thus defined by two maps $f_1\colon U \to W$ and $f_2\colon U \to W$ which satisfy the property that for any $u \in U$, $f_1(u) < f_2(u)$.

The intuition is that $u \in U$ implicitly defines two endpoints. In order to define the required map of $W_{can} \to W$, we must define an image in W for each endpoint. With reference to the construction described above, each endpoint comes from (at least) one of the two copies of U. We start by defining $h'\colon U_1 \sqcup U_2 \to W$ in the following manner: if $u \in U_i$, then $h'(u) = f_i(u)$.

i) the preceding construction can be quotiented by the equivalence relation α. Indeed, if $(u, v) \in \alpha$, with $u \in U_i$ and $v \in U_j$, this means that $(u, v)\varphi(\mathbf{a}_{i,j})$, which in turn means that the i-th endpoint of u coincides with the j-th endpoint of v, and $h'(u) = f_i(u) = f_j(v) = h'(v)$;

ii) the map $h\colon W_{can} \to W$ obtained after quotienting by α is strictly increasing: this can be shown using a reasoning similar to the previous one, where α is replaced by β.

In this way, we obtain a map $h\colon W_{can} \to W$ which makes the following diagram commutative:

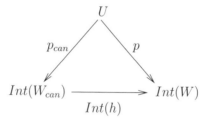

iii) the map h such that the triangle commutes is uniquely defined.

Indeed, let us assume that two maps $h, h'\colon W_{can} \to W$ make the diagram commutative; we would then have:

$$Int(h) \circ p_{can}(u) = f(u) \text{ and } Int(h') \circ p_{can}(u) = f(u)$$

Any $w \in W_{can}$ comes from (at least) one endpoint of U. Let then $w \in W_{can}$ and $u \in U_i$ (u is an i-th endpoint) such that $w = p_{can}(u)$. Then, the commutativity of the triangle implies that $h(u) = h'(u)$.

DEFINITION 9.4.– *A scenario (N, C) is reduced if $C(i, j) = \mathbf{1}'$ implies $i = j$, which means that the equality does not appear as a label between distinct vertices.*

The next propositions state that the concept of weak representation is equivalent to a generalized concept of algebraically closed and reduced scenario.

Consider a weak representation (U, φ) of $\mathbf{A}_2$. For each pair (u, v) of elements of U, there exists a unique element $C(u, v)$ of $\mathbf{B}_2$ such that $(u, v) \in \varphi(C(u, v))$ (recall that the map φ lists the set of pairs which are labeled by each basic relation). We thus obtain from (U, φ) a pair (U, C), where U is a (possibly infinite) set and $C: U \times U \to \mathbf{B}_2$ is a labeling of pairs of elements by basic relations.

PROPOSITION 9.5.– *Let (U, C) be a pair formed by a set U and a map $C: U \times U \to \mathbf{B}_2$ such that the following conditions hold*:

1) $C(v, u) = C(u, v)^{-1}$;
2) $C(u, v) = \mathbf{1}'$ if, and only if, $u = v$;
3) $C(u, v) \subseteq C(u, w) \circ C(w, v)$.

Let $\varphi: \mathbf{B}_2 \to \mathcal{P}(U \times U)$ be defined by: $\varphi(r) = \{(u, v) \mid C(u, v) = r\}$. Then, (U, φ) extends to a weak representation of $\mathbf{A}_2$.

DEFINITION 9.5.– *An algebraically closed, reduced, generalized scenario is a pair (U, C) satisfying the conditions of proposition 9.5.*

PROPOSITION 9.6.– *The concept of weak representation is equivalent to that of its associated generalized scenario.*

Conversely, let us describe explicitly how a weak representation can be deduced from a generalized scenario which is algebraically closed and reduced.

Given (U, C), let $R_b = C^{-1}(b)$, for $b \in \mathbf{B}_2$, and, for $a \in \mathbf{A}_a$, let us define $R_a = \bigcup_{b \in a} R_b$. Let $B \subseteq \mathbf{B}_2$ be the image of C. Then, the set of R_b, for $b \in B$ forms a partition of $U \times U$. In particular, the set of R_a satisfies the following conditions:

1) $R_{b-1} = R_b^{-1}$;
2) $R_{1'} = \Delta_U$;
3) $R_b \circ R_c \subseteq R_{boc}$.

Then the associated weak representation is simply the map which associates R_a with $a \in \mathbf{A}_n$.

EXAMPLE 9.5.– Let us start from the weak representation which is associated with the network represented in the left part of Figure 9.4. We have a set $U = \{u, v, w\}$ with three elements. Let $U_1 = \{u_1, v_1, w_1\}$ and $U_2 = \{u_2, v_2, w_2\}$ be two copies of U. Since $(u, w) \in \varphi(\mathrm{m})$ and $\mathrm{m} = \mathbf{a}_{2,1}$, the pair (u_2, w_1) belongs to the equivalence relation α, and it is the only pair in this case. Thus, we have a set of five equivalence classes $\{u_1, v_1, \{u_2, w_1\}, v_2, w_2\}$ for W_{can}.

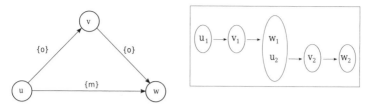

Figure 9.4. *A weak representation of Allen's algebra (on the left), and the linear order associated with it by the canonical construction (on the right)*

Since (u, v) and (v, w) are contained in $\varphi(\mathsf{o})$, it follows from $\mathsf{o} \in \mathbf{b}_{1,1}$ and $\mathsf{o} \in \mathbf{b}_{2,2}$ that $u_1 \prec_{can} v_1$, $v_1 \prec_{can} w_1$, $u_2 \prec_{can} v_2$, and $v_2 \prec_{can} w_2$.

Thus, we have in W_{can}, the ordering $u_1 \prec_{can} v_1 \prec_{can} \{w_1, u_2\} \prec_{can} v_2 \prec_{can} w_2$.

The canonical map p_{can} is the map which sends u on (u_1, u_2), v on (v_1, v_2), and w on (w_1, w_2) (Figure 9.4).

Let us give an example of the universality property.

EXAMPLE 9.6.– Let $W = \mathbb{R}$, and let us consider the configuration formed in W by the set of three intervals $I = \{[0, 5], [1, 6], [5, 8]\}$.

The bijection which associates u, v, and w with the elements $[0, 5]$, $[1, 6]$, and $[5, 8]$ of I, respectively, defines an isomorphism of the weak representation considered in the previous example with the one associated to this configuration.

Clearly, the map $h: W_{can} \to W$ defined by $u_1 \mapsto 0, v_1 \mapsto 1, u_2 \mapsto 5, v_2 \mapsto 6$, and $w_2 \mapsto 8$ makes the triangle below commutative, as claimed by the universal property:

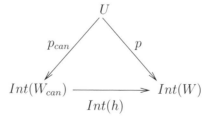

9.2.3. *Weak representations of the n-interval algebra*

Remarkably, the techniques we have used for the study of weak representations of Allen's interval algebra extend to the algebras of generalized intervals without fundamental changes.

9.2.3.1. *From configurations to weak representations*

First of all, we define a configuration for $\mathbf{A}_n$: it consists of a linear order W and a (non-empty) set of n-intervals on W (thus, W is assumed to have at least n elements).

A weak representation of $\mathbf{A}_n$ is naturally associated to such a configuration: the set U is the set I of all n-intervals in the configuration; the map φ associates to each element $b \in \mathbf{B}_n$, the set of pairs of n-intervals which belong to the (n, n)-relation b.

In this way, we get a canonical way of associating a weak representation of $\mathbf{A}_n$ with a configuration of n-intervals.

9.2.3.2. *From weak representations to configurations*

Conversely, given a weak representation of $\mathbf{A}_n$, there exists a canonical configuration which is associated with it, and this configuration has a property of universality.

We will now describe the construction of this canonical configuration. It differs only minimally from the construction described for Allen's interval algebra.

In what follows, we denote by i, j, k, l integers in the set $\{1, \ldots, n\}$.

DEFINITION 9.6.– *In the algebra* $\mathbf{A}_n$:

– *let $\mathbf{a}_{i,j}$ be the set of (n, n)-relations for which the i-th boundary of the first n-interval coincides with the j-th boundary of the second n-interval, or more concisely — using the encoding of (n, n)-relations defined in Chapter 3, section 3.2 — the set of (n, n)-relations whose i-th coordinate is $(2j - 1)$;*

– *let $\mathbf{b}_{i,j}$ be the set of (n, n)-relations for which the i-th boundary of the first n-interval strictly precedes the j-th boundary of the second n-interval, in short, the set of (n, n)-relations whose i-th coordinate is less than $(2j - 1)$.*

EXAMPLE 9.7.– When $n = 1$ or $n = 2$:

– if $n = 1$, $\mathbf{a}_{1,1}$ contains only the relation eq, and $\mathbf{b}_{1,1}$, the relation $<$;

– if $n = 2$, we get the definitions already used for Allen's interval algebra.

PROPOSITION 9.7.– *The following properties hold*:

1) $\mathbf{a}_{i,i} \geq \mathbf{1}'_{n,n}$, and $\bigcap_{i=1}^{i=n} \mathbf{a}_{i,i} = \mathbf{1}'_{n,n}$;

2) $\mathbf{a}_{i,i}^{-1} = \mathbf{a}_{i,i}$;

3) $\mathbf{a}_{i,j} \circ \mathbf{a}_{j,k} = \mathbf{a}_{i,k}$;

4) $\mathbf{a}_{i,j} \circ \mathbf{b}_{j,k} \circ \mathbf{a}_{k,l} = \mathbf{a}_{i,l}$;

5) $\mathbf{b}_{i,j} \circ \mathbf{b}_{j,k} = \mathbf{b}_{i,k}$;

6) $\mathbf{b}_{i,j} \cdot \mathbf{a}_{j,i}^{-1} = \mathbf{0}$;

7) $\mathbf{1} = \mathbf{b}_{i,j} + \mathbf{b}_{j,i}^{-1} + \mathbf{a}_{i,j}$;

8) *if $i < j$, then $\mathbf{1}'_{n,n} \in \mathbf{b}_{i,j}$.*

Proof. The argument below, which is not strictly a proof, gives the gist of the contents of this proposition.

1) if a first and second n-interval coincide, their i-th boundaries are the same for any i; if conversely, these boundaries coincide for any i ranging from 1 to n, then both n-intervals are the same;

2) the coincidence of the i-th boundary of the second interval with the j-th boundary of the first interval amounts to the coincidence of the j-th boundary of the first interval with the i-th boundary of the second interval;

3) if the i-th boundary of a first interval coincides with the j-th boundary of a second interval, and the latter with the k-th boundary of a third interval, then the i-th boundary of the first interval coincides with the k-th boundary of the third interval;

4) if the i-th boundary of a first interval coincides with the j-th boundary of a second interval, that the latter precedes the k-th boundary of a third interval which itself coincides with the l-th boundary of a fourth interval, then the i-th boundary of the first interval precedes the l-th boundary of the fourth interval;

5) if the i-th boundary of a first interval precedes the j-th boundary of a second interval, and the latter precedes the k-th boundary of a third interval, then the i-th boundary of the first interval precedes the k-th boundary of the third interval;

6) one cannot have simultaneously the fact that the i-th boundary of a first interval precedes the j-th of a second interval, and the fact that j-th boundary of the second precedes the i-th of the first;

7) for any pair of n-intervals, and any pair i, j, either the i-th boundary of the first interval precedes the j-th boundary of the second, or the j-th boundary of the second interval precedes the i-th boundary of the first, or else both boundaries coincide;

8) if $i < j$, the i-th boundary of an n-interval precedes its j-th boundary.

$\square$

9.2.4. Constructing the canonical configuration

Consider a weak representation (U, φ) of the n-interval algebra $\mathbf{A}_n$. We can now describe the construction of the canonical configuration which is associated with it. The steps to be followed are quite similar to those described above in the case of Allen's interval algebra.

9.2.4.1. Constructing the set of boundaries

Let $W' = U_1 \sqcup \ldots U_n$ be the disjoint union of n copies of U. Consequently, $W' \times W'$ is the disjoint union of $U_i \times U_j$, for $1 \leq i$ and $j \leq n$.

Let α be the binary relation defined on W' in the following manner: if $u \in U_i$ and $v \in U_j$, we have $(u, v) \in \alpha$ if, and only if, $(u, v) \in \varphi(\mathbf{a}_{i,j})$.

The relation α is an equivalence relation: this can easily be proved using proposition 9.7.

Let $W_{can} = W'/\alpha$ be the quotient set. By construction, we have n maps $p_i \colon U \to W_{can} (1 \leq i \leq n)$ induced by the map which sends U in the i-th copy U_i:

$$p_i \colon U \to U_i \to (U_1 \sqcup \ldots U_n) \to W_{can}$$

9.2.4.2. *Constructing a linear order*

Let the binary relation β on W' be defined in the following manner: if $u \in U_i$ and $v \in U_j$, we have $(u, v) \in \beta$ if, and only if, $(u, v) \in \varphi(\mathbf{b}_{i,j})$.

The following statements can easily be proved by again using proposition 9.7:

– α is a congruence with respect to β, which implies that β defines a binary relation $\prec_{can}$ on W_{can};

– the relation $\prec_{can}$ is a strict linear order on W_{can};

– if $i < j$, where $(1 \leq i, j \leq n)$, then $p_i(u) \prec_{can} p_j(u)$, which implies that for any $u \in U$, $p_{can}(u) = (p_1(u), \ldots, p_n(u))$ is an n-interval of W_{can}.

9.2.4.3. *Universality of the construction*

We thus have a canonical map $p_{can} \colon U \to Int_n(W_{can})$, where $Int_n(W_{can})$ denotes the set of n-intervals on W_{can}.

This map is injective, and thus identifies U with a subset of n-intervals of W_{can}. Moreover, it has a universality property:

PROPOSITION 9.8.– *Let* (W, I) *be a configuration whose associated weak representation is isomorphic to* (U, φ). *Then, there exists an injective map* $h \colon W_{can} \to W$ *such that the following triangle is commutative.*

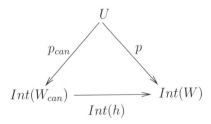

The proof of universality for "ordinary" intervals given previously can easily be transposed to the case of n-intervals.

9.3. Classifying the weak representations of $\mathbf{A}_n$

In what follows, we will make use of notions of category theory (see Appendix B). Our aim is not to get into technical details, but only to show that the categorical point of view provides a new and potentially fruitful outlook on the constructions described in the previous sections.

9.3.1. *The category of weak representations of* $\mathbf{A}_n$

Let us consider the category whose objects are the weak representations of $\mathbf{A}_n$. By definition, such an object is a pair (U, φ), where U is a non-empty set, and φ: $\mathbf{A}_n \to \mathcal{P}(U \times U)$. Informally speaking, to each basic (n, n)-relation, φ associates the set of pairs of elements of U which are labeled by this (n, n)-relation.

We now define the morphisms of the category:

DEFINITION 9.7.– *Let* $\mathcal{U} = (U, \varphi)$ *and* $\mathcal{V} = (V, \psi)$ *be two weak representations of* $\mathbf{A}_n$. *A morphism* $\mathcal{U} \to \mathcal{V}$ *is a map* $h: U \to V$ *such that for any* $a \in \mathbf{A}_n$, *and for any pair of elements* (u, v) *of* U, *we have* $(h(u), h(v)) \in \psi(a)$ *if* $(u, v) \in \varphi(a)$.

In other words, a map h defines a morphism if two elements of U and their images by h in V are labeled in the same way.

EXAMPLE 9.8.– Let us consider the case where $n = 1$. As seen above, a weak representation of the algebra $\mathbf{A}_1$ is a linearly ordered set.

The condition of being a morphism here reduces to the fact that, if $u < v$, then $h(u) < h(v)$, hence that h is a strictly increasing map.

In particular, a morphism in the category WR_1 of linear orders is an injective map. Actually, this is a general property: any n:

PROPOSITION 9.9.– *In the category* WR_n, *morphisms are injective maps.*

Proof. If u and v are two distinct elements, then the pair (u, v) is not labeled by the equality relation, so that the same is true for the pair $(h(u), h(v))$. □

NOTATION.– In what follows, WR_n will denote the category of weak representations of $\mathbf{A}_n$.

9.3.1.1. *From linear orders to n-intervals*

If we start with objects of the category WR_1, that is, linear orders, it is quite easy to build objects of the category WR_n, (for $n \geq 1$): we consider the n-intervals on these linear orders (provided that there are any, thus that the subjacent set contains at least n elements).

Consider the situation in detail. Assume that $n \geq 1$, and let W be a linear order (containing at least n elements). Let $Int_n(W)$ be the set of n-intervals of W.

$Int_n(W)$ is thus the set of all strictly increasing sequences of n-elements of W. But we claim that it is provided with a structure which is in fact an object of the category WR_n. Indeed, given two arbitray elements of $Int_n(W)$, there exists exactly one basic (n,n)-relation, hence a basic relation of $\mathbf{A}_n$ which describes the relative position of these n-intervals. We may also see the fact that such a relation exists as providing a map φ, which to each basic (n,n)-relation, associates the set of pairs of corresponding elements of W. Clearly, by construction, the axioms defining a weak representation are satisfied.

If we remember that a linear order is nothing other than a weak representation of $\mathbf{A}_1$, we may see Int_n as associating with each object of WR_1 (at least with each object of size at least n) an object of WR_n.

What about the morphisms of the two categories? If $h\colon W \to W'$ is a morphism in WR_1, that is a strictly increasing map between the two linear orders W and W', it will send increasing sequences onto increasing sequences, hence it defines a map of the n-intervals of W to those of W'. Moreover, in the category WR_n, this map defines a morphism of the object $Int_n(W)$ to the object $Int_n(W')$: intuitively, this results from the fact that h, which preserves the ordering, also preserves the (n,n) relations between n-intervals.

Ultimately, we have:

PROPOSITION 9.10.– *For any $n \geq 1$, $Int_n()$ defines a functor $Int_n\colon WR_1 \to WR_n$.*

9.3.1.2. *The case of Allen's intervals*

At this stage, we may pause and analyze what this result means in the case of ordinary intervals.

EXAMPLE 9.9.– Let us start from a linear order with four elements: $W = \{a, b, c, d\}$ (the order is the alphabetical order). Then $U = Int_2(W)$, the set of 2-intervals, i.e. intervals in Allen's sense, contains six elements. The associated weak representation (U, φ) describes the relations between these six elements. For example, we have:

$$\varphi(s) = \{([a,b],[a,c]), ([a,b],[a,d]), ([a,c],[a,d]), ([b,c],[b,d])\}$$

EXAMPLE 9.10.– Let us consider a linear order with five elements: $W = \{a, b, c, d, e\}$. In this case, $U = Int_2(W)$, the set of 2-intervals contains 10 elements. Among these

10 elements, let us denote by u, v, and w the three intervals $u = [a, c]$, $v = [b, d]$, and $w = [c, e]$.

The map of Allen's interval algebra into $\mathcal{P}(U \times U)$ makes $Int_2(W)$ a weak representation whose values are sets of pairs of elements of U.

Let $V = \{u, v, w\}$. For each basic relation r of Allen's interval, consider the subset of pairs in $\varphi(r)$ whose elements belong to V, and let $\varphi|_V$ denote the corresponding map of Allen's interval algebra to $\mathcal{P}(V \times V)$. Clearly, the pair $(V, \varphi|_V)$ is a weak representation of Allen's interval algebra, and this restriction operation is general. Moreover, we can easily check that the canonical injection $V \hookrightarrow U$ induces a morphism in the category WR_2.

Let ψ denote the map $\varphi|_V$.

We thus obtain a weak representation (V, ψ) which is entirely characterized by the fact that $\psi(\mathsf{o}) = \{(u, v), (v, w)\}$ and $\psi(\mathsf{m}) = \{(u, w)\}$. We recognize it as the weak representation $V = \{u, v, w\}$ of example 9.3.

9.3.2. Reinterpretating the canonical construction

In section 9.2.3.2, we described the canonical construction which, given a weak representation, associates with it a configuration which we called the canonical configuration.

More precisely, this canonical configuration consists of a linear order of W_{can} and a canonical map $p_{can}\colon U \to Int_n(W_{can})$.

We may now reinterpret this construction in terms of categories. First of all, the linear order W_{can} is an object of the category WR_1.

Next, consider a morphism $h\colon (U, \varphi) \to (V, \psi)$ in the category W_n. Recall that h is then an injective map $h\colon U \to V$ such that "the labelings are preserved". It can be easily checked — we will not do it here — that h induces an injective map on the associated canonical configurations, and that all the properties defining a functor are satisfied. We denote this functor[1] by $Bnd_n\colon WR_n \to WR_1$.

Consequently, we now have two functors connecting the categories WR_n and WR_1:

$$Int_n\colon WR_1 \to WR_n \text{ and } Bnd_n\colon WR_n \to WR_1$$

---

1 Bnd stands for "boundaries".

We will see below that the pair (Int_n, Bnd_n) is a pair of *adjoint functors* (the reader may refer to Appendix B, section B.4.2). More precisely, Bnd_n is left-adjoint to Int_n. The situation of *adjunction* is a very important phenomenon in mathematics, and many phenomena of duality can be expressed by using it.

Let us illustrate the situation with an example, in the case where $n = 2$.

EXAMPLE 9.11.– We start with an object of WR_1, namely the linear order W with five elements considered in example 9.3.

$U = Int_2(W)$ is a weak representation containing 10-intervals, among which u, v, and w are the three intervals considered in example 9.10.

Intuitively, the construction of the canonical configuration associated with U corresponds to making explicit the implicit boundaries of the intervals in U. Now clearly, U and V define the same set of endpoints, so that $Bnd_2(U)$ and $Bnd_2(V)$ correspond to the same linear order with five elements, as can easily be checked. Correspondingly, the injective morphism of V in U (a morphism in the category WR_2) has an image which is the identity morphism in the category WR_1.

We conclude that applying successively the functors Int_2, then Bnd_2, to W results in an object $Bnd_2(Int_2(W))$ which is isomorphic to W.

Let us now start from the weak representation (V, ψ), which contains three intervals. Its image under Bnd_2 is the linear order with five points, the three initial intervals being identified with the intervals u, v, and w. Applying the Int_2 functor, we obtain the weak representation containing all ten intervals in this 5-element order. We would have obtained the same result if we had started with the weak representation (U, φ) itself.

Here, the result of applying successively Bnd_2, then Int_2 is an object of the category WR_2 which contains the initial object — a weak representation which explicitly contains all the intervals implicitly present in the situation.

In addition, as already noticed, the image by Int_2 of the weak representation (U, φ) (a weak representation strictly containing (V, ψ)) is isomorphic to that of (V, ψ).

We have here a concrete example of the fact that $Int_2(Bnd_2(V))$ is what is called as *closed* weak representation. The composed functor $Int_2 \circ Bnd_2$ sends an arbitrary weak representation to its closure, which is the smallest closed weak representation containing it.

The previous example is typical of the general situation, for any $n \geq 1$. To prove this fact, we will use the general properties of a situation of adjunction. Prior to that, let us informally summarize the main points which we have noted about this example, of which we will see that they can be extended to the general case:

1) we have two functors $Int_n\colon WR_1 \to WR_n$ and $Bnd_n\colon WR_n \to WR_1$;

2) the composed functor $(Bnd_n \circ Int_n)\colon WR_1 \to WR_1$ associates with a given linear order a linear order which is isomorphic to it;

3) the composed functor $Int_n \circ Bnd_n\colon W_n \to W_n$ associates with a weak representation a representation containing it, which is the closure of the initial representation;

4) a closed representation explicitly contains all the boundaries of the n-intervals which it involves;

5) the canonical map $p_{can}\colon U \to Int_n(Bnd_n(U))$ defines a natural transformation $\varepsilon_{can}\colon \mathbf{1}_{WR_n} \to (Int_n \circ Bnd_n)$.

We will also see that the concept of closure well deserves its name: it has all the properties of an abstract closure relation.

9.3.3. *The canonical construction as adjunction*

We now know enough about adjunction to show how the canonical construction appears as the construction of a functor which is left-adjoint to the natural functor $Int_n\colon WR_1 \to WR_n$.

Let W be a linear order, and $\mathcal{U} = (U, \varphi)$ a weak representation of the n-interval algebra $\mathbf{A}_n$.

First of all, it can be easily checked that the construction of $W_{can} = Bnd_n(U)$, which is an object of WR_1 associated with an object U of WR_n, can be extended to define a functor $Bnd_n\colon WR_n \to WR_1$; if $f\colon \mathcal{U} \to \mathcal{V}$ is a morphism in WR_n, where $\mathcal{V} = (V, \psi)$, then f is defined by an injective map $h\colon U \to V$, and the canonical construction induces an injection $Bnd_n(f)$ of the linear order $Bnd_n(\mathcal{U})$ into $Bnd_n(\mathcal{V})$.

On the other hand, for any weak representation $\mathcal{U}$, the canonical construction makes it possible to define an injective morphism $p_{can}\colon \mathcal{U} \to Int_n(Bnd_n(\mathcal{U}))$.

1) we have already noted that this morphism has the universal property: for any linear order W, and any morphism $f\colon Bnd_n(\mathcal{U}) \to W$, there exists a unique arrow $g\colon (\mathcal{U}) \to Int_n(W)$ such that the triangles of Figure 9.5 are commutative;

2) for any $g\colon \mathcal{U} \to Int_n(W)$, there exists a unique $f\colon Bnd_n(\mathcal{U})W$ such that the same triangles are commutative.

The map $\eta_{\mathcal{U}}\colon \mathcal{U} \to Int_n(Bnd_n(\mathcal{U}))$ is the natural inclusion of $\mathcal{U}$ in its closure $Int_n(Bnd_n(\mathcal{U}))$.

In the general situation of adjunction, the composed functor $(Bnd_n \circ Int_n)$ is called the *interior* functor. Here, $Bnd_n(Int_n(W))$ is none other than W itself. So, ε_W is the

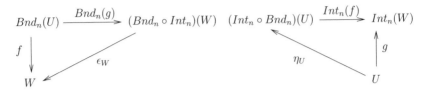

Figure 9.5. *The adjunction* $(Bnd_n, Int_n, \varepsilon, \eta)$. *In this case,* ε_w *is the identity, and* η_U *is an injection of* U *in its closure* $(Int_n \circ Bnd_n)(U)$

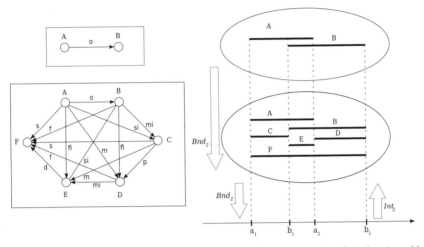

Figure 9.6. *The functors* Bnd_2 *and* Int_2. *Above, a weak representation* (V, ψ), *where* $V = \{A, B\}$ *and* $\psi(o) = \{A, B\}$. *The functor* Bnd_2 *associates a linear order with four elements to this object; the functor* Int_2 *associates with the latter a weak representation (in the middle)* (U, φ) *with six elements:* $U = \{A, B, \ldots, F\}$. *The weak representation* (U, φ) *is the closure of* (V, ψ)

identical map (which is strictly increasing) of W on itself. In particular, all objects of $W R_1$ are closed.

Figure 9.6 summarizes those points on a typical example, for $n = 2$; a weak representation (V, ψ) has two elements; its image under Bnd_2 is a linear order with four elements, whose image under Int_2 is a weak representation (U, φ) with six elements; (U, φ) is the closure of (V, ψ).

The concept of closure of a weak representation naturally results in a notion of equivalence for weak representations:

DEFINITION 9.8.– *Two weak representations are* equivalent *if their closures are isomorphic.*

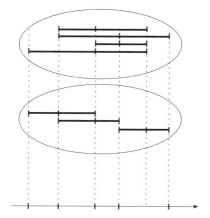

Figure 9.7. *Two weak representations of* $\mathbf{A}_3$ *(the objects correspond to 3-intervals) which are equivalent*

EXAMPLE 9.12.– The two weak representations of $\mathbf{A}_2$ in Figure 9.6 are equivalent.

EXAMPLE 9.13.– Figure 9.7 represents the two weak representations of $\mathbf{A}_3$. The first contains four objects, and the second contains three objects. These are two equivalent weak representations.

9.3.3.1. *Closed weak representations*

We have just seen that, in the adjunction defined by the pair (Bnd_n, Int_n), the non-trivial concept is the notion of the closure $Int_n(Bnd_n(\mathcal{U}))$ of a weak representation $\mathcal{U}$.

DEFINITION 9.9.– *A weak representation* $\mathcal{U}$ *of* $\mathbf{A}_n$ *is a* closed *weak representation if, and only if,* $\eta_\mathcal{U}: \mathcal{U} \to Int_n(Bnd_n(\mathcal{U}))$ *is an isomorphism.*

Intuitively, the concept corresponds to the fact that all the n-intervals which are implicitly defined by a weak representation considered are explicitly present in U.

When a weak representation is finite (i.e. U is a finite set), a simple criterion makes it possible to test whether a given weak representation is closed: in this case, $Bnd_n(\mathcal{U})$ is a finite linear order; let k be the number of its elements; then, $Int_n(Bnd_n(\mathcal{U}))$ contains $k(k-1)/2$ elements, and the weak representation is closed if, and only if, this number equals the number of elements of U.

According to general results that are valid in all situations of adjunction, the pair of adjoint functors (Bnd_n, Int_n) defines an equivalence of categories between the category WR_1 and the subcategory of WR_n containing those weak representations which are closed.

Representations are weak representations with additional properties. Now, these properties imply that they are closed weak representations:

PROPOSITION 9.11.– *A representation of* $\mathbf{A}_n$ *is a closed weak representation.*

Proof. The proof is not difficult. The intuition is that any n-tuple of boundaries, where each boundary is *a priori* associated with several distinct n-intervals, can in fact be defined by just one single n-interval, which is the same for all n endpoints.   □

9.3.3.2. $\aleph_0$ *categoricity*

According to proposition 9.11, representations of $\mathbf{A}_n$ are among the closed weak representations. Moreover:

LEMMA 9.5.– *If* $\mathcal{U}$ *is a representation of* $\mathbf{A}_n$, *then* $Bnd_n(\mathcal{U})$ *is a representation of* $\mathbf{A}_1$.

Proof. We know that the representations of $\mathbf{A}_1$ correspond to those linear orders which are dense and unlimited on the right and left. Hence it will be enough to show that, if $\mathcal{U} = (U, \varphi)$ is a representation of $\mathbf{A}_n$, then $W_{can} = Bnd_n(\mathcal{U})$ is dense and unlimited on the left and right.

i) *Density*. Let w and w' be two distinct elements of W_{can}. Let us assume for example that $w \prec w'$, and that w is associated with an i-th boundary u, and w' to a k-th boundary $v (1 \leq i, k \leq n)$. Thus, we have in this case $(u, v) \in \varphi(\mathbf{b}_{i,k})$.

According to proposition 9.7, we have $\mathbf{b}_{i,j} \circ \mathbf{b}_{j,k} = \mathbf{b}_{i,k}$. Since the weak representation considered is in fact a representation, we deduce that $\varphi(\mathbf{b}_{i,k}) = \varphi(\mathbf{b}_{i,j}) \circ \varphi(\mathbf{b}_{j,k})$, and so there exists a $w \in U$ such that $(u, w) \in \varphi(\mathbf{b}_{i,j})$ and $(w, v) \in \varphi(\mathbf{b}_{j,k})$.

Let w'' be the image in W_{can} of the j-th boundary of w (in other words, the element defined from the copy of w located in U_j, which is the j-th copy of U). Then we can deduce from the above that $w \prec w'' \prec w'$, which shows that the property of density holds.

ii) *The order is unlimited on the right and on the left*. Let $w \in W_{can}$, and assume that w is the image of $u \in U_i$ for some i. If $i < n$, the image of the n-th boundary of u is an element w' of W_{can} such that $w \prec w'$. Otherwise, we have $\mathbf{b}_{i,j} \circ \mathbf{b}_{i,j}^{-1} = 1$. Since we are considering a representation, we infer that in particular $\Delta_U \subseteq \varphi(\mathbf{b}_{i,j}) \circ \varphi(\mathbf{b}_{i,j})^{-1}$. Consequently, we can find $v \in U$ such that $(u, v) \in \varphi(\mathbf{b}_{i,j})$, and the image w' of v in W_{can} is such that $w \prec w'$. So, W_{can} is unlimited on the right.

A similar reasoning shows that it is unlimited on the left as well.   □

We can conclude from the preceding discussion that the representations of the n-interval algebra correspond — using the pair of adjoint functors (Bnd_n, Int_n) — to representations of the Point algebra. However, a theorem of Cantor [CHA 77, HOD 93] gives a characterization of the latter:

THEOREM 9.1.– *Any countable dense linear order which is unlimited on the left and on the right is isomorphic to the order $\mathbb{Q}$ of the rational numbers.*

As a consequence, we have the following result:

THEOREM 9.2.– *Let n be an integer greater than or equal to 1. Any countable representation of the n-interval algebra is isomorphic to the representation $Int_n(\mathbb{Q})$.*

This result generalizes a result which was known for Allen's interval algebra thanks to Ladkin's thesis [LAD 87]. There, the proof is based on the use of the classical technique of elimination of quantifiers.

Obviously, the relation algebras we consider have no finite representations, and all their countable representations are isomorphic. These two properties taken together constitute what is called the property of $\aleph_0$-categoricity. As a consequence, the associated first order theories are decidable:

COROLLARY 9.1.– *Let n be an integer greater than or equal to 1. The first order theory associated with the n-interval algebra is decidable.*

9.4. Extension to the calculi based on linear orders

In Chapters 3 and 4, we have considered several temporal or spatial formalisms which can be characterized as formalisms based on linear orders. The simplest calculus among them is the Point calculus. We may characterize Allen's calculus as derived from this calculus by considering sequences of length two, and more generally characterize the n-interval calculus as derived from it by considering sequences of length n. We may also consider sequences of a length belonging to a subset S of the positive integers, to obtain the calculus of S-intervals.

On the other hand, formalisms like the Cardinal direction calculus, the Rectangle calculus, the n-point calculus or the n-rectangle calculus are derived by using products.

We will see that basically all the discussion previously presented in this chapter, concerning the classification of the weak representations of the associated algebras, and the link between weak representations and configurations, can be extended to a wide family of formalisms based on linear orders.

9.4.1. *Configurations*

Let us recall that a configuration for the n-interval calculus consists of a linear order W and a set I of n-intervals. Similarly, we now define a precise meaning for the term "configuration" for each of the following calculi: the S-interval calculus (where S is a subset of positive integers), the n-point calculus, and n-block calculus.

DEFINITION 9.10.– *(Configurations)*

    – let S be a finite subset of positive integers. A configuration of S-intervals $C = (I, W)$ consists of a linear order W and a subset I of p-intervals in W, where $p \in S$;

    – let n be a positive integer. A configuration of n-points $C = (P, W_1, \ldots, W_n)$ consists of n linear orders $W_1, \ldots, W_n$ and a subset P of points of $W_1 \times \cdots \times W_n$;

    – let n be a positive integer. A configuration of n-blocks $C = (U, W_1, \ldots, W_n)$ consists of n linear orders $W_1, \ldots, W_n$ and a subset B of $Int(W_1) \times \cdots \times Int(W_n)$, where $Int(W)$ denotes the set of 2-intervals in W.

9.4.2. *Description languages and associated algebras*

For each of the three families of calculi — the S-interval calculi, for $S \subset \mathbb{N}$, the n-point calculi ($n \geq 1$), and the n-block calculi ($n \geq 1$) — languages based on relation algebras will be used to give qualitative representations of configurations in terms of weak representations of this algebra.

DEFINITION 9.11.– *(Basic relations)*

    – S-intervals: Let S be a finite set of positive integers. Then, $\mathbf{B}_S$ is the union of $\mathbf{B}_{p,q}$, for $p, q \in S$. When S contains only one element n, we simply denote the corresponding set of basic relations by $\mathbf{B}_n$. Thus, $\mathbf{B}_1$ corresponds to points, and $\mathbf{B}_2$ corresponds to the set of Allen's basic relations;

    – n-points: for $n \geq 1$, $\mathbf{B}_{Points_n}$ is the set $\mathbf{B}_1^n$ of n-tuples of $\mathbf{B}_1$, which represent the qualitative positions of two points in the n-dimensional Euclidean space. The corresponding calculus is the n-point calculus [BAL 99b];

    – n-blocks: for $n \geq 1$, $\mathbf{B}_{Blocks_n}$ is the set $\mathbf{B}_2^n$ of n-tuples of $\mathbf{B}_2$, which represent the qualitative positions of two blocks in the n-dimensional Euclidean space. The corresponding calculus is the n-block calculus [BAL 99c, BAL 99a].

Let us define what we mean by "representing a configuration" for each of these languages:

    – if $C = (I, W)$ is a configuration of S-intervals, and if i and j are two elements of I, there exists $p, q \in S$ such that i is a p-interval and j is a q-interval in W, hence a well-defined basic (p, q)-relation $C(i, j)$ such that $(i, j) \in C(i, j)$. The pair $(I, C : I \times I \to \mathbf{A}_S)$ thus defined satisfies the conditions required for defining a weak representation of the algebra $\mathbf{A}_S$;

– if $\mathcal{C} = (P, W_1, \ldots, W_n)$ is a configuration of n-points, and if $x = (x_1, \ldots, x_n), y = (y_1, \ldots, y_n)$ are two elements of P, we have for each i, where $1 \leq i \leq n$, one of the three relations $x_i < y_i, x_i = y_i$ or $x_i > y_i$. The corresponding n-tuple of basic relations is a basic relation $C(x, y)$ in the n-point algebra. Here again, the pair $(P, C \colon P \times P \to \mathbf{B}_{Points})$ thus defined satisfies the conditions required for defining a weak representation of the algebra $\mathbf{A}_{Points}$;

– if $\mathcal{C} = (U, W_1, \ldots, W_n)$ is a configuration of n-blocks, the situation is similar to the previous one: each block x is a product $x = x_1 \times \ldots x_n$, where x_i is an interval (in Allen's sense) in W_i, for each i ($1 \leq i \leq n$). For any pair of elements x, y of B, and any i, where $1 \leq i \leq n$, we have a well-defined basic relation in Allen's algebra $C_i(x, y)$ describing the relation of x_i with respect to y_i. Let $C(x, y) = (C_1(x, y), \ldots, C_n(x, y))$ be the n-tuple of relations obtained in this way. Then, the pair $(B, C \colon B \times B \to \mathbf{B}_{Blocks})$ defines a weak representation of $\mathbf{A}_{Blocks}$.

9.4.3. Canonical constructions

For all the formalisms we are considering — recall that the n-interval calculi, including Allen's calculus and the Point calculus, are among them — we now consider the category of weak representations of the corresponding algebra $\mathbf{A}$.

The construction which associates a weak representation to a configuration is a generalization of the construction which, given a linear order W, associates to it the weak representation $Int_n(W)$ consisting of the n-intervals in W.

We will now see that, as was the case for n-intervals, we can conversely define a construction which, given a weak representation of an algebra belonging to one of the three families of formalisms, associates with it a configuration, in a canonical way; moreover, this configuration has a universal property. We will not give a detailed description of the construction and be content with giving an outline of it (the reader may refer to [LEB 07] for more details).

9.4.3.1. The case of S-intervals

Let (U, φ) be a weak representation of $\mathbf{A}_S$. The gist of the construction is that, since an element of U is a p-interval, for some p in S, this element defines a strictly increasing sequence of p boundaries in some linear order. So, we will consider p copies of U: the first copy will provide the first boundaries, the second copy will provide the second boundaries, and so on.

We now express this intuitive content in algebraic terms.

First of all, let us consider the neutral element $\mathbf{1}'$ of composition in $\mathbf{A}_S$. This element is a sum: $\mathbf{1}' = \sum_{p \in S} \mathbf{1}'_p$.

Each $1'_p$ is an atom in $\mathbf{A}_S$. Let us consider $\varphi(1'_p)$: this is a set of pairs (u, u), where $u \in U_p$, for a subset U_p of U, (which we may refer to as to the subset of p-intervals), and U is the disjoint union of U_p, for $p \in S$.

We will now build W (a set of boundaries) by using the elements of U. Each element of U_1 (if any) brings a contribution of one boundary to W; each element of U_2 brings two, and so on.

We thus arrive at the following definition (where $s = \max(S)$):

$$W' = (U_1 \sqcup U_2 \ldots \sqcup U_s) \sqcup (U_2 \ldots \sqcup U_s) \sqcup \ldots (U_s)$$

In this direct union, the first term corresponds to the first boundaries, the second term to the second boundaries (so that the points in U_1 no longer make a contribution to W), the third to the third boundaries, and so on. The only subset contributiong s-th boundaries is U_s.

Let $W'(i, p)$ denote the copy of U_p used in the i-th term of W'. Hence $i \leq p \leq s$, and $W'(i, p)$ corresponds to the i-th boundaries in the p-intervals.

Clearly, W' fully lists all the points in U. Of course, there is the possibility that the same point appears several times, as the i-th boundary of an element and as the j-th boundary of another. But then the algebraic structure points out this fact:

DEFINITION 9.12.– *Let $\mathbf{a}^{p,q}_{i,j}$ be the subset of (p,q)-relations of $\mathbf{B}_{p,q}$ whose i-th coordinate is $(2j-1)$.*

Consequently, a pair (u, v) belongs to an atomic relation of $\mathbf{a}^{p,q}_{i,j}$ if the i-th point of u coincides with the j-th point of v. In this case, we must identify these two points.

DEFINITION 9.13.– *Let W be the quotient set of W' by the following relation: $u \in W'(i, p)$ is equivalent to $v \in W'(j, q)$ if, and only if, $(u, v) \in \varphi(\mathbf{a}^{p,q}_{i,j})$.*

In order for this definition to make sense, the relation $\varphi(\mathbf{a}^{p,q}_{i,j})$ has to be an equivalence relation. This is indeed the case:

LEMMA 9.6.– *The following holds true in the algebra $\mathbf{A}_S$:*

1) $\mathbf{a}^{p,p}_{i,i} \supseteq 1'_p$;
2) $(\mathbf{a}^{p,q}_{i,j})^{-1} = \mathbf{a}^{q,p}_{j,i}$;
3) $\mathbf{a}^{p,q}_{i,j} \circ \mathbf{a}^{q,r}_{j,k} = \mathbf{a}^{p,r}_{i,k}$.

Proof. Since the relations $\mathbf{a}^{p,q}_{i,j}$ are convex, it is enough (according to proposition 3.9) to check that, with respect to composition, their largest and smallest elements behave as stated by the lemma. An easy calculation shows that they do. □

Using the lemma, and the fact that φ corresponds to a weak representation (and hence that the image of the composition *contains* the composition of images), $\varphi(a_{i,j}^{p,q})$ is an equivalence relation: it is reflexive, symmetrical, and transitive.

EXAMPLE 9.14.– Let us consider the example of Figure 9.8. Here $S = \{2, 3\}$, and $U_2 = \{A\}, U_3 = \{B, C\}$. We must take two copies of U_2 and three copies of U_3, so we have $2 + 6 = 8$ points in W'. We use lower case letters and subscripts to denote the same element in the various copies of U (the subscript i means that we consider the i-th term, which corresponds to i-th boundaries). In this case, the general construction is as follows:

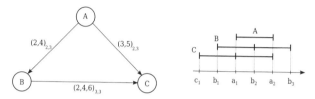

Figure 9.8. *Construction of the configuration associated to a weak representation in the case of $\{2, 3\}$-intervals*

$W'(1, 2) = \{a_1\}, W'(1, 3) = \{b_1, c_1\}, W'(2, 2) = \{a_2\}, W'(2, 3) = \{b_2, c_2\}$, and $W'(3, 3) = \{b_3, c_3\}$. Since $(A, C) \in \varphi((3, 5)_{2,3})$, and $(3, 5)_{2,3} \in a_{1,2}^{2,3}$, a_1 and c_2 define the same point in W. For similar reasons, a_2 and c_3 coincide in W, and these are the only identifications that have to be made. Consequently, W contains six elements, which may be represented by the set of elements $\{a_1, a_2, b_1, b_2, b_3, c_1\}$.

Once the set of subjacent points has been obtained, we have to define a linear order on the resulting set. Once again, the algebra provides the necessary information:

DEFINITION 9.14.– *Let $b_{i,j}^{p,q}$ be the subset of (p, q)-relations of $\mathbf{B}_{p,q}$ whose i-th coordinate is strictly less than $(2j - 1)$.*

We define an ordering on W' in the following manner: $u \in W'(i, p)$ precedes $v \in W'(j, q)$ if, and only if, $(u, v) \in \varphi(b_{i,j}^{p,q})$.

LEMMA 9.7.– *The following holds in $\mathbf{A}_S$:*

1) $a_{i',i}^{p',p} \circ b_{i,j}^{p,q} \circ a_{j,j'}^{q,q'} = b_{i',j'}^{p',q'}$;
2) $b_{i,j}^{p,q} \cap (b_{j,i}^{q,p})^{-1} = \emptyset$;
3) $b_{i,j}^{p,q} \circ b_{j,k}^{q,r} = b_{i,k}^{p,r}$.

Using this lemma, we get the fact that the precedence defines a relation on the set W of equivalence classes; moreover, the relation induced on these equivalence classes is irreflexive and transitive (properties 2 and 3). It is thus a strict order on W.

Moreover, this order is linear, because of the following result:

LEMMA 9.8.– *The following holds*:
1) $\mathbf{B}_{p,q} = \mathbf{b}_{i,j}^{p,q} \sqcup \mathbf{a}_{i,j}^{p,q} \sqcup (\mathbf{b}_{j,i}^{q,p})^{-1}$;
2) *in particular*, $\mathbf{1}'_p \in \mathbf{b}_{i,j}^{p,p}$ *if* $i < j$, $\mathbf{1}'_p \in \mathbf{a}_{i,i}^{p,p}$, *and* $\mathbf{1}'_p \in (\mathbf{b}_{i,j}^{p,p})^{-1}$ *if* $i > j$.

Proof. For any atomic (p, q)-relation a, if the i-th coordinate of a is strictly greater than $(2j - 1)$, then the j-th odd integer, which determines j-th coordinate of a^{-1}, is located to the left of the i-th boundary, hence the j-th coordinate of $a^{-1}1$ is strictly less than $2i - 1$.

As $\mathbf{1}'_p = (1, 3, \dots, 2p - 1)$, the last statement is obvious.   □

Ultimately, we have equipped W with the structure of a linear order. Moreover, as U_p has p canonical maps in W', we obtain for each p in S, a sequence of length p of maps of U_p in W. This sequence is *strictly increasing*, so that it defines a p-interval, because clearly if $u \in U_p$, then $(u, u) \in \varphi(\mathbf{1}'_p)$, hence the corresponding element in $W'(i, p)$ precedes that in $W'(j, p)$ if $i < j$, because of the last statement of the lemma.

In other words, the image of each element of U_p in W is a p-interval. Let ι be the corresponding map $\iota: U \to Int_S(W)$. Clearly, ι is injective, since the intersection of the equivalence relations which take part to the quotients is the identical relation. We may thus identify U with a set of S-intervals of W, i.e. an S-configuration in W. Finally, it is clear that this S-configuration is surjective.

This ends the construction.

PROPOSITION 9.12.– *There exists a well-defined construction which, to each weak representation $\mathcal{U} = (U, \varphi)$ of $\mathbf{A}_s$, associates a linear order W and a canonical injective map $\iota: U \to Int_S(W)$ so that U is identified with a surjective S-configuration in W.*

EXAMPLE 9.15.– Let us consider example 9.13 again. Since we have $(A, B) \in \varphi((2, 4)_{2,3})$, and that $(2, 4)_{2,3} \in \mathbf{b}_{1,2}^{2,3}$ (the first coordinate 2 is less than the second odd number 3), we conclude that $a_1 \prec b_2$. The order we get is $c_1 \prec b_1 \prec a_1 \prec b_2 \prec a_2 \prec b_3$. The canonical map ι sends A to the 2-interval (a_1, a_2), B to the 3-interval (b_1, b_2, b_3), and C to the 3-interval (c_1, a_1, a_2).

9.4.4. *The construction in the case of* $\mathbf{A}_{Points_n}$

Let (U, φ) be a weak representation of $\mathbf{A}_{Points_n}$. Here, each element of U has to correspond to a point in a product set. So we will use n copies of U, one for each projection.

For $1 \leq i \leq n$, let $\mathbf{a}_i$ be the set of atomic relations of $\mathbf{B}_{Points_n}$ whose i-th coordinate is eq. Clearly, it is an equivalence relation. Consequently, due to the fact that φ corresponds to a weak representation, $\varphi(\mathbf{a}_i)$ is itself an equivalence relation on U.

Let W_i be the quotient set of W' by $\varphi(\mathbf{a}_i)$. For each i, there exists a canonical map of U on W_i, hence a map $\varphi : U \rightarrow W_1 \times \cdots \times W_n$. This map is injective, because the intersection of all $\mathbf{a}_i$ is $\mathbf{1}'$, whose image by φ is the identity relation on U.

Up to now, each element of W_i is a set with no additional structure. We now show how to define an order structure on this set.

Firstly, for $1 \leq i \leq n$, let $\mathbf{b}_i$ be the set of atomic relations $\mathbf{B}_{Points_n}$ whose i-th coordinate is the basic relation $\prec$.

Using the fact that composition can be computed componentwise, the following result can easily be proved:

LEMMA 9.9.– *The following identities hold*:

1) $\mathbf{a}_i \circ \mathbf{b}_i \circ \mathbf{a}_i = \mathbf{b}_i$;
2) $\mathbf{b}_i \cap \mathbf{b}_i^{-1} = \emptyset$;
3) $\mathbf{b}_i \circ \mathbf{b}_i = \mathbf{b}_i$;
4) $\mathbf{b}_i \circ \mathbf{b}_i^{-1} = \mathbf{b}_i^{-1} \circ \mathbf{b}_i = \mathbf{B}_{Points_n}$.

This enables us to define a precedence relation on W_i: (the equivalence class of) u precedes (that of) v if, and only if, $(u, v) \in \varphi(\mathbf{b}_i)$.

Using the lemma, we see that precedence is well defined, and that it induces a strict ordering on W_i which is obviously a linear ordering.

EXAMPLE 9.16.– Let us consider the example of Figure 9.9, where the relations considered are those of the Cardinal direction calculus (see Chapter 4). We easily see that $\mathbf{a}_1$, which is the set of relations for which the first projections coincide, is $\{\mathsf{n}, \mathsf{eq}, \mathsf{s}\}$; similarly, $\mathbf{a}_2$ is $\{\mathsf{e}, \mathsf{eq}, \mathsf{w}\}$. Thus, the classes of A and B coincide in W_1, while the classes of B and D coincide in W_2, and these are the only non-trivial equivalences. Hence both W_1 and W_2 have three elements. In addition, $\mathbf{b}_1$ is $\{\mathsf{nw}, \mathsf{w}, \mathsf{sw}\}$ and $\mathbf{b}_2$ is $\{\mathsf{ne}, \mathsf{e}, \mathsf{se}\}$. We thus obtain the ordering $c_1 \prec a_1 \prec d_1$ on W_1 and the ordering $c_2 \prec b_2 \prec a_2$ on W_2.

9.4.4.1. *The case of* $\mathbf{A}_{Blocks_n}$

In this case, the two types of construction — the one corresponding to 2-intervals (intervals in Allen's sense) and that corresponding to products — have to be combined. The construction is left to the reader.

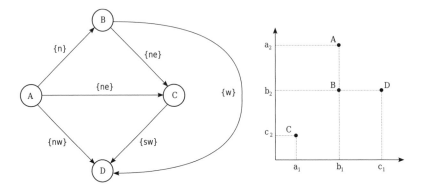

Figure 9.9. *Constructing the configuration associated to a weak representation of the cardinal direction algebra*

9.5. Weak representations and configurations

For all the formalisms based on linear orders which we have considered so far in this chapter, we have seen that any configuration resulted in a weak representation of the algebra associated to the calculus, and that conversely, a canonical configuration is associated to any weak representation.

In particular, for all these formalisms, we have the following theorem, where **A** denotes the algebra of the formalism:

THEOREM 9.3.– *Let U be a weak representation of* **A**. *Then, there exists a configuration whose description is U. In particular, any algebraically closed scenario is consistent.*

Proof. Only Part 2 needs a proof. An algebraically closed scenario is clearly equivalent to an algebraically closed reduced scenario. Now the latter is equivalent to a finite weak representation of **A**. □

9.5.1. *Other qualitative formalisms*

All the formalisms based on linear orders that we have considered satisfy the following properties:

– their associated algebra **A** is a Boolean algebra with inversion and composition operators;

– **A** is characterized by its composition table, provided that the equality relation is atomic;

– in most cases, this algebra is a relation algebra;

– any algebraically closed scenario is consistent.

It only became progressively apparent that these properties do not extend to all qualitative formalisms. A clarification of the complex situations which can arise when some of them fail to hold has not yet been fully accomplished [LIG 03, REN 04].

9.5.2. *A non-associative algebra: INDU*

We have already noted (Chapter 4, section 4.11.4) that the algebra associated with the INDU formalism is not associative (see also [LIG 03]).

Hence the INDU algebra is not a relation algebra, but only an algebra which satisfies all the axioms of relation algebras except for the axiom of associativity for composition. We will examine these algebras, called non-associative algebras, in Chapter 11. The phenomenon of non-associativity was independently discovered by [EGE 99] for another qualitative algebra.

The natural interpretation of the INDU algebra in terms of intervals on the real line, where relations are interpreted in terms of relative interval durations, is a weak representation of the algebra; but, it is not a representation. Indeed, let $(Int(\mathbb{R}), \varphi)$ denote this weak representation. Consider, for example, the intervals $[0, 3]$ and $[4, 6]$. This pair is in the relation $m^=$: $([0, 3], [4, 6]) \in \varphi(m^=)$. In the algebra, we have $m^= \circ m^= = p^=$. So we have:

$$\varphi(m^= \circ m^=) \supseteq \varphi(m^=) \circ \varphi(m^=)$$

but we do not have the converse inclusion, since we cannot find an interval I of length 2 such that $([0, 3], I) \in \varphi(m^=)$ and $(I, [4, 6]) \in \varphi(m^=)$: there is no room between 3 and 4 for an interval of length 2.

9.5.3. *Interpreting Allen's calculus on the integers*

The phenomenon identified for the weak representation associated to the INDU calculus — namely, that this weak representation is not a representation — actually does not have any exceptional character. Consider, for instance Allen's algebra; let us interpret the intervals in terms of intervals of integers, hence as pairs of integers $(m, n) \in \mathbb{Z} \times \mathbb{Z}$ (with $m < n$). Under these conditions, the natural interpretation of the algebra is not a representation of the algebra, but only a weak representation: this is clear, since we do not have the density property that being a representation would imply; or we may also note that, for example, $([1, 2], [3, 4]) \in \varphi(\mathsf{p})$, but that there is no integer interval I such that $([1, 2], I) \in \varphi(\mathsf{p})$ and $(I, [3, 4]) \in \varphi(\mathsf{p})$, although we have $\mathsf{p} \circ \mathsf{p} = \mathsf{p}$ in Allen's Interval algebra.

9.5.4. *Algebraically closed but inconsistent scenarios: the case of cyclic intervals*

Consider the following constraint network on the Cyclic interval algebra (Figure 9.10): it has four vertices $\{V_1, V_2, V_3, V_4\}$, with the constraints m on the arcs (V_1, V_2), (V_2, V_3), and (V_3, V_1) and ppi on the arcs (V_1, V_4), (V_2, V_4), and (V_3, V_4).

In other words, the three directed arcs V_1, V_2, and V_3 are arranged to entirely cover the circle by placing themselves one behind the other, without encroaching on each other, and the intruder V_4 tries to find some free space on the circle. It is intuitively clear that in the absence of one of the four arcs, the scenario is achievable, but that it is not achievable if all are present.

More precisely, on the one hand, we easily check that the four 3-element subnetworks of the network, which is a reduced scenario, are consistent: for the subnetwork containing the vertices V_1, V_2, and V_3, there is a unique model formed by three arcs (A, B), (B, C), and (C, A), where A, B, and C are three distinct points such that the sequence A, B, C corresponds to the counterclockwise orientation. For the other three subnetworks with three elements, the network consists of one m constraint and two ppi constraints, for which a solution is easy to find.

As a consequence, this network is 3-consistent, hence algebraically closed. But it is not consistent, since any model for the subnetwork $\{V_1, V_2, V_3\}$ is formed by three intervals which entirely cover the circle, so that there is no room left for a fourth interval which would not touch the first three (Figure 9.10).

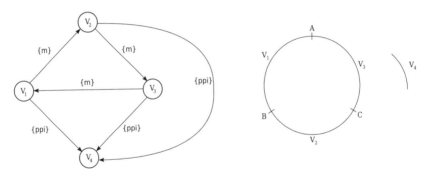

Figure 9.10. *The network on the left is 3-consistent: if one of the four vertices is left out, a scenario satisfying all constraints is easily found. But it is not consistent: V_1, V_2, and V_3 entirely cover the circle, leaving no free room for V_4*

This example shows that there are weak representations for the Cyclic interval calculus which do not correspond to any configuration.

9.5.5. *Weak representations of* RCC–8

Let us now consider the RCC–8 formalism.

Here, any algebraically closed scenario is consistent, i.e. corresponds to configurations, in a sense to be specified. The proof of this fact is due to Nebel

[NEB 94a]. The result has been extended by Renz [REN 98a, REN 02a, REN 02b], who precisely shows which models can be built in Euclidean spaces.

More generally, the non-empty subsets of a set provide weak representations of RCC−5, and the regular closed sets of a topological space provide weak representations of RCC−8.

The links between the models of RCC−8 and those of the RCC theory will be discussed later in Chapter 10.

For the moment, let us only note that algebraically closed scenarios may have qualitatively distinct models: consider, for example, the network with three vertices where all three constraints are the basic relation PO. Clearly (Figure 9.11), at least two qualitatively distinct configurations of regions can be found which correspond to this weak representation: the first has three regions which meet pairwise but do not have a common point; the second has three regions sharing a common subregion.

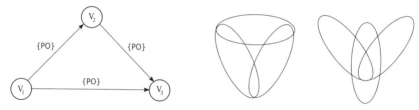

Figure 9.11. *A weak representation of* RCC−8 *(on the left) may correspond to qualitatively distinct configurations (in the center and on the right)*

Our next aim will be to describe a method for building configurations associated to a finite weak representation of RCC−8. For the moment, we start with the simpler case of finite weak representations of RCC−5.

9.5.5.1. *Set-theoretic models of* RCC−5

Intuitively, the RCC−5 calculus describes configurations of regions in purely set-theoretic terms. This motivates the following definition of a configuration (of sets) for RCC−5:

DEFINITION 9.15.– *A configuration (of sets) for* RCC−5 *is a pair* (W, P), *where* W *is a non-empty set and* $P \subseteq W \times W$ *is a family of non-empty subsets of* W.

Clearly, any configuration of sets gives rise to a weak representation of the RCC−5 algebra. The above example also shows that qualitatively distinct configurations may result in the same weak representation.

Let us give a precise definition of the basic relations of RCC−5 when regions are interpreted as non-empty sets. Let A and B be two non-empty subsets of a set W. Table 9.1 defines the five basic relations in terms of the three predicates $A \cup B = \emptyset$, $A \subseteq B$, and $A \supseteq B$.

	$A \cap B = \emptyset$	$A \subseteq B$	$A \supseteq B$
DR	1	0	0
PO	0	0	0
PP	0	1	0
PPI	0	0	1
EQ	0	1	1

Table 9.1. *Definition of the basic* RCC−5 *relations between two non-empty subsets A and B (1 denotes the Boolean value* **true** *and 0 the Boolean value* **false**)

LEMMA 9.10.– *Let W be a non-empty set. The five binary relations defined by the conditions given in Table 9.1 on the non-empty subsets of W is a set of relations which has the JEPD property.*

Proof. The proof is straightforward: if $A \cap B = \emptyset$, we cannot have neither $A \subseteq B$ since then $A \cap B = A = \emptyset$, nor $A \supseteq B$ since A is non-empty. So we are left with four logical possibilities.   □

Let $\mathbf{B}_{RCC5}$ denote the set $\{\mathsf{DR}, \mathsf{PO}, \mathsf{PP}, \mathsf{PPI}, \mathsf{EQ}\}$ considered as a set of five relation symbols, and let $\mathbf{A}_{RCC5}$ denote the algebra of subsets of $\mathbf{B}_{RCC5}$ equipped with the inversion and composition operations.

As in the case of RCC−8, we associate a lattice (represented in Figure 9.12) to the set of basic relations; to refer to intervals in this lattice, we make conventions similar to those described in section 4.14 for RCC−8. Under these conditions, the composition table of RCC−5 is given in Table 9.2.

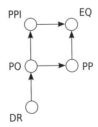

Figure 9.12. *The lattice of basic relations of* RCC−5

∘	DR	PO	PP	PPI
DR	[DR, EQ]	[DR, PP]	[DR, PP]	DR
PO	[DR, PPI]	[DR, EQ]	[PO, PP]	[DR, PPI]
PP	DR	[DR, PP]	PP	[DR, EQ]
PPI	[DR, PPI]	[PO, PPI]	[PO, EQ]	PPI

Table 9.2. *Composition table of* RCC−5

PROPOSITION 9.13.− *Let W be a non-empty set and $U \subseteq \mathcal{P}(W)$, a family of non-empty subsets of W. Let $C: U \times U \rightarrow \mathbf{B}_{RCC5}$ be the map which, to each pair (A, B) of elements of P, associates the basic relation defined by the conditions of Table 9.1. Then, (U, C) is a weak representation of the algebra $\mathbf{A}_{RCC5}$.*

Any configuration of sets thus defines a weak representation of $\mathbf{A}_{RCC5}$:

What about the converse situation: given a weak representation of $\mathbf{A}_{RCC5}$, can we find a configuration of sets such that the weak representation associated to is isomorphic to the initial representation? The answer is positive, as follows from [NEB 94a] in particular, but here, contrary to what was the case for Allen's calculus, several choices are possible in general, and there is no canonicity for the acceptable configurations. Intuitively, this is due to the fact that binary constraints specify the conditions of pairwise intersection between subsets, but do not say anything about the intersections of three or more subsets.

We will give an elementary method to show the existence of such configurations for finite weak representations, by using the approach first described in [LIG 99]. The construction is based on the interpretation of the RCC−5 relations in terms of propositional and modal logics introduced by Bennett [BEN 94, BEN 95, BEN 96b] (this interpretation will be described below in Chapter 13).

9.5.5.2. *Possibility conditions and constraints*

Let (U, φ) be a finite weak representation of RCC−5. We may see (U, φ) as an algebraically closed reduced scenario whose vertices are the elements of U. Let us recall that $\varphi(b)$, for $b \in \mathbf{A}_{RCC5}$, is the set of pairs of elements of U labeled by the constraint b.

Let us choose a subset S of pairs (u, v) in $U \times U$ in the following manner: this set contains all the pairs in $\varphi(\mathsf{PP})$; in the case of PO and DR, which are symmetrical relations, $\varphi(\mathsf{PO})$ ($\varphi(\mathsf{DR})$ respectively) contains (u, v) if, and only if, it contains (v, u), we only include one of these two pairs in the set. In other words, we select a directed graph associated with (U, φ) such that the label PPI does not appear (we reverse the arrow if necessary), and we consider the set S of arrows obtained in this way.

For each $u \in U$, let X_u be a Boolean variable. For each pair of $s = (u, v) \in S$, we introduce worlds w in the following manner:

– if $s = (u, v) \in \varphi(\mathsf{DR})$, we introduce two worlds: a world where X_u is true and a world where X_v is true;

– if $s = (u, v) \in \varphi(\mathsf{PO})$, we introduce three worlds: a world where $X_u \wedge X_v$ is true, a world where $X_u \wedge \neg X_v$ is true, and a world where $X_v \wedge \neg X_u$ is true;

– if $s = (u, v) \in \varphi(\mathsf{PP})$, we introduce two worlds: a world where $X_u \wedge X_v$ is true and a world where $X_v \wedge \neg X_u$ is true.

The conditions introduced for the truth-values on the worlds considered here are called *possibility conditions* by Bennett. Moreover, for each element of S, we introduce *constraints* on the Boolean variables:

– if $s = (u, v) \in \varphi(\mathsf{DR})$, we enforce the constraints $X_u \rightarrow \neg X_v$ and $X_v \rightarrow \neg X_u$;

– if $s = (u, v) \in \varphi(\mathsf{PP})$, we enforce the constraints $X_u \rightarrow X_v$ and $\neg X_v \rightarrow \neg X_u$.

There is no new constraint when $s = (u, v) \in \varphi(\mathsf{PO})$.

The possibility conditions and constraints are summarized in Table 9.3.

	Possibility conditions	Constraints
DR	X_u, X_v	$X_u \rightarrow \neg X_v, X_v \rightarrow \neg X_u$
PO	$X_u \wedge X_v, X_u \wedge \neg X_v, X_v \wedge \neg X_u$	
PP	$X_u \wedge X_v, X_v \wedge \neg X_u$	$X_u \rightarrow X_v, \neg X_v \rightarrow \neg X_u$

Table 9.3. *Possibility conditions and constraints for* RCC−5

EXAMPLE 9.17.– Consider the following network: $U = \{1, 2, 3\}$, and $C(1, 2) = \mathsf{PP}, C(1, 3) = \mathsf{DR}$, and $C(2, 3) = \mathsf{PO}$. It is algebraically closed, hence it defines a weak representation.

Referring to the construction described above, we may choose for S the set $\{(1, 2), (1, 3), (2, 3)\}$.

Then for $(1, 2)$, which is labeled by PP, we introduce two worlds w_1 and w_2; the possibility conditions state that X_1 and X_2 are true in w_1 and $X_2 \wedge \neg X_1$ is true in w_2.

Now, for $(1, 3)$, which is labeled by DR, we introduce two worlds w_3 and w_4; we must have X_1 true in w_3 and X_3 true in w_4.

Finally, for $(2, 3)$, which is labeled by PO, we introduce three worlds w_5, w_6, and w_7 such that $X_2 \wedge X_3$ is true in w_5, $X_2 \wedge \neg X_3$ is true in w_6, and $X_3 \wedge \neg X_2$ is true in w_7.

The constraints due to $(1,2)$ are $X_1 \rightarrow X_2$ and $\neg X_2 \rightarrow \neg X_1$, and those due to $(1,3)$ are $X_1 \rightarrow \neg X_3$ and $X_3 \rightarrow \neg X_1$.

This first stage of the construction may be summarized in the following manner:

1) start with an empty set of worlds W;

2) for each condition of possibility, we add to W a new world in which the corresponding condition of possibility (which involves two Boolean variables) is true;

3) the set W obtained in this way will be the underlying set for the configuration we are trying to build.

At the end of this first stage, we obtain a partial valuation of the Boolean variables X_u which intuitively says whether the subset u contains w, for each world $w \in W$.

EXAMPLE 9.18.– Consider again the previous example. Table 9.4 describes the partial valuation obtained at the end of the first stage of the construction.

	w_1	w_2	w_3	w_4	w_5	w_6	w_7
X_1	1	0	1				
X_2	1	1			1	1	0
X_3				1	1	0	1

Table 9.4. *The initial partial valuation resulting from the application of the possibility conditions (1 denotes the value **true**)*

We proceed with the construction by iterating the following steps until we get a complete valuation (i.e. such that it has a truth-value for each (variable, world) pair):

1) apply the constraints to the current partial valuation;

2) if a pair (variable, world) does not have a value, select a truth-value arbitrarily.

EXAMPLE 9.19.– Let us proceed with the example. After a first application of the constraints, we get the truth-values shown in Table 9.5.

	w_1	w_2	w_3	w_4	w_5	w_6	w_7
X_1	1	0	1	0	0		0
X_2	1	1	1		1	1	0
X_3	0		0	1	1	0	1

Table 9.5. *The partial valuation after a first application of the constraints*

At this juncture, three values have not been instantiated. Let us for example choose the value **true** for X_3 in w_2. Applying the constraints, we get the fact that X_1 has to be false in w_2, which is the case. Now for X_2 in w_4, let us choose the value **false**. All constraints are satisfied. We still have to choose a value for X_1 in w_6, for instance **false**.

The resulting valuation, represented in Table 9.6, is now complete, and all the required constraints are satisfied.

	w_1	w_2	w_3	w_4	w_5	w_6	w_7
X_1	1	0	1	0	0	0	0
X_2	1	1	1	0	1	1	0
X_3	0	1	0	1	1	0	1

Table 9.6. *The final valuation at the end of the construction*

At the end of the construction, we obtain a configuration by associating to each $u \in U$ the subset of W formed by worlds for which X_u has the value **true**. The left side of Figure 9.13 represents the configuration obtained in this way for our running example.

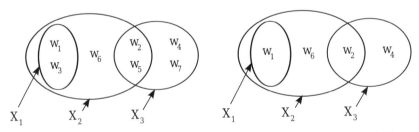

Figure 9.13. *Two configurations corresponding to the network of example 9.16: on the left, the configuration obtained at the end of the construction; on the right, a simplified configuration*

NOTE 9.1.– If we examine the configuration we have obtained, we note that the worlds w_1 and w_3 behave exactly in the same way (the columns for these two worlds are the same in Table 9.6); moreover, the same is true of the worlds w_2 and w_5, and of the worlds w_4 and w_7. We may thus merge w_1 and w_3, w_2 and w_5, and w_4 and w_7, respectively, to obtain a configuration containing only four points. This configuration is shown in the right part of Figure 9.13.

PROPOSITION 9.14.– *If (U, φ) is a finite weak representation of $\mathbf{A}_{RCC5}$, the previous construction always terminates successfully, and it provides a configuration whose associated representation is the initial weak representation.*

The Boolean variables $(X_u)_{u\in U}$ define a map $U \to \mathcal{P}(W)$ which explicitly associates a subset of W with each element of U.

Proof. The main point of the proof consists in showing that the application of the constraints does not lead to a contradiction, i.e. to a situation which would result in allocating to a variable X_u, in a world w, a truth-value which is the opposite of the one it already has been allocated previously.

Now the constraints are of three possible types:

1) $X_u \to X_v$ (if (u, v) is labeled by PP);
2) $\neg X_u \to \neg X_v$ (for the same labeling);
3) $X_u \to \neg X_v$ (if (u, v) is labeled by PP).

Assume that a chain of applications of the constraints leads us to conclude that some variable X_u is true in some world, whereas another leads us to conclude that it is false in the same world.

The first chain is necessarily a sequence of application of constraints of type 1), $X_{u_0} \to \ldots X_u$ resulting from the relation PP. Since this relation is transitive, this means that (u_0, u) is labeled by PP.

For the second chain, there are two possibilities: either a chain of type $X_{u_0} \to \cdots \neg X_u$, or a chain of type $\neg X_{u_0} \to \cdots \neg X_u$.

In the first case, we necessarily have a sequence of constraints of type 1), followed by a single constraint of type 3), followed by a sequence of constraints of type 2): $X_{u_0} \to \cdots X_{u_k} \to \neg X_{u_1} \cdots \neg X_u$. But this means that (u_0, u_k) is labeled by PP, (u_l, u) is labeled as PPI, and that the (u_k, u_l) is labeled as DR. We conclude that u_0 should be a subset of two disjoint subsets u_k and u_l, which is a contradiction.

In the second case, we have a chain of constraints of type 3), and, using the transitivity of PP, we again end up in a contradiction. $\square$

9.5.5.3. *Topological models of* RCC-8

The RCC-8 calculus adds the topological concept of boundary to the RCC-5 calculus. We are led to define a configuration as follows:

DEFINITION 9.16.– *A (topological) configuration for* RCC-8 *is a pair* (W, P), *where* W *is a non-empty topological space and* P *is a family of non-empty subsets of* W *which are regular closed sets.*

Let us recall (the reader may refer to Appendix A) that a closed regular set of a topological space W is a non-empty subset $V \subseteq W$ which is closed and equal to the closure of its interior.

We intend to prove the following result:

PROPOSITION 9.15.– *Let W be a topological space. On the set of non-empty regular closed sets of W, the eight relations defined in Table 9.7 is a set of binary relations which has the JEPD property.*

DC(A, B)	iff	$A \cap B = \emptyset$
EC(A, B)	iff	$(A \cap B \neq \emptyset) \wedge (\mathring{A} \cap \mathring{B} = \emptyset)$
PO(A, B)	iff	$(\mathring{A} \cap \mathring{B} \neq \emptyset) \wedge (\mathring{A} \not\subseteq B) \wedge (\mathring{B} \not\subseteq A)$
TPP(A, B)	iff	$(A \subseteq B) \wedge (A \not\subseteq \mathring{B}) \wedge (B \not\subseteq A)$
NTPP(A, B)	iff	$(A \subseteq \mathring{B}) \wedge (B \not\subseteq A)$
EQ(A, B)	iff	$(A \subseteq B) \wedge (B \subseteq A)$
TPPI(A, B)	iff	TPP(B, A)
NTPPI(A, B)	iff	NTPP(B, A)

Table 9.7. *Topological relations between two non-empty regular closed sets A and B*

The proof makes use of the following lemma:

Figure 9.14. *If a closed set B is not regular, one can simultaneously have $\mathring{A} \cap \mathring{B} = \emptyset$, $A \cap B \neq \emptyset$ and $\mathring{A} \cap B \neq \emptyset$*

LEMMA 9.11.– *Let A and B be two non-empty regular closed sets. If $\mathring{A} \cap \mathring{B} = \emptyset$ and $A \cap B \neq \emptyset$, then $A \cap \mathring{B} = B \cap \mathring{A} = \emptyset$.*

Proof. Indeed, let us assume, for example, that $B \cap \mathring{A}$ is not empty, and let x be a point of this set. Then, since B is closed and regular, any closed set containing $\mathring{B}$ contains B and x. Since $\mathring{A}$ and $\mathring{B}$ are disjoint, $W \setminus \mathring{A}$ is such a closed set. So it contains x, which contradicts the fact that $x \in \mathring{A}$.   □

NOTE 9.2.– If A and B are not regular, this property is no longer true. Figure 9.14 illustrates a case where B is not regular; we have simultaneously $\overset{\circ}{A} \cap \overset{\circ}{B} = \emptyset$ and $A \cap B \neq \emptyset$ with $\overset{\circ}{A} \cap B \neq \emptyset$.

LEMMA 9.12.– *Let A and B be two non-empty regular closed sets. Consider the four conditions $A \cap B = \emptyset$, $\overset{\circ}{A} \cap \overset{\circ}{B} = \emptyset$, $A \subseteq B$, and $B \supseteq A$. Then, the only logical possibilities for the truth-values of these conditions are those given in Table 9.8.*

	$A \cap B = \emptyset$	$\overset{\circ}{A} \cap \overset{\circ}{B} = \emptyset$	$A \subseteq B$	$A \supseteq B$
DC	1	1	0	0
EC	0	1	0	0
PO	0	0	0	0
PP	0	0	1	0
PPI	0	0	0	1
EQ	0	0	1	1

Table 9.8. *Topological relations between two non-empty regular closed sets A and B (1 denotes the Boolean value* **true** *and 0 denotes the Boolean value* **false**)

Proof. If the first condition is true, the second one is also true. But this is also the same case for the third condition, since $A \subseteq B$ is equivalent to $A \cap B = A$ and A is not empty; this is the case for the fourth condition by symmetry. So we are left with only one possibility among the eight *a priori* logical possibilities.

Let us consider the remaining eight possibilities where the first condition is false. If the second condition is true, lemma 9.11 implies that the third and fourth ones are false. Indeed, if we had for example $A \subseteq B$, hence $\overset{\circ}{A} \subseteq \overset{\circ}{B}$, then $\overset{\circ}{A} \cap \overset{\circ}{B} = \overset{\circ}{A}$ would be non-empty (since its closure must be A), which contradicts lemma 9.11. So we are left with only one of the four logical possibilities.

We are left with four logical possibilities where $A \cap B \neq \emptyset$ and $\overset{\circ}{A} \cap \overset{\circ}{B} \neq \emptyset$; these are the possibilities shown in Table 9.8. □

The relation PP may in turn be refined into two relations NTPP and TPP, so that PPI is refined into the two inverse relations NTPPI and TPPI: by definition, we have $\mathsf{NTPP}(A, B)$ if $\mathsf{PP}(A, B)$ and $A \subseteq \overset{\circ}{A}$, and $\mathsf{TPP}(A, B)$ if $\mathsf{PP}(A, B)$ and $A \not\subseteq \overset{\circ}{B}$.

PROPOSITION 9.16.– *Let W be a topological space. On the set of non-empty regular closed sets of W, the eight relations defined by Table 9.8 are a set of binary relations with the JEPD property.*

From the above discussion, we deduce the following proposition:

PROPOSITION 9.17.– *Let W be a topological space. Let U be a set of non-empty regular closed subspaces of W. If the basic relations of* RCC−8 *are interpreted by φ as indicated in Table 9.7, then (U, φ) is a weak representation of* $\mathbf{A}_{RCC8}$.

9.5.6. *From weak representations to configurations*

Let us now consider consider the converse situation: given a weak representation (U, φ) of the RCC−8 algebra, can we find a topological space W and a subset $P \subseteq \mathcal{P}(W)$ of non-empty regular closed subsets of W in such a way that U is isomorphic to the weak representation associated with the configuration (P, W)?

A finite weak representation of the RCC−8 algebra corresponds to an algebraically closed scenario. In this case, the answer is positive. The proof is based on the possibility of translating the constraint networks on RCC−8 in terms of formulas of modal logic [BEN 94, BEN 96b, REN 99b]. We will come back to this topic in Chapter 13.

9.5.7. *Finite topological models*

In particular, a finite weak representation corresponds to a configuration in a particular type of finite topological space called a *quasi-saw space*.

DEFINITION 9.17.– *A finite topological space is a* quasi-saw *space if it can be defined by a preorder in which each element has at most two successors, which are not comparable.*

The reader may refer to Appendix A for the topology associated with a preorder. In particular, the closure and interior operators are defined in the following way:

DEFINITION 9.18.– *Let W be a preorder equipped with the preorder topology.*

– the closure of a subset A is the set of elements which precedes an element of A:
$\overline{A} = \{x \in A \mid (\exists y \in A)x \leq y\}$;

– the interior of a set A is the set of elements of A whose successors are all themselves in A: $\overset{\circ}{A} = \{x \in A \mid (\forall y \in A)x \leq y \rightarrow y \in A\}$.

THEOREM 9.4.– *Any finite weak representation (U, φ) of* RCC−8 *corresponds to a configuration of non-empty regular closed sets in a quasi-saw topological space: there exists a quasi-saw finite topological space W and a map which associates to each $u \in U$ a non-empty regular closed set of W in such a way that for any basic relation b of* RCC−8 *and any pair $(u, v) \in U^2$, the relation between the image of u and that of v is the relation b if, and only if, $(u, v) \in \varphi(b)$ ([REN 98a]).*

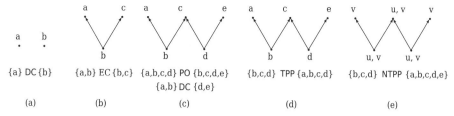

Figure 9.15. *Each of the basic relations of* RCC$-$8 *can be realized in a quasi-saw topological space*

EXAMPLE 9.20.– In particular, each basic relation (that is, each scenario with two elements) can be realized in a quasi-saw space. Figure 9.15 illustrates quasi-saw realizations for each basic relation. For example:

– for DC, we have in (a) a realization in a space with two elements; but this space is not connected; a connected realization is illustrated in (c), with $A = \{a, b\}, B = \{d, e\}$;

– for PO, we have in (c): $A = \{a, b, c, d\}$ and $B = \{b, c, d, e\}$, hence $\overset{\circ}{A} = \{a, b, c\}, \overset{\circ}{B} = \{c, d, e\}$;

– for TPP, we have in (d): $A = \{b, c, d\}$ and $B = \{a, b, c, d\}$, hence $\overset{\circ}{A} = \{c\}, \overset{\circ}{B} = \{a, b, c\}$;

– for NTPP, we have in (d): $A = \{b, c, d\}$ and $B = \{a, b, c, d, e\}$, hence $\overset{\circ}{A} = \{c\}, = \{a, b, c, d, e\}$.

9.5.7.1. *An explicit construction of finite models*

The reader can find in [LIG 99] the description of an explicit construction of a configuration associated with a given weak representation of RCC$-$8. This construction is similar to the one described previously for weak representations of RCC$-$5. It is based on the translation of relations in terms of modal logic ([BEN 96b], see also Chapter 13).

9.5.8. *Models in Euclidean space*

In applications such as geographical knowledge bases, we are interested in the existence of configurations in specific topological spaces, for example, in Euclidean spaces, with regions having specific properties, such as connectedness. Now some RCC$-$8 networks which can be realized as sets of connected regions in the 3D Euclidean space are not representable in the 2D Euclidean space [LEM 96].

Renz [REN 98a] proves the following result:

THEOREM 9.5.– *For the* RCC$-$8 *algebra the following holds*:

– any weak representation of RCC−8 *can be realized in the Euclidean space of dimension* $n \geq 1$ *by regions which are unions of polytopes;*

– any weak representation of RCC−8 *can be realized by polytopes (hence by connected regions) in the Euclidean spaces of dimension* $n \geq 3$.

9.6. Historical note

The works of Ladkin and Maddux [LAD 88, LAD 94] have popularized the use of algebraic methods in the field of qualitative temporal reasoning. Hirsch [HIR 97a, CRI 04] considers the complexity problems in the more general context of relation algebras.

The concept of a weak representation (not to be confused with the concept of weak representation used by Jónsson [JÓN 59, HIR 02]) was introduced by Ligozat in 1990 [LIG 90]. Ligozat uses it to study the weak representations of the n-interval algebras, for $n \geq 1$, and to prove decidability results, as shown in this chapter. The extension of these results to product formalisms and S-intervals is described in [LIG 01].

The field of qualitative spatial reasoning has evolved with a delay compared to that of qualitative temporal reasoning. The approach of the Leeds school focusses on an axiomatic point of view; it has explored in depth the expressiveness properties of spatial formalisms (see for example [GOT 94]). Fundamental questions which, due to the fact that they all have a positive response for Allen's interval algebra, had taken some time to be considered in a clear way, have been examined during the 1990s; they include the question of determining whether the standard models are representations, or only weak representations, and whether algebraic closure implies 3-consistency. A significant work has also been done to automate the computation of the composition tables for formalisms having a large number of basic relations; the work of Bennett on the interpretation of the RCC−5 and RCC−8 formalisms in terms of intuitionistic or modal logic are related to this attempt. They led to the determination of polynomial classes for these formalisms [REN 97, REN 99a]. The RCC−5 and RCC−8 models will be dealt with in more detail in Chapter 10.

The concept of weak representation has recently been proposed as an adequate means of providing a general abstract framework for the concept of a qualitative formalism. We will come back to this topic in Chapter 11.

Chapter 10

Models of RCC−8

10.1. "Disks in the plane"

The most common representation of the basic relations of RCC−8 is the one where disks in the Euclidean plane are used to illustrate the eight relations, as shown in (Figure 10.1).

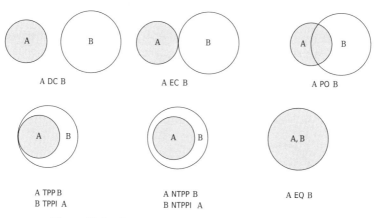

Figure 10.1. *The eight basic relations of* RCC−8 *between two disks in the plane*

The pair (U, φ), where U is the set of closed disks in the plane, and φ the map which, to each of the eight basic relation symbols, associates the set of pairs of disks satisfying this relation, is a weak representation of the RCC−8 algebra.

The composition table (Table 4.6) expresses a set of implications, such as: if for three disks x, y, z we have $(x, z) \in$ NTPP and $(z, y) \in$ TPPI, then the relation between x and y is one of the five relations other than EQ, TPPI, and NTPPI. But it can be easily checked that conversely, if the relation between two disks x and y is one of these five relations, for example PO, then we may find a disk z so that we have $(x, z) \in$ NTPP and $(z, y) \in$ TPPI y.

Hence we have the following theorem:

THEOREM 10.1.– *The natural weak representation of the* RCC-8 *algebra by disks in the plane is a representation.*

This is a positive result which shows that the RCC-8 algebra is actually a relation algebra, since we may consider it as a binary relation algebra (see Appendix B), that is an algebra whose elements are *bona fide* binary relations.

We may ask the question for the 1D analog of this weak representation: is it a representation?

Consider the Cyclic interval calculus, which we introduced in Chapter 4 (section 4.13). Clearly, the pair (U, φ), where U is the set of oriented intervals on the circle, and φ the map which, to each basic relation symbol of RCC-8, associates the set of pairs of intervals which satisfy this relation, is again a weak representation of the RCC-8 algebra.

But it is not a representation. Indeed, let us consider (Figure 10.2) the case of two intervals x and y such that $(x$ moi $y)$. In this case, the corresponding relation in RCC-8 is PO. According to the composition table (Table 4.6), PO belongs to the composition (NTPP$\circ$TPPI). However, we cannot find an interval z such that x NTPP z and z TPPI

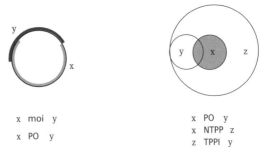

x moi y

x PO   y

x PO   y

x NTPP z

z TPPI y

Figure 10.2. *Two intervals x and y such that x moi y, hence x PO y; however, we cannot find an interval z such that x NTPP z and z TPPI y, since such an interval z would contain the whole circle: what is possible in 2D (see the right side of the figure) is not possible in 1D*

y, since such an interval z would contain both x and y, where x and y are two intervals whose union is the whole circle.

One of the advantages of the RCC−8 formalism is that it provides a simple language to describe the configurations of regions in the plane. But in many applications, for example in geographical ones, we cannot consider circular regions alone. The aim of the RCC language, of which RCC−8 is a sublanguage, is to provide a means of expression which includes the possibility of considering sums, differences, and complements of regions. This is the context we will consider in this chapter.

Structure of the chapter

Since the RCC−8 formalism is a sublanguage of the RCC theory, we will consider the study of weak representations of RCC−8 in the context of RCC-models. In the RCC theory, we are provided with operations which allow us to build new regions from given regions: to a given region, we may associate its complement, and to a pair of regions, their sum and their product (the latter may be empty).

A representation is a weak representation which satisfies additional properties. To begin with, we examine some related properties for weak representations. We then discuss the question of deciding whether there are RCC models which provide RCC−8 representations, and, since the answer is negative, of determining to what extent the composition table expresses necessary and sufficient conditions. This issue was solved by Li and Ying [LI 03b], and we present their results, which use a translation (due to Stell [STE 00]) of RCC models in algebraic terms. Lastly, we present the generalization of the RCC theory also proposed by Li and Ying [LI 04a] which makes it possible to consider a more significant variety of models, including the models considered by Galton [GAL 99] which were discussed in Chapter 4.

10.2. Models of a composition table

10.2.1. *Complements on weak representations*

To make things precise, let us consider a finite relation algebra $\mathbf{A}$ whose elements correspond to the subsets of a finite set of basic relations $\mathbf{B}$.

Recall that a weak representation (U, φ) of $\mathbf{A}$ consists of a non-empty set U and a map $\varphi \colon \mathbf{A} \to \mathcal{P}(U \times U)$ such that the following properties are satisfied:

 – φ is a morphism of Boolean algebras;
 – $\varphi(\mathbf{1}') = \Delta_U$;
 – for any $x \in A$, $\varphi(x^{\smile}) = \varphi(x)^{-1}$;
 – for all $x, y \in A$, $\varphi(x;y) \supseteq \varphi(x) \circ \varphi(y)$.

The properties which we deal with may be considered in the more general context of the *composition table* of the algebra $\mathbf{A}$, rather than of the algebra itself. If $\mathbf{B}$ contains n basic relations, the composition table has n rows and n columns indexed by $\mathbf{B}$, the entry in row a and column b being the composition $(a \circ b)$ of the basic relations a and b. The composition table τ is then simply a map $\tau \colon \mathbf{B} \times \mathbf{B} \to 2^{\mathbf{B}}$.

10.2.2. *Properties of weak representations*

We will examine several properties which a weak representation may possess.

First of all, let us recall that a weak representation defines a partition of $U \times U$ indexed by the elements of $\mathbf{B}$ whose image is non-empty, or in other words, an equivalence relation on $U \times U$ defined by the condition: (u, v) and (u', v') are equivalent if there exists $b \in \mathbf{B}$ such that $(u, v) \in \varphi(b)$ and $(u', v') \in \varphi(b)$.

In what follows, we will when necessary distinguish between the map $\varphi \colon \mathbf{B} \to \mathcal{P}(U \times U)$ and the map $2^{\varphi} \colon \mathbf{A} \to \mathcal{P}(U \times U)$, the latter being defined as usual by the condition $2^{\varphi}(r) = \cup_{b \in r} \varphi(b)$. If we identify $\mathbf{B}$ with the subset of $\mathbf{A}$ formed by subsets containing a single element, we may consider that 2^{φ} extends the map φ.

Assume that a composition table $\tau \colon \mathbf{B} \times \mathbf{B} \to \mathbf{A}$ is given. In this chapter, we will mainly consider the composition tables of RCC-5 and RCC-8.

NOTE 10.1.– It may be convenient to consider (U, φ) as a graph (or a constraint network) whose vertices are the elements of U and whose arcs are labeled by elements of $\mathbf{B}$. The labeling of the arcs of the graph can be made explicit by denoting by $b_{i,j}$ the unique element of $\mathbf{B}$ which labels (i, j).

The fundamental property of weak representations — namely the fact that for all $a, b \in \mathbf{B}, \varphi(\tau(a, b)) \supseteq \varphi(a) \circ \varphi(b)$ — corresponds to the fact that for any 3-tuple (i, j, k) of vertices, the label $b_{i,k}$ of the arc (i, k) is one of the basic relations appearing in the entry $\tau(b_{i,j}, b_{j,k})$ of the composition table.

Let us consider the following properties:

1) for all $b \in \mathbf{B}, \varphi(b) \neq \varnothing$;

2) for all $b \in \mathbf{B}$ there exists $i, j \in U$ such that $(i, j) \in \varphi(b)$;

3) the map $2^{\varphi} \colon \mathbf{A} \to \mathcal{P}(U \times U)$ is injective;

4) for all $a, b \in \mathbf{B}, \varphi(\tau(a, b)) \subseteq \varphi(a) \circ \varphi(b)$;

5) for all $a, b, c \in \mathbf{B}$, if $c \in \tau(a, b)$, then $(\varphi(a) \circ \varphi(b)) \cap (c) \neq \varnothing$;

6) for all $a, b, c \in \mathbf{B}$, if $(\varphi(a) \circ (b)) \cap \varphi(c) \neq \varnothing$, then $c \in \tau(a, b)$;

7) for all $a, b \in \mathbf{B}, \varphi(\tau(a, b)) \supseteq \varphi(a) \circ (b)$.

Clearly, condition 2) makes the meaning of condition 1) explicit, hence 1) and 2) are equivalent. Condition 3) is also equivalent to 1) and 2), due to the fact that the set of $\varphi(b)$, for $\varphi(b) \neq \varnothing$, is a partition of $U \times U$.

Let us note that strictly speaking, condition 4) should read: for all $a, b \in \mathbf{B}$, $2^{\varphi}(\tau(a, b)) \subseteq \varphi(a) \circ \varphi(b)$, since in general $\tau(a, b)$ is a subset of $\mathbf{B}$.

Alternatively, this condition can be expressed in terms of graphs in the following manner: if (i, j) is labeled by a basic relation appearing in the entry $\tau(a, b)$, then there is a vertex k such that (i, k) is labeled by a and that (k, j) is labeled by b.

For weak representations, the conjunction of properties 1) and 4) expresses the fact that it is a representation.

Condition 5) may be read in the following way: if c appears in the entry $\tau(a, b)$, then we can find three vertices (i, j, k) of the graph such that (i, j) carries the label a, (j, k) the label b, and (i, k) the label c. In other words, for any entry $\tau(a, b)$ of the table, each element of $\tau(a, b)$ has at least one *witness* in the graph which justifies its presence. In particular, this condition is met by representations:

LEMMA 10.1.– *Conditions 1) and 4) imply condition 5). Condition 5) implies condition 1).*

Proof. If a, b, c are such that $c \in \tau(a, b)$, condition 4) implies that $\varphi(c)$ is included in $\varphi(a) \circ \varphi(b)$. As $\varphi(c)$ is not empty according to 1), we can find an arc (i, j) labeled by c. This arc is contained in $\varphi(a) \circ \varphi(b)$, and so there exists k such that (i, k) is labeled by a and (k, j) by b, and (i, j, k) provides the witness requested by condition 5).

If we assume that $\mathbf{B}$ contains a symbol eq interpreted as the equality relation, we have $\tau(a, \text{eq}) = a$, therefore according to 5), $\varphi(a) \neq \varnothing$, for any $a \in \mathbf{B}$. □

Condition 6) expresses a condition which is the converse of condition 5): if there are three vertices i, j, k such that (i, k), (k, j), and (i, j) are labeled, respectively, by $a, b, c \in \mathbf{B}$, then c has to be present in the entry $\tau(a, b)$. But it is almost straightforward to see that this is condition 7), a condition which expresses what we have called the *algebraic closure* property.

LEMMA 10.2.– *Conditions 6) and 7) are equivalent.*

Proof. Firstly, condition 7) implies condition 6): indeed, if a, b, c are such that $(\varphi(a) \circ \varphi(b)) \cap \varphi(c) \neq \varnothing$, this means that there is an arc (i, j) labeled by c, and a vertex k such that (i, k) is labeled by a and (k, j) by b. This implies that $(i, j) \in \varphi(a) \circ \varphi(b)$, and so according to condition 7), that the label c is one of the elements of $\tau(a, b)$.

Conversely, condition 6) implies condition 7): if $(i, j) \in \varphi(a) \circ \varphi(b)$, this means that there exists k such that (i, k) is labeled by a and (k, j) by b. Let c be the label of (i, j). The conditions of 6) are satisfied by a, b, c, and thus $c \in \tau(a, b)$, which implies that (i, j) is labeled by one of the elements of $\tau(a, b)$, which can be expressed as $(i, j) \in \varphi(\tau(a, b))$. □

The gist of the preceding discussion can be summarized in terms of three properties:

– the property of *injectivity*, which can be expressed by 1), 2), or 3). It means that each basic symbol $b \in \mathbf{B}$ appears at least once in the graph;

– the condition of *existence of witnesses* for the elements of the table, expressed by condition 5);

– the condition of *algebraic closure*, expressed by 6) or equivalently by 7), which is part of the defining properties of a weak representation.

It should be noted that the existence of witnesses is a condition that is much weaker than condition 4). Consider for example the case of the Point algebra. We have seen previously that a weak representation of this algebra is a linear order. Condition 5) simply demands that this total order should contain at least three elements. On the other hand, condition 4) implies that this order is dense and unlimited on the right and on the left.

Condition 5) reflects the following intuitive idea: if a basic element $c \in \mathbf{B}$ appears in the composition table as a possible result of the composition of a with b, this is because elements may be found in U which justify the presence of c in this entry of the composition table. This property is related to the concept of *weak composition* of binary relations, whose definition we recall here:

DEFINITION 10.1.– *Let U be a non-empty set and $(R_i)_{i \in I}$ a partition of $U \times U$. The weak composition of the relations R_i and R_j, denoted by $R_i \diamond R_j$, is the union of the smallest family $(R_k)_{k \in J \subseteq I}$ of relations such that $R_i \diamond R_j \subseteq \cup_{k \in J} R_k$.*

In other words, we want to express the composition of two relations of the family in terms of unions of members of this family. As, generally, there is no reason why this composition should be expressible as a union of the relations of the partition, we just use the best approximation possible: whenever a pair $(i, j) \in U \times U$ belongs to the composition $R_i \circ R_j$, we add to $R_i \diamond R_j$ the element of the partition which contains it.

We are thus certain of approximating the *bona fide* composition in the most economical way.

If we consider now the case of a weak representation (U, φ) associated to a set $\mathbf{B}$ of basic relations, condition 5) expresses this same idea of minimality. Taken together with condition 7), it asserts that the table we are considering describes the weak composition of the relations $(\varphi(b))_{b \in \mathbf{B}}$. We will discuss this point in more detail in Chapter 11.

Given a finite set of basic relations $\mathbf{B}$ and a composition table τ, the following definitions are commonly used in the literature on this topic (in particular, they are used in [LI 03b]):

DEFINITION 10.2.– *A* model *of* $(\mathbf{B}, \tau)$ *is an injective weak representation of* $A = 2^{\mathbf{B}}$. *A model is* consistent *if condition 5) holds, that is, if any entry of the table has a witness. A model is* extensional *if condition 4) holds, that is, if it is a representation of the algebra* $\mathbf{A}$.

10.2.3. *Models of the composition table of* RCC−8

10.2.3.1. *Closed disks in the plane*

In the introduction of this chapter, we saw that the interpretation of RCC−8 in terms of relations between closed disks in the plane defines a representation of the RCC−8 algebra:

PROPOSITION 10.1.– *Let* U_{disk} *be the set of closed disks in the Euclidean plane and let* $\varphi_{disk}(b)$ *be the usual interpretation for each basic relation* b *of* RCC−8. *Then,* $(U_{disk}, \varphi_{disk})$ *is a representation of the* RCC−8 *algebra.*

10.2.3.2. *Egenhofer's model*

Another model has been introduced by Egenhofer in [EGE 91a]. For this model, U_{Jordan} is the set of regions in the Euclidean plane bounded by Jordan curves (or equivalently, which are homeomorphic to a closed disk in the plane) and the interpretation of RCC−8 relations is the natural interpretation.

Recall that a Jordan curve $\gamma \colon S^1 \to \mathbb{R}^2$ is, by definition, a continuous map of the unit circle S^1 in the plane which is injective (its image is a simple closed curve), and which consequently defines a homeomorphism of the circle S^1 on $\gamma(S^1)$.

According to Jordan's theorem[1], such a curve separates the plane into two disjoint parts, of which only one (called the interior part) is bounded. This means that $\mathbb{R}^2 \setminus \gamma(S^1)$ has two connected components, of which one part, called the interior of the curve, is bounded. The other part is called the exterior of the curve.

---

1 A nice "elementary" proof of this theorem can be found in [HEN 76]. This theorem was initially stated in 1887 by the French mathematician Camille Jordan (1838–1922) in his "Cours d'analyse" (A course in mathematical analysis).

Then U_{Jordan} can be defined in a precise way as the set of topological closures of the interiors of all Jordan curves in the plane. The interpretation of RCC−8 relations is again the usual interpretation.

The weak representation thus obtained is a consistent model. In fact, as was previously conjectured [LI 03b], it has been proved to be a representation of RCC−8 [LI 03a]. This model is widely referred to as *Egenhofer's model*.

THEOREM 10.2.– $(U_{Jordan}, \varphi_{Jordan})$ *is an extensional model of the composition table of* RCC−8 *(i.e. a representation of the* RCC−8 *algebra).*

The proof of this result given in [LI 03a] uses the fact that the RCC−8 relations are invariable by homeomorphism, which implies that, in order to study a pair (x, y) of regions (which are homeomorphic to closed disks in the plane), we may assume that one of the regions is a closed disk. In each of the 94 cases the problem can be reduced to, a suitable region z is built after a detailed examination of all possible configurations.

10.3. The RCC theory and its models

The RCC−8 formalism has its origins in two independent directions of research: one is Egenhofer's "9-intersection" calculus, the other stems from the development of region calculi by the Leeds school based on the RCC theory. From the viewpoint of the latter, RCC−8 appears as a simpler sublanguage of the more encompassing RCC theory. It is therefore natural to ask the questions: what are the models of the RCC theory which result in models of the composition table of RCC−8, and what are the properties of the corresponding weak representations?

The work of Li and Ying [LI 03b], which uses an algebraic characterization of RCC models due to Stell [STE 00], answers these questions. Before describing their results in detail, we may anticipate on them by mentioning that they imply that no RCC model provides a *representation* of RCC−8. More precisely, for each entry of the composition table of RCC−8, the models which would be suitable for an extensional interpretation can be characterized, and there are entries in the table for which no extensional interpretation is feasible.

The intuition behind this negative result is that the extensional models of RCC−8 require that the corresponding regions do not allow some "unpleasant" configurations, while the axioms of RCC, which make it possible to build regions by sum and non-empty product, tend to introduce such situations.

10.3.1. *Composition tables relative to a logical theory*

Let us consider a first order logical theory Θ in which a finite set Σ of binary relation symbols (for example, the eight symbols DC, EC, PO, TPP, NTPP, TPPI, NTPPI, EQ of RCC−8) are defined, and such that the relations associated to these symbols have the JEPD property (their interpretations are pairwise disjoint, and the union of these interpretations is the universal relation $U \times U$).

Under these assumptions, the associated composition table (this is called the consistency-based definition of the composition table) is the following: $\tau(R, S)$, for $R, S \in \Sigma$, is the smallest subset $\{T_1, \ldots, t_k\}$ of Σ such that the formula:

$$\forall x \forall y \forall z [R(x, z) \wedge S(z, y) \rightarrow (T_1(x, y) \vee \ldots \vee T_k(x, y))]$$

is a valid formula (i.e. it is true in any model of Θ). The associated composition table is also referred to as the *weak composition table* associated with Θ.

By construction, it is clear that any model of theory Θ is *ipso facto* a model of the associated composition table, but there is no guarantee that this model is consistent, or *a fortiori* extensional.

10.3.2. *The* RCC *theory*

The RCC theory is an example of this situation. Recall that this theory is based on a binary *connection* relation C between entities interpreted as regions. Intuitively, at least as a first approximation, two regions are connected if their topological closures have a non-empty intersection. However, the very aim of the theory is to develop a point-free approach to spatial reasoning in which regions are primitive concepts.

The eight RCC−8 relations are defined from the connection relation as shown in Table 10.1.

$DC(x, y)$	$\neg C(x, y)$
$P(x, y)$	$\forall z [C(z, x) \rightarrow C(z, y)]$
$PP(x, y)$	$P(x, y) \wedge \neg P(y, x)$
$EQ(x, y)$	$P(x, y) \wedge PA(y, x)$
$O(x, y)$	$\exists z [P(z, x) \wedge P(z, y)]$
$PO(x, y)$	$O(x, y) \wedge \neg P(x, y) \wedge \neg P(y, x)$
$EC(x, y)$	$C(x, y) \wedge \neg O(x, y)$
$DR(x, y)$	$\neg O(x, y)$
$TPP(x, y)$	$PP(x, y) \wedge \exists z [EC(z, x) \wedge EC(z, y)]$
$NTPP(x, y)$	$PP(x, y) \wedge \neg \exists z [EC(z, x) \wedge EC(z, y)]$
$TPPI(x, y)$	$TPP(y, x)$
$NTPPI(x, y)$	$NTPP(y, x)$

Table 10.1. *Definition of* RCC−8 *relations from* C

In the RCC theory, C is assumed to be reflexive and symmetrical. Under these conditions, it can be easily checked that the eight relations defined in Table 10.1 have the JEPD property.

A *model* of the RCC theory consists of:

– a non-empty set U;

– a distinguished element t $\in U$;

– a one element set $\{b\}$ disjoint from U;

– a binary relation C on U;

– a unary operation compl: $U \setminus \{t\} \rightarrow U \setminus \{t\}$;

– two binary operations sum: $U \times U \rightarrow U$ and prod: $U \times U \rightarrow U \cup \{b\}$.

The elements of U are interpreted as non-empty regions. The element t corresponds to the *universal* region. The element b represents the empty set which may be the result of the product of two regions. The compl, sum, and prod operations are intended to represent the complement, sum, and product operations of two regions.

The data $(U, C, t, b, \text{compl}, \text{sum}, \text{prod})$ has to satisfy the following conditions:

1) $(\forall x \in U)C(x, x)$;

2) $(\forall x, y \in U)[C(x, y) \rightarrow (y, x)]$;

3) $(\forall x \in U)C(x, t)$;

4) $(\forall x \in U)(\forall y \in U - \{t\})[C(x, \text{compl}(y)) \leftrightarrow \neg\text{NTPP}(x, y)]$;

5) $(\forall x \in U)(\forall y \in U - \{t\})[O(x, \text{compl}(y)) \leftrightarrow \neg P(x, y)]$;

6) $(\forall x, y, z \in U)[C(x, \text{sum}(y, z)) \leftrightarrow C(x, y) \vee C(x, z)]$;

7) $(\forall x, y, z \in U)[\text{prod}(y, z) \in U \rightarrow [C(x, \text{prod}(y, z)) \leftrightarrow (\exists w \in U)[P(w, y) \wedge P(w, z) \wedge C(x, w)]]]$;

8) $(\forall x, y \in U)[\text{prod}(x, y) \in U \leftrightarrow O(x, y)]$.

Conditions 1) and 2) express the fact that the interpretation of the relation C is reflexive and symmetrical. The symbol t denotes the universal region, to which every region is connected, as expressed by Condition 3).

Condition 4) expresses part of the definition of the complement of a region y other than the universal region: a non-empty region x is contained in y in a non-tangential way (hence it is "well inside" y) if, and only if, it is not connected to the complement of y.

Condition 5) completes this definition: x is contained in y (possibly sharing a part of its own border with the border of y, which corresponds to the relations TPP and $NTPPA$) if, and only if, it does not overlap (relation O) the complement of y.

Condition 6) defines the sum of two regions y and z: it is characterized by the fact that an arbitrary region x is connected to this sum if, and only if, it is connected to y or to z.

Conditions 7) and 8) define the product of two regions y and z: if this product is a region (left part of condition 7)), then an arbitrary region is connected to it if, and only if, it is connected to a subregion common to y and z; and finally, condition 8) states that the product of two regions is a region if, and only if, these two regions overlap (relation O).

10.3.2.1. *Strict models*

The axioms of RCC do not imply that the interpretation of the relation EQ is the identity relation. Besides, as we will see below, there are natural RCC models for which this interpretation is a non-trivial equivalence relation.

DEFINITION 10.3.– *A model of* RCC *is a* strict *model if the interpretation of* EQ *is the identity relation:* $(\forall x, y \in U)[\mathsf{P}(x, y) \wedge \mathsf{P}(y, x) \rightarrow x = y]$.

In the case of strict models, we have the following property, which implies that the composition of two basic relations of RCC−8 is non-empty:

PROPOSITION 10.2.– *Let* $(U, \mathsf{C}, \mathsf{t}, \mathsf{b}, \mathsf{compl}, \mathsf{sum}, \mathsf{prod})$ *be a strict model of* RCC. *Then, for any region* $x \in U$ *other than* t, *and for any basic relation* R, *there exists* y *such that* $R(x, y)$.

10.3.3. *Strict models and Boolean connection algebras*

Let us consider a model of RCC. The complement, the sum, and the product operations provide the set of regions of this model with an algebraic structure which strongly resembles the algebraic structure of a Boolean algebra. Moreover, this structure is equipped with a binary relation C.

We owe Stell [STE 00] a precise characterization of the type of structure obtained in this way, which he calls a *Boolean connection algebra*. Stell shows that this algebraic notion is equivalent to that of a strict model of RCC.

Stell's proof of this equivalence is based on two converse constructions which we now describe.

10.3.3.1. *From strict models to algebras*

Given a strict model of RCC, the first construction derives a Boolean connection algebra from it:

Assume that $(U, \mathsf{C}, \mathsf{t}, \mathsf{b}, \mathsf{compl}, \mathsf{sum}, \mathsf{prod})$ is a strict model of RCC; let $A = U \cup \{\mathsf{b}\}$. We define two operations $\vee$ and $\wedge$ on A in the following manner: $x \vee y = \mathsf{sum}(x, y)$ if $x, y \in U$, and $x \vee \mathsf{b} = x$, $\mathsf{b} \vee y = y$, $x \wedge y = \mathsf{prod}(x, y)$ if $x, y \in U$, and $x \wedge \mathsf{b} = \mathsf{b}, \mathsf{b} \wedge y = \mathsf{b}$.

We also define a unary operation on A by setting $x' = \mathsf{compl}(x)$ if $x \in U \setminus \{\mathsf{t}\}$, $\mathsf{t}' = \mathsf{b}$, and $\mathsf{b}' = \mathsf{t}$.

Stell shows that $(A, \mathsf{t}, \mathsf{b}, ', \wedge, \vee)$ makes of A a Boolean algebra (for which t is the largest element, b the smallest, and $'$ is complementation). Moreover, this Boolean algebra is equipped with a binary relation C on $A \setminus \{\mathsf{t}\}$.

DEFINITION 10.4.– *Let* $A = (A, \top, \bot, ', \vee, \wedge)$ *be a Boolean algebra containing more than two elements. Let* $U = A - \{\bot\}$ *and* $U^- = U - \{\top\}$, *and* C *a binary relation on* U. *The structure* $A = (A, \top, \bot, ', \vee, \wedge, \mathsf{C})$ *is a* generalized Boolean connection algebra *if it satisfies conditions 1), 2), and 3); it is a* Boolean connection algebra *if it also satisfies condition 4):*

1) C *is reflexive and symmetrical;*
2) $(\forall x \in U^-)\mathsf{C}(x, x')$;
3) $(\forall x, y, z \in U)$, *we have* $\mathsf{C}(x, y \vee z)$ *if, and only if,* $\mathsf{C}(x, y)$ *or* $\mathsf{C}(x, z)$;
4) $(\forall x \in U^-)(\exists y \in U)\neg\mathsf{C}(x, y)$.

EXAMPLE 10.1.– Consider the algebra B_5 defined in [LI 03b]. It corresponds to the configuration $\mathcal{C}_5$ of regions in the plane shown in Figure 10.3, which contains five regions; the first four are a disk A, a ring B surrounding A, two disjoint disks C and D which do not meet B. A bounded region is then considered, for example, a rectangle M strictly containing the four previous regions (hence the border of M is not connected to the four regions), and the fifth region E is the complement of $A \cup B \cup C \cup D$ with respect to M.

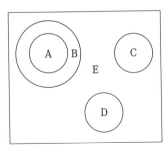

Figure 10.3. *The generalized connection algebra* B_5: *it is the finite Boolean algebra with the five atoms* a, b, c, d, e *equipped with the connection relation* C *corresponding to the connection relation between* A, B, C, D, E; *for instance, b is connected to a and e, and e to b, c, and d*

The sum of the five regions is the rectangle M, and their pairwise products are either empty or 1D.

The algebra B_5 is the abstract algebra representing the Boolean combinations of these five regions, together with their connection relations. More precisely, B_5 is the Boolean algebra containing five atoms a, b, c, d, and e. The connection relation C, restricted to these five atoms, is the smallest reflexive and symmetrical relation such that C(a, b), C(b, e), C(c, e), and C(d, e).

The relation C is then extended to the set of subsets of $\{a, b, c, d, e\}$ in a natural way: C(x, y) is true if, and only if, x contains an atom a_x and y an atom a_y such that C(a_x, a_y), i.e. two regions are connected if, and only if, one of the components of the first is connected to a component of the second.

It is straightforward to check that the algebra B_5 obtained in this way is a generalized Boolean connection algebra. It is not a connection algebra, since condition 4) is not satisfied: for example, $x = (b + c + d + e)$ is connected to any element of B_5 other than 0.

A weak representation $\mathcal{W}_5 = (U_5, \varphi_5)$ of RCC–8 is associated to the configuration $\mathcal{C}_5$. This weak representation may be seen as describing the set U_5 of 31 non-empty regions that are Boolean combinations of the five elementary regions A, B, C, D, E. We may also obtain it by using the definition of the RCC–8 relations shown in Table 10.1.

PROPOSITION 10.3.– *The weak representation $\mathcal{W}_5$ is injective. Moreover, it satisfies condition 5) of section 10.2.2: any entry of the composition table has a witness in $\mathcal{W}_5$.*

Proof. Checking the injectivity property is straightforward: for example, one notes that DC(a, c), EC(a, c), PO$(a + b, a + c)$, TPP$(b, a + b)$ and NTPP$(a, a + b)$, which is enough to conclude that the image of each basic relation under φ_5 is non-empty.

Checking property 5) requires an exhaustive description, but it does not involve any difficulty. For example, let us show that the five entries of the composition table of RCC–8 which correspond to the composition of EC with DC have witnesses in the weak representation $\mathcal{W}_5$:

Indeed, one has EC $\circ$ DC = $\{DC, EC, PO, TPPI, NTPPI\}$. Now, it can be easily checked that:

- EC(a, b), DC(b, c) and DC(a, c);
- EC(b, e), DC(e, a) and DC(b, a);
- EC$(b + c, a)$, DC$(a, c + d)$ and PO$(b + c, c + d)$;

– $\mathsf{EC}(a+c, b+d), \mathsf{DC}(b+d, c)$ and $\mathsf{TPPI}(a+c, c)$;

– $\mathsf{EC}(a+b, e), \mathsf{DC}(e, a)$ and $\mathsf{NTPPI}(a+b, a)$. □

Let us now come back to the construction for associating an algebraic structure with a model of RCC. The first main result is that, if the model is a strict model, then the structure obtained as described above is a Boolean connection algebra:

PROPOSITION 10.4.– *([STE 00]) If* $(U, \mathsf{C}, \mathsf{t}, \mathsf{b}, \mathsf{compl}, \mathsf{sum}, \mathsf{prod})$ *is a strict model of* RCC, *then* $(A, \mathsf{t}, \mathsf{b}, ', \wedge, \vee, \mathsf{C})$ *a Boolean connection algebra.*

Proof. We refer the reader to Stell's paper for a proof of this result. The difficult part of the proof, once the fact that the construction provides a complemented lattice has been established, consists in proving that this lattice is *distributive*. In order to do so, one shows that for any 3-tuple of elements x, y, z, both $\mathsf{P}((x \vee y) \wedge z, (x \wedge z) \vee (y \wedge z))$ and $\mathsf{P}((x \wedge z) \vee (y \wedge z), (x \vee y) \wedge z)$ simultaneously hold, hence $\mathsf{EQ}((x \vee y) \wedge z, (x \wedge z) \vee (y \wedge z))$ holds. Since the model is assumed to be a strict one, this implies that $(x \vee y) \wedge z = (x \wedge z) \vee (y \wedge z)$. □

10.3.3.2. *From a Boolean connection algebra to a strict model*

Conversely, let $A = (A, \top, \bot, ', \vee, \wedge, \mathsf{C})$ be a Boolean connection algebra. Let $U = A \setminus \{\bot\}$, $\mathsf{b} = \bot$, $\mathsf{t} = \top$. For all $x, y \in U$, and $z \in U \setminus \{\top\}$, set $\mathsf{sum}(x, y) = x \vee y$, $\mathsf{prod}(x, y) = x \wedge y$, and $\mathsf{compl}(z) = z'$.

Then $(U, \mathsf{C}, \mathsf{t}, \mathsf{b}, \mathsf{complsum}, \mathsf{prod})$ is a strict model of RCC.

As a consequence of the equivalence between strict models and Boolean connection algebras, when strict models of RCC are considered, the language of models or that of lattices may be used indifferently. For instance, $x \preceq y$ may be used for $P(x, y)$, $x \prec y$ for $PP(x, y)$, and so on.

10.3.4. *Consistency of strict models*

We have seen that, by construction, a model of RCC provides a model of the composition table of RCC−8. To what extent is this model consistent? Li and Ying show that any strict model yields a consistent model, or, in other words, an injective weak representation having the property of existence of witnesses. The proof of this result uses the structural properties of Boolean connection algebras, as well as the existence of a finite weak representation, namely the weak representation $\mathcal{W}_5$ described previously. The weak representation $\mathcal{W}_5$ "provides" witnesses for the entries of the composition table of RCC−8.

THEOREM 10.3.– *Any strict* RCC *model provides a consistent model of the composition table of* RCC−8.

Proof. Consider a strict model of RCC, or, equivalently, a Boolean connection algebra (A, C). Then A contains other elements than $\top$ and $\bot$. Because of proposition 10.2, elements m, c, d can be found in the set $A - \{\top, \bot\}$ such that the relations $\mathsf{DC}(m, c), \mathsf{DC}(m, d)$, and $\mathsf{DC}(c, d)$ hold. Let a be such that $\mathsf{NTPP}(a, m)$, and consider $b = m - a$ and $e = (a \vee b \vee c \vee d)'$.

The Boolean algebra generated by $\{a, b, c, d, e\}$ is isomorphic to B_5. In addition, if it is equipped with the restriction of the relation C, it can be easily checked that it is a generalized Boolean connection algebra, which is isomorphic to B_5. Consequently, proposition 10.3 implies that any entry of the composition table of RCC−8 has a witness in the model. □

10.4. Extensional entries of the composition table

Let us recall the extensionality condition 4):

$$(\forall a, b \in \mathbf{B})\varphi(\tau(a, b)) \subseteq (a) \circ \varphi(b)$$

A 3-tuple $(a, c, b) \in \mathbf{B}^3$ such that $c \in \tau(a, b)$, — that is, such that c is one of the basic relations contained in the entry in row a and column b of the composition table — is called a *triad*[2].

In order for a weak representation (U, φ) to verify condition 4), the condition should be verified for all triads, i.e. for each triad (a, b, c), we should have:

$$(\forall u, v \in U)(u, v) \in \varphi(c) \rightarrow (\exists w \in U)((u, w) \in \varphi(a) \wedge (w, v) \in \varphi(b))$$

The paper by Li and Ying [LI 03b] gives a very thorough analysis of the entries of the composition table of RCC−8 which will not be reproduced in detail here. We will be content with describing the main concepts and results of the paper.

The question of the extensionality of the RCC−8 table was raised by Bennett [BEN 94]. A first realization was that it is not possible for an RCC model to satisfy all the extensionality conditions if the universal region is accepted on the same footing as other regions. Indeed, the composition table states that EC is one of the possible results of the composition of DC with itself. But if two regions x and y are such that their union is the universal region, it is clear that we cannot find a region z such that z is disjoint from x and y.

In view of this fact, Bennett ([BEN 97b], p. 147) proposed to consider the universal region separately, adding: "All the exceptions to extensional composition that I am aware of involve u [the universal region]; so it seems that an extensional interpretation could be achieved with respect to a modified theory without a universal region. The

---

2 In Hirsch and Hodkinson [HIR 02], (a, b, c) is called a *consistent 3-tuple* of atoms if $(a, c^{\smile}, b)$ is a triad.

domain of this new theory would then be more homogeneous and more similar to that of the Allen relations, where intervals are always bounded".

Li and Ying show that this idea cannot be implemented in the context of the RCC theory, since there are irreducible triads which cannot be extensionally interpreted, no matter what we do. Moreover, their analysis leads a clear description of the extent to which each individual triad may deviate from the extensionality condition.

In what follows, we will give a brief summary of the properties of triads discussed in [LI 03b], and of the results contained in the paper.

10.4.1. *Properties of the triads of a composition table*

We are interested in the following property 4):

$$(\forall u, v \in U)(u, v) \in \varphi(c) \rightarrow (\exists w \in U)((u, w) \in \varphi(a) \wedge (w, v) \in \varphi(b))$$

A similar property 8) reads:

$$(\forall u, v \in U)(u, v) \in \varphi(c) \wedge (u \vee v \neq \top \rightarrow$$
$$(\exists w \in U)((u, w) \in \varphi(a) \wedge (w, v) \in \varphi(b)) \wedge (u \vee v \vee w \neq \top)$$

This property is weaker than 4): if 4) is satisfied, then 8) is also satisfied. It is strictly less strong: the triad (DC, EC, DC) which does not satisfy 4), satisfies condition 8).

However, even condition 8) is not true for all triads, irrespective of the model of RCC considered. A counterexample is the following [LI 03b]:

Let (U, φ) be an RCC model. Then let $u, v, w \in U$ such that $\varphi(\mathsf{DC})(u, v)$, $\varphi(\mathsf{DC})(v, w)$, and $\varphi(\mathsf{DC})(u, w)$. We have $\varphi(\mathsf{PO})(u + v, v + w)$. But it is clear that we cannot find $t \in U$ such that $\varphi(\mathsf{EC})(u + v, t)$ and $\mathsf{TPP}(t, v + w)$, and so the triad (EC, PO, TPP) does not satisfy condition 8).

Let us consider a specific triad, that is, a 3-tuple of basic relations (a, c, b) such that $c \in \tau(a, b)$, where τ is the composition table of RCC−8.

DEFINITION 10.5.– *([LI 03b, DÜN 01b]) Given a triad:*

   – *c is below $\tau(a, b)$ with respect to an RCC model (U, φ) if condition 4) is satisfied;*

   – *c is weakly below $\tau(a, b)$ with respect to an RCC model (U, φ) if condition 8) is satisfied, while c is not below $\tau(a, b)$.*

DEFINITION 10.6.– *A model (U, φ) satisfies the* interpolation condition *if the image of the relation NTPP has the following density property*:

$$(\forall u, v \in U)[\varphi(\mathsf{NTPP})(u, v) \rightarrow (\exists w \in U)(\varphi(\mathsf{NTPP})(u, w) \wedge \varphi(\mathsf{NTPP})(w, v))]$$

Using these definitions, the triads of the composition table can be distributed into six mutually exclusive classes. For a given triad (a, c, b):

1) either c is below $\tau(a, b)$ for any RCC model;

2) or c is weakly below $\tau(a, b)$ for any RCC model;

3) or c is below $\tau(a, b)$ if, and only if, the model considered satisfies the interpolation condition;

4) or c is neither below $\tau(a, b)$, nor weakly below $\tau(a, b)$, irrespective of the model considered;

5) or c is below $\tau(a, b)$ with respect to an RCC model (U, φ) if, and only if, this model satisfies the condition:

$$(\forall u, v \in U)[\varphi(\mathsf{NTPP})(u, v) \rightarrow (\exists w \in U)(\varphi(\mathsf{EC})(u, w) \wedge \varphi(\mathsf{NTPP})(w, v))]$$

6) or c is under $\tau(a, b)$, with respect to an RCC model (U, φ), if, and only if, this model satisfies the condition:

$$(\forall u, v \in U)[\varphi(\mathsf{NTPP})(u, v) \rightarrow (\exists w \in U)(\varphi(\mathsf{TPP})(u, w) \wedge \varphi(\mathsf{TPP})(w, v))]$$

EXAMPLE 10.2.– The triad $(\mathsf{DC}, \mathsf{DC}, \mathsf{DC})$ belongs to the first class. Indeed, if two elements u, v of some model of RCC are such that $\varphi(\mathsf{DC}(u, v))$, we know that $(u + v) \neq \top$, hence that the complement $(u+v)'$ of $(u+v)$ exists. We may thus find w such that $\varphi(\mathsf{NTPP}(w, (u + v)'))$. As a consequence, we have $\varphi(\mathsf{DC}(u, w))$ and $\varphi(\mathsf{DC}(w, v))$.

EXAMPLE 10.3.– The triad $(\mathsf{DC}, \mathsf{EC}, \mathsf{DC})$ belongs to the second class. Firstly, it does not belong to the first class, since, if two elements u, v of some RCC model are such that $\varphi(\mathsf{EC}(u, v))$, there is the possibility that v is precisely the complement of u, in which case we cannot find w such that $\varphi(\mathsf{DC}(u, w))$ and $(\mathsf{DC}(w, v))$ are simultaneously true.

However, if v is not the complement of u, we have $u + v \neq \top$, which, as in the previous case, allows us to choose w such that $\varphi(\mathsf{DC}(u, w))$ and $\varphi(\mathsf{DC}(w, v))$.

EXAMPLE 10.4.– The triad $(\mathsf{NTPP}, \mathsf{NTPP}, \mathsf{NTPP})$ belongs to the third class, by the very definition of the interpolation condition. The triad $(\mathsf{EC}, \mathsf{NTPP}, \mathsf{NTPP})$ belongs to the fifth class, here again by the very definition of this class; and similarly, the triad $(\mathsf{TPP}, \mathsf{NTPP}, \mathsf{TPP})$ belongs to the sixth class.

EXAMPLE 10.5.– The triad $(\mathsf{DC}, \mathsf{EC}, \mathsf{EC})$ belongs to the fourth class. Indeed, this class is characterized by the fact that condition 8) is not satisfied, i.e. that the following formula is true:

$$(\exists u, v \in U)[(u, v) \in \varphi(c) \wedge (u + v) \neq \top \wedge$$
$$(\forall w \in U)((u, w) \notin \varphi(a) \vee (w, v) \notin \varphi(b))]$$

Let us show that such is the case for this triad: let t be an element of U other than $\top$, and let v be such that $v \in \varphi(\mathsf{NTPP}(v, t))$. Let $u = (t - v)$. Then $v \in \varphi(\mathsf{EC}(u, v))$. If w is an arbitrary element such that $\varphi(\mathsf{EC}(w, v))$, we necessarily have $u \wedge w \neq \bot$, hence $v \in \varphi(\mathsf{DC}(u, w))$ cannot be true.

10.4.1.1. *An assessment for the triads of* RCC−8

At the end of a complete examination of the 178 triads which occur in the composition table of RCC−8, Li and Ying come to the conclusion that there are 92 triads belonging to the first class and 35 to the second. These 127 triads satisfy the extensionality property in a full sense (class 1) or in a restricted sense (class 2). The remaining triads can be divided into 4 triads of class 3, 35 triads of class 4, 8 triads of class 5, and 4 triads of class 6.

Why is it not possible to find extensional models of RCC? According to Li and Ying, this impossibility is related to the fact that the RCC theory allows us to build regions which are not connected, as well as regions containing "holes". This can be contrasted to the model of closed disks in the plane, or to Egenhofer's model with regions bounded by Jordan curves: both types of regions are connected and do not contain holes. Incidently, the notion of a hole can be defined in the RCC theory:

DEFINITION 10.7.− *The relation* $\mathsf{H}(u, v)$ *(*u *is a hole in* v*) is defined by* $u + v \neq \top \wedge \varphi(\mathsf{EC})(u, v) \wedge (\forall w \in U)(\varphi(\mathsf{EC})(w, u) \rightarrow \varphi(\mathsf{O})(u, v))$.

The presence of holes excludes extensionality:

PROPOSITION 10.5.− *A model of* RCC *for which* $\varphi(\mathsf{H})$ *is non-empty cannot be extensional.*

Similarly, a model that allows us to consider regions made up of two disjoint regions, or of two regions which are externally connected, cannot be extensional:

PROPOSITION 10.6.− *An* RCC *model which has three pairwise disjoint elements* u, v, w *such that* $u + v \in U$ *and* $v + w \in U$ *cannot be extensional.*

10.4.2. *Topological models of* RCC

What are the topological spaces which can provide RCC theory models? An answer to this question is given by Gotts [GOT 96].

THEOREM 10.4.− *Let* X *be a non-empty, connected and regular topological space. Let* U *be the set of non-empty regular closed sets of* X. *Then* $(U, \mathsf{C}, \mathsf{t}, \mathsf{b}, \mathrm{compl}, \mathrm{sum}, \mathrm{prod})$ *is a model of* RCC, *where:*

1) *for all* $(u, v) \in U^2$, $\mathsf{C}(u, v)$ *is true if, and only if,* $u \cap v \neq \emptyset$;

2) $t = X$;

3) b = ∅;

4) compl(u) = $Cl(X \setminus u)$;

5) sum(u, v) = $u \cup v$;

6) prod(u, v) = $Cl(Int(u \cap v))$.

NOTE 10.2.– The union of two non-empty regular closed sets is a non-empty regular closed set, since the set-theoretic union operator commutes with topological closure. Consequently, the interpretation of the sum is the set-theoretic union.

On the other hand, the complement and product operations cannot be interpreted directly in set-theoretic terms. The complement $X \setminus u$ of a closed set u is open, and so in general is not closed (in a connected space, besides, only the universal region is simultaneously open and closed). However, the closure $Cl(X \setminus u)$, which is the smallest closed set containing $X \setminus u$, is a closed approximation of this complement; while the union of u and $Cl(X \setminus u)$ is the entire space, as befits a complement, their intersection, the boundary of u, is in general non-empty. If u is regular, $Cl(X \setminus u)$ is also regular.

A similar difficulty arises with the product: the intersection of two regular closed sets u and v is in general not a regular closed set. However, there is a smaller regular closed set contained in u and v, which is precisely $Cl(Int(u \cap v))$ (where Int denotes the interior operator) (Figure 10.4).

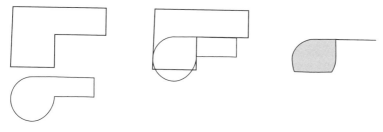

Figure 10.4. *Two regular closed regions in the plane (on the left); in the middle, the two regions are partially superposed; their intersection (on the right) is a closed region which is not regular (it contains a cusp of dimension 1); the largest regular closed subset contained in the two regions is the region in gray*

10.4.3. *Pseudocomplemented lattices*

Topological models of RCC may be built using closed regions. But they may also be built in terms of open regions. Let us now examine the latter choice: instead of non-empty regular closed sets, we consider non-empty regular open sets in a topological space.

Now the definition of the connection relation C is the following: two open sets u and v are connected if their closures have a non-empty intersection:

$C(u, v)$ iff $Cl(u) \cap Cl(v) \neq \emptyset$

The interpretation of regions in terms of open sets raises problems which are dual to those we encountered in the case of closed sets: the product may be interpreted in set-theoretic terms, but the same is not true for the sum and the complement.

Indeed, the intersection of two non-empty regular open sets is a regular open set; hence the product is interpreted as the intersection.

The complement of a regular open set is a closed set, and so in general is not an open set. However, there exists a largest regular open set contained in this complement, namely, the interior of the complement of A (Figure 10.5, on the right).

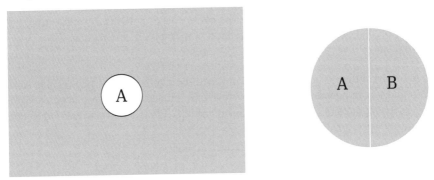

Figure 10.5. *The complement of a regular open set A is a closed set; the largest regular open set disjoint from A is the interior of this complement (on the left); the union of two open half-disks A and B (on the right) is an open disk where a diameter has been removed, which is open, but is not regular, because it has a "crack" in it. The interior of its closure is the smallest regular open set containing A and B*

The union of two regular open sets is in general not a regular open set. For example, in the left side of Figure 10.5, the union of two open half-disks A and B is the open disk where a diameter has been removed, which, although it is open, is not regular, since it has a "crack" in it. However, there is a smallest regular open set containing u and v: it is the open disk which is the interior of the closure of the union of A and B. Hence we will interpret the sum of u and v as $Int(Cl(u \cup v))$.

Now the two operations used to define the complement and sum can be reduced to the use of a unique operation: the operation of pseudocomplementation.

DEFINITION 10.8.– *In a topological space X, the* pseudocomplement A^* *of an open set A is the interior of the complement of A:* $A^* = Int(X \setminus A)$.

Consequently, the pseudocomplement of an open set u is such that $u \cap u^* = \emptyset$, but $u \cup u^*$ is not necessarily the entire space.

Let us recall that the closure and interior operations are dual of each other: we have, for any u, the identity $u \setminus Cl(X \setminus u) = Int(u)$. Hence the interior of the closure of u is u^{**}, and the regular open sets of a topological space are characterized as the fixed elements of the operation $u \mapsto u^{**}$.

The definition extends to arbitrary distributive lattices:

DEFINITION 10.9.− *A distributive lattice L is a* pseudocomplemented *lattice, or a* Brouwer lattice, *if every element x of L has a pseudocomplement x^*, i.e. an element x^* which is the greatest element y of L such that $x \wedge y = 0$.*

The set of all regular open sets in a topological space X, equipped with the set-theoretic maps $(u, v) \mapsto u \sqcap v = u \cap v$ and $(u, v) \mapsto u \sqcap v = Int(Cl(u \cup v))$ is a Boolean algebra whose largest element is the entire space and the smallest element is the empty set.

The complement of an open set u, where the term "complement" is used in its meaning for Boolean algebras, is the open set $Int(X \setminus U)$, which is the pseudocomplement of u in terms of pseudocomplemented lattices.

More generally, in a pseudocomplemented distributive lattice, the map $x \mapsto x^{**}$ is an idempotent map (actually it is a closure operation) whose elements are by definition, the *skeletal* elements of the lattice. This concept generalizes the concept of regular open set for the lattice of open sets of a topological space.

The set of skeletal elements of a pseudocomplemented lattice form a Boolean algebra, in which $x \sqcap y = x \wedge y$, $x \sqcup y = (x \vee y)^{**}$, and the complement of x is its pseudocomplement x^*.

The elements x such that $x^{**} = \top$ are called the *dense* elements of the lattice. In any pseudocomplemented distributive lattice, x^{**} is skeletal, and $(x \vee x^*)$ is dense; since for any x we have $x = x^{**} \wedge (x \vee x^*)$, we may conclude that any element of such a lattice is the intersection of a skeletal element and of a dense element.

Recall that a topological space X is *connected* if the only open and closed sets are the empty set and the whole space X. In other words, there are no open set U and V other than $\emptyset$ and X such that $U \cap V = \emptyset$ and $U \cup V = X$.

This definition extends in an obvious way to pseudocomplemented distributive lattices: such a lattice is connected, if and only if, there are no elements x, y other than $\bot$ and $\top$ such that $x \sqcap y = \bot$ and $x \sqcup y = \top$.

When a topological space X is connected, the pseudocomplement $U^* = Int(Cl(U))$ of a non-empty regular open set U is *always distinct* from the set-theoretic complement of U, since this set-theoretic complement is closed, and we would then have an open-closed set other than $\emptyset$ or X. So we have $U \cup U^* \neq X$. If we want to have $U \cup V^* = X$, other than by taking $V^* = X$ — hence $V = \emptyset$ — with a regular non-empty open set V, we have to find a non-empty open set V inside U that does not have a common boundary with U. This is the intuitive idea behind the following definition:

DEFINITION 10.10.– *A pseudocomplemented distributive lattice is* inexhaustible *if for any skeletal element x other than $\perp$, there is a skeletal element y other than $\perp$ such that $x \vee y^* = \top$.*

In the case of the open sets of a topological space, this means that for any non-empty regular open set U there is a non-empty regular open set V such that the interior of the complement of V and U cover the whole space.

10.4.4. *Pseudocomplementation and connection*

The results of Stell [STE 00] and Li and Ying [LI 04a] state that the concepts of pseudocomplemented distributive lattices and connection algebra are closely related:

THEOREM 10.5.– *Let T be a connected pseudocomplemented distributive lattice containing more than two skeletal elements. If T is inexhaustible, the Boolean algebra of its skeletal elements, equipped with the relation C, defined by:*

$$\mathsf{C}(x, y) \text{ if, and only if, } x^* \vee y^* \neq \top$$

is a Boolean connection algebra. Conversely, if the Boolean algebra of skeletal elements of T contains more than two elements, and if the relation C makes this Boolean algebra a Boolean connection algebra, then T is connected and inexhaustible.

This result applies to topological spaces:

COROLLARY 10.1.– *Let X be a topological space containing more than two non-empty regular open sets. Let $R(X)$ be the set of regular open sets of X. If U and V are two non-empty regular open sets, define $\mathsf{C}(U, V)$ by the condition $Cl(U) \cap Cl(V) \neq \emptyset$. Let $\mathsf{sum}(U, V) = Int(Cl(U \cup V))$, $\mathsf{prod}(U, V) = U \cap V$, and $\mathsf{compl}(U) = Int(X - U)$. Then $(R(X), \{\emptyset\}, X, \mathsf{compl}, \mathsf{sum}, \mathsf{prod}, \mathsf{C})$ is a model of RCC if, and only if, X is connected and inexhaustible.*

10.4.5. *Non-strict models*

Stell's results make it possible to characterize the strict models of RCC algebraically. As the preceding discussion shows, the use of the set of non-empty regular open sets in an appropriate topological space provides a good intuitive support for understanding the more general lattice-based considerations.

Now Li and Ying [LI 03b] go further and show that candidates for the construction of models may be selected in a much more liberal fashion: intuitively, all open sets which are not "too big", i.e. whose regularization (that is, the interior of their closure) is not the entire space, may be used.

We will now describe how this idea is implemented by Li and Ying. Let T be a pseudocomplemented distributive lattice. Let T^d be the set of elements x of the lattice other than $\top$ such that $x^{**} \neq \top$.

Note that the skeletal elements of the lattice are elements of T^d: if $x \neq \top$, and if $x^{**} = x, x \in T^d$, and in addition $\top \in T^d$ by definition.

On T^d, a binary sum $\sqcup$ is defined by the condition that $x \sqcup y = x \vee y$ if $(x \cup y)^{**} \neq \top$ and by $x \sqcup y = \top$ otherwise. In addition, a connection relation C is defined on $T^d \setminus \bot$ by the condition that $C(x, y)$ is true if, and only if, $x^* \vee y^* \neq \top$.

Let us note that these definitions take us outside skeletal elements: even if x and y are skeletal, the element $x \vee y$ is not skeletal in general, as can easily be seen in the case of topological spaces.

We consider the elements of T^d other than $\bot$. Using the definitions of RCC−8 relations in terms of C, we get the following algebraic characterizations:

Let $x, y \in T^d \setminus \{\bot\}$. Then:
- $P(x, y)$ if, and only if, $y^* \leq x^*$;
- $O(x, y)$ if, and only if, $x \wedge y > \bot$;
- $NTPP(x, y)$ if, and only if, $x^* \vee y^{**} = \top$.

We then have the following theorem ([LI 03b], theorem 2.2):

THEOREM 10.6.– *Let T be a pseudocomplemented distributive lattice, and let $S(T)$ be the Boolean algebra of its skeletal elements. Let $U = T^d \setminus \{\bot\}$, $n = \bot$, $u = \top$, and for all $x, y \in U$, and $z \in U \setminus \{\top\}$, let $sum(x, y) = x \sqcup y$, $prod(x, y) = x \wedge y$, $compl(z) = z^*$. Let $C(x, y)$ be the condition $x^* \vee y^* \neq \top$. If the lattice has more than two skeletal elements, then $(U, \{n\}, u, compl, sum, prod, C)$ is a model of RCC if, and only if, the lattice T is connected and inexhaustible.*

The previous result applies to topological spaces:

COROLLARY 10.2.– *Let X be a topological space containing more than two non-empty regular open sets. Let $R(X)$ be the set of non-empty open sets of X whose topological* *closure is not the entire space, along with X. If U and V are two non-empty open sets, define* $\mathsf{C}(U, V)$ *by the condition* $Cl(U) \cap Cl(V) \neq \emptyset$. *Let* $\mathsf{sum}(U, V) = U \cup V$ *if the closure of* $U \cup V$ *is not* X, *and* $\mathsf{sum}(U, V) = X$ *otherwise; let* $\mathsf{prod}(U, V) = U \cap V$, *and* $\mathsf{compl}(U) = Int(X \setminus U)$. *Then the 7-tuple* $(R(X), \{\emptyset\}, X, \mathsf{compl}, \mathsf{sum}, \mathsf{prod}, \mathsf{C})$ *is a model of* RCC *if, and only if,* X *is closed and inexhaustible.*

Let us return to the general case, and recall that $\mathsf{EQ}(x, y)$ is defined as the conjunction of conditions $\mathsf{P}(x, y)$ (that is, $y^* \leq x^*$) and $\mathsf{P}(y, x)$. Since in any pseudocomplemented lattice we have for all x the identity $x^{***} = x^*$ (which is true in particular for topological spaces), we always have $\mathsf{EQ}(x, x^{**})$. In other terms, the element x and its "regularization" play the same role.

Thus, one has a natural construction of non-strict models of RCC, i.e. models for which EQ is not the identity relation. However, it is an equivalence relation, and it can be easily checked that taking the quotient by this relation yields a strict model of RCC. This model plays the same role with respect to the RCC theory as the non-strict model from which it is derived.

Li and Ying's conclusion on the matter of strict and non-strict models is that, since the RCC theory is a first order theory which does not differentiate between two regions belonging to the relation EQ, the restriction to strict models does not imply any loss of generality.

10.4.6. *Models based on regular closed sets*

The preceding discussion of models of RCC in terms of pseudocomplemented distributive lattices corresponds, in the case of topological spaces, to considering regions which are non-empty open sets. Now the alternative way, considering regions which are non-empty closed sets, corresponds for lattices to the dual concept of *pseudosupplemented* distributive lattices. Let us briefly describe the main stages of this alternative approach.

The set of closed sets of a topological space X is a distributive lattice. Any closed set Y has a pseudosupplement, namely the closure of its complement $K(Y) = X \setminus Y$; this closure is the smallest closed set Y^* such that $Y \cup Y^* = X$. Since $Y^* = Cl(K(Y))$, $Y^{**} = Cl(Int(Y))$. In particular, the closed sets which are fixed under the map $Y \mapsto Y^{**}$ are the regular closed sets.

Recall that a topological space is *regular* if it satisfies the following axiom: for any closed set Z and any point $x \notin Z$, there are two disjoint open sets U and V such that $x \in U$ and $Z \subseteq V$.

An equivalent definition is the following: for any open set U and $x \in U$, there exists an open set V containing x such that the closure $Cl(V)$ of V is contained in U.

In [GOT 96], Gotts shows that the regular and connected topological spaces provide models of RCC if we define a region as a non-empty regular closed set, and the relation C by the condition that $C(Y, Z)$ is true if, and only if, $Y \cap Z \neq \emptyset$.

More generally in a distributive lattice T, the pseudosupplement of x is it the smallest element x^* such that $x \vee x^* = \top$. A pseudosupplemented distributive lattice is a distributive lattice where any element has a pseudosupplement.

Gotts's result may be seen as a particular case of corollary 10.4 below.

10.5. The generalized RCC theory

The classical RCC theory discussed so far has some limitations:

– the presentation of the theory by means of a single primitive connection relation does not allow a clear separation of what pertains to mereology — the "part of" relation — and what pertains to topology;

– the models of the theory are intrinsically infinite, due to axioms of inexhaustibility or regularity; however, for several applications, such as geographical ones, it would be quite beneficial to have discrete models (of raster type) which could be related to the continuous models (of vector type);

– such models as the "egg-yolk" models ([COH 96], see also section 7.4.10) should be subsumable by a general theory.

In [LI 04a], Li and Ying propose to solve these problems by defining generalized RCC theories based on Stell's algebraic approach, as presented earlier. More precisely, they describe a theory called GRCC, which generalizes RCC. The theory has the advantage of clearly separating a mereological part from a topological part. In this way, the theory answers objections raised by Smith [SMI 96]. One of the advantages of this separation is that the two parts — the mereological and the topological one — can be modified independently in order to adapt them to various circumstances such as, for example, the representation of uncertainty.

We give a brief sketch of the construction of the GRCC theory.

Following [LI 04a], we then describe how the GRCC theory generalizes the approach of the representation of discrete space proposed by Galton [GAL 99] described in Chapter 4 (section 4.15). We conclude the chapter by presenting the construction by Li and Ying of an interesting example of non-standard model of RCC, i.e. a model which is not associated with the non-empty regular closed sets of a topological space.

Let us first describe the construction of the GRCC theory.

10.5.1. *The mereological component: variations of a set-theoretic theme*

The mereological part of the GRCC theory is the first order theory with identity using a predicate P ("part of") which is a partial ordering (it is reflexive, antisymmetric, and transitive): this is expressed by axioms [10.1], [10.2], and [10.3] of Table 10.2. The expression $P(x, y)$ may be read as "x is a part of y".

The mereology obtained in this way is the *ground mereology* denoted by **M** in [VAR 96].

$P(x, x)$	[10.1]
$(P(x, y) \land P(y, x)) \rightarrow x = y$	[10.2]
$(P(x, y) \land P(y, z)) \rightarrow P(x, z)$	[10.3]
$\neg P(x, y) \rightarrow \exists z(P(z, x) \land \neg O(z, y))$	[10.4]
$\exists z \forall t(O(t, z) \leftrightarrow (O(t, x) \lor O(t, y)))$	[10.5]
$O(x, y) \rightarrow \exists z \forall t(P(t, z) \leftrightarrow (P(t, x) \land P(t, y)))$	[10.6]
$\exists z(P(z, x) \land \neg O(z, y)) \rightarrow \exists z \forall t(P(t, z) \leftrightarrow (P(t, x) \land \neg O(t, y)))$	[10.7]
$\exists z \forall x P(x, z)$	[10.8]
$\forall x \exists y(P(y, x) \land \neg PP(z, y))$	[10.9]
$\exists x \phi(x) \rightarrow \exists z \forall t(O(t, z) \leftrightarrow \exists x(\phi(x) \land O(t, x)))$	[10.10]

Table 10.2. *Axioms used for the mereologic theories (I)*

Based on P, the relations PP (proper part), O (overlap), PO (partial overlap), and DR (disjunction) are defined as follows:

$PP(x, y) \overset{\text{def}}{=} P(x, y) \land \neg P(y, x)$;

$O(x, y) \overset{\text{def}}{=} \exists z P(z, x) \land P(z, y)$;

$PO(x, y) \overset{\text{def}}{=} O(x, y,)P(x, y) \land \neg P(x, y) \land \neg P(y, x)$;

$DR(x, y) \overset{\text{def}}{=} O(y, x)$.

In other words, PP is the strict order associated with the partial order P. The relation O expresses the fact that two regions have a lower bound (they share a common sub-region). This is trivially true if one contains the other; the relation PO excludes this possibility. The relation DR expresses the fact that two regions do not have a common lower bound (they do not contain a common region).

More axioms may be added to these axioms.

Axiom [10.4], known as the *axiom of supplementation*, states that if a region x is not contained in a region y, we can find in x a region which does not have any common subregion in common with y.

The **M** theory with axiom [10.4] added to it is called the *extensional mereology* **EM**. In this mereology, the relation O is *extensional*, i.e. a region is *characterized* by the set of regions with which it shares a common subregion:

$$\forall z(O(z,x) \leftrightarrow O(z,y)) \leftrightarrow x = y \qquad\qquad [10.11]$$

The theory used for constructing the GRCC theory adds four axioms to **EM**; each one of them states the existence of a region having specific properties.

10.5.1.1. *Sums*

Axiom [10.5] states that given two regions, there exists a third region which is intuitively their sum: this sum is such that an arbitrary region shares a subregion with it (relation O) if, and only if, this arbitrary region shares a subregion with one of the two regions. Because of the extensionality of O, this region is unique; it is called the *sum* of x and y, denoted by $x + y$.

10.5.1.2. *Products*

Similarly, axiom [10.6] states the existence of a region, except that now this existence is conditional: provided that two regions x and y share a common subregion, there exists a subregion whose subregions are those regions which are subregions of both x and y. If this region exists, then it is unique; it is called the *product* of x and y, denoted by $x \times y$. The product of two regions is thus defined only for regions satisfying the relation O. Intuitively, $x \times y$ is the smallest subregion common to x and y.

10.5.1.3. *Differences*

As was the case for products, axiom [10.7] states a conditional existence. Let x and y be two regions; the condition is that region x contains a subregion which does not have any common subregion with y. Under these conditions, axiom [10.7] states the existence of a well-defined region whose subregions are exactly those of x which do not share a subregion with y. This region is the *difference* of x and y, denoted by $x - y$.

10.5.1.4. *Universal region*

Axiom [10.8] states the existence of a *universal* region, denoted by u, which contains every region.

The theory obtained in this way is called the *closed extensional mereology* or **CEM** in the literature [VAR 96].

10.5.1.5. *Complements*

Note that for any region x other than the universal region u, the pair (u, x) satisfies the condition on the left part of axiom [10.7]. Indeed, there exists a region z which "makes it possible to distinguish x and u by using O", so that $P(z, u)$ and $\neg O(z, x)$. Hence there is a well-defined region $u - x$, called the *complement* of x, denoted by $\tilde{x}$.

The complement of x is hence the unique region $\tilde{x}$ characterized by the condition:

$$\forall t (P(t, \tilde{x}) \leftrightarrow \neg O(t, x))$$

As stated earlier, one of the motivations for the introduction of the GRCC theory is the possibility to deal with discrete models. To this end, the axiom of atomicity [10.9] will be used. This axiom states that any region contains a subregion known as an atomic subregion, i.e. which has no subregion other than itself.

If this axiom is added to **CEM**, the resulting theory is the **ACEM** theory.

The entire discussion can be concisely expressed in algebraic terms, by using the concepts of quasi-Boolean algebras and atomic algebras: a *quasi-Boolean* algebra is a Boolean algebra from which its bottom element has been removed; a Boolean algebra is *atomic* if any element other than the bottom element contains an atom.

Li and Ying prove the following theorem:

THEOREM 10.7.– *Any model of* **CEM** *(of* **ACEM**, *respectively) is isomorphic to a quasi-Boolean algebra (an atomic quasi-Boolean algebra, respectively).*

This fundamental result is based on the existence of two converse constructions, which are basically those the reader could expect: firstly, given a model (U, P), consider the algebra whose underlying set is $U \cup \{\bot\}$, where $\bot$ is a new element which will be used as the bottom element. The universal region u is used as the top element. For pairs of elements (x, y) in U, $x \vee y$ is defined as $x + y$, and $x \wedge y$ as $x \times y$. On U, P defines the order relation of the Boolean lattice. Similarly, if $x \in U$ is not the universal region u, its complement x' is defined as $\tilde{x}$. What remains to be done is to suitably extend the operations to the whole of $U \cup \{\bot\}$, and to prove that a Boolean algebra is obtained in this way.

Conversely, given a Boolean algebra, a model is obtained by leaving out its bottom element and by restricting the operations in a natural way.

Because of this isomorphism, the notations of the RCC theory or those of lattice theory may be used indifferently; in particular, the following are equivalent pairs of notations:

P(x, y) and $x \leq y$;

PP(x, y) and $x < y$;

O(x, y) and $x \wedge y > \bot$;

DR(x, y) and $x \wedge y = \bot$;

PO(x, y) and $x \wedge y > \bot \wedge \nleq y \wedge x \ngeq y$.

NOTE 10.3.– Recall that a Boolean algebra is *complete* if any set of elements has a least upper bound and a greatest lower bound.

Quasi-Boolean algebras corresponding to *complete* Boolean algebras correspond to the mereological theory known as the *extended extensional mereology*, denoted by **GEM**. This theory uses an infinite number of axioms associated with the first order formulas ϕ in which x is a free variable, as explained below.

The intuition is a simple one: consider a condition that may be satisfied by regions. If this condition can be expressed by using a first-order formula ϕ, and if there exists at least one region satisfying this condition (remember that there is no "empty region"), then the intuition is there is a region which is exactly the union, or the "fusion" of all the sub-regions which satisfy this condition. Consequently, condition [10.10] is called the axiom schema of fusion.

The **EM** theory to which the axiom schema of fusion has been added is known as the **GEM** theory. It not only contains the **EM** theory, but also the **CEM** theory. If the axiom of atomicity is added to it, the resulting theory is known as the **AGEM** theory.

Theorem 10.7 is the "finitary" analog of a theorem which states that any model of **GEM** (of **AGEM**, respectively) is isomorphic to a complete quasi-Boolean algebra (a complete and atomic quasi-Boolean algebra, respectively).

10.5.2. *The topological component*

The theory described up to now does not contain a topological component. To make it a mereotopological theory, a new relation called the *connection relation*, denoted by C, is added to it. This relation is reflexive (axiom [10.12]) and symmetrical (axiom [10.13]):

Axiom [10.14] establishes a link between purely mereological concepts and the new concept of connection: if x is a sub-region of y, then any region which is connected to x must also be connected to y.

The theory obtained by adding the preceding axioms to **CEM** is called the *ground mereotopology* and is denoted by **CEMT**.

$C(x, x)$	[10.12]
$C(x, y) \rightarrow C(y, x)$	[10.13]
$P(x, y) \rightarrow \forall t C(t, x) \rightarrow C(t, y)$	[10.14]
$C(t, x + y) \leftrightarrow (C(t, x) \vee C(t, y))$	[10.15]
$\exists z \neg P(z, x) \rightarrow C(x, \tilde{x})$	[10.16]
$\exists xy PP(x, y)$	[10.17]
$\exists z \neg PP(z, x) \rightarrow (\exists z \neg C(z, x)$	[10.18]
$\exists x \phi(x) \rightarrow \exists z \forall t (C(t, z) \leftrightarrow \exists x (\phi(x) \wedge C(t, x)))$	[10.19]

Table 10.3. *Axioms for the mereotopological theories (II)*

Using C, the relations DC, EC, TPP, and NTPP can now be defined as follows:

$$DC(x, y) \overset{\text{def}}{=} \neg C(x, y);$$

$$EC(x, y) \overset{\text{def}}{=} C(x, y) \wedge \neg O(x, y);$$

$$TPP(x, y) \overset{\text{def}}{=} PP(x, y) \wedge \exists z(EC(z, x) \wedge EC(z, y));$$

$$NTPP(x, y) \overset{\text{déf}}{=} PP(x, y) \wedge \neg \exists z(EC(z, x) \wedge EC(z, y)).$$

Three more axioms are still to be added to define the GRCC theory.

The first (axiom [10.15]) characterizes the connection relation of a region with respect to the sum of two regions.

The second (axiom [10.16]) states a property of connectedness of the universe: any region other than the universal region is connected to its complement. This is the analog of connectedness for topological spaces: a space is connected if it is not the union of two open sets, where both sets are non-empty.

The theory **CEMT** to which the two previous axioms have been added has a trivial model, namely the Boolean algebra $\{\bot, \top\}$ with two elements: in this case, there is a unique region $\top$ which also happens to be the universal region. To exclude this model, axiom [10.17] is added to the axioms.

10.5.2.1. *Extensionality*

We have seen (axiom [10.11]) that the relation O is extensional in the **EM** theory. It can be shown that in the **CEMT** theory, axiom [10.16] is equivalent to the extensionality of EC: a region is fully characterized by the set of regions to which it is externally connected ([LI 03b], theorem 3.1).

Another axiom relating the mereologic aspect and topology is axiom [10.18] which states that if x is not the universal region, a region can be found that is not connected to it.

In the **CEMT** theory, Li and Ying show that this axiom is equivalent to the fact that C is extensional ([LI 03b], theorem 3.2).

10.5.3. *The GRCC theory*

The GRCC theory is hence the **CEMT** theory to which axioms [10.15], [10.16], and [10.17] have been added.

Recall that a generalized Boolean connection algebra (section 10.4) is a Boolean algebra whose set of elements other than $\perp$ is equipped with a reflexive and symmetrical relation C, such that any $x \neq \top$ is connected to its complement, and that $C(x, y + z)$ is equivalent to $C(x, y)$ or $C(x, z)$.

The equivalence between models of **CEM** and quasi-Boolean algebras implies the equivalence of models of GRCC and generalized Boolean connection algebras. It may also be noted that the definition of a Boolean connection algebra adds an extra condition corresponding to axiom [10.18].

Steel's result shows that the models of the RCC correspond precisely to those of the GRCC theory to which axiom [10.18] has been added. Hence the GRCC theory is a generalization of the RCC theory.

10.5.4. *Constructing generalized Boolean connection algebras*

10.5.4.1. *Pseudocomplements and open sets*

The construction described above of Boolean connection algebras, given pseudocomplemented distributive lattices (theorem 10.5), can also be used for generalized Boolean connection algebras.

More precisely, we have the following theorem which generalizes theorem 10.5:

THEOREM 10.8.– *Let T be a pseudocomplemented distributive lattice. Let $x \mapsto x^*$ denote pseudocomplementation. Let $S(T)$ be the Boolean algebra of skeletal elements. On $S(T) \setminus \{\perp\}$, consider the relation C defined by $C(x, y)$ if, and only if, $x^* \vee y^* \neq \top$, and assume that $S(A)$ contains at least two elements. Then $(S(T), C)$ is a generalized Boolean connection algebra (a Boolean connection algebra, respectively) if, and only if, T is connected (connected and inexhaustible, respectively).*

As seen before, in the case of topological spaces, this situation corresponds to the lattice of open sets. The skeletal elements of this lattice are then the regular open sets. Let a topological space be inexhaustible if its lattice of open sets is inexhaustible. The preceding theorem implies the following generalization of corollary 10.1:

COROLLARY 10.3.– *Let X be a topological space; assume that the set of non-empty regular open sets contains more than two elements. Define the relation C by the condition $C(U,V)$ on this set if, and only if, $Cl(U) \cap Cl(V) \neq \emptyset$. Let $U + V$, $U \times V$ and $\tilde{U}$ denote the interior of $Cl(U \cup V)$, the intersection of U and V, and interior of the complement of U, respectively. Then the set of non-empty regular open sets of X equipped with C is a model of GRCC (a model of RCC, respectively) if, and only if, X is connected (connected and inexhaustible, respectively).*

10.5.4.2. *Pseudosupplements and closed sets*

Similarly, the construction defined by Stell [STE 00] of models from pseudosupplemented distributive lattices can be applied in the context of generalized Boolean connection algebras. In particular, the lattice of closed sets of a topological space is pseudosupplemented particular, which implies:

COROLLARY 10.4.– *Let X be a connected topological space. Assume that the set of non-empty regular closed sets contains more than two elements. Define the relation C on this set[3] by the condition $C(Y,Z)$ if, and only if, $Y \cap Z \neq \emptyset$. Let $Y + Z$, $Y \times Z$ and $\hat{Y}$ be $Y \cup Z$, the closure the interior of $Y \cap Z$, and the closure of the complement of Y, respectively. Then the set of non-empty regular closed sets of X equipped with C is a model of GRCC model. Moreover, if X is regular[4], it is a model of RCC.*

10.5.5. *An application to finite models*

Li and Ying also show that Galton's theory, presented in Chapter 4, section 4.15, is in essence a particular case of the GRCC theory. Indeed, it is based on a binary primitive adjacency relation on a set X of cells which is a reflexive and symmetrical relation. A region in X is a non-empty subset of X. The set X is assumed to contain more than two elements.

The adjacency relation **A** satisfies the following condition, for any pair of regions a and b: if $a \cup b = X$, then there exist cells $x \in a$ and $y \in b$ such that $\mathbf{A}(x,y)$.

---

3 For an arbitrary topological space X, Li and Ying propose to call this relation the *canonical connection relation* on X.

4 A topological space is regular if for any pair (x, Y), where x is a point and Y is a closed set such that $x \notin Y$, there exist two disjoint open sets containing x and Y, respectively (see Appendix A).

The definition of the connection relation **C** between two regions states that two regions are connected if, and only if, each one contains a cell such that these two cells are adjacent.

The theory is clearly an atomic theory.

Clearly, the fusion property [10.10] is satisfied. Axiom [10.19], which is the analog of [10.10] where the relation C is replaced by O, is also satisfied.

Lastly, Galton's theory satisfies the following axiom, which expresses the fact that if two regions are connected, then each one of them contains an atom such that the resulting two atoms are connected:

$$\mathsf{C}(a,b) \rightarrow \exists xy(\mathsf{at}(x) \wedge \mathsf{at}(y) \wedge \mathsf{P}(x,a) \wedge \mathsf{P}(y,b) \wedge \mathsf{C}(x,y)) \qquad [10.20]$$

In this axiom, $\mathsf{at}(x) \overset{\text{déf}}{=} \neg\exists z\mathsf{PP}(z,x)$.

These axioms completely characterize Galton's theory:

THEOREM 10.9.– *Galton's theory of adjacency spaces is equivalent to the* GRCC *theory to which the axioms [10.9, 10.10, 10.19], and [10.20] have been added.*

10.6. A countable connection algebra

Model theory shows that there is only one *countable* Boolean algebra without atoms up to isomorphism. This algebra is not complete. On the other hand, the Boolean algebra formed by the regular closed sets of a topological space is complete. Consequently, the models of RCC obtained from regular connected topological spaces, which are without atoms and complete, are not countable.

However, Li and Ying show how to build a countable Boolean connection algebra, which is moreover *minimal* in the following sense: it can be embedded in any Boolean connection algebra.

We give the outline of this construction below.

10.6.1. *An interval algebra*

To start with, a Boolean algebra is constructed, using half-open subintervals of the interval $[0, 1)$. Each interval has a level which is an integer k, such that the length of the interval is $1/2^k$ (there are 2^k intervals for level k).

At level 0, there is only one interval of length 1, the interval $[0, 1)$. By definition, the address of this interval is the empty string ε. Similarly, each interval of level k has an address, which is a finite string of length k on 0 and 1. Intuitively, 0 denotes the left part and the right part of a current interval.

At level 1, there are two intervals of length 1/2, [0, 1/2) (whose address is 0) and [1/2, 1) (whose address is 1). At level 2, there are four intervals of length 1/4, [0, 1/4) (its address is 00), [1/4, 1/2) (its address is 01), [1/2, 3/4) (its address is 10), and [3/4, 1) (its address is 11).

One proceeds in the same way for each level $k \geq 0$. The addresses of intervals form a binary tree. If $s \in \{0, 1\}^*$ is the address of an interval $[u, u + 1/2^k)$ at level k, the address of $[u, u + 1/2^{k+1})$ is the string $s0$, and that of $[u + 1/2^{k+1}, u + 1/2^k)$ the string $s1$.

Denote by X_k the set of intervals of level k. Let $X_\omega = \bigcup_{k=0}^{\infty} X_k$.

Let B_k be the Boolean algebra generated in the algebra of all subsets of $[0, 1)$ by the elements of X_k. An element B_k is hence a (possibly empty) union of intervals of X_k.

In order to define a Boolean connection algebra, one has to define a connection relation, and to show that this relation satisfies all required conditions.

10.6.2. Defining a connection relation

10.6.2.1. Motivation

In order to motivate definitions which otherwise could be seen as arbitrary, we start with the description of a construction which anticipates the way the connection algebra is going to be used.

Let (U, C) be a model of RCC. Choose a region x_0 other than $\top$ or $\bot$. Let x_1 be its complement, which is also distinct from $\top$ and $\bot$ (Figure 10.6).

We thus have in particular $\mathsf{C}(x_0, x_1)$.

According to the properties of RCC, a region x_{00} can be found in x_0 such that $\mathsf{NTPP}(x_{00}, x_0)$. Let x_{01} be the complement of x_{00} in x_0, i.e. in the Boolean notation, the region $x_0 \wedge (x_{00})'$.

The same operation is now applied to x_1: a region x_{10} can be found in x_1 such that $\mathsf{NTPP}(x_{10}, x_1)$. Let x_{11} be the complement of x_{10} in x_1, i.e. the region $x_1 \wedge (x_{10})'$.

At this stage, illustrated by Figure 10.6, it is clear that the adjacency relations are the following:

    – x_0 is adjacent to x_1;

    – x_{00} is adjacent to x_{01};

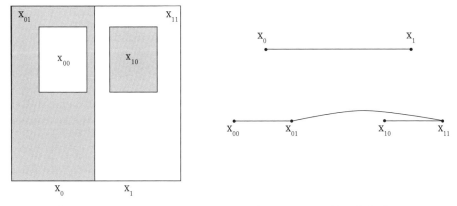

Figure 10.6. *Constructing the connection algebra, for the strings of length 2; the region x_{11} (the rectangle on the right with the rectangular hole x_{10}) is adjacent to the 2 gray regions x_{10} and x_{01}. The adjacency relations of these regions are shown on the right side of the figure*

– x_{10} is adjacent to x_{11};
– x_{01} is adjacent to x_{11}.

The construction whose first two steps we have outlined may be continued according to the following principle: if the region x_s is defined for a string s on $\{0, 1\}$, then:

– x_{s0} is a subregion of x_s such that $\mathsf{NTPP}(x_{s0}, x_s)$;
– x_{s1} is the complement of x_{s0} in x_s.

In particular, due to the way it has been defined, each new region x_{s0} is entirely "cut off" from any exterior connection except for the "ring" constituted by x_{s1}. For its part, x_{s1} is connected to $x_{\bar{s}1}$, where $\bar{s}$ is the string obtained from s by replacing the last digit of s by 1 if this digit is 0, and by 0 if it is 1.

10.6.2.2. *Constructing the connection relation*

Let us now come back to the half-open intervals of X_ω, which are in one-to-one correspondence with the strings of finite length on $\{0, 1\}$, or, in other terms, with the nodes of the complete binary tree.

Let us denote by x_s, for $s \in \{0, 1\}^*$, the interval whose address is s.

Based on the preceding construction of regions, an adjacency relation A is defined in the following manner:

For each string s:
– $\mathsf{A}(x_s, x_s)$;

  – $A(x_{s0}, x_{s1})$ (x_{s0} is adjacent to its complement in x_s);
  – $A(x_{s1}, x_{t1})$ if A (x_s, x_t) (the rings around two adjacent regions are adjacent).

Clearly, the relation defined in this way is reflexive and symmetrical, hence it is an adjacency relation on X_ω. For any $k \in \mathbb{N}$, the set X_k equipped with the restriction of A is an adjacency space. Hence a connection relation C_k can be deduced on the algebra of non-empty subsets of X_k. In other words, the structure (B_k, C_k) is a generalized Boolean connection algebra.

Li and Ying show that the *inductive limit* of X_k (as a set, this is simply the union of underlying sets) is a Boolean connection algebra (B_ω, C_ω). Their proof involves a detailed study of the adjacency relations on the algebra B_ω. In particular, the following proposition is proved:

PROPOSITION 10.7.– *If s and t are two distinct strings, and if $A(x_s, x_t)$, then s and t are of the same length, and there exists a string u and an integer $n \geq 0$ such that $\{s, t\} = \{u01^n, u11^n\}$.*

EXAMPLE 10.6.– Consider the regions of Figure 10.7. The region x_{111} is adjacent to x_{011} ($u = \epsilon, n = 2$), to the region x_{101} ($u = 1, n = 1$), and to the region x_{110} ($u = 11, n = 0$). Proposition 10.7 implies that those are the only regions—in addition to x_{111} itself — which are adjacent to x_{111}.

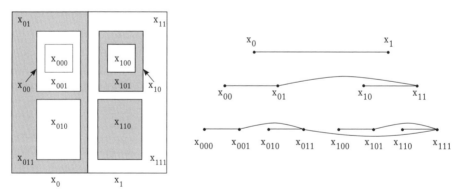

Figure 10.7. *Constructing of the connection algebra, for the strings of length 3; the region x_{111} (the rectangle on the right with the two rectangular holes x_{10} and x_{110} in it) is adjacent to the three gray regions x_{110}, x_{101}, and x_{011}. The adjacency relations are shown on the right part of the figure*

The connection relation has the property that, for each level k, it coincides with the adjacency relation:

PROPOSITION 10.8.– *Let s and t be two strings of the same length. Then, $\mathsf{C}_\omega(x_s, x_t)$ if, and only if, $\mathsf{A}_\omega(x_s, x_t)$.*

10.6.3. *Minimality of the algebra (B_ω, C_ω)*

Consider now the construction of regions which was introduced as a motivation.

Let (U, C) be a model of RCC, or equivalently, a Boolean connection algebra $(\mathbf{A}, \mathsf{C})$. Clearly, for each level $k \geq 2$, the algebra of regions x_s, where s is a string of length ≥ 2 is isomorphic to the generalized Boolean connection algebra B_k. By taking the inductive limit, we obtain a subalgebra of $\mathbf{A}$ which is isomorphic to B_ω. In that sense, B_ω is thus a *minimal* Boolean connection algebra:

THEOREM 10.10.– *Any Boolean connection algebra $(\mathbf{A}, \mathsf{C})$ contains a subalgebra which is isomorphic to $(\mathbf{B}_\omega, \mathsf{C}_\omega)$.*

10.7. Conclusions

Starting with an examination of the weak representations of the RCC−8 algebra, we have described recent results about models of the RCC theory. Those models, in general, do not allow an extensional interpretation of the composition table of RCC−8, and the work of Li and Ying provides a detailed description of this negative result by giving a very precise discussion of the circumstances in which entries of the composition table may be interpreted extensionally.

It should be mentioned here that another method of trying to obtain an extensional composition table would be to refine the basic relations. However, according to [DÜN 01a], for any model of RCC, the relation algebra generated by the basic relations of RCC−8 contains at least 25 atoms; for the model consisting of the regular closed sets of the Euclidean space $\mathbb{R}^n$, we know ([LI 05]) that this relation algebra contains an infinite strictly decreasing sequence of relations. This seems to suggest that obtaining an extensional interpretation by refinement may not be possible.

We have also given an overview of the state of knowledge concerning more generally the models of the RCC theory, both in its original form, as defined by the Leeds school, as well as in its generalizations. Stell's results about the equivalence between strict models of RCC and Boolean connection algebras has played a pivotal role in this respect. A clear distinction between mereological aspects (corresponding to the Boolean algebra structure) and topology (represented by the connection relation) clarifies the nature of these models, and proves to be a convenient tool for the development of generalizations.

In our view, two main points have emerged from the discussion:

– on the one hand, structures which are more general than topological spaces — namely pseudocomplemented distributive lattices (or pseudosupplemented distributive lattices) — constitute adequate domains for constructing models of RCC, the lattices of open sets (or closed sets) of a topological space only being a particular case: indeed, there are useful models which do not arise from topological spaces;

– on the other hand, structures which are more general than Boolean algebra are useful for constructing models of the calculus for regions which have a great practical significance, namely finite or discrete which naturally arise when the regions considered are regions of raster type (sets of pixels). The introduction of the generalized RCC calculus (GRCC) by Li and Ying provides a framework which is sufficiently general to describe both the "classical" continuous models of RCC (in geographical terms, "vectorial" models) and finite or discrete models. In particular, the GRCC formalism allows us to give an account of Galton's [GAL 99] "adjacency spaces". The GRCC calculus corresponds to structures known as generalized Boolean connection algebras.

General results of the theory of models imply that any topological space which is not reduced to a point, and which does not contain isolated points, is necessarily uncountable if it is connected and regular. The use of classical model-theoretic techniques for the construction of models from given models (sub-structures, inductive limits, localization) allows Li and Ying to show that any Boolean connection algebra contains a countable algebra. The study of models formed by pixels in the pixelated plane also allows them to define effective algorithms for determining the relations between two regions of the plane (in which regions are represented as quad-trees of finite depth).

The algebraic approach also provides a tool for a systematic development of the study of vague or imprecise regions (early work in this direction is represented by the *egg-yolk theory*). Here, Boolean algebras are replaced by the structures corresponding to *rough sets*, namely *regular double Stone algebras*.

Lastly, the description of spatial structures with different resolutions, and the management of multiresolution spatial data is a fundamental theme in the field of GIS and Artificial Intelligence, as testified by the ubiquity of the issues of granularity and generalization. The corresponding algebraic concept is that of families of Boolean connection algebras indexed by a lattice of resolution levels. The reader may refer to [LI 04a] for more information about this topic.

Chapter 11

A Categorical Approach of Qualitative Reasoning

11.1. "Waiting in line"

I am waiting in a line of ten people, and I am getting bored. Qualitative reasoning being on my mind, I decide to set up the basis for a qualitative formalism by dividing the line into three categories:

– myself (the identity relation);

– the two people who are just in front of and behind me (the proximity relation);

– the remaining people in the line (the remoteness relation).

In this way, I have defined three basic relations for a qualitative formalism which divides the world into three categories: myself, the two persons next to me, and everyone else. If this formalism is adopted, it leads to the partition of the set of pairs of individuals in the line into three relations: the diagonal relation Δ, the relation P (for "proximate"), and the relation R (for "remote"). These three relations have the JEPD property.

This formalism may be used to describe the state of the waiting line at a given time. It can also be used to reason about the relations between people: for example, I may be convinced by examining the various possible cases that, if $(x, y) \in P$ (x is near y) and $(y, z) \in P$ (y is near z), then either $(x, z) \in R$ or $(x, y \in \Delta$.

The set of rules we get in this way can be summarized in a composition table, as shown in Table 11.1.

This composition table corresponds to *weak* composition: indeed, x near y and y near z imply the fact that x is far from z, or coincides with z, but the converse

$\circ$	Δ	P	R
Δ	Δ	P	R
P	P	$R \cup \Delta$	$P \cup R$
R	R	$P \cup R$	$\Delta \cup P \cup R$

Table 11.1. *The composition table for P and R*

implication is not true: the fact that x is far from z does not imply that some y can be found which is at the same time near x and z. Hence (provided the line contains more than three people), the composition of relation P with itself is strictly contained in the union of relations R and Δ.

With this example of a universe U containing ten people, and the partition of $U \times U$ into three binary relations, we have a simple instance of the main topic of this chapter: a *partition scheme*.

The reader is now familiar with many examples of qualitative formalisms. Let us recall some of them (Chapter 4):

– temporal formalims: Allen's calculus [ALL 83] as a typical instance, together with other calculi such as the Point calculus [VIL 86], the Point-and-interval calculus [DEC 91], the generalized interval calculi (Chapter 3), and the INDU calculus [PUJ 99b];

– spatial formalisms:

- formalisms of Allen type, such as the Directed interval calculus [REN 01b], the Cardinal direction calculus [LIG 98b], which is also a particular case of the n-point calculus [BAL 99b], the Rectangle calculus [BAL 98a], and more generally the n-block calculi [BAL 99c];

- formalisms associated with axiomatic systems of the RCC type, including the RCC−5 and RCC−8 calculi;

- varied formalisms, such as the Cyclic interval calculus [BAL 00a], the formalisms of $2n$-star type [MIT 02], and the Preference calculi [DÜN 02].

A quick examination of these formalisms shows that all of them implement similar ideas, and that they share many common properties.

Consider the prototypical example of Allen's calculus: it uses a finite set of basic relations; disjunctions of these basic relations, called (disjunctive) relations, are used to represent and reason about incomplete knowledge. A relation has a well-defined inverse relation, and the relations may be composed, which provides them with an algebraic structure; the resulting algebra, called Allen's interval algebra, is a relation algebra in the sense of Tarski [TAR 41].

In practice, knowledge is represented by temporal networks which are labeled directed graphs whose vertices represent intervals and whose labels represent relations. The reasoning mechanism is based on constraint propagation, and the fundamental problem consists in determining whether a given network is consistent (a problem which is NP-complete in the general case [VIL 86]). When a network is consistent, finding an instantiation of it amounts to finding a consistent atomic subnetwork, which, in Allen's case, can be done in a purely algebraic way.

It is therefore natural to ask the general question: "What are the properties that extend to the various qualitative calculi?" This question was examined in [LIG 04a], and it became apparent that in fact many "nice" properties of Allen's calculus do not extend to other calculi. For example:

– as already noted in [EGE 99, LIG 04a], the algebras associated with some formalisms are not relation algebras in Tarski's sense, but more general algebras, called "non-associative" algebras by Maddux [MAD 82, HIR 02] (relation algebras then correspond to the particular case where these "non-associative" algebras are associative[1]). For example, the INDU algebra is a semi-associative algebra, but not an associative algebra. The same is true of the algebra studied by Egenhofer and Rodriguez [EGE 99];

– the natural models of a formalism are not necessarily representations of the associated algebra. It is a well-known fact, for example, that composition in Allen's interval algebra only expresses necessary and sufficient conditions provided that the intervals belong to a dense linear order which is unlimited on the left and on the right. However, some more general linear orders may be adequate models of time — for example, the integers as a model of discrete time — and an interval calculus of Allen type can be developed in this context. The corresponding model if no longer a representation of Allen's algebra, but it is still a weak representation of it;

– for some algebras, such as the Containment algebra [LAD 94] or the algebra of the Cyclic interval calculus [BAL 00a], there exist atomic constraints networks which are algebraically closed but not consistent.

– in the case of Allen's calculus, any consistent atomic network with n nodes is k-consistent, for $k < n$. Here again, similar results do hold for many formalisms. The study of the weak representations of the algebra of the formalism provides useful indications to understand why that is so.

If we want to go beyond the presentation of specific qualitative formalisms in order to study general properties, a first step consists in providing a general definition for them. Hopefully, this will facilitate a better understanding of the phenomena, and the development of general methods applicable to whole classes of formalisms rather than to isolated ones.

---

1 It would be more satisfactory to refer to them as to not "necessarily associative algebras".

In the following, we propose an answer to the question: "What is a qualitative formalism?" To our knowledge, this answer covers the vast majority of the formalisms we have been considering.

We will see that within the general framework we propose, the concept of a weak representation of a non-associative algebra is pivotal. This will lead us to use the language of category theory — as already done in Chapter 9. We will show how the language can be used in particular for clarifying the notion of consistency.

Our presentation is based on [LIG 04b] and [LIG 05a].

11.2. A general construction of qualitative formalisms

Most of the spatial or temporal qualitative formalisms are based on considering a set of non-empty binary relations on a universe U, which form a partition of $U \times U$: this is the JEPD (*jointly exhaustive, pairwise disjoint*) property.

Our starting point for a general definition is the concept of a *partition scheme*.

11.2.1. *Partition schemes*

Let U be a non-empty set, called the universe, which is the set of the entities that the qualitative formalism deals with (for example, temporal entities such as points, intervals, or spatial entities such as points, regions, etc.). We consider a partition of $U \times U$, that is, a family $(R_i)_{i \in I}$ of pairwise disjoint, non-empty binary relations whose union is the set $U \times U : U \times U = \bigcup_{i \in I} R_i$.

The relations R_i are called the *basic relations* of the partition scheme. In most cases, the calculus uses a finite number of basic relations, hence the set of indexes I is a finite set. However, this is not necessarily the case. For example, the TCSP formalism defined by Dechter, Meiri, and Pearl (Chapter 6, section 6.2) uses a set of basic relations which is the set of intervals on the real line (including half-open intervals and infinite intervals)[2].

The intuitive idea is that, among all the possible relations between two entities, the partition chooses a (finite) set of "qualitative", jointly exhaustive, and mutually exclusive relations, which will serve as the basis for describing particular situations. For example, in the case of Allen's calculus, where U is the set of bounded and closed

---

2 In this case, U is the set of points represented by the real line, and, for an interval α on the real line, R_α is the set of pairs of points (t, t') such that $(t' - t) \in \alpha$.

intervals on the real line, the 13 basic relations only distinguish between the relative orderings of the bounding points of two intervals, and these 13 relations are used to describe an arbitrary configuration of such intervals.

We make some relatively weak assumptions in connection with these data. Firstly, we assume that there exists a distinguished element i_0 in the set I of subscripts such that the associated relation R_{i_0} is the identity relation (also called the diagonal relation):

$$R_{i_0} = \Delta = \{(u, v) \in U \times U \mid u = v\} \tag{11.1}$$

Furthermore, we assume that the partition is globally invariant under inversion. This means that there exists a map $\smile : I \to I$ such that the inverse of each relation of the partition is itself one of the relations of the partition:

$$(\forall i \in I)(\exists j \in I) \ R_i^{-1} = R_{i^\smile} \tag{11.2}$$

DEFINITION 11.1.– *A partition scheme is a pair* $(U, (R_i)_{i \in I})$, *where U is a non-empty set and* $(R_i)_{i \in I}$ *is a partition of $U \times U$ which satisfies conditions [11.1] and [11.2].*

11.2.2. *Description of configurations*

A partition scheme can be used to describe configurations of entities in U, that is, to describe sets $V \subseteq U$ of elements of U. By definition, given such a set, each pair $(u, v) \in V \times V$ belongs to one of the relations R_i for a well-defined i. We may think of V as the set of vertices of a graph, and the map $\nu : V \times V \to I$ as a labeling of the arcs of the graph by basic relations. Clearly, $\nu(u, u)$ is the identical relation R_{i_0}, and $\nu(v, u)$ is the inverse of the relation $\nu(u, v)$.

More generally, we may express constraints between entities by means of Boolean expressions using the basic relations. In particular, networks labeled by disjunctions of basic relations are interpreted as conjunctions of disjunctive relations.

11.2.3. *Weak composition*

Constraint propagation uses the composition of relations. Recall that the composition $R \circ S$ of two binary relations R and S is defined by:

$$(R \circ S) = \{(u, v) \in U \times U \mid (\exists w \in U)(u, w) \in R \ \& \ (w, v) \in S\} \tag{11.3}$$

Now generally, there is no reason why the composition of two basic relations could be expressed as a basic relation (this is generally not the case, even for Allen's calculus), or as a disjunction of basic relations. The concept of weak composition corresponds to an approximation of the *bona fide* composition by the smallest union of basic relations which contain this composition. More precisely, the weak composition of two basic relations R_i and R_j, denoted by $R_i \diamond R_j$, is defined in the following way:

$$(R_i \diamond R_j) = \bigcup_{k \in J} R_k \text{ where } k \in J \text{ if, and only if, } (R_i \circ R_j) \cap R_k \neq \emptyset \quad [11.4]$$

The weak composition of two relations is hence the best approximation possible for the composition if the only available "building blocks" are the basic relations provided by the partition scheme. Note that weak composition is relative to a particular partition scheme, so that it is not to a purely relational concept like that of composition.

At this level of generality, some unpleasant phenomena may occur. For instance, even assuming that the relations R_i are non-empty, there is no guarantee that $R_i \diamond R_j$ is also non-empty. Nevertheless, in full generality, weak composition is an upper-bounding approximation of composition:

LEMMA 11.1.– *For all $i, j \in I : R_i \diamond R_j \supseteq R_i \circ R_j$.*

Proof. Any $(u, v) \in R_i \circ R_j$ belongs to a (unique) R_k for a well-defined k. Since R_k has a common element with $R_i \circ R_j$, R_k necessarily belongs to $R_i \diamond Rj$. □

LEMMA 11.2.– *For all $i, j, k \in I : (R_i \diamond R_j) \cap R_k = \emptyset$ if, and only if, $(R_i \circ R_j) \cap R_k = \emptyset$.*

Proof. In view of lemma 11.1, one direction of the equivalence is obvious. Conversely, if $(R_i \diamond R_j) \cap R_k$ is not empty, then, since $(R_i \diamond R_j)$ is a union of R_l, this set contains R_k. However, by the definition of weak composition, this means that R_k meets $R_i \circ R_j$. □

The interaction between weak composition and inverse easily follows from the properties of composition:

LEMMA 11.3.– *For all $i, j \in I : (R_i \diamond R_j)^{-1} = R_j^{-1} \diamond R_i^{-1}$*

11.2.4. *Weak composition and seriality*

In many cases, the basic relations have the property of being *serial* relations. Let us recall that a relation R is serial if the following condition holds:

$$(\forall u \in U)(\exists v \in U) \text{ such that } (u, v) \in R \qquad [11.5]$$

LEMMA 11.4.– *If the relations R and S are serial, then $R \circ S$ is serial (hence it is non-empty).*

Proof. If R and S are serial, then, given an arbitrary $u \in U$, choose w such that $(u, w) \in R$, then choose v such that $(w, v) \in S$. Then $(u, v) \in (R \circ S)$.   □

Consequently, since the basic relations are non-empty, the composition of two basic relations is non-empty.

LEMMA 11.5.– *If the basic relations are serial, then* $\forall i \in I : \bigcup_{j \in I}(R_i \diamond R_j) = U \times U$.

Proof. We have to prove that, for any index i, and any pair (u, v), there is an index j such that (u, v) belongs to $R_i \diamond R_j$. We know that $(u, v) \in R_k$, for some well-defined k. Since R_i and R_k are serial, for any t, there exist x and y such that $(t, x) \in R_i$ and $(t, y) \in R_k$. Consequently, $(x, y) \in R_i^{-1} \circ R_k$, so $R_i^{-1} \circ R_k$ is non-empty.

Moreover, there exists a well-defined j such that $(x, y) \in R_j$. Hence (t, y) is simultaneously in R_k and $R_i \circ R_j$. This implies that $R_k \subseteq (R_i \diamond R_j)$, hence that $(u, v) \in (R_i \diamond R_j)$.   □

11.3. Examples of partition schemes

EXAMPLE 11.1.– *The linear order with two elements.* Let $U = \{a, b\}$ be a set with two elements. Let $R_0 = \{(a, a), (b, b)\}$, $R_1 = \{(a, b)\}$, and $R_2 = \{(b, a)\}$. The set U, in other words, is linearly ordered by R_1 (and by R_2). Then $R_1 \circ R_1 = R_2 \circ R_2 = \emptyset$, $R_1 \circ R_2 = \{(a, a)\}$, and $R_2 \circ R_1 = \{(b, b)\}$. Hence $R_1 \diamond R_1 = \emptyset$, $R_2 \diamond R_2 = \emptyset$, $R_1 \diamond R_2 = R_0$, and $R_2 \diamond R_1 = R_0$.

EXAMPLE 11.2.– *The linear order with three elements.* Let $U = \{a, b, c\}$ be a set with three elements. Let $R_0 = \{(a, a), (b, b), (c, c)\}$, $R_1 = \{(a, b), (b, c), (a, c)\}$, and $R_2 = \{(b, a), (c, b), (c, a)\}$. Here, the set U is linearly ordered by R_1 (and by R_2). Then $R_1 \circ R_1 = \{(a, c)\}$, $R_2 \circ R_2 = \{(c, a)\}$, $R_1 \circ R_2 = R_2 \circ R_1 = \{(a, a), (b, b), (a, b), (b, a)\}$. Hence $R_1 \diamond R_1 = R_1$, $R_2 \diamond R_2 = R_2$, and $R_1 \diamond R_2 = R_2 \diamond R_1 = U \times U$.

EXAMPLE 11.3.– *The Point algebra.* In the case of the Point algebra, U is the set of rational numbers $\mathbb{Q}$, R_1 is the ordinary order on $\mathbb{Q}$, denoted by $<$. R_2 is the inverse of R_1. Since this order is dense and unlimited on the right and on the left, $R_1 \circ R_1 = R_1$, $R_2 \circ R_2 = R_2$, and $R_2 \circ R_1 = R_1 \circ R_2 = U \times U$: in this case, weak composition is the same as composition.

EXAMPLE 11.4.– indexalgebra!Allen's Interval*Allen's interval algebra.* Here, U is the set of pairs $(q_1, q_2) \in \mathbb{Q} \times \mathbb{Q}$ such that $q_1 < q_2$. The basic relations are defined in the usual way. Here again, weak composition and composition coincide.

EXAMPLE 11.5.– *Allen's calculus on the integers.* Now U is the set of pairs of integers $(n_1, n_2) \in \mathbb{Z} \times \mathbb{Z}$ such that $n_1 < n_2$, and the basic relations are defined as before. In this case, composition and weak composition differ. For example, although $p \diamond p = p$, the pair $([0, 1], [2, 3])$ belongs to p, but it does not belong to $p \circ p$, which shows that $p \diamond p = p$ is strictly greater than $p \circ p = p$.

11.4. Algebras associated with qualitative formalisms

11.4.1. *Algebras associated with partition schemes*

We now adopt the viewpoint of *abstract* algebras (see for example, Appendix B): an algebra is a set provided with a family of operations.

For each $i \in I$, let us introduce a symbol r_i (which denotes the relation R_i) and consider the set $\mathbf{B} = \{r_i \mid i \in I\}$. Let $\mathbf{A}$ be the Boolean algebra of all subsets of $\mathbf{B}$. Let $\mathbf{0}$ and $\mathbf{1}$ denote the bottom element and the top element of $\mathbf{A}$, respectively. Denote the union, intersection, and complement operations by $+$, $\cdot$, and $-$, respectively. Let $\mathbf{1}'$ denote the set $\{r_{i0}\}$. Let $r_i^{\smile} = r_{i\smile}$.

On the set $\mathbf{B}$, weak composition defines an operation usually denoted by ";" in this context. The table of this binary operation is called the (weak) composition table of the formalism. This operation on the basic symbols extends to all subsets in the usual way:

$$\text{for } a, b \in A, (a; b) = \bigcup_{i,j}(r_i; r_j), \text{ where } r_i \in a \text{ and } r_j \in b \qquad [11.6]$$

The abstract algebra $\mathbf{A}$ described above is called the algebra associated to the partition scheme. Since the preceding definitions reflect the behavior of "concrete" binary relations, the abstract algebra obtained in this way would be a relation algebra in Tarski's sense provided that composition would coincide with weak composition. In the general case, we get a more general type of algebra called a *non-associative algebra* [MAD 82, HIR 02]:

DEFINITION 11.2.– *A non-associative algebra A is an 8-tuple* $\mathbf{A} = (A, +, -, \mathbf{0}, \mathbf{1}, ;, \smile, \mathbf{1}')$ *such that* $(A, +, -, \mathbf{0}, \mathbf{1})$ *is a Boolean algebra, and that:*

1) $(x^{\smile})^{\smile} = x$;
2) $\mathbf{1}'; x = x; \mathbf{1}' = x$;
3) $x; (y + z) = x; y + x; z$;
4) $(x + y)^{\smile} = x^{\smile} + y^{\smile}$;
5) $(x - y)^{\smile} = x^{\smile} - y^{\smile}$;
6) $(x; y)^{\smile} = y^{\smile}; x^{\smile}$;
7) $(x; y).z^{\smile} = \mathbf{0}$ *if, and only if,* $(y; z).x^{\smile} = \mathbf{0}$.

A non-associative algebra is a relation algebra *if* ; *is an associative operation.*

Maddux [MAD 82] also defines intermediate classes between the class of relation algebras (**RA**) and the class of non-associative algebras (**NA**), namely the classes of *weakly associative* algebras (**WA**) and the class of *semi-associative* algebras (**SA**). These classes of algebras form a hierarchy:

$$\textbf{NA} \supseteq \textbf{WA} \supseteq \textbf{SA} \supseteq \textbf{RA} \supseteq \qquad\qquad [11.7]$$

Semi-associative algebras are those non-associative algebras which satisfy the following condition:

$$\text{for any } a, (a; \mathbf{1}); \mathbf{1} = a; \mathbf{1} \qquad\qquad [11.8]$$

PROPOSITION 11.1.– *The algebra associated with a partition scheme is a non-associative algebra. If the basic relations of the partition scheme are serial relations, this algebra is a semi-associative algebra.*

Proof. We must check that conditions (1) to (7) of the definition are satisfied. A preliminary remark is that it is enough to check them for basic relations. The first six conditions are easily checked. The seventh condition is a consequence of lemma 11.2. In addition, if the basic relations are serial, the condition of semi-associativity is satisfied because, according to lemma 11.5, we have $(x; \mathbf{1}) = \mathbf{1}$ for any basic relation x.   □

11.4.2. *Examples*

Let us review some of the examples considered above. The composition tables of example 11.1 and example 11.2 are shown in Table 11.2, where the symbols "$\prec$" and "$\succ$" are used for r_1 and r_2 (since r_0 is a unit for weak composition, the corresponding rows and columns are omitted).

$\circ$	r_1	r_2
r_1	0	$1'$
r_2	$1'$	0

$\circ$	$\prec$	$\succ$
$\prec$	$\prec$	1
$\succ$	1	$\succ$

Table 11.2. *Weak composition table of examples (11.1) (left) and (11.2) (right)*

Note that the weak composition table associated with example 11.2 coincides with that of the Point calculus (example 11.3).

11.4.3. *Associativity*

The non-associative algebras resulting from partition schemes are generally not associative. For example, the algebra of example 11.1 is not associative, since we have

$((r_1; r_2); r_2) = (\mathbf{1}'; r_2) = r_2$, whereas $(r_1; (r_2; r_2)) = (r_1; \mathbf{0}) = \mathbf{0}$. The weak axiom of associativity [MAD 82] is satisfied, but not that of semi-associativity, since we have for example, $(r_1; \mathbf{1}); \mathbf{1} = \mathbf{1}$ whereas $r_1; (\mathbf{1}; \mathbf{1}) = r_1 + \mathbf{1}'$.

When weak composition coincides with composition, the family $(R_i)_{i \in I}$ is an algebra of binary relations, hence it is an associative algebra.

However, this sufficient condition is not necessary, as shown by example 11.2: although the associated partition scheme has a weak composition which does not coincide with composition, its associated álgebra is the Point algebra, which is an associative algebra.

An example of an algebra which is semi-associative but non-associative is the INDU algebra [BAL 03] (semi-associativity is a consequence of the fact that the basic relations of INDU are serial).

11.5. Partition schemes and weak representations

We have seen that a qualitative formalism can be defined from a partition scheme. A non-associative algebra is associated with such a scheme: it is an algebra which satisfies all axioms of a relation algebra, except possibly for the associativity property.

Conversely, what is the relationship of the partition scheme with respect to the algebra? The answer is that it is a weak representation[3] of this algebra.

The concept of weak representation has been discussed in detail in Chapter 9. It extends to non-associative algebras in a natural way:

DEFINITION 11.3.– *Let* **A** *be a non-associative algebra*[4]. *A weak representation of* **A** *is a pair* (U, φ), *where* U *is a non-empty set, and* φ *is a map of* **A** *in* $\mathcal{P}(U \times U)$, *such that:*

1) φ *is a homomorphism of Boolean algebras;*
2) $\varphi(\mathbf{1}') = \Delta = \{(x, y) \in U \times U \mid x = y\};$
3) $\varphi(a^\smile)$ *is the inverse of* $\varphi(a);$
4) $\varphi(a; b) \supseteq \varphi(a) \circ \varphi(b).$

---

3 It may be appropriate in this regard to note that the concept of a weak representation we use in this book should not be confused with the concept of weak representability used by Jónsson [JÓN 59, HIR 02].

4 We assume in this definition that we are dealing with a simple algebra, see [HIR 02].

A weak representation is a *representation* if:

1) φ is injective;

2) $\varphi(a;b) = \varphi(a) \circ \varphi(b)$.

11.5.1. *The weak representation associated with a partition scheme*

Let us return to the initial situation where we have a universe U a partition of $U \times U$ which define a partition scheme. Consider the pair (U, φ), where $\varphi \colon \mathbf{A} \to \mathcal{P}(U \times U)$ is defined on the basic symbols by:

$$\varphi(r_i) = R_i \qquad\qquad [11.9]$$

and is extended to the Boolean algebra in the usual manner:

$$\text{for } a \in \mathbf{A} \text{ let } \varphi(a) = \bigcup_{r_i \in a} \varphi(r_i) \qquad\qquad [11.10]$$

PROPOSITION 11.2.– *Given a partition scheme U, let φ be the map defined above. Then, the pair (U, φ) is a weak representation of* **A**.

Proof. The only point requiring a proof is axiom [11.4]. For basic symbols, we have $\varphi(r_i; r_j) = R_i \diamond R_j$, by definition, and $\varphi(r_i) \circ \varphi(r_j) = R_i \circ R_j$. According to lemma 11.1, the first relation contains the second. This fact extends to disjunctive relations. $\qquad\square$

As an easy consequence, we get the following corollary:

COROLLARY 11.1.– *The weak representation associated to a partition scheme is a representation if, and only if, weak composition coincides with composition.*

11.6. A general definition of qualitative formalisms

We can now give an answer to our initial question: "What is a qualitative formalism?"

DEFINITION 11.4.– *A qualitative formalism is a 3-tuple* $(\mathbf{A}, U, \varphi)$ *where:*

– **A** *is a non-associative algebra;*

– (U, φ) *is a weak representation of* **A**.

11.6.1. *The pivotal role of weak representations*

We have seen that a partition scheme defines an algebra. This algebra is a non-associative algebra. It may or may not be a relation algebra. If the partition scheme is serial, it is semi-associative.

Moreover, the initial partition scheme defines a weak representation of the algebra.

In what follows, we highlight the dual nature of weak representations: on the one hand, they can be seen as representing constraints, in the form of algebraically closed, normalized and atomic constraint networks; on the other hand, they can also be seen as interpretations of qualitative formalisms. Because of this dual nature, the concept of consistency can be expressed in a natural way in terms of morphisms between weak representations. This is a further reason for getting interested in the category of weak representations of the algebra associated with a qualitative calculus.

11.6.2. *Weak representations as constraints*

Let (N, ν) be a constraint network, and for each basic element $a \in \mathbf{A}$, consider the set $\rho(a) = \{(i, j) \in N \times N \,|\, \nu(i, j) = a\}$. We thus define a map of $\mathbf{A}$ to the set of subsets of $N \times N$, whose interpretation is as follows: for each basic element a, $\rho(a)$ is the set of arcs whose labels contain a. If the network is atomic, an arc is labeled by a unique basic element, and the family of sets $\rho(a)$ which are non-empty defines a partition of $N \times N$ indexed by a subset of the basic elements of $\mathbf{A}$. If the network is normalized, this partition satisfies conditions [11.1] and [11.2], which characterize a partition scheme. If it is algebraically closed, then (N, ρ), where ρ is naturally extended to $\mathbf{A}$, i.e. by setting $\rho(b) = \sum_{a \in b} \rho(a)$, is a weak representation of $\mathbf{A}$ with N as its universe.

Conversely, for any weak representation of (U, φ), we may interpret U as a set of vertices, and $\varphi(r_i)$ as the set of arcs labeled by r_i. Any arc is labeled by a basic relation in such a way that (v, u) is labeled by $r_i^{\smile}$ if (u, v) is labeled by r_i. In addition, for all u, v, w, the composition of the label of (u, w) with that of (w, v) contains the label of (u, v). Consequently, a weak representation defines an atomic, normalized and algebraically closed constraint network[5].

To consider a weak representation in terms of constraint networks amounts to considering it from an *intensional* viewpoint, as expressing constraints on the possible instantiations of variables of the network. But weak representations can also be

---

5 At least if N is a finite set; otherwise, it defines a natural generalization of the concept for infinite universes.

considered as *extensional* entities: indeed, as becomes apparent with partition schemes, they can be viewed as interpretations.

11.6.3. *Weak representations as interpretations*

Many standard interpretations of temporal formalisms are particular cases of weak representations of the algebra of the formalism; in several cases, they are even representations of this algebra. Such is the case for the interpretation of Allen's interval algebra in terms of pairs of ordered points in the rational line $\mathbb{Q}$ or in the real line $\mathbb{R}$. However in many cases, weak representations, rather than representations, are the main focus of the calculus. We have mentioned this fact for the interpretation of Allen's calculus in terms of intervals on the integers (example 11.5). Another example for Allen's interval algebra is its extension to unbounded intervals [CUK 04], which amounts to considering intervals on $\{\infty\} \cup \mathbb{Q} \cup \{-\infty\}$, or equivalently on $[0, 1] \cap \mathbb{Q}$. We may note that in this case the partition scheme is not serial. For this interpretation, the consistency problem of constraint networks appears in a novel context.

The appearance of the seriality property in this discussion should not be a surprise. Indeed, recall that a constraint network is k-consistent if any consistent instantiation of $k - 1$ variables can be extended to a consistent instantiation with k-variables. In particular, a network is 2-consistent if any instantiation of a variable extends to two variables. Consequently, a partition scheme is serial if, and only if, the (possibly infinite) network U is 2-consistent. Many formalisms have consistent networks which are not 2-consistent. For example, in the case of Allen's calculus on the integers, the network with two elements $\{v_1, v_2\}$ whose constraint $\nu(v_1, v_2)$ is d, is consistent, but it is not 2-consistent: if v_2 is instantiated by an interval of length 1, an instantiation for v_1 satisfying the constraint cannot be found.

11.7. Interpretating consistency

The above discussion shows that a weak representation may be considered in two ways: either as a particular case of (an atomic, normalized and algebraically closed) constraint network, or as an interpretation in some universe. Now the basic problem for a constraint network is the question of its consistency with respect to a given interpretation.

Intuitively, a network $\mathcal{N} = (N, \nu)$ is consistent (with respect to a qualitative calculus $(\mathbf{A}, U, \varphi)$) if it has an atomic refinement $\mathcal{N}' = (N, \nu')$ which is itself consistent, i.e. such that the variables N of $\mathcal{N}$ may be interpreted in terms of elements of U in such a way that the relations prescribed by ν' hold in U. More precisely, (N, ν') is algebraically closed, normalized, and atomic. Let us consider the associated weak representation (N, ρ). Then, the consistency of the network with regard to the weak representation (U, φ) means that there exists an instantiation $h: N \to U$ such that, for any atom $a \in \mathbf{A}, (i, j) \in \rho(a)$ implies that $(h(i), h(j)) \in \varphi(a)$. Consequently, the consistency of a network appears as a particular case of compatibility between two weak representations of the same algebra. In other words, consistency is a property involving two weak representations.

DEFINITION 11.5.– *Let $\mathcal{N} = (N, \rho)$ and $\mathcal{U} = (U, \varphi)$ be two weak representations of $\mathbf{A}$. Then, $\mathcal{N}$ is* consistent *with respect to $\mathcal{U}$ if there exists a map $h: N \to U$ such that the diagram of Figure 11.1 commutes, i.e. for any $a \in \mathbf{A}, (i, j) \in \rho(a)$ implies that $(h(i), h(j)) \in \varphi(a)$. A constraint network $\mathcal{N}$ is* consistent *(with respect to $\mathcal{U}$) if it has an atomic refinement which is a consistent weak representation with respect to $\mathcal{U}$.*

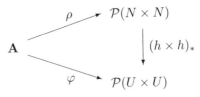

Figure 11.1. *The general concept of consistency*

This generalization of the concept of consistency highlights the fact that it is a relation between two weak representations, one being interpreted in intensional terms, while the other is used in an extensional manner, as a universe of interpretation.

EXAMPLE 11.6.– *The Point algebra.* A weak representation of this algebra is a linearly ordered set. Let $(N, \prec_N)$ and $(U, \prec_U)$ be two weak representations. Then, $(N, \prec_N)$ is consistent with respect to $(U, \prec_U)$ if, and only if, there exists a strictly increasing map $h: N \to U$.

EXAMPLE 11.7.– *Allen's interval algebra.* Any weak representation of this algebra is consistent with respect to the standard representation $(Int(\mathbb{Q}), \varphi)$.

11.7.1. *Inconsistent weak representations*

In view of this discussion, what does the fact that weak representations are not consistent (with respect to the standard interpretation of the calculus) mean? We know that there are examples of algebraically closed atomic networks which are not consistent, for example, for the Cyclic interval calculus or the INDU calculus [LIG 04a]. In those cases, the universe of interpretation of the calculus (such as the oriented intervals on a circle, or the intervals with constraints on their relative durations) has too many structural constraints between its relations for the network to take them into account. It seems that characterizing those cases where this kind of phenomenon occurs remains an open problem.

11.8. The category of weak representations

Let **A** be the algebra of a qualitative formalism. The preceding discussion shows the significance of weak representations, but also shows that of morphisms between two weak representations. Hence a natural move consists in using once again the language of category theory, as done already in Chapter 9, and considering the category of weak representations of **A**.

The concept of consistency, as we have seen, reduces to the existence of a morphism: if $\mathcal{U}$ and $\mathcal{V}$ are two objects of the category of weak representations of **A**, then $\mathcal{U}$ is consistent with respect to $\mathcal{V}$ if $\mathrm{Hom}(\mathcal{U}, \mathcal{V})$ is non-empty.

A morphism is defined by a map $h\colon U \to V$ which has the following property: if the label of the pair $(u_1, u_2) \in U \times U$ is the basic relation a, then its image $(h(u_1), h(u_2))$ in $V \times V$ is also labeled by a. This may be written as $(\forall a \in \mathsf{B})(x, y) \in \varphi(a) \to (h(x), h(y)) \in \psi(a)$.

An illuminating way of visualizing a weak representation (U, φ) is to see it as a partition of $U \times U$ indexed by (a subset) of the basic relations of **A**. Then the condition is that each equivalence class of the partition of $U \times U$ is sent by h to the equivalence class of $V \times V$ with the same label.

The map h is necessarily injective, since a pair of elements of U which is not labeled by the identical relation, cannot be sent on a pair labeled by the identical relation. If there exists a morphism $h\colon U \to V$, it makes of U a subobject of V.

Obviously, the identical map is a morphism, so that any weak representation is consistent with respect to itself. If $f\colon \mathcal{U} \to \mathcal{V}$ and $g\colon \mathcal{V} \to \mathcal{W}$ are two morphisms, the map $(g \circ f)\colon \mathcal{U} \to \mathcal{W}$ is itself a morphism. It can be easily seen that all the properties defining a category are satisfied. The composition of two morphisms is a morphism, and the identical morphism is a neutral element for composition.

EXAMPLE 11.8.– Let us consider the Point algebra again. A linear order U is consistent with respect to a linear order V if U can be embedded into V. In the case of finite linear orders, this is true if, and only if, V has at least as many elements as V. An example of two incomparable linear orders for the consistency relation is that of $\mathbb{N}$ equipped with the standard ordering, and the same set equipped with the opposite ordering. Both are weak representations of the Point algebra, but none of them can be embedded into the other, since the first has a smallest element, whereas the second does not.

11.8.1. *The algebra of partial orders*

The algebra of partial orders M_4 has four basic relations $\{\prec, \succ, eq, \|\}$, where the fourth relation corresponds to two elements being incomparable. A weak representation of M_4 is basically a partial order. More precisely, consider such a weak representation (U, φ). Let R be the binary relation $\varphi(\prec)$ on U. It can be easily seen that R is a partial ordering on U, so that U equipped with R is a partial order.

Conversely, any partial ordering R on a set U provides a weak representation (U, φ) of M_4: Let $\varphi(eq)$ be the diagonal relation Δ on U, let $R = \varphi(\prec)$, $R^\smile = \varphi(\succ)$, and $\varphi(\|) = U \times U \setminus (\Delta \cup R \cup R^\smile)$.

The two constructions which we have just outlined are converse of each other.

What about the representations of M_4? It can be shown [LIG 04a] that if $U = \mathbb{Q} \times \mathbb{Q}$ is equipped with the product ordering, then (U, φ) is a *representation* of M_4, which implies that M_4 is a relation algebra, a fact which may also be checked directly.

In the category of weak representations of M_4, the concept of consistency is related to the theory of dimension of partial orders.

In order to make this relationship explicit, we need the following concepts: if (P, R) and (Q, S) are two partial orders, a map $h \colon P \to Q$ is an *embedding* of (P, R) in (Q, S) if h is injective, and if $(u, v) \in R$ implies $(h(u), h(v)) \in S$. It is a *full embedding* if for all $u, v \in P$, we have $(u, v) \in R$ if, and only if, $(h(u), h(v)) \in S$.

Then, it can be easily seen that $h \colon P \to Q$ induces a morphism of (P, R) to (Q, S) — as weak representations of M_4, or in other words that (P, R) is consistent with respect to (Q, S) — if, and only if, h is a full embedding.

The dimension of a partial order (P, R) is by definition the smallest integer n such that (P, R) can be fully embedded in $\mathbb{Q}^n$. In other words, a weak representation of M_4 (i.e. a partial order) has a dimension which is the smallest integer n for which it is consistent with respect to $\mathbb{Q}^n$.

11.8.2. *On the relativity of consistency*

The above discussion highlights two important aspects of qualitative reasoning:

– It is good practice to clearly separate two notions of algebra when dealing with qualitative reasoning: the first notion is that of the *abstract* algebra associated to a given calculus — a non-associative algebra, and in several cases, a relation algebra; the second notion is that of the concrete algebra of relations generated by the interpretations of the symbols of the abstract algebra, which is a particular weak representation of it.

– There are generally numerous weak representations of the same algebra, which implies that a consistency problem makes sense only with respect to a well-defined weak representation of this algebra.

Consequently, the two notions of algebra have to be carefully differentiated, even if making no difference between them may be safe as is most often the case for Allen's interval algebra.

A telling example is that of the RCC−5 algebra, also known as the Containment algebra [RAN 92a, LAD 94]. Under the name of RCC−5, it refers to topological interpretations (actually, to set-theoretic interpretations, see Chapters 9 and 10). As the Containment algebra, it is considered by Ladkin and Maddux in the context of intervals on the real line. But both terms refer to the same abstract algebra characterized by its composition table. As pointed out by Düntsch [DÜN 03], many calculi involve interpretations of the composition table of RCC−5 which are not representations, but only weak representations of the algebra. In its realization as the Containment algebra, the algebra is a subalgebra of Allen's interval algebra which may be interpreted in terms of intervals on the real line. Ladkin and Maddux [LAD 94] show that there exist scenarios (algebraically closed atomic networks, hence weak representations) of this algebra which are not consistent with respect to this interpretation. But they are consistent with respect to other weak representations of the algebra, for example, in terms of regions in the plane, or as intervals on a circle.

11.8.3. *Semi-strong weak representations*

The question of defining suitable properties for characterizing a qualitative formalism is considered in Mossakowski *et al.* [MOS 06] in the context of category theory. The authors define a notion of weak representation which is more general than the one we use, since it does not assume the image of $1'$ to be the identity relation. A weak representation which has this property is said to be *diagonal-preserving*.

The authors of [MOS 06] also define a notion of *strong* representation; they note that the weak representations associated with a partition scheme are not in general strong representations, but only *semi-strong* representations:

DEFINITION 11.6.– *Let* **A** *be an atomic non-associative algebra. A weak representation* (U, φ) *of* **A** *is* semi-strong *if it satisfies the following condition*:

$$(a; b) = \vee \{c \mid c \text{ is atomic, and } (\varphi(x) \circ \varphi(y)) \cap \varphi(a) \neq \emptyset\}$$

The reader will recognize here condition 5) of section 10.2.2, in Chapter 10, which expresses that, in the weak representation considered, each entry of the composition table has a *witness*. Clearly, by construction, the weak representation associated with a partition scheme satisfies this condition.

Based on this fact, [MOS 06] proposes the following definition of a qualitative formalism:

DEFINITION 11.7.– *A qualitative formalism consists of a non-associative algebra and of a* semi-strong *weak representation of this algebra.*

We have seen that the question of determining under what conditions the algebraic closure property can be used to determine the consistency of constraint networks may be expressed in terms of the existence of morphisms in the category of weak representations of the corresponding algebra. Now in a category, a weakly terminal object is an object T such that for any other object X of the category, there exists a morphism of X to T. Therefore, for such weak representations, the method of algebraic closure can be used to decide the consistency of a constraint network.

11.9. Conclusions

Starting from the general question: "What is a qualitative formalism?", we have introduced here a general framework for defining qualitative calculi: in short, a qualitative calculus consists of a non-associative algebra and of a weak representation of this algebra.

The fact that, for nearly two decades, Allen's calculus had been considered as the paradigmatic example of a qualitative calculus might have suggested that the algebras associated with qualitative calculi are necessarily relation algebras, and that their domains of interpretation must be necessarily representations of these algebras.

These assumptions have proved not to reflect the general situation: firstly, some formalisms (see [EGE 99, LIG 04a]) involve non-associative algebras; then, for many calculi, the domains of interpretation may vary, and they are not necessarily representations.

The abstract definition of a qualitative formalism highlights the fact that some constraint networks on the one hand, and the domains of interpretation on the other hand, are essentially of the same nature: they are weak representations of the algebra. This fact was known before, and it has been implicitly used, for example, for building representations of a relation algebra by incrementally enriching algebraically closed networks [HIR 02] using Ehrenfeucht-Fraïssé games.

However, the framework we have outlined suggests that any new calculus could be examined from a uniform perspective, and that a standard set of questions should be asked: What are the properties of its algebra? What are the weak representations considered? Are these interpretations representations? Under what conditions is a weak representation consistent with respect to a given interpretation?

The definition of consistency in terms of the existence of a morphism in the category of weak representations makes apparent the algebraic character of the notion. The consideration of algebras such as the algebras associated with partial orders shows that non-trivial theories — such as the dimension theory of partial orders — are related to the notion of relative consistency for weak representations.

Chapter 12

Complexity of Constraint Languages

12.1. "Sudoku puzzles"

Who nowadays has not heard about sudoku puzzles? A sudoku puzzle (Figure 12.1) consists of a 9×9 grid which is divided into nine 3×3 subgrids known as regions. Some of the boxes initially contain digits, and the objective is to fill in the empty boxes with digits in such a way that each of the rows, columns, and regions contains all digits from 1 to 9.

Why consider sudoku puzzles? The answer is that they represent a typical example of a constraint satisfaction problem on a finite domain (the nine digits) which, moreover, uses a relation of high arity.

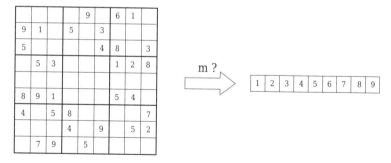

Figure 12.1. *A sudoku puzzle: on the left, a grid U_{grid}, divided into nine regions; on the right, the template U_{sudo}; the objective consists in finding a map m: $U_{grid} \rightarrow U_{sudo}$ extending the partial map defined in the puzzle, so that each row, each column, and each region is mapped to distinct digits*

In fact, sudoku puzzles show how easily humans, in certain conditions, are able to handle the concept of n-ary relations, for fairly high values of n: for sudoku puzzles, the relevant relation is the 9-ary relation on the digits from 1 to 9 which states that "each digit is different from the others!". More precisely, sudoku puzzles use a *relational structure* $(U_{sudo}, D, P_1, \ldots, P_n)$, which we will refer to as to the sudoku *template*:

– U_{sudo} is the set $\{1, \ldots, 9\}$, called the universe of the structure;

– D is the "all are different" 9-ary relation: $D(x_1, \ldots, x_9)$ means that the set $\{x_1, \ldots, x_9\}$ is precisely the set $\{1, \ldots, 9\}$;

– $P_i (i = 1, \ldots, 9)$ is the unary relation which states that an integer is equal to i: $P_i(x)$ is true if, and only if, $x = i$.

What does solving a sudoku puzzle mean? An instance of the puzzle corresponds to a universe which is a grid U_{grid} of 81 boxes, some of which are already filled in by digits. This can be expressed by considering that each predicate P_i, for $(i = 1, \ldots, 9)$, is interpreted as a subset of boxes of the grid. The objective of the player is to complete this interpretation, which means to define a map m of U_{grid} to U_{sudo} such that:

– for a box already containing a given digit, m has this digit as a value;

– if nine boxes belong to the 9-ary relation on the set of boxes U_{grid}, still denoted by the symbol D whose interpretation is that those boxes either belong to the same row, or to the same column, or to the same region, then their images in U_{sudo} (the nine integers that m associates with them) belong to the interpretation of D in U_{sudo} (they are all different).

As usually in logics, we may consider that D and P_i, for $1 \leq i \leq 9$, are relation symbols of which we have two interpretations: one in the template U_{sudo}, and another the grid U_{grid}. A solution of (an instance of) the sudoku puzzle is then simply a map $m: U_{grid} \rightarrow U_{sudo}$ of the grid into the template which is a *morphism of relational structures*, i.e. which preserves the relations D and P_i.

How is this discussion related to qualitative temporal and spatial reasoning? Recall for instance what a consistency problem is for the Point algebra.

In that case, we have a template which is the relational structure whose universe is $U_{\mathbb{Q}} = \mathbb{Q}$, and whose eight binary relations are $<, \text{eq}, >, \leq, \geq, \neq, 0$, and 1 — we leave their precise descriptions to the reader.

An instance of the consistency problem in this case can be seen as a relational structure, whose universe is the set N of vertices of a constraint network, and a set of binary relations on this universe: the labeling of the arcs of the network, indeed, defines an interpretation of each of the eight symbols in terms of sets of pairs of vertices. Now solving the problem consists in finding a map m of N to $U_{\mathbb{Q}}$ such that the images of the eight binary relations on vertices are contained in the corresponding relations on the template $U_{\mathbb{Q}}$; again, this may be expressed by saying that m is a *morphism* of the structure corresponding to the instance to the template with universe $U_{\mathbb{Q}} = \mathbb{Q}$.

Obviously, this is just a different way of stating that the two problems — the sudoku puzzle and the consistency problem — are CSPs, the first CSP having a finite universe, while the second one corresponds to a structure with an infinite universe. But the interesting aspect of focussing on relational structures stems from a link established by Jeavons and his collaborators [JEA 95a, JEA 95b, JEA 97, JEA 98, COH 00, BUL 00, COH 06a] between, on the one hand, the complexity of the constraint satisfaction problem, and on the other hand the existence of (unary, binary, ternary, etc.) structure-preserving operations on the relational structure called *polymorphisms*.

12.2. Structure of the chapter

When dealing with qualitative formalisms involving binary relations, we emphasized the role played by the relation algebra (or more generally the non-associative algebra) associated to the formalisms. In this chapter, we will consider another way to use the algebraic structure, where we do not restrict ourselves to the relations initially given on the structure: we consider instead all the relations generated by them, in a sense to be made precise. This approach was developed by Jeavons and his collaborators (we refer the reader to [COH 06a] for bibliographical references).

The approach was initially developed for constraint satisfaction problems on finite domains, starting with domains with two elements only (these are known as Boolean domains). More recently this approach has been extended to formalisms whose domains are relational structures with infinite universes [BOD 03b, BOD 06, BOD 07b, BOD 09]. As we have seen before, many temporal or spatial formalisms are of this type (Allen's calculus, the Generalized interval calculi, the n-point calculi, the n-block calculi, etc.).

In this chapter, we will recall the basic principles of the approach developed by Jeavons *et al.* as well as its typical results in the finite case: besides relating the complexity properties to the existence of specific properties of algebras related to the CSP, it also allows us to study the issue of local vs. global consistency: typical results will be the fact that, for such-and-such calculus, strong k-consistency implies global consistency.

Based on the work of Bodirsky and Chen, we will then describe some of the techniques developed in order to apply this approach to several classical formalisms such as the Point calculus, Allen's calculus, the RCC-5 formalism, and the Rectangle calculus [BOD 07b, BOD 09].

An important theme in the study of complexity in general, and of CSPs in particular, is that of *dichotomy results*. Generally, in the case of CSPs, a dichotomy result states that, for a given domain U of variables, any instance of a problem is either of polynomial complexity, or is an NP-complete problem. For example, this is true for CSPs whose domain of variables contains two or three elements. The same is also true for Allen's interval algebra, as shown by the complete classification of tractable sub-algebras obtained by Krokhin *et al.* [KRO 03] (see Chapter 2, section 2.3).

We end this chapter with a description of another approach of the study of complexity of constraint satisfaction problems. This constructive approach studies the complexity of the combination of two formalisms whose complexity is known. We describe the relation between the concept of independence and the refinement technique introduced by Renz [REN 99a, REN 07a].

12.3. Constraint languages

Recall that if U is an arbitrary set, the set of relations on U is $\bigcup_{n \geq 1} \mathcal{P}(U^n)$. If R is a relation, its arity is the integer n such that $R \subseteq U^n$. On recalling the example of sudoku puzzles, or that of the Point calculus, the reader should be able to accept the following definition:

DEFINITION 12.1.– *Let U be a set. A* constraint language Σ *on U (U is called the domain of the language) consists of a set Σ of relations on U. If Σ is a constraint language on U, then the pair (U, Σ) is called a* relational structure.

Intuitively, a constraint language is just a set of "names" of relations on a given domain. A relational structure is a constraint language on a domain, together with the interpretations of those names as relations on this domain. The set of symbols Σ is the *signature* of the relational structure.

EXAMPLE 12.1.– The constraint language of sudoku puzzles has the set $\{1, \ldots, 9\}$ as its domain, and as relations, one relation D of arity 9, and nine relations $P_1, \ldots, P_9$ of arity 1.

The constraint language of the time point algebra has $\mathbb{Q}$ as its domain, and eight binary relations as relations.

A constraint language can be used to state the associated *constraint satisfaction problems* (CSP):

DEFINITION 12.2.– *Let Σ be a constraint language on U. The* constraint satisfaction problem $CSP(\Sigma)$ *is the following decision problem*:
 – *an* instance *of the problem consists of a 3-tuple $(V, U, \mathcal{C})$, where*:
  - *V is a set of variables,*
  - *$\mathcal{C}$ is a finite set of constraints,*

- each constraint $C \in \mathcal{C}$ is a pair (s, R), where $s = (v_1, \ldots, v_n)$ is an n-tuple of variables called scope *of the constraint, and $R \in \Sigma$ is an n-ary relation on U called the* relation *of the constraint,*

– the problem consists in deciding whether there is a solution, *i.e. a map m: $V \to U$ such that for any constraint $(s, R) \in \mathcal{C}$, where $s = (v_1, \ldots, v_n)$, one has $(m(v_1), \ldots, m(v_n)) \in R$.*

Given an instance $(V, U, \mathcal{C})$ of the constraint satisfaction problem, V can be considered as a relational structure of signature Σ: for each relation $R \in \Sigma$, of arity n, the interpretation of R in V is the union of n-tuples of variables s for which $(s, R) \in \mathcal{C}$. Conversely, any relational structure of universe V and relations Σ defines a constraint satisfaction problem.

Using this equivalence, the constraint satisfaction problem associated to $(V, U, \mathcal{C})$ is equivalent to deciding whether there exists a morphism m of the structure defined by this instance on the structure associated with the constraint language.

12.4. An algebraic approach of complexity

The main intuition of the algebraic approach of constraint satisfaction problems, introduced by Jeavons *et al.* [COH 00, BULL 00, COH 06a], is that the complexity of the constraint satisfaction problem $CFP(K)$, where K is fixed, is related to the expressiveness of relations of K. If the latter have a strong expressive power, and make it possible to express many relations, we may expect the problem to be a difficult one. On the other hand, consider all the operations on the structure K, i.e. all maps $K^n \to K$, for $n \geq 0$. Among these maps, some preserve the relations of K, in a sense to be made precise. We may expect that a strong expressiveness of the relations tends to restrict the set of operations which preserve them. If this is the case, having few operations preserving the relations will be related to high complexity, and vice versa.

In this chapter, we will provide the basic elements for giving a precise meaning to these intuitive considerations. We will show how, in the case of finite structures, they allow a precise characterization of the complexity of the constraint satisfaction problem.

So far, we have focussed on the issue of complexity. Now a specificity of the domain of constraint satisfaction problems is the existence of algorithmic procedures, such as those based on the notion of k-consistency, which can be used as filters when considering partial solutions. Typically, for some classes of problems, strong k-consistency, for some integer k, will be sufficient to guarantee consistency. The algebraic approach provides tools for studying this phenomenon, and it also allows us to characterize new instances of such local-to-global consistency properties.

In general, the problems considered in temporal and spatial qualitative reasoning are not finite CSPs: the universes of the Σ-structure which we consider are infinite. However, Bodirsky and Chen [BOD 07b] have shown that many techniques used in the finite case can be adapted if the structure considered is infinite, provided it is $\aleph_0$-categorical. Let us recall that this property, which appeared as a consequence of the description of weak representations in Chapter 9, implies that there is only one countable model of the structure up to isomorphism. We will give a brief outline of the adaptation of these techniques for Allen's interval algebra, the Rectangle algebra, as well as for formalisms such as the RCC-5 and RCC-8 calculi (which are not $\aleph_0$-categorical).

12.5. CSPs and morphisms of relational structures

The main idea of this section is that solving a constraint satisfaction problem corresponds to determining if there exists a morphism of two Σ-structures. Here, Σ is a (finite) set of relational symbols (in terms of constraint networks, these symbols are the labels used to label the arcs or hyperarcs of the network).

12.5.1. *Basic facts about CSPs*

Recall that a *constraint satisfaction problem* or CSP is defined by a set N of variables and a set of constraints on these variables. The constraint satisfaction problem consists in determining if there exists an assignment of values to these variables such that all the constraints of C are satisfied.

We have opened this chapter with the example of the sudoku puzzles, for which the set of variables is a set of 81 boxes, and where the possible values of these variables are the digits $\{1, \ldots, 9\}$. The constraints are of two types: on the one hand, unary constraints corresponding to an initial partial assignment of values to the variables, and on the other hand, a 9-ary constraint of distinctiveness.

A standard example of a finite constraint satisfaction problem is the n-queens problem: on a chessboard of $n \times n$ squares, the problem consists in placing n queens in such a way that none of them threatens[1] another one (the usual chessboard corresponds to $n = 8$). This problem becomes a finite CSP if we associate a variable $v_i, 1 \leq i \leq n$ with each column and indicate the position of a queen by giving her row number. Here the set of values is the set $\{1, \ldots, n\}$.

---

[1] A queen threatens another piece if this piece is located in the same row, or the same column, or on the same diagonal as the queen itself.

The 3-coloring problem is another example. This problem, given an undirected graph (N, E) whose set of vertices is N and the set of edges E, consists in determining if the vertices of the graph can be colored by three colors, let us say R, B, J, (red, blue, yellow), such that two adjacent vertices have different colors. In other words, we have to decide whether there exists $h\colon N \to \{R, B, J\}$ such that $(x, y) \in E$ implies $h(x) \neq h(y)$.

In these three examples, the set of values that may be taken by the variables is a finite set: they are called finite CSPs.

The domains of application of the CSP techniques, in addition to temporal and spatial reasoning, are quite numerous: we may mention graph theory (colorization, partitioning), databases (confinement of conjunctive queries), computational algebra (polynomial equations and inequalities), complexity theory, operational research (linear programming, integer programming), typing of programming languages, etc.

12.5.2. CSPs and morphisms of structures

Let Σ be a relational signature, i.e. a set of relational symbols (an *arity* $v(r)$ is hence associated to each relation symbol $r \in \Sigma$). A Σ-*structure* consists of a domain U, and of a $v(r)$-ary relation r^U on U: $r^U \subseteq U^{v(r)}$ for each symbol $r \in \Sigma$.

If U and V are two Σ-structures, a morphism $h\colon U \to V$ is a map $h\colon U \to V$ of the domain of U to that of V such that, for any $r \in \Sigma, (u_1, \ldots, u_{v(r)}) \in r^U$ implies $(h(u_1), \ldots, h(u_{v(r)})) \in r^V$.

EXAMPLE 12.2.– *Sudoku puzzles.* As explained above, sudoku puzzles correspond to the signature $\Sigma = (D, P_1, \ldots, P_9)$, where the symbol D has arity 9, while the other 9 symbols are unary. The sudoku template is the Σ-structure with universe $\{1, \ldots, 9\}$, for which $D(x_1, \ldots, x_9)$ is true if the set $\{x_1, \ldots, x_9\}$ has exactly 9 elements, and $P_i(x)$ is true if, and only if, $x = i$.

An instance of the sudoku puzzle is defined by a relational structure on the same signature, whose universe is a set of 81 boxes subdivided into 9 rows, 9 columns, and 9 regions; the symbol D is interpreted to mean that 9 boxes are either in the same row, or in same column, or in the same region, and the symbol P_i means that a box contains the value i".

Solving a specific sudoku puzzle is then equivalent to finding a morphism of the associated Σ-structure to the sudoku template.

EXAMPLE 12.3.– *Graph coloring.* Consider the signature $\Sigma = \{e\}$, where e denotes a binary relation. An undirected graph (N, E) defines a Σ-structure $\mathcal{N}$ of domain N, where e^N is defined as the set of pairs $(x, y) \in N^2$ such that $\{x, y\} \in E$.

In addition, consider the following Σ-structures: the first structure $\mathcal{K}_2$ has a domain $K_2 = \{0,1\}$ with $e^{K_2} = V^2 \setminus \Delta$; e is interpreted as the relation of difference; the second structure $\mathcal{K}_3$ has a domain $K_3 = \{0,1,2\}$ with $e_3^K = V^2 \setminus \Delta$ (of three elements, at least two are distinct).

It can be easily checked that finding a 2-coloring (a 3-coloring, respectively) of an undirected graph corresponds to finding a morphism of U to K_2 (to K_3, respectively).

More generally:

DEFINITION 12.3.– *Let Σ be a finite relational signature, and K, a Σ-structure. Given a Σ-structure U, the constraint satisfaction problems $CSP(K)$ consists in deciding whether there exists a morphism of U to K. The Σ-structure K is called the* template *of the problem.*

For instance, the 2-colorability problem (the 3-colorability problem, respectively) for a graph is CSP(K_2) (CSP(K_3), respectively).

EXAMPLE 12.4.– Consider the signature $\Sigma = \{e\}$ again, where e denotes a binary relation. A directed graph (N, C) defines a Σ-structure $\mathcal{N}$ of domain N, where e^N is interpreted as the set C of the arcs of the directed graph.

Consider the Σ-structure $(\mathbb{Q}, <)$ whose domain is $\mathbb{Q}$, where the interpretation of e is the usual relation of precedence on $\mathbb{Q}$.

It can be easily seen that there exists a morphism of $\mathcal{N}$ to $(\mathbb{Q}, <)$ if, and only if, the graph is acyclic. Hence the acyclicity problem for a directed graph is CSP($(\mathbb{Q}, <)$).

EXAMPLE 12.5.– Let us again consider the structure PA which is defined by the 9-tuple $(\mathbb{Q}, \leq, <, =, \neq, \geq, >, \mathbf{1}, \mathbf{0})$ (where the last two symbols denote the universal relation and the empty relation, respectively) — a structure which we have considered in the previous chapters — as a representation of the Point algebra.

Then as noted in the beginning of this chapter, CSP(PA) is precisely the general consistency problem for the Point algebra: namely, given a network labeled by the set of eight relation symbols, is there an assignment of variables to values in $\mathbb{Q}$ such that the constraints expressed by the network are satisfied?

12.5.3. *Polymorphisms and invariant relations*

Let $\mathcal{U}$ be a Σ-structure of domain U.

12.5.3.1. *Operations, substructures, and products*

Recall that an n-ary *operation* on U is a map $f \colon U^n \to U$.

If $\mathcal{U}$ is a Σ-structure of domain U, and V, a subset of U, then the Σ-structure of domain V such that for any $r \in \Sigma$, we have $r^V = r^U \cap V^{v(r)}$, is called the *substructure induced* on V, denoted by $\mathcal{U}|_V$.

For any pair of Σ-structures $\mathcal{U}$ and $\mathcal{V}$, the product $U \times V$, equipped with the "product" interpretation of the relation symbols, is a Σ-structure called the product of $\mathcal{U}$ and $\mathcal{V}$; it is denoted by $\mathcal{U} \times \mathcal{V}$; for each $r \in \Sigma$, $((x_1, y_1), \ldots (x_{v(r)}, y_{v(r)})) \in r^{U \times V}$ if, and only if, $(x_1, \ldots, x_{v(r)}) \in r^U$ and $(y_1, \ldots, y_{v(r)}) \in r^V$.

12.5.3.2. *Polymorphisms*

DEFINITION 12.4.– *Let $\mathcal{U}$ be a Σ-structure of domain U. Let $k \geq 1$. A polymorphism φ of $\mathcal{U}$ is a morphism $\varphi \colon \mathcal{U}^k \to \mathcal{U}$.*

In other words, polymorphisms are operations which preserve the relational structure. They play a fundamental role in the study of CSPs and their complexity.

EXAMPLE 12.6.– If $\mathcal{U}$ is a Σ-structure, and $k \geq 1$, an integer, the k canonical projections $\mathrm{pr}_i \colon \mathcal{U}^k \to \mathcal{U}$ $(1 \leq i \leq k)$ are polymorphisms.

EXAMPLE 12.7.– For the Σ-structure $(\mathbb{Q}, \leq, <)$, the ternary operation called the *median* defined by $m(x, y, z) = b$ if $\{x, y, z\} = \{a, b, c\}$, with $a \leq b \leq c$, is a polymorphism.

12.5.4. *pp-Definable relations and preservation*

A relational structure is by definition equipped with a set of relations Γ. A polymorphism, also by definition, preserves all the relations of Γ. Does it preserve other relations?

DEFINITION 12.5.– *A relation is* pp-definable *(definable by positive primitive formulas) if it can be defined by a first order formula with equality using only existential quantification and conjunction.*

NOTATION.– If $\mathcal{U}$ is a relational structure, $\langle \mathcal{U} \rangle$ denotes the set of relations which are pp-definable from $\mathcal{U}$.

This set of relations is also called the *clone of relations* generated by Γ. It coincides with the set of relations that can be obtained by using the joint and projection operators of database theory.

EXAMPLE 12.8.– Let R and S be two binary relations. The relations R^t and $(R \circ S)$ are pp-definable from $\{R, S\}$. Indeed, $R^t(x, y)$ is defined by the atomic formula $R(y, x)$, and $(R \circ S)(x, y)$ is defined by the formula $(\exists z) R(x, z) \wedge S(z, y)$.

The projections of a relation R are also pp-definable from R; for example, if R is a ternary relation: $pr_1(R)(x)$ is defined by $(\exists x_2 x_3) R(x_1, x_2, x_3)$.

The k-ary relation $\Delta_k = \{(x, \ldots, x) \in U^k\}$ is defined by the formula $x_1 = \cdots = x_k$, hence it is pp-definable.

PROPOSITION 12.1.– *A pp-definable relation is preserved by all polymorphisms.*

pp-definability and complexity are related in a fundamental way:

PROPOSITION 12.2.– *If U and V are two relational structures, and if every relation of U is pp-definable from V, then there is a polynomial reduction of $CSP(U)$ to $CSP(V)$.*

For finite relational structures, the property of preservation of proposition 12.1 characterizes pp-definable relations:

THEOREM 12.1.– *Let U be a relational structure on a finite universe U. Then, a relation is pp-definable from U if, and only if, it is preserved by all polymorphisms.*

12.5.5. *A Galois correspondence*

Given a relational structure and a set of relations Γ on its universe U, let $\mathrm{Pol}(\Gamma)$ be the set of operations which preserve all the relations of Γ. Conversely, given a set F of operations on U, let $\mathrm{Inv}(F)$ be the set of relations which are preserved by all the operations of F.

The pair of maps $(\mathrm{Pol}, \mathrm{Inv})$ defines a *Galois correspondence* (see Appendix B) between the relations on U and the operations on U [PÖS 79, BOD 07c].

For any set of relations Γ, we have the inclusion $\langle \Gamma \rangle \subseteq \mathrm{Inv}(\mathrm{Pol}(\Gamma))$. But in the general case this inclusion is strict.

However, in the finite case, theorem 12.1 is equivalent to the following statement:

THEOREM 12.2.– *Let U be a relational structure with a finite universe U. Then, $\langle \Gamma \rangle = \mathrm{Inv}(\mathrm{Pol}(\Gamma))$.*

Since the knowledge of the polymorphisms of a relational structure U determines that of $\langle U \rangle$, the relative complexity of two problems is reflected in terms of the polymorphisms of the corresponding structures:

THEOREM 12.3.– *Let $\mathcal{U}$ and $\mathcal{V}$ be two relational structures. If $\mathrm{Pol}(\mathcal{V}) \subseteq \mathrm{Pol}(\mathcal{U})$, then $CSP(\mathcal{U})$ can be polynomially reduced to $CSP(\mathcal{V})$.*

Recall that the general intuition is that a language is complex if it is very expressive, and hence accepts few polymorphisms. In particular:

PROPOSITION 12.3.– *([BOD 07c]) Let $\mathcal{U}$ be a relational structure with a universe having at least two elements. If $\mathrm{Pol}(\mathcal{U})$ contains only the projections, then $CSP(\mathcal{U})$ is NP-difficult.*

12.6. Clones of operations

If $\mathcal{U}$ is a relational structure, the set $\mathrm{Pol}(\mathcal{U})$ is an example of a clone of operations:

DEFINITION 12.6.– *A set of operations $\mathcal{P}$ on a set U is a* clone of operations *if it has the following properties*:

– $\mathcal{P}$ *contains all projections, i.e. the operations $pr_i^n \colon U^n \to U (1 \leq i \leq n)$ defined by $pr_i^n(u_1, \ldots, u_n) = u_i$;*

– $\mathcal{P}$ *is stable by composition, where the composition of $f \colon U^n \to U$ with a sequence $(g_1, \ldots, g_n)$ of m-ary operations is the m-ary operation h defined by:*

$$h(u_1, \ldots, u_m) = f(g_1(u_1, \ldots, u_m), \ldots, g_n(u_1, \ldots, u_m))$$

For finite structures, the study of complexity reduces to the study of idempotent clones, i.e. of clones that contain only idempotent polymorphisms.

DEFINITION 12.7.– *A map $f \colon U^n \to U$ is idempotent if $f(u, \ldots, u) = u$.*

THEOREM 12.4.– *Let U be a finite relational structure. There exists a finite relational structure $\mathcal{U}_1$ where all the polymorphisms are idempotent such that $CSP(\mathcal{U})$ and $CSP(\mathcal{U}_1)$ are polynomially equivalent.*

In the Boolean case, that is when the universe U contains two elements, there is a precise characterization of idempotent clones.

NOTATION.– Let $U = \{0, 1\}$ be the Boolean algebra with two elements, where $0 < 1$. The operations $\wedge$ and $\vee$ are two binary operations. The ternary operations maj (for majority) and min (for minority) are defined by:

$$\mathrm{maj}(0, 0, 1) = \mathrm{maj}(0, 1, 0) = \mathrm{maj}(1, 0, 0) = 0$$
$$\mathrm{maj}(1, 1, 0) = \mathrm{maj}(1, 0, 1) = \mathrm{maj}(0, 1, 1) = 1$$
$$\mathrm{min}(0, 0, 1) = \mathrm{min}(0, 1, 0) = \mathrm{min}(1, 0, 0) = 1$$
$$\mathrm{min}(1, 1, 0) = \mathrm{min}(1, 0, 1) = \mathrm{min}(0, 1, 1) = 0$$

THEOREM 12.5.– *[BOD 07b] An idempotent clone on the set $\{0, 1\}$ either contains only the projections, or it contains one of the four operations $\wedge, \vee$, maj, and min.*

COROLLARY 12.1.– *Let $\mathcal{U}$ be a relational structure whose universe contains two elements, and such that $\mathrm{Pol}(\mathcal{U})$ is idempotent. If none of the four operations $\wedge$, $\vee$, maj, and min is a polymorphism, then $CSP(\mathcal{U})$ is NP-complete.*

This result extends to arbitrary clones. Let $c_i\colon U \to U (0 \leq i \leq 1)$ such that $c_i(u) = i$.

THEOREM 12.6.– *[BOD 07b] Let $\mathcal{U}$ be a relational structure whose universe contains two elements. If none of the six operations $\wedge$, $\vee$, maj, min, c_0 and c_1 is a polymorphism, then $CSP(\mathcal{U})$ is NP-complete.*

12.6.1. *The Boolean case*

The complexity of Boolean problems was determined by Schaeffer [SCH 78] who proved the following theorem:

THEOREM 12.7.– *[Schaeffer's dichotomy theorem] Let $\mathcal{U}$ be a relational structure on the universe $U = \{0, 1\}$. Then $CFP(\mathcal{U})$ is polynomial if at least one of the following conditions is satisfied:*

1) *every relation contains $(0, \ldots, 0)$;*

2) *every relation contains $(1, \ldots, 1)$;*

3) *every relation is equivalent to a conjunction of binary clauses;*

4) *every relation is equivalent to a conjunction of Horn clauses (i.e. clauses with most one positive literal);*

5) *every relation is equivalent to a conjunction of co-Horn clauses (i.e. clauses with at most one negative literal);*

6) *every relation can be defined by a system of linear equations on the finite field $\mathbb{F}_2$.*

Otherwise, $CFP(\mathcal{U})$ is NP-complete.

It is conjectured that CSP(Γ) has the dichotomy property, namely: for any finite relational structure Γ, the CSP(γ) problem is either polynomial or NP-complete. Schaeffer's theorem shows that this is true for Boolean universes. The same result also holds for universes with three elements [BUL 02].

While theorem 12.6 gives a sufficient condition for NP-completeness, Schaeffer's theorem fully characterizes it. Let us now describe the correspondence between the conditions of these two results.

To say that the constant unary map c_0 (c_1, respectively) of $\{0, 1\}$ to itself preserves R precisely means that R contains $(0, \ldots, 0)$ $((1, \ldots, 1),$ respectively). Thus, we see that condition 1) (condition 2), respectively) of theorem 12.7 is equivalent to the operation c_0 (c_1, respectively) being a polymorphism.

It can also be shown that the operation min preserves a relation on $\{0, 1\}$ if, and only if, this relation is the set of solutions of a system of linear equations on the finite field $\mathbb{F}_2$. Hence condition 6) of theorem 12.7 is equivalent to min being a polymorphism.

Conditions 4) and 5) are related to the existence of polymorphisms which allow to apply the so-called hyper-arc consistency procedure, which is polynomial, to solve the CSP problem. We will not develop the topic here and we refer the reader to Chapter 4 of [BOD 07b] for more details.

As for condition 3), the ternary operation maj is majority function, a particular case of *quasi-unanimity* functions. The general results we describe below in the next section imply that in this case, the 3-consistency procedure can be applied to compute globally consistent instances.

12.7. From local consistency to global consistency

Properties of local consistency play a significant role in many constraint satisfaction problems. Recall that by definition, a constraint network with n vertices is k-consistent if any partial solution on $(k - 1)$ vertices extends to a solution on k vertices. It is strongly k-consistent if it is k'-consistent for $k' \leq k$. It is globally consistent if it is strongly n-consistent.

When (strong) k-consistency for some k implies global consistency, we speak of a "local-to-global" property: the idea is that it is enough to test the consistency "locally" on subsets of variables to solve the consistency problem.

In the case of finite structures, Jeavons, Cohen, and Cooper [JEA 98] show that the local-to-global property is related to the existence of certain types of operations.

DEFINITION 12.8.– *A map* $f \colon U^n \to U$ *of arity at least 3 is a* near-unanimity *operation if, for all* $u, v \in U$, *it satisfies*:

$$f(v, u, u, \ldots, u) = f(u, v, u, u, \ldots, u) = \cdots = f(u, u, \ldots, v) = u$$

The main result is the following theorem:

THEOREM 12.8.– *Let* $\mathcal{U} = (U, \Gamma)$ *be a finite relational structure. For any integer* $k \geq 3$, *the following conditions are equivalent*:

1) *every relation R of Γ is preserved by some near-unanimity operation v of arity k;*

2) *strong k-consistency implies global consistency.*

We have mentioned above that this result applies in particular to the Boolean case: when the considered structure admits the ternary operation of majority maj, strong 3-consistency implies global consistency. We refer the reader to [JEA 98] for an in-depth presentation and many examples.

Theorem 12.8 remains true when infinite universes are considered. A direct application of its use in this case is to the STP (*simple temporal problems*) calculus (section 6.2). Let us recall that the corresponding constraints are of type $x_i - x_j \leq d$, where the set U is $\mathbb{Q}$ and where $d \in \mathbb{Q}$. The ternary operation of median respects these constraints, which means that the theorem can be applied. We thus obtain a proof of the fact that strong 3-consistency implies global consistency for STP . This result was initially proved in [DEC 91].

12.8. The infinite case

The approach that we have sketched for finite structures does not *a priori* extend directly to infinite relational structures. However, most of the spatial or temporal qualitative formalisms are interpreted in infinite universes.

The approach we have described so far makes a crucial use of the fact that pp-definable relations on a given algebraic structure are characterized by the polymorphisms of this structure. Now, for infinite universes, the identity $\langle \Gamma \rangle = $ Inv(Pol(Γ) is not necessarily true, as shown by the following counterexample ([COH 06a], example 8.55):

EXAMPLE 12.9.– Let $\Gamma = \{R_1, R_2, R_3\}$ on the set of natural integers $\mathbb{N}$ be defined as follows: R_1 is the quaternary relation $R_1 = \{(a, b, c, d) \,|\, a = b \text{ or } c = d\}$, $R2$ the unary relation $R_2 = \{(1)\}$, and R_3 the binary relation $R_3 = \{(a, a+1) \,|\, a \in \mathbb{N}\}$. It can be shown that the only polymorphisms of this relational structure are the projections, so that Inv(Pol(Γ)) is the set of *all* relations on $\mathbb{N}$. However, there exist relations, like the unary relation defining the set of even integers, which do not belong to $\langle \Gamma \rangle$.

12.8.1. *Homogeneous and $\aleph_0$-categorical structures*

A class of infinite structures which has a good behavior is the class of countable structures which are *homogeneous*, i.e. such that any isomorphism of a finite sub-structure of this structure extends to an automorphism of the structure itself.

EXAMPLE 12.10.– Let $(\mathbb{Q}, <)$ be the linear order of rational numbers. Any strictly increasing injective map $f: \{q_1, \ldots, q_k\} \rightarrow \mathbb{Q}$, where $\{q_1, \ldots, q_k\} \subset \mathbb{Q}$ can be extended to an automorphism of $\mathbb{Q}$. hence the relational structure $(\mathbb{Q}, <)$ is homogeneous.

These structures allow the elimination of quantifiers. Moreover, if their signature contains a finite number of symbols for each arity, they are $\aleph_0$-categorical: their first order theory has only one countable model up to isomorphism.

As above, adding relations which have a positive primitive definition to $\mathcal{U}$ does not change the complexity of CSP($\mathcal{U}$).

Bodirsky and Nešetřil show that the characterization of the pp-definable relations in terms of invariants of its polymorphisms still holds for $\aleph_0$-categorical structures:

THEOREM 12.9.– *[BOD 03b] Let $\mathcal{U} = (U, R_1, \ldots, R_k)$ be a relational structure, where U is a countable infinite set. If this structure is $\aleph_0$-categorical, then we have $\langle \Gamma \rangle =$* Inv(Pol(Γ)).

In other words, for these structures, a relation is *pp*-definable if, and only if, it is preserved by all polymorphisms.

EXAMPLE 12.11.– The intersection, inversion, and composition operations are pp-definable, and hence, for any subset S of Allen's interval algebra, the subalgebra S' generated by S is contained in $\langle S \rangle$. As a consequence, CSP(S) and CSP(S') are of polynomially equivalent complexities: in order to study complexity in Allen's algebra, we may restrict ourselves to subalgebras.

Theorem 12.9 shows that the study of the polymorphisms of relational structures whose universe is the set of bounded and closed intervals of $\mathbb{Q}$, and whose relations are subalgebras of Allen's relations, can be used for the classification of tractable subsets. In what follows, based on [BOD 09], we describe the relations between the properties of local consistency and global consistency more precisely.

12.8.2. *Quasi near-unanimity operations*

We have seen the role played by near-unanimity functions in the study of finite problems. Here, the relevant notion is that of *quasi near-unanimity* functions (or QNU functions):

DEFINITION 12.9.– *An operation $f \colon U^k \to U$, for $k \geq 3$, is* quasi near-unanimity *if for all x, y, it satisfies $f(x, \ldots, x, y) = f(x, \ldots, x, y, x) = \cdots = f(y, x, \ldots, x) = f(x, \ldots, x)$.*

For example, the median function is a ternary QNU function. Moreover, this function defines a polymorphism of the structure $(\mathbb{Q}, \leq, <)$.

Proof. Let us show that the relation $\leq$ is preserved by the median function. Let $(q_1, q_1'), (q_2, q_2'), (q_3, q_3')$ such that $q_i, \leq q_i', 1 \leq i \leq 3$. After carrying out a permutation of indexes if necessary, we may assume that $q_1 \leq q_2 \leq q_3$, which implies that the median of (q_1, q_2, q_3) is q_2. Under these conditions, q_2' and q_3' are on the right of q_2, and hence the median of (q_1', q_2', q_3') is also necessarily on the right of q_2.   □

Let $\mathcal{U} = (U, \Gamma)$ be a relational structure. Γ is a set of relations on the universe U. We may associate with $\mathcal{U}$ an algebra $\mathsf{Al}(\mathcal{U})$, whose domain is U, and whose operations are the polymorphisms of $\mathcal{U}$ (hence we introduce a symbol to name each of them).

The algebra $\mathsf{Al}(\mathcal{U})$ is *locally closed*: this means that if $f \colon U^K \to U$ is a k-ary operation such that for any finite part $A \subseteq U$, there exists a function $g \in \mathsf{Al}(\mathcal{U})$ such that $f(u) = g(u)$ for any $u \in A^k$, then f is an operation of $\mathsf{Al}(\mathcal{U})$.

DEFINITION 12.10.– *A polymorphism f of a $\aleph_0$-categorical structure $\mathcal{U}$ is* oligopotent *if the unary function $u \mapsto f(u, \ldots, u)$ is contained in the locally closed clone generated by the automorphisms of $\mathcal{U}$.*

DEFINITION 12.11.– *A structure $\mathcal{U}$ is k-decomposable if any relation of $\mathcal{U}$ can be defined by a conjunction of at most k-ary pp-definable relations of $\mathcal{U}$.*

We have the following theorems:

THEOREM 12.10.– *[BOD 06, BOD 08] Let $k \geq 3$. A $\aleph_0$-categorical relational structure $\mathcal{U}$ of bounded maximal arity has a k-ary oligopotent quasi near-unanimity polymorphism if, and only if, any strongly k-consistent instance of the $CSP(\mathcal{U})$ is globally consistent.*

THEOREM 12.11.– *[BOD 07a] Let $k \geq 3$. A $\aleph_0$-categorical relational structure $\mathcal{U}$ has a k-ary quasi near-unanimity oligopotent polymorphism if, and only if, it is $(k-1)$-decomposable.*

12.8.3. *Application to the point algebra*

The Point algebra corresponds to the structure with universe $\mathbb{Q}$ equipped with the eight binary relations $\leq, <, \geq, >, =, \neq, \emptyset$ and $\mathbb{Q}^2$. For this algebra, Koubarakis [KOU 97] has shown that strong 5-consistency implies global consistency. Using theorem 12.10, this implies the following theorem:

THEOREM 12.12.– *The Point algebra has a quasi near-unanimity oligopotent polymorphism of arity 5, but no quasi near-unanimity oligopotent polymorphism of arity 4.*

A direct proof of this result is given in [BOD 07b]; it uses the properties of partial orders.

A detailed study of fragments of the Point algebra is also presented in the same paper.

12.8.4. *Application to the* RCC−5 *calculus*

Let X be an infinite countable set. The relational structure considered here, denoted by B_1, has a universe which is the set $P(X)\setminus\{\emptyset\}$ of non-empty subsets of X. The basic relations considered are DR, PO, PP, PPI, and EQ which are defined in the usual manner. For example, DR(u, v) is true if the two sets u and v are disjoint, PP(u, v) is true if $u \subset v$, etc.

The relational structure obtained from B_1 by adding the 2^5 disjunctive relations corresponds to the constraint satisfaction problem for RCC−5, which is NP-complete.

The relational structure B_1 is not $\aleph_0$-categorical. However, Bodirsky and Chen show that the techniques described in this chapter can be applied to study its complexity, by replacing it with a structure which is $\aleph_0$-categorical,

This structure is constructed by using the class of all finite substructures of B_1 up to isomorphism. A technique due to Fraïssé is applied. Here is an overview of the construction, as described in [BOD 09].

DEFINITION 12.12.– *(Age of a relational structure) The* age *of a relational structure U is the class of all finite substructures which can be embedded in U.*

EXAMPLE 12.12.– Let $(\mathbb{N}, <)$ be the natural integers equipped with the usual strict ordering. The finite substructures of this structure are the finite linear orders, which are characterized up to isomorphism by their cardinal. The corresponding age is hence a countable class.

Now, let $(\mathbb{Q}, <)$ be the rational numbers with their usual ordering. The corresponding age is the same class, namely that of finite linear orders.

DEFINITION 12.13.– *(Amalgamation class) A class of finite structures C is an* amalgamation class *if it is non-empty, if it is stable by isomorphism and by taking induced substructures, and if it has the amalgamation property: for all $A, B, C \in C$, and embeddings $i: A \to B$ and $j: A \to C$, there exist $D \in C$ and embeddings $g: B \to D$ and $h: C \to D$ which coincide with A, i.e. $gi = hj$.*

THEOREM 12.13.– *(Fraïssé, [FRA 00]) A countable class of finite relational structures of countable signature U is the age of a homogeneous countable structure if, and only* *if, it is an amalgamation class. In this case, this countable structure is unique up to isomorphism and is known as the Fraïssé limit of $\mathcal{U}$.*

EXAMPLE 12.13.– The class of finite linear orders is an amalgamation class. Its Fraïssé limit is the homogeneous structure $(\mathbb{Q}, <)$. The structure $(\mathbb{N}, <)$ has the same age as $(\mathbb{Q}, <)$, but is not homogeneous. For example, the embedding $i \colon \{1, 3\} \to \{4, 5\}$ does not extend to an automorphism.

Let $\mathcal{C}$ be the class of finite induced substructures of $\mathcal{B}_1$. Bodirsky and Chen show that this class is an amalgamation class. Consequently, it has a Fraïssé limit $\mathcal{B}_0$, which is $\aleph_0$-categorical. Moreover, it can be easily shown that $\mathrm{CSP}(\mathcal{B}_1) = \mathrm{CSP}(\mathcal{B}_0)$.

The next step consists in proving that, for any $k \geq 5$, there exists a quasi near-unanimity oligopotent polymorphism for the structure $\mathcal{B}_0$. We refer the reader to the paper for more details.

It follows that the property of "local-to-global" consistency holds for the basic relations of RCC-5, and also for the expansions of this language by disjunctions of negations of equalities with a bounded number of variables.

12.8.5. *Application to pointizable relations of Allen's algebra*

12.8.5.1. *Interpretations*

Let Σ and T be two relational signatures. Let $\mathcal{U}$ be a Σ-structure, and $\mathcal{V}$, a T-structure.

DEFINITION 12.14.– *[HOD 97] The σ-structure $\mathcal{U}$ has a* first order interpretation *in the T-structure $\mathcal{V}$) if there exists a natural integer d, called the* dimension *of the interpretation, together with:*

— *a first order T-formula $\delta(x_1, \ldots, x_d)$ called the* domain formula;

— *for each m-ary relation symbol R in Σ, a T-formula $\Phi_R(\bar{x}_1, \ldots, \bar{x}_m)$, where $\bar{x}_i$ denotes disjoint n-tuples of distinct variables; Φ_R is called the* defining formula *associated to R;*

— *a surjective map $h \colon \delta(\mathcal{V}^d) \to U$, called the* coordinate map.

such that for each relation R of $\mathcal{U}$ and for all $\bar{a}_i \in \delta(\mathcal{V}^d)$:

$$\mathcal{U} \models R(h(\bar{a}_1), \ldots, h(\bar{a}_m)) \Leftrightarrow \mathcal{V} \models \phi_R(h(\bar{a}_1)), \ldots, \bar{a}_m)$$

EXAMPLE 12.14.– *Fractions.* The standard construction of rational numbers as pairs of integers whose second element is non-zero corresponds to an interpretation of $\mathbb{Q}$ of dimension 2. Here, $\mathcal{U} = (\mathbb{Q}, =_{\mathbb{Q}})$, and $\mathcal{V}$ is the structure $(\mathbb{Z}, =_{\mathbb{Z}})$.

The domain formula here is $\delta(x_1, x_2) = \neg(x_2 =_Z 0)$. The defining formula $x_1.x_4 =_Z x_2.x_3$ is associated with the equality relation $=_Q$. The domain formula defines $\delta(\mathbb{Z}^2)$ as the set of pairs of integers whose second element is non-zero. The coordinate map surjectively sends this set on the set of rational fractions, which appear as equivalence classes of pairs of integers whose second element is non-zero.

EXAMPLE 12.15.– *Allen's interval algebra.* Here, intervals are seen as pairs of rational numbers, whose second element is strictly smaller than the first. More precisely, the structure $\mathcal{U} = (Int(\mathbb{Q}), \mathbf{B}_2)$, where $\mathbf{B}_2$ is the set of basic relation symbols, is interpreted in terms of pairs of rational numbers, that is elements of $V = (\mathbb{Q}, =, \neq)$. The domain formula $\delta(x_1, x_2)$ is $x_1 < x_2$. The coordinate map is the identity map which sends (x_1, x_2) with $x_1 < x_2$ to $(x_1, x_2) \in Int(\mathbb{Q})$. For each basic relation, there is a defining formula associated to it. For example, $x_2 = x_3$ is the defining formula associated to the relation $\mathsf{m}(x_1, x_2, x_3, x_4)$.

EXAMPLE 12.16.– *The Rectangle algebra.* Similarly, the structure corresponding to the rectangle algebra has a 2D interpretation in Allen's interval algebra. The domain formula is **true** (there is no restriction on considering an orthoaxial rectangle as a pair of intervals); the coordinate map is the identity, and the defining formulas define the basic relations of the calculus, which are pairs of Allen basic relations.

First order interpretations preserve the property of $\aleph_0$-categoricity:

PROPOSITION 12.4.– *[HOD 97] If V is $\aleph_0$-categorical, then any structure which a first order interpretation in V is $\aleph_0$-categorical as well.*

This result holds in particular for Allen's interval algebra and for the Rectangle algebra. More generally, it also implies the $\aleph_0$-categoricity of the formalisms "based on linear orders" considered in Chapter 9, which gives an alternative proof of this result.

12.8.6. *Applications to the study of complexity*

An interpretation is *primitive positive* if its domain formula δ, as well as all defining formulas ϕ_R, are primitive positive.

PROPOSITION 12.5.– *[BOD 07b] Let V be a $\aleph_0$-categorical relational structure, and let $\mathcal{U}$ be a structure which has a primitive positive interpretation in V. If strong k-consistency implies global consistency for CSP(V), then $\mathcal{U}$ has a k-ary quasi near-unanimity polymorphism.*

This proposition, together with an additional argument which we will not elaborate here — and which ensures that the polymorphism whose proposition states the existence is oligopotent — can be applied to the pointizable relations of Allen's interval algebra, resulting in a proof of the following theorem:

THEOREM 12.14.– *For pointizable relations of Allen's interval algebra, strong 5-consistency implies global consistency.*

A similar argument can be applied for the Rectangle algebra: for basic relations of the Rectangle algebra, strong 5-consistency implies global consistency.

12.9. Disjunctive constraints and refinements

The global approach of the complexity of CSPs — in which, for a given formalism, the question is to determine the complexity of the corresponding consistency problem — has been complemented by constructive, or incremental, approaches [COH 00, BRO 00b, BRO 02]. Typically, we consider two "simple" formalisms, for example, whose corresponding CSP is tractable, and we study the complexity of a formalism obtained by appropriately "combining" these simple formalisms. Combining two formalisms is accomplished by using disjunctive constraints, as explained below. At the present state of knowledge, two provisional conclusions emerge from this work: on the one hand, combining simple formalisms is no guarantee that their composition remains simple; on the other hand, a suitable concept of independence makes it possible to build formalisms in an interesting way while preserving 'simplicity" at the same time.

12.9.1. *Disjunctive constraints*

DEFINITION 12.15.– *Let R_1 be an n-ary relation and R_2 an m-ary relation on the same set U. Then, the disjunction of R_1 and R_2 is the (m + n)-ary relation defined by*:

$$R_1 \vee R_2 = \{(u_1, \ldots, u_{m+n}) \mid (u_1, \ldots, u_n) \in R_1) \vee (u_{n+1}, \ldots, u_{n+m} \in R_2)\}$$

This definition naturally extends to two constraint languages Γ and Δ on the same domain U:

DEFINITION 12.16.– *Let Γ and Δ be two constraint languages on the same domain U. Then, the constraint language $\Gamma \stackrel{\vee}{\times} \Delta$ is defined by*:

$$\Gamma \stackrel{\vee}{\times} \Delta = \Gamma \Delta \vee \{R_1 \vee R_2 \mid R_1 \in \Gamma, R_2 \in \Delta\}$$

NOTATION.– Let Δ be a constraint language. $\Delta^{\vee 1}$ denotes the language Δ, $\Delta^{\vee 2}$ the language $\Delta \stackrel{\vee}{\times} \Delta$, and more generally, for $n \geq 3$, we define $\Delta^{\vee(n+1)} = \Delta^{\vee n} \stackrel{\vee}{\times} \Delta$. Lastly, we set $\Delta^* = \bigcup_{i=1}^{\infty} \Delta^{\vee i}$.

EXAMPLE 12.17.– Let Λ be the set of relations on $\{0, 1\}$ which can be defined by a single literal. This language is obviously tractable (in linear time).

The language $\Lambda^{\vee 2}$ contains all Boolean constraints defined by clauses containing at most two literals. Hence CSP($\Lambda^{\vee 2}$) is the 2-SAT problem, which is tractable.

The language $\Lambda^{\vee 3}$ is that of Boolean constraints defined by clauses containing at most three literals. Hence CSP($\Lambda^{\vee 3}$) is the 3-SAT problem, which is NP-complete.

In particular, this example shows that the composition of tractable formalisms by using disjunction may be tractable or not.

12.9.2. Guaranteed satisfaction property

DEFINITION 12.17.– *A set Γ of constraints has the* guaranteed satisfaction property *if any finite part $C \subseteq \Gamma$ is consistent.*

A first result of preservation of tractability is the following:

THEOREM 12.15.– *[COH 00] Let Γ and Δ be two sets of constraints. If Γ has the guaranteed satisfaction property, then CSP($\Gamma \stackrel{\times}{\vee} \Delta$) also has the guaranteed satisfaction property, and is therefore tractable.*

EXAMPLE 12.18.– The set Λ of Boolean constraints defined by a single literal of example 12.17 contains the set Γ_0 of constraints defined by a single *negative* literal. The latter obviously has the guaranteed satisfaction property, since the assignment of value **false** to all variables is a solution.

Theorem 12.15 implies that the set of constraints $\Gamma_0 \stackrel{\times}{\vee} \Lambda^*$ also has this property, and hence that CSP($\Gamma_0 \stackrel{\times}{\vee} \Lambda^*$) is tractable. These are constraints defined by clauses containing at least one negative literal, which correspond to relations that all contain $(0, \ldots, 0)$: this is precisely the first class of relations of Schaeffer's theorem (theorem 12.7).

Symmetrically, if Γ_1 is the set of constraints defined by a single positive literal, $\Gamma_1 \stackrel{\times}{\vee} \Lambda^*$ corresponds to constraints which can be defined by clauses containing at least one positive literal, which corresponds to the second class of Schaeffer's theorem.

EXAMPLE 12.19.– Let Γ be the set of constraints which can be defined by the negation of a linear equality on the set of real numbers $\mathbb{R}$, i.e. expressions of the form $\Sigma a_i x_i \neq b$, where a_i and b are real numbers.

Here again, it is clear that Γ has the guaranteed satisfaction property: an instance of the problem corresponds to considering $\mathbb{R}^n$ from which a finite number of hyperplanes is excluded, which is a non-empty subset of $\mathbb{R}^n$.

Consequently, for any set of constraints Δ on the real numbers, the constraint language $\Gamma \stackrel{\times}{\vee} \Delta^*$ has the guaranteed satisfaction property, and hence the CSP($\Gamma \stackrel{\times}{\vee} \Delta^*$) is tractable.

This applies in particular to the language Δ, which contains the constraints of Γ and the constraints defined by a single weak inequality, i.e. an expression of the form $\Sigma a_i x_i \leq b$, where a_i and b are real numbers.

The corresponding constraint language $\Gamma \stackrel{\times}{\vee} \Delta^*$ contains constraints such as:

$$x_1 + x_3 + x_5 \neq 7$$
$$(3x_1 + x_5 - 4x_3 \neq 7) \vee (2x_1 + 3x_2 - 4x_3 \neq 4) \vee (x_2 + x_3 + x_5 \leq 7)$$
$$(3x_1 + x_5 - 4x_3 \neq 7) \vee (2x_1 + 3x_2 - 4x_3 \leq 4) \vee (x_2 + x_3 + x_5 \leq 7)$$
$$(4x_1 + x_3 \neq 3) \vee (5x_2 - 3x_5 + x_4 \neq 6)$$

12.9.3. The k- independence property

To go further, Cohen *et al.* introduce the more refined concept xof k-independence.

NOTATION.– Let Γ and Δ be two sets of constraints. Then, $CSP_{\Delta \leq k}(\Gamma \cup \Delta)$ denotes the subproblem of $CSP(\Gamma \cup \Delta)$ formed by all the instances of the problem which contain at most k constraints belonging to Δ.

DEFINITION 12.18.– *Let Γ and Δ be two constraint languages on a set U. Then Δ is k-independent with respect to Γ if the following condition is satisfied: any of instance of $CSP(\Gamma \cup \Delta)$ with set of constraints C has a solution provided that any instance of $CSP_{\Delta \leq k}(\Gamma \cup \Delta)$ with constraints $C' \subseteq C$ has a solution.*

This means that the satisfiability of an arbitrary set of constraints of Δ can be determined by considering only k of these constraints simultaneously, even for arbitrary constraints of Γ.

Under these conditions, one has the following theorem:

THEOREM 12.16.– *[COH 00, BRO 02] Let Γ and Δ be two constraints languages on a set U such that the $CSP_{\Delta \leq 1}(\Gamma \cup \Delta)$ is tractable. The constraint language $\Gamma \stackrel{\times}{\vee} \Delta^*)$ is tractable if Δ is 1-independent with respect to Γ. Otherwise, it is NP-complete.*

This result implies in particular [COH 00] that the Boolean constraints defined by Horn clauses, or symmetrically, by clauses containing at most one negative literal, are tractable, which corresponds to two classes of Schaeffer's theorem.

Another significant example is the following:

EXAMPLE 12.20.– Let U be the set of real numbers, or the set of rational numbers. Let Γ be the constraint language on U containing the constraints defined by a single weak inequality. Let Δ be the language of constraints on U defined by a single negation of a weak equality.

Then the $\text{CSP}_{\Delta \leq 1}(\Gamma \cup \Delta)$ is tractable: it can be determined in polynomial time whether a set C of inequalities is consistent, by using Khachian's linear programming algorithm [KHA 79] or Karmarkar's algorithm [KAR 84]. Then, for a constraint C which is a negation of an equality, it can be determined in polynomial time whether $C \cup \{C\}$ is consistent, by using this algorithm to determine if C implies the negation of C.

The fact that Δ is 1-independent with respect to Γ is a consequence of the geometrical interpretation of constraints in terms of excluded half-spaces and hyperplanes [KOU 96].

The theorem can be applied, which shows that the set of *linear Horn relations* $\Gamma \overset{\times}{\vee} \Delta^*$ is tractable.

12.9.4. *Refinements*

Let $\mathbf{B}$ be a set of binary relations which is a partition of $U \times U$ (hence a JEPD set of basic relations). Given a subset $S \subseteq 2^B$, we consider the CSP(S): an instance of this problem consists of a set V of variables on U, i.e. variables which can be instantiated by elements of U, and of a finite set of constraints $(x, y) \in R$, where $x, y \in V$ and $R \in S$.

A *refinement* of a constraint $R(x, y)$ is a constraint $R'(x, y)$, where $R' \subseteq R$. A refinement of a set of constraints Θ is a set of constraints Θ' such that each constraint of Θ' is a refinement of a constraint of Θ. Intuitively, a refinement consists of a set of possible reinforcements of each constraint of S.

Let us consider a set of constraints Θ whose variables are $x_1, \ldots, x_n$.

DEFINITION 12.19.– *Let* $S, T \in 2^B$. *We say that* S *can be reduced to* T *by refinement if, for any relation* $R \in S$, *there exists a relation* $R_T \in T$ *with* $R_T \subseteq R$, *and if any algebraically closed set of constraints* Θ *on* S *can be refined to a set* Θ' *by replacing* $R(x_i, x_j) \in \Theta$ *with* $R_T(x_i, x_j) \in \Theta'$ *for* $i < j$, *such that the algebraic closure algorithm applied to* Θ *does not produce an inconsistency.*

EXAMPLE 12.21.– Let us start with a very simple example. It involves constraints which are relations of Allen's interval algebra. The set S is the set of relations $\{\{p, m\}, \{pi, mi\}, o, s, d, f, oi, if, di, fi, eq\}$. We have noted in Chapter 4 (section 4.10.3.1) that any algebraically closed network on S can be refined by replacing $\{p, m\}$ with p and $\{pi, mi\}$ with pi, and by not changing the other basic relations, resulting in a network on the set $\mathbf{B}_2$ of Allen basic relations, and that the algebraic closure of this refined network does not contain the empty relation.

The set S can thus be reduced to the set of basic relations by refinement.

The previous example has only an illustrative interest. But the importance of the notion of refinement is due to the following theorem:

PROPOSITION 12.6.– *If the algebraic closure algorithm is a decision procedure for the consistency problem of T, and if S can be reduced to T by refinement, the algebraic closure algorithm is also a decision procedure for the consistency problem of S.*

Hence, if we know that algebraic closure can be used to decide consistency for a set of relations T, we can extend this result to a set of more complex relations S, provided that we know of suitable refinements.

12.9.4.1. *Automating the search for refinements*

Given a set of relations S, possible refinements of S can be described by refinement matrices:

DEFINITION 12.20.– *A refinement matrix M of S is a Boolean matrix which has a row for each element of S and a column for each (disjunctive) relation, such that $M[S][R]$, for $S \in S$ and $R \in 2^B$, is true if, and only if, S can be refined to R.*

EXAMPLE 12.22.– The refinement considered in example 12.21 is described by a refinement matrix which has 11 rows, one for each element of S, and 2^{13} columns. The row corresponding to $\{p, m\}$ contains the value true only for the column corresponding to p, and similarly that corresponding to $\{pi, mi\}$ contains the value true only for the column corresponding to pi. The other rows coincide with those of the *basic* refinement matrix, for which $M[S][R]$ is true if, and only if, $R = S$.

The refinement method developed by Renz [REN 99a] is based on the fact that, given a set of relations T for which the algebraic closure is a decision procedure, a set S, and a refinement matrix M of S to T, it is possible to determine *in an automated way* if there exists a refinement specified by M such that S can be reduced to T by refinement.

Indeed, if applying the algebraic closure algorithm to a network obtained by a refinement specified by a matrix M produces an inconsistency, this means that there exists a 3-tuple of constraints on S whose refinement by algebraic closure produces the empty relation. For checking that this cannot occur, we are thus led to testing a finite number of 3-tuples and a finite number of refinement options, for a finite number of relations.

Data: A set S and a refinement matrix M of S
Result: **failure** if the refinements specified by M can make an algebraically
        closed 3-tuple of relations of S inconsistent, **success** otherwise
$changes \leftarrow$ **true**
while $changes$ **do**
    | $Ma \leftarrow M$
    | **for each** *algebraically closed 3-tuple* $t = (R_{i,j}, R_{j,k}, R_{i,k})$ *of relations on*
    | S **do**
    | | **for each** *refinement* $t' = (R'_{i,j}, R'_{j,k}, R'_{i,k})$ *of* S *with*
    | | $Ma[R_{i,j}][R'_{i,j}] = Ma[R_{j,k}][R'_{j,k}] = Ma[R_{i,k}][R'_{i,k}] =$ **true do**
    | | | $t'' \leftarrow$ ALGEBRAIC-CLOSURE(t')
    | | | **if** $t'' = (R''_{i,j}, R''_{j,k}, R''_{i,k})$ *contains the empty relation* **then**
    | | | | **return** *failure*
    | | | **else**
    | | | | $M[R_{i,j}][R''_{i,j}] \leftarrow true$
    | | | | $M[R_{j,k}][R''_{j,k}] \leftarrow true$
    | | | | $M[R_{i,k}][R''_{i,k}] \leftarrow true$
    | | | **end**
    | | **end**
    | | **if** $M = Ma$ **then**
    | | | $changes \leftarrow$ **false**
    | | **end**
    | **end**
end
return *success*

Figure 12.2. *The* CHECK-REFINEMENTS *algorithm*

The CHECK-REFINEMENTS algorithm (Figure 12.2) provides an implementation of this idea:

THEOREM 12.17.– *Let* S, T *be two sets of relations, and* M *a refinement matrix of* S. *If the outcome of the* CHECK-REFINEMENTS *algorithm is* **success**, *the* GET-REFINEMENTS *algorithm returns a refinement matrix* M'. *If for each relation* $S \in S$, *there exists a relation* $S_T \in T$ *such that* $M'[S][S_T]$ *is true, then* S *can be reduced to* T *by refinement.*

Still, the task of determining a suitable refinement matrix is not automated. However, a simple heuristic method consists in eliminating the identity relations.

12.9.4.2. *Applications*

Renz shows that the refinement method can be applied for Allen's interval algebra to show that algebraic closure is a decision procedure for pre-convex relations. This can be deduced from the similar fact for pointizable relations (see section 1.3.2.2).

Indeed, the CHECK-REFINEMENTS and GET-REFINEMENTS algorithms can be applied to the pair S, T, where the class S is the class of pre-convex relations, and T is that of pointizable relations.

The refinement considered in this case is defined in the following way:

– to each 2D pre-convex relation, associate the sub-relation formed by the set of its 2D atoms;

– leave pre-convex relation of dimension less than 2 untouched.

Clearly, this refinement produces pointizable relations: if a pre-convex relation R is 2D, its convex closure $C(R)$ is obtained by adding 0 or 1D atoms to it; the characterization of pointizable relations (proposition 2.5) shows that the set $C(R)$ from which all basic relations with odd coordinate have been removed is pointizable; but this is exactly the set of 2D relations atoms of R, hence the result.

It is moreover clear that pre-convex relations of dimension less than 2 are pointizable.

In this case, the outcome of the CHECK-REFINEMENTS algorithm is **success**, so that the existence of refinement described above implies that the class of pre-convex relations can be reduced by refinement to that of pointizable relations, for which the algebraic closure method is known to be a decision procedure for consistency.

The same idea is applied in [REN 99a] to show that the two classes of RCC−8 denoted by C_8 and Q_8 (see section 4.14.4) can be reduced to $\hat{\mathcal{H}}_8$ by refinement. Since the algebraic closure method is a decision procedure for the latter, the same is true for these two classes.

The refinement used in this case is what is called the *identity refinement*, defined by the refinement matrix $M^{\neq}$: $M^{\neq}[S][T]$ is true if, and only if, $T = S \setminus \{\text{EQ}\}$.

Actually, for RCC−8 the refinement method achieves more than that, because of the following theorem:

THEOREM 12.18.– *The three classes $\hat{\mathcal{H}}_8$, C_8, and Q_8 can be reduced by refinement to the set of basic relations of RCC−8.*

For each of the three classes, a map of this class to the basic relations can be found so that an appropriate refinement is defined. As a consequence, for an algebraically closed network whose relations belong to one of these classes, a consistent scenario can be determined in $O(n^2)$ time (theorem 21 of [REN 99a]).

12.10. Refinements and independence

The principle of the refinement method is to replace constraints by stronger constraints without changing the consistency problem. In the case of disjunctive relations, one proceeds in the opposite direction, by adding constraints, and, under the assumption of 1-independence, one can still show that the consistency problem is not changed.

Broxvall, Jonsson, and Renz [BRO 00b] show that under certain conditions, the refinement technique can be used to obtain sets of 1-independent constraints.

In order to do this, particular refinements are considered:

DEFINITION 12.21.– *Let R be a disjunctive relation. The R-refinement matrix of a set of relations S is defined by the condition: $M^R[S][S']$ is true if, and only if, $S' = S \cap R$ and $S' \neq \emptyset$, or $S' = S$.*

DEFINITION 12.22.– *Let S be a set of disjunctive relations, and R a disjunctive relation. We say that R is a* refinement *of S if the outcome of* CHECK-REFINEMENTS (S, M^R) *is* success.

THEOREM 12.19.– *Let $S \subseteq 2^B$ be a set of relations for which algebraic closure is a decision procedure for consistency, and let M^R be a refinement matrix. If the outcome of* CHECK-REFINEMENTS (S, M^R) *is* success, *then R is 1-independent of S.*

This theorem allows us to test the 1-independence of a relation R relative to a set S in an automated way, by using the CHECK-REFINEMENTS (S, M^R) algorithm. If the algorithm terminates on a success, we may conclude to the independence of R relative to S. Otherwise, we cannot in general conclude (although no counterexample seems to be known). But in many cases, the following conjecture is holds:

CONJECTURE.– *Let $S \subseteq 2^B$ be a set of relations for which the algebraic closure is a decision procedure for consistency, and let M^R be a refinement matrix. Then* CHECK-REFINEMENTS $(S, M^R.)$ *algorithm terminates on a success if, and only if, R is 1-independent of S.*

There is a particular case where this conjecture can be proved. In order to describe it, let us introduce the following definition:

DEFINITION 12.23.– *Let $S \subseteq 2^B$ and $R \in S$. We say that the algebraic closure makes R* explicit *if, for any algebraically closed instance Θ of $CSP(S)$, we have the following property: if we have $R(h(x), h(y))$ for every solution $h: V \to U$ of Θ, then $S(x, y) \in \Theta$ and $S \subseteq R$.*

THEOREM 12.20.– *Let* $S \subseteq 2^B$ *and assume that* $R \in S$ *is 1-independent of* S. *Then,* CHECK-REFINEMENTS (S, M^R) *terminates on a success if, and only if, the algebraic closure makes the negation of* R *explicit.*

This applies in particular to the case where the algebraic closure procedure computes the minimal network:

Let $S \subseteq 2^B$ for which the algebraic closure procedure computes the minimal network, and let M^R be a refinement matrix. Then, CHECK-REFINEMENTS (S, M^R) terminates on a success if, and only if, R is 1-independent of S.

12.11. Historical note

As already mentioned above, Jeavons *et al.* have introduced the approach which systematically relates complexity issues to algebraic properties of clones associated to constraint satisfaction problems [JEA 95a, JEA 95b, JEA 97, JEA 98]. The extension to problems with infinite domain was studied in a series of works by Bodirsky, Nešetřil, Chen, Dalmau [BOD 03b, BOD 07b, BOD 08].

In addition, the work of Hirsch [HIR 96] has contributed to the development of a model-theoretic approach of temporal and spatial reasoning, with a specific focus on the concepts of homogeneity and interpretation.

The discovery of the properties of disjunctive linear constraints has been made independently by Jonsson and Bäckström [JON 98] and by Koubarakis [KOU 96] (see Appendix C). The development of the concept of refinement, and the impetus for using methods making a systematic use of this concept for finding tractable classes are due to Renz [REN 99a, REN 07a].

Chapter 13

Spatial Reasoning and Modal Logic

13.1. "The blind men and the elephant"

The Buddha tells the story of the blind men and the elephant (*Udana 68-69*): a king of the town of Savatthi ordered all the blind people of his kingdom to be brought to his palace and divided into several groups. An elephant was brought in, and each group was asked to describe what it looked like. "An elephant", said those who had touched the head, "is like a big jar". "It looks like a pillar", said those who had touched the foot. "No", said those who had touched the trunk, "it is like a plow". "Not at all", "it looks like a brush", said the blind men who had touched the tip of the tail. And so on it went, without the blind people being able to reach an agreement.

The blind men of Savatthi could only get a local view of the elephant. Modal logics are languages which, according to a "slogan" of Blackburn *et al.* give a *local* perspective

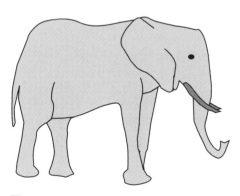

Figure 13.1. *What does an elephant look like?*

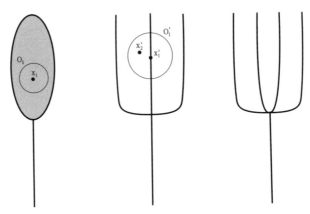

Figure 13.2. *A spoon (on the left) and a fork (in the middle); if player I chooses y_2 in v_1 outside the fork, player II cannot reply with a point of u_1 outside the spoon. On the other hand, player I cannot show that the fork on the right differs from that in the middle*

about relational structures ([BLA 01], slogan 2 of the preface). A local perspective can only be partial, as illustrated by the anecdote, but how far can it go in the description of space?

The work of the Amsterdam school [AIE 01] provides an illustration of the expressive possibilities of modal languages. In particular, van Benthem and Aiello show how a two player-game, where the first player tries to show that the two objects are different, whereas the other maintains that they are similar (the game is an Ehrenfeucht-Fraïssé game), makes it possible to take a decision in just one round: a spoon is definitely qualitatively different from a fork.

The game is played by two players: player I intends to show that the two objects are different, and player II maintains that they are similar (Figure 13.2). Player I chooses a point x_1 inside the spoon (on the left), so that there is a small neighborhood O_1 around this point which is entirely contained in the spoon. Player II starts with a point x_1' of the fork, and chooses a small neighborhood O_1' of this point. It is now the turn of player I: he chooses x_2' which belongs to the neighborhood O_1' chosen by player II, but which does not belong to the fork. It is now player II's turn to reply with a point x_2 inside O_1, but no matter what player II does, this point is necessarily in the spoon, and x_2 is in the spoon, whereas x_2' is not in the fork. Thus player I has won the game: he has shown that a spoon and a fork are qualitatively different.

On the other hand, using the same rules, player II, who has forks with four prongs, and player I, who insists on using forks with three prongs, cannot conclude that the two kinds of forks are different: no matter what player I does, player II is always able to find a response, so that player I cannot show by using the game that his three-pronged forks are different from those of player II.

13.2. Space and modal logics

In 1995, commenting on the question of reasoning by using formalisms which are sufficiently expressive, but which all the same allow us to reason efficiently, Bennett [BEN 96a] proposed to use modal logics to this aim. Egenhofer's formalism, according to him, allows a limited kind of reasoning. By contrast, the RCC theory, which is a first order logical theory, has a much greater expressive power, but the reasoning which it allows is much more difficult to implement.

Accordingly, Bennett introduces the use of modal logics for the representation of spatial knowledge, by considering an interpretation of these logics in which a propositional variable does not refer to a truth-value, but to a region — more precisely, to a subspace of a topological space.

This kind of interpretation goes back to the 1930s and 1940s, i.e. to a time which precedes by many years the introduction by Kripke of the semantics of "possible worlds" for modal logics. The fundamental result proved by McKinsey and Tarski [MCK 44] states that the S4 logic is the logic of any regular metric space without isolated points.

Although it has been somewhat marginalized by the success of the possible worlds semantics since the 1950s, the topological tradition was revived and developed towards the end of the last century, particularly by the Amsterdam school, notably by van Benthem, Aiello, and others [AIE 03, AIE 02c, AIE 02b, PRA 07, BEN 07b]. This has led to the development of the domain of *spatial logic*, which proposes a systematic investigation of the relationship between logical languages and geometrical structures in a broad sense [PRA 07]. Besides the fact that many of the questions arising in the field of temporal logic have a counterpart in spatial logic, the development of this branch of logic, to a significant extent, owes its existence to its direct relation with qualitative spatial reasoning. As is the case for the latter, the applications to Artificial Intelligence, GIS, database theory, but also to image processing, theoretical physics or philosophy are powerful motivations.

In this chapter, we will present some salient features of what particularly concerns the development of logics of modal type for spatial reasoning. For more details and for most of the proofs, the reader may refer to original articles, as well as to synthetic volumes on the topic [BEN 07b, AIE 07].

13.3. The modal logic S4

13.3.1. *Language and axioms*

Recall that the language of classical modal logic is that of the propositional calculus enriched with a modal operator $\Box$. The system of modal logic considered here is the system S4, which is the system of minimal logic **K** equipped with two additional axioms: axiom T: $\Box\varphi \rightarrow \varphi$, and axiom 4: $\Box\varphi \rightarrow \Box\Box\varphi$.

Consequently, a system of axioms for the logic S4 is the following:

K: $\Box(\varphi \rightarrow \psi) \rightarrow (\Box\varphi \rightarrow \Box\psi)$

T: $\Box\varphi \rightarrow \varphi$

4: $\Box\varphi \rightarrow \Box\Box\varphi$

The theorems of S4 are obtained from these axiom schemes and the two rules of inference:

– the *modus ponens* MP: from two theorems $(\varphi \rightarrow \psi)$ and φ, we may deduce that φ is a theorem;

– the *rule of necessitation* RN: if φ is a theorem, then $\Box\varphi$ is also a theorem.

It can be easily shown that S4 may also be defined by using the following alternative formal system:

– **Axioms**

N: $\Box\top$

R: $(\Box\varphi \wedge \Box\psi) \leftrightarrow \Box(\varphi \wedge \psi)$

T: $\Box\varphi \rightarrow \varphi$

4: $\Box\varphi \rightarrow \Box\Box\varphi$

– **Rules of inference**

MP (modus ponens): from two theorems φ and $\varphi \rightarrow \psi$, we may deduce ψ.

M: from the theorem $\varphi \rightarrow \psi$, we may deduce that $\Box\varphi \rightarrow \Box\psi$ is a theorem.

13.3.2. *Kripke models*

The classical semantics in terms of possible worlds uses Kripke models:

DEFINITION 13.1.– *A modal frame is a pair* $M = (W, R)$, *where*:

– *W is a non-empty set of worlds*;

– $R \subseteq W \times W$ *is a binary relation on* W.

DEFINITION 13.2.– *A Kripke model is a 3-tuple* $M = (W, R, V)$ *where*:

– (W, R) *is a modal frame*;

– $V \subseteq W \times V$ *is a valuation, i.e. a map of the set of propositional variables to the set of subsets of* W.

A modal frame is hence a relational structure (which can also be seen as a directed graph whose set of vertices is W). Intuitively, for each propositional variable, a valuation gives the set of worlds in which this variable is true. If $M = (W, R, V)$ is a Kripke model, we say that M is based on the frame (M, R). A valuation V may also be seen as a binary relation on the product of the set of propositional variables by W, or as a map of W in all the subsets of propositional variables: then, for each world, the valuation indicates the variables which are true in this world.

A valuation V extends to the set of formulas in a unique way. Equivalently, given a model, we can define the concept of satisfaction of a formula φ in the following manner ($M \models_w \varphi$ reads "φ is true in world $w \in M$"):

1) for any propositional variable p, $M \models_w p$ if, and only if, $w \in V(p)$;

2) $M \models_w \neg\varphi$ if, and only if, we do not have $M \models_w \varphi$;

3) $M \models_w (\varphi \wedge \psi)$ if, and only if, we simultaneously have $M \models_w \varphi$ and $M \models_w \psi$;

4) $M \models_w (\varphi \vee \psi)$ if, and only if, at least one of the two conditions $M \models_w \varphi$ and $M \models_w \psi$ is satisfied;

5) $M \models_w (\varphi \rightarrow \psi)$ if, and only if, $M \models_w \varphi$ implies that $M \models_w \psi$;

6) $M \models \Box\varphi$ if, and only if, for any $w' \in W$ such that $(w, w') \in R$, we have $M \models w'\varphi$;

7) $M \models \Diamond\varphi$ if, and only if, there exists a world $w' \in W$ which is reachable from w, i.e. such that $(w, w') \in R$, such as $M \models w'\varphi$.

A classical result states that the logic S4 is complete with respect to the class of models whose binary relation is a preorder, i.e. a reflexive (axiom T) and transitive (axiom 4) relation: if a model M is a preorder, any theorem of S4 is valid in M, and conversely, any valid formula for the class of models which are preorders is a theorem of S4.

The topological interpretation is an alternative way to define the semantics of the logic S4.

This interpretation is suggested by the comparison of the axioms of S4 with the properties of the interior operator in topology:

$$Int(\emptyset) = \emptyset \qquad\qquad \text{N}: \Box\top$$
$$Int(A \cap B) = Int(A) \cap Int(B) \qquad \text{R}: (\Box\varphi \wedge \Box\psi) \leftrightarrow (\varphi \wedge \psi)$$
$$Int(A) \subseteq A \qquad\qquad \text{T}: \Box\varphi \leftarrow \varphi$$
$$Int(Int(A)) = Int(A) \qquad\qquad 4: \Box\varphi \leftarrow \Box\Box\varphi$$

The modal approach of reasoning about space is based on the topological interpretation.

13.4. Topological models

DEFINITION 13.3.– *A topological model $M = (X, Int_X, \nu)$ consists of a topological space (X, Int_X) and a valuation ν which associates a subset of X with each propositional variable.*

In other words, a topological model is defined by an arbitrary topological space and a map which, to any propositional variable, associates a topological subspace. The propositional variables are thus interpreted as regions in a topological space.

A valuation extends in a unique way to the set of formulas by setting:

$- \nu(\neg\varphi) = X \setminus \nu(\varphi);$
$- \nu(\varphi \vee \psi) = \nu(\varphi) \cup \nu(\psi);$
$- \nu(\varphi \vee \psi) = \nu(\varphi) \cap \nu(\psi);$
$- \nu(\Box\varphi) = Int(\nu(\varphi));$

The intuition behind these definitions is to interpret the operator $\Box$ as an interior operator. The interior of a set Y is characterized by the fact that any interior point has an open neighborhood entirely contained in Y.

Equivalently, we define the concept of satisfaction of a formula φ at a point x of a topological model:

– for any propositional variable p, $M \models_x p$ if, and only if, $x \in V(p)$;

– $M \models_x \neg\varphi$ if, and only if, we do not have $M \models_x \varphi$;

– $M \models_x (\varphi \wedge \psi)$ if, and only if, we simultaneously have $M \models_x \varphi$ and $M \models_x \psi$;

– $M \models_x (\varphi \vee \psi)$ if, and only if, at least one of the two conditions $M \models_x \varphi$ and $M \models_x \psi$ is satisfied;

– $M \models_x (\varphi \wedge \psi)$ if, and only if, $M \models_x \varphi$ implies that $M \models_x \psi$;

– $M \models_x \Box\varphi$ if, and only if, there exists an open set U containing x such that for all $y \in U$ we have $M \models_y \varphi$;

– $M \models_x \Diamond\varphi$ if, and only if, any open set U containing x contains a point y such that $M \models_y \varphi$.

We see that the operator $\Diamond$, which is the dual of $\Box$, associates its topological closure to a region.

Figure 13.3 [AIE 02b] illustrates the way in which the modal language can be used to explore a given region, in this case, the image of a spoon in the plane: if p denotes the spoon, $\Box p$ is its interior, $p \wedge \neg\Box p$ its boundary, $\Diamond\Box p$ the closure of its interior, $p \wedge \neg\Diamond\Box p$ is the handle of the spoon, where the point of contact is not included, and $\Diamond\Box p \wedge (p \wedge \neg\Diamond\Box p)$ is the point of contact between the spoon and its handle.

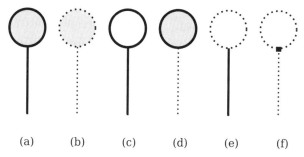

Figure 13.3. *Regions associated to formulas (a–f):*
(a) p. (b) □ p. (c) p∧¬□ p. (d) ◇□ p. (e) p∧¬◇□ p. (f) ◇□ p ∧◇(p ∧ ¬◇□ p)

13.4.1. *Topological games*

A *topological game* is played between two players I and II, on two topological models (X, Ω_X, ν) and $(X', \Omega_{X'}, \nu')$. Player I tries to show that the models are *different*, whereas player II tries to show that they are similar.

The game starts with two given points, one on each model. These points are the initial current points. A game of length n is played in n rounds; in each round, player I makes the initial move, with the intent to prove II wrong: he chooses one of the models, and an open set containing the current point of the model; then player II tries to reply by choosing an open set in the other model containing the current point of that model; next, player I plays again, selecting a point in the open set just chosen by player II, which becomes the current point; finally, player II has to reply by selecting a point in the open chosen originally by player I; in this way, the two players construct two sequences of related points; player II wins if all corresponding pairs of points in the sequence satisfy the same atomic formulas, otherwise player I wins.

13.4.2. *The rules of the game*

More precisely, a game is played in the following manner:
– we start the game with two models (X, Ω_X, ν) and $(X', \Omega_{X'}, \nu')$;
– we select $x_1 \in X$ and $x_1' \in Y$; the are the initial current points;
– we fix a number of rounds n;
– for each round:
  1) player I chooses one of the models X_I and an open neighborhood O_I containing the current point in this model;
  2) player II chooses an open neighborhood O_{II} in the other model, such that this open neighborhood contains the current point x_{II} in this model;
  3) player I chooses a point $\bar{x}_{II}$ II in the open neighborhood O_{II} of model X_{II};

4) player II replies by choosing $\bar{x}_I$ I in the open neighborhood O_I of X_I;

5) the points $\bar{x}_I$ and $\bar{x}_{II}$ become the new current points in their respective models.

To summarize, player I chooses a model twice in each new round, thereby forcing II to reply in the other model. Then, two choices of an open neighborhood, and two choices of a point are made during a round.

13.4.3. *End of game*

An n-round game finishes after n rounds:

– after n rounds, we have two sequences:

$$\{x_1, O_1, x_2, O_2, \ldots, O_{n-1}, x_n\}$$
$$\{x'_1, O'_1, x'_2, O'_2, \ldots, O'_{n-1}, x'_n\}$$

– player II wins (after n rounds) if for any $i \in [1, n]$, the points x_i and x'_i satisfy the same atomic formulas;

– if player II has lost before the end of n rounds, then player I wins;

– a *winning strategy* for player II is a function which indicates what player II must do to win, no matter how player I decides to play;

– a *winning strategy* for player I is a function which indicates what player I must do to win, no matter how player II decides to play.

13.4.4. *Examples of games: example 1*

The first example (Figure 13.4) is quite similar to the one presented in the introduction of this chapter. The initial data (a) consists of two models X and X'

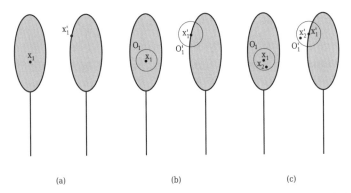

(a)   (b)   (c)

Figure 13.4. *A game in which player I wins in one round. The starting point is (a). In (b), player I chooses an open neighborhood O_1 containing x_1 which is entirely contained in the spoon; player II must then choose an open neighborhood containing x'_1, that is O'_1; player I then chooses x'_2 in O'_2 which is not in the spoon; now the reply x_2 by player II in O_1 can only be in the spoon on the left: player II loses the game*

(two "spoons"), and two points x_1 on X and x_1' on X'. The first point is inside the spoon X, the second on the edge of the spoon X'.

In this case, player I wins in one round: he chooses an open neighborhood O_1 containing x_1 which is entirely contained inside X (Figure 13.4 (b)). Player II must then choose an open neighborhood containing x_1'. Regardless of what he does, this open neighborhood contains points of the interior of the complement of X', so that player I can choose one of them, say x_2'. But then the reply of player II is a point x_2 of X which, being in O_1, is necessarily in X. So x_2 is in X, while x_2' is not in X': player I wins.

In one round, the game thus makes it possible to distinguish an interior point like x_1 from a point of the border such as x_1'. If the models considered correspond to the propositional variable p, p is true in x_1 and x_1', whereas it is always true in x_2, but not in x_2'.

Actually, there exists a formula which is true in x_1 and false in x_1', namely the formula $\Box p$ (which expresses the existence of an open neighborhood containing x entirely contained in the interpretation of p).

13.4.5. *Example 2*

Here the initial points are a point of the handle, for X, and a point on the edge of the spoon, for X' (Figure 13.5 (a)). This time, player I chooses an open neighborhood O_1 around x_1 which does not meet the interior of the spoon (b). Player II must then

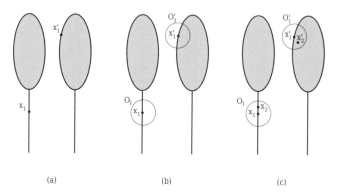

(a)   (b)   (c)

Figure 13.5. *A game where I wins in two rounds. The starting point is (a). In (b), player I chooses an open neighborhood O_1 containing x_1 and not meeting the interior of the spoon; the open neighborhood containing x_1' that player II has to choose necessarily contains points of this interior, and player I chooses one of them, say x_2'(c); the reply x_2 by player II in O_1 has to belong to the handle of the spoon, and the situation of x_2 and x_2' is the same as that of the previous example: player II will lose in the following round*

choose an open neighborhood containing x_1'. Necessarily, this open set will contain points which belong to the interior of the spoon. Player I will then choose one of these points, say x_2'. In order reply, player II must choose x_2 in the spoon and in O_1. It must thus choose a point of the handle. But by doing this, he finds himself in the situation of example 1, so that player I will win in the following round.

There also exist formulas which make it possible to distinguish x_1 and x_1': for example the formula $\lozenge\square p$, which is true in x_1' (it expresses that any neighborhood of x_1' meets the interior of the spoon) and false in x_1.

13.4.6. *Example 3*

Here, x_1 is the junction point between the handle and the spoon (Figure 13.6), and x_1' is a point on the boundary of the spoon. This time, player I chooses an open neighborhood around x_1' which is small enough that it does not contain any point of the handle of the spoon. Player II must then choose an open neighborhood around x_1. Regardless of what he does, this open neighborhood will contain a point x_2 of the handle, and this is the point chosen next by player I. If player II replies with an interior point x_2', he will lose in the following round (this is the situation of example 1). If he chooses a point x_2' on the boundary, we are brought back to the situation of example 2. Consequently, there exists a winning strategy for player I which allows him to distinguish the two configurations in a maximum of three rounds.

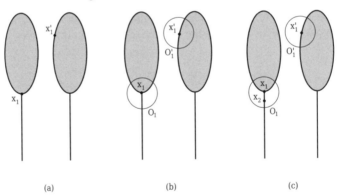

(a)   (b)   (c)

Figure 13.6. *A game where I wins in three rounds. The starting point is (a). In (b), player I chooses an open neighborhood O_1' containing x_1' and not meeting the handle of the spoon; the open neighborhood containing x_1 which player II must choose necessarily contains points of the handle, and player I chooses one of them, say x_2 (c); the reply x_2' by player II in O_1' can only be either in the interior of the spoon, which would bring us to a situation where player II loses in one round, or on its boundary, and then player II loses in two rounds*

In this case, the formula $\lozenge(p \wedge \neg\square p)$ makes it possible to distinguish the two cases: it is true in x_1, and false in x_1'.

We see a general scheme appearing in our examples if we consider on the one hand the number of rounds necessary for player I to prove the topological differences, and on the other hand the complexity of the formulas for distinguishing between the two models:

– one round: $\Box p$;

– two rounds: $\neg \Diamond \Box p$;

– three rounds: $\Diamond (p \wedge \neg \Diamond \Box p)$.

13.4.6.1. *Modal rank of a formula*

DEFINITION 13.4.– *The modal rank of a formula φ of modal logic, denoted by $\mathrm{rm}(\varphi)$, is defined in the following manner:*

– *the modal rank of a propositional variable is 0;*

– *the modal rank of $\neg \varphi$ is the modal rank of φ;*

– *the modal rank of $(\varphi \wedge \psi)$, $(\varphi \vee \psi)$, and $(\varphi \rightarrow \psi)$ is the maximum of the modal ranks of φ and ψ;*

– *the modal rank of $\Box \varphi$ and $\Diamond \varphi$ is the modal rank of φ incremented by 1.*

EXAMPLE 13.1.– The modal rank of $p \wedge \neg \Box p, \Box p$ is 1, that of $\Diamond \Box p, p \wedge \neg \Diamond \Box p$ is 2, and that of $\Diamond (p \wedge \neg \Diamond \Box p)$ is equal to 3.

13.4.7. *Games and modal rank of formulas*

More precisely, let $TG(X, X', n, x_1, x_1')$ be a topological game with n rounds on two topological models X and X', with x_1 and x_1' as initial points on the models X and X', respectively.

THEOREM 13.1.– *Player II has a winning strategy for the topological game $TG(X, X', n, x_1, x_1')$ if, and only if, x_1 and x_1' satisfy the same modal formulas with modal rank less than or equal to n.*

Proof. The reader may refer to [AIE 02c, AIE 02b]. We will just give an outline of the principal stages of the proof.

The existence of a winning strategy for player II implies that a formula of modal rank $\leq n$ is true at x_1 if, and only if, it is true at x_1'.

The proof is by induction on n:

– the result is obvious for $n = 0$;

– for $n \geq 1$, φ is a Boolean combination of formulas of the form $\Box \psi$, where ψ is of modal rank $\leq n - 1$;

– let us assume that $X \models_{x_1} \Box\psi$ (we may assume that player I starts playing in this model);

– as a consequence, there exists an open neighborhood $O \ni x_1$ which is entirely contained in the region defined by ψ;

– let us assume that player I starts the game by choosing O; then player II can use his strategy σ to choose $O' \ni x_1'$, where ψ is true everywhere;

– for any choice of $u' \in O'$ by player I, player II can reply by choosing $u \in O$, which ends the first round;

– the remaining strategy σ' is still a winning strategy for player II in $TG(X, X', n - 1, u, u')$;

– according to the induction hypothesis, $X \models_u \psi$ implies $X' \models_{u'} \psi$, and this is true for any $u' \in O'$, hence $X' \models_{x_1'} \Box\psi$.

Conversely:

– if $n = 0$, player II wins from the start;

– again, one reasons by induction on n, using the fact that, up to logical equivalence, there is only a finite number of logical formulas with modal rank at most k;

– let $\Psi_{n-1}(z)$ be the conjunction of all formulas of modal rank $(n - 1)$ which are true in z;

– a suitable open neighborhood O can then be defined.   □

NOTE 13.1.– Player I may find it advantageous to choose open neighborhoods which are as small as possible, because this will restrict the choices of player II. But player II may also find it advantageous to choose open neighborhoods which are as small as possible, to restrict the choices of player I.

If there exists a winning strategy for player I (player II, respectively), there exists a winning strategy for which the sequence of successive open neighborhoods is decreasing.

13.4.8. *McKinsey and Tarski's theorem*

It is straightforward to check that S4 is correct for the topological interpretation: if φ is a theorem of S4 (S4 $\vdash \varphi$) then φ is a *topologically valid* formula, i.e. it is true in any topological space. The converse is true, so that we have a result of completeness:

THEOREM 13.2.– *If a formula φ is valid in any topological space, then φ is a theorem of S4: one has* S4 $\vdash \varphi$.

A formula is hence a theorem of S4 if it is valid in any topological space, i.e. valid in any model based on a topological space.

Actually, McKinsey and Tarski's result is much stronger:

THEOREM 13.3.– *(McKinsey and Tarski) [MCK 44] If φ is valid in a* separable *and* dense-in-itself[1] *metric topological space, then φ is a theorem of S4.*

NOTE 13.2.– The result of completeness for a topological space X implies that, if φ *is not* a theorem of S4, then we can find a model based on X such that φ is false in at least one point of X.

The real line $\mathbb{R}$, the rational line $\mathbb{Q}$, and the Cantor space $\mathbf{C}$ are separable and dense-in-themselves metric spaces. McKinsey and Tarski's theorem implies that formulas which are valid in all the models based on one of these spaces are theorems of S4.

Detailed direct proofs of the completeness for $\mathbb{R}$, $\mathbb{Q}$, and $\mathbf{C}$ (as well as outlines of proof in [BEN 07b]) can be found in [BEZ 05, BEN 07c], and [AIE 03], respectively. For the completeness of S4 on the Cantor space, the reader is referred to [MIN 05].

13.4.8.1. *Canonical models*

In the case of classical temporal logics, a standard method of proof of completeness is based on constructing *canonical models*, or Henkin models (see for example [BES 92], Chapter 3).

Henkin's construction has been adapted to the topological context by Aiello, van Benthem, and Bezhanishvili [AIE 03, BEN 07b]. In what follows, we give a rough description of their construction of a canonical model.

In accordance with the usual practice, one starts with the notion of a *maximal consistent* set of formulas of S4.

DEFINITION 13.5.– *A set Γ of formulas is* S4-consistent *if there is no finite subset of formulas $\{\varphi_1, \ldots, \varphi_n\}$ such that $\neg(\varphi_1 \wedge \ldots \wedge \varphi_n)$ is a theorem of* S4. *It is* maximal consistent *if there is no consistent set strictly containing it.*

Maximal consistent sets are characterized by the fact that, for such a set Γ, an arbitrary formula φ is either in Γ or has its negation $\neg\varphi$ in Γ.

The construction of the canonical model proceeds in the following manner:

– the set of points of the topological space of the canonical model is the set of maximal consistent sets of formulas;

– a base of open sets consists of the maximal consistent sets containing $\Box\varphi$, where φ is the set of all formulas;

---

1 A topological space is dense-in-itself if it does not contain isolated points.

– to each propositional variable p, the valuation associates the set of maximal consistent sets containing p.

It can then be shown that the characterization of validity in this model, as it has been defined for propositional formulas, extends in fact to arbitrary formulas: an arbitrary formula is valid at a point of the canonical model (i.e. at a maximal consistent set) if, and only if, this maximal consistent set contains the formula.

As a consequence, if φ is not a theorem of S4, $\{\neg\varphi\}$ can be extended into a maximal consistent set which does not contain φ, so that φ is not valid at this "point": thus φ is falsified at a point of the canonical model.

A further consequence of this proof is that, for a given formula, the construction can be done by using only the formula and its subformulas, so that a non-theorem can be falsified in a finite topological model.

13.4.9. *Topological bisimulations*

The notion of equivalence between two topological spaces corresponds to that of homeomorphism. The notion of modal equivalence corresponds to that of *topological bisimulation*.

Let M and M' be two topological models.

DEFINITION 13.6.– *A topological bisimulation is a binary relation $\sim$ between M and M', i.e. $\sim \subseteq M \times M'$ such that, if $x \sim x'$:*

– *(base condition) p is true at x if, and only if, p is true at x';*

– *(forth condition) if U is an open set containing x, there is an open set U' containing x' such that each point of U' has a corresponding bisimilar point in U;*

– *(back condition) if U' is an open set containing x', there is an open set U containing x such that each point of U has a corresponding point in U'.*

The forth condition can be expressed as: if $x \in U \in \Omega_X$, then $(\exists U' \in \Omega_{X'})(x' \in U'$ and $\forall y' \in U'(\exists y \in U)(y \sim y'))$; the back condition can be expressed in a similar way.

EXAMPLE 13.2.– $U \xhookrightarrow{i} X$, where U is an open set X, is a topological bisimulation:

– the relation $\sim$ is the identity relation on U;

– $x \sim x' = x$ means that $x \in U$;

– if V is an open set containing x, $V \cap U$ satisfies the forth condition;

– if $V \cap U$ is an open set in U containing x, $V \cap U$ satisfies the back condition.

13.4.9.1. *Topological bisimilarity as modal equivalence*

THEOREM 13.4.– *If $\sim$ is a topological bisimulation, and if $s \sim t$, then s and t satisfy the same modal formulas.*

The particular case of the inclusion of an open set in a topological space illustrates the *local* character of topological validity: to determine if φ is true at point x, it is sufficient to know what is true in an *arbitrarily small* neighborhood of x. Indeed, let U be an open set of X, where $M = (X, \Omega_X, \nu)$ is a topological model. By definition, the submodel $(M \mid U)$ of the model M is the subspace U as a topological space, together with the valuation ν_U defined by $\nu_U(p) = \nu(p) \cap U$. Now we have the following proposition:

PROPOSITION 13.1.– *For any $x \in U$, we $M \models_x \varphi$ if, and only if, $(M \mid U) \models_x \varphi$.*

For topological models, topological bisimulations play a role which is analogous to the one played by homeomorphisms for topological spaces. The concept of equivalence defined in this way is generally much coarser than that defined by homeomorphism. It can be shown [BEN 96c, BLA 01] that, for *finite* topological models, the following property holds:

PROPOSITION 13.2.– *If two finite models M and M' are such that the same modal formulas are satisfied in $x \in M$ and $x' \in M'$, then there exists a topological bisimulation $\sim$ between M and M' such that $x \sim x'$.*

13.4.10. *Expressiveness*

We now move on to the question of expressiveness: what are the properties that can be expressed by using the basic language of modal logic?

Firstly, we have negative results: for instance, McKinsey and Tarski's theorem implies that there exists no modal formula characterizing the fact that a topological space is metrizable or dense-in-itself.

The result we have just seen for bisimulations can similarly be used to get negative results: if a property is invariable by bisimulation, it cannot be expressed by using the basic modal language.

EXAMPLE 13.3.– The connectedness property cannot be expressed by using the modal language S4: if X is the space formed by two disjoint disks U and V, then the inclusion of U in X is a topological bisimulation. However, X is not connected (Figure 13.7).

13.4.11. *Relational and topological models*

We have described two semantics for the modal language of S4: a relational semantics in terms of Kripke models, and a topological one. Now the two semantics can be related in an explicit way.

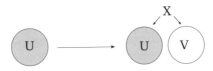

Figure 13.7. *A bisimulation which does not preserve the property of connectedness*

Indeed, a modal frame for S4 is a preorder (the relation R is reflexive and transitive). Hence W may be equipped with the preorder topology, for which a base of open sets consists of the ↑-saturated subsets (see Appendix A):

DEFINITION 13.7.– *Let X be a subset of W:*

  – *X is ↑-saturated if $x \in X$ and xRy imply that $y \in X$;*
  – *X is ↓-saturated if $x \in X$ and yRx imply that $y \in X$.*

For the preorder topology, the closure of A is the set of points dominated (in the broad sense) by at least a point in A, while its interior is the set of points of A such that all points dominating them are in A.

DEFINITION 13.8.– *An* Alexandroff space *is a topological space where the following equivalent conditions are satisfied:*

  – *any intersection of open sets is open;*
  – *any point has a smaller open neighborhood.*

Clearly, the topological space (W, Ω_X) associated with a preorder W by the previous construction is an Alexandroff space: the smallest open set containing a point $x \in W$ is the set of points y such that xRy. By reflexivity, this set contains x. By transitivity, it is ↑-saturated.

A preorder is an order if the relation is antisymmetric: we may have xRy and yRx only if $x = y$. This implies that for two distinct points x and y, either the smallest open neighborhood of x does not contain y, or the smallest open neighborhood of y does not contain x. In other words, in this case, the topological space associated with W satisfies the T_0 separation axiom.

A map $f: W \to W'$ between two preorders (W, R) and (W', R') is increasing if xRy implies $f(x)R'f(y)$. It can be easily checked that an increasing map induces a continuous map between the associated topological spaces.

13.4.12. *From topological models to Kripke models*

Conversely, we may associate with any topological space a preorder on the set of its points, namely the relation of *specialization*:

DEFINITION 13.9.– *Let X be a topological space, and $x, y \in X$. We say that x is a specialization of y if $x \in Cl(\{y\})$ (the closure of y contains x).*

Equivalently, x is a *specialization* of y if any open set containing x necessarily contains y.

Clearly, this relation is reflexive and transitive. We thus obtain a modal frame which is a preorder.

If U is an open set, and if $x \in U$ is a specialization of y, then $y \in U$: any open set is ↑-saturated for this relation. The topology associated with the preorder defined by specialization is in general finer than the initial topology of the topological space considered. If this topological space is an Alexandroff space, then the two topologies coincide, since in that case, any ↑-saturated set for specialization is an open set.

LEMMA 13.1.– *Let $f \colon X \to Y$ be a map between two topological spaces. If f is continuous, then it preserves the specialization relation; if X is an Alexandroff space, the converse is true.*

Proof. Let us show that, if $f \colon X \to Y$ is continuous, then it preserves the specialization relation. Let us assume that this is not the case, so that there is a specialization x of y in X such that $f(x)$ is not a specialization of $f(y)$: this means that there is an open set $V \subseteq Y$ containing $f(x)$ but not $f(y)$. Now the inverse image $f^{-1}(V)$ is an open set containing x, so it has to contain y, hence $f(y) \in V$, a contradiction.

Conversely, let us assume that f preserves the specialization relation. Let V be an open set of Y. Let us show that $U = f^{-1}(V)$ is open. If not, there exists a point $x \in U$ such that any neighborhood of x meets $X \setminus U$. In particular, the smallest open set containing x meets $X \setminus U$ at a point y. By definition, x is a specialization of y, therefore $f(x)$ is a specialization of $f(y)$: this means that any open set containing $f(x)$, the open set V in particular, should contain $f(y)$, which is not the case.   □

The preceding discussion can be used to show that there is a functor from the category of Alexandroff topological spaces to the category of preorders which is an equivalence of categories. This functor associates to an Alexandroff space the pre-order corresponding to the relation of specialization, and it associates to a continuous map the increasing map between the associated preorders. The inverse functor associates with a preorder the topological space whose open sets are the ↑-saturated subsets, and it associates with an increasing map, the continuous map it defines between the associated topological spaces.

The preorder defined by the specialization relation is an order (i.e. antisymmetric) if, and only if, the topological space verifies the T_0 separation axiom. Consequently, the functors described above define an equivalence of categories between the category of Alexandroff topological spaces satisfying the T_0 axiom and the category of partial orders.

For the Alexandroff spaces — characterized by the fact that any point has a smaller open neighborhood — we have the correspondence below:

preorders $\leftrightarrow$ Alexandroff spaces

orders $\leftrightarrow$ Alexandroff spaces satisfying T_0

In particular, any finite topological space is an Alexandroff space. The category of finite topological spaces with continuous maps as morphisms, is hence equivalent to the category of finite preorders with increasing maps as morphisms, and the subcategory of finite topological spaces satisfying T_0 to the category of finite partial orders.

The reader is referred to [AIE 01] for more information about the correspondence between Kripke models and topological models, and the results that can be derived from it. Among these consequences, let us mention here the fact that the canonical model described above is compact and dense-in-itself, which implies that S4 is also the logic of compact and dense-in-themselves topological spaces.

13.4.13. *An extended language:* $S4_u$

We have seen that some important topological properties cannot be expressed by a formula of modal logic S4. In order to increase the expressiveness of the language, we introduce a new operator **U** which will allow us to go beyond the purely local character of the basic language: the intuitive significance of $U\varphi$ is "φ is true everywhere".

The dual operator **E** is then interpreted as an existence operator: E_φ means that φ is true somewhere.

The bimodal language $S4_u$ is thus obtained by adding to the language two operators **U** and **E**, together with:

– axioms for **U** and its dual **E**: these are the axioms of $S5$;

– an axiom which connects the two systems, namely: $\mathbf{U}p \rightarrow \Box p$.

Using this new language, it is now possible to express the property of connectedness [SHE 99, AIE 02b] by the formula $\mathbf{U}(\Diamond p \rightarrow \Box p) \rightarrow (\mathbf{U}p \vee \mathbf{U}\neg p)$.

13.5. Translating the RCC-8 predicates

Bennett [BEN 94, BEN 96b] has shown how the modal language $S4_u$ can be used to define the predicates of RCC-8; this translation is shown in Table 13.1.

Relation	Formula
$\mathsf{C}(p,q)$	$\mathbf{E}(p \wedge q)$
$\mathsf{DC}(p,q)$	$\neg\mathbf{E}(p \wedge q)$
$\mathsf{EC}(p,q)$	$\mathbf{E}(p \wedge q) \wedge \neg\mathbf{E}(\Box p \wedge \Box q)$
$\mathsf{PO}(p,q)$	$\mathbf{E}(\Box p \wedge \Box q) \wedge \mathbf{E}(\Box p \wedge \neg q) \wedge \mathbf{E}(\neg p \wedge \Box q)$
$\mathsf{TPP}(p,q)$	$\mathbf{U}(p \rightarrow q) \wedge \mathbf{E}(p \wedge \Diamond\neg q) \wedge \mathbf{E}(\neg p \wedge q)$
$\mathsf{NTPP}(p,q)$	$\mathbf{U}(p \rightarrow \Box q) \wedge \mathbf{E}(\neg p \wedge q))$
$\mathsf{EQ}(p,q)$	$\mathbf{U}(p \leftrightarrow q)$

Table 13.1. *Translation of the* RCC-8 *relations*

We then have the theorem:

THEOREM 13.5.– *[BEN 94, BEN 96b, WOL 00b] An* RCC-8 *formula is satisfiable in a topological model if, and only if, its translation is satisfiable in a topological space, or equivalently, in a finite Alexandroff space.*

Wolter and Zakharyaschev [WOL 00b,WOL 03] show how this result can be extended to a language they call BRCC-8 in which Boolean terms can be used to denote regions. For instance, this language has formulas such as NTPP$(A, B \sqcup C)$ (whose interpretation is that region A is a non-tangential part of the union of regions B and C).

We have already mentioned (section 9.5.7) that Renz [REN 98a] has shown that the translation of a satisfiable RCC-8 formula can be satisfied in a simple kind of Alexandroff topological space known as a *quasi-saw* space. Moreover, the number of closed points of this space can be upper bounded by the length of the translation of the formula. Here again, this result can be extended to the BRCC-8 language [WOL 00b].

13.6. An alternative modal translation of RCC-8

Besides Bennett's translation, an alternative bimodal translation of the RCC-8 language has been proposed by Nutt [NUT 99]. In this translation, the bimodal logic has an interior operator of type S4, denoted by $\Box$, and an operator which satisfies the axioms of the minimal modal logic **K**, denoted by $\Box_K$; $\Diamond_K$ denotes the operator which is dual to $\Box_K$.

Nutt defines constraints called arbitrary constraints, which generalize the RCC-8 constraints. These arbitrary constraints are translated in terms of the bimodal logic, and one has the following theorem:

THEOREM 13.6.– *Let C be an arbitrary constraint. Then C is satisfiable if, and only if, its translation $\pi(C)$ in the bimodal $(\Box, \Box_K)$-logic is satisfiable.*

In particular, the basic RCC−8 relations have the following translations:

$$\pi(\mathsf{DC}(x,y)) = \Box_K \Box \neg (x \wedge y)$$
$$\pi(\mathsf{EC}(x,y)) = \Box_K \Box \neg (\Box x \wedge \Box y) \wedge \Diamond_K \Diamond (x \wedge y)$$
$$\pi(\mathsf{PO}(x,y)) = \Diamond_K \Diamond (\Box x \wedge \Box y) \wedge \Diamond_K \Diamond (x \wedge \neg y) \wedge \Diamond_K \Diamond (\neg x \wedge y)$$
$$\pi(\mathsf{EQ}(x,y)) = \Box_K \Box (x \to y) \wedge \Box_K \Box (y \to x)$$
$$\pi(\mathsf{TPP}(x,y)) = \Box_K \Box (x \to y) \wedge \Diamond_K \Diamond (x \wedge \neg \Box y)$$
$$\pi(\mathsf{NTPP}(x,y)) = \Box_K \Box (x \to \Box y)$$

13.7. Generalized frames

One of the classical techniques in modal logics is the use of *generalized frames*. The idea is to restrain the interpretation of propositional variables to specific subclasses of subsets. In the topological context, this corresponds to the fact that these variables are interpreted in specific classes of subspaces.

This theme has also been developed by the Amsterdam school [AIE 01].

The subfamilies considered include the *serial* subsets of $\mathbb{R}$, which are defined as finite unions of convex subsets of $\mathbb{R}$ (hence unions of points or intervals). The class of serial subsets is stable under Boolean operations, under the interior and the closure operators, so that a semantics can be defined using this particular topological model. Since there are fewer possibilities of falsification, the set of valid formulas for this model contains the set of theorems of S4. The inclusion can be shown to be strict, so that new formulas which are not theorems of S4 become valid in this model, in particular:

– Grzegorczyk axiom $\Box(\Box(\varphi \to \Box\varphi) \to \varphi) \to \varphi$;
– the $\mathbf{BD_2}$ axiom $(\neg\varphi \wedge \Diamond\varphi) \to \Diamond\Box\varphi$;
– the $\mathbf{BW_2}$ axiom $\neg(\varphi \wedge \psi \wedge \Diamond(\varphi \wedge \neg\psi) \wedge (\neg\varphi \wedge \psi) \wedge (\neg\varphi \wedge \neg\psi))$.

NOTE 13.3.– For the Kripke semantics, the Grzegorczyk axiom corresponds to the fact that the relational frame is a Noetherian (partial) order, i.e. an order in which any accessibility chain originating from a given world is stationary: for any world $w \in W$, the existence of an infinite chain $(w = w_0, w_1, \ldots, w_n, \ldots)$ such that $w_i R w_{i+1}$, for any $i \geq 0$, implies that $w_i = w_{i+1}$ for if i is large enough [BLA 01]. The $\mathbf{BD_2}$ ($\mathbf{BW_2}$, respectively) axioms express that the depth (the width, respectively) of this frame is at most 2.

Aiello *et al.* show that these three axioms added to those of S4 axiomatize the logic thus obtained.

Similarly, they consider the set of all regions in $\mathbb{R}^2$ formed by finite unions of products $X_1 \times X_2$ of convex sets X_1, X_2 in $\mathbb{R}$. This set of regions, called *chequered* regions, is stable under Boolean operations, and under the interior and closure operators. Hence it can be used to define a semantics for the formulas of S4 by limiting the interpretation to chequered regions [AIE 01]. The valid formulas for this interpretation are axiomatized by the addition of the Grzegorczyk axiom to S4, and of conditions expressing that the Kripke models have a maximum depth of 3, and a maximum width of 4. The results can be extended to $\mathbb{R}^n$, for $n \geq 3$.

13.8. Complexity

Up to now, we have mentioned complexity issues only incidently. The initial result on this topic concerns the system S4 itself: it states that deciding whether a formula of S4 is valid is a PSPACE-complete problem [LAD 77].

The language $S4_u$ of the logic S4 augmented with the operators **U** and **E**, and interpreted on the class of all topological spaces (on the class of Alexandroff topological spaces, respectively) still has the same complexity:

THEOREM 13.7.– *[SHE 99, ARE 00] A formula of* $S4_u$ *is satisfiable in at least one topological space if, and only if, it is satisfiable in at least one Alexandroff topological space. The corresponding problem is* PSPACE-*complete.*

Similarly, the satisfiability of Nutt's arbitrary topological constraints is a PSPACE-complete problem.

The reader will find in [KON 08] a panorama of recent results concerning the complexity of topological spatial logics. The authors examine the question of the property of *connectedness*. Recalling that a formula of $S4_u$ is satisfiable in at least one *connected* topological space if, and only if, it is satisfiable in at least one connected Alexandroff topological space, or in an arbitrary separable and dense-in-itself topological space ([SHE 99]), they show that the corresponding problem is again a PSPACE-complete problem.

In the same chapter, the question of complexity of logical languages when the interpretation of variables is restricted to certain types of subspaces — in particular, to regular closed subspaces — is also examined. The language associated to the RCC−8 calculus is a particular case of this type of logics. As Renz showed in [REN 98a], we know that, in this case, a formula is satisfiable for an interpretation in terms of closed regular sets if, and only if, it is satisfiable in terms of connected closed regular sets, or in terms of closed regular sets of $\mathbb{R}^n$, for any $n \geq 1$, and that the corresponding problem is NP-complete.

In the particular interpretation of RCC−8 known as Egenhofer's model, the variables are interpreted as simple regions in the plane $\mathbb{R}^2$, where a *simple* region is a region which is homeomorphic to the closed disk.

The complexity of determining whether an RCC−8 formula is satisfiable in Egenhofer's model was determined by Schaefer *et al.* [SCH 03] who relate this problem to the *weak realizability* problem for graphs (intuitively, the possibility of drawing a graph in the plane with no sides intersecting except the ones which join vertices fixed in advance). These authors prove the following result:

THEOREM 13.8.– *The problem of the satisfiability of an* RCC−8 *formula in Egenhofer's model is NP-complete.*

13.9. Complements

13.9.1. *Analogs of Kamp operators*

Similar to the situation in temporal logic, where, besides the unary modal operators **F**, **P**, **G**, and **H**, binary operators such as the operator $\mathcal{U}$ (*until*) have been introduced by Kamp, it is natural to consider a binary operator $\mathcal{U}$ in the spatial domain, whose significance is the following: $\mathcal{U}(p, q)$ is true at point x, if there is an open neighborhood U of x in which p is true everywhere, and such that q is true at each point of the boundary of U. The reader will find more information on this topic in [BEN 07b].

13.9.2. *Space and epistemic logics*

An interesting point to mention is the relationship between epistemic logics and spatial logics [PAR 07]. This point is also discussed in [BEN 07b]: in a typical scenario, one considers observers placed in a geometrical space, the accessibility relation being conditioned by the properties of that space. A case in point is Balbiani *et al.*'s paper [BAL 10], which uses Flatland [ABB 63] as its geometrical space: observers living in this flat space have a field of vision limited to a half-plane, so that they only have a partial knowledge about the world and about the knowledge of the other observers.

13.9.3. *Other extensions*

Let us also mention here the *metric* extensions of spatial logics [KUT 03, WOL 05, SHE 06]. The interested reader may also refer to [LEB 07] for an introduction to this domain, as well as to the interpretations of modal systems in various types of geometrical universes (such as affine spaces and projective spaces).

Chapter 14

Applications and Software Tools

14.1. Applications

The development of research in the field of qualitative reasoning about time and/or space has been uninterruptedly motivated by the existence of many types of applications, be they effective or only potential. As regards time, Allen's work has been designed from the very start in view of its natural language processing and planning applications. The same holds in the spatial domain for the research based on the RCC formalism, which was early on used to describe, for example, the functioning of a hydraulic force pump, or the biological process of phagocytosis.

In this chapter, rather than describing in detail a — necessarily — limited subset of applications of qualitative reasoning, we will instead try to draw a general map of them, by listing pointers to the various applicative domains. We will refer the reader to the papers or books pointed to, as well to synthetic publications such as [FIS 05], which devote a separate chapter to each of the following domains of application of temporal reasoning: temporal databases, planning, law, natural language, medicine, and qualitative simulation.

14.1.1. *Applications of qualitative temporal reasoning*

– planning and scheduling [ALL 83, ALL 91a, ALL 91b, ELK 96, CES 02, FOX 03, FOX 05];

– diagnosis [NÖK 89], including the diagnosis of breakdowns in telecommunication networks [OSM 99a, OSM 00];

– meteorology [HUA 00];

– legal reasoning [VIL 05];

– medical information systems [BEE 91, KER 05];

– knowledge representation [MYL 90];

– temporal databases [CHO 05];

– constraint databases [REV 02];

– computer aided software and hardware verification [ALU 99];

– trajectory calculus [WEG 05b, WEG 07];

– multimedia [BUC 92, AND 96, ADA 00, SUK 04];

– natural language processing [ALL 84, MEU 05];

– representating tense and aspect in natural language [ALL 84, BES 89b, SCH 00];

– temporal structure of narratives and discourse analysis [NAK 87, NAK 88a, NAK 88b, LAS 91, LAS 93, ASH 05];

– multidocument news summarization [BAR 02];

– tracking and recognition of moving objects [BEN 04, BEN 08b];

– automatic categorization of events from textual data, search for event-driven knowledge on the Internet and application to question-answering systems [SAQ 04, HAR 05, MOL 05].

14.1.2. *Applications of spatial qualitative reasoning*

– GIS (geographic information systems) [BEN 96a, BEN 08a, COH 07];

– spatio-temporal databases [KOU 03];

– vague and rough location, granularity [GAL 98, BIT 98, WOR 98, BIT 02, BIT 08];

– geospatial operations in object-oriented databases [FRE 00];

– representing and reasoning about terrain silhouettes [CHE 05];

– spatial query languages [SVE 91, HUA 92, HAD 92, CLE 94];

– document structure recognition [AIE 02a];

– bio-spatial knowledge [COH 01], ecology (formalizing the concept of ecological niche) [SMI 99a, SMI 99b];

– specification of the syntax and semantics of visual languages [COH 94, HAA 95, GOO 96];

– qualitative simulation, common sense reasoning about physical systems [RAN 89, RAN 92b, CLA 05];

– robot navigation and exploration, cognitive mapping [KUI 91, LIU 04, WAG 04, REM 04, KUI 08];

– piano mover's problem [FAL 95];

– high level vision [COH 06b];

– interior design [BHA 09b] (design of intelligent environments);

– topological map learning [WAL 09];

– visibility and alignment-based localization and navigation [FOG 09];

– spatial cognition in sea navigation [WOL 08];

– route modeling [WER 00]; planning of actions using conceptual neighborhoods [DYL 07];

– hydrology [WÜR 00a, WÜR 00b, BEN 07a, LEB 07];

– land use recognition [LEB 99,BER 08, LEB 07];

– digital fingerprint recognition [BEN 07a];

– automated updating of geographical databases using satellite images [COT 05];

– automated document structure recognition [WAL 99];

– semantics of spatial prepositions [HER 86, AUR 93, SAB 95], representating spatial concepts in natural language [SLA 03];

– sketch interpretation, sketch-based reasoning [EGE 97, HAA 97, FOR 01, SCH 01, FOR 04, FER 03];

– automated translation of sketches or maps into route descriptions [FRA 98], scene generation from natural language descriptions [TAP 04];

– using space for representating semantics [GÄR 04, ADA 09];

– using space as a metaphor for structuring knowledge [LEH 94, RAL 96].

14.1.3. *Spatio-temporal applications*

Applications which deal with dynamic scenes, moving objects, and so on, come under the spatial as well as the temporal domains:

– modeling of spatio-temporal change [JIN 03];

– spatio-temporal granularity [HOR 01, MAU 06];

– representation of events from video entries [FER 00, KÖH 04], scene analysis [BHA 09a], and automatic surveillance [DEE 09];

– search for establishment of relations between successive video scenes [SAN 02, SAN 03];

– applications of the direction calculus between the regions for the detection of risk events in the context of security [LIG 09];

– generation of "smart" cards from accounts [LIG 07];

– archeology [JEA 07];

– trajectory calculus [WEG 05b, WEG 07];

– moving objects [BEN 04, BEN 08b].

14.2. Software tools

14.2.1. *The Qualitative Algebra Toolkit (QAT)*

The QAT [CON 06c] has been developed with the aim of providing software tools for working on arbitrary qualitative formalisms without having to develop the basic tools from scratch for each new formalism. This is possible because of the similar algebraic structures of many qualitative formalisms. The QAT offers the user ready-to-use tools, once the specification of the formalism has been provided to the system.

The Qualitative Algebra Toolkit (QAT) software is being developed at the University of Artois, France. It is a Java library designed to offer generic tools for the definition and the manipulation of qualitative algebras and constraint networks on these algebras.

The QAT is composed of of three packages: the ALGEBRA package, the QCN (*qualitative constraint networks*) package, and the SOLVER package.

14.2.1.1. *The* ALGEBRA *package*

This package allows the user to define arbitrary qualitative algebras (binary, ternary, or of arbitrary arity) using an XML file.

The XML file specifying an algebra has to satisfies a DTD containing the definitions of the elements which define the algebraic structure of the calculus: set of basic relations, diagonal elements, rotation table, permutation table, and composition table.

The package contains ready-to-use files for several formalisms frequently used in the literature (Allen's interval algebra, Point algebra, Cyclic point algebra, Cyclic interval algebra, Rectangle algebra, INDU algebra, n-point algebra, RCC-5 and RCC-8 algebras, and Cardinal direction algebra).

The package contains tools for defining and manipulating relations.

It also contains a module which, for binary relations, provides specifically tailored methods which are more effective than those used for arbitrary arities.

14.2.1.2. *The* QCN *package*

This package is used to define and manipulate qualitative constraint networks on a qualitative algebra. Again, the definition of the network is provided by the user as an XML file. The package also supports the automated generation of random instances of constraint networks.

14.2.1.3. *The* SOLVER *package*

This package contains tools for solving the main problems of interest when dealing with qualitative constraint networks: the consistency problem, the problem of finding one or all solutions, the problem of determining the minimal network.

All these methods are generic: they may be applied on arbitrary qualitative calculi.

Most of the usual solving methods are implemented, including the standard generate-and-test methods, search methods based on back-track and forward checking, and local propagation methods.

The user can configure these different methods by choosing among a range of heuristics. These heuristics are related to the choice of the variables or the constraints to be scanned, and of the basic relations to be be considered in a constraint during a search. Indeed, it has been shown that constraint ordering and value ordering can greatly affect the performance of a backtracking algorithm.

Several versions of the algebraic closure algorithm are provided (PC-1, PC2, PCMix).

The QAT is an open platform which also allows the user to define and test new heuristics.

Besides the three main packages, the QAT also contains additional applicative packages. For instance, the CAMPAIGN package implements tools for making benchmarks, while the MERGING package contains classes for merging the temporal or spatial information of several constraint networks.

14.2.2. *The SparQ toolbox*

SparQ is a software toolbox for qualitative reasoning. It has been developed in the context of a project on spatial cognition, and has been sponsored by the DFG (*Deutsche Forschungsgemeinschaft*). The aim of the project is to make the qualitative formalism techniques developed in the research community available in a single homogeneous framework.

SparQ is explicitly designed for two types of users: application designers or researchers working in a domain other than that of qualitative reasoning, who are offered access to qualitative reasoning techniques in an easy-to-use manner, and researchers in the domain, who are provided with an implementation toolbox of key techniques which facilitates the experimentation and development of new calculi.

SparQ contains two parts: part 1 is devoted to the specification of formalisms, the second is a functional part, designed as an open set, which comprises three modules:

a QUALIFY module, a COMPUTE-RELATION module, and a CONSTRAINT-REASONING module. Other planned modules are a NEIGHBORHOOD-REASONING module and a QUANTIFY module.

SparQ comprises a set of C libraries and a main program written in Lisp. It is a freeware released under the GNU (General Public License).

14.2.2.1. *The* QUALIFY *module*

Given a (spatial) configuration and a qualitative formalism, the function of this module is to describe the configuration by using the basic relations of the formalism.

An option allows the user either to generate a complete description (option *all*), which will contain n^2 basic relations if the configuration comprises of n objects, or to restrict the description to only contain the relations between the first object (in the binary case), or the first two objects (in the ternary case), and all other objects (option *first2all*).

The available objects are points (a real value), intervals (two real values, where the first is strictly less than the second), points in the plane (two real coordinate values), directed points in the plane (a point and a direction vector, hence four real values), and dipoles (pairs of points in the plane). Concretely, the result appears as a list of n-tuples — in the binary case, of 3-tuples containing the identifier of the first object, the relation name, and the identifier of the second object.

For example, if the formalism is Allen's calculus, and if the configuration contains three intervals $A = (0, 2)$, $B = (1, 4)$, and $C = (3, 4)$, calling QUALIFY with the option *first2all* results in the relation o between A and B, and the relation p between A and C. Using Lisp-like notations, we thus get the list $((A \circ B)(A \text{ p } C))$. With the option *all*, we would have got $((A \circ B)(A \text{ p } B)(B \text{ fi } C))$.

14.2.2.2. *The* COMPUTE-RELATION *module*

The function of this module is to compute the relations resulting from an operation of the calculus. Hence results are lists of relations, or sets of lists. The operations may be operations of the calculus (inversion and composition in the binary case, ternary or n-ary composition in general), closure operations (such as the computation of the smallest subclass generated by a set of relations), and set-theoretic operations (computing complements, intersections, unions, or differences).

14.2.2.3. *A SparQ session*

A typical interaction with SparQ uses a syntax in which the user specifies a functional module (for example, COMPUTE-RELATION, whose function is to compute a relation), a formalism (for example *allen*), and an operation (for example, composition) followed by the appropriate parameters (in the case of composition, the name of two relations of the calculus).

In this case, the user will input:

(compute-relation allen compositon o d)

(the syntax used is the lisp syntax); the output of the system will be the list of relations (o s d).

14.2.2.4. *The* CONSTRAINT-REASONING *module*

Given a constraint network, this module allows the user to carry out a particular operation on it. This operation may be the computation of its algebraic closure (the algorithm used is the AC-3 algorithm of [MAC 77]), or the search for an atomic refinement (a scenario) of the network which is an algebraically closed scenario (this operation is called *scenario-consistency*).

SparQ contains a module (under development) for testing the consistency of a network for formalisms whose domain of interpretation is defined in terms of real algebraic objects (this means that these objects are defined by algebraic equations on the field of real numbers). This test for consistency is based on the use of Gröbner bases [COX 98]. This functionality can be used to build composition tables, by proving the inconsistency of unfeasible scenarios.

14.2.2.5. *Available formalisms*

The main formalisms available are Allen's calculus, the Cardinal relation calculus, the dependency calculus [RAG 05a, RAG 05b], the Dipole calculi [SCH 95, MOR 00, MOR 05], the Single cross calculus [FRE 92a] and the Double cross calculus [FRE 92a], the Flip-flop calculus and its refinement $\mathcal{LR}$ [LIG 93a, SCI 04], the geometrical alignment calculus [DYL 04], the $\mathcal{OPRA}_m$ calculi [MOR 05, MOR 06], the Point calculus, several versions of the Qualitative trajectory calculus [WEG 04] (see section 15.3.1), and the RCC−8 and RCC−5 calculi.

14.2.3. *The GQR system*

GQR (an acronym for *Generic Qualitative Reasoner*) [GAN 08] is a solver for binary qualitative constraint networks developed at the University of Freiburg im Breisgau, Germany. The primary focus of the designers of this reasoning software is on *genericity* and *extensibility*, while preserving *efficiency* and *scalability*.

14.2.3.1. *General principles*

Given a qualitative formalism defined in a purely syntactic way by its set **B** of basic relations, and its inversion and composition operations, as well as a constraint network on the algebra **A** of relations (subsets of **B**), the aim of the software is to efficiently determine whether this network is consistent.

A network is represented as an adjacency matrix whose entries are bit vectors encoding the relations.

GQR implements Mackworth's variant of the path consistency algorithm [MAC 77, DEC 03]. It then uses chronological backtracking, making use of known tractable subclasses of the calculus to reduce the branching factor.

The two main phases of the computation — the enforcement of path consistency and the chronological backtracking search — involve choices for which several heuristics have been proposed in the literature. For the first, the heuristics based on weight and cardinality have been implemented; for the second, the cardinality heuristics for variable selection has been used.

In contrast to the two projects SparQ (encoded in Java) and QAT (programmed in LISP), the GQR software is encoded in C++.

The main formalisms implemented are the Point algebra, the Cardinal direction algebra (for points), Allen's interval algebra, the RCC-5 and RCC-8 formalisms, and the $\mathcal{OPRA}_4$ calculus.

14.2.3.2. *Genericity and extensibility*

Genericity means that the user should be able to use the system to define and test new formalisms at will. As a consequence, he/she is offered the possibility of defining formalisms by using textual files or XML files. The user is also allowed to define and use his/her own heuristics.

In addition, the software can be used to check the algebraic properties of a formalism, and (at least partially) to compile composition tables.

14.2.3.3. *Efficiency and scalability*

The techniques used in the implementation include Hogge's method used in [LAD 97] by Ladkin and Reinefeld, the use of a queue data structure as in Van Beek and Manchak's implementation of the path consistency method [BEE 96], and the use of caching techniques for computing inversion and composition [LAD 97].

The authors of [GAN 08] describe a comparison between the performances of GQR and those of two softwares designed specifically for particular calculi, namely

Nebel's software [NEB 96] for Allen's interval algebra, and Renz and Nebel's software [REN 98b] for RCC−8. Both are encoded in the C language. The conclusion of their experiments is that the behavior of GQR — a generic system — although slower than that of these specialized systems, is satisfactory for easy problems, but will have to be improved in order to deal with difficult problems efficiently.

14.2.3.4. *Applications using GQR*

GQR has been used for the SailAway project [WOL 08], which makes use of $\mathcal{OPRA}_4$, a formalism having 272 basic relations. It has also been used for the evaluation of algorithms for customizing qualitative calculi for specific applications [REN 07b].

GQR is a free software released under the GNU *General Public License*.

Chapter 15

Conclusion and Prospects

15.1. Introduction

To conclude, we present briefly some recent directions of research which, judging from the current activity in the field, seem to represent promising domains of investigation for the future of qualitative temporal and spatial reasoning.

15.2. Combining qualitative formalisms

Combining several qualitative formalisms is one of the themes which has emerged in recent years: on the one hand, it is natural to represent spatio-temporal phenomena by combining a formalism for time and a formalism for space; on the other hand, spatial formalisms are usually restricted to a single type of spatial relation (topology, orientation, qualitative distance, etc.), and the combination of several different aspects seems to be a natural way toward more expressive formalisms.

The general problem of combination is described by Westphal and Wölfl [WES 08]. First, one has to set apart the case where the two formalisms involve relations that are semantically independent. Such is the case, for example, of the cardinal direction calculus, which may be seen as the product of two "copies" of the Point calculus, or the Rectangle calculus, which may be seen as the product of two copies of Allen's calculus. In concrete terms, this independence, or orthogonality, results in the fact that the basic relations of the new formalism are pairs of basic relations of the component formalisms.

15.2.1. *Tight or loose integration*

In most cases, however, the relations of the two formalisms will be interdependent. The INDU calculus is a case in point: if a temporal interval has a duration strictly less than that of another one, the corresponding Allen relation cannot be one of the relations fi, fi, fi, or eq. Conversely, if one of the latter holds between two intervals, then the first interval has a duration at least equal to that of the second one. This is the reason why the INDU formalism does not have $3 \times 13 = 39$, but only 25 basic relations.

The interaction between the two types of relations can be made explicit by using *interdependence tables*. For example, Table 15.1 gives the interdependence tables[1] of the relative duration constraint on intervals and Allen's relations.

Duration	Allen	Allen	Duration
eq	p, m, o, eq, pi, mi, oi	s, d, f	<
<	p, m, o, s, d, f, pi, mi, oi	si, di, fi	>
>	p, m, o, si, di, fi, pi, mi, oi	eq	eq

Table 15.1. *The interdependence tables for the combination of Allen's calculus with the relative duration constraint on intervals. The table on the left represents the implication of relative durations in terms of Allen's relation; the table on the right, the implication of Allen's relations in terms of relative durations (we have omitted the cases where Allen's relations do not imply any constraint in terms of relative durations)*

In addition to the INDU formalism, another example of combination is studied in an article by Gerevini and Renz [GER 02b]. There, the RCC−8 calculus is refined by considering the relative sizes of the regions. The situation is hence the spatial analog of that of the INDU calculus. We may thus consider that what the authors are doing is combining RCC−8 with the Point calculus — the symbols <, eq, and > of the latter being interpreted as "smaller", "of the same size" and "larger", respectively.

However, INDU and the approach of [GER 02b] represent two different ways to approach the combination of formalisms. In INDU, the Point algebra is used to refine the partition of binary relations associated to Allen's interval algebra, and to build thus a *new* qualitative formalism. In this case, Westphal and Wölfl [WES 08] propose to use the term of *tight* integration of two formalisms. By contrast, [GER 02b] is an example of *loose* integration: there, one reasons about pairs of relations (r, s) between entities, where r is a relation of the first formalism and s a relation of the second one. No attempt is made to build a new calculus. The viewpoint here is closer to the use of "virtual relations" in the INDU lattice (see Chapter 4, section 4.11).

---

1 There is one interdependence table for each direction of implication.

Consequently, Gerevini and Renz use bi-labeled networks known as *biconstraint networks*, and they propose the *bipath consistency* algorithm as a generalization of the algorithms enforcing algebraic closure for a unique network. In essence, this algorithm propagates the two types of constraints in parallel to enforce algebraic closure on each network, and uses the interdependence tables to transfer information between the two networks. Ultimately, the network obtained after execution is algebraically closed for each formalism, and, if the label of an arc (i, j) is (r, s), the constraints r and s are compatible.

A comparison of the two approaches is presented in [WES 08, WES 09b, WÖL 09]. Tight integration has a greater expressive power in general. A series of empirical experiments carried out by the authors suggest that loose integration is efficient when there is a great number of basic relations, or when tractable classes are known for each formalism, and can be made use of for reasoning. By contrast, for calculi with a small number of basic relations, or for which no tractable subclasses are known, it would seem that preference should be given to tight integration.

15.2.2. RCC−8 *and the Cardinal direction calculus*

Another example of combination is considered in [RAG 08]. It consists of the combination of RCC−8 with the Cardinal direction calculus (between points). Here, the entities considered are closed disks in the plane, and the relations are RCC−8 relations between the disks as regions on the one hand, and on the other hand cardinal relations between the centers of these disks, which are points in the plane. The two relation systems are interdependent: for instance, if the centers of two disks coincide, the only possible RCC−8 relations are NTPP, NTPPI, and EQA. Composition cannot be computed componentwise: for example, the weak composition of $(\mathsf{EC}, \mathsf{n})$ and $(\mathsf{EC}, \mathsf{n})$ is the relation $(\mathsf{DC}, \mathsf{n})$, which is finer than $(\mathsf{EC} \diamond \mathsf{EC}, \mathsf{n})$.

15.2.3. RCC−8, *the Rectangle calculus, and the Cardinal direction calculus between regions*

In the example of the combination of RCC−8 with the Cardinal direction calculus, there is a small number of basic relations in each of the formalisms. This is no longer the case in [LIU 09], where Liu, Li, and Renz study the combination of RCC−8 with the Rectangle calculus, as well as of RCC−8 with the Cardinal direction calculus between regions, which is more expressive than the Rectangle calculus. In particular, they show that the consistency problem for basic relations of RCC−8 and of the Rectangle calculus is polynomial, but that the similar problem for RCC−8 and the Cardinal direction calculus between regions is NP-complete. The results of their paper generalize in particular those of a previous paper by Li [LI 07].

15.2.4. *The lattice of partition schemes*

A partition scheme on a given domain U is a partition of U^2, or equivalently, an equivalence relation on U^2 which satisfies additional properties. It is well known [COH 81] that the equivalence relations on a given set have a lattice structure.

EXAMPLE 15.1.– The partition scheme which defines the Point calculus has $U = \mathbb{R}$ as its domain. The map sgn: $U^2 \rightarrow \{-, 0, +\}$ which associates the sign of $(u - v)$ to the pair $(u, v) \in U^2$ is surjective, and the three equivalence classes constituting the partition scheme are $\mathsf{sgn}^{-1}(-), \mathsf{sgn}^{-1}(0)$, and $\mathsf{sgn}^{-1}(+)$. We have a partition scheme since:

  – Δ is an equivalence class, since $\Delta = \mathsf{sgn}^{-1}(0)$;
  – due to the fact that $\mathsf{sgn}(v, u) = -\mathsf{sgn}(u, v)$, the inverse of $\mathsf{sgn}^{-1}(+)$ is $\mathsf{sgn}^{-1}(0)$.

Condotta, Kaci, and Schwind [CON 09] show that partition schemes on the same universe have a largest common refinement, and that there exists a smallest partition scheme of which they are a common refinement. Thus, formalisms can be combined not only by refinement, but also by generalization. These authors use the two basic operations of the lattice of partition schemes for studying the fusion of constraint networks which are defined on different qualitative formalisms. Hence we can use both the existence of a *greatest common refinement* of these formalisms as well the existence of a *smallest generalization*, called in [CON 09] the *common abstraction* of these formalisms.

15.3. Spatio-temporal reasoning

Representating motion and change implies simultaneously dealing with time and space.

15.3.1. *Trajectory calculi*

A way of representing some types of motion consists in reducing them to static entities. The notion of trajectory, for example, associates a spatial object to a spatio-temporal event. Now the *trajectory calculi* of Van de Weghe [WEG 04] integrate directional knowledge with variational knowledge in the spirit of qualitative physics: their basic relations may denote direction of motion (e.g. left or right) and information about increase or decrease of the distance, as well as about the relative speed of moving objects.

More precisely, trajectory calculi consider mobile points on the line or in the plane, and use parameters to describe the situation of two moving points at two successive points in time t and $t + 1$ (Figure 15.1). According to the calculus considered, given two points A and B, the basic relations use one or more of the three following parameters:

Figure 15.1. *Trajectory calculi, in dimensions 1 and 2; on the left, we can write that $A(-,+,-)$ B in the QTC-B12 calculus (A approaches B, B moves away from A, and the speed of A is less than that of B. On the right, in the QTC-C22 calculus, $A(-,+,-,+,-)$ B (A approaches B, B moves away from A, A moves toward the left half-plane, B toward the right half-plane, and the speed of A is less than that of B*

– the fact that one of the points approaches $(-)$, moves away from $(+)$, or remains at the same distance from the other (0);

– the relative speed of the two points: the speed of A is smaller $(-)$, larger $(+)$, or equal (0) to that of B;

– in dimension 2, the fact that each point moves toward the left half-plane $(-)$, towards the right half-plane $(+)$, or moves while staying on the line $(A, B)(0)$.

More precisely, let $A_t, A_{t+1}, B_t, B_{t+1}$ be the respective positions of A and B at t and $t + 1$. Denoting distance by d, we consider the quantity $d(A_{t+1}, B_t) - d(A_t, B_t)$.

By definition, A approaches B if this quantity is negative, and moves away from it if it is positive. A remains at the same distance from B if it is zero.

According to the dimension considered and the parameters taken into account, Van de Weghe obtains the calculi summarized in Table 15.2.

Name	Dim.	vdist (A/B)	vdist (B/A)	dir(A)	dir(B)	cspeed(A/B)	num
QTC-B11	1	yes	yes			no	9
QTC-B12	1	yes	yes			yes	17
QTC-B21	2	yes	yes	no	no	no	9
QTC-B22	2	yes	yes	no	no	yes	27
QTC-C21	2	yes	yes	yes	yes	no	81
QTC-C22	2	yes	yes	yes	yes	yes	243

Table 15.2. *QTC calculi. For each calculus, and each parameter, the table indicates if this parameter is taken into account by the calculus. Dim denotes the dimension, vdist(A/B) the variation of the distance of A with respect to B, vdist(B/A) the variation of the distance of B with respect to A; dir(A) and dir(B) indicate toward which half-plane A and B are moving, respectively; cspeed(A/B) indicates whether the speed of A is smaller than, equal to, or greater than that of B; num is the number of basic relations of the calculus*

NOTE 15.1.– In the QTC-B12 formalism, there are only 17 basic relations, because some of the 27 3-tuples of $\{-, 0, +\}^3$ are excluded. For example, *in dimension 1*, if A and B are stationary, their speeds are equal, which excludes the 3-tuples $(0, 0, -)$ and $(0, 0, +)$; if one of the points is stationary and that the other is not, the speed of the second is higher than that of the first: this excludes another eight 3-tuples.

EXAMPLE 15.2.– Figure 15.1 illustrates the situation in dimension 1 (on the left) and dimension 2 (on the right). On the left, the relation of A with B is $(-, +, -)$ in the QTC-B12 calculus; on the right, the relation is $(-, +, -, +, -)$ in the QTC-C22 calculus.

A paper by Van de Weghe *et al.* [WEG 05a] describes a way of obtaining a "condensed" composition table for the QTC-C21 calculus by using a method which is similar to that used by Freksa [FRE 92a] for Allen's composition table. The question of conceptual neighborhoods is discussed in [WEG 05b]. A qualitative trajectory calculus in the context of networks is described in [BOG 06], and extended to evolutionary networks in [DEL 08].

15.3.2. *Reasoning about space-time*

Muller [MUL 98b] takes a radically different approach, which consists of directly reasoning about regions in space-time.

The reader is also referred to Muller's thesis [MUL 98a], which describes in detail the construction of a spatio-temporal logic, and shows how it can be applied to define notions of continuity, to describe motion, as well as to relate the formal system to natural language semantics.

The construction of the logical language starts from the mereotopological component of Asher and Vieu's system [ASH 95], which uses a connection relation C between spatio-temporal regions. It adds to it a temporal order relation, denoted by $<$, which corresponds to the intuition that a region in space-time has a lifetime[2] which entirely precedes that of another, and a temporal connection relation, denoted by $\lesssim$, whose intuitive meaning is that the temporal projections of the regions share at least one common point.

A region of time-space can be visualized as the graph of a function which associates a spatial region to every point in time.

15.3.2.1. *Continuity*

Muller gives a definition of the continuity of a spatio-temporal region which can be informally stated as follows:

---

2 Intuitively, the lifetime of a region in space-time corresponds to its projection on the time axis.

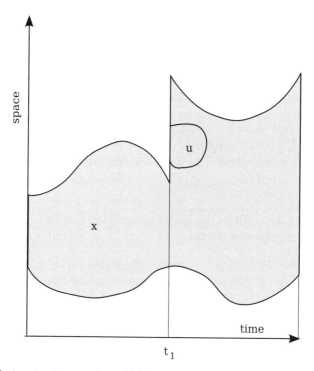

Figure 15.2. *A region in space-time which is not continuous in Muller's sense [MUL 98b]: the temporal slice x and the subregion u are contemporary (their projections share the point t_1), but they are not connected to each other*

– a spatio-temporal region w is continuous if, and only if, for any "temporal slice" x of w and any part u of w, if x and u are contemporary, then x and u are connected.

Figure 15.2 represents a situation where this continuity property is not verified: the spatio-temporal region w contains a temporal slice x (the regularization of the part of the region preceding the point t_1) and a part u which are *contemporary* (their temporal projections have point t_1 in common), but are not connected).

The notion of continuity is an important one if the notion of conceptual neighborhood — for instance for RCC−8 relations — is to be based on a concept of continuous change. Galton [GAL 97, GAL 00] and Davis [DAV 01] have shown how various definitions of the distance between regions, and their associated notions of continuity, influence the structure of conceptual neighborhoods. Davis [DAV 01] studies the continuity of Boolean operations, and shows that continuity in the sense of Muller corresponds to the Hausdorff metric.

15.3.3. *Combining space and time*

However, most of the spatio-temporal formalisms in the literature are obtained by combining spatial and temporal formalisms.

Bennett *et al.* study a way of "temporalizing" RCC−8 in the context of multimodal logics [BEN 02a]. More precisely, they introduce the **PSTL** (*Propositional Spatio-Temporal Logic*) logic which is the Cartesian product of the **PTL** logic[3] and the logic $S4_u$, and show that several temporal extensions of RCC−8 (based on points as well as on intervals) can be embedded in decidable fragments of this logic.

The reader can also refer to [WOL 00a].

Gerevini and Nebel [GER 02a] study the combination of RCC−8 constraints (for space) and Allen constraints (for time).

EXAMPLE 15.3.− The set of formulas $[I: (X\{DC, EC\}Y)]$, $[I: (Y\{TPP\}Z)]$, $[J: (X\{PO\}Y)]$, $[J: (Y\{DC\}Z)]$ expresses relations of the RCC−8 type enforced on three regions X, Y, and Z during two intervals I and J.

Gerevini and Nebel show that, even when restricted to using only basic relations and the universal relation for each of the two formalisms, the consistency problem is NP-complete. On the other hand, complexity does not increase if a persistence constraint on the size of the regions as well as continuity constraints are introduced.

Another aspect of the combination of space and time is the phenomenon of periodicity, or more generally of eventual periodicity (the latter refers to behaviors which, after some finite stretch of time, repeat the same spatio-temporal motive). Spatio-temporal constraint networks of this type, called *ultimately periodic networks*, are studied in [CON 06a]. They represent a temporal extension of the STP formalism of Dechter, Meiri, and Pearl (see section 6.2) which expresses spatio-temporal constraints of this type on points moving on a line, or between series of events.

15.4. Alternatives to qualitative reasoning

The question of legitimacy of qualitative reasoning itself has been raised for the last few years, at least as far as the efficiency of this type of reasoning is concerned: can we be sure that representing and reasoning in the qualitative reasoning framework is advantageous in terms of efficiency? Could we gain in efficiency by solving the main problem of consistency in a more classical framework, such as first order logic, a

---

3 The **PTL** logic is a propositional modal logic equipped with the operators S (*since*) and U (*until*); hence, in particular, it has an operator $\bigcirc$ (next), defined as $U(\bot, \varphi)$.

description logic, a finite CSP, or by using the powerful techniques recently developed for solving the SAT problem?

In [WES 09a], Westphal and Wölfl examine those questions, based on empirical experiment carried out with currently available software tools; their conclusion is that qualitative techniques keep their advantage with respect to techniques using a translation in terms of first order logic or description logics: reasoning systems in both domains are clearly less efficient than methods using constraint propagation.

15.4.1. *Translation in terms of finite CSP*

Qualitative constraint networks can be encoded in terms of finite CSPs [REN 01a, BRA 04, CON 06b]. Here is a brief description of the process, assuming that we deal with a formalism whose basic relations are the elements of a set $\mathbf{B}$.

Let $\mathcal{N} = (N, C)$ be a constraint network with variables $\{V_1, \ldots, V_n\}$. The idea is to replace this binary constraint network by a network of unary and ternary constraints on new variables $X_{i,j}$ with $1 \leq i < j \leq n$, which intuitively correspond to the arcs $(V_i, V_j)(i < j)$ of the original network. We thus have $\frac{n(n-1)}{2}$ variables in this new network.

The unary constraints associate the subset $C(i, j)$ of $\mathbf{B}$ to each variable $X_{i,j}$.

As for the non-trivial ternary constraints, they involve 3-tuples of variables $(X_{i,j}, X_{i,k}, X_{k,j})$, for $1 \leq i < j < k \leq n$, and associate the set $TC = \{(a, b, c) \in \mathbf{B}^3 \mid a \in (b \diamond c)\}$ to each 3-tuple. In other words, the elements of TC are the 3-tuples (a, b, c) of basic relations such that (b, a, c) is a *triad*, in the sense given to this term in Chapter 10, section 10.4. TC thus represents the (weak) composition table of the calculus.

We thus have $\frac{(n-1)^3 - (n-1)}{6}$ 3-tuples of variables which have to satisfy the constraint TC.

Let $\mathsf{T}_{\mathsf{DCN}}(\mathcal{N})$ be the constraint network thus obtained.

EXAMPLE 15.4.– The translation of the network with three vertices of Figure 15.3 (on the left) is the network on the right, for which the three unary domain constraints are shown, the only ternary constraint being the constraint TC on the 3-tuple $(X_{1,3}, X_{1,2}, X_{2,3})$.

The translation of the network with four vertices of Figure 15.4 (on the left) is the network on the right, which has six vertices. The constraint TC involves four 3-tuples $(X_{1,3}, X_{1,2}, X_{2,3}), (X_{1,4}, X_{1,2}, X_{2,4}), (X_{1,4}, X_{1,3}, X_{3,4})$, and $(X_{2,4}, X_{2,3}, X_{3,4})$.

The following proposition is proved in [CON 06b]:

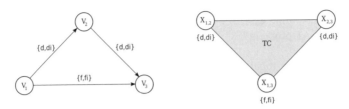

Figure 15.3. *A network on Allen's algebra (on the left) and its translation in terms of finite CSPs. Both networks are consistent*

PROPOSITION 15.1.– *Let $\mathcal{N} = (N, C)$ be a constraint network. If $\mathcal{N}$ is consistent, then $T_{DCN}(\mathcal{N})$ is consistent.*

The converse statement is not true, and we only have:

PROPOSITION 15.2.– *Let $\mathcal{N} = (N, C)$ be a constraint network. If $T_{DCN}(\mathcal{N})$ is consistent, then $\mathcal{N}$ contains a subnetwork which is an algebraically closed scenario.*

As a consequence, the converse is true only for calculi where any non-zero algebraically closed scenario — in other terms, any weak representation — is consistent.

EXAMPLE 15.5.– The network of Figure 15.3 (on the left) is a consistent network. The same holds for the network on the right. For example, $X_{1,2} = $ d, $X_{2,3} = $ di, $X_{1,3} = $ fi is a solution of the latter.

The network on the left side of Figure 15.4 is an example of a network which is algebraically closed but inconsistent. Hence its translation (on the right) is inconsistent.

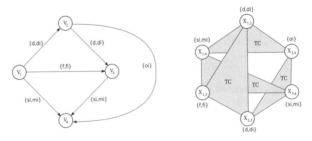

Figure 15.4. *A network on Allen's algebra (on the left) and its translation in terms of a finite CSP. The network on the left is algebraically closed but is inconsistent*

The domain of finite CSPs has very effective methods of resolution, and we could hope to benefit from them by translating qualitative networks in terms of finite CSPs. In [WES 09b], Westphal and Wölfl describe an analysis of the comparative efficiency of qualitative solvers as opposed to that of finite CSP solvers. For the latter, the solver used is the *Mistral* software library [HEB 08]. Their empirical study examines five calculi: RCC−8, Allen's calculus, RCC−23 [BEN 97b], $\mathcal{OPRA}_2$, and $\mathcal{OPRA}_4$. The results suggest that qualitative methods are at an advantage for calculi having a small number of basic relations. By contrast, for calculi having a high number of basic relations, such as those of the $\mathcal{OPRA}$ family, finite CSP-based methods get the upper hand.

15.4.2. *Translation into an instance of the SAT problem*

Finally, one can try to make use of the progress in solving the SAT problem by translating the finite CSPs in terms of instances of the SAT problem. Among the various methods which have been devised to this aim — whose description can be found in [WAL 00] — the authors of [WES 09b] choose the *1D support scheme* of Pham *et al.* [PHA 06]. Given a finite CSP, the translation proceeds in the following manner:

– for each variable $X_{i,j}$, and for each element of $b \in \mathbf{B}$ of the corresponding unary constraint, we introduce a Boolean variable $X_{i,j}^b$ whose intuitive meaning is "variable $X_{i,j}$ takes the value b";

– we then successively express the following three conditions:
1) variable $X_{i,j}$ takes at least one of the values of $C(i,j) \subseteq \mathbf{B}$ as its value;
2) variable $X_{i,j}$ takes at most one of the values of $C(i,j)$ as its value;
3) for any 3-tuple $(X_{i,j}, X_{i,k}, X_{k,j})$, if $X_{i,k}$ takes b as its value and $X_{k,j}$ takes c as its value, then the value of $X_{i,j}$ is one of the elements of $(b \diamond c)$.

In terms of logical formulas, this can be written as follows:
– for each (i,j), if $C(i,j) = \{b_1, \ldots, b_k\}$, we have:

$$X_{i,j}^{b_1} \vee \ldots \vee X_{i,j}^{b_k}$$

– for each (i,j) and each pair (b,c) of distinct elements of $C(i,j)$, we have:

$$\neg(X_{i,j}^b \wedge X_{i,j}^c) \text{ or equivalently } \neg X_{i,j}^b \vee \neg X_{i,j}^c$$

– for any 3-tuple (i,j,k) with $i < k < j$, and for all (b,c), where $b \in C(i,k), c \in C(k,j)$, if $(C(i,k) \diamond C(k,j)) \cap C(i,j) = \{a_1, \ldots, a_m\}$, we have:

$$(X_{i,k}^b \wedge X_{k,j}^c) \rightarrow (X_{i,j}^{a_1} \vee \ldots \vee X_{i,j}^{a_m})$$

or equivalently:

$$\neg X_{i,k}^b \vee \neg X_{k,j}^c \vee X_{i,j}^{a_1} \vee \ldots \vee X_{i,j}^{a_m}$$

The propositional formula obtained in this way is equivalent to the finite CSP problem. This translation leads to a significant increase of the number of variables, since, if B is the size of $\mathbf{B}$, and n the number of variables of the finite CSP, we get $O(n^2.B)$ variables and $O(n^3.B^2)$ clauses.

In the same series of experiments, the authors of [WES 09b] also report evaluating this approach by making use of the MiniSat solver [EÉN 03]. Their conclusion is that the translation into an instance of the SAT problem proves to be robust in difficult cases where the qualitative method of algebraic closure gives poor approximations of consistency, but that it is also very costly in terms of computation time and space.

15.5. To conclude — for good

In spite of its size, this book has totally left out — or only superficially dealt with — a number of topics. However, as such, we hope it will have given the reader a taste for qualitative temporal and spatial reasoning, as well as the desire to explore the field further, and perhaps also to contribute to it.

Appendix A

Elements of Topology

A.1. Topological spaces

DEFINITION A.1.– *A topological space is a pair* (X, Ω), *where* Ω *is a collection of subsets of* X *such that*:

- $\emptyset$ *and* $X \in \Omega$;
- *if* $A, B \in \Omega$, *then* $A \cap B \in \Omega$;
- *any union of elements of* Ω *belongs to* Ω.

The elements of X are the *points*, and those of Ω are called as the *open sets* of the topological space.

EXAMPLE A.1.– Some examples of topologies are as follows:

1) the *discrete* topology (X, Ω_X) on a set X is the topology for which any subset of X is an open set: $\Omega_X = \mathcal{P}(X)$;

2) the *coarse* topology on X is the topology whose only open sets are $\emptyset$ and X itself;

3) the open sets of the real line $\mathbb{R}$ are the unions of open intervals (a, b), where $a, b \in \mathbb{R}$, with $a < b$;

4) let $X = (0, +\infty)$ and $\Omega = \{\emptyset, X\} \cup_{a \geq 0} (a, +\infty)$. We thus define a topological space structure on $X = (0, +\infty)$;

5) the pair (X, Ω), where $X = \{a, b\}$, and $\Omega = \{\emptyset, X, \{a\}\}$, is a finite topological space containing two points. It can be visualized as an ordinary point b together with an infinitesimal direction a;

6) the pair (X, Ω), where $X = \{a, b, c, d\}$, $\Omega = \{\emptyset, X, \{a\}, \{b\}, \{a, c\}, \{a, b, c\},$ $\{a, b\}\}$ defines another finite topological space containing four points.

DEFINITION A.2.– *Let* (X, Ω) *be a topological space; a subset* Y *of* X *is* closed *if, and only if,* $X \setminus Y$ *is open.*

Clearly:

1) $\emptyset$ and X are closed;

2) if Y and Z are closed, $Y \cup Z$ is also closed;

3) any intersection of closed sets is a closed set.

DEFINITION A.3.– *A* neighborhood *of a point* $x \in X$ *is any subset containing an open set containing* x.

A.1.1. *Interior, exterior, boundary*

DEFINITION A.4.– *Let* X *be a topological space, and let* A *be a subset of* X. *The* closure $Cl(A)$ *of* A *is the smallest closed set containing* A *(equivalently, the intersection of all closed sets containing* A*). The* interior $Int(A)$ *of* A *is the largest open set contained in* A *(equivalently, the union of all open sets contained in* A*). The* boundary *of* A *is the set* $Cl(A) \setminus Int(A)$.

A.1.2. *Properties of the closure operator*

For all subsets A and B:

1) $A \subseteq Cl(A)$;

2) if $A \subseteq B$, then $Cl(A) \subseteq Cl(B)$;

3) $Cl(Cl(A)) = Cl(A)$;

4) $Cl(A \cup B) = Cl(A) \cup Cl(B)$.

The first three properties characterize a *closure operator*. An operator having the fourth property as well is a *topological closure operator*.

NOTE A.1.– Obviously, $Cl(A \cap B) \subseteq Cl(A) \cap Cl(B)$ since the second term is a closed set containing A and B, but equality does not hold in general. For example, if $A = [0, 1), B = \{1\}$, then $A \cap B = \emptyset$, $Cl(A) = [0, 1], Cl(B) = \{1\}$, and thus $Cl(A \cap B) = \emptyset$, whereas $Cl(A) \cap Cl(B) = \{1\}$.

A.1.3. *Properties of the interior operator*

For all subsets A and B:

1) $Int(A) \subseteq A$;
2) if $A \subseteq B$, then $Int(A) \subseteq Int(B)$;
3) $Int(Int(A)) = Int(A)$;
4) $Int(A \cap B) = Int(A) \cap Int(B)$.

This time, $Int(A \cup B) \subseteq Int(A) \cup Int(B)$, but equality does not hold in general. For example, if $A = \mathbb{R} \setminus \{1\}$, and $B = \{1\}$, we have $A \cup B = \mathbb{R}, Int(A) = A, Int(B) = \emptyset$, hence $Int(A \cup B) = \mathbb{R}$, whereas $Int(A) \cup Int(B) = \mathbb{R} \setminus \{1\}$.

A.1.4. *Closure, interior, complement*

We thus have three operators on the subsets of a topological set: the closure, the interior, and the complement operators.

First of all, the closure operator and the interior operator are dual to each other. Let X be a topological space. Let K denote the complement operator: $K(A) = X \setminus A$.

LEMMA A.1.– *For any subset A of X, $Cl(A) = K(Int(K(A)))$ and $Int(A) = K(Cl(K(A)))$.*

Proof. If $x \in A$, then $x \ni K(A)$, and *a fortiori*, $x \ni Int(K(A))$, hence $x \in K(Int(K(A)))$. This shows that $K(Int(K(A)))$ is a closed set containing A: it thus contains $Cl(A)$, hence $K(Int(K(A))) \supseteq Cl(A)$. Conversely, let $x \in K(Int(K(A)))$, hence $x \ni Int(K(A))$. As x is not in the interior of $K(A)$, any open set U containing x meets A, hence $x \in Cl(A)$. This proves the first identity. The second identity is equivalent to the first. $\square$

LEMMA A.2.– *For any subset A of X, $Cl(Int(Cl(Int(A)))) = Cl(Int(A))$.*

Proof. For any B, we have $B \subseteq Cl(B)$. Hence in particular $Int(A) \subseteq Cl(Int(A))$. The subset $Int(A)$ of $Cl(Int(A))$ is open, and consequently contained in the interior of $Cl(Int(A))$: $Int(A) \subseteq Int(Cl(Int(A)))$. This implies for the closures that $Cl(Int(A)) \subseteq Cl(Int(Cl(Int(A))))$. Conversely, we have $Int(Cl(Int(A))) \subseteq Cl(Int(A))$. Since $Cl(Int(A))$ is closed, it contains the closure of $Int(Cl(Int(A)))$, and so we have $Cl(Int(A)) \supseteq Cl(Int(Cl(Int(A))))$. $\square$

A.1.5. *Defining topological spaces in terms of closed sets*

In a dual way, topological spaces can be defined in terms of closed sets.

DEFINITION A.5.– *A topological space is a pair* (X, Φ), *where* Φ *is a collection of subsets of* X *such that*:

- $\emptyset$ *and* $X \in \Phi$;
- *if* $X, Y \in \Phi$, *then* $X \cup Y \in \Phi$;
- *any intersection of elements of* Φ *is in* Φ.

The elements of Φ are called the *closed sets* of the topological space. By definition, a subset of X is open if its complement is closed.

A.1.6. *Defining topological spaces in terms of operators*

DEFINITION A.6.– *A topological space is a pair* (X, Cl), *where* X *is a set and* Cl *is an operator* Cl *on the collection of subsets of* X, *called the closure operator, such that*:

1) $Cl\emptyset = \emptyset$;
2) $A \subseteq Cl(A)$;
3) $Cl(Cl(A)) = Cl(A)$;
4) $Cl(A \cup B) = Cl(A) \cup Cl(B)$.

Under these conditions:

DEFINITION A.7.– *A closed set* F *of* X *is a subset which is invariant under the closure operation, i.e. such that* $Cl(F) = F$.

An equivalent definition can also be given in terms of an interior operator:

DEFINITION A.8.– *A topological space is a pair* (X, Int), *where* X *is a set and* Int *is an operator on the collection of subsets of* X, *called the interior operator, such that*:

1) $Int\emptyset = \emptyset$;
2) $Int(A) \subseteq A$;
3) $IntIntA = IntA$;
4) $Int(A \cap B) = ClA \cap ClB$.

DEFINITION A.9.– *An open set* U *of* X *is a subset which is invariant under the interior operator, i.e.* $Int(U) = U$.

It can be easily seen that the four definitions of a topological space are equivalent.

A.1.7. *Pseudocomplement of an open set*

If U is an open set, let $U^* = Int(K(U))$. The open set U^* is the largest open set which does not meet U. This set is called the *pseudocomplement* of U.

Because of lemma A.1, $U^{**} = Int(K(IntK(U))) = Int(Cl(U))$. Lemma A.2 implies that, for any open set U, we have the identity $U^{***} = U^*$.

We deduce from above that the map $U \mapsto U^{**} = Int(Cl(U))$ has the properties of a closure operator:

1) $U^{**} \supseteq U$;

2) if $U \subseteq V$, then $U^{**} \subseteq V^{**}$;

3) $U^{****} = U^{**}$.

The invariable open sets under this closure operator are the regular open sets, which are characterized by the fact that they coincide with the interior of their closure.

EXAMPLE A.2.– Let us consider the open sets $U = (0, 1) \cup (1, 2)$ and $V = (2, 3)$ in $\mathbb{R}$. We have $U^{**} = (0, 2)$, $V^{**} = (2, 3)$. The open set V is regular. The open set U is not regular (it has a 1D hole at point 1). Note that $(U \cup V)^{**} = (0, 3)$, whereas $U^{**} \cup V^{**} = (0, 2) \cup (2, 3)$. Hence the closure operator $U \mapsto U^{**}$ is *not* a *topological* closure operator, since $(U \cup V)^{**} \neq U^{**} \cup V^{**}$.

A.1.8. *Pseudosupplement of a closed set*

If F is a closed set, we can, *mutatis mutandis*, develop the same type of construction: the closed set $F^{\circ} = Cl(K(F))$ is the smallest closed set whose union with F covers the whole space. It is called as the *pseudosupplement* of F.

The map $F \mapsto F^{\circ\circ} = Cl(Int(F))$ is an interior operator, whose fixed elements are the regular closed sets, which are characterized as coinciding with the closure of their interior.

We thus have:

1) $F^{\circ\circ} \subseteq F$;

2) If $F \subset F'$, then $F^{\circ\circ} \subset F'^{\circ\circ}$;

3) $F^{\circ\circ\circ\circ} = F^{\circ\circ}$.

EXAMPLE A.3.– Let us consider the closed sets $F = [0, 1] \cup \{2\}$ and $F' = [1, 2]$ in $\mathbb{R}$. We have $F^{\circ\circ} = [0, 1]$, $F'^{\circ\circ} = [1, 2]$. The closed set F' is regular. The closed set F is not regular (it has a component of dimension 0 at point 2). Note that $F \cap F' = \{1\} \cup \{2\}$, hence $(F \cap F')^{\circ\circ} = \emptyset$. On the other hand, $F^{\circ\circ} \cap F'^{\circ\circ} = \{1\}$. Hence the interior operator $F \mapsto F^{\circ\circ}$ is *not* a *topological* interior operator.

A.1.9. Regular sets

Let $(X, \mathcal{O}_X)$ be a topological space.

DEFINITION A.10.– *A regular open set $A \subseteq X$ is an open set $A \in \mathcal{O}_X$ which coincides with the interior of its closure. A regular closed set $B \subseteq X$ is a closed set which coincides with the closure of its interior.*

For example, X and $\varnothing$ are regular open and closed sets.

A.1.10. Axioms of separation

The concept of separation takes many aspects. However, the following axioms are standard:

DEFINITION A.11.– *(T_0) A topological space is T_0, or Kolmogorov, if given two distinct points, at least one of them is contained in an open set not containing the other.*

DEFINITION A.12.– *(T_1) A topological space is T_1, or Fréchet, if, given two distinct points, each of them is contained in an open set not containing the other.*

DEFINITION A.13.– *(T_2) A topological space is T_2, or Hausdorff, if two distinct points have disjoint open sets containing each one of them.*

DEFINITION A.14.– *(T_3) A topological space X is T_3 if for any closed set A of X and any point $x \in X \setminus A$ there are disjoint open sets U_A containing A and U_x containing x. A topological space is* regular *if it is Hausdorff and T_3 (and thus T_2)*[1].

DEFINITION A.15.– *(T_4) A topological space X is T_4, or* normal, *if any pair of closed sets A and B such that $A \cap B = \emptyset$ have disjoint open sets U_A and U_B containing each one of them.*

DEFINITION A.16.– *(T_5) A topological space X is T_5, or* completely normal *if for any pair of subsets A and B such that $A \cap Cl(B) = \emptyset$ and $B \cap Cl(A) = \emptyset$, there exist two disjoint open sets U_A and U_B containing A and B, respectively.*

A.1.11. Bases of a topology

DEFINITION A.17.– *A family of open sets Σ is a* base *for a topology Ω if any non-empty open set is a union of elements of Σ.*

---

1 The coarse topology is T_3, but it is not T_2.

EXAMPLE A.4.– The open intervals of $\mathbb{R}$ constitute a base of the usual topology of $\mathbb{R}$.

Similarly:

EXAMPLE A.5.– Let us consider the plane $\mathbb{R}^2$. Let:

 – Σ^2 be the set of open disks;

 – Σ^∞ be the set of open orthoaxial squares;

 – Σ^1 be the set of open squares whose axes are parallel to the first or the second bisectors.

Then each one of the above families of sets is a base of the usual topology of $\mathbb{R}^2$.

A.1.12. *Hierarchy of topologies*

Consider two topologies Ω_1 and Ω_2 on the same set X.

DEFINITION A.18.– Ω_1 *is finer than* Ω_2 *(or,* Ω_2 *is coarser than* Ω_1*) if* $\Omega_1 \supseteq \Omega_2$.

EXAMPLE A.6.– On any set:

 – the *coarse* topology is the coarsest topology on a set;

 – the *discrete* topology is the finest topology on a set.

Equivalent bases:

 – two bases on a set are *equivalent* if they define the same topology.

For example, the bases Σ^2, Σ^∞, and Σ^1 on $\mathbb{R}^2$ are equivalent.

A.1.13. *Preorder topology*

Let $(X, \preceq)$ be a preorder, i.e. a set X equipped with a binary relation $\preceq$ which is reflexive and transitive.

DEFINITION A.19.– *The subsets of* X *of the form* $\{x \in X \mid a \preceq x\}$*, for* $a \in X$ *form the base of a topology on* X *called the* preorder topology.

In this topology, it is clear that any point a has a smallest open neighborhood, namely $\{x \in X \mid a \preceq x\}$.

DEFINITION A.20.– *A topological space is an* Alexandroff space *if each point has a smallest neighborhood.*

The topological spaces associated with a pre-order are therefore Alexandroff spaces.

EXAMPLE A.7.– The preorder topology on the set $X = \{a, b, c, d\}$ where $d \preceq c \preceq a$, and $d \preceq b$, has a base of open sets $\{a\}, \{b\}, \{a, c\}, \{a, b, c, d\}$. It has three additional open sets: $\emptyset, \{a, b\}$, and $\{a, b, c\}$. This is the topological space with four points considered in example A.1.

EXAMPLE A.8.– Define on the set of integers $\mathbb{Z}$ a preorder relation such that for any k, we have $2k \preceq 2k - 1$ and $2k \preceq 2k + 1$. The topological space thus defined (Figure A.1) is known as the *digital line* or *Khalimsky line* $\mathbf{K}^1$.

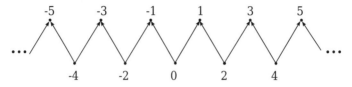

Figure A.1. *The Khalimsky line*

A.1.14. *Constructing topological spaces*

Constructing new structures from simpler elements is a widely encountered situation in mathematics. Topology is no exception. Among the basic constructions, we recall the most important ones for our subject: constructing subspaces, products, quotients, and direct sums.

DEFINITION A.21.– *Let (X, Ω) be a topological space, and Y a subset of X. The topology Ω_Y induced on Y has open sets $V \cap Y$, where $V \in \Omega$.*

A.1.14.1. *Products of topological spaces*

Let (X, Ω) and (Y, Θ) be two topological spaces.

DEFINITION A.22.– *The Cartesian product $X \times Y$ is the topological space whose set of points is $X \times Y$, and whose base of open sets is the set of all $U \times V$, where U is an open set of X and V an open set of Y.*

PROPOSITION A.1.– *The canonical projections are continuous.*

EXAMPLE A.9.–

– the product of $\mathbb{R}$ by $\mathbb{R}$ is homeomorphic to $\mathbb{R}^2$;

– the torus is homeomorphic to $S^1 \times S^1$, the product of two circles;

– the *Khalimsky plane* is the product of $\mathbf{K}^2 = \mathbf{K}^1$ by itself equipped with the product topology. Those points whose both coordinates are even (odd, respectively) are closed (open, respectively). All other points are neither open nor closed.

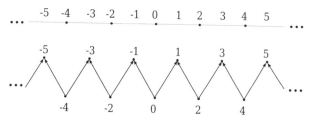

Figure A.2. *The Khalimsky line as a quotient space*

A.1.14.2. *Quotients of topological spaces*

Let (X, Ω) be a topological space, and R an equivalence relation on X.

DEFINITION A.23.– *The quotient X / R is the topological space whose set of points is X / R, and whose open sets are the sets U such that $pr^{-1}(U)$ is open in X.*

The canonical projection $X \to X / R$ is continuous (by construction). Actually, the quotient topology is *the finest topology* for which the canonical projection is continuous.

EXAMPLE A.10.– Consider (Figure A.2) the partition of the real line whose equivalence classes are the even integers, and the open intervals $(2k, 2k + 2)$, for $k \in \mathbb{Z}$. The real line is equipped with the usual topology. Then the quotient space of the line by this equivalence relation is the Khalimsky line.

A.1.14.3. *Disjoint unions*

Let (X_1, Ω_1) and (X_2, Ω_2) be two topological spaces.

DEFINITION A.24.– *The disjoint union of X and Y is the space $X_1 \sqcup X_2$:*
– *the points of $X_1 \sqcup X_2$ are the elements of the disjoint union of X_1 and X_2;*
– *a subset U is open if, and only if, $U \cap X_1$ and $U \cap X_2$ are open.*

The disjoint union topology is *the finest topology* for which the canonical injections are continuous.

A.1.15. *Continuous maps*

DEFINITION A.25.– *Let (X, Ω_X) and (Y, Ω_Y) be two topological spaces. Then the map $f: X \to Y$ is continuous if for any $V \in \Omega_Y, f^{-1}(V) \in \Omega_Y$.*

In other words, the inverse image of any open set is an open set.

EXAMPLE A.11.– In particular:

  – the identity $id_X \colon X \to X$ is continuous;

  – if $Y \subseteq X$ is an arbitrary subset of X, the canonical injection $j \colon Y \to X$ is continuous.

PROPOSITION A.2.– *The composition of two continuous maps is continuous.*

A.1.16. *Homeomorphisms*

For topological spaces, the adequate concept of equivalence is that of a homeomorphism. In the same way as two sets are cannot be distinguished *qua* sets if there exists a bijection between them, two topological spaces are indistinguishable if, in addition to their underlying sets being in a one-to-one correspondence, this correspondence also identifies the two topological structures:

DEFINITION A.26.– *A map $f \colon X \to Y$ is a homeomorphism if it is continuous, bijective, and if the inverse map $f^{-1} \colon Y \to X$ is also continuous (f is said to be bicontinuous).*

EXAMPLE A.12.– Consider (Figure A.3) the unit sphere, which can be defined in $\mathbb{R}^3$ by the equation $X^2 + Y^2 + Z^2 = 1$. Let $P = (0, 0, 1)$ be the north pole. Any point M on the sphere other than P defines a line which is not parallel to the horizontal plane $Z = 0$, and which cuts this plane at exactly one point N. Conversely, given a point N in the plane $Z = 0$, there exists a unique line connecting N with P, and this line cuts the sphere at exactly one point M distinct from P.

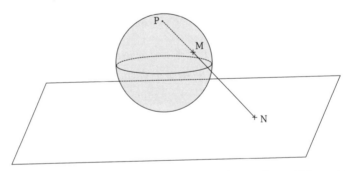

Figure A.3. *A homeomorphism between the sphere — from which a point has been removed — and the plane*

The two maps $M \mapsto N$ and $N \mapsto M$ are clearly continuous and each one is the inverse of the other. Thus, they define a homeomorphism between the Euclidean plane and the sphere from which the pole has been removed.

DEFINITION A.27.– *A* homeomorphism *is an invertible map f such that f and f^{-1} are continuous.*

EXAMPLE A.13.–

- the identical map is a homeomorphism;
- the composition of two homeomorphisms is a homeomorphism;
- the inverse of a homeomorphism is a homeomorphism.

DEFINITION A.28.– *Two topological spaces X and Y are* homeomorphic *if there exists a homeomorphism $f \colon X \to Y$.*

A.2. Metric spaces

A *metric* (or distance function) on a set X is a function $\rho \colon X \times X \to \mathbb{R}^{+} = \{x \in \mathbb{R} \mid x \geq 0\}$ such that:

1) $\rho(x, y) = 0$ if, and only if, $x = y$;
2) $\rho(x, y) = \rho(y, x)$;
3) $\rho(x, y) \leq \rho(x, z) + \rho(z, y)$ (triangle inequality).

For example, $(x, y) \mapsto |x - y|$ on $\mathbb{R}$, $(x, y) \mapsto \sqrt{\sum(x_i - y_i)^2}$ on $\mathbb{R}^n$, and $(x, y) \mapsto \sum |x_i - y_i|$ on $\mathbb{R}^n$ are metrics.

A.2.1. *Minkowski metrics*

In the Euclidean space $\mathbb{R}^n$, the Minkowski metric ρ_p, where $p \geq 1$, is defined by:

$$\rho_p(x, y) = \sqrt[p]{\sum_{i=1}^{n} |x_i - y_i|^p}$$

By convention, the metric ρ_∞ is defined by $\rho_\infty(x, y) = sup_{i=1,\ldots n} |x_i - y_i|$.

A metric space is a pair (X, ρ), where X is a set and ρ is a metric on X. The metric $|x - y|$ on $\mathbb{R}$ and more generally, the metrics $\sqrt{\sum_{i=1}^{n}(x_i - y_i)^2}$ on $\mathbb{R}^n$, for $n > 1$, are called Euclidean metrics.

A.2.2. *Balls and spheres*

Let (X, ρ) be a metric space, $a \in X$ a point in X, and r a positive real number.

The open ball, the closed ball, and the sphere with center a and radius r, respectively, are defined, as follows:

$$B_r(a) = \{x \in X \mid \rho(a, x) < r\}$$
$$D_r(a) = \{x \in X \mid \rho(a, x) \leq r\}$$
$$S_r(a) = \{x \in X \mid \rho(a, x) = r\}$$

For example, $D_n = D_1(0)$ in $\mathbb{R}^n$ is the unit n-disk. $S_{n-1} = S_1(0)$ in $\mathbb{R}^n$ is the unit $(n-1)$-sphere (it is assumed that the metric is the Euclidean metric).

A.2.3. Bounded sets

A subset A of a metric space (X, ρ) is a bounded set if there exists a real number $d > 0$ such that $\rho(x, y) < d$ for all $x, y \in A$. The lower bound of the set of d satisfying this property is called the diameter of A, denoted by $diam(A)$.

Equivalently, a set A is bounded if there exists a ball containing it.

A.2.4. Topology of a metric space

Let (X, ρ) a metric space. Let Ω be the collection of subsets of X consisting of the empty set and all unions of open balls. Then (X, Ω) is a topological space, and Ω is called the metric topology on (X, ρ).

A topological space is a metrizable space if its topology can be generated by a metric.

For example, the usual topology on $\mathbb{R}$ is generated by the metric $(x, y) \mapsto |x - y|$. A coarse topological space is not metrizable if it contains more than one point. A finite space is metrizable if, and only if, it is discrete.

A.2.5. Equivalent metrics

Two metrics ρ_1 and ρ_2 on the same set are equivalent if they define the same topology on X. A necessary and sufficient condition for this to be true is that there exist two real constants $c, C > 0$ such that: $c\rho_1(x, y) \leq \rho_2(x, y) \leq C\rho_1(x, y)$.

For example, the three metrics:

$$(x, y) \mapsto \sqrt{((x_1 - y_1)^2 + (x_2 - y_2)^2)}$$
$$(x, y) \mapsto |x_1 - y_1| + |x_2 - y_2|$$
$$(x, y) \mapsto sup(|x_1 - y_1|, |x_2 - y_2|)$$

on $\mathbb{R}^2$ are equivalent.

A.2.6. *Distances between subsets*

Let (X, ρ) be a metric space. If $A \subseteq X$ is a subset of X and $b \in X$, the distance from b to A is by definition, the number $\rho(b, A) = inf\{\rho(b, a) \,|\, a \in A\}$.

If $A, B \subseteq X$ are two subsets of X, the Hausdorff distance between A and B is defined by $d_\rho(A, B) = max\{sup_{a \in A}\rho(a, B), sup_{b \in B}\rho(b, A)\}$.

A.2.7. *Convergence of a sequence*

Recall that for $X = \mathbb{R}^n (n \geq 1)$:

$- U \subseteq X$ is open if, and only if, for any $x \in U$, there exists $\epsilon > 0$ such that the open ball $B_\epsilon(x)$ is contained in U;

$- Y$ is closed if its complement $X \setminus Y$ is open.

DEFINITION A.29.– *A sequence* $\{x_n\}_{n \in \mathbb{N}}$ *converges toward l if, and only if, for any $\epsilon > 0$, the ball $B_\epsilon(l)$ contains all the terms of the sequence except for a finite number of them.*

A.3. Connectedness and convexity

A.3.1. *Connectedness*

Intuitively, a topological space is connected if it is in one piece.

DEFINITION A.30.–

– a topological space X is connected if the only open sets which are also closed sets are $\emptyset$ and X;

– a subset A of X is connected if A, equipped with the induced topology, is a connected topological space.

For example, in Figure A.4, region (a) is the only region which is not connected.

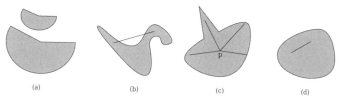

(a)   (b)   (c)   (d)

Figure A.4. *Region (a) is not connected; regions (b) and (c) are connected, but not convex; region (c) is star-shaped with respect to p; region (d) alone is a convex region*

Connectedness is preserved under topological closure and continuous maps:

– the topological closure of a connected subset is connected;

– the continuous image of a connected subset is connected. Hence connectedness is a topological property.

A.3.2. *Connected components*

The various connected "pieces" of a topological space X are called its connected components:

DEFINITION A.31.– *A connected component of a topological space X is a connected subset of X which is maximal for the inclusion relation.*

We have in particular the following properties:

– connected components are closed;

– the number of connected components of a topological space is a topological property.

EXAMPLE A.14.– A subset of $\mathbb{R}$ is connected if, and only if, it is an interval.

A.3.3. *Convexity*

A.3.3.1. *The betweenness relation*

The notion of betweenness can be formalized by a ternary relation $B(x, y, z)$ (which reads "y is between x and z"). Among the axioms that can be considered for a betweenness relation B, consider the following [GÄR 00]:

1) if $B(x, y, z)$, then x, y, and z are distinct;
2) if $B(x, y, z)$, then $B(z, y, x)$;
3) if $B(x, y, z)$, then we do not have $B(y, x, z)$;
4) if $B(x, z, y)$ and $B(z, y, t)$, then $B(x, z, t)$;
5) if $B(x, y, z)$ and $B(y, t, z)$, then $B(x, y, t)$.

In an undirected graph, if $B(x, y, z)$ is defined by the condition that y is on the shortest path between x and z, then all the axioms above are satisfied, except axiom 4.

The standard practice in a metric space (X, ρ) is to define B as follows:

DEFINITION A.32.– $B(x, y, z)$ *if, and only if,* $\rho(x, z) = \rho(x, y) + \rho(y, z)$.

Then all five axioms are satisfied.

In Euclidean geometry, the *line* defined by two distinct points x and y can be characterized as the set containing x, y, and all the points t for which we have $B(x, t, y)$, $B(t, x, y)$, and $B(x, y, t)$. Similarly, *planes* defined by a line and a point which is not located on the line can be characterized using the betweenness relation B.

A general definition of convexity can be deduced from that of the betweenness relation:

DEFINITION A.33.– *A convex* subset A *in a space* X *equipped with a betweenness relation* B *is a subset* A *such that* $x, y \in A$ *implies that all points between* x *and* y *are also in* A: $\forall x, y \in X$, *if* $x \in A$, $y \in A$, *and* $B(x, t, y)$, *then* $t \in A$.

More generally, a subset is *star-shaped* with respect to a point x of A if for any $y \in A$, all the points between x and y are also in A.

Consequently, a subset is convex if, and only if, it is star-shaped with respect to each one of its points.

EXAMPLE A.15.– In particular:

- the whole space X is convex;
- the projections of a convex set in $\mathbb{R}^n$ are convex;
- the product of a convex set in $\mathbb{R}^m$ and a convex set in $\mathbb{R}^n$ is a convex set in $\mathbb{R}^{m+n}$.

Convexity is not a topological concept. Intuitively, bending, stretching, or twisting a convex subspace can make it lose its convexity.

Convexity in Euclidean space implies connectedness: if $A \subseteq \mathbb{R}^n$ is convex, then A is connected. Obviously, the converse statement is false. For example, the circle S^1 is connected, but not convex.

Appendix B

Elements of Universal Algebra

B.1. Abstract algebras

An (abstract) *algebra* consists of a set A, called the *support* of the algebra, and a set of *operations* on A. An *operation* o is by definition a map $o: A \times \ldots A \rightarrow A$ of the product of n copies of A with values to A; such an operation is an n-ary operation. In the particular case where $n = 0$, a 0-ary operation simply consists of an element of A; a 0-ary operation is called a *constant* (operation).

For an algebra, the list of its operation symbols, together with the map assigning to each symbol the arity of the associated operation, is called the *signature* of the algebra. Various axioms are typically satisfied by the operations.

EXAMPLE B.1.– The set of integers $\mathbf{Z}$, equipped with the binary addition operation $+$ and the unary operation $-$ which associates with each integer the opposite integer, as well as the constant 0, is a type of algebra called the abelian group. The signature of this algebra is $(+, -, 0)$, with $(2, 1, 0)$ as the associated arities. The axioms satisfied by the operations include associativity for addition, its commutativity, and the fact that the sum of x and $-x$ is equal to 0, for any $x \in A$.

EXAMPLE B.2.– A *lattice* is an algebra A of signature $(\vee, \wedge)$, where $\vee$ and $\wedge$ are two binary operations which satisfy the following properties:

1) $\wedge$ and $\vee$ are commutative and associative;
2) $\wedge$ and $\vee$ are idempotent: for any $x \in A$, we have:

$x \wedge x = x$ and $x \vee x = x$

3) $\wedge$ and $\vee$ are related by the property of absorption: for any $x, y \in A$, we have:

$x \wedge (x \vee y) = x$ and $x \vee (x \wedge y) = x$

Alternatively, a lattice can be defined in terms of partially ordered sets or POSs.

DEFINITION B.1.– *A lattice is a partially ordered set* $(A, \preceq)$ *such that, for all* x, y *in* A, *the set* $\{x, y\}$ *has a greatest lower bound inf*(x, y) *and a least upper bound sup*(x, y).

One goes over from this definition to the one above by setting $x \vee y = \sup(x, y)$ and $x \wedge y = \inf(x, y)$. In the reverse direction, one defines $x \preceq y$ by the condition that $x \vee y = y$ (or equivalently $x \wedge y = x$).

A lattice A is a *complete* lattice if, and only if, any part of A has a greatest lower bound and a least upper bound.

A lattice is *distributive* if the operation $\vee$ is distributive with respect to $\wedge$, or, equivalently, if $\wedge$ is distributive with respect to $\vee$.

A lattice is *complemented* if it has a smallest element 0, a largest element 1, and if for each $x \in A$ there exists y, called the *complement* of x, such that $x \vee y = 1$ and $x \wedge y = 0$.

B.2. Boolean algebras

B.2.1. *Boolean algebras of subsets*

Consider an arbitrary set B. The collection A of all subsets of B has a set of natural operations: a binary operation, the union $\cup$, a unary operation $-$, the complement, and two constants, namely the empty set $\emptyset$ and the whole set B.

More generally, given a basic set B, let us consider a non-empty family A of subsets of B which has the following properties:

– if X and Y are in A, then $X \cup Y$ is also in A;

– if X is in A, then its complement $-X = B \setminus X$ is also in A.

In this case, which generalizes the previous one, the empty set and the basic set B belong[1] to A.

Such a family is called a *field of sets* on B.

If A is a field of sets on B, then $(A, \cup, -, \emptyset, B)$ is an algebra of signature $(\cup, -, \emptyset, B)$ which satisfies a set of axioms which define Boolean algebras:

---

1 Since B is not empty, it contains at least one set X, which is its complement. But the union of these two sets is the set B, which is in A, as well as its complement, the empty set.

B.2.2. *Boolean algebras*

DEFINITION B.2.– *A* Boolean algebra *is an algebra of signature* $(+, -, 0, 1)$, *such that the following axioms are satisfied (the abbreviation $x.y$ stands for $-(-x + -y)$):*

– *the binary operation + is associative, commutative, and idempotent:*

$$(x + y) + z = x + (y + z) \qquad\qquad \text{[B.1]}$$

$$x + y = y + x \qquad\qquad \text{[B.2]}$$

$$x + x = x \qquad\qquad \text{[B.3]}$$

– *the unary operation − satisfies:*

$$-(-x) = x \qquad\qquad \text{[B.4]}$$

$$x + (-x) = 1 \qquad\qquad \text{[B.5]}$$

$$-1 = 0 \qquad\qquad \text{[B.6]}$$

– *the operation · is distributive with respect to +:*

$$x \cdot (y + z) = x \cdot y + x \cdot z \qquad\qquad \text{[B.7]}$$

– *0 is a neutral element for +*

$$0 + x = x \qquad\qquad \text{[B.8]}$$

An alternative definition for Boolean algebras can be given in terms of lattices:

DEFINITION B.3.– *A* Boolean algebra *is a distributive and complemented lattice.*

The correspondence between the two definitions associates the operations $\vee, \wedge$, the complement operation, the smallest element, and the largest element, respectively, to the symbols $+, \cdot, -, 0,$ and 1, respectively.

An *atom* is by definition an element a which is not 0 and such that there does not exist y with $0 \preceq y \preceq a$. A Boolean algebra is *atomic* if, for any $x \neq 0$, there exists an atom a such that $a \preceq x$.

B.2.3. *Stone's representation theorem*

A field of sets is a Boolean algebra, if the symbols $+, -, 0,$ and 1, respectively, are interpreted as the union, the complement, the empty set, and the set B, respectively. The issue of representability consists in asking whether, conversely, any Boolean algebra can be interpreted as a field of subsets of some set.

Stone's representation theorem states that this is indeed the case.

In full generality, Stone's theorem states that, for any Boolean algebra A, there exists a topological space $S(A)^2$, and a subset B of $S(A)$ (namely, the subsets of $S(A)$ which are both open and closed) such that A is isomorphic to the algebra of subsets of B.

For finite Boolean algebras, i.e. whose support is a finite set, the topological space $S(A)$ is the set B of atoms of A, and Stone's theorem amounts to the statement that there exists a one-to-one correspondence between the algebra and the algebra of subsets of B. Specifically, the map from A to the algebra of subsets of B is the map which, to each element x of A, associates the set of atoms y such that $y \preceq x$. The inverse map associates to each subset of B (a finite set of atoms) its least upper bound.

This result implies in particular that a finite Boolean algebra contains 2^k elements, for a well-determined k, and that any finite Boolean algebra having the same number of elements is isomorphic to it.

B.3. Binary relations and relation algebras

B.3.1. *Binary relations*

Recall that, given a set U, a binary relation on U is by definition a subset of $U \times U$. Binary relations on a set U include:

– the empty relation $\varnothing$;
– the universal relation $U \times U$;
– the equality relation or diagonal relation $\Delta = \{(x,x) \mid x \in U\}$;
– the difference relation: $\Delta' = \{(x,y) \mid x \neq y\}$.

A binary relation R on U can be visualized as an directed graph whose vertices are the elements of U: there is an arc (x, y), where $x, y \in U$, if, and only if, $(x, y) \in R$. Then many of the usual properties of a binary relation can be expressed in terms of the associated graph:

Reflexive: each vertex of the graph has a loop;

Irreflexive: no vertex of the graph has a loop;

Symmetrical: if (x, y) is an arc, then (y, x) is also an arc;

Antisymmetrical: if there is an arc $x \rightarrow y$, with $x \neq y$, then (y, x) is not an arc;

Transitive: if (x, y) and (y, z) are arcs, the (x, z) is an arc;

Functional: if (x, y) and (x, z) are arcs, then $y = z$.

---

2 The points of this space are the ultrafilters on A.

B.3.2. *Inversion and composition*

The set of binary relations on a set U is a Boolean algebra, and thus has the operations of a Boolean algebra. But in addition, owing to the fact that they are binary relations, it also has the inversion and composition operations:

The inverse R^{-1} of the relation R is the relation containing the set of pairs (y, x), where $(x, y) \in R$.

The composition of R and S, denoted by $R \circ S$ contains (x, y) if there exists an element z such that $(x, z) \in R$ and $(z, y) \in S$. In terms of graphs, we can go from x to y by initially following an arc of R, then one of S^3.

The inversion and composition operations have the following properties:

– inversion is an involution, i.e. $(R^{-1})^{-1} = R$;
– composition is associative: $(R \circ S) \circ T = R \circ (S \circ T)$;
– Δ is a neutral element for composition: $(R \circ \Delta) = (\Delta \circ R) = R$;
– $(R \circ S)^{-1} = S^{-1} \circ R^{-1}$.

In addition, the triangle axiom is also satisfied: for any 3-tuple of relations, the three conditions $(R \circ S) \cap T = \varnothing$, $(R^{-1} \circ T) \cap S = \varnothing$, and $(T \circ S^{-1})R = \varnothing$ are equivalent.

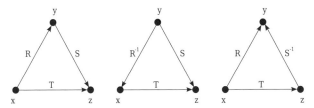

Figure B.1. *The triangle axiom: the triangles are simultaneously either consistent, or inconsistent. This expresses the fact that the three conditions*
$(R \circ S) \cap T = \varnothing$, $(R^{-1} \circ T) \cap S = \varnothing$, *and* $(T \circ S^{-1}) \cap R = \varnothing$ *are equivalent*

B.3.2.1. *About the triangle axiom*

The triangle axiom expresses an almost obvious fact, contrary to what may be assumed at first sight: indeed, referring to Figure B.1, saying for instance that $(R \circ S \cap T) = \varnothing$ means that if x, y, z can be found in U such that $(x, y) \in R$ and $(y, z) \in S$, then we can assert that $(x, z) \ni T$. Now, $(x, y) \in R$ is equivalent to $(y, x) \in R^{-1}$, and $(y, z) \in S$ to $(z, y) \in S^{-1}$. Hence all three triangles are simultaneously consistent or inconsistent.

---

3 If R and S are functional and correspond to functions f_R and f_S, care should be taken that the relation $R \circ S$, which is also functional, corresponds to the function $f_S \circ f_R$.

B.3.3. *Proper relation algebras*

In the case of Boolean algebras, we considered fields of sets which were "concrete" Boolean algebras, whose elements are sets rather than abstract elements. Proper relation algebras are to relation algebras what fields of sets are to Boolean algebras: their elements are *bona fide* binary relations on a set U.

Let U be a set. A *field of binary relations* on U is any subset of all binary relations on U closed under union and complementation relative to a fixed relation W on $U \times U$.

DEFINITION B.4.– *A proper relation algebra (PRA) on U is a field of binary relations on U which is closed under inversion and composition, and which has a neutral element for composition.*

DEFINITION B.5.– *If $\mathcal{R}$ is a set of binary relations, the proper relation algebra generated by $\mathcal{R}$, denoted by $\lfloor \mathcal{R} \rfloor$, is the smallest PRA containing all the relations of $\mathcal{R}$.*

It can be easily seen that under these conditions, the relation W is necessarily an equivalence relation on U. When $W = U \times U$, we say that the proper relation algebra is *square*.

B.3.4. *Relation algebras*

Relation algebras were introduced by Tarski [TAR 41] to axiomatize the properties of proper relation algebras:

DEFINITION B.6.– *A relation algebra $(A, +, -, 0, 1, 1', \smile, ;)$ is an algebra of signature $(+, -, 0, 1, 1', \smile, ;)$ such that the following conditions are satisfied*:

– $(A, +, -, 0, 1)$ *is a Boolean algebra;*
– ; *is an associative binary operation, i.e.*:

$$x; (y; z) = (x; y); z \qquad\qquad [\text{B.9}]$$

– *the following properties hold*:

$$(x + y); z = x; z + y; z \qquad\qquad [\text{B.10}]$$

$$x; 1' = x \qquad\qquad [\text{B.11}]$$

$$(x^{\smile})^{\smile} = x \qquad\qquad [\text{B.12}]$$

$$(x + y)^{\smile} = x^{\smile} + y^{\smile} \qquad\qquad [\text{B.13}]$$

$$(x; y)^{\smile} = y^{\smile}; x^{\smile} \qquad\qquad [\text{B.14}]$$

– *the Piercean law holds*:

$$(x; y) \cdot z^{\smile} = 0 \quad if,\ and\ only\ if, \quad (y; z) \cdot x^{\smile} = 0 \qquad\qquad [\text{B.15}]$$

B.3.4.1. *Composition tables*

When a relation algebra A is finite, it is atomic. Its structure as a Boolean algebra is then determined in a unique way. In order to completely determine its structure as a relation algebra, it is sufficient to describe the inverse and composition operations on the atoms. This can be done by using the *composition table* of the algebra, whose rows and columns correspond to atoms, and where the entry in row a and column b is $(a \circ b)$.

B.3.5. *Representations*

Any proper relation algebra is a relation algebra, if $1'$ is interpreted as the diagonal relation on U, $\smile$ as the transposition, and ; as the composition of binary relations.

The problem of representation consists in determining whether a given relation algebra can be considered as a proper relation algebra. This is not the case, as shown initially by Lyndon [LYN 50]: there are relation algebras which are not isomorphic to a proper relation algebra.

More precisely, we define a representation of a relation algebra in the following manner:

DEFINITION B.7.– *A representation (U, φ) of a relation algebra* A *consists of a non-empty set U and of a map φ of the support A of* A *to a proper relation algebra on U such that the following conditions are satisfied*:

1) φ is injective;

2) φ is a homomorphism of Boolean algebras;

3) $\varphi(\alpha; \beta) = \varphi(\alpha) \circ \varphi(\beta)$;

4) $\varphi(\alpha^{\smile})$ is the inverse of $\varphi(\alpha)$.

A *representable* relation algebra is an algebra which has at least one representation. Lyndon's results imply that there are non-representable relation algebras. The smallest non-representable relation algebra is an algebra with 16 elements [MCK 70].

B.4. Basic elements of the language of categories

B.4.1. *Categories and functors*

A category $\mathcal{C}$ comprises objects $Obj(\mathcal{C})$ and arrows (or morphisms) $Fl(\mathcal{C})$. Each arrow has a source and a target which are objects of the category.

EXAMPLE B.3.– The category *Ens* of sets has sets as objects, and the maps between sets as arrows. The category *Top* of topological spaces has topological spaces as objects and the continuous maps as arrows.

For any pair of objects A, B of a category $\mathcal{C}$, $Hom_{\mathcal{C}}(A, B)$ or simply $Hom(A, B)$ denotes the set of arrows with source A and target B. For $A = B$, there exists a particular arrow denoted by id_A.

Two arrows can be composed if the target of the first is the source of the second: for any 3-tuple of objects A, B, C, composition $\circ$ associates with arrows $f \in Hom(A, B)$ and $g \in Hom(B, C)$ an arrow $(g \circ f) \in Hom(A, C)$. This composition is associative, and id_A is a neutral element.

EXAMPLE B.4.– Let $\mathcal{X} = (X, \preceq)$ be a preorder, i.e. a set X equipped with a binary relation $\preceq$ on X which is reflexive and transitive. Then $\mathcal{X}$ defines a category in the following manner: the objects of this category are the elements of X, and $Hom(x, y) = \{*\}$ is a set with a unique element $*$ if $x \preceq y$ otherwise $Hom(x, y) = \varnothing$. Owing to reflexivity, $Hom(x, x)$ is a set with one element, for any $x \in X$, and, by transitivity, if $x \preceq y$ and $y \preceq z$, composition $Hom(x, y) \times Hom(y, z) \rightarrow Hom(x, z)$ associate $*$ to the pair $(*, *)$.

The previous example is an example of a *small category*, which is by definition a category whose collections of objects and arrows are sets (we will not enter into the technical complexities related to the foundations of the theory of categories, and will refer the reader to standard references such as [MAC 71]) for more details.

Many examples of categories appear as the result of building upon existing categories to which structure is added or removed. For example, a topological space $(X, \mathcal{O}_X)$ is a set X to which a topological structure of open sets $\mathcal{O}_X$ is added. Similarly, a vector space is a set equipped with operations such as addition, multiplication by a scalar, and so on.

In all these cases, there is a way back from the "richer" category to the " poorer" one by "forgetting" the extra structure. For example, starting with a topological space, i.e. an object of the category *Top*, we can forget about the topological structure and only retain the set X. We can thus associate an object of *Ens* with each object of *Top*. This "forgetfulness" on objects extends to arrows: if $f\colon X \rightarrow Y$ is an arrow of *Top* (hence a continuous map), we can forget about continuity, and only retain the map $f s$ from X to Y, which is an arrow in *Ens*.

What we have just described in an informal way is known as the *forgetful functor*, that we will denote by $Fgt\colon Top \rightarrow Ens$.

More generally, a *functor* $F\colon \mathcal{C} \rightarrow \mathcal{D}$ associates with each object A of $\mathcal{C}$, an object $F(A)$ of $\mathcal{D}$, and with any arrow $f\colon A \rightarrow B$, an arrow $F(f)\colon F(A) \rightarrow F(B)$, such that the following conditions are satisfied:

1) for any object A, $F(id_A) = id_F(A)$;

2) if $f\colon A \rightarrow B$ and $g\colon C \rightarrow D$, then $F(g) \circ F(f) = F(g \circ f)$.

EXAMPLE B.5.– Let $\mathcal{C}$ be a category. The map which, for each object A of $\mathcal{C}$, associates A to itself, and for each arrow $f: A \to B$, associates f to itself, is a functor, known as the identity functor of $\mathcal{C}$ and denoted by $\mathbf{1}_\mathcal{C}$.

DEFINITION B.8.– *A functor $F: \mathcal{C} \to \mathcal{D}$ is a* full *functor if for any pair (A, B) of objects of $\mathcal{C}$, the map $Hom_\mathcal{C}(A, B) \to Hom_\mathcal{D}(F(A), F(B))$ is surjective; it is* faithful *if it is injective; it is* essentially surjective *if for any object D of $\mathcal{D}$, an object C of $\mathcal{C}$ can be found such that D is isomorphic to $F(C)$.*

EXAMPLE B.6.– Let $\mathcal{X}$ and $\mathcal{Y}$ be two preorders. Let us denote the corresponding categories by using the same symbols (example B.4). Then, an increasing map of $\mathcal{X}$ in $\mathcal{Y}$ obviously defines a functor of $\mathcal{X}$ in $\mathcal{Y}$.

A functor thus intuitively corresponds to a mapping between categories. We will need what corresponds to the notion that two categories are essentially the same, namely the notion of the equivalence of two categories.

B.4.2. *Adjoint functors*

Functors allow transitions from one category to another. The concept of a map between two functors is known as a *natural transformation*:

Let $F, G: \mathcal{C} \to \mathcal{D}$ be two functors of category $\mathcal{C}$ with values in $\mathcal{D}$.

DEFINITION B.9.– *A natural transformation $\eta: F \to G$ associates with each object A of $\mathcal{C}$ a morphism η_A, which is called the component of η in A, such that for any morphism $f: A \to B$, we have the identity*:

$$\eta_B \circ F(f) = G(f) \circ \eta_A$$

i.e. the diagram below is commutative. We say that η is a *natural isomorphism* if for any object A of $\mathcal{C}$, η_A is an isomorphism in $\mathcal{D}$.

$$\begin{array}{ccc} F(A) & \xrightarrow{\eta_A} & G(A) \\ F(f) \downarrow & & \downarrow G(f) \\ F(B) & \xrightarrow{\eta_B} & G(B) \end{array}$$

In category theory, the equivalence of two categories, which corresponds to the intuitive concept of the fact that the two categories are essentially the same, is defined in the following way:

DEFINITION B.10.– *An equivalence of categories between two categories C and D consists of two functors $F: C \to D$ and $G: D \to D$ and two natural isomorphisms ϵ: $FG \to 1_D$ and $\eta: 1_C \to GF$.*

An easy criterion for the existence of an equivalence between two categories is the following:

PROPOSITION B.1.–*A functor $F: C \to D$ can be extended to an equivalence of categories if, and only if, it is full, faithful, and essentially surjective.*

DEFINITION B.11.– *An adjunction consists of (F, G, ϵ, η), where $F: D \to C$ is a functor called the* left adjoint functor *and $G: C \to D$ is a functor called the* right adjoint functor, *a natural isomorphism $\Phi: Hom_C(F, -) \to Hom_D(-, G)$, a natural transformation $\epsilon: F \circ G \to 1_C$ called the counit, and a natural transformation η: $1_D \to G \circ F$ called the unit, such that the following conditions are satisfied:*

– *for any morphism $f: F(B) \to A$, there exists a unique morphism in D, say $\Phi_{B,A}(f) = g: B \to G(A)$, such that $\epsilon_A \circ F(g) = f$ and $G(f) \circ \eta_B = g$;*
– *for any morphism $g: B \to G(A)$, there exists a unique morphism in C, say $\Phi_{A,B}^{-1}(g) = f: F(B) \to A$, such that $\epsilon_A \circ F(g) = f$ and $G(f) \circ \eta_B = g$.*

The two conditions are summarized by the statement that the two diagrams of Figure B.2 commute.

Figure B.2. *The adjunction is a data (F, G, ϵ, η) such that: given f, there exists a unique g such that the two diagrams commute and, given g, a unique F such that the same condition is satisfied*

EXAMPLE B.7.– We have introduced previously the example of the forgetful functor $Fgt: Top \to Ens$ which forgets the topological structure on a topological space $(A, \mathcal{O}A)$.

Given a set A, let *Coa(A)* be the topological space formed by A equipped with the coarse topology, and *Dis(A)* the topological space formed by the same A equipped with the discrete topology.

It can be easily seen that *Coa* and *Dis* define two functors *Coa, Dis*: *Ens* → *Top* — the only condition to check is that in each case the relevant maps are continuous.

We then have:
– the functor *Coa* is right adjoint to the forgetful functor *Fgt*;
– the functor *Dis* is left adjoint to the forgetful functor *Fgt*.

In the previous example, the equivalence associated with the first adjunction simply expresses the obvious equivalence of the category of sets with the category of topological spaces with the coarse topology. The equivalence associated with the second adjunction, unsurprizingly, expresses the equivalence of the category of sets with the category of discrete topological spaces.

B.4.3. *Galois connections*

Let $\mathcal{X}$ and $\mathcal{Y}$ be two preorders, and $F\colon X \to Y, G\colon Y \to X$ be two increasing maps. We say that (F, G) defines a Galois connection if, for any $x \in X$ and $y \in Y$, we have $F(x) \preceq_Y y$ if, and only if, $x \preceq_X G(y)$.

When such a pair (F, G) defines a Galois connection, $GF\colon \mathcal{X} \to \mathcal{X}$ is a closure operator, i.e. an operator which satisfies the following conditions:
1) $x \preceq_X GF(x)$;
2) $GFGF(x) \preceq_X GF(x)$;
3) if $x \preceq_X x'$, then $GF(x) \preceq_X x'$.

Similarly, $FG\colon \mathcal{Y} \to \mathcal{Y}$ is an interior operator, i.e. an operator which satisfies the dual conditions of the preceding conditions:
1) $FG(y) \preceq_Y y$;
2) $FG(y) \preceq_Y FGFG(y)$;
3) if $y \preceq_Y y'$, then $FG(y) \preceq_X y'$.

Two elements x and x' of a preorder are isomorphic, which is denoted by $x \cong x'$, if both $x \preceq x'$ and $x' \preceq x$ hold. If the preorder is a partial order, which means that $\preceq$ is an antisymmetric relation, then $x = x'$. In the general case, the fact that (F, G) is a Galois connection implies that, for any $x \in X$, one has $GFGF(x) \cong GF(x)$ and similarly for any $y \in Y$, $FGFG(y) \cong FG(y)$.

Since GF is a closure operator, there is a natural definition of *closed* elements: $x \in X$ is *closed* if it is isomorphic to its closure $GF(x)$. Similarly, in Y, an *element y* is *open* if it is isomorphic to $FG(y)$.

An important aspect of a Galois connection (F, G) is that the maps F and G define a *bijection* between the equivalence classes of the subpreorder of closed objects of $\mathcal{X}$ and of the subpreorder of open objects in $\mathcal{Y}$.

EXAMPLE B.8.– Let O and A be two sets, and I a binary relation in $O \times A$. Consider $\mathcal{C} = \mathcal{P}(O)$ and $Y = \mathcal{P}(A)$, which are, respectively, the collection of subsets of O and that of subsets of A; let us order the first collection using $\subseteq$ and the second using $\supseteq$.

For $C \subseteq O$ and $D \subseteq A$, define $F(C) = \{a \in A \mid (\forall o \in C), (o, a) \in I\}$ and $G(D) = \{o \in O \mid (\forall a \in D), (o, a) \in I\}$.

Then (F, G) induces an isomorphism between the lattice of closed objects of O and the lattice of closed objects of A.

Appendix C

Disjunctive Linear Relations

DLRs (*Disjunctive Linear Relations*) have been introduced independently by Koubarakis [KOU 96, KOU 01] and Jonsson and Bäckström [JON 98], and applied to temporal and qualitative spatial reasoning. In this appendix, we give a short summary of Jonssson and Bäckström's paper [JON 98].

C.1. DLRs: definitions and satisfiability

In what follows, we consider a finite set of n real-valued variables $X = \{x_1, \ldots, x_n\}$.

DEFINITION C.1.– *A linear polynomial α is a polynomial of degree one $a_1 x_1 + \ldots + a_n x_n$, where $a_i \in \mathbb{Z}$, for $1 \leq i \leq n$.*
A disequation on X is an expression of the form $\alpha \neq c$, where c is an integer.
A linear equation on X is an expression of the form $\alpha = c$, where c is an integer.
A linear relation on X is an expression of the form $\alpha\, r\, c$, where r is one of the relations $<, \leq, >, \geq, =, \neq$.
A convex linear relation on X is an expression of the form $\alpha\, r\, c$, where r is one of the relations $<, \leq, >, \geq, =$.

DEFINITION C.2.– *A disjunctive linear relation (DLR) on X is a finite set of linear relations.*

The idea behind these definitions is that we consider subsets of $\mathbb{R}^n$ defined by constraints which are disjunctions of linear relations (represented by DLRs), the problem being to decide under what conditions these sets are non-empty. This point will be clarified by the definition of a satisfiable set of DLRs.

EXAMPLE C.1.– The set $\gamma = \{3x_1 + 2x_2 - x3 \leq 7, 11x_2 - 7x_3 \neq 0, x_3 = 8\}$ is a disjunctive linear relation.

NOTATION.– Let γ be a DLR. $\mathcal{C}(\gamma)$ denotes the set of convex linear relations contained in γ, and $\mathcal{NC}(\gamma)$ be the set of inequations contained in γ. We thus have $\gamma = \mathcal{C}(\gamma) \cup \mathcal{NC}(\gamma)$, for any DLR γ (a disjoint union).

DEFINITION C.3.– *A DLR γ is* convex *if $\gamma = \mathcal{C}(\gamma)$. It is* inequational *if $\gamma = \mathcal{NC}(\gamma)$. It is* homogeneous *if it is convex or inequational; otherwise it is* heterogeneous*. A DLR γ is a unit DRL if it contains only one element. It is a Horn DLR if $\mathcal{C}(\gamma)$ contains at most one element.*

EXAMPLE C.2.– The DLR $\gamma = \{3x_1 + 2x_2 - x_3 \leq 7, 11x_2 - 7x_3 \neq 0, x_3 = 8\}$ is heterogeneous. We have $\mathcal{C}(\gamma) = \{3x_1 + 2x_2 - x_3 \leq 7, x_3 = 8\}$ and $\mathcal{NC}(\gamma) = \{11x_2 - 7x_3 \neq 0\}$. It is not a Horn DLR.

EXAMPLE C.3.– The three DLRs $\gamma_1 = \{3x_1 - 5x_2 \leq 15\}$, $\gamma_2 = \{-3x_1 - 5x_2 \leq -30\}$, and $\gamma_3 = \{x_2 \leq 9\}$ are unitary and convex.

DEFINITION C.4.– *Let $X = \{x_1, \ldots, x_n\}$ be a set of variables, and $\Gamma = \{\gamma_1, \ldots, \gamma_k\}$ be a set of DLRs on X. Γ is* satisfiable *if there exists an instantiation $m\colon X \to \mathbb{R}$ of the variables such that for each $\gamma \in \Gamma$ at least one of the linear relations of γ is satisfied (then m is said to be a* solution *of Γ).*

DEFINITION C.5.– *Given a set Γ of DLRs on X, the $DLRSAT$ problem consists in determining whether Γ is satisfiable.*

NOTE C.1.– If α is a linear polynomial, the condition $\alpha = c$ defines a hyperplane (a line in $\mathbb{R}^2$, a plane in $\mathbb{R}^3$) in $\mathbb{R}^n$. The condition $\alpha \neq c$ defines the complement of this hyperplane, which consists of two open half-spaces, $\alpha > c$ and $\alpha < c$. The conditions $\alpha \leq c$ and $\alpha \geq c$ defined the closed half-spaces which are the topological closures of those open half-spaces.

EXAMPLE C.4.– Consider the set $\Gamma = \{\gamma_1, \gamma_2, \gamma_3\}$ of example C.3. It is satisfiable, and the set of its solutions is the set of points inside the gray triangle represented in Figure C.1.

C.2. Linear programming

The study of the DLRSAT problem is based on relating it to a linear programming problem. Let us recall the basic definitions of the latter.

DEFINITION C.6.– *Let A be a $(m \times n)$-matrix of integers, and $x = (x_1, \ldots, x_n)$ a vector of n real variables. An instance of the* linear programming problem *consists in*

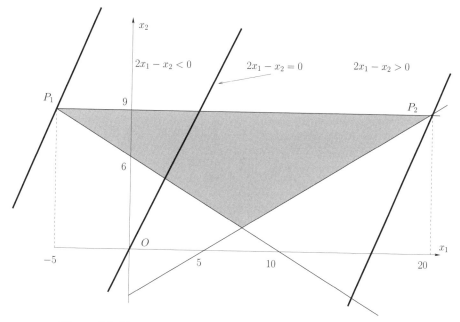

Figure C.1. *Linear programming: minimizing and maximizing* $2x_1 - x_2$

minimizing the quantity $c^t x$ under the condition that $Ax \leq b$, where b is an m vector of integers, and c an n-vector of integers. More precisely, given A, b, and c, we have:

1) *either to find an assignment of values to the variables $x_1, \ldots, x_n$ such that the condition $Ax \leq b$ is satisfied, and that $c^t\ x$ is minimal under these conditions;*

2) *or to assert that such an assignment does not exist;*

3) *or to assert that under these conditions $c^t x$ does not have a lower bound.*

The problem defined in this way is a minimization problem. A maximization problem is defined in a similar way for the same data.

EXAMPLE C.5.– Let us consider the following data: $A = \begin{pmatrix} 3 & -5 \\ -3 & -5 \\ 0 & 1 \end{pmatrix}$,

$b^t = (15, -30, 9)$, and $c = (2, -1)$. The associated linear programming problems consist of minimizing (maximizing, respectively) the quantity $2x_1 - x_2$ under the conditions defined by the three DLRs of example C.3. In this case, considering the graphic representation shows that the minimization problem has a solution (point P_1 of the figure), and similarly for the maximization problem (point P_2).

EXAMPLE C.6.– Consider now the data: $A = \begin{pmatrix} 3 & -5 \\ -3 & -5 \\ -3 & 5 \end{pmatrix}$,

$b^t = (15, -30, 30)$, and $c = (2, -1)$. The set of solutions of $Ax \leq b$ is represented in Figure C.2. The minimization problem still has a unique solution (point P_3), but the maximization problem does not: the set of values of $2x_1 - x_2$ does not have an upper bound.

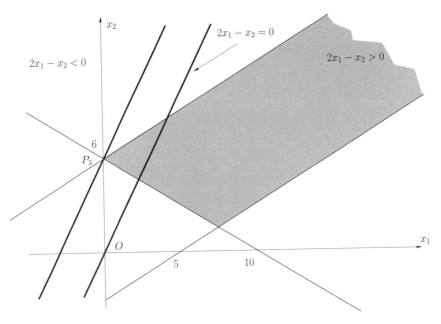

Figure C.2. *Linear programming: minimizing $2x_1 - x_2$*

The linear programming problem can be solved by using Dantzig's simplex algorithm, which is exponential. But it is in fact solvable in polynomial time, as shown by Khachiyan [KHA 79] and Karmarkar [KAR 84].

C.3. Complexity of the satisfiability problem

The main result concerning the satisfiability problem of a set of DLRs is summed up in two statements: on the one hand, this problem is NP-complete for arbitrary DLRs; on the other hand, it is polynomial for Horn DLRs.

A key notion in proving those results is the following:

DEFINITION C.7.– *Let Γ be a set of DLRs which is satisfiable. A DLR γ blocks Γ if, for each inequation $d \in \mathcal{NC}(\gamma)$, the set $\Gamma \cup \{d\}$ is not satisfiable.*

Intuitively, this means the following: γ contains some inequations $d_1, \ldots, d_k$. Let $\bar{d}_1, \ldots, \bar{d}_k$ be the associated equations ($\neq$ is replaced with =). To say that γ blocks a satisfiable set Γ means that the set of solutions is contained in the intersection of the hyperplanes defined by $\bar{d}_1, \ldots, \bar{d}_k$.

In particular, if γ blocks Γ, but if $\Gamma \cup \{\gamma\}$ is satisfiable, there necessarily exists a *convex* linear relation δ in γ, such that $\Gamma \cup \{\delta\}$ is satisfiable: all $d_i, 1 \leq i \leq k$ can be falsified, as δ is satisfied.

The link to linear programming can now be established. A consequence of the polynomiality of linear programming problems is the following lemma:

LEMMA C.1.– *Let A be a $(m \times n)$-matrix, b an m-vector, and $x = (x_1, \ldots, x_n)$ an n-vector of real-valued variables. Let α be a linear polynomial on $x_1, \ldots, x_n$, and c an integer. The problem of determining whether the system $Ax \leq b$, with $\alpha \neq c$ has a solution, is a polynomial problem.*

Proof. We consider the two problems LV_1 (LP_2, respectively) of minimizing (maximizing, respectively) α under the condition $Ax \leq b$. If none of them has a solution, the system is not satisfiable. If both give the same optimal value for α and if this value is c, it is also not satisfiable since any solution of LV_1 and LP_2 gives the value c to α. In other cases, the system is clearly satisfiable.   □

A set of constraints such that $Ax \leq b$ defines an intersection of half-spaces which is by definition what is called a (generalized) polyhedron. Any non-empty polyhedron is a convex subset of $\mathbb{R}^n$.

Using the fact that, for Horn DLRs, we may restrict ourselves to use only $\leq$ and $\neq$, the previous lemma has the following consequence:

LEMMA C.2.– *Let Γ be a set of convex unit $DLRs$ which is satisfiable, and let γ be a DLR. The problem of determining whether γ blocks Γ can be solved in polynomial time.*

A fundamental result is the following purely geometrical lemma:

LEMMA C.3.– *Let S be a convex subset of $\mathbb{R}^n$. If $H_1, \ldots, H_k$ are distinct hyperplanes, and if $S \subseteq \bigcup_{i=1}^{i=k} K_k$, then there exists $i \in \{1, \ldots, k\}$ such that $S \subseteq H_i$.*

For example, in the plane, this means that if a convex set is contained in a finite union of distinct lines, it has to be contained in one of them. Indeed, assume it is not;

consider a minimal subset of these lines, which implies that each one of them, H_i, contains an element x_i of S which is contained in none of the other lines. If $x_1 \in H_1$ and $x_2 \in H_2$ are such points in S, the same is true of the segment $[x_1, x_2]$. As no line of the family can contain both x_1 and x_2, any line of the family meets this segment in one point at most. It is therefore impossible that the union of the lines contains the entire segment.

The same principle of proof can be used in any dimension.

The preceding result yields a sufficient condition for the satisfiability of a set of Horn DLRs:

LEMMA C.4.– *Let Γ be a set of Horn DLRs. Let C be the set of elements of Γ which are convex, and $D = \Gamma \setminus C = \{\gamma_1, \ldots, \gamma_k\}$. If C is satisfiable and if none of the γ_is blocks C, then Γ is satisfiable.*

Indeed, for each γ_i, we can find an inequation $d_i \in \gamma_i$ such that $\Gamma \cup \{d_i\}$ is satisfiable, since γ_i does not block Γ.

In addition, the following lemma justifies the use of an operation on which the decision algorithm will be based:

LEMMA C.5.– *Let Γ be a set of Horn DLRs. Let C be the set of elements of Γ which are convex. If there exists a heterogeneous DLR $\gamma \in \Gamma$ such that γ blocks C, then Γ is satisfiable if, and only if, $(\Gamma \setminus \{\gamma\}) \cup C(\gamma)$ is satisfiable.*

Proof. If $(\Gamma \setminus \{\gamma\}) \cup C(\gamma)$ is satisfiable, i.e. when the linear relations of γ are replaced by a subset of them, namely those which are convex, it is clear that Γ, which enforces broader constraints, is *a fortiori* satisfiable. Conversely, the fact that Γ is satisfiable cannot be attributed to one of the inequations of γ, as γ blocks C. Therefore, $C(\gamma)$ must be satisfied. □

The SAT algorithm (Figure C.3) which can be used to decide the satisfiability of Horn DLR is based on the operation described in lemma C.5.

It can be easily seen that the SAT algorithm accepts a set of Horn DLRs if, and only if, this set is satisfiable. Moreover, in this algorithm, the number of recursive calls is obviously bounded by the number of heterogeneous DLRs contained by the input. Since according to lemma C.2, the blocking property can be tested in polynomial time, one gets the fundamental theorem:

THEOREM C.1.– *The satisfiability problem of a set of Horn DLRs can be solved in polynomial time.*

Data: A set Γ of Horn DLRs
Result: **accept** if Γ is satisfiable, **reject** otherwise
$A \leftarrow \bigcup\{\mathcal{C}(\gamma) \mid \gamma \in \Gamma \text{ is convex}\}$
if *A is not satisfiable* **then**
  | return *reject*
end
if *there exists $\gamma \in \Gamma$ which blocks A and is disequational* **then**
  | return *reject*
end
if *there exists $\gamma \in \Gamma$ which blocks A and is heterogeneous* **then**
  | SAT$((\Gamma \setminus \{\gamma\}) \cup \mathcal{C}(\gamma))$
end
return *accept*

Figure C.3. *The SAT algorithm (after [JON 98])*

The above theorem implies in particular that the satisfiability problem of a finite set of DLRs belongs to the NP class: if Γ is such a satisfiable set, then each DLR in this set contains a linear relation whose conjunction is satisfiable. Now the satisfiability of these DLRs is decidable in polynomial time. As in addition, a simple reduction of the 3-colorability problem in the DLR language shows that the problem is NP-difficult, one gets the following theorem:

THEOREM C.2.– *The satisfiability problem of a set of DLRs is NP-complete.*

Bibliography

[ABB 63] ABBOTT E., *Flatland - A Romance of Many Dimensions*, Basil Blackwell, Oxford, England, 1963.

[ADA 00] ADALI S., CONSOLE L., SAPINO M.L., SCHENONE M., TERENZIANI P., "Representing and reasoning with temporal constraints in multimedia presentations", in *Proceedings of TIME 2000*, Cape Breton, Nova Scotia, Canada, IEEE-Computer Society, USA, p. 3-12, 2000.

[ADA 09] ADAMS B., RAUBAL M., "A metric conceptual space algebra", in HORNSBY K.S., *et al.* (eds.), p. 51-68, 2009.

[AIE 01] AIELLO M., VAN BENTHEM J., BEZHANISHVILI G., Reasoning about Space: The Modal Way, Report no. PP-2001-18, University of Amsterdam, The Netherlands, 2001.

[AIE 02a] AIELLO M., MONZ C., TODORAN L., "Document understanding for a broad class of documents", *International Journal on Document Analysis and Recognition*, vol. 5, no. 1, p. 1-16, 2002.

[AIE 02b] AIELLO M., VAN BENTHEM J., *Logical Patterns in Space*, CSLI, Stanford, USA, 2002.

[AIE 02c] AIELLO M., VAN BENTHEM J., "A modal walk through space", *Journal of Applied Non-Classical Logics*, vol. 12, no. 3-4, p. 319-364, 2002.

[AIE 03] AIELLO M., VAN BENTHEM J., BEZHANISHVILI G., "Reasoning about space: the modal way", *Journal of Logic and Computation*, vol. 13, no. 6, p. 889-920, 2003.

[AIE 07] AIELLO M., PRATT-HARTMANN I., VAN BENTHEM J. (eds.), *Handbook of Spatial Logics*, Springer Netherlands, Amsterdam, The Netherlands, 2007.

[ALL 83] ALLEN J.F., "Maintaining knowledge about temporal intervals", *Communications of the Association for Computing Machinery*, vol. 26, no. 11, p. 832-843, 1983.

[ALL 84] ALLEN J.F., "A general model of action and time", *Artificial Intelligence*, vol. 23, no. 2, 1984.

[ALL 85] ALLEN J.F., HAYES P.J., "A commonsense theory of time", in *Proceedings of the Ninth International Joint Conference on Artificial Intelligence (IJCAI '85)*, Los Angeles, California, Morgan Kaufmann, USA, p. 528-531, 1985.

[ALL 91a] ALLEN J.F., "Planning as temporal reasoning", in *Proceedings of the Second International Conference on Principles of Knowledge Representation and Reasoning*, Morgan Kaufmann, USA, p. 3-14, 1991.

[ALL 91b] ALLEN J., KAUTZ H., PELLAVIN R., TENENBERG J., *Reasoning about Plans*, Morgan Kaufmann, USA, 1991.

[ALU 99] ALUR R., "Timed automata", *Theoretical Computer Science*, vol. 126, p. 183-235, 1999.

[AND 96] ANDRÉ E., RIST T., "Coping with temporal constraints in multimedia presentation planning", in *Proceedings of AAAI '96*, Portland, Oregon, AAAI Press/The MIT Press, USA, p. 142-147, 1996.

[ANG 98] ANGER F., MITRA D., RODRIGUEZ R., "Temporal constraint networks in non-linear time", in *Proceedings of the ECAI-98 Workshop on Spatial and Temporal Reasoning (W22)*, Brighton, UK, p. 33-39, 1998.

[ANG 00] ANGELSMARK O., JONSSON P., "Some observations on durations, scheduling and Allen's algebra", in DECHTER R. (ed.), p. 484-488, 2000.

[ARE 00] ARECES C., BLACKBURN P., MARX M., "The computational complexity of hybrid temporal logics", *Logic Journal of the IGPL*, vol. 8, p. 653-679, 2000.

[ASH 95] ASHER N., VIEU L., "Toward a geometry of common sense: a semantics and a complete axiomatization of mereotopology", in *International Joint Conference on Artificial Intelligence (IJCAI)*, Montreal, Canada, Morgan Kaufmann, USA, p. 846-852, 1995.

[ASH 05] ASHER N., VIEU L., "Subordinating and coordinating discourse relations", *Lingua*, vol. 115, no. 4, p. 591-610, Elsevier, Amsterdam, The Netherlands, 2005.

[AUR 93] AURNAGUE M., VIEU L., "A three-level approach to the semantics of space", in ZELINSKY-WIBBELT C. (ed.), *The Semantics of Prepositions—from Mental Processing to Natural Language Processing*, Mouton de Gruyter, Berlin, Germany, 1993.

[BAD 06] BADALONI S., GIACOMIN M., "The algebra IA^{fuz}: a framework for qualitative fuzzy temporal reasoning", *Artificial Intelligence*, vol. 170, no. 10, p. 872-908, 2006.

[BAL 98a] BALBIANI P., CONDOTTA J.-F., FARIÑAS DEL CERRO L., "A model for reasoning about bidimensional temporal relations", in *Proceedings of KR-98*, Morgan Kauffmann, USA, p. 124-130, 1998.

[BAL 98b] BALBIANI P., CONDOTTA J.-F., FARIÑAS DEL CERRO L., OSMANI A., "A model for reasoning about generalized intervals", in GIUNCHIGLIA F. (ed.), *Proceedings of the Eighth International Conference on Artificial Intelligence: Methods, Systems, Applications (AIMSA '98)*, LNAI 1480, Springer, Germany, p. 50-61, 1998.

[BAL 99a] BALBIANI P., CONDOTTA J.-F., FARIÑAS DEL CERRO L., "A new tractable subclass of the rectangle algebra", in *Proceedings of IJCAI-99*, Stockholm, Sweden, Morgan Kaufmann, USA, p. 442-447, 1999.

[BAL 99b] BALBIANI P., CONDOTTA J.-F., FARIÑAS DEL CERRO L., "Spatial reasoning about points in a multi-dimensional setting", in *Proceedings of the IJCAI-99 Workshop on Spatial and Temporal Reasoning*, Stockholm, Sweden, p. 105-113, 1999.

[BAL 99c] BALBIANI P., CONDOTTA J.-F., FARIÑAS DEL CERRO L., "A tractable subclass of the block algebra: constraint propagation and preconvex relations", in *Proceedings of the Ninth Portuguese Conference on Artificial Intelligence (EPIA '99)*, LNAI, 1695, Springer, Germany, p. 75-89, 1999.

[BAL 00a] BALBIANI P., OSMANI A., "A model for reasoning about topological relations between cyclic intervals", in *Proceedings of KR-2000*, Breckenridge, Colorado, Morgan Kaufmann, USA, p. 378-385, 2000.

[BAL 00b] BALBIANI P., CONDOTTA J.-F., LIGOZAT G., "Reasoning about generalized intervals: Horn representation and tractability", in GOODWIN S., TRUDEL A. (eds.), *Proceedings of the Seventh International Workshop on Temporal Representation and Reasoning (TIME-00)*, Cape Breton, Nova Scotia, Canada, IEEE Computer Society, USA, p. 23-30, 2000.

[BAL 03] BALBIANI P., CONDOTTA J.-F., LIGOZAT G., "On the consistency problem for the $\mathcal{INDU}$ calculus", in *Proceedings of TIME-ICTL-2003*, IEEE Computer Society, Cairns, Australia, p. 203-211, 2003.

[BAL 06] BALBIANI P., CONDOTTA J.-F., LIGOZAT G., "On the consistency problem for the $\mathcal{INDU}$ calculus", *Journal of Applied Logic*, vol. 4, p. 119-140, 2006.

[BAL 10] BALBIANI P., GASQUET O., SCHWARZENTRUBER F., "Knowledge in flatland", in *Atelier RTE (Représentation du Temps et de l'Espace)*, Caen, France, 2010.

[BAR 00] BARBER F., "Reasoning on interval and point-based disjunctive metric constraints in temporal contexts", *Journal of Artificial Intelligence Research*, vol. 12, no. 1, p. 35-86, AI Access Foundation, 2000.

[BAR 02] BARZILAY R., ELHADAD N., MCKEOWN K., "Inferring strategies for sentence ordering in multidocument news summarization", *Journal of Artificial Intelligence Research*, vol. 17, p. 35-55, 2002.

[BAR 08] BARKOWSKY T., KNAUFF M., LIGOZAT G., MONTELLO D.R. (eds.), *Spatial Cognition V: Reasoning, Action, Interaction, (International Conference on Spatial Cognition 2006)*, Bremen, Germany, September 2006, Revised Selected Papers, *Lecture Notes in Computer Science*, vol. 4387, Springer, Germany, 2008.

[BEE 90a] VAN BEEK P., "Reasoning about qualitative temporal information", in *Proceedings of AAAI-90*, Boston, USA, p. 728-734, 1990.

[BEE 90b] VAN BEEK P., COHEN R., "Exact and approximate reasoning about temporal relations", *Computational Intelligence*, vol. 6, p. 132-144, 1990.

[BEE 91] VAN BEEK P., "Temporal query processing with indefinite information", *Artificial Intelligence in Medicine*, vol. 3, p. 325-339, 1991.

[BEE 92] VAN BEEK P., "Reasoning about qualitative temporal information", *Artificial Intelligence*, vol. 58, no. 1-3, p. 297-326, December 1992.

[BEE 96] VAN BEEK P., MANCHAK D.W., "The design and experimental of algorithms for temporal reasoning", *Journal of Artificial Intelligence Research*, vol. 4, p. 1-18, 1996.

[BEN 94] BENNETT B., "Spatial reasoning with propositional logic", in *Proceedings of KR '94*, Morgan Kaufmann, USA, p. 51-62, 1994.

[BEN 95] BENNETT B., "Modal logics for qualitative spatial reasoning", *Bulletin of the IGPL*, vol. 4, no. 1, p. 1-22, 1995.

[BEN 96a] BENNETT B., "The application of qualitative spatial reasoning to GIS", in ABRAHART R. (ed.), *Proceedings of the First International Conference on GeoComputation*, vol. I, p. 44-47, Leeds, England, 1996.

[BEN 96b] BENNETT B., "Modal logics for qualitative spatial reasoning", *Journal of the Interest Group on Pure and Applied Logic*, vol. 4, no. 1, p. 23-45, 1996.

[BEN 96c] VAN BENTHEM J., *Exploring Logical Dynamics, Studies in Logic, Language and Information*, CSLI Publications & Cambridge University Press, USA, 1996.

[BEN 97a] BENNETT B., ISLI A., COHN A., "When does a composition table provide a complete and tractable proof procedure for a relational constraint language?", in *Proceedings of the IJCAI-97 Workshop on Spatial and Temporal Reasoning*, Nagoya, Japan, p. 75-81, 1997.

[BEN 97b] BENNETT B., Logical representations for automated reasoning about spatial relationships, PhD thesis, The University of Leeds, School of Computer Studies, Leeds, England, 1997.

[BEN 02a] BENNETT B., COHN A., WOLTER F., ZAKHARYASCHEV M., "Multi-dimensional modal logic as a framework for spatio-temporal reasoning", *Applied Intelligence*, vol. 17, no. 3, p. 239-251, 2002.

[BEN 02b] BENNETT B., "What is a forest? On the vagueness of certain geographic concepts", *Topoi*, vol. 20, p. 189-201, 2002.

[BEN 04] BENNETT B., MAGEE D.R., COHN A.G., HOGG D.C., "Using spatio-temporal continuity constraints to enhance visual tracking of moving objects", in LÓPEZ DE MÁNTARAS R., SAITTA L. (eds.), p. 922-926, 2004.

[BEN 07a] BEN ALOUI N., GLOTIN H., HEBRARD P., PAPINI O., "Vers une approche qualitative pour la reconnaissance des empreintes digitales", in *Plate-forme AFIA, Atelier Représentation et raisonnement sur le temps et l'espace (RTE)*, Grenoble, France, July 2007.

[BEN 07b] VAN BENTHEM J., BEZHANISHVILI G., "Modal logics of space", in AIELLO M., *et al.* (eds.), p. 217-298, 2007.

[BEN 07c] VAN BENTHEM J., BEZHANISHVILI G., TEN CATE B., SARENAC D., "Multimodal logics of products of topologies", *Studia Logica*, vol. 84, p. 369-392, 2007.

[BEN 08a] BENNETT B., "Spatial reasoning", in KEMP K.K. (ed.), *Encyclopedia of Geographic Information Science*, SAGE Publications, Thousand Oaks /London/New Delhi/Singapore, p. 426-432, 2008.

[BEN 08b] BENNETT B., MAGEE D.R., COHN A.G., HOGG D.C., "Enhanced tracking and recognition of moving objects by reasoning about spatio-temporal continuity", *Image and Vision Computing*, vol. 26, no. 1, p. 67-81, Elsevier, 2008.

[BEN 08c] BENNETT B., MALLENBY D., THIRD A., "An ontology for grounding vague geographic terms", in *Proceeding of the 2008 conference on Formal Ontology in Information Systems*, IOS Press, Amsterdam, The Netherlands, p. 280-293, 2008.

[BER 08] BERTAUX A., BRAUD A., BER F.L., "Mining complex hydrobiological data with Galois lattices", *CoRR*, vol. abs/0811.0971, 2008.

[BES 89a] BESTOUGEFF H., LIGOZAT G., "On relations between intervals", *Information Processing Letters*, vol. 32, p. 177-182, 1989.

[BES 92] BESTOUGEFF H., LIGOZAT G., *Logical Tools for Temporal Knowledge Representation*, Ellis Horwood, 1989.

[BES 96] BESSIÈRE C., "A simple way to improve path consistency processing in interval algebra networks", in *Proceedings of AAAI-1996*, Portland, Oregon, AAAI Press/The MIT Press, p. 375-380, 1996.

[BET 98a] BETTINI C., DYRESON C.E., EVANS W.S., SNODGRASS R.T., WANG X.S., "A glossary of time granularity concepts", in ETZION O., JAJODIA S., SRIPADA S. (eds.), *Temporal Databases - Research and Practice, LNCS*, vol. 1399, Springer, Berlin, p. 406-413, 1998.

[BET 98b] BETTINI C., WANG X.S., JAJODIA S., "A general framework for time granularity and its application to temporal reasoning", *Annals of Mathematics and Artificial Intelligence*, vol. 22, no. 1-2, p. 29-58, 1998.

[BET 02] BETTINI C., WANG X.S., JAJODIA S., "Solving multi-granularity temporal constraint networks", *Artificial Intelligence*, vol. 140, p. 107-152, 2002.

[BEZ 05] BEZHANISHVILI G., GEHRKE M., "Completeness of S4 with respect to the real line: revisited", *Annals of Pure and Applied Logic*, vol. 131, no. 1-3, p. 287-301, 2005.

[BHA 09a] BHATT M., DYLLA F., "A qualitative model of dynamic scene analysis and interpretation in ambient intelligence systems", *International Journal of Robotics and Automation*, vol. 24, no. 3, 2009.

[BHA 09b] BHATT M., DYLLA F., HOIS J., "Spatio-terminological inference for the design of ambient environments", in HORNSBY K.S., *et al.* (eds.), p. 371-391, 2009.

[BIL 04] BILLEN R., CLEMENTINI E., "A model for ternary projective relations between regions", in BERTINO E., CHRISTODOULAKIS S., PLEXOUSAKIS D., CHRISTOPHIDES V., KOUBARAKIS M., BÖHM K., FERRARI E. (eds.), *EDBT, LNCS*, vol. 2992, Springer, Berlin, p. 310-328, 2004.

[BIL 05] BILLEN R., CLEMENTINI E., "Semantics of collinearity among regions", in MEERSMAN R., TARI Z., HERRERO P., MÉNDEZ G., CAVEDON L., MARTIN D., HINZE A., BUCHANAN G., PÉREZ M.S., ROBLES V., HUMBLE J., ALBANI A., DIETZ J.L.G., PANETTO H., SCANNAPIECO M., HALPIN T.A., SPYNS P., ZAHA J.M., ZIMÁNYI E., STEFANAKIS E., DILLON T.S., FENG L., JARRAR M., LEHMANN J., DE MOOR A., DUVAL E., AROYO L. (eds.), *OTM Workshops*, vol. 3762, *LNCS*, Springer, Berlin, p. 1066-1076, 2005.

[BIT 98] BITTNER T., STELL J.G., "A boundary-sensitive approach to qualitative location", *Annals of Mathematics and Artificial Intelligence*, vol. 24, no. 1-4, p. 93-114, 1998.

[BIT 02] BITTNER T., STELL J.G., "Vagueness and rough location", *GeoInformatica*, vol. 6, no. 2, p. 99-121, 2002.

[BIT 08] BITTNER T., STELL J.G., "Approximation", in SHEKHAR S., XIONG H. (eds.), *Encyclopedia of GIS*, Springer, Berlin/Heidelberg, p. 21-25, 2008.

[BLA 01] BLACKBURN P., DE RIJKE M., VENEMA Y., *Modal Logic, Cambridge Tracts in Theoretical Computer Science, No. 53*, Cambridge University Press, Cambridge, UK, 2001.

[BOD 03a] BODENHOFER U., "A unified framework of opening and closure operators with respect to arbitrary fuzzy relations", *Soft Computing*, vol. 7, no. 4, p. 220-227, 2003.

[BOD 03b] BODIRSKY M., NEŠETŘIL J., "Constraint satisfaction with countable homogeneous templates", in BAAZ M., MAKOWSKY J.A. (eds.), *CSL, Lecture Notes in Computer Science*, vol. 2803, Springer, Berlin/Heidelberg, p. 44-57, 2003.

[BOD 06] BODIRSKY M., DALMAU V., "Datalog and constraint satisfaction with infinite templates", in DURAND B., THOMAS W. (eds.), *STACS, Lecture Notes in Computer Science*, vol. 3884, Springer, Berlin/Heidelberg, p. 646-659, 2006.

[BOD 07a] BODIRSKY M., CHEN H., "Oligomorphic clones", *Algebra Universalis*, vol. 57, no. 1, p. 109-125, 2007.

[BOD 07b] BODIRSKY M., CHEN H., "Qualitative temporal and spatial reasoning revisited", in DUPARC J., HENZINGER T.A. (eds.), *CSL, Lecture Notes in Computer Science*, vol. 4646, Springer, Berlin/Heidelberg, p. 194-207, 2007.

[BOD 07c] BODIRSKY M., CHEN H., *The Right-Hand Side Complexity of Constraint Satisfaction: A Short Course Script for the ESSLLI 2007 Course Complexity of Constraint Satisfaction,* Dublin, Ireland, 2007.

[BOD 08] BODIRSKY M., DALMAU V., "Datalog and constraint satisfaction with infinite templates", *CoRR*, vol. abs/0809.2386, 2008.

[BOD 09] BODIRSKY M., CHEN H., "Qualitative temporal and spatial reasoning revisited", *Journal of Logic and Computation*, vol. 19, no. 6, p. 1359-1383, 2009.

[BOG 06] BOGAERT P., DE WEGHE N.V., COHN A.G., WITLOX F., MAEYER P.D., "The qualitative trajectory calculus on networks", in BARKOWSKY T., *et al.* (eds.), p. 20-38, 2006.

[BOS 02] BOSCH A., TORRES M., MARIN R., "Reasoning with disjunctive fuzzy temporal constraint networks", in *Proceedings of TIME 2002*, IEEE Computer Society, p. 36-45, 2002.

[BOU 09] BOUTILIER C. (ed.), *IJCAI 2009, Proceedings of the 21st International Joint Conference on Artificial Intelligence*, Pasadena, California, USA, July 11–17, 2009.

[BRA 85] BRACHMAN R., LEVESQUE H. (eds.), *Readings in Knowledge Representation*, Morgan Kaufmann, Stanford, USA, 1985.

[BRA 04] BRAND S., "Relation variables in qualitative spatial reasoning", in BIUNDO S., FRÜHWIRTH T.W., PALM G. (eds.), *KI*, vol. 3238, *Lecture Notes in Computer Science*, Springer, Berlin, p. 337-350, 2004.

[BRO 99] BROXVALL M., JONSSON P., "Towards a complete classification of tractability in point algebras for non-linear time", in *Principles and Practice of Constraint Programming (CP '99)*, vol. 1713, *Lecture Notes in Computer Science*, Springer, Berlin/Heidelberg, p. 129-143, 1999.

[BRO 00a] BROXVALL M., JONSSON P., "Disjunctive temporal reasoning in partially ordered models of time", in *Proceedings of AAAI-2000*, Austin, Texas, USA, p. 464-469, 2000.

[BRO 00b] BROXVALL M., JONSSON P., RENZ J., "Refinements and independence: a simple method for identifying tractable disjunctive constraints", in DECHTER R. (ed.), p. 114-127, 2000.

[BRO 02] BROXVALL M., JONSSON P., RENZ J., "Disjunctions, independence, refinements", *Artificial Intelligence*, vol. 140, no. 1-2, p. 153-173, Elsevier Science Publishers Ltd., 2002.

[BUC 92] BUCHANAN M.C., ZELLWEGER P., "Scheduling multimedia documents using temporal constraints", in RANGAN P.V. (ed.), *NOSSDAV, Lecture Notes in Computer Science*, vol. 712, Springer, Berlin/Heidelberg, p. 237-249, 1992.

[BUL 00] BULATOV A.A., KROKHIN A.A., JEAVONS P., "Constraint satisfaction problems and finite algebras", in *Proceedings of the 27th International Conference on Automata, Languages and Programming (ICALP '00)*, LNCS 1853, Springer, Berlin/Heidelberg, p. 272-283, 2000.

[BUL 02] BULATOV A.A., "A dichotomy theorem for constraints on a three-element set", in *Proceedings of the 43rd Symposium on Foundations of Computer Science (FOCS 2002)*, Vancouver, Canada, IEEE Computer Society, p. 649-658, 2002.

[CES 02] CESTA A., ODDI A., SMITH S.F., "A constraint-based method for project scheduling with time windows", *Journal of Heuristics*, vol. 8, no. 1, p. 109-136, Kluwer Academic Publishers, 2002.

[CHA 77] CHANG C.C., KEISLER H.J., *Model Theory*, North-Holland, Amsterdam/New York, 1977.

[CHE 91] CHEESEMAN P., KANEFSKY B., TAYLOR W.M., "Where the *really* hard problems are", in *Proceedings of the 12th International Conference on Artificial Intelligence (IJCAI-91)*, Sydney, Australia, Morgan Kaufmann, USA, p. 331-337, 1991.

[CHE 05] CHEVRIAUX Y., SAUX E., CLARAMUNT C., "A landform-based approach for the representation of terrain silhouettes", in SHAHABI C., BOUCELMA O. (eds.), *GIS*, ACM, USA, p. 260-266, 2005.

[CHO 05] CHOMICKI J., TOMAN D., "Temporal databases", in FISHER M., *et al.* (eds.), p. 429-467, 2005.

[CIC 04] CICERONE S., DI FELICE P., "Cardinal directions between spatial objects: the pairwise-consistency problem", *Information Sciences*, vol. 164, no. 1-4, p. 165-188, 2004.

[CLA 81] CLARKE B.L., "A calculus of individuals based on connection", *Notre Dame Journal of Formal Logic*, vol. 22, no. 3, p. 204-217, 1981.

[CLA 85] CLARKE B.L., "Individuals and points", *Notre Dame Journal of Formal Logic*, vol. 26, no. 1, p. 61-75, 1985.

[CLA 00] CLARAMUNT C., "Extending Ladkin's algebra on non-convex intervals towards an algebra on union-of-regions", in *ACM-GIS*, p. 9-14, 2000.

[CLA 05] CLANCY D., KUIPERS B., "Time in qualitative simulation", in FISHER M., *et al.* (eds.), p. 655-664.

[CLE 94] CLEMENTINI E., SHARMA J., EGENHOFER M.J., "Modeling topological spatial relations: strategies for query processing", *Computers & Graphics*, vol. 18, no. 6, p. 815-822, 1994.

[CLE 09] CLEMENTINI E., A conceptual framework for modeling spatial relations, PhD thesis, INSA Lyon, France, 2009.

[COH 81] COHN P., *Universal Algebra*, D. Reidel Publishing Company, Dordrecht/Boston/London, 1981.

[COH 94] COHN A.G., GOODAY J.M., "Defining the syntax and the semantics of a visual programming language in a spatial logic", in ANGER F.D., LOGANANTHARAJ R. (eds.), *Proceedings of the AAAI-94 Spatial and Temporal Reasoning Workshop*, Seattle, USA, 1994.

[COH 96] COHN A., GOTTS N., "The 'egg-yolk' representation of regions with indeterminate boundaries", in BURROUGH P.A., FRANK A.U. (eds.), *Geographic Objects with Indeterminate Boundaries*, Taylor and Francis Ltd., London/Bristol, p. 171-187, 1996.

[COH 97] COHN A.G., BENNETT B., GOODAY J., GOTTS N.M., "Representing and reasoning with qualitative spatial relations about regions", in STOCK (ed.), *Spatial and Temporal Reasoning*, Kluwer Academic Publisher, Dordrecht, p. 97-134, 1997.

[COH 00] COHEN D., JEAVONS P., JONSSON P., KOUBARAKIS M., JEAVONS P., "Building tractable disjunctive constraints", *Journal of the Association for Computing Machinery*, vol. 47, p. 826-853, 2000.

[COH 01] COHN A.G., "Formalising bio-spatial knowledge", in WELTY C., SMITH B. (eds.), *Proceedings 2nd International Conference on Formal Ontology in Information Systems (FOIS '01)*, ACM, p. 198-209, 2001.

[COH 06a] COHEN D., JEAVONS P., "The complexity of constraint languages", in ROSSI F., VAN BEEK P., WALSH T. (eds.), *Handbook of Constraint Programming (Foundations of Artificial Intelligence)*, Chapter 8, Elsevier Science Inc., The Netherlands, p. 245-280, 2006.

[COH 06b] COHN A., HOGG D., BENNETT B., DEVIN V., GALATA A., MAGEE D., NEEDHAP C., SANTOS P., "Cognitive vision: integrating symbolic qualitative representations with computer vision", in CHRISTENSEN H.I., NAGEL H.-H. (eds.), *Cognitive Vision Systems: Sampling the Spectrum of Approaches*, *LNCS*, vol. 3948, Chapter 14, Springer, Berlin/Heidelberg, p. 221-246, 2006.

[COH 07] COHN A.G., RENZ J., "Qualitative spatial reasoning", in VAN HARMELEN F., LIFSCHITZ V., PORTER B. (eds.), *Handbook of Knowledge Representation*, Elsevier, Amsterdam, The Netherlands, 2007.

[CON 00] CONDOTTA J.-F., "The augmented interval and rectangle networks", in *Proceedings of the Seventh International Conference on Principles of Knowledge (KR 2000)*, Morgan Kaufmann, Breckenridge, Colorado, USA, p. 571-579, 2000.

[CON 06a] CONDOTTA J.-F., LIGOZAT G., SAADE M., TRIPAKIS S., "Ultimately periodic simple temporal problems (UPSTPs)", in *Proceedings of TIME 2006*, IEEE Computer Society, USA, p. 69-77, 2006.

[CON 06b] CONDOTTA J.-F., D'ALMEDA D., LECOUTRE C., SAIS L., "From qualitative to discrete constraint networks", in *Workshop on Qualitative Constraint Calculi held with KI 2006*, Bremen, Germany, p. 54-64, 2006.

[CON 06c] CONDOTTA J.-F., LIGOZAT G., SAADE M., "A generic toolkit for n-ary qualitative temporal and spatial calculi", in *Proceedings of the 13th International Symposium on Temporal Representation and Reasoning (TIME '06)*, Budapest, Hungary, p. 78-86, 2006.

[CON 09] CONDOTTA J.-F., KACI S., SCHWIND N., "Merging qualitative constraint networks defined on different qualitative formalims", in HORNSBY K.S., *et al.* (eds.), p. 106-123, 2009.

[COR 01] CORMEN T.H., LEISERSON C.E., RIVEST R.L., STEIN C., *Introduction to Algorithms*, MIT Press and McGraw-Hill, USA, 2001.

[COT 05] COTTERET G., Extraction d'éléments curvilignes guidée par des mécanismes attentionnels pour des images de télédétection: approche par fusion de données, PhD thesis, Paris-Sud University, France, 2005.

[COX 98] COX D.A., LITTLE J.B., O'SHEA D., *Using Algebraic Geometry*, GTM, Springer, New York, 1998.

[CRI 04] CRISTANI M., HIRSCH R., "The complexity of constraint satisfaction problems for small relation algebras", *Artificial Intelligence*, vol. 156, no. 2, p. 177-196, 2004.

[CUK 04] CUKIERMAN D., DELGRANDE J.P., "A theory for convex interval relations including unbounded intervals", in BARR V., MARKOV Z. (eds.), *Proceedings of the FLAIRS Conference*, AAAI Press, USA, 2004.

[DAV 01] DAVIS E., "Continuous shape transformation and metrics on regions", *Fundamenta Informaticae*, vol. 46, no. 1-2, p. 31-54, 2001.

[DEC 89] DECHTER R., MEIRI I., PEARL J., "Temporal constraint networks", in *Proceedings of KR 1989*, Toronto, Canada, Morgan Kaufmann, USA, p. 83-93, 1989.

[DEC 91] DECHTER R., MEIRI I., PEARL J., "Temporal constraint networks", *Artificial Intelligence*, vol. 49, no. 1-3, p. 61-95, 1991.

[DEC 00] DECHTER R. (ed.), *Proceedings of the 6th International Conference on Principles and Practice of Constraint Programming (CP 2000)*, Lecture Notes in Computer Science, vol. 1894, Springer, Berlin/Heidelberg, Singapore, September 2000.

[DEC 03] DECHTER R., *Constraint Processing*, Morgan Kaufmann, USA, 2003.

[DEE 09] DEE H.M., HOGG D.C., COHN A.G., "Scene modeling and classification using learned spatial relations", in HORNSBY K.S., *et al.* (eds.), p. 295-311, 2009.

[DEL 08] DELAFONTAINE M., VAN DE WEGHE N., BOGAERT P., DE MAEYER P., "Qualitative relations between moving objects in a network changing its topological relations", *Information Sciences*, vol. 178, no. 8, p. 1997-2006, Elsevier Science Inc., Amsterdam, The Netherlands, 2008.

[DRA 98] DRAKENGREN T., JONSSON P., "A complete classification of tractability in Allen's algebra relative to subsets of basic relations", *Artificial Intelligence*, vol. 106, no. 2, p. 205-219, 1998.

[DU 05a]   Du S., Qin Q., Li B., "Fuzzy description of topological relations I: a unified fuzzy 9-intersection model", in Wang L., Chen K., Ong Y.S. (eds.), *Advances in Natural Computation, Lecture Notes in Computer Science*, vol. 3612, Springer-Verlag, Berlin/Heidelberg, p. 1261-1273, 2005.

[DU 05b]   Du S., Qin Q., Li B., "Fuzzy description of topological relations II: computation methods and examples", in Wang L., Chen K., Ong Y.S. (eds.), *Advances in Natural Computation, Lecture Notes in Computer Science*, vol. 3612, Springer-Verlag, Berlin/Heidelberg, p. 1274-1279, 2005.

[DUB 96]   Dubois D., Fargier H., Prade H., "Possibility theory in constraint satisfaction problems: handling priority, preference and uncertainty", *Applied Intelligence*, vol. 6, p. 287-309, 1996.

[DÜN 01a]   Düntsch I., Schmidt G., Winter M., "A necessary relation algebra for mereotopology", *Studia Logica*, vol. 69, p. 380-409, 2001.

[DÜN 01b]   Düntsch I., Wang H., McCloskey S., "A relation-algebraic approach to the region connection calculus", *Theoretical Computer Science*, vol. 255, p. 63-83, 2001.

[DÜN 02]   Düntsch I., Roubens M., "Tangent circle algebras", in de Zwart H. (ed.), *Relational Methods in Computer Science, Lecture Notes in Science*, vol. 2561, Springer-Verlag, Berlin/Heidelberg, p. 300-314, 2002.

[DÜN 03]   Düntsch I., Relation Algebras and Their Application in Qualitative Spatial Reasoning, Report no. CS-03-07, Brock University, St. Catarines, Ontario, Canada, 2003.

[DYL 04]   Dylla F., Moratz R., "Exploiting qualitative spatial neighborhoods in the situation calculus", in Freksa C., *et al.* (eds.), p. 304-322, 2004.

[DYL 07]   Dylla F., Wallgrün J.O., "Qualitative spatial reasoning with conceptual neighborhoods for agent control", *Journal of Intelligent and Robotic Systems*, vol. 48, no. 1, p. 55-78, Kluwer Academic Publishers, 2007.

[EGE 89]   Egenhofer M.J., "A formal definition of binary topological relationships", in Litwin W., Schek H.J. (eds.), *FODO*, vol. 367, *Lecture Notes in Computer Science*, Springer, Berlin/Heidelberg, p. 457-472, 1989.

[EGE 90]   Egenhofer M.J., Herring J., "A mathematical framework for the definition of topological relations", in *Fourth International Symposium on Spatial Data Handling*, Zurich, Switzerland, p. 803-813, 1990.

[EGE 91a]   Egenhofer M.J., "Reasoning about binary topological relations", in Günther O., Schek H.-J. (eds.), p. 143-160, 1991.

[EGE 91b]   Egenhofer M.J., Franzosa R.D., "Point set topological relations", *International Journal of Geographical Information Systems*, vol. 5, p. 161-174, 1991.

[EGE 97]   Egenhofer M.J., "Query processing in spatial-query-by-sketch", *Journal of Visual Languages and Computing*, vol. 8, no. 4, p. 403-424, 1997.

[EGE 99]   Egenhofer M., Rodriguez A., "Relation algebras over containers and surfaces: an ontological study of a room space", *Spatial Cognition and Computation*, vol. 1, no. 2, p. 155-180, 1999.

[ELK 96] EL-KHOLY A., RICHARDS B., "Temporal and resource reasoning in planning: the parc PLAN approach", in *Proceedings of ECAI-96*, Budapest, Hungary, John Wiley and Sons, Chichester, UK, p. 614-618, 1996.

[ERW 97] ERWIG M., SCHNEIDER M., "Vague regions", in SCHOLL M., VOISARD A. (eds.), *SSD*, vol. 1262, *Lecture Notes in Computer Science*, Springer, Berlin/Heidelberg, p. 298-320, 1997.

[EUZ 96] EUZENAT J., "An algebraic approach for granularity in qualitative space and time representation", in *Proceedings of IJCAI-95*, Montreal, Canada, Morgan Kaufmann, USA, p. 894-900, 1996.

[EUZ 01] EUZENAT J., "Granularity in relational formalisms with application to time and space", *Computational Intelligence*, vol. 17, no. 4, p. 703-737, 2001.

[EVA 07] EVANS A., WATERS T., "Mapping vernacular geography: web-based GIS tools for capturing 'fuzzy' or 'vague' entities", *International Journal of Technology, Policy and Management*, vol. 7, no. 2, p. 134-150, 2007.

[EÉN 03] EÉN N., SÖRENSEN N., "An extensible SAT-solver", in *SAT-2003*, LNCS 2919, Springer, Berlin/Heidelberg, p. 502-518, 2003.

[FAL 95] FALTINGS B., "Qualitative spatial reasoning using algebraic topology", in FRANK A.U., KUHN W. (eds.), *Proceedings of COSIT '95*, *LNCS*, 988, Springer, Berlin/Heidelberg, p. 17-30, 1995.

[FER 00] FERNYHOUGH J., COHN A., HOGG D., "Constructing qualitative event models automatically from video input", *Image and Vision Computing*, vol. 18, p. 81-103, 2000.

[FER 03] FERGUSON R.W., BOKOR J.L., MAPPUS IV R.L., FELDMAN A., "Maintaining spatial relations in an incremental diagrammatic reasoner", in KUHN W., WORBOYS M.F., TIMPF S. (eds.), *COSIT*, vol. 2825, *Lecture Notes in Computer Science*, Springer, Berlin/Heidelberg, p. 136-150, 2003.

[FIS 00] FISHER P., "Sorites paradox and vague geographies", *Fuzzy Sets and Systems*, vol. 113, no. 1, p. 7-18, Elsevier North-Holland, The Netherlands, 2000.

[FIS 05] FISHER M., GABBAY D., VILA L. (eds.), *Handbook of Temporal Reasoning in Artificial Intelligence*, vol. 1, Elsevier, Amsterdam, The Netherlands, 2005.

[FOG 09] FOGLIARONI P., WALLGRÜN J.O., CLEMENTINI E., TARQUINI F., WOLTER D., "A qualitative approach to localization and navigation based on visibility information", in HORNSBY K.S., *et al.* (eds.), p. 312-329, 2009.

[FOR 01] FORBUS K.D., FERGUSON R.W., USHER J.M., "Towards a computational model of sketching", in *Proceedings of IUI '01*, Santa Fe, New Mexico, ACM, USA, p. 77-83, 2001.

[FOR 04] FORBUS K.D., USHER J.M., CHAPMAN V., "Qualitative spatial reasoning about sketch maps", *AI Magazine*, vol. 25, no. 3, p. 61-72, 2004.

[FOX 03] FOX M., LONG D., "PDDL2.1: an extension to PDDL for expressing temporal planning domains", *Journal of Artificial Intelligence Research*, vol. 20, p. 61-124, 2003.

[FOX 05] FOX M., LONG D., "Time in planning", in FISHER M., *et al.* (eds.), p. 495-536.

[FRA 92a] FRANK A.U., "Qualitative spatial reasoning about distances and directions in geographic space", *Journal of Visual Languages and Computing*, vol. 3, p. 343-371, 1992.

[FRA 92b] FRANK A.U., CAMPARI I., FORMENTINI U. (eds.), *Proceedings of the International Conference GIS - From Space to Territory: Theories and Methods of Spatio-Temporal Reasoning in Geographic Space*, vol. 639, *Lecture Notes in Computer Science*, Pisa, Italy, Springer, Berlin/Heidelberg, 1992.

[FRA 98] FRACZAK L., Descriptions d'itinéraires: de la référence au texte, PhD thesis, Paris-Sud University, 1998.

[FRA 00] FRAÏSSÉ R., *Theory of Relations*, English translation, CLOTE P. (revised edition), North-Holland, Amsterdam, The Netherlands, 2000.

[FRE 91] FREKSA C., "Conceptual neighborhood and its role in temporal and spatial reasoning", in *Proceedings of the IMACS International Workshop on Decision Support Systems and Qualitative Reasoning*, Toulouse, France, p. 181-187, 1991.

[FRE 92a] FREKSA C., "Temporal reasoning based on semi-intervals", *Artificial Intelligence*, vol. 54, p. 129-227, 1992.

[FRE 92b] FREKSA C., "Using orientation information for qualitative spatial reasoning", in FRANK A.U., *et al.* (eds.), p. 162-178, 1992.

[FRE 00] FREYTAG J.C., FLASZA M., STILLGER M., "Implementing geospatial operations in an object-relational database system", in *SSDBM*, p. 209-219, 2000.

[FRE 05] FREKSA C., KNAUFF M., KRIEG-BRÜCKNER B., NEBEL B., BARKOWSKY T. (eds.), "Spatial Cognition IV: Reasoning, Action, Interaction", International Conference Spatial Cognition 2004, Revised Selected Papers, vol. 3343, *Lecture Notes in Computer Science*, Frauenchiemsee, Germany, Springer, Berlin/Heidelberg, 2005.

[GAL 97] GALTON A., "Continuous change in spatial regions", in HIRTLE S.C., FRANK A.U. (eds.), p. 1-13, 1997.

[GAL 98] GALTON A., "Modes of overlap", *Journal of Visual Languages and Computing*, vol. 9, no. 1, p. 61-79, 1998.

[GAL 99] GALTON A., "The mereotopology of discrete space", in FREKSA C., MARK D.M. (eds.), *COSIT*, vol. 1661, *Lecture Notes in Computer Science*, Springer, Berlin/Heidelberg, p. 251-266, 1999.

[GAL 00] GALTON A., *Qualitative Spatial Change*, Oxford University Press, Oxford, UK, 2000.

[GAL 01] GALTON A., "Dominance diagrams: a tool for qualitative reasoning about continuous systems", *Fundamenta Informaticae*, vol. 46, no. 1-2, p. 55-70, 2001.

[GAN 08] GANTNER Z., WESTPHAL M., WÖLfl S., "GQR- a fast reasoner for binary qualitative constraint calculi", in *Proceedings of the AAAI '08 Workshop on Spatial and Temporal Reasoning*, Chicago, USA, 2008.

[GAR 79] GAREY M.R., JOHNSON D.S., *Computers and Intractability: A Guide to the Theory of NP-Completeness*, Freeman W.H., 1979.

[GÄR 00] GÄRDENFORS P., *Conceptual Spaces: The Geometry of Thought*, The MIT Press, 2000 (hardcover edition).

[GÄR 04] GÄRDENFORS P., *Conceptual Spaces: The Geometry of Thought*, Bradford/MIT Press, Cambridge/London, 2004 (paperback edition).

[GER 93] GEREVINI A., SCHUBERT L., SCHAEFFER S., "Temporal reasoning in timegraph I-II", *Association for Computing Machinery Sigart Bulletin*, vol. 4, no. 3, p. 21-25, 1993.

[GER 95] GEREVINI A., CRISTANI M., "Reasoning with inequations in temporal constraint networks", in *Proceedings of the IJCAI-95 Workshop on Spatial and Temporal Reasoning*, Montreal, Canada, 1995.

[GER 02a] GEREVINI A., NEBEL B., "Qualitative spatio-temporal reasoning with RCC-8 and Allen's interval calculus: computational complexity", in VAN HARMELEN F. (ed.), p. 312-316, 2002.

[GER 02b] GEREVINI A., RENZ J., "Combining topological and size information for spatial reasoning", *Artificial Intelligence*, vol. 137, no. 1-2, p. 1-42, 2002.

[GOD 95] GODO L., VILA L., "Possibilistic temporal reasoning based on fuzzy temporal constraints", in *Proceedings of IJCAI-95*, Montreal, Canada, Morgan Kaufmann, USA, p. 1916-1922, 1995.

[GOL 93] GOLUMBIC M.C., SHAMIR R., "Complexity and algorithms for reasoning about time: a graph-theoretic approach", *Journal of the Association for Computing Machinery*, vol. 40, no. 5, p. 1108-1133, 1993.

[GOO 96] GOODAY J.M., COHN A.G., "Visual language syntax and semantics: a spatial logic approach", in MARRIOTT K., MEYER B. (eds.), *Proceedings Workshop on Theory of Visual Languages*, Gubbio, Italy, 1996.

[GOO 98] GOODCHILD M., MONTELLO D., FOHL P., GOTTSEGEN J., "Fuzzy spatial queries in digital spatial data libraries", in *Proceedings of the IEEE World Congress on Computational Intelligence*, p. 205-210, 1998.

[GOT 94] GOTTS N.M., "How far can we C? Defining a 'doughnut' using connection alone", in DOYLE J., SANDEWALL E., TORASSO P. (eds.), *Principles of Knowledge Representation and Reasoning: Proceedings of the 4th International Conference (KR'94)*, Bonn, Germany, Morgan Kaufmann, San Francisco, USA, 1994.

[GOT 96] GOTTS N., An axiomatic approach to topology for information systems, Report no. TR-96-25, School of Computer Studies, University of Leeds, UK, 1996.

[GOY 97] GOYAL R.K., EGENHOFER M.J., "The direction-relation matrix: a representation for directions relations between extended spatial objects", in *The Annual Assembly and the Summer Retreat of University Consortium for Geographic Information Systems Science*, Bar Harbor, USA, 1997.

[GOY 00] GOYAL. R.K., Similarity assessment for cardinal directions between extended spatial objects, PhD thesis, The University of Maine, USA, 2000.

[GOY 01] GOYAL R.K., EGENHOFER M.J., "Similarity of cardinal directions", in JENSEN C.S., *et al.* (eds.), p. 36-58, 2001.

[GUE 94] GUESGEN H.W., HERTZBERG J., PHILPOTT A., "Towards implementing fuzzy Allen relations", in *Proceedings of the ECAI Workshop on Spatial and Temporal Reasoning*, Amsterdam, The Netherlands, p. 49-55, 1994.

[GUE 01] GUESGEN H.W., HERTZBERG J., "Algorithms for buffering fuzzy raster maps", in RUSSELL I., KOLEN J.F. (eds.), *Proceedings of the FLAIRS Conference*, AAAI Press, USA, p. 542-546, 2001.

[GUE 02a] GUESGEN H.W., "From the egg-yolk to the crambled-egg theory", in HALLER S.M., SIMMONS G. (eds.), *Proceedings of the FLAIRS Conference*, AAAI Press, USA, p. 476-480, 2002.

[GUE 02b] GUESGEN H.W., "Reasoning about distance based on fuzzy Sets", *Applied Intelligence*, vol. 17, no. 3, p. 265-270, 2002.

[GÜN 91] GÜNTHER O., SCHEK H.-J. (eds.), *Advances in Spatial Databases, Proceedings of the Second International Symposium, SSD '91*, vol. 525, *Lecture Notes in Computer Science*, Springer, Zurich, Switzerland, Berlin/Heidelberg, 1991.

[GÜS 89] GÜSGEN H., Spatial Reasoning Based on Allen's Temporal Logic, Report no. TR 89-049, ICSI, Berkeley, USA, 1989.

[HAA 95] HAARSLEV V., "Formal semantics of visual languages using spatial reasoning", in *Proceedings of the 1995 IEEE Symposium on Visual Languages*, p. 156-163, 1995.

[HAA 97] HAARSLEV V., WESSEL M., "Querying GIS with animated spatial sketches", in *Proceedings of the 1997 IEEE Symposium on Visual Languages*, p. 201-208, 1997.

[HAD 92] HADZILACOS T., TRYFONA N., "A model for expressing topological integrity constraints in geographic databases", in FRANK A.U., *et al.* (eds.), p. 252-268, 1992.

[HAR 81] HARD A., SIVIK L., "NCS-natural color system: a Swedish standard for color notation", *Color Research and Application*, vol. 6, p. 129-138, 1981.

[HAR 02] VAN HARMELEN F. (ed.), *Proceedings of the 15th Eureopean Conference on Artificial Intelligence, ECAI 2002*, Lyon, France, IOS Press, Amsterdam, The Netherlands, 2002.

[HAR 05] HARABAGIU S., BEJEAN C., "Question answering based on temporal inference", in *Proceedings of the AAAI-2005 Workshop on Inference for Textual Question Answering*, Pittsburgh, USA, 2005.

[HEB 08] HEBRARD E., "Mistral, a constraint satisfaction library", in *Proceedings of the Third International CSP Solver Competition*, 2008.

[HEL 23] HELLY E., "Über Mengen konvexer Körper mit gemeinschaften Punkten", *Jahresbericht der Deutschen Mathematiker-Vereinigung*, vol. 32, p. 175-176, 1923.

[HEN 76] HENLE M., *A Combinatorial Introduction to Topology*, Dover Publications, New York, 1976.

[HEN 02] HENTENRYCK P.V. (ed.), *Proceedings of the 8th International Conference on the Principles and Practice of Constraint Programming (CP 2002)*, vol. 2470, *Lecture Notes in Computer Science*, Ithaca, USA, Springer, Berlin/Heidelberg, 2002.

[HER 86] HERSKOVITS A., *Language and Spatial Cognition — An Interdisciplinary Study of the Prepositions in English*, Cambridge University Press, Cambridge, UK, 1986.

[HIR 96] HIRSCH R., "Relation algebras of intervals", *Artificial Intelligence*, vol. 83, p. 1-29, 1996.

[HIR 97a] HIRSCH R., "Expressive power and complexity in algebraic logic", *Journal of Logic and Computation*, vol. 7, no. 3, p. 309-351, 1997.

[HIR 97b] HIRTLE S.C., FRANK A.U. (eds.), *Proceedings of the International Conference on Spatial Information Theory: A Theoretical Basis for GIS (COSIT '97)*, Laurel Highlands, USA, *Lecture Notes in Computer Science*, vol. 1329, Springer, Berlin/Heidelberg, 1997.

[HIR 02] HIRSCH R., HODKINSON I., *Relation Algebras by Games Studies in Logic and the Foundations of Mathematics No. 147*, North-Holland, The Netherlands, 2002.

[HOB 85] HOBBS J.R., "Granularity", in *Proceedings IJCAI-85*, Los Angeles, USA, p. 432-435, 1985.

[HOD 93] HODGES W., *Model Theory*, Cambridge University Press, Cambridge, UK, 1993.

[HOD 97] HODGES W., *A Shorter Model Theory*, Cambridge University Press, Cambridge, UK, 1997.

[HOR 00] HORN W. (ed.), *ECAI 2000, Proceedings of the 14th European Conference on Artificial Intelligence*, Berlin, Germany, IOS Press, The Netherlands, 2000.

[HOR 01] HORNSBY K., "Temporal zooming", *Transactions in GIS*, vol. 5, no. 3, p. 255-272, 2001.

[HOR 09] HORNSBY K.S., CLARAMUNT C., DENIS M., LIGOZAT G. (eds.), *Proceedings of the 9th International Conference on Spatial Information Theory (COSIT 2009)*, Aber Wrac'h, France, *Lecture Notes in Computer Science*, vol. 5756, Springer, Berlin/Heidelberg, 2009.

[HUA 92] HUANG Z., SVENSSON P., HAUSKA H., "Solving spatial analysis problems with GeoSAL, a spatial query language", in HINTERBERGER H., FRENCH J.C. (eds.), *Proceedings of the 6th International Working Conference on Scientific and Statistical Database Management, Monte Verita, Switzerland, 1992*, Institut für. Wissenschaftliches Rechnen Eidgenössische Technische Hochschule Zürich, Switzerland, p. 1-17, 1992.

[HUA 00] HUANG X., ZHAO F., "Relation-based aggregation: finding objects in large spatial datasets", *Intelligent Data Analysis*, vol. 4, no. 2, p. 129-147, IOS Press, The Netherlands, 2000.

[ISL 00] ISLI A., COHN A.G., "A new approach to cyclic ordering of 2D orientations using ternary relation algebras", *Artificial Intelligence*, vol. 122, no. 1-2, p. 137-187, 2000.

[JEA 95a] JEAVONS P.G., COHEN D.A., GYSSENS M., "A unifying framework for tractable constraints", in *Proceedings of CP-95*, *LNCS*, 976, Springer, Berlin/Heidelberg, p. 276-291, 1995.

[JEA 95b] JEAVONS P.G., COOPER M., "Tractable constraints on ordered domains", *Artificial Intelligence*, vol. 79, no. 2, p. 327-339, 1995.

[JEA 97] JEAVONS P.G., COHEN D.A., GYSSENS M., "Closure properties of constraints", *Journal of the Association for Computing Machinery*, vol. 44, p. 527-548, 1997.

[JEA 98] JEAVONS P.G., COHEN D.A., COOPER M., "Constraints, consistency and closure", *Artificial Intelligence*, vol. 101, no. 1-2, p. 251-265, 1998.

[JEA 07] JEANSOULIN R., PAPINI O., "Under water archaeological knowledge analysis and representation in the VENUS project: a preliminary draft", in GEORGOPOULOS A. (ed.), *XXI international CIPA Symposium*, vol. XXXVI-5/C53, *The International Archives of Photogrammetry, Remote Sensing and Spatial Information Sciences*, ICOMOS/ISPRS Committee for Documentation of Cultural Heritage, p. 394-399, September 2007.

[JEN 01] JENSEN C.S., SCHNEIDER M., SEEGER B., TSOTRAS V.J. (eds.), *Advances in Spatial and Temporal Databases, 7th International Symposium, SSTD 2001, Redondo Beach, CA, USA, July 12–15, 2001, Proceedings*, vol. 2121, *Lecture Notes in Computer Science*, Springer, Berlin/Heidelberg, 2001.

[JIN 03] JIN P., YUE L., GONG Y., "Semantics and modeling of spatiotemporal changes", in MEERSMAN R., TARI Z., SCHMIDT D.C. (eds.), *CoopIS/DOA/ODBASE*, vol. 2888, *Lecture Notes in Computer Science*, Springer, Berlin/Heidelberg, p. 924-933, 2003.

[JÓN 52] JÓNSSON B., TARSKI A., "Boolean algebras with operators, Part II", *American Journal of Mathematics*, vol. 74, p. 127-162, 1952.

[JÓN 59] JÓNSSON B., "Representation of modular lattices and relation algebras", *Transactions of the American Mathematical Society*, vol. 92, p. 449-464, 1959.

[JON 98] JONSSON P., BÄCKSTRÖM C., "A unifying approach to temporal constraint reasoning", *Artificial Intelligence*, vol. 102, no. 1, p. 143-155, 1998.

[JON 99] JONSSON P., DRAKENGREN T., BÄCKSTRÖM C., "Computational complexity of relating time points with intervals", *Artificial Intelligence*, vol. 109, no. 1-2, p. 273-295, 1999.

[KAE 05] KAELBLING L.P., SAFFIOTTI A. (ed.), *IJCAI-05, Proceedings of the 19th International Joint Conference on Artificial Intelligence*, Professional Book Center, Edinburgh, Scotland, UK, 2005.

[KAR 84] KARMARKAR N., "A new polynomial time algorithm for linear programming", *Combinatorica*, vol. 4, p. 373-395, 1984.

[KAU 91] KAUTZ H.A., LADKIN P.B., "Integrating metric and qualitative temporal reasoning", in *Proceedings of the Ninth National Conference on Artificial Intelligence (AAAI '91)*, vol. , p. 241-246, Anaheim, USA, 1991.

[KER 05] KERAVNOU E., SHAHAR Y., "Temporal reasoning in medicine", in FISHER M., *et al.* (eds.), p. 587-653, 2005.

[KHA 79] KHACHIYAN L., "A polynomial algorithm in linear programming", *Soviet Mathematics - Doklady*, vol. 20, p. 191-194, 1979.

[KHA 01] KHATIB L., MORRIS P., MORRIS R., ROSSI F., "Temporal constraint reasoning with preferences", in *Proceedings of IJCAI-01*, Seattle, USA, Morgan Kaufmann Publishers, USA, p. 322-327, 2001.

[KNA 97] KNAUFF M., RAUH R., RENZ J., "A cognitive assessment of topological spatial relations: results from an empirical investigation", in HIRTLE S.C., FRANK A.U. (eds.), p. 193-206, 1997.

[KNA 98] KNAUFF M., RAUH R., SCHLIEDER C., STRUBE G., "Mental models in spatial reasoning", in FREKSA C., HABEL C., WENDER K.F. (eds.), *Spatial Cognition*, vol. 1404, *Lecture Notes in Computer Science*, Springer, Berlin/Heidelberg, p. 267-292, 1998.

[KÖH 04] KÖHLER C., OTTLIK A., NAGEL H.-H., NEBEL B., "Qualitative reasoning feeding back into quantitative model-based tracking", in LÓPEZ DE MÁNTARAS R., SAITTA L. (eds.), p. 1041-1042, 2004.

[KON 89] KONG T., ROSENFELD A., "Digital topology: introduction and survey", *Computer Vision, Graphics, and Image Processing*, vol. 48, p. 357-393, 1989.

[KON 08] KONTCHAKOV R., PRATT-HARTMANN I., WOLTER F., ZAKHARYASCHEV M., "Topology, connectedness, and modal logic", in ARECES C., GOLDBLATT R. (eds.), *Advances in Modal Logic 7*, College Publications, p. 151-176, 2008.

[KOU 92] KOUBARAKIS M., "Dense time and temporal constraints with ≠", in NEBEL B., RICH C. (eds.), *Proceedings of the 3rd International Conference on Principles of Knowledge Representation and Reasoning (KR '92)*, Cambridge, USA, Morgan Kaufmann, USA, p. 24-35, 1992.

[KOU 96] KOUBARAKIS M., "Tractable disjunctions of linear constraints", in FREUDER E.C. (ed.), *Proceedings of the Second International Conference on Principles and Practice of Constraint Programming (CP 1996)*, Cambridge, USA, *Lecture Notes in Computer Science*, vol. 1118, Springer, Berlin/Heidelberg, p. 297-307, 1996.

[KOU 97] KOUBARAKIS M., "From local to global consistency in temporal constraint networks", *Theoretical Computer Science*, vol. 173, no. 1, p. 89-112, 1997.

[KOU 01] KOUBARAKIS M., "Tractable disjunctions of linear constraints: basic results and applications to temporal reasoning", *Theoretical Computer Science*, vol. 266, no. 1-2, p. 311-339, 2001.

[KOU 03] KOUBARAKIS M., SELLIS T.K., FRANK A.U., GRUMBACH S., GÜTING R.H., JENSEN C.S., LORENTZOS N.A., MANOLOPOULOS Y., NARDELLI E., PERNICI B., SCHEK H.-J., SCHOLL M., THEODOULIDIS B., TRYFONA N. (eds.), "Spatio-Temporal Databases: The Chorochronos Approach", *Lecture Notes in Computer Science*, vol. 2520, Springer, Berlin/Heidelberg, 2003.

[KRO 92] KRONHEIMER E.H., "The topology of digital images", *Topology and its Applications*, vol. 46, p. 279-303, 1992.

[KRO 03] KROKHIN A., JEAVONS P., JONSSON P., "Reasoning about temporal relations: the tractable subalgebras of Allen's interval algebra", *Journal of the Association for Computing Machinery*, vol. 50, no. 5, p. 591-640, ACM Press, 2003.

[KRO 04] KROKHIN A.A., JEAVONS P., JONSSON P., "Constraint satisfaction problems on intervals and length", *SIAM Journal on Discrete Mathematics*, vol. 17, no. 3, p. 453-477, 2004.

[KUI 91] KUIPERS B.J., BYUN Y.-T., "A robot exploration and mapping strategy based on a semantic hierarchy of spatial representations", *Journal of Robotics and Autonomous Systems*, vol. 8, p. 47-63, 1991.

[KUI 08] KUIPERS B., "Cognitive robot mapping: an introduction", in JEFFERIES M.E., YEAP W.-K. (eds.), *Robotics and Cognitive Approaches to Spatial Mapping*, *Springer Tracts in Advanced Robotics*, vol. 38, Springer, Berlin/Heidelberg, p. 239-242, 2008.

[KUL 01] KULIK L., "A geometric theory of vague boundaries based on supervaluation", in MONTELLO D.R. (ed.), p. 44-59, 2001.

[KUT 03] KUTZ O., WOLTER F., STURM H., SUZUKI N.-Y., ZAKHARYASCHEV M., "Logics of metric spaces", *ACM Transactions on Computational Logic*, vol. 4, no. 2, p. 260-294, 2003.

[LAD 77] LADNER R., "The computational complexity of provability in systems of modal logic", *SIAM Journal on Computing*, vol. 6, p. 467-480, 1977.

[LAD 86] LADKIN P.B., "Time representation: a taxonomy of interval relations", in *Proceedings of AAAI-86*, Philadelphia, USA, AAAI Press/The MIT Press, USA, p. 360-366, 1986.

[LAD 87] LADKIN P.B., The Logic of time representation, PhD thesis, University of California, Berkeley, USA, 1987.

[LAD 88] LADKIN P.B., MADDUX R.D., On Binary Constraint Networks, Report no. KES.U.88.8, Kestrel Institute, Palo Alto, USA, 1988.

[LAD 92] LADKIN P., REINEFELD A., "Effective solution of qualitative constraint problems", *Artificial Intelligence*, vol. 57, p. 105-124, 1992.

[LAD 94] LADKIN P.B., MADDUX R.D., "On binary constraint problems", *Journal of the Association for Computing Machinery*, vol. 41, no. 3, p. 435-469, 1994.

[LAD 97] LADKIN P.B., REINEFELD A., "Fast algebraic methods for interval constraint problems", *Annals of Mathematics and Artificial Intelligence*, vol. 19, no. 3-4, p. 383-411, 1997.

[LAS 91] LASCARIDES A., ASHER N., "Discourse relations and defeasible knowledge", in *Proceedings of the 29th Annual Meeting of the Association of Computational Linguistics (ACL '91)*, Berkeley, USA, p. 55-62, 1991.

[LAS 93] LASCARIDES A., ASHER N., "Temporal interpretation, discourse relations, and commonsense entailment", *Linguistics and Philosophy*, vol. 16, p. 437-493, Springer, 1993.

[LEB 99] LE BER F., MANGELINCK L., NAPOLI A., "Représentation de relations et classification de structures spatiales", *Revue d'Intelligence Artificielle*, vol. 13, no. 2, p. 441-467, 1999.

[LEB 07] LE BER F., LIGOZAT G., PAPINI O. (eds.), *Raisonnements sur l'espace et le temps*, Hermès-Lavoisier, Paris, 2007.

[LEH 94] LEHMANN F., COHN A.G., "The egg/yolk reliability hierarchy: semantic data integration using sorts with prototypes", in *Proceedings of the Conference on Information Knowledge Management*, ACM Press, USA, p. 272-279, 1994.

[LEM 96] LEMON O., "Semantical foundations of spatial logics", in *Proceedings of the Fifth International Conference on Principles of Knowledge Representation and Reasoning (KR '96)*, Cambridge, USA, Morgan Kaufmann, USA, p. 212-219, 1996.

[LEŚ 92] LEŚNIEWSKI S., *Collected Works*, Kluwer, The Netherlands, 1992.

[LI 03a] LI S., YING M., "Extensionality of the RCC-8 composition table", *Fundamenta Informaticae*, vol. 55, no. 3-4, p. 363-385, 2003.

[LI 03b] LI S., YING M., "Region connection calculus: its models and composition table", *Artificial Intelligence*, vol. 145, no. 1-2, p. 121-146, 2003.

[LI 04a] LI S., YING M., "Generalized region connection calculus", *Artificial Intelligence*, vol. 160, no. 1-2, p. 1-34, 2004.

[LI 04b] LI Y., LI S., "A fuzzy sets theoretic approach to approximate spatial reasoning", *IEEE Transactions on Fuzzy Systems*, vol. 12, no. 6, p. 745-754, 2004.

[LI 05] LI Y., LI S., YING M., "Relational reasoning in the region connection calculus", *CoRR*, vol. abs/cs/0505041, 2005.

[LI 07] LI W., "Combining topological and directional information for spatial reasoning", in VELOSO M.M. (ed.), p. 435-440, 2007.

[LIG 90] LIGOZAT G., "Weak representations of interval algebras", in *Proceedings of AAAI-90*, Boston, USA, AAAI Press/The MIT Press, p. 715-720, 1990.

[LIG 91] LIGOZAT G., "On generalized interval calculi", in *Proceedings of AAAI-91*, Anaheim, USA, AAAI Press/The MIT Press, p. 234-240, 1991.

[LIG 93a] LIGOZAT G., "Models for qualitative spatial reasoning", in ANGER F.D., GÜSGEN H., VAN BENTHEM J. (eds.), *Proceedings of the IJCAI-93 Workshop on Spatial and Temporal Reasoning*, Chambéry, France, 1993.

[LIG 93b] LIGOZAT G., "Qualitative triangulation for spatial reasoning", in FRANK A., CAMPARI I. (eds.), *Proceedings of the International Conference on Spatial Information Theory: A Theoretical Basis for GIS, (COSIT '93)*, Marciana Marina, Elba, Italy, *LNCS*, 716, Springer, Berlin/Heidelberg, p. 54–68, 1993.

[LIG 94a] LIGOZAT G., "Temporal reasoning made simpler", in *Proceedings of IEA/AIE 94*, Austin, Texas, USA, p. 123-130, 1994.

[LIG 94b] LIGOZAT G., "Tractable relations in temporal reasoning: pre-convex relations", in ANGER F.D., GÜSGEN H., LIGOZAT G. (eds.), *Proceedings of the ECAI-94 Workshop on Spatial and Temporal Reasoning*, Amsterdam, The Netherlands, p. 99-108, 1994.

[LIG 96] LIGOZAT G., "A new proof of tractability for ORD-Horn relations", in *Proceedings of AAAI-96*, Portland, Oregon, USA, AAAI Press/The MIT Press, p. 395-401, 1996.

[LIG 97] LIGOZAT G., "Figures for thought: temporal reasoning with pictures", in *Proceedings of the AAAI-97 Workshop on Spatial and Temporal Reasoning, 14th National Conference on Artificial Intelligence*, Providence, Rhode Island, USA, 1997.

[LIG 98a] LIGOZAT G., "'Corner' relations in Allen's algebra", *CONSTRAINTS: An International Journal*, vol. 3, p. 165-177, 1998.

[LIG 98b] LIGOZAT G., "Reasoning about cardinal directions", *Journal of Visual Languages and Computing*, vol. 1, no. 9, p. 23-44, 1998.

[LIG 99] LIGOZAT G., "Simple models for simple calculi", in FREKSA C., MARK D. (eds.), *Proceedings of COSIT '99*, *LNCS*, 1661, Springer Verlag, Berlin/Heidelberg, p. 173-188, 1999.

[LIG 01] LIGOZAT G., "When tables tell it all", in MONTELLO D.R. (ed.), p. 60-75, 2001.

[LIG 03] LIGOZAT G., MITRA D., CONDOTTA J.-F., "Spatial and temporal reasoning: beyond Allen's calculus", in *Proceedings of the AAAI Spring Symposium on Foundations and Applications of Spatio-Temporal Reasoning (FASTR)*, 2003.

[LIG 04a] LIGOZAT G., MITRA D., CONDOTTA J.-F., "Spatial and temporal reasoning: beyond Allen's calculus", *AI Communications*, vol. 17, no. 4, p. 223-233, 2004.

[LIG 04b] LIGOZAT G., RENZ J., "What is a qualitative calculus? A general framework", in *Proceedings of PRICAI'04, LNCS*, 3157, Auckland, New Zealand, p. 53-64, 2004.

[LIG 05a] LIGOZAT G., "Categorical methods in qualitative reasoning: the case for weak representations", in COHN A.G., MARK D.M. (eds.), *COSIT, Lecture Notes in Computer Science*, vol. 3693, Springer, Berlin/Heidelberg, p. 265-282, 2005.

[LIG 05b] LIGOZAT G., CONDOTTA J.-F., "On the relevance of conceptual spaces for spatial and temporal reasoning", *Spatial Cognition and Computation*, vol. 5, no. 1, p. 1-27, 2005.

[LIG 07] LIGOZAT G., NOWAK J., SCHMITT D., "From language to pictorial representations", in VETULANI Z. (ed.), *Proceedings of the Language and Technology Conference (L&TC '07)*, Wydawnictwo Poznańskie, Poznań, Poland, September 2007.

[LIG 09] LIGOZAT G., VETULANI Z., OSIŃSKI J., "Spatio-temporal aspects of the monitoring of complex events", in GUESGEN H.W., BHATT M. (ed.), *Proceedings of IJCAI-09 Workshop on Spatial and Temporal Reasoning (W32)*, Pasadena, California, USA, p. 44-51, 2009.

[LIU 04] LIU J., DANESHMEND L., *Spatial Reasoning and Planning: Geometry, Mechanisms, and Motion*, Advanced Information Processing, Springer Verlag, New York/Berlin/Heidelberg, 2004.

[LIU 06] LIU K., SHI W., "Computing the fuzzy topological relations of spatial objects based on induced fuzzy topology", *International Journal of Geographical Information Science*, vol. 20, no. 8, p. 857-883, 2006.

[LIU 09] LIU W., LI S., RENZ J., "Combining RCC-8 with qualitative direction calculi: algorithms and complexity", in BOUTILIER C. (ed.), p. 854-859, 2009.

[LIU 10] LIU W., ZHANG X., LI S., YING M., "Reasoning about cardinal directions between extended objects", *Artificial Intelligence*, vol. 174, no. 12-13, p. 951-983, 2010.

[LYN 50] LYNDON R., "The representation of relational algebras", *Annals of Mathematics*, vol. 51, no. 3, p. 707-729, 1950.

[LÜC 08] LÜCKE D., MOSSAKOWSKI T., WOLTER D., "Qualitative reasoning about convex relations", in FREKSA C., NEWCOMBE N.S., GÄRDENFORS P., WÖLFL S. (eds.), *Spatial Cognition, Lecture Notes in Computer Science*, vol. 5248, Springer, Berlin/Heidelberg, p. 426-440, 2008.

[MAC 71] MACLANE S., *Categories for the Working Mathematician*, Springer Verlag, New York, Berlin, Heidelberg, 1971.

[MAC 77] MACKWORTH A.K., "Consistency in networks of relations", *Artificial Intelligence*, vol. 8, p. 99-118, 1977.

[MAD 82] MADDUX R., "Some varieties containing relation algebras", *Transactions of the American Mathematical Society*, vol. 272, no. 2, p. 501-526, 1982.

[MÁN 04] LÓPEZ DE MÁNTARAS R., SAITTA L. (eds.), *Proceedings of the 16th European Conference on Artificial Intelligence (ECAI 2004), including Prestigious Applicants of Intelligent Systems (PAIS 2004)*, Valencia, Spain, IOS Press, The Netherlands, 2004.

[MAU 06] MAU I., HORNSBY K.S., BISHOP I.D., "Modeling geospatial events and impacts through qualitative change", in BARKOWSKY T., *et al.* (eds.), p. 156-174, 2006.

[MCK 44] MCKINSEY J., TARSKI A., "The algebra of topology", *Annals of Mathematics*, vol. 45, p. 141-191, 1944.

[MCK 70] MCKENZIE R., "Representations of integral relational algebras", *Michigan Mathematical Journal*, vol. 17, p. 279-287, 1970.

[MEI 91] MEIRI I., "Combining qualitative and quantitative constraints in temporal reasoning", in DEAN T., MCKEOWN K. (eds.), *Proceedings of the 9th National Conference on Artificial Intelligence*, AAAI Press/The MIT Press, California, USA, p. 260-267, 1991.

[MEI 96] MEIRI I., "Combining qualitative and quantitative constraints in temporal reasoning", *Artificial Intelligence*, vol. 87, no. 1-2, p. 343-385, 1996.

[MEU 05] TER MEULEN A., "Temporal reasoning in natural language", in FISHER M., *et al.* (eds.), p. 559-585, 2005.

[MIN 05] MINTS G., ZHANG T., "A proof of topological completeness for S4 in (0, 1)", *Annals of Pure and Applied Logic*, vol. 133, no. 1-3, p. 231-245, 2005.

[MIT 02] MITRA D., "Qualitative reasoning with arbitrary angular directions", in *Proceedings of the AAAI-02 W20 Workshop on Spatial and Temporal Reasoning*, Edmonton, Canada, 2002.

[MOE 88] MOENS M., STEEDMAN M., "Temporal ontology and temporal reference", *Computational Linguistics*, vol. 14, no. 2, p. 15-28, 1988.

[MOL 05] MOLDOVAN D.I., CLARK C., HARABAGIU S.M., "Temporal context representation and reasoning", in KAELBLING L.P., SAFFIOTTI A. (eds.), p. 1099-1104, 2005.

[MON 74] MONTANARI U., "Networks of constraints: fundamental properties and applications to picture processing", *Information Sciences*, vol. 7, p. 95-132, 1974.

[MON 01] MONTELLO D.R. (ed.), *Proceedings of the International Conference on Spatial Information Theory: Foundations of Geographic Information Science (COSIT 2001)*, Morro Bay, USA, *Lecture Notes in Computer Science*, vol. 2205, Springer, Berlin/Heidelberg, 2001.

[MON 03] MONTELLO D., GOODCHILD M., GOTTSEGEN J., FOHL P., "Where's downtown?: behavioral methods for determining reference of vague spatial queries", *Spatial Cognition and Computation*, vol. 3, no. 2-3, p. 185-204, 2003.

[MOR 91] MORRIS A.R., AL-KHATIB L., "An interval-based temporal relational calculus for events with gaps", *Journal of Experimental and Theoretical Artificial Intelligence*, vol. 3, 1991.

[MOR 93a] MORMANN T., "Natural predicates and the topological structure of conceptual spaces", *Synthese*, vol. 95, p. 219-240, 1993.

[MOR 93b] MORRIS R., SHOAFF W.D., KHATIB L., "Path consistency in a network of non-convex intervals", in *Proceedings of IJCAI-93*, Chambéry, France, Morgan Kaufmann Publishers, USA, p. 655-660, 1993.

[MOR 95] MORRIS R., LIGOZAT G., KHATIB L., "Generating scenarios from specifications of repeating events", in *Proceedings of the Second International Workshop on Temporal Representation and Reasoning (TIME)*, FLAIRS, Melbourne Beach, Florida, 1995.

[MOR 00] MORATZ R., RENZ J., WOLTER D., "Qualitative spatial reasoning about line segments", in HORN W. (ed.), p. 234-238, 2000.

[MOR 05] MORATZ R., DYLLA F., FROMMBERGER L., "A relative orientation algebra with adjustable granularity", in *Proceedings of the IJCAI-05 Workshop on Agents in Real-Time and Dynamic Environments*, Edinburgh, Scotland, July 2005.

[MOR 06] MORATZ R., "Representing relative direction as a binary relation of oriented points", in BREWKA G., CORADESCHI S., PERINI A., TRAVERSO P. (eds.), *ECAI*, vol. 141, *Frontiers in Artificial Intelligence and Applications*, IOS Press, The Netherlands, p. 407-411, 2006.

[MOS 06] MOSSAKOWSKI T., SCHRÖDER L., WÖLFL S., "A categorical perspective on qualitative constraint calculi", in *Qualitative Constraint Calculi: Application and Integration, Workshop Proceedings*, p. 28-39, 2006.

[MUL 98a] MULLER P., Éléments d'une théorie du mouvement pour la formalisation du raisonnement spatio-temporel de sens commun, PhD thesis, IRIT, University of Paul Sabatier, Toulouse, 1998.

[MUL 98b] MULLER P., "A qualitative theory of motion based on spatio-temporal primitives", in COHN A.G., SCHUBERT L., SHAPIRO S.C. (eds.), *Proceedings of the 6th International Conference on Principles of Knowledge Representation and Reasoning (KR'98)*, Morgan Kaufmann, USA, p. 131-141, 1998.

[MYL 90] MYLOPOULOS J., BORGIDA A., JARKE M., KOUBARAKIS M., "Telos: representing knowledge about information systems", *ACM Transactions on Information and System Security*, vol. 8, no. 4, p. 325-362, 1990.

[NAK 87] NAKHIMOVSKY A., "Temporal reasoning in natural language understanding: the temporal structure of the narrative", in *EACL*, p. 262-269, 1987.

[NAK 88a] NAKHIMOVSKY A., "Aspect, aspectual class, and the temporal structure of narrative", *Computational Linguistics*, vol. 14, no. 2, p. 29-43, 1988.

[NAK 88b] NAKHIMOVSKY A., RAPAPORT W.J., "Discontinuities in narratives", in *Proceedings of the 12th International Conference on Computational Linguistics (COLING)*, Budapest, Hungary, John von Neumann Society for Computing Sciences, p. 465-470, 1988.

[NEB 94a] NEBEL B., "Computational properties of qualitative spatial reasoning: first results", in *Proceedings of KI '95, LNCS*, 981, Springer, Berlin/Heidelberg, p. 233-244, 1994.

[NEB 94b] NEBEL B., BÜRCKERT H., "Reasoning about temporal relations: a maximal tractable subclass of Allen's interval algebra", in *Proceedings of AAAI-94*, Seattle, Washington, AAAI Press/The MIT Press, p. 356-361, 1994.

[NEB 94c] NEBEL B., BÜRCKERT H.-J., "Reasoning about temporal relations: a maximal tractable subclass of Allen's interval algebra", in *Proceedings of the 12th National Conference of the American Association for Artificial Intelligence*, (Extended version published in *Journal of the ACM*), MIT Press, Cambridge, USA, p. 356-361, 1994.

[NEB 95] NEBEL B., BÜRCKERT H.-J., "Reasoning about temporal relations: a maximal tractable subclass of Allen's interval algebra", *Journal of the Association for Computing Machinery*, vol. 42, no. 1, p. 43-66, 1995.

[NEB 96] NEBEL B., "Solving hard qualitative temporal reasoning problems: evaluating the efficienty of using the ORD-Horn class", in *Proceedings of the 12th Conference on Artificial Intelligence (ECAI '96)*, Budapest, Hungary, John Wiley and Sons, UK, p. 38-42, 1996.

[NEB 97] NEBEL B., "Solving hard qualitative temporal reasoning problems: evaluating the efficiency of using the ORD-Horn class", *Constraints*, vol. 1, no. 3, p. 175-190, 1997.

[NÖK 88] NÖKEL K., Convex Relations Between Time Intervals, Report no. SR-88-17, Universität Kaiserslautern, 1988.

[NÖK 89] NÖKEL K., "Temporal matching: recognizing dynamic situations from discrete measurements", in *Proceedings of IJCAI-89*, Detroit, Michigan, Morgan Kaufmann, USA, p. 1255-1260, 1989.

[NUT 99] NUTT W., "On the translation of qualitative spatial reasoning problems into modal logics", in BURGARD W., CHRISTALLER T., CREMERS A. (eds.), *Proceedings of KI-99, LNAI 1701*, p. 113-124, 1999.

[OSM 99a] OSMANI A., Diagnostic de pannes dans les réseaux de télécommunications : approche à base de modèles et raisonnement temporel, PhD thesis, University of Paris XIII, 1999.

[OSM 99b] OSMANI A., "Introduction to reasoning about cyclic intervals", in IMAM I., KODRATOFF Y., EL-DESSOUKI A., ALI M. (eds.), *Multiple Approaches to Intelligent Systems, Proceedings of IEA/AIE-99*, LNCS 1611, Springer, Berlin/Heidelberg, p. 698-706, 1999.

[OSM 00] OSMANI A., LÉVY F., "A constraint-based approach to simulate faults in telecommunication networks", in LOGANANTHARAJ R., PALM G. (eds.), *Proceedings of IEA/AIE, Lecture Notes in Computer Science*, vol. 1821, Springer, Berlin/Heidelberg, p. 463-473, 2000.

[PAL 04] PALSHIKAR G., "Fuzzy region connection calculus in finite discrete space domains", *Applied Soft Computing*, vol. 4, p. 13-23, 2004.

[PAR 07] PARIKH R., MOSS L.S., STEINSVOLD C., "Topology and epistemic logic", in AIELLO M., *et al.* (eds.), p. 299-341, 2007.

[PHA 06] PHAM D.N., THORNTON J., SATTAR A., "Towards an efficient SAT encoding for temporal reasoning", in BENHAMOU F. (ed.), *Proceedings of CP 2006, Lecture Notes in Computer Science*, vol. 4204, Springer, Berlin/Heidelberg, p. 421-436, 2006.

[PÖS 79] PÖSCHEL R., KALUŽNIN L.A., *Funktionen- und Relationenalgebren*, DVW, Berlin, 1979.

[PRA 07] PRATT-HARTMANN I., AIELLO M., VAN BENTHEM J., "What is spatial logic?", in AIELLO M., *et al.* (eds.), p. 1-11, 2007.

[PUJ 99a] PUJARI A.K., KUMARI G.V., SATTAR A., "INDU: an interval and duration network", in *Australian Joint Conference on Artificial Intelligence*, p. 291-303, 1999.

[PUJ 99b] Pujari A.K., Sattar A., "A new framework for reasoning about points, intervals and durations", in Thomas D. (ed.), *Proceedings of the 16th International Joint Conference on Artificial Intelligence (IJCAI '99)*, Stockholm, Sweden, Morgan Kaufmann, USA, p. 1259-1267, 1999.

[RAG 05a] Ragni M., Scivos A., "Dependency calculus: reasoning in a general point relation algebra", in *Proceedings of the 28th German Conference on Artificial Intelligence (KI 2005)*, Koblenz, Germany, p. 49-63, September 2005.

[RAG 05b] Ragni M., Scivos A., "Dependency calculus reasoning in a general point relation algebra", in Kaelbling L.P., Saffiotti A. (eds.), p. 1577-1578, 2005.

[RAG 08] Ragni M., Wölfl S., "Reasoning about topological and positional information in dynamic settings", in Wilson D., Lane H.C. (ed.), *Proceedings of the FLAIRS Conference*, AAAI Press, USA, p. 606-611, 2008.

[RAL 96] Ralha C.G., A framework for dynamic structuring of information, PhD thesis, School of Computer Studies, University of Leeds, UK, 1996.

[RAN 89] Randell D.A., Cohn A.G., "Modeling topological and metrical properties in physical processes", in Brachman H.J.L.R.J., Reiter R. (eds.), *Proceedings of the 1st International Conference on Principles of Knowledge Representation and Reasoning*, Toronto, Canada, Morgan Kaufmann, USA, p. 357-368, 1989.

[RAN 92a] Randell D., Cui Z., Cohn T., "A spatial logic based on regions and connection", in Neumann B. (ed.), *Proceedings of KR-92*, San Mateo, Morgan Kaufmann, CA, p. 165-176, 1992.

[RAN 92b] Randell D.A., Cohn A.G., Cui Z., "Naive topology: modeling the force pump", in Struss P., Faltings B. (eds.), *Advances in Qualitative Physics*, MIT Press, USA, p. 177-192, 1992.

[RAU 97] Rauh R., Schlieder C., Knauff M., "Präferierte mentale Modelle beim räumlich-relationalen Schließen: Empirie und kognitive Modellierung", *Kognitionswissenschaft*, vol. 6, no. 1, p. 21-34, 1997.

[REI 66] Reichenbach H., *Elements of Symbolic Logic*, The Free Press, New York, 1966.

[REM 04] Remolina E., Kuipers B., "Towards a general theory of topological maps", *Artificial Intelligence*, vol. 152, no. 1, p. 47-104, 2004.

[REN 92] Renegar J., "On the computational complexity and geometry of the first order theory of the reals. Parts I–III", *Journal of Symbolic Computation*, vol. 13, no. 3, p. 255-352, 1992.

[REN 97] Renz J., Nebel B., "On the complexity of qualitative spatial reasoning: a maximal tractable fragment of the region connection calculus", in *Proceedings of the 15th International Joint Conference on Artificial Intelligence (IJCAI '97)*, Nagoya, Japan, Morgan Kaufmann, USA, p. 522-527, 1997.

[REN 98a] Renz J., "A canonical model of the region connection calculus", in *Proceedings of the 6th International Conference on Principles of Knowledge Representation and Reasoning (KR'98)*, Trento, Italy, Morgan Kaufmann, USA, p. 330-341, 1998.

[REN 98b]   RENZ J., NEBEL B., "Efficient algorithms for qualitative spatial reasoning", in *Proceedings of the 13th European Conference on Artificial Intelligence (ECAI '96)*, Budapest, Hungary, John Wiley & Sons, Chichester, UK, p. 562-566, 1998.

[REN 99a]   RENZ J., "Maximal tractable fragments of the region connection calculus: a complete analysis", in DEAN T. (ed.), *Proceedings of the 16th International Joint Conference on Artificial Intelligence (IJCAI '99)*, Stockholm, Sweden, Morgan Kaufmann, USA, p. 448-455, 1999.

[REN 99b]   RENZ J., NEBEL B., "On the complexity of qualitative spatial reasoning", *Artificial intelligence*, vol. 108, p. 69-123, 1999.

[REN 01a]   RENZ J., NEBEL B., "Efficient methods for qualitative spatial reasoning", *Journal of Artificial Intelligence Research*, vol. 15, p. 289-318, 2001.

[REN 01b]   RENZ J., "A spatial odyssey of the interval algebra: 1. directed intervals", in *Proceedings of the 17th International Joint Conference on Artificial Intelligence, IJCAI 2001*, Seattle, Washington, Morgan Kaufmann, USA, p. 51-56, 2001.

[REN 02a]   RENZ J., "A canonical model of the region connection calculus", *Journal of Applied Non-Classical Logics*, vol. 12, no. 3-4, p. 469-494, 2002.

[REN 02b]   RENZ J., *Qualitative Spatial Reasoning with Topological Information, Lecture Notes in Computer Science*, vol. 2293, Springer, Berlin/Heidelberg, 2002.

[REN 04]   RENZ J., LIGOZAT G., "Problems with local consistency for qualitative calculi", in *Proceedings of ECAI '04*, Valencia, Spain, IOS Press, The Netherlands, p. 1047-1048, 2004.

[REN 07a]   RENZ J., "Qualitative spatial and temporal reasoning: efficient algorithms for everyone", in VELOSO M.M. (ed.), p. 526-531, 2007.

[REN 07b]   RENZ J., SCHMID F., "Customizing qualitative spatial and temporal calculi", in ORGUN M.A., THORNTON J. (eds.), *Australian Conference on Artificial Intelligence, Lecture Notes in Computer Science*, vol. 4830, Springer, Berlin/Heidelberg, p. 293-304, 2007.

[REV 02]   REVESZ P.Z., *Introduction to Constraint Databases*, Springer, Berlin/Heidelberg, 2002.

[ROS 01]   ROSSI F., SPERDUTI A., KHATIB L., MORRIS P., MORRIS R., "Learning preferences on temporal constraints: a preliminary report", in *Proceedings of the 8th International Symposium on Temporal Representation and Reasoning (TIME-01)*, IEEE Computer Society, Civdale del Friuli, Italy, p. 63-68, 2001.

[ROS 02]   ROSSI F., SPERDUTI A., VENABLE K.B., KHATIB L., MORRIS P.H., MORRIS R.A., "Learning and solving soft temporal constraints: an experimental study", in HENTENRYCK P.V. (ed.), p. 249-263, 2002.

[SAB 95]   SABLAYROLLES P., "The semantics of motion", in *7th Conference of the European Chapter of the Association for Computational Linguistics (EACL 1995)*, Belfield, Dublin, Ireland, p. 281-283, 1995.

[SAN 02]   SANTOS P., SHANAHAN M., "Hypothesising object relations from image transitions", in VAN HARMELEN F. (ed.), p. 292-296, 2002.

[SAN 03] SANTOS P., SHANAHAN M., "A logic-based algorithm for image sequence interpretation and anchoring", in *Proceedings of the 18th International Joint Conference on Artificial intelligence (IJCAI '03)*, San Francisco, California, Morgan Kaufmann, USA, p. 1408-1410,2003.

[SAQ 04] SAQUETE E., MARTÍNEZ-BARCO P., MUÑOZ R., GONZÁLEZ J.L.V., "Splitting complex temporal questions for question answering systems", in *Proceedings of the 42nd Meeting of the Association of Computational Linguistics (ACL 2004)*, Barcelona, Spain, p. 566-573, 2004.

[SCH 78] SCHAEFER T.J., "The complexity of satisfiability problems", in *STOC '78: Proceedings of the Tenth Annual ACM Symposium on the Theory of Computing*, ACM, New York, NY, USA, p. 216-226, 1978.

[SCH 95] SCHLIEDER C., "Reasoning about ordering", in *Proceedings of COSIT '95, LNCS*, vol. 988, Springer, Berlin/Heidelberg, p. 341-349, 1995.

[SCH 00] SCHUBERT L.K., HWANG C.H., "Episodic logic meets Little Red Riding Hood: a comprehensive natural representation for language understanding", in IWAŃSKA Ł.M., SHAPIRO S.C. (eds.), *Natural Language Processing and Knowledge Representation: Language for Knowledge and Knowledge for Language*, MIT Press, Cambridge, USA, p. 111-174, 2000.

[SCH 01] SCHLAISICH I., EGENHOFER M.J., "Multimodal spatial querying: what people sketch and talk about", in STEPHANIDIS C. (ed.), *The 9th International Conference on Human-Computer Interaction (HCI 2001)*, New Orleans, USA, Lawrence Erlbaum, p. 732-736, 2001.

[SCH 03] SCHAEFER M., SEDGWICK E., ŠTEFANKOWIČ D., "Recognizing string graphs in NP", *Journal of Computer and System Sciences*, vol. 67, p. 365-380, 2003.

[SCH 06] SCHOCKAERT S., AHN D., DE COCK M.D., KERRE E.E., "Question answering with imperfect temporal information", in LARSEN H.L., PASI G., ARROYO D.O., ANDREASEN T., CHRISTIANSEN H., (eds.), *Flexible Query Answering Systems, Seventh International Conference, (FQAS 2006)*, Milan, Italy, *Lecture Notes in Computer Science*, vol. 4027, Springer, Springer, Berlin/Heidelberg, p. 647-658, 2006.

[SCH 08a] SCHOCKAERT S., DE COCK M.D., "Temporal reasoning about fuzzy intervals", *Artificial Intelligence*, vol. 172, no. 8-9, p. 1158-1193, 2008.

[SCH 08b] SCHOCKAERT S., DE COCK M.D., CORNELIS C., KERRE E.E., "Fuzzy region connection calculus: an interpretation based on closeness", *International Journal of Approximate Reasoning*, vol. 48, no. 1, p. 332-347, 2008.

[SCH 09] SCHOCKAERT S., DE COCK M.D., KERRE E.E., "Spatial reasoning in a fuzzy region connection calculus", *Artificial Intelligence*, vol. 173, no. 2, p. 258-298, 2009.

[SCI 00] SCIVOS A., Einführung in eine Theorie der ternären RST-Kalküle für qualitatives räumliches Schließen, PhD thesis, Albert-Ludwigs-Universität Freiburg, Mathematische Fakultät, 2000.

[SCI 01] SCIVOS A., NEBEL B., "Double-crossing: decidability and computational complexity of a qualitative calculus for navigation", in MONTELLO D.R. (ed.), p. 431-446, 2001.

[SCI 04] SCIVOS A., NEBEL B., "The finest of its class: the natural point-based ternary calculus $\mathcal{LR}$ for qualitative spatial reasoning", in FREKSA C., *et al.* (eds.), p. 283-303, 2004.

[SEL 95] SELMAN B., "Stochastic and phase transitions: AI meets physics", in MELLISH C. (ed.), *Proceedings of the 14th International Joint Conference on Artificial Intelligence (IJCAI '95)*, Montreal, Quebec, Canada, Morgan Kaufmann, USA, p. 998-1002, 1995.

[SHE 99] SHEHTMAN V., "'Everywhere' and 'here'", *Journal of Applied Non-Classical Logics*, vol. 9, no. 2-3, p. 369-379, 1999.

[SHE 06] SHEREMET M., TISHKOVSKY D., WOLTER F., ZAKHARYASCHEV M., "From topology to metric: modal logic and quantification in metric spaces", in GOVERNATORI G., HODKINSON I.M., VENEMA Y. (eds.), *Advances in Modal Logic*, College Publications, p. 429-448, 2006.

[SHI 07] SHI W., LIU K., "A fuzzy topology for computing the interior, boundary, and exterior of spatial objects quantitatively in GIS", *Computational Geosciences*, vol. 33, no. 7, p. 898-915, Pergamon Press, 2007.

[SKI 01] SKIADOPOULOS S., KOUBARAKIS M., "Composing cardinal direction relations", in JENSEN C.S., *et al.* (eds.), p. 299-320, 2001.

[SKI 02] SKIADOPOULOS S., KOUBARAKIS M., "Consistency checking for qualitative spatial reasoning with cardinal directions", in HENTENRYCK P.V. (ed.), p. 341-355, 2002.

[SKI 04] SKIADOPOULOS S., KOUBARAKIS M., "Composing cardinal direction relations", *Artificial Intelligence*, vol. 152, no. 2, p. 143-171, 2004.

[SKI 05] SKIADOPOULOS S., KOUBARAKIS M., "On the consistency of cardinal direction constraints", *Artificial Intelligence*, vol. 163, no. 1, p. 91-135, 2005.

[SLA 03] SLACK J., VAN DER ZEE E. (eds.), *Representing Direction in Language and Space*, Oxford Linguistics, Oxford University Press, UK, 2003.

[SMI 96] SMITH B., "Mereotopology — a theory of parts and boundaries", *Data Knowledge Engineering*, vol. 20, p. 287-303, 1996.

[SMI 99a] SMITH B., VARZI A.C., "The formal structure of ecological contexts", in BOUQUET P., SERAFINI L., BRÉZILLON P., BENERECETTI M., CASTELLANI F. (eds.), *CONTEXT*, *Lecture Notes in Computer Science*, vol. 1688, Springer, Berlin/Heidelberg, p. 339-350, 1999.

[SMI 99b] SMITH B., VARZI A.C., "The niche", *Noûs*, vol. 33, no. 2, p. 198-222, 1999.

[STA 01] STAAB S., "From binary temporal relations to non-binary ones and back", *Artificial Intelligence*, vol. 128, no. 1-2, p. 1-29, 2001.

[STE 00] STELL J., "Boolean connection algebras: a new approach to the region-connection calculus", *Artificial Intelligence*, vol. 122, p. 111-136, 2000.

[SUK 04] SUKTHONG N., "Spatial and temporal reasoning in multimedia information retrieval and composition with XDD", *IEEE Sixth International Symposium on Multimedia Software Engineering (ISMSE '04)*, IEEE Computer Society, p. 201-208, 2004.

[SVE 91] SVENSSON P., HUANG Z., "Geo-SAL: a query language for spatial data analysis", in GÜNTHER O., SCHEK H.J. (eds.), p. 119-140, 1991.

[TAN 06] TANG X., FANG Y., KAINZ W., "Fuzzy topological relations between fuzzy spatial objects", in WANG L., JIAO L., SHI G., LI X., LIU J. (eds.), *Fuzzy Systems and Knowledge Discovery, Third International Conference (FSKD 2006), Lecture Notes in Computer Science*, vol. 4223, Springer, Berlin/Heidelberg, p. 324-333, 2006.

[TAN 07] TANG X., KAINZ W., ZHANG H., "Some topological invariants and a qualitative topological relation model between fuzzy regions", in LEI J. (ed.), *Fourth International Conference on Fuzzy Systems and Knowledge Discovery (FSKD 2007)*, IEEE Computer Society, vol. 1, Haikou, Hainan, China, p. 241-246, 2007.

[TAP 04] TAPPAN D., Knowledge-based spatial reasoning for automated scene generation from text descriptions, PhD thesis, New Mexico State University, Las Cruces, USA, 2004.

[TAR 41] TARSKI A., "On the calculus of relations", *Journal of Symbolic Logic*, vol. 6, no. 3, p. 73-89, 1941.

[VAR 96] VARZI A., "Parts, wholes, and part-whole relations: the prospects of mereotopology", *Data Knowledge Engineering*, vol. 20, no. 3, p. 259-286, 1996.

[VAR 01] VARZI A., "Vagueness in geography", *Philosophy and Geography*, vol. 4, no. 1, p. 49-65, 2001.

[VEL 07] VELOSO M.M. (ed.), *Proceedings of the 20th International Joint Conference on Artificial Intelligence (IJCAI 2007)*, Hyderabad, India, 6-12 January 2007.

[VIJ 02] VIJAYA KUMARI G., INDU: Interval-Duration Network. A Unified Framework for Reasoning with Time Intervals and their Duration, PhD thesis, University of Hyderabad, India, 2002.

[VIL 82] VILAIN M.B., "A system for reasoning about time", in *Proceedings of the Second National Conference on Artificial Intelligence (AAAI-82)*, Pittsburgh, Pennsylvania, AAAI Press/The MIT Press, USA, p. 197-201, 1982.

[VIL 86] VILAIN M.B., KAUTZ H., "Constraint propagation algorithms for temporal reasoning", in *Proceedings of the fifth National Conference on Artificial Intelligence (AAAI-86)*, Pittsburgh, Pennsylvania, AAAI Press/The MIT Press, USA, p. 377-382, 1986.

[VIL 89] VILAIN M., KAUTZ H.A., VAN BEEK P.G., "Constraint propagation algorithms for temporal reasoning: a revised report", in WELD D., DE KLEER J. (eds.), *Readings in Qualitative Reasoning about Physical Systems*, Morgan Kaufmann, USA, 1989.

[VIL 94] VILA L., GODO L., "On fuzzy constraint satisfaction problems", *Mathware and Soft Computing*, vol. 1, no. 3, p. 315-334, 1994.

[VIL 05] VILA L., YOSHINO H., "Time in automated legal reasoning", in FISHER M., *et al.* (eds.), p. 537-557.

[WAG 04] WAGNER T., HÜBNER K., "An egocentric qualitative spatial knowledge representation based on ordering information for physical robot navigation", in NARDI D., RIEDMILLER M., SAMMUT C., SANTOS-VICTOR J. (eds.), *RoboCup 2004, Lecture Notes in Computer Science*, vol. 3276, Springer, Berlin/Heidelberg, p. 134-149, 2004.

[WAL 75] WALTZ D., "Understanding line drawings of scenes with shadows", in WINSTON P.H. (ed.), *The Psychology of Computer Vision*, Chapter 2, McGraw-Hill Book Company, New York, NY, USA, p. 19-92, 1975.

[WAL 99] WALISCHEWSKI H., "Learning regions of interest in postal automation", in *Fifth International Conference on Document Analysis and Recognition (ICDAR 1999)*, IEEE Computer Society, Bangalore, India, p. 317-320, 1999.

[WAL 00] WALSH T., "SAT v CSP", in DECHTER R. (ed.), p. 441-456, 2000.

[WAL 09] WALLGRÜN J.O., "Exploiting qualitative spatial constraints for multi-hypothesis topological map learning", in HORNSBY K.S., *et al.* (eds.), p. 141-158, 2009.

[WEG 04] VAN DE WEGHE N., Representing and reasoning about moving objects: a qualitative approach, PhD thesis, Ghent University, Belgium, 2004.

[WEG 05a] VAN DE WEGHE N.V., KUIJPERS B., BOGAERT P., MAEYER P.D., "A qualitative trajectory calculus and the composition of its relations", in RODRÍGUEZ M.A., CRUZ I.F., EGENHOFER M.J., LEVASHKIN S. (eds.), *GeoS, Lecture Notes in Computer Science*, vol. 3799, Springer, Berlin/Heidelberg, p. 60-76, 2005.

[WEG 05b] VAN DE WEGHE N., DE MAEYER P., "Conceptual neighborhood diagrams for representing moving objects", in AKOKA J., LIDDLE S.W., SONG I.-Y., BERTOLOTTO M., COMYN-WATTIAU I., CHERfi S.S.-S., VAN DEN HEUVEL W.-J., THALHEIM B., KOLP M., BRESCIANI P., TRUJILLO J., KOP C., MAYR H.C. (eds.), *ER (Workshops), Lecture Notes in Computer Science*, vol. 3770, Springer, Berlin/Heidelberg, p. 228-238, 2005.

[WEG 07] VAN DE WEGHE N., BOGAERT P., COHN A.G., DELAFONTAINE M., TEMMERMAN L.D., NEUTENS T., MAEYER P.D., WITLOX F., "How to handle incomplete knowledge concerning moving objects", in GOTTFRIED B. (ed.), *BMI*, vol. 296, *CEUR Workshop Proceedings*, CEUR-WS.org, p. 91-101, 2007.

[WER 00] WERNER S., KRIEG-BRÜCKNER B., HERRMANN T., "Modeling navigational knowledge by route graphs", in FREKSA C., BRAUER W., HABEL C., WENDER K.F. (eds.), *Spatial Cognition*, vol. 1849, *Lecture Notes in Computer Science*, Springer, p. 295-316, 2000.

[WES 08] WESTPHAL M., WÖLfl S., "Bipath consistency revisited", in *Proceedings of the ECAI Workshop on Spatial and Temporal Reasoning*, Patras, Greece, 2008.

[WES 09a] WESTPHAL M., WÖLfl S., "Confirming the QSR promise", in *Proceedings of the AAAI Spring Symposium on Benchmarking of Qualitative Spatial and Temporal Reasoning Systems, AAAI Technical Report SS-09-02*, Stanford, California, USA, 2009.

[WES 09b] WESTPHAL M., WÖLfl S., "Qualitative CSP, finite CSP, and SAT: comparing methods for qualitative constraint-based reasoning", in BOUTILIER C. (ed.), p. 628-633, 2009.

[WOL 00a] WOLTER F., ZAKHARYASCHEV M., "Spatio-temporal representation and reasoning based on RCC-8", in *Proceedings of the Seventh International Conference on Principles of Knowledge Representation and Reasoning (KR 2000)*, Breckenridge, Colorado, USA, Morgan Kaufmann, USA, p. 3-14, 2000.

[WOL 00b] WOLTER F., ZAKHARYASCHEV M., "Spatial reasoning in RCC-8 with Boolean region terms", in HORN W. (ed.), p. 244-250, 2000.

[WOL 03] WOLTER F., ZAKHARYASCHEV M., "Qualitative spatiotemporal representation and reasoning: a computational perspective", in *Exploring Artificial Intelligence in the New Millennium*, Morgan Kaufmann, USA, p. 175-215, 2003.

[WOL 05] WOLTER F., ZAKHARYASCHEV M., "A logic for metric and topology", *Journal of Symbolic Logic*, vol. 70, no. 3, p. 795-828, 2005.

[WOL 08] WOLTER D., DYLLA F., WÖLfl S., WALLGRÜN J.O., FROMMBERGER L., NEBEL B., FREKSA C., "SailAway: spatial cognition in sea navigation", *Künstliche Intelligenz*, vol. 22, no. 1, p. 28-30, Springer, Berlin/Heidelberg, 2008.

[WÖL 09] WÖLFL S., WESTPHAL M., "On combinations of binary qualitative constraint calculi", in BOUTILIER C. (ed.), p. 967-973, 2009.

[WOR 95] WORBOYS M.F., *GIS: A Computing Perspective*, Taylor & Francis, London, UK, 1995.

[WOR 98] WORBOYS M.F., "Imprecision in finite resolution spatial data", *GeoInformatica*, vol. 2, no. 3, p. 257-279, 1998.

[WÜR 00a] WÜRBEL E., JEANSOULIN R., PAPINI O., "Revision: an application in the framework of GIS", in *Proceedings of the Seventh International Conference on Principles of Knowledge Representation and Reasoning (KR 2000)*, Breckenridge, Colorado, USA, Morgan Kaufmann, USA, p. 505-515, 2000.

[WÜR 00b] WÜRBEL E., JEANSOULIN R., PAPINI O., "Révision: une application dans le contexte des Systèmes d'Information Géographiques", in *Actes de la Conférence Reconnaissance des Formes et Intelligence Artificielle (RFIA 2000)*, Paris, France, p. 195-204, 2000.

[YOR 03] YORKE-SMITH N., VENABLE K.B., ROSSI F., "Temporal reasoning with preferences and uncertainty", in GOTTLOB G., WALSH T. (eds.), *Proceedings of the International Joint Conference on Artificial Intelligence (IJCAI 2003)*, Acapulco, Mexico, Morgan Kaufmann, USA, p. 1385-1386, 2003.

[ZHA 08] ZHANG X., LIU W., LI S., YING M., "Reasoning with cardinal directions: an efficient algorithm", in FOX D., GOMES C.P. (eds.), *Proceedings of the Twenty-Third AAAI Conference on Artificial Intelligence (AAAI 2008)*, Chicago, Illinois, AAAI Press, USA, p. 387-392, 2008.

Index

A

a-cut, 194, 196
adjunction, 278-281, 460, 461
age (of a structure), 379
algebra
    Allen's, 9, 11-13, 20-22, 28-30, 39,
        48, 52, 60, 61, 76, 78, 79,
        82-85, 99, 104, 105, 113, 121,
        123, 125, 172, 174, 175, 179,
        191, 224-226, 234, 237-243,
        245-247, 252, 253, 255-257,
        259, 262-266, 271-273, 277,
        283, 285, 291, 304, 345, 355,
        356, 359, 366, 368, 377,
        380-382, 385, 387, 416, 420,
        421, 424, 432
    Boolean, 20, 78, 93, 111, 125, 261,
        265, 290, 307, 316, 317, 319,
        325-327, 332-335, 337, 338,
        341, 342, 350, 352, 353, 373,
        452-457
    Boolean connection, 315-319, 326,
        335-338, 340-342
    connection, 315-319, 326, 335-342

    containment, 345, 359
    fuzzy interval, 188, 189, 191, 193,
        198
    generalized Boolean connection,
        317, 319, 335, 336, 340-342
    non-associative, 125, 291, 345,
        346, 350-354, 358-360, 365
    relation, 20, 60, 78, 261, 284, 290,
        291, 306, 307, 341, 350-352,
        354, 358, 360, 365, 454, 456,
        457
    semi-associative, 125, 345, 351
algebraically closed, 21, 22, 24, 44, 45,
    47, 48, 58, 61, 83, 96, 99, 106, 114,
    131, 135, 153, 154, 172, 194, 238,
    239, 252, 253, 255-257, 345,
    354-356, 359, 360
algorithm
    Check-Refinements, 387
    Combined-Metric-Allen, 168
    ConsAtom, 26, 27
    CSPAN, 12
    linear programming, 202, 385
    SAT, 468, 469